The Government Contracts Reference Book

The Government Contracts Reference Book

A Comprehensive Guide to the Language of Procurement

SECOND EDITION

Ralph C. Nash, Jr.
Steven L. Schooner
Karen R. O'Brien

The George Washington University
WASHINGTON DC

LAW SCHOOL

GOVERNMENT CONTRACTS PROGRAM

Library of Congress Catalog Card Number: 97-75247
ISBN 0-935165-54-1

Contents

Preface to the Second Edition

Since 1992, when we published the first edition of *The Government Contracts Reference Book*, there has been a revolution in Government procurement. Numerous statutory and regulatory changes have been made, and the terminology of Government contracting has changed along with the policy. We have reflected all of this new terminology (through the end of 1997) in this new edition.

The purpose of the book remains the same: to give concise, comprehensive information to the practitioner of the art of Government contracting. Looking up a key term, the reader can find a definition followed by a summary of where the term is used in the statutes or regulations dealing with the procurement process. We have also included references to those places in the literature where the term is more fully discussed. The book is not designed to stand alone; it is a *first* reference, pointing the user to additional sources as needed. The book makes it clear what we have known for a long time: Government contracting is complex, and the rules cannot be gleaned from a single source such as the Federal Acquisition Regulation. They can only be learned by constant reading of reference materials and textbooks — not to mention decisions of the courts, boards of contract appeals, and General Accounting Office. Navigating the waters of Government procurement is an arduous task, and this book is intended as an aid in that journey.

This edition not only updates terms from the first edition but also incorporates many new ones — a total of over 1,500 (as compared to

1,100 in the first edition). A reference work in a constantly changing field, however, is never "complete," and we welcome contributions from you, our readers, regarding what we might include in the next edition.

Finally, we would like to acknowledge the valuable input of our research assistants, Michael C. Boteler and Agnes Rodriguez. Significant research work was also done by Claude Hooker.

How to Use This Reference Book

To Find the Term You're Looking For

Alphabetization

This book uses the word-by-word (as opposed to letter-by-letter) mode of alphabetizing, with hyphens, commas, and other punctuation treated as word spaces. For example:

PERFORMANCE

PERFORMANCE-BASED SERVICE CONTRACTING

PERFORMANCE BOND

Numbers within terms are treated as words. 8(a) PROGRAM is alphabetized as EIGHT A PROGRAM, for example, and A-76 POLICY as A SEVENTY SIX POLICY.

Acronyms and Abbreviations

Because many terms in Government contracting have acronyms or abbreviations, and because these shortened forms are often as familiar as the full terms, common-use acronyms and abbreviations have been included in the book's entry titles:

COST-PLUS-FIXED-FEE (CPFF) CONTRACT

QUALIFIED PRODUCTS LIST (QPL)

Virtually all entry titles, however, are terms spelled out in full (REQUEST FOR PROPOSALS (RFP) as opposed to RFP, for example). If you want to look up an acronym or abbreviation but don't know what it stands for, you can find the full term in Acronyms and Abbreviations Used in This Reference Book. You can also refer to this listing if you need to look up one of the handful of acronyms (FAR, DOD, DOE, GSA, NASA, and a few others) that have been used in the text without full-term introduction in order to save space.

To Locate Additional Information

Cross-References

In order to gain a better understanding of one term, it will sometimes be helpful to refer to the book's entry on another term. The book's cross-referencing system has therefore been designed to guide you to entries that provide additional detail, discuss closely related concepts, or define terminology that must be read with a precise meaning. Cross-references are in ALL CAPITALS.

References to Other Sources

All the entries in *The Government Contracts Reference Book* will lead you to pertinent information to be found in various other documents.

Most entries cite other documents (frequently the Federal Acquisition Regulation (FAR)) as the source for the capsule definitions provided or for other statements made.

In addition to the FAR, regulations cited in this book include the Department of Defense FAR Supplement (DFARS), the Department of Energy Acquisition Regulation (DEAR), and the National Aeronautics and Space Administration (NASA) FAR Supplement (NFS). References to these regulations are current as of December 15, 1997; in some cases, proposed changes pending at that time are noted. This reference book is not, however, a substitute for federal procurement statutes or their implementing regulations. The regulations should be consulted directly before making binding decision about federal contracting matters.

Many of the book's entries treat or cite procurement-related statutes. In most cases, reference is made to the current (1991) version of the U.S. Code. Pertinent court and board of contract appeals decisions are referenced as well, following *The Bluebook: A Uniform System of Citation* style.

Also cited in this reference book are some 50 texts, scores of articles from more than 30 different periodicals, and many other types of documents issued by both Government and private industry (pamphlets, booklets, study reports, manuals, and so forth). All appear in the entries in italics, often with "see" or "see also" references to signal that they provide useful information beyond that synopsized in this book.

About the Authors

Ralph C. Nash, Jr., is a widely recognized author and lecturer in the Government contracts field. A professor emeritus of law at The George Washington University Law School, he founded the University's Government Contracts Program in 1960 and served as its director from 1960 to 1966 and from 1979 to 1984. In addition to teaching, he does consulting work for Government agencies, private corporations, and law firms. He is a member of the Public Contracts Section of the American Bar Association, is a member of the Procurement Round Table, and is a fellow and serves on the board of advisers of the National Contract Management Association. He served as a member of the Department of Defense Advisory Panel on Streamlining and Codifying Acquisition Laws (Section 800). Professor Nash is the author of *Government Contract Changes* and is the coauthor of several texts including *Formation of Government Contracts*, *Administration of Government Contracts*, *Cost-Reimbursement Contracting*, *Competitive Negotiation: The Source Selection Process*, *Patents and Technical Data*, and *Construction Contracting*. He received an A.B., magna cum laude, from Princeton University and a J.D. from The George Washington University Law School.

Steven L. Schooner is the associate administrator for procurement law and legislation at the Office of Federal Procurement Policy (OFPP). Prior to joining OFPP, Mr. Schooner practiced Government contracts law in the Commercial Litigation Branch of the Department of Justice. He previously served as a commissioner at the Armed Services Board of Contract Appeals and practiced with private law firms. He received a

B.A. from Rice University, a J.D. from the College of William and Mary, and an LL.M., with highest honors, from The George Washington University. An Army Reserve officer, he is an adjunct professor in the Contract Law Department of the Judge Advocate General's School of the Army, in Charlottesville, Virginia. He is a fellow of the National Contract Management Association (NCMA), a certified professional contracts manager (CPCM), and an associate editor of the American Bar Association's *Public Contract Law Journal.* He speaks frequently on a broad range of procurement-related topics and has authored and coauthored numerous articles in professional journals including *Public Contract Law Journal*, *Business Lawyer*, *Construction Lawyer*, and *Army Lawyer*.

Karen R. O'Brien is the director of publications at The George Washington University Law School's Government Contracts Program. Ms. O'Brien has assisted Professors Nash and Cibinic with *Formation of Government Contracts*, *Administration of Government Contracts*, *Competitive Negotiation: The Source Selection Process*, and *Cost-Reimbursement Contracting*. Previously, she was a captain in the Army Judge Advocate General's Corps, assigned primarily in the areas of criminal law (both at the trial and appellate level) and Government contract law. She was the legal adviser to the principal assistant responsible for contracting in Southwest Asia. She was a staff attorney for the Department of Defense Advisory Panel on Streamlining and Codifying Acquisition Laws (Section 800). She is a member of the Public Contracts Section of the American Bar Association. She received a B.A. in accounting, magna cum laude, from Niagara University and a J.D., cum laude, from Vermont Law School.

A

A-76 POLICY The policy of the executive branch, first promulgated by the Bureau of the Budget in 1955, that the Government should generally rely on the private sector for commercially available goods and services. Detailed guidance on determining whether commercial activities should be performed under contract with commercial sources or in-house using Government facilities and personnel is contained in OMB Circular No. A-76 (revised), *Performance of Commercial Activities*, Aug. 16, 1983, most recently amended Feb. 28, 1991; its *Revised Supplemental Handbook* (Apr. 1, 1996); and FAR Subpart 7.3. The policy recognizes that some functions are inherently Governmental (see INHERENTLY GOVERNMENTAL FUNCTIONS) and must be performed by Government personnel; it also states that the Government should contract out if certain criteria are met and should give appropriate consideration to relative cost in deciding between Government performance and performance under contract. OMB Circular No. A-76 and the FAR provide that in comparing the costs of Government and contractor performance, agencies must base the contractor's cost of performance on firm offers. See Cibinic & Nash, chap. 3, Sec. IV., *Formation of Government Contracts* (3d ed. 1998); Gamboa, *Depot Maintenance & Manufacturing by Government Facilities: What Impact on Privatization?*, 1995 A.B.A. Sec. Pub. Cont. L.; Nash, *Reforming the Procurement Process: Part I—The Proposals Are Coming*, 7 N&CR ¶ 7 (Feb. 1993); Perfilio, *Contracting Out: A Road Map*, 30 A.F. L. Rev. 69 (1988); Catania, *Contracting Out: Management and Labor at War under Section 7106 of the Civil Service Reform Act*, 16 Pub. Cont. L.J. 287 (1986).

ABSTRACT OF BIDS See ABSTRACT OF OFFERS.

ABSTRACT OF OFFERS The record of all BIDS received on an unclassified sealed bid procurement. FAR 14.403 requires the BID OPENING officer to personally and publicly open all bids received and have them recorded on Standard Form 1409, Abstract of Offers, FAR 53.301-1409, or Standard Form 1410, Abstract of Offers—

Construction, FAR 53.301-1410. The bid opening officer must complete the abstract and certify its accuracy as soon after bid opening as possible. Because they are available for public inspection, abstracts will not contain information about failure to meet minimum standards of RESPONSIBILITY, apparent collusion of bidders (see COLLUSIVE BIDDING), or other matters properly exempt from public disclosure. When bid items are too numerous to warrant complete recording, abstract entries for individual bids may be limited to item numbers and corresponding prices.

ACAT See ACQUISITION CATEGORIES.

ACCELERATED PERFORMANCE See ACCELERATION.

ACCELERATED PROCEDURE A procedure for the accelerated disposition of appeals before an agency BOARD OF CONTRACT APPEALS (BCA) that is required by the CONTRACT DISPUTES ACT OF 1978 at 41 U.S.C. § 607(f). This procedure is sometimes referred to as the "Rule 12.3 procedure" because it is implemented by Uniform Rule 12.3 (see UNIFORM RULES). The accelerated procedure may be elected only by the contractor and originally applied to claims of $50,000 or less. This limit was raised to claims of $100,000 by the FEDERAL ACQUISITION STREAMLINING ACT OF 1994, Pub. L. No. 103-355. However, a number of the BCA rules have not been amended to reflect the $100,000 statutory requirement. Uniform Rule 12.1(c) explains that the contractor must make the election to proceed pursuant to Rule 12.3 within 60 days of receipt of the notice of docketing "unless such period is extended by the Board for good cause." The BCA has 180 days after the election to issue a decision on the appeal. Under this procedure the parties are encouraged to waive pleadings, discovery and briefs; and a concise written decision will normally be rendered by a single judge with such concurrence as may be required by the rules of the BCA. The decision may be given orally at the close of the hearing followed by the written decision. For claims of $50,000 or less, a contractor may elect an alternate expedited procedure (see EXPEDITED PROCEDURES). Neither procedure is available if the contractor appeals the DECISION OF THE CONTRACTING OFFICER to the U.S. COURT OF FEDERAL CLAIMS. See Churchill et al., *Report of the Federal Contract Claims and Remedies Committee on Ways of Expediting Appeals Before the Boards of Contract Appeals*, 16 Pub. Cont. L.J. 161 (1986).

ACCELERATION Speeding up work to complete performance earlier than anticipated. If a contractor accelerates on its own initiative to ensure completion within the contract schedule, the additional costs of that acceleration are not recoverable from the Government. In addition, the Schedules for Construction Contracts clause at FAR 52.236-15 permits the contracting officer to order acceleration without compensation if the contractor has fallen behind schedule. Compensable acceleration occurs when the Government orders accelerated performance that is not required to meet the current contract schedule. This generally occurs constructively (as a type of CONSTRUCTIVE CHANGE) when the Government requires the contractor to meet the current contract schedule in the face of an EXCUSABLE DELAY. Such a delay entitles the contractor to a schedule extension, and an order to meet the original schedule is equivalent to an order to complete the work in advance of schedule. A constructive acceleration thus typically entails an excusable delay, Government knowledge of the delay, some Government statement or act construed as an acceleration order, notice by the contractor that the order is a constructive change, and incurring of additional costs of accelerated effort. See Cibinic & Nash, *Administration of Government Contracts* 450–62 (3d ed. 1995).

ACCEPTANCE OF OFFER The formal act of the recipient of an OFFER, typically the Government, that results in a legally binding contract. The standard forms (SFs) for issuing solicitations—SF 33, Solicitation, Offer, and Award, FAR 53.301-33 and SF 1442, Solicitation, Offer, and Award (Construction, Alteration, or Repair), FAR 53.301-1442—contain a block for the signature of the CONTRACTING OFFICER signifying acceptance. Acceptance is also made by sending a NOTICE OF AWARD. When the Government issues a PURCHASE ORDER, under SIMPLIFIED ACQUISITION PROCEDURES, acceptance is made by the contractor, either by signing the purchase order or by beginning performance. FAR 13.302-3. Acceptance is generally binding at the time of transmission of the acceptance document (the MAILBOX RULE). See Cibinic & Nash, chap. 2, Sec. I., *Formation of Government Contracts* (3d ed. 1998).

ACCEPTANCE OF WORK The act of an AUTHORIZED REPRESENTATIVE of the Government by which the Government, for itself or as an agent of another, (1) assumes ownership of existing identified supplies tendered or (2) approves specific services rendered as partial or complete performance of a contract. FAR 46.101. Acceptance of supplies or services is the responsibility of the CONTRACTING OFFICER. FAR 46.502. Acceptance constitutes acknowledgment that the supplies or services conform to applicable contract quality and quantity requirements. FAR 46.501. Acceptance may take place before delivery, at the time of delivery, or after delivery, depending on the TERMS AND CONDITIONS of the contract. Neither supplies nor services are ordinarily accepted before completion of Government contract QUALITY ASSURANCE actions. Acceptance is usually evidenced by execution of an acceptance certificate on an inspection and receiving report (see MATERIAL INSPECTION AND RECEIVING REPORT) or commercial shipping document/packing list. FAR 46.501. Acceptance has unusual legal significance in Government contracting because the Inspection of Supplies—Fixed-Price clause (FAR 52.246-2) and the Inspection of Construction clause (FAR 52.246-12) make acceptance conclusive on the Government except for LATENT DEFECTs, FRAUD, GROSS MISTAKEs AMOUNTING TO FRAUD, and any right of the Government under warranties (see WARRANTY). See Cibinic & Nash, *Administration of Government Contracts* 833–99 (3d ed. 1995); Bednar, chap. 19, *Construction Contracting* 815–24 (1991); Hedlund, *The Relationship of Government Contract Warranties to Inspection and Acceptance*, 29 A.F. L. Rev. 103 (1988).

ACCESSORY ITEM An item that facilitates or enhances the operation of PLANT EQUIPMENT but is not essential for its operation. FAR 45.501. With regard to management of GOVERNMENT PROPERTY in the possession of contractors, FAR 45.505-5 requires that a contractor maintain the property record of accessory items as part of the record of the associated plant equipment.

ACCORD AND SATISFACTION A method of resolving an issue whereby the parties agree (enter into an EXECUTORY ACCORD) to (1) give and accept something ("satisfaction") in settlement of the issue and (2) perform the agreement. If the performance is not rendered, the other party has the election to pursue its rights under the original contract. If the performance is rendered, the new contract discharges the original contract. *Restatement (Second) of Contracts* § 281 (1981). In an alternative form of settlement agreement, the SUBSTITUTED CONTRACT, the old contract is discharged at the time of entering into the new contract. *Restatement (Second) of Contracts* § 279 (1981). Decisions on Government contracts frequently do not distinguish between these two types of settlement agreements but refer to them both as accord and satisfaction. Accord and satisfaction is normally accomplished by execution of a bilateral MODIFICATION and payment by the Government in accordance with the modification. See Cibinic & Nash, *Administration of Government Contracts* 1219–21 (3d ed. 1995).

ACCOUNTING CLASSIFICATION REFERENCE NUMBER (ACRN) A two-position control code used in all contracts assigned for contract administration to DLA's DEFENSE CONTRACT MANAGEMENT COMMAND or to the plant cognizance representatives of the military departments and agencies. It provides a method of relating the long-line accounting classification citation number to detailed line-item scheduled information. DFARS 204.7101. The ACRN may be any discrete two-position alphanumeric code assigned to each accounting classification within each contract (except that the letters "I" and "O" are not used). The code is shown as a detached prefix to the long-line accounting classification number, usually in the Accounting and Appropriation Data block of the contract. DFARS 204.7107(d).

ACCRUAL BASIS ACCOUNTING An accounting method in which revenue is recorded when earned and costs and BALANCE SHEET items are recorded when commitments are made. The accrual basis of accounting, rather than the CASH BASIS ACCOUNTING method, is used by organizations with more complex dealings. Under the accrual basis, costs are incurred when an obligation to pay arises, and such costs are recorded as accrued even though actual payment is not required until later. The overwhelming majority of Government contractors use the accrual basis. See Cibinic & Nash, *Cost-Reimbursement Contracting* 638 (2d ed. 1993).

ACCUMULATING COSTS Collecting cost data in an organized manner, such as through a system of accounts. FAR 31.001. CAS 401, 48 C.F.R. § 9904.401-20, requires that a contractor's practices in estimating costs in order to price a proposal be consistent with the COST ACCOUNTING PRACTICEs the contractor uses in accumulating contract costs, and that, conversely, the contractor's practices in accumulating actual contract costs be consistent with practices used in pricing the related proposal.

ACCURATE, COMPLETE, AND CURRENT The standard that COST OR PRICING DATA must meet when submitted in accordance with the TRUTH IN NEGOTIATIONS ACT. When the data are required, contractors must certify as soon as practicable after reaching agreement, that, to the best of their knowledge and belief, the data submitted to the contracting officer meet the standard as of the date the contractor and the Government agreed on a price or another date agreed to by the parties. FAR 15.403-4; FAR 15.406-2. If, before agreement on price, the contracting officer learns that any cost or pricing data submitted are inaccurate, incomplete, or noncurrent (see DEFECTIVE

COST OR PRICING DATA), the contracting officer should bring the information to the attention of the contractor so that the data can be corrected, completed, or made current. After contract award, the Government is entitled to a PRICE ADJUSTMENT, including PROFIT or FEE, of any significant amount by which the price was increased because the data were inaccurate, incomplete, or noncurrent. FAR 15.407-1(b)(1). See the Price Reduction for Defective Cost or Pricing Data clause at FAR 52.215-22. See also Cibinic & Nash, *Administration of Government Contracts* 119–31 (3d ed. 1995); Wall, *Surviving Commercial Pricing Rules*, 23 Pub. Cont. L.J. 553 (1994); Allen & Johnson, *Escaping the Maze of TINA: No Way Out?,* 10 Computer L. 22 (1993).

ACQUISITION Acquiring by contract, with appropriated funds, supplies or services (including construction) by and for the use of the Federal Government through purchase or LEASE, whether the supplies or services already exist or must be created, developed, demonstrated, and evaluated. FAR 2.101. Acquisition begins at the point when agency needs are established and includes description of the agency's requirements, solicitation and selection of sources, AWARD of contracts, contract financing, contract performance, contract administration, and those technical and management functions directly related to the process of fulfilling agency needs by contract. The procurement statutes generally use the synonymous term PROCUREMENT. However, "acquisition" is generally used in the FAR to describe this activity. See Cibinic & Nash, chap. 1, Sec. I., *Formation of Government Contracts* (3d ed. 1998); Cibinic & Nash, *Administration of Government Contracts* 18–29 (3d ed. 1995).

ACQUISITION CATEGORIES (ACATs) The division by DOD of its major programs into a series of categories, each with corresponding levels of scrutiny. ACAT I programs are major defense acquisition programs (MDAPs), which generally are defined as programs estimated by the Under Secretary of Defense (Acquisition and Technology) (USD(A&T)) to require eventual expenditure for research, development, test, and evaluation of more than $355 million (in FY96 constant dollars) or procurement of more than $2.135 billion (in FY96 constant dollars). ACAT I programs have two subcategories: (1) ACAT ID for which the milestone decision authority (MDA) is USD(A&T); the "D" in ID refers to the Defense Acquisition Board, which advises the USD(A&T) at major decision points; and (2) ACAT IC for which the MDA is the DOD component head or, if delegated, the DOD component acquisition executive (CAE); the "C" in IC refers to component. ACAT IA programs are major automated information systems (MAISs), which generally are estimated to require program costs for any single year in excess of $30 million (FY96 constant dollars), total program in excess of $120 million (FY96 constant dollars). ACAT IA programs have two subcategories: (1) ACAT IAM for which the MDA is the Office of the Secretary of Defense (OSD) chief information officer (CIO); the "M" in IAM refers to Major Automated Information Systems Review Council (MAISRC); and (2) ACAT IAC for which the MDA is the DOD component chief information officer (CIO); the "C" in IAC refers to component. ACAT II programs are those acquisition programs that do not meet the criteria for an ACAT I program, but do meet the criteria for a major system. A major system is defined generally as a program estimated by the DOD component head to require eventual expenditure for research, development, test, and evaluation of more than $75 million in FY80 constant dollars (approximately $140 million in FY96 constant dollars), or for procurement of more than $300 million in FY80 constant dollars (approximately $645 million in FY96 constant dollars). The MDA is the DOD CAE. ACAT III programs are those acquisition programs that do not meet the criteria for an ACAT I, an ACAT IA, or an ACAT II program. The MDA is designated by the CAE and shall be at the lowest appropriate level. Jones, *Glossary: Defense Acquisition Acronyms and Terms* (8th ed., Defense Systems Management College).

ACQUISITION COST The price level or value of the supplies or services to be purchased under a contract. Before issuing the solicitation, the contracting officer must include in the ACQUISITION PLAN an estimate of the ACQUISITION COST. See FAR Part 7. Estimates can range from simple budgetary estimates to complex estimates based on inspection of the product itself and review of such items as DRAWINGS, SPECIFICATIONs, and prior DATA. Ideally, the acquisition cost estimate will be made in conjunction with the budgeting process so that sufficient funds can be obtained to carry out the procurement. The estimate can be made using data on the class of products or services being procured, data from past procurement of the same or similar products or services, or any other relevant data. Nash & Cibinic, *Competitive Negotiation: The Source Selection Process* 25 (1993).

ACQUISITION FORECASTING Public announcement of annual contract opportunities pursuant to the Business Opportunity Development Reform Act of 1988, 15 U.S.C. § 631 et seq. NASA defines "contract opportunity" as planned new contract awards exceeding

$25,000 and, as required by statute, issues a publicly available forecast and semiannual update of expected contract opportunities for the FISCAL YEAR. Opportunities for SMALL BUSINESS CONCERNs, particularly those owned by socially and economically disadvantaged individuals, are included. NFS Subpart 18-7.72.

ACQUISITION INSTRUMENT IDENTIFICATION A system of identifying numbers to be assigned to NASA contracts and related instruments. NFS Subpart 18-4.71. The basic number will remain unchanged throughout the life of the instrument. It consists of no more than 11 alphanumeric characters. A five-position prefix combines "NAS" (except for certain reimbursable contracts, which use "DEN") with a two-position identifier of the installation responsible for the contract. A hyphen is inserted after the prefix and is followed by a six-position set of serial numbers assigned by each installation, without regard to fiscal year or type of contract. (As an exception, "(F)" appears in the final position for facilities contracts.) The two-position installation identifier used in the prefix is also used to begin solicitation numbers, but the rest of the solicitation identifying numbers are installation-unique. PURCHASE ORDERs, including blanket purchase orders, use a simplified identification system. NFS 18-4.7103. See also PROCUREMENT INSTRUMENT IDENTIFICATION NUMBERS.

ACQUISITION LIFE CYCLE See ACQUISITION PROCESS.

ACQUISITION PLAN A plan addressing all technical, business, management, and other significant considerations that will control an acquisition. It summarizes ACQUISITION PLANNING deliberations and must identify milestones for decisions in the ACQUISITION PROCESS. FAR 7.105 contains detailed guidance on the contents of written acquisition plans. See also DFARS 207.105; GSAR 507.105; NFS 18-7.105. See Cibinic & Nash, chap. 3, Sec. I., *Formation of Government Contracts* (3d ed. 1998).

ACQUISITION PLANNING The process by which the efforts of all personnel responsible for an acquisition are coordinated and integrated through a comprehensive plan for fulfilling the agency need in a timely manner and at a reasonable cost. Acquisition planning includes developing the overall strategy for managing the acquisition. FAR 7.101. This planning process is conducted pursuant to the statutory requirement in 10 U.S.C. § 2305(a)(1)(A)(ii) and 41 U.S.C. § 253a(a)(1)(B) that agencies conduct advance procurement planning. Its purpose is to ensure that FULL AND OPEN COMPETITION is obtained to the greatest extent feasible and that COMMERCIAL ITEMs are procured to the maximum extent practicable. FAR Part 7 prescribes policies and procedures for (1) developing ACQUISITION PLANs, (2) determining whether to use commercial or Government resources for acquisition of supplies or services, (3) deciding whether it is more economical to lease equipment than to purchase it, and (4) determining whether functions are inherently Governmental (see INHERENTLY GOVERNMENTAL FUNCTIONS). Some agencies prescribe extensive additions or modifications to the FAR guidance. See, for example, DFARS Subpart 207.1 and NFS Subpart 18-7.1. See Cibinic & Nash, chap. 3, *Formation of Government Contracts* (3d ed. 1998); Nash, *Reform at the Beginning of the Acquisition Process: The Contracting/Technical Team*, 11 N&CR ¶ 6 (Jan. 1997); Nash & Cibinic, chap. 1, *Competitive Negotiation: The Source Selection Process* (1993).

ACQUISITION PROCESS A basic framework for managing a DOD system ACQUISITION PROGRAM, from identification of a mission need for the system to be acquired through production, implementation, and improvement of that system. This term was used in DOD Directive 5000.2, *Defense Acquisition Management Policies and Procedures*, Feb. 23, 1991, but is no longer used in the new guidance on DOD acquisition procedures, DOD Regulation 5000.2-R, *Mandatory Procedures for Major Defense Acquisition Programs (MDAPs) and Major Automated Information System (MAIS) Acquisition Programs*, Mar. 15, 1996.

ACQUISITION PROGRAM A directed, funded effort that is designed to provide a new, improved, or continuing weapon system or automated information system capability in response to a validated operational need. Acquisition programs are divided into categories, which are established to facilitate decentralized decisionmaking and execution and compliance with statutory requirements. Policies and procedures for DOD acquisition programs are contained in DOD Directive 5000.1, *Defense Acquisition*, Mar. 15, 1996, and DOD Regulation 5000.2-R, *Mandatory Procedures for Major Defense Acquisition Programs (MDAPs) and Major Automated Information System (MAIS) Acquisition Programs*, Mar. 15, 1996. These regulations emphasize that acquisition programs should be structured with great flexibility but contain elaborate guidance on policies and procedures that must be followed by PROGRAM MANAGERs.

ACQUISITION PROGRAM BASELINE (APB) A DOD document that contains the most important cost, schedule, and performance parameters (both objectives and thresholds) for a program. It is approved by the milestone decision authority, and signed by the program manager and his/her direct chain of supervision. For example, the APB for ACQUISITION CATEGORY ID programs is signed by the program manager, program executive officer, component acquisition executive, and defense acquisition executive. Jones, *Glossary: Defense Acquisition Acronyms and Terms* (8th ed., Defense Systems Management College).

ACQUISITION REFORM NETWORK (ARNet) A website created as a joint project of the NATIONAL PERFORMANCE REVIEW, OFFICE OF FEDERAL PROCUREMENT POLICY, NATIONAL CONTRACT MANAGEMENT ASSOCIATION, The Council for Excellence in Government, The National Academy of Public Administration, and Lawrence Livermore National Laboratory, with the objective of "foster[ing] and propagat[ing] measurable breakthrough improvements in the way the Government obtains goods and services." ARNet's homepage is located at <http://www.arnet.gov> and includes links to reference materials, acquisition opportunities, and acquisition training materials. In addition, proposed rules are available at ARNet for electronic review and comment. See Cibinic, *Surfing the Procurement "Net,"* 9 N&CR ¶ 65 (Dec. 1995).

ACQUISITION REVIEW The process by which agency procurement executives oversee development of procurement systems, evaluate system performance in accordance with approved criteria, enhance career management of the procurement workforce, and certify to the agency heads that procurement systems meet approved criteria. Exec. Order No. 12352, 47 Fed. Reg. 12125 (Mar. 17, 1982). OMB Memorandum M-89-21, "Improving Management Controls Over Government Procurement," requires senior procurement executives to review their agencies' procurement office operations, identify and correct any problems, and report the results to the OFFICE OF FEDERAL PROCUREMENT POLICY. Acquisition reviews cannot be conducted by officials from within the reviewed agency but, rather, must be performed by outside officials. Procurement executives are responsible for enforcing the results and recommendations of reviews if problems are found. See Kestenbaum & Straight, *A Protocol for Conducting Acquisition Reviews*, 25 Nat'l Cont. Mgmt. J., Issue No. 1, p. 27 (1993).

ACQUISITION SAVINGS Savings of contractors resulting from the application of a VALUE ENGINEERING CHANGE PROPOSAL to contracts awarded by the same contracting office or its successor for essentially the same unit. FAR 48.001. Acquisition savings include (1) INSTANT CONTRACT SAVINGS, (2) CONCURRENT CONTRACT SAVINGS, and (3) FUTURE CONTRACT SAVINGS. Savings of the Government are called COLLATERAL SAVINGS. See Cibinic & Nash, *Administration of Government Contracts* 413–17 (3d ed. 1995).

ACQUISITION STRATEGY The conceptual framework for conducting a MAJOR SYSTEM acquisition. The term encompasses the broad concepts and objectives that direct and control the overall development, production, and deployment of a system. OMB Circular No. A-109, *Major System Acquisitions*, Apr. 5, 1976, establishes the requirements for developing an acquisition strategy. Such a strategy must be written, must be tailored to the particular needs of the system acquisition program, and must set forth an overall plan for satisfying the mission need in the most effective, economical, and timely manner. The contents of an ACQUISITION STRATEGY are the same as those of an ACQUISITION PLAN, subject to any requirements peculiar to the major system acquisition. FAR 34.004.

ACQUISITION STREAMLINING The effort of a procuring agency that results in more efficient and more effective use of resources to design, develop, produce, or deploy quality systems. FAR 7.101. The objective of acquisition streamlining is to reduce the time and cost required for acquiring systems and to improve the quality of those systems by ensuring that solicitations and contracts contain only those necessary SPECIFICATIONs, STANDARDs, and related documents that have been tailored (see TAILORING) for application at the most appropriate time in the acquisition cycle. FAR 10.002. See *Defense Management: Efforts to Streamline Acquisition Management Structure*, GAO/NSIAD-91-15 (Dec. 1990). Acquisition streamlining has also been addressed to shortening the time for and reducing the resources used in the SOURCE SELECTION process. See Edwards, *Streamlining Source Selection by Improving the Quality of Evaluation Factors*, 8 N&CR ¶ 56 (Oct. 1994); Nash, *Acquisition Streamlining: Revamping the Competitive Negotiation Process,* 4 N&CR ¶ 38 (June 1990). Streamlining techniques are being tested by DOD (see DOD Regulation 5000.2-R, *Mandatory Procedures for Major Defense Acquisition Programs (MDAPs) and Major Automated Information System (MAIS) Acquisition Programs,* Mar. 15, 1996, ¶ 3.3.5.1).

ACTIVITY BASED COSTING (ABC) A set of managerial accounting methods used to identify and describe COST OBJECTIVEs, the activities they create and the amount of resources the activities consume. It is a technique to quantitatively measure the cost and performance of activities, resources, and cost objects, including when appropriate, overhead. ABC identifies organizational activities, traces costs to these activities, and then uses various cost drivers to trace the cost of activities to products. These cost drivers, such as the number of persons performing work or the number of setups required per product, reflect the consumption of activities by the products. ABC is a tool for management designed to translate cost data and provide a reliable information source on which to base managerial decisions. See DOD, *ABC Guidebook* (June 9, 1995).

ACTUAL CASH VALUE The cost of replacing damaged property with property of like kind and quality and in the physical condition of the damaged property immediately before the damage. FAR 31.001. CAS 416, 48 C.F.R. § 9904.416-50, states that in measuring actual losses to be covered by a contractor's SELF INSURANCE program, the amount of loss must be measured, in part, by the actual cash value of the property destroyed. 48 C.F.R. § 9904.416-50(a)(3).

ACTUAL COST An amount expended by a contractor to perform work, as determined on the basis of incurred costs as distinguished from forecasted costs. 48 C.F.R. § 9904.401-30; FAR 31.001. Actual costs include STANDARD COSTs properly adjusted for applicable VARIANCEs. They are those costs sustained in fact, on the basis of costs incurred, as distinguished from projected or estimated costs. The actual cost history of producing the same or a similar product is a fact taken into account when COST ANALYSIS is performed. Actual costs are also used, as a general rule, to establish the amount of an EQUITABLE ADJUSTMENT when it is determined after the work has been performed. See HISTORICAL COST.

ACTUARIAL ASSUMPTION A prediction of future conditions affecting PENSION PLAN costs (such as mortality rate, employee turnover, compensation levels, pension fund earnings, and changes in values of pension funds assets). FAR 31.001. CAS 412, 48 C.F.R. § 9904.412-40(b)(2), provides that, in accounting for pension costs and allocating them to COST OBJECTIVEs, actuarial assumptions must be separately identified and take into account past as well as anticipated experience. It also states that their validity shall be evaluated solely with respect to that assumption. 48 C.F.R. § 9904.412(b)(2).

ACTUARIAL COST METHOD A technique that uses ACTUARIAL ASSUMPTIONs to measure the present value of future pension benefits and pension fund administrative expenses, and that assigns the cost of such benefits and expenses to cost accounting periods. FAR 31.001. Under CAS 412, 48 C.F.R. § 9904.412-40, a cost method used in determining and measuring component costs of a defined-benefit PENSION PLAN must measure separately (1) the normal cost of the cost accounting period, (2) a part of any unfunded ACTUARIAL LIABILITY, (3) an interest equivalent on the unamortized portion of such liability, and (4) an adjustment for any ACTUARIAL GAIN AND LOSS.

ACTUARIAL GAIN AND LOSS The effect on PENSION PLAN costs resulting from differences between ACTUARIAL ASSUMPTIONs and actual experience. FAR 31.001. CAS 413, 48 C.F.R. § 9904.413-20, provides guidance on adjusting pension costs by measuring actuarial gains and losses and assigning them to cost accounting periods. It requires that actuarial gains and losses be (1) calculated annually and assigned to the cost accounting period for which the actual valuation is made and to subsequent periods, and (2) identified separately from unfunded actuarial liabilities. It permits them to be amortized through subsequent pension contributions or offset by gains and losses in subsequent cost accounting periods. 48 C.F.R. § 9904.413-50(a)(1).

ACTUARIAL LIABILITY Pension costs attributable, under the ACTUARIAL COST METHOD in use, to the years preceding the date of a particular actuarial valuation. FAR 31.001. As of such date, the actuarial liability represents the excess of the present value of the future benefits and administrative expenses over the present value of future contributions, for the normal cost for all PENSION PLAN participants and beneficiaries. The excess of the actuarial liability over the value of the assets of a pension plan is the unfunded actuarial liability. Pension plan costs applicable to prior years that were specifically unallowable (see ALLOWABLE COST) under then-existing Government contracts must be separately identified and excluded from unfunded actuarial liability. 48 C.F.R. § 9904.412-50(a)(2).

ADDENDUM An alteration of a SOLICITATION issued by the contracting agency to all potential OFFERORs prior to the time for receipt of BIDs or PROPOSALs. This term is no longer used; the FAR uses the term AMENDMENT.

ADEQUATE COMPETITION The level of competition required to justify AWARD ON INITIAL PROPOSALS in competitive negotiated procurement (see NEGOTIATION) prior to the COMPETITION IN CONTRACTING ACT. In general, this was a sufficient amount of competition to ensure that the award price was a FAIR AND REASONABLE PRICE. The term is no longer used in federal procurement, but the concept of a sufficient amount of competition to ensure fair and reasonable prices is still found in FAR 13.003(b) dealing with the SET-ASIDE of simplified acquisitions for small business.

ADEQUATE EVIDENCE Information sufficient to support the reasonable belief that a particular act or omission has occurred, for purposes of SUSPENSION of a contractor. FAR 9.403. FAR 9.407-1(b) requires agency officials to consider the amount of evidence, its credibility, whether there is corroboration of important allegations, and what inferences can reasonably be drawn.

ADEQUATE PRICE COMPETITION The degree of competition that precludes the contracting officer from obtaining COST OR PRICING DATA under the TRUTH IN NEGOTIATIONS ACT. Adequate price competition can be found in any of three circumstances. FAR 15.403-1(c)(1)(i) provides that adequate price competition exists when (1) two or more responsible (see RESPONSIBILITY) offerors, competing independently, submit priced offers responsive to the SOLICITATION's expressed requirements; (2) award is to be made to the offeror with the greatest value or the lowest evaluated price; and (3) there is no finding that the price is unreasonable. FAR 15.403-1(c)(1)(ii) provides that adequate price competition exists when only one offer was received, if it is determined by the contracting officer and approved at a level above the contracting officer that (1) there was a reasonable expectation, based on MARKET RESEARCH, that two or more responsible offerors, competing independently, would submit priced offers responsive to the solicitation's requirements; and (2) the single offer was submitted in the expectation of competition. FAR 15.403-1(c)(1)(iii) provides that adequate price competition exists when PRICE ANALYSIS clearly demonstrates that a proposed price is reasonable in comparison with current prices or recent prices for the same or similar items purchased in comparable quantities, under comparable terms and conditions of contracts that resulted from adequate price competition. See Cibinic & Nash, chap. 9, Sec. I., *Formation of Government Contracts* (3d ed. 1998).

ADJECTIVAL RATINGS A notational scoring system in which adjectives are used to describe the quality of an offeror's PROPOSAL. Proposals may be rated using such terms as Outstanding, Highly Acceptable, Excellent, Good, Fair, and Poor; or Acceptable, Marginally Acceptable, and Unacceptable. See Cibinic & Nash, chap. 6, Sec. II., *Formation of Government Contracts* (3d ed. 1998); Nash & Cibinic, *Competitive Negotiation: The Source Selection Process* 157–58 (1993). See also COLOR CODING.

ADJUSTMENT An alteration of the contract price to reflect some changed circumstances in the performance of the contract. See EQUITABLE ADJUSTMENT and PRICE ADJUSTMENT.

ADMINISTRATIVE CHANGE A unilateral contract change, in writing, that does not affect the substantive rights of the parties (for example, a change in the paying office or the appropriation data). FAR 43.101. See also MODIFICATION.

ADMINISTRATIVE CONTRACTING OFFICER (ACO) A CONTRACTING OFFICER engaged in administering contracts. FAR 2.101. An ACO does most of his or her work after the PROCURING CONTRACTING OFFICER has awarded the contract but generally does not have the authority to enter into MODIFICATIONs. An ACO functions at and through a contract administration office and performs contract administration functions involving, among other things, contractors' employee compensation structures and insurance plans, postaward orientation, FORWARD PRICING RATE AGREEMENTs, ADVANCE AGREEMENTs, ALLOWABLE COSTs, DISPUTEs, COST ACCOUNTING STANDARDS, PROGRESS PAYMENTs, COST OVERRUNs, modifications, traffic management, tax exemption and duty-free entry certificates, LABOR RELATIONS, QUALITY ASSURANCE, safety requirements, property administration, engineering surveillance, acceptance and rejection of WAIVERs and DEVIATIONs, VALUE ENGINEERING programs, CONTRACTOR PURCHASING SYSTEM REVIEW, consent to subcontracts, and monitoring of small business subcontracting plan compliance. FAR 42.302. A number of agencies do not separate the procuring and administrative contracting officer functions, but hold a single contracting officer responsible for both the award and administration of a contract. See Cibinic & Nash, *Administration of Government Contracts* 34 (3d ed. 1995).

ADMINISTRATIVE DISPUTE RESOLUTION ACT A 1990 Act, 5 U.S.C. § 571 et seq., of five years' duration, that required all federal agencies to adopt a policy favoring the use of ALTERNATIVE DISPUTE RESOLUTION (ADR) procedures, in lieu of litigation, to settle claims and disputes. One such procedure, ARBITRATION, was allowed, for the first time, in situations in which all parties agreed to its use but the Government was given the right to reject the arbitration award. The Act also amended the CONTRACT DISPUTES ACT OF 1978 to authorize contracting officers to use ADR. The Act was made permanent in 1996 by the ADMINISTRATIVE DISPUTE RESOLUTION ACT OF 1996, Pub. L. No. 104-320. At that time the provision permitting arbitration was amended to allow Government agencies to use binding arbitration. See Cibinic, *The Administrative Dispute Resolution Act: Making a Mountain out of a Molehill*, 5 N&CR ¶ 34 (June 1991); Parrette, *The Contract Disputes Act and the Administrative Dispute Resolution Act: A Richness of Remedies, Finally Ready for Trial,* 20 Pub. Cont. L.J. 293 (1991).

ADMINISTRATIVE DISPUTE RESOLUTION ACT OF 1996 A 1996 Act, Pub. L. No. 104-320, that reauthorized ALTERNATIVE DISPUTE RESOLUTION in the federal administrative process. In addition, section 12 of the Act enlarged the BID PROTEST jurisdiction of the U.S. COURT OF FEDERAL CLAIMS, granting the court jurisdiction to hear both pre- and postaward bid protests. Further, section 12 of the Act statutorily provided jurisdiction to the district courts to hear bid protests (see SCANWELL ACTION) until January 1, 2001, unless extended by Congress.

ADMINISTRATIVE JUDGE A member of a BOARD OF CONTRACT APPEALS (BCA) functioning under the CONTRACT DISPUTES ACT (CDA) OF 1978. 41 U.S.C. § 607(b)(1). The term was created by the BCAs and is synonymous with the statutory term "member of an agency board." Commonly confused with the title "administrative law judge" (see Keyes, *Government Contracts Under the Federal Acquisition Regulation* (2d ed. 1997)) the position of administrative judge was created by the CDA under Title 41, not by the Administrative Procedure Act under Title 5. Unlike administrative law judges, the BCAs' administrative judges are contract law specialists with five years or more of public contract law experience and are not subject to reassignment by the Office of Personnel Management. The Commerce Clearing House *Board of Contract Appeals Decisions* includes a loose-leaf binder containing brief biographies of the various administrative judges. [Commerce Clearing House, 4025 West Peterson Avenue, Chicago, IL 60646]

ADMINISTRATIVE SETOFF See SETOFF.

ADVANCE ACQUISITION An exception to the FULL FUNDING policy that allows acquisition of LONG-LEAD-TIME ITEMS (advanced long-lead acquisition) or economic order quantities (see ECONOMIC ORDER QUANTITY) in a FISCAL YEAR previous to that in which the related end item is to be acquired. FAR 17.101. Advance acquisitions may include materials, parts, and components, as well as costs associated with the further processing of those materials, parts, and components. DOD is authorized to make use of this technique in multiyear procurement by 10 U.S.C. § 2306b(h)(2).

ADVANCE AGREEMENT An agreement as to the allowability of costs, negotiated by a contracting officer and a contractor before the costs are incurred. See ALLOWABLE COST. FAR 31.109 provides guidance on the negotiation of such agreements and suggests their use to avoid possible subsequent DISALLOWANCE or DISPUTE based on unreasonableness or nonallocability (see REASONABLENESS OF COST and ALLOCABLE COST) of special or unusual costs. Advance agreements may be negotiated either before or during a contract. The advance agreement must be (1) in writing, (2) executed by both contracting parties, and (3) incorporated into applicable current and future contracts. It must contain a statement of its applicability and duration. Advance agreements may be negotiated with a particular contractor for a single contract, for a group of contracts, or for all contracts with a contracting office, an agency, or several agencies. See Cibinic, *Advance Agreements: What Do the Changes Mean?,* 8 N&CR ¶ 11 (Feb. 1995); Cibinic & Nash, *Cost-Reimbursement Contract* 629–32 (2d ed. 1993).

ADVANCE APPROPRIATION Appropriations that are enacted normally in the current year, scored after the budget year (for example, in each one, two, or more later years, depending on the language), and available for obligation in the year scored and subsequent years if specified in the language. Advance appropriations may be accompanied by regular annual appropriations to provide funds available for obligation in the budget year as well as in subsequent years. See also MULTIYEAR APPROPRIATION. GAO, *Principles of Budgeting for Capital Asset Acquisitions*, 8 Budget of the United States Government, Fiscal Year 1998 (1997).

ADVANCE FUNDING BUDGET AUTHORITY provided in an APPROPRIATION act that allows funds to be obligated or committed to a specific purpose and spent during that FISCAL YEAR even though the appropriation is actually for the next fiscal year. Advance funding generally is used to avoid requests for supplemental appropriations for entitlement programs late in a fiscal year, when the appropriations for the current fiscal year are too low. Jones, *Glossary: Defense Acquisition Acronyms and Terms* (8th ed., Defense Systems Management College).

ADVANCE PAYMENT An advance of money made by the Government to a contractor before costs have been incurred on a contract. Such payments are expected to be liquidated from payments due on the contract or contracts for which they made. FAR 32.102. Agencies may authorize advance payments in negotiated and sealed bid contracts if appropriate under the procurement statutes (41 U.S.C. § 255 and 10 U.S.C. § 2307) or under Pub. L. No. 85-804, 50 U.S.C. §§ 1431–1435, which provides for EXTRAORDINARY CONTRACTUAL ACTIONs. FAR 32.401. Agencies should authorize advance payments sparingly, as they are the least preferred method of contract FINANCING. See FAR 32.402(b). However, advance payments may be appropriate for research and development with educational institutions and for the management and operation of Government-owned plants. FAR 31.403. For advance payments to be authorized, the statutes provide that (1) the contractor must give adequate security, (2) the payments must not exceed the unpaid contract price, and (3) the agency head or a designee must determine that advance payment is in the public interest or facilitates the NATIONAL DEFENSE. FAR 32.402 contains detailed guidance on these requirements. When advance payments are used, the Advance Payments clause in FAR 52.232-12 is required. FAR 32.412. See Cibinic & Nash, *Administration of Government Contracts* 1144–45 (3d ed. 1995).

ADVANCE PROCUREMENT AUTHORITY Authority provided in an appropriations act to obligate and disburse during a FISCAL YEAR from the succeeding year's appropriation. The funds are added to the BUDGET AUTHORITY for the current fiscal year and deducted from the budget authority of the succeeding fiscal year. This may be used in major acquisition programs to obtain components whose long-lead times require purchase early in order to reduce the overall procurement lead time of the major end item. Advance procurement of long-lead components is an exception to the DOD "full funding" policy.

Jones, *Glossary: Defense Acquisition Acronyms and Terms* (8th ed., Defense Systems Management College).

ADVANCE PROCUREMENT PLANNING See ACQUISITION PLANNING.

ADVANCED CONCEPT TECHNOLOGY DEMONSTRATION (ACTD) An acquisition of military hardware using mature technology to demonstrate that an urgent military need can be met. ACTDs are not acquisition programs that have been approved under the procedures of DOD Directive 5000.1, *Defense Acquisition*, Mar. 15, 1996. Thus, if the demonstration shows that the new hardware is effective and the military service determines that additional quantities should be acquired, new approvals must be obtained. See ¶ 2.7 of DOD Regulation 5000.2-R, *Mandatory Procedures for Major Defense Acquisition Programs (MDAPs) and Major Automated Information System (MAIS) Acquisition Programs*, Mar. 15, 1996.

ADVERTISED PROCUREMENT The preferred form of procurement before the passage of the COMPETITION IN CONTRACTING ACT. This term was synonymous with FORMAL ADVERTISING and is now called SEALED BIDDING. See Shnitzer, *Government Contract Bidding* 3-2 through 3-14 (3d ed. 1987 & Supp. 1991).

ADVERTISEMENT Any single message prepared for placement in communications media, regardless of the number of placements. FAR 5.501. FAR Subpart 5.5 provides guidance on the use of paid advertisements by Government agencies as a means of informing potential offerors of contracting opportunities with the Government. NASA does not permit the use of paid advertisements for procurement purposes. NFS 18-5.502. FAR 31.205-1 places strict limitations on the allowability of the ADVERTISING costs incurred by contractors. See ALLOWABLE COST and RECRUITMENT COSTS.

ADVERTISING The use of media to promote the sale of products or services, recruit personnel required for performing contractual obligations, acquire scarce items for contract performance, and dispose of scrap or surplus materials acquired for contract performance. FAR 31.205-1. Advertising media include but are not limited to conventions, exhibits, free goods, samples, magazines, newspapers, trade papers, direct mail, dealer cards, window displays, outdoor advertising, radio, and television. The advertiser must have control over the form and content of what will appear, the media in which it will appear, and the time when it will appear. Advertising costs are allowable in contracts with commercial organizations only when specifically required by the contract or used to recruit personnel for a contract, acquire scarce items, or dispose of scrap. FAR 31.205-1(d). See Cibinic & Nash, *Cost-Reimbursement Contracting* 758–64 (2d ed. 1993).

ADVERTISING MATERIAL Material designed to acquaint the Government with a prospective contractor's present products or potential capabilities, or to determine the Government's interest in buying these products. FAR 15.601. FAR 15.603(b) provides that such materials are not UNSOLICITED PROPOSALs.

ADVISORY AND ASSISTANCE SERVICES Services acquired by contract from non-Governmental sources to support or improve organizational policy development, decisionmaking, management and administration, program and/or project management and administration, or research and development activities. FAR 37.201. Acquisition of advisory and assistance services is a legitimate way to improve Government services and operations. Such services may be used at all organizational levels to help managers achieve maximum effectiveness or economy in their operations. FAR 37.203. However, the acquisition of such services shall not be used to (1) perform work of a policy, decisionmaking or management nature, (2) bypass personnel ceilings or competitive employment practices, (3) give preference to former Government employees, (4) aid or influence legislation, or (5) obtain professional or technical advice that is readily available within the Federal Government. FAR 37.203(c). 41 U.S.C. § 419 also limits the use of advisory and assistance services for the evaluation or analysis of PROPOSALs. See FAR 37.204. Advisory and assistance services may take the form of information, advice, opinions, alternatives, conclusions, recommendations, training, or direct assistance. FAR 37.201. Such services are treated in OMB Circular No. A-120 (revised), *Guidelines for the Use of Advisory and Assistance Services*, Jan. 4, 1988; OFPP Policy Letter No. 89-1, *Conflict of Interest Policies Applicable to Consultants*, Dec. 8, 1989; and DOD Directive 4205.2, *Acquiring and Managing Contracted and Assistance Services*, Feb. 10, 1992. The FEDERAL ACQUISITION STREAMLINING ACT OF 1994 added 10 U.S.C. § 2304b and 41 U.S.C. § 253I, limiting the use of TASK ORDER CONTRACTs for advisory and assistance services. These provisions preclude the award of such contracts for a period longer than five years and require multiple award contracts for contracts that exceed three years in duration or $10,000,000. FAR 16.504(a)(4)(vi) requires the use of the Multiple Awards for Advisory and Assistance Services clause in FAR 52.216-28 when multiple awards will be made.

AEROSPACE INDUSTRIES ASSOCIATION OF AMERICA (AIA) A nonprofit trade association representing the nation's manufacturers of commercial, military, and business aircraft, helicopters, aircraft engines, missiles, spacecraft, and related components and equipment. AIA's professional staff works through councils and committees made up of volunteers from member companies who develop policy on significant issues and present industry's point of view. AIA speaks for industry on such issues as procurement policy, legislative affairs, civil aviation, environmental concerns, technology development, and internationalization of the industry. [AIA, 1250 Eye Street, NW, Suite 1200, Washington, DC 20005; (202) 371-8400]

AFFILIATES Associated business concerns or individuals if, directly or indirectly, (1) either one controls or can control the other or (2) a third party controls or can control both. FAR 2.101. In determining whether a company qualifies as a SMALL BUSINESS CONCERN, the sales and employees of an affiliate are combined with the sales and employees of the company being evaluated. FAR 19.101 contains a detailed definition of this term when it is used to determine the SIZE STATUS of a firm. Purchases from affiliates are MAKE ITEMs rather than BUY ITEMs. Affiliates are also subject to DEBARMENT or SUSPENSION. FAR Subpart 9.4. See Cibinic & Nash, chap. 10, Sec. I., *Formation of Government Contracts* (3d ed. 1998).

AFFILIATION See AFFILIATES.

AFFINITY GROUP In the context of federal INFORMATION TECHNOLOGY, any interagency group focused on a business or technology area with common information technology or customer requirements. The functions of an affinity group can include identifying common program goals and requirements; identifying opportunities for sharing information to improve quality and effectiveness; reducing costs and burden on the public; and recommending protocols and other standards, including security standards, to the National Institute of Standards and Technology for Governmentwide applicability, for action in accordance with the Computer Security Act of 1987, as amended by the Information Technology Act. Exec. Order No. 13011, 61 Fed. Reg. 37657 (July 16, 1996).

AFFIRMATIVE ACTION A contractual requirement under the Equal Opportunity clause, FAR 52.222-26, to take positive steps to ensure that applicants and employees are given equal opportunity without regard to their race, color, religion, sex, or national origin. Detailed requirements for steps to be taken in a company's hiring practices to ensure that their workforce is representative of the local area are set forth in DEPARTMENT OF LABOR (DOL) regulations at 41 C.F.R. § 60-2. Generally, a contractor must (1) make a utilization analysis of its workforce, (2) determine that there is underutilization of minority groups that are not employed in representative percentages, (3) establish a set of goals and timetables to reach representative percentages, and (4) adopt policies for recruitment and training that will assist in achieving the goals. See Cibinic & Nash, chap. 10, Sec. VI., *Formation of Government Contracts* (3d ed. 1998); Heggs et al., *Practitioner's Viewpoint: What to Expect After Adarand*, 25 Pub. Cont. L.J. 451 (1996); Newman & Margery, *Affirmative Action and the Construction Industry*, 25 Pub. Cont. L.J. 433 (1996).

AFFIRMATIVE ACTION PROGRAM A contractor's program that complies with DEPARTMENT OF LABOR regulations in 41 C.F.R. § 60-1 and § 60-4 to ensure equal employment opportunities to minorities and women. FAR 22.801. Under such program a contractor must use best efforts to bring its employment of minorities and women to a level commensurate with the number of minorities and women in the community through AFFIRMATIVE ACTION. Such efforts include establishing employment goals, adopting a timetable for reaching such goals, and recruiting and training minorities and women. See Cibinic & Nash, chap. 10, Sec. VI., *Formation of Government Contracts* (3d ed. 1998).

AGENCY Any executive department, military department or defense agency, or other agency or independent establishment of the executive branch. FAR 9.403. This term has a variety of meanings depending on the context in which it is used. See Cibinic & Nash, chap. 1, Sec. I., *Formation of Government Contracts* (3d ed. 1998). See FAR 24.101 for a slightly different definition of the term.

AGENCY HEAD See HEAD OF THE AGENCY.

AGENCY RECORD A document in the possession of a Government agency that is subject to the provisions of the FREEDOM OF INFORMATION ACT. The Act contains no definition of "agency record," but the term has been interpreted broadly in litigation. See Nash & Rawicz, *Intellectual Property in Government Contracts*, vol. 3, 164–83 (3d ed. 1997).

AGENCY-PECULIAR PROPERTY Government-owned personal property that is peculiar to the mission of one agency. FAR 45.301. DFARS 245.301 defines the term as used in DOD; NFS 18-45.301, as used by NASA. Agency-peculiar material excludes Government material, SPECIAL TEST EQUIPMENT, SPECIAL TOOLING, and FACILITIES.

AGGREGATION See BUNDLING.

AGREEMENT A written instrument of understanding, negotiated between an agency or contracting activity and a contractor, containing contract clauses that will apply to future contracts. See FAR Subpart 16.7. The two types of agreements described in the FAR are BASIC AGREEMENTs and BASIC ORDERING AGREEMENTs (BOAs). Agreements are not contracts that are legally binding on the parties because the Government makes no promise to purchase any supplies or services. However, agreements facilitate the making of future contracts because they spell out all standard TERMS AND CONDITIONS of such future contracts.

AIR FREIGHT FORWARDER An indirect air carrier that is responsible for the transportation of property, from the point of receipt to the point of destination, and utilizes for the whole or any part of such transportation the services of a direct air carrier or its agent, or of another air freight forwarder. FAR 47.401. Agencies may use air freight forwarders that are engaged in international air transportation for U.S. Government-financed movements of property. See FAR 47.404.

ALL-DISPUTES CLAUSE A disputes clause that gives the BOARDs OF CONTRACT APPEALS (BCAs) jurisdiction to hear all disputes "RELATING TO THE CONTRACT." The current Disputes clause in FAR 52.233-1 is an all-disputes clause. The adoption of such a clause was one of the major innovations included in the CONTRACT DISPUTES ACT OF 1978. Its main benefit is that it precludes the contractor from having to file CLAIMs on one contract in both the agency BCA and the court (called FRAGMENTATION OF REMEDIES).

ALLOCABLE COST A cost that is assignable or chargeable to one or more COST OBJECTIVEs in accordance with the relative benefits received or other equitable relationships defined or agreed upon by contractual parties. FAR 31.201-4 provides that a cost is allocable to a Government contract if it (1) is incurred specifically for the contract, (2) benefits both the contract and other work and can be distributed in reasonable proportion to the benefits received, or (3) is necessary to the overall operation of the business, although a direct relationship to any particular cost objective cannot be shown. See generally Cibinic & Nash, *Cost-Reimbursement Contracting* 658–726 (2d ed. 1993). See Cibinic, *Confusion Between Allocability and Allowability*, 5 N&CR ¶ 14 (Mar. 1991).

ALLOCATED CONFIGURATION IDENTIFICATION (ACI) A DOD term for currently approved performance-oriented specifications governing the development of CONFIGURATION ITEMs (CIs) that are part of a higher-level CI, in which each specification defines the functional characteristics that are allocated from those of the higher-level CI; establishes the tests required to demonstrate achievement of its allocated functional characteristics; delineates necessary interface requirements with other CIs; and establishes design constraints, if any, such as component or part standardization, use of inventory items, and logistic support requirements. Jones, *Glossary: Defense Acquisition Acronyms and Terms* (8th ed., Defense Systems Management College).

ALLOCATION BASE A numerical measure to which costs can be assigned in a methodical fashion from an indirect pool to COST OBJECTIVEs. CAS 410, 48 C.F.R. § 9904.410-40, provides guidance on the calculation of the allocation base for GENERAL AND ADMINISTRATIVE EXPENSEs, stating a preference for a cost input base. See Lynch, *Allocation of Home Office Expenses to Segments and Business Unit G&A Expenses Final Cost Objectives*, 22 Pub. Cont. L.J. 339 (1993).

ALLOCATION OF COST The assignment of an item of cost, or a group of items of cost, to one or more COST OBJECTIVEs; the term includes both direct assignment of cost and the reassignment of a share from an INDIRECT COST POOL. FAR 31.001. Substantial guidance on the proper allocation of costs is contained in the COST ACCOUNTING STANDARDS at 48 C.F.R. chap. 99. See ALLOCABLE COST. See also Cibinic & Nash, *Cost-Reimbursement Contracting* 658–726 (2d ed. 1993); Schooner, *Allowability Versus Allocability of Government and Administrative Expenses: Recent Guidance from the Federal Circuit*, Army Law. 60 (Oct. 1994).

ALLOCATION OF FUNDS In DOD, the process by which the Assistant Secretary of Defense (Comptroller) subdivides APPORTIONMENTs among the Secretaries of the military departments, by which the Secretaries further subdivide the funds among their heads of operating agencies, and by which the heads of operating agencies in turn subdivide (suballocate) the funds among their subordinate commanders. Hill, *The Dollars and Sense of Government Contract Funding*, 1988 A.B.A. Sec. Pub. Cont. L. 54-55.

ALLOCATION OF WORK The assignment of work to a source without following the normal competitive processes. FAR Subpart 8.7 requires the allocation of certain specified work to nonprofit agencies for the BLIND OR SEVERELY DISABLED.

ALLOTMENT In DOD, the process by which commanders, major commanders, or special operating agencies distribute their allocated funds (see ALLOCATION OF FUNDS) to themselves, to installation commanders, or to other subordinate organizations. This process may continue into as many suballotments as necessary. Hill, *The Dollars and Sense of Government Contract Funding*, 1988 A.B.A. Sec. Pub. Cont. L. 55.

ALLOWABLE COST A cost that the Government will permit to be recovered (reimbursed by the Government) for the performance of a contract. FAR 31.201-2 provides that the factors to be considered in determining whether a cost is allowable include (1) reasonableness (see REASONABLENESS OF COST), (2) allocability (see ALLOCABLE COST), (3) standards promulgated by the COST ACCOUNTING STANDARDS BOARD, (4) GENERALLY ACCEPTED ACCOUNTING PRINCIPLES and practices appropriate to the particular circumstances, (5) the terms of the contract, and (6) any limitations set forth in FAR Subpart 31.2. FAR 31.205 contains detailed guidance on the allowability of 52 categories of "selected costs." Costs, including directly associated costs, that are expressly unallowable must be identified and excluded from any billing, claim, or proposal applicable to a Government contract. FAR 31.201-6. See 10 U.S.C. § 2324 and 41 U.S.C. § 256 for special rules and sanctions that apply to allowable costs. See generally Cibinic & Nash, chap. 5, *Cost-Reimbursement Contracting* (2d ed. 1993). See also Cibinic, *Allocability and Allowability: More Alphabet Confusion in the Federal Circuit*, 8 N&CR ¶ 15 (Mar. 1994); Cibinic, *Confusion Between Allocability and Allowability*, 5 N&CR ¶ 14 (Mar. 1991).

ALTERNATIVE DISPUTE RESOLUTION (ADR) Any procedure or combination of procedures voluntarily used, in lieu of litigation, to resolve issues in controversy, including but not limited to settlement negotiations, conciliation, facilitation, MEDIATION, fact finding,

MINITRIALs, and ARBITRATION. FAR 33.201. ADR is used when the contracting officer and the contractor cannot resolve a dispute through normal contracting procedures. These techniques are now recognized and encouraged by the ADMINISTRATIVE DISPUTE RESOLUTION ACT, 5 U.S.C. §§ 571–584, as implemented by FAR Subpart 33.2. See Dauber, *The Ties that Bind: Nonbinding Arbitration in Federal Administrative Agencies*, 9 Admin. L.J. Am. U. 165 (1995). The techniques are intended to resolve disputes without the time, expense, and cost of formal litigation, whether before a court or an agency BOARD OF CONTRACT APPEALS. ADR is sometimes called alternate dispute resolution. It includes any alternative to full-scale litigation, whether mandatory or voluntary, binding or nonbinding, structured or unstructured. ADR is often conducted with the understanding that the record of the proceeding will be kept confidential and that—if the selected method's conclusions are not acceptable to either party—the normal litigation process may be begun or resumed. See Gomez et al., *ADR in Government Contracting: Trend or Revolution?*, 39 Gov't Contractor ¶ 210 (Apr. 30, 1997); Shapiro & Rumbaugh, *Alternative Dispute Resolution: Recent Initiatives and Techniques for the Professional*, 37 Cont. Mgmt. 4 (Jan. 1997); Nash, *Alternative Dispute Resolution: When Should It Be Done?*, 10 N&CR ¶ 26 (June 1996); Arnavas & Hornyak, *Alternative Dispute Resolution/Ed. II*, 96-11 Briefing Papers (Oct. 1996); MacPherson, *In Your Face ADR: New York City's Construction Contract Dispute Procedure*, 25 Pub. Cont. L.J. 301 (1996); Reba & Jockisch, *The Corps of Engineers Board of Contract Appeals Use of Alternative Dispute Resolution*, 24 Pub. Cont. L.J. 453 (1995); McMichael & Sheridan, *Federal Push for Alternative Dispute Resolution*, 31 Procrmt. Law. 3 (Fall 1995); Mackey, *ADR Can Banish Due Process From Public Contract Disputes*, 30 Procrmt. Law. 3 (Sum. 1995); Rosenberg & Folberg, *Alternative Dispute Resolution: An Empirical Analysis*, 46 Stan. L. Rev. 1487 (July 1994); Lamari, *The Role of Alternative Dispute Resolution in Government Construction Contract Disputes*, 23 Hofstra L. Rev. 205 (1994); Cibinic, *Alternative Dispute Resolution: The Nitty Gritty*, 7 N&CR ¶ 67 (Dec. 1993); Nash, *Alternative Dispute Resolution: An Update*, 7 N&CR ¶ 25 (May 1993); Cibinic, *The Alternative Dispute Resolution Act: Making a Mountain out of a Molehill*, 5 N&CR ¶ 34 (June 1991); Brittin, *Alternative Dispute Resolution in Government Contract Appeals*, 19 Pub. Cont. L.J. 210 (1990); Arnavas & Duffy, *Alternative Dispute Resolution*, 88-8 Briefing Papers (July 1988); Page & Lees, *Roles of Participants in the Mini-Trial*, 18 Pub. Cont. L.J. 54 (1988); Administrative Conference of the United States, *Sourcebook: Federal Agency Use of Alternative Means of Dispute Resolution* (Office of the Chairman, 1987).

ALTERNATIVE SOURCE SELECTION PROCEDURES Procedures, used by a Government agency to solicit COMPETITIVE PROPOSALS, that do not conform to the detailed requirements of the FAR. This term was used in FAR 15.613 prior to FAC 97-02, September 30, 1997. It is no longer used in the FAR but FAR 15.101 permits using "any one or a combination of source selection approaches." See DOD "Four Step" procedure in DFARS 215.613-70. Generally, these procedures provide for limited discussion with offerors prior to SOURCE SELECTION and NEGOTIATION with the winning contractor after selection.

AMBIGUITY Contract language that is capable of being understood to have more than one meaning. The test for determining whether the language is ambiguous is whether reasonable persons would find the contract subject to more than one interpretation. A PATENT AMBIGUITY is obvious, since it arises from defective, contradictory, obscure, or senseless language. In contrast, a LATENT AMBIGUITY arises from language that appears clear and intelligible but that—because of some extrinsic fact or extraneous evidence—requires interpretation or a choice between two or more possible meanings. *Black's Law Dictionary* 79–80 (6th ed. 1990). See also CONTRA PROFERENTEM. Contractors frequently receive EQUITABLE ADJUSTMENTs for latent ambiguities, but they are held to a DUTY TO SEEK CLARIFICATION of patent ambiguities. See Cibinic & Nash, chap. 2, *Administration of Government Contracts* (3d ed. 1995), for complete guidance on the process of contract interpretation. See also Nash, *Postscript: Contractor Reliance When Specifications Are Ambiguous*, 8 N&CR ¶ 28 (May 1994); Nash, *Ambiguities: They Can't Be Proved by Subsequent Clarification of the Language*, 5 N&CR ¶ 25 (May 1991); Gottleib, *Latent & Patent Conditions*, 27 Cont. Mgmt. 20 (Aug. 1987).

AMENDMENT An alteration to a SOLICITATION. FAR 14.208, FAR 15.206. The FAR distinguishes between amendments and MODIFICATIONs: amendments alter solicitations and modifications alter contracts. Standard Form 30, Amendment of Solicitation/Modification of Contract, FAR 53.301-30, must be used to change sealed bid solicitations, FAR 14.208(a), and may be used to change negotiated solicitations, FAR 15.210. Detailed instructions on the proper response upon receipt of an amendment are set forth in the solicitation provisions Amendments to Invitation for Bids in FAR 52.214-3 and Instructions to Offerors—Competitive Acquisition in FAR 52.215-1. In normal legal terminology an amendment is a formal legal document altering a contract by mutual agreement (hence signed by both parties). FAR 43.103 discusses such documents using the terms "bilateral modification" (see MODIFICATION) and SUPPLEMENTAL AGREEMENT. See Cibinic & Nash, chaps. 5, Sec. I. & chap. 6, Sec. III., *Formation of Government Contracts* (3d ed. 1998); Cibinic, *Sealed Bidding: Constructive Receipt of Amendments*, 11 N&CR ¶ 4 (Jan. 1997).

AMENDMENT WITHOUT CONSIDERATION A contract alteration that benefits the contractor but contains no CONSIDERATION to the Government. Authority to make such alterations is conferred by Pub. L. No. 85-804, 50 U.S.C. §§ 1431–1435, as implemented by Exec. Order No. 10789, 23 Fed. Reg. 8897 (Nov. 14, 1958), as amended. Procedures for use of this authority are set forth in FAR Part 50, EXTRAORDINARY CONTRACTUAL ACTION.

AMERICAN INSTITUTE OF ARCHITECTS (AIA) A national professional society, founded in 1857, whose members are licensed architects, graduate architects, and retired architects. AIA promotes design excellence and fosters professionalism and accountability through professional development programs and achievement awards. It also maintains a 30,000-volume library and publishes reference books and standard documents on legal, contract, and accounting forms. The organization maintains a Government Affairs department. [AIA, 1735 New York Avenue, N.W., Washington, DC 20006; (202) 626-7300]

AMERICAN SOCIETY OF CIVIL ENGINEERS (ASCE) A national professional society of engineers founded in 1852. ASCE supports research, offers continuing education courses and technical specialty conferences, and presents achievement awards. It also offers bibliographic information retrieval services. [ASCE, 345 E. 47th Street, New York, NY 10017; (212) 705-7496]

AMERICAN SUBCONTRACTORS ASSOCIATION (ASA) A national trade association, founded in 1966, whose members are construction subcontractors of trades and specialties such as foundations, concrete, masonry, steel, mechanical, drywall, electrical, painting, plastering, roofing, and acoustical. ASA works with other segments of the construction industry to promote ethical practices, beneficial legislation, and business education. It maintains a Government Relations committee. [ASA, 1004 Duke Street, Alexandria, VA 22314; (703) 684-3450]

AMORTIZATION An accounting procedure that gradually reduces the cost value of a limited-life or intangible asset through periodic charges to income. *Barron's Finance and Investment Handbook* (3d ed. 1990). When the purchase method of accounting for a BUSINESS COMBINATION is used, allowable amortization is limited to the amounts that would have been allowed had the combination not taken place. FAR 31.205-52. In measuring and allocating the COST OF CAPITAL COMMITTED TO FACILITIES in accordance with CAS 414, 48 C.F.R. § 9904.414, contractors must take into account INTANGIBLE CAPITAL ASSETs subject to amortization.

ANNOUNCEMENT OF OPPORTUNITY (AO) A NASA BROAD AGENCY ANNOUNCEMENT generally used to solicit PROPOSALs for on-board flight experiments. Special proposal preparation, evaluation, and selection regulations are found in NFS Subpart 18-72.3, NASA Acquisitions of Investigations. AOs are publicized in the same manner as other solicitations and also through a mailing list maintained by the Office of Space Science and Applications, Code S, at NASA Headquarters.

ANNUAL APPROPRIATION See APPROPRIATION.

ANNUAL FUNDING The current congressional practice of including in authorizations and APPROPRIATIONs authority and funds to cover the needs of an agency for only one fiscal year at a time. FAR 17.101. This practice is used, with rare exceptions, for all types of appropriations. It can lead to inefficient procurement on a year-to-year basis but can be overcome by the use of OPTIONs, multiple year contracting (see MULTIPLE YEAR CONTRACT) or MULTIYEAR CONTRACTING. See GAO, *Principles of Federal Appropriations Law*, vol. I, chap. 2 (2d ed. 1991).

ANNUAL RECEIPTS The average annual gross revenue of a concern. In some instances, the qualification of a company as a SMALL BUSINESS CONCERN is determined by its annual receipts. For companies in business over three years, the amount is determined by averaging the receipts for the last three fiscal years. For a company in business for less than three complete fiscal years, total receipts for the period it has been in business are divided by the number of weeks including fractions of a week that it has been in business, and multiplied by 52. FAR 19.101 contains a detailed definition of the types of revenues that are included in annual receipts. See also STANDARD

INDUSTRIAL CLASSIFICATION. See Cibinic & Nash, chap. 10, Sec. I., *Formation of Government Contracts* (3d ed. 1998).

ANSWER In a contract DISPUTE, a formal pleading presented to a court by the DEFENDANT, or to a BOARD OF CONTRACT APPEALS by the RESPONDENT, in response to a COMPLAINT filed by the PLAINTIFF, or appellant (see APPELLANT BEFORE BOARD OF CONTRACT APPEALS and APPELLANT BEFORE FEDERAL CIRCUIT COURT OF APPEALS). This statement is normally filed by the Government because the plaintiff, or appellant, is normally the contractor.

ANTICIPATORY REPUDIATION Statements or acts of a contractor before an actual BREACH OF CONTRACT that indicate that the contractor does not intend or is unable to complete, or continue to perform under, the contract. *Black's Law Dictionary* 93 (6th ed. 1990). Anticipatory repudiation is sometimes called "anticipatory breach." It will generally not be found unless the contractor, by statements, actions, or refusal to provide adequate assurance of performance, clearly manifests the intention not to perform. Generally in this case the Government need not wait for the performance period to run in order to terminate the contract for default (see TERMINATION FOR DEFAULT). See Cibinic & Nash, *Administration of Government Contracts* 953–54 (3d ed. 1995); Cibinic, *Anticipatory Repudiation: We're Out of Here*, 5 N&CR ¶ 15 (Mar. 1991); U.C.C. § 2-610, § 2-611.

ANTI DEFICIENCY ACT A statute prohibiting Government agencies from obligating the Government, by contract or otherwise, in excess of or in advance of appropriations, unless authorized by some specific statute. Codified at 31 U.S.C. § 1341 et seq. since 1982, the Act prevents Government employees from involving the Government in expenditures or liabilities beyond those contemplated and authorized by Congress. As a result, the Government uses clauses such as the Limitation of Cost clause at FAR 52.232-20 to limit its liability in COST-REIMBURSEMENT CONTRACTs. Government officers and employees can be fined or imprisoned for violating the Act. The Act's salient features include (1) prohibitions against authorizing or incurring obligations or expenditures in excess of amounts apportioned by the OFFICE OF MANAGEMENT AND BUDGET (OMB) or permitted by agency regulations and (2) establishment of procedures for determining responsibility for violations and for reporting them to the Congress and, through OMB, to the President. Jones, *Glossary: Defense Acquisition Acronyms and Terms* (8th ed., Defense Systems Management College).

See GAO, *Principle of Federal Appropriations Law*, chap. 6, vol. II, Part C (2d ed. 1991); Cibinic, *The Anti-Deficiency Act and Implied Warranty of Specifications: Strange Bedfellows*, 3 N&CR ¶ 8 (Jan. 1989).

ANTI-KICKBACK ACT OF 1986 An Act, 41 U.S.C. §§ 51–58, to deter subcontractors from making payments and contractors from accepting payments for the purpose of improperly obtaining or rewarding favorable treatment. FAR 3.502-2. The Act prohibits any person from providing KICKBACKs, soliciting kickbacks, or including the amount of the kickback in the contract price. It imposes criminal penalties for engaging in these prohibited practices, provides for recovery of civil penalties by the United States, requires the reporting of suspected violations, and calls for the inclusion of contract provisions regarding the Act. FAR 3.502-2. The Act is implemented through the use of the Anti-Kickback Procedures clause in FAR 52.203-7. See Arnavas, *The New Anti-Kickback Act*, 87-9 Briefing Papers (Aug. 1987). See also COPELAND ANTI-KICKBACK ACT.

ANTI-LOBBYING ACT A 1919 Act, 18 U.S.C. § 1913, providing that no money appropriated by Congress may be used to pay for any personal service, ADVERTISEMENT, communication, or other device intended or designed to influence a member of Congress to favor or oppose any legislation or APPROPRIATION. The Act does not prohibit requests, through proper official channels, for legislation and appropriations deemed necessary for the efficient conduct of the public business. The Act includes criminal fines and imprisonment as penalties for violations. The BYRD AMENDMENT, an Act passed in 1989, prohibits the use of appropriated funds to influence Government personnel (in both the legislative and executive branches). This Act, implemented in FAR Subpart 3.8, requires certifications and disclosures on contracts exceeding $100,000. See also LOBBYING COSTS.

ANTITRUST VIOLATION A violation of a U.S. law intended to ensure that markets operate competitively. 10 U.S.C. § 2305(b)(9) and 41 U.S.C. § 253b(i) require that such violations be reported to the Attorney General. Any agreement or mutual understanding among competing firms that restrains the natural operation of market forces is suspect. FAR 3.303. See Kovacic, *Expanded Antitrust Scrutiny Requires Greater Caution*, 30 Procmt. Law. 23 (Sri. 1995); Chierichella & Perry, *Mergers & Acquisitions of Government Contractors: Special Considerations & Due Diligence Concerns*, 23 Pub. Cont. L.J. 471 (1994); Yao & DeSanti, *Antitrust Analysis of Defense Industry Mergers*,

23 Pub. Cont. L.J. 379 (1994); Hershey, *Avoiding Antitrust Problems: A Guide for Government Contractors*, 34 Cont. Mgmt. 4 (Jan. 1994); Kattan, *The Declining Defense Sector & Federal Antitrust Enforcement*, 23 Pub. Cont. L.J. 21 (1993); Nash, *Postscript: Antitrust Violations in Government Contracting*, 7 N&CR ¶ 4 (Jan. 1993); Kovacic, *The Antitrust Government Contracts Handbook*, 1990 A.B.A. Sec. of Antitrust L.; Nash, *Antitrust Violations in Government Contracting*, 3 N&CR ¶ 66 (Sept. 1989); Eger, *Contractor Team Arrangements under the Antitrust Laws*, 17 Pub. Cont. L.J. 595 (1988); Dameron & Sherry, *Son of Scanwell: Antitrust Challenges to Government Contracts Awards and Related Actions*, 17 Pub. Cont. L.J. 500 (1988). See CLAYTON ACT; SHERMAN ACT.

APPARENT AUTHORITY Obvious, evident, or manifest authority that a reasonably prudent person, using diligence and discretion, would, in view of a principal's conduct, naturally suppose the principal's agent to possess. *Black's Law Dictionary* 96 (6th ed. 1990). The Federal Government is not bound by unauthorized agents with apparent authority; only properly designated CONTRACTING OFFICERs, or their representatives acting within the limits of their designated authority, can obligate the Government. Therefore, anyone dealing with the Government should ascertain whether a person who purports to act for the Government has the authority to do so, and not rely on a mere appearance of authority. However, BOARDs OF CONTRACT APPEALS and courts have frequently found that Government employees have IMPLIED AUTHORITY. See Cibinic & Nash, *Administration of Government Contracts* 30–47 (3d ed. 1995).

APPARENT CLERICAL MISTAKE See CLERICAL MISTAKE.

APPEAL FILE A file containing all documents pertaining to a DISPUTE, which Uniform Rule 4 (see UNIFORM RULES) requires the CONTRACTING OFFICER to assemble. Frequently called the RULE 4 FILE, it represents one of the more significant differences between appeals before a BOARD OF CONTRACT APPEALS (BCA) and litigation before the U.S. COURT OF FEDERAL CLAIMS. The Rule 4 procedure, applying only to BCA appeals, is intended to make all pertinent documents immediately available to the contractor and the BCA. The rule gives the contractor an opportunity to supplement this appeal file. Rule 4 requires and encourages both parties to present relevant documents in support of their respective cases and facilitates the production of documents as an aid to further discovery. It operates as an automatic, first-round discovery order without eliminating customary discovery proceedings; documents contained in the appeal file are considered, without further action by the parties, as part of the record on which the BCA will render its decision. See Federal Bar Ass'n, *Manual for Practice Before the Boards of Contract Appeals* III-C (1981).

APPEAL FROM A CONTRACTING OFFICER'S DECISION The document that a contractor must file before a BOARD OF CONTRACT APPEALS (BCA) to obtain review of a DECISION OF THE CONTRACTING OFFICER. Contractors must file their appeals with the agency BCA and furnish a copy to the contracting officer within 90 days of receiving a contracting officer's decision. 41 U.S.C. § 606; FAR 33.211. The notice of appeal should include (1) a statement of intent to appeal, (2) reference to a contract and the agency involved so that the BCA can identify the DISPUTE, and (3) signature by an AUTHORIZED REPRESENTATIVE. GENERAL SERVICES ADMINISTRATION BOARD OF CONTRACT APPEALS (GSBCA) Rule 5 directs the contractor to include also "a brief account of the circumstances giving rise to the appeal." The contractor may begin an appeal on the basis of DEEMED DENIAL jurisdiction; if the contracting officer fails to render a decision within 60 days of a CLAIM, the CONTRACT DISPUTES ACT OF 1978 deems that the contracting officer has denied the claim, and the contractor may appeal. 41 U.S.C. § 605(c)(5). In lieu of appealing to the BCA, the contractor may bring a DIRECT ACCESS suit within 12 months in the U.S. COURT OF FEDERAL CLAIMS. See Cibinic & Nash, *Administration of Government Contracts* 1304–16 (3d ed. 1995); Cibinic, *Appealing Contracting Officer Decisions: Starting Off With a "Clean Slate,"* 8 N&CR ¶ 43 (July 1994). See also COMPLAINT.

APPEAL FROM THE RULING OF A COURT OR BOARD A document, filed by either the contractor or the Government, requesting that the U.S. COURT OF APPEALS FOR THE FEDERAL CIRCUIT review a decision of a BOARD OF CONTRACT APPEALS (BCA) or of the U.S. COURT OF FEDERAL CLAIMS. A BCA's decision is final unless either the HEAD OF THE AGENCY (with prior approval of the Attorney General) or a contractor appeals the decision within 120 days after receipt of a copy. 41 U.S.C. § 607. Appeals from rulings of the U.S. COURT OF FEDERAL CLAIMS must be filed within 60 days. 28 U.S.C. § 2107. Under the EQUAL ACCESS TO JUSTICE ACT, 5 U.S.C. § 504, the Government cannot appeal a BCA's award of ATTORNEY'S FEES.

APPELLANT BEFORE BOARD OF CONTRACT APPEALS The contractor who files an APPEAL FROM A CONTRACTING OFFICER'S DECISION before a BOARD OF CONTRACT APPEALS (BCA). Since all appeals are from a DECISION OF THE CONTRACTING OFFICER, regardless of whether the DISPUTE arises from a contractor or a Government CLAIM, the contractor is always the appellant. The Government thus becomes the RESPONDENT. In spite of the use of these titles, the Board conducts a DE NOVO review of the dispute. The contractor, or appellant, may be represented before the BCA by an attorney, by a corporate officer, or, in some instances, by himself or herself. See, for example, ARMED SERVICES BOARD OF CONTRACT APPEALS Rule 26. Sole-proprietor contractors can handle their own appeals, partnerships can be represented by a partner, and corporations can be represented by a corporate officer. Of course, any of these types of contractors may retain an attorney, provided that the attorney has been admitted to practice in a state's highest court.

APPELLANT BEFORE FEDERAL CIRCUIT COURT OF APPEALS The party bringing an appeal before the U.S. COURT OF APPEALS FOR THE FEDERAL CIRCUIT, the court authorized by the CONTRACT DISPUTES ACT OF 1978 to review the decisions of the BOARDs OF CONTRACT APPEALS or the U.S. COURT OF FEDERAL CLAIMS. The appellant must have been one of the litigants in the forum from which the appeal is taken. If the appellant is the Government, it will be represented by the DEPARTMENT OF JUSTICE, even if agency counsel represented it before the Board or the U.S. Court of Federal Claims.

APPLICABLE CONDITIONS Those conditions that could significantly affect an acquisition, such as requirements for compatibility with existing or future systems or programs and any cost, schedule, and capability or performance constraints. FAR 7.105(a)(2). Applicable conditions are a mandatory element of the ACQUISITION PLAN prepared by the CONTRACTING OFFICER, and they identify the constraints that must be imposed on the end product of the procurement. Precise identification of such constraints early in the procurement process enables the agency to explore options to reduce or eliminate them if they appear detrimental to the planned procurement. Many constraints, however, must be accepted as an inherent element of a procurement. Nash & Cibinic, *Competitive Negotiation: The Source Selection Process* 23–24 (1993).

APPLIED RESEARCH An effort that (1) normally follows BASIC RESEARCH but may not be severable from it; (2) attempts to determine and exploit the potential of scientific discoveries or improvements in technology, materials, processes, methods, devices or techniques; and (3) attempts to advance the state of the art. FAR 35.001. Applied research does not include DEVELOPMENT—those efforts whose principal aim is design, development, or test of specific items or services to be considered for sale. However, applied research generally attempts to find practical applications for the results of basic research.

APPORTIONMENT A periodic distribution made by the OFFICE OF MANAGEMENT AND BUDGET of amounts available for OBLIGATION in an APPROPRIATION or fund account. Apportionments divide amounts available for obligation by specific time periods (usually quarters), activities, projects, or objects, or by a combination of these. The amounts so apportioned limit the amount of obligations that may be incurred during the SEGMENT. Apportionment is intended to prevent the need for deficiency or supplemental appropriations and to ensure that there is no need for drastic curtailment of the activity for which the appropriation is made. That is, apportionment should prevent an agency from spending its entire appropriation before the end of the FISCAL YEAR and requiring Congress to grant an additional appropriation or else allow activity to grind to a halt. GAO, *Principles of Federal Appropriations Law*, vol. II, chap. 6, Part C (2d ed. 1991).

APPROPRIATED FUNDS Funds made available by Congress for specified purposes, including formation of contracts.

APPROPRIATION An act of Congress permitting federal agencies to incur OBLIGATIONs and to make payments out of the Treasury for specified purposes. Appropriation acts make funds available for obligation for one FISCAL YEAR (annual appropriations), for a specified number of years (multiyear appropriations), or for an unlimited period (no-year appropriations). General appropriations are for broad categories of work (such as research and development, procurement, operation and maintenance), while specific appropriations are for specific projects (most frequently construction projects). Contractors are limited by the amounts in a specific appropriation but not by those in a general appropriation. See 31 U.S.C. § 1301 et seq.; GAO, *Principles of Federal Appropriations Law*, vol. I, chap. 2 (2d ed. 1991). An appropriation bill is a measure before a legislative body to authorize the expenditure of public moneys and to stipulate the amount, manner, and purpose of the various items of expenditure. *Black's Law Dictionary*

101–2 (6th ed. 1990). See Cibinic & Nash, chap. 1, Sec. II., *Formation of Government Contracts* (3d ed. 1998); Manos, *The Antideficiency Act Without an M Account: Reasserting Constitutional Control*, 23 Pub. Cont. L.J. 337 (1994); Efros, *Statutory Restrictions on Funding of Government Contracts*, 10 Pub. Cont. L.J. 254 (1978).

APPROVAL A contracting officer's written notification to a contractor that the Government agrees with a proposed course of conduct. FAR 9.301 defines this term as it relates to the acceptance of test results when the contract requires FIRST ARTICLE TESTING.

APPROVED PURCHASING SYSTEM A contractor's purchasing system that has been reviewed and approved in accordance with the CONTRACTOR PURCHASING SYSTEM REVIEW. FAR 44.101. A contractor with an approved purchasing system is required to get far less prior consent of the contracting officer for subcontracts that it issues during contract performance. See FAR 44.201.

APPROVING AUTHORITY An agency official or contract adjustment board authorized to approve EXTRAORDINARY CONTRACTUAL ACTIONs under Pub. L. No. 85-804, 50 U.S.C. § 1431 et seq., and Exec. Order No. 10789, 23 Fed. Reg. 8897 (Nov. 14, 1958), as amended. FAR 50.001.

ARBITRATION A dispute resolution technique whereby parties voluntarily refer disputes to an impartial third party (an arbitrator or panel of arbitrators, typically made up of experts in the field) for a decision based on the presentation of evidence and arguments. Arbitration frequently proves more expeditious and less expensive than litigation. In binding arbitration, the parties agree in advance to be bound by the arbitrator's determination and award. Nonbinding arbitration differs in that the parties may consider the determination a recommendation rather than a final judgment. Arbitration, binding and nonbinding, has frequently been used between contractors and subcontractors. The Government, however, was not permitted to use binding arbitration (31 U.S.C. § 3702(a); 8 Comp. Gen. 96 (1928)) until 1990, when such use was authorized by the ADMINISTRATIVE DISPUTE RESOLUTION ACT (with the proviso that the HEAD OF THE AGENCY be permitted to vacate any arbitration award). 5 U.S.C. § 580(c). The Act was amended in 1996 to permit an agency to use binding arbitration after the head of the agency, in consultation with the Attorney General, has issued guidance. 5 U.S.C. § 575(c). See Hoffman, *Mandatory Arbitration: Alternative Dispute Resolution or*

Coercive Dispute Suppression?, 17 Berkeley J. Empl. & Lab L. 131 (1996); Deen, *Arbitration Improves the Justice System*, 50 Disp. Resol. J. 57 (Jan. 1995); Gibbens et al., *Recent Developments: The Uniform Arbitration Act*, 1995 J. Disp. 383 (1995); Zielke, *Arbitrating Miller Act Claims and Problems in Enforcing an Award Under the Federal Arbitration Act*, 24 Pub. Cont. L.J. 401 (1995); Turian, *Drafting Fee Arbitration Provisions*, 40 Prac. Law. 23 (Dec. 1994); Bernstein, *Understanding the Limits of Court-Connected ADR: A Critique of Federal Court-Annexed Arbitrant Programs*, 141 U. Pa. L. Rev. 2169 (June 1993); Lee, *Hiring the Cheapest Piper: Arbitration of Subcontract Disputes by Boards of Contract Appeals*, 34 Pub. Cont. L.J. 105 (1993); Margulies, chap. 14, *Construction Contracting* 1021–72 (1991); Behre, *Arbitration: A Permissible or Desirable Method for Resolving Disputes Involving Federal Acquisition and Assistance Contracts?,* 16 Pub. Cont. L.J. 66 (1986). See also ALTERNATIVE DISPUTE RESOLUTION.

ARCHITECT-ENGINEER (A-E) CONTRACT A Government contract for ARCHITECT-ENGINEER SERVICES. Such contracts are entered into using special SOURCE SELECTION procedures as required by the BROOKS ACT (ARCHITECT-ENGINEER PROCUREMENT). See FAR Subpart 36.6. These procedures are conducted in two phases. In the first phase, the agency prepares a "final selection list" of firms, in order of preference, that are considered the most qualified to perform the services based on all relevant criteria except the fee to be paid for the services. In the second phase, the contracting officer negotiates the contract with the most preferred firm on the selection list. If a satisfactory contract cannot be negotiated with this firm, the contracting officer is then permitted to negotiate with the next in the rankings. See Cibinic & Nash, chap. 7, Sec. III., *Formation of Government Contracts* (3d ed. 1998); Braude, chap. 15, *Construction Contracting* (1991); Ness & Medill-Jones, *A-E Government Contracts*, 88-11 Constr. Briefings (Oct. 1988).

ARCHITECT-ENGINEER (A-E) SERVICES Services in the field of architect-engineering, including (1) professional services of an architectural or engineering nature that are associated with research, development, design, construction, alteration, or repair of real property and are required by law to be performed by a registered, licensed, or certified architect or engineer; (2) such other professional services, as determined by the contracting officer, that logically or justifiably require performance by a registered or licensed architect or engineer; and (3) incidental services that members of the architectural or engineering professions or those in their employ may logically or justifiably perform in conjunction with professional architect-engineer services. FAR 36.102. If these services are acquired under a separate contract, the procedures set forth in the BROOKS ACT (ARCHITECT-ENGINEER PROCUREMENT) must be followed. However, they can also be acquired as part of a DESIGN-BUILD contract. See Braude, chap. 15, *Construction Contracting* 1075–1110 (1991); Ness & Medill-Jones, *A-E Government Contracts*, 88-11 Constr. Briefings (Oct. 1988). See also ARCHITECT-ENGINEER CONTRACT.

AREA OF GENERAL ECONOMIC DISTRESS Pursuant to the President's Executive Order on EMPOWERMENT CONTRACTING, an area defined, for all urban and rural communities, as a census tract that has a poverty rate of at least 20 percent or any designated Federal Empowerment Zone, Supplemental Empowerment Zone, Enhanced Enterprise Community, or Enterprise Community. Further, the Secretary of Commerce may designate, as an area of general economic distress, any additional rural or Indian reservation area after considering the unemployment rate, the degree of poverty, the extent of out-migration, and the rates of business formation and business growth. Exec. Order No. 13005, 61 Fed. Reg. 26069 (May 24, 1996). See also LABOR SURPLUS AREA.

AREA WIDE CONTRACT A master contract for utility services entered into between the General Services Administration and a utility service supplier, under the authority of 40 U.S.C. § 481, to cover the utility service to all federal agencies from that supplier for a period not to exceed 10 years. FAR 41.101. Federal agencies, including DOD, are covered when an authorization attached to the area wide contract is completed and accepted by the supplier and executed by the agency and the supplier. FAR 41.204. See FAR Subpart 41.2 for procedures to be followed in contracting for utility services when an area wide contract is in place and when there is no such contract.

"ARISING UNDER THE CONTRACT" Falling within the scope of a contract clause and therefore providing a REMEDY (usually an EQUITABLE ADJUSTMENT) for some event that occurred during contract performance. Prior to the enactment of the CONTRACT DISPUTES ACT (CDA) OF 1978, BOARDs OF CONTRACT APPEALS (BCAs) had jurisdiction only over DISPUTEs that were found to arise under the contract. Other cases were required to be resolved by the Court of Claims. The CDA abolished this rule by granting the BCAs jurisdiction over all disputes "RELATING TO THE CONTRACT." "Arising under the contract" still has significance, however, because the standard Disputes clause in FAR 52.233-1 provides that the contractor has a DUTY TO PROCEED only with regard to claims that meet the "arising under" test.

ARMED SERVICES BOARD OF CONTRACT APPEALS (ASBCA) DOD's BOARD OF CONTRACT APPEALS (BCA). As the largest BCA, the ASBCA employed 28 ADMINISTRATIVE JUDGEs (most agency BCAs consist of the minimum required three administrative judges) and maintained a pending docket of 1325 active appeals on October 1, 1997. Its docket reached a high of 2503 appeals on October 1, 1987. In addition to formal litigation of disputes, the Board makes ALTERNATIVE DISPUTE RESOLUTION procedures available at the request of the parties. Whereas most BCAs include one administrative judge who serves as the Board's chair and another who serves as vice chair, the ASBCA, because of its size, has three vice chairs. The ASBCA resolves disputes involving DOD, NASA, the DEPARTMENT OF STATE, the Agency for International Development, the DEPARTMENT OF HEALTH AND HUMAN SERVICES, and other agencies. Although ASBCA offices are located in Falls Church, Virginia, the Board's administrative judges travel across the country and around the world to give contractors the opportunity to litigate their disputes. See Dingman, *Primary Jurisdiction and the Armed Services BCA*, 10 Geo. Mason U. L. Rev. 473 (1988); Nash, *The Armed Services Board of Contract Appeals: A Status Report*, 1 N&CR ¶ 31 (Apr. 1987); Williams, *A Brief Look at the Armed Services Board of Contract Appeals*, 22 Pub. Cont. Newsl. 3 (Fall 1986).

ARMED SERVICES PRICING MANUAL (ASPM) A two-volume manual, issued in 1986 and 1987, based on the policies and procedures of the FAR and the DFARS, which contained instructional material covering the entire range of CONTRACT PRICING. The ASPM has been replaced by a series of five desk reference pricing guides. See FAR 15.404-1(a)(7). (The Contract Pricing Reference Guides include *Price Analysis*, *Quantitative Techniques for Contract Pricing*, *Cost Analysis, Advanced Issues in Contract Pricing*, and *Federal Contract Negotiation Techniques*.) The ASPM used detailed discussions and examples to illustrate the application of pricing policies to pricing problems, but it was not directive in nature. The first volume dealt with contract pricing in general, whereas the second focused specifically on PRICE ANALYSIS. The ASPM contained a topical index, appendices, a list of acronyms, and a short glossary. It was used for training in classrooms and on the job and also as a reference.

ARMED SERVICES PROCUREMENT ACT (ASPA) The statute governing the procurement procedures followed by DOD, NASA, and the Coast Guard. It was originally enacted in 1947 and is now codified at 10 U.S.C. § 2302 et seq. It has been modified numerous times, with the most sweeping changes enacted in the COMPETITION IN CONTRACTING ACT in 1984 and the FEDERAL ACQUISITION STREAMLINING ACT OF 1994. See Cibinic & Nash, chap. 1, Sec. I., *Formation of Government Contracts* (3d ed. 1998). NASA derives its procurement authority from the ASPA, but that does not modify its civilian agency role as established by the Space Act. 42 U.S.C. § 2452.

ARMED SERVICES PROCUREMENT REGULATION (ASPR) The original regulation issued under the ARMED SERVICES PROCUREMENT ACT (ASPA) to promulgate the procedures to be followed by DOD. During its existence the ASPR was a top-level regulation that was by far the most complete procurement regulation in the Federal Government. It was in effect from 1948 to 1984. It was renamed the DEFENSE ACQUISITION REGULATION (DAR) in 1978. In 1984, the DAR was replaced by the current FEDERAL ACQUISITION REGULATIONS (FAR) SYSTEM combining defense and civilian agency regulations. Many of the DAR/ASPR clauses, provisions, and textual explanations survived the merger and were incorporated in simplified form into the FAR; many of those that failed to survive were put in the original DOD FAR SUPPLEMENT.

ARMS EXPORT CONTROL ACT (AECA) A 1968 Act, 22 U.S.C. § 2751 et seq., setting forth the U.S. policy of facilitating the common defense by controlling the export of products and technology through the requirement for mandatory licensing of exports, to friendly countries only, of data, research, development, production, procurement, and LOGISTICS support. The AECA provides for FOREIGN MILITARY SALES for purposes including internal security, legitimate self-defense, maintenance or restoration of international peace and security, and participation in regional or collective arrangements.

ARNET See ACQUISITION REFORM NETWORK.

AS-BUILT DRAWINGS See RECORD DRAWINGS.

AS-PLANNED DRAWINGS Drawings that show how a construction contractor or subcontractor plans to perform the work under contract. Such drawings are updated as changes, delays, and other eventualities occur during performance and thus eventually take the form of "as-built" or RECORD DRAWINGS. They are often used, in conjunction with record drawings, to prove DELAY.

ASIAN-PACIFIC AMERICANS U.S. citizens whose origins are in Japan, China, the Philippines, Vietnam, Korea, Samoa, Guam, the United States Trust Territory of the Pacific Islands, the Northern Mariana Islands, Laos, Cambodia, Taiwan, Burma, Thailand, Malaysia, Indonesia, Singapore, Brunei, Republic of the Marshall Islands, or the Federated States of Micronesia. FAR 19.001(b)(2). These persons are "to be considered" socially and economically disadvantaged for the purpose of determining the ownership of a SMALL DISADVANTAGED BUSINESS CONCERN, FAR 19.001(b). Paragraph (c) of the Utilization of Small, Small Disadvantaged and Women-Owned Small Business Concerns clause in FAR 52.219-8 states that, for purposes of implementing the Government's policies, the contractor shall presume that these individuals are socially and economically disadvantaged.

ASSET An amount recorded on a contractor's BALANCE SHEET representing the value of property owned by or debts owed to the contractor. Assets may be cash, near-cash (accounts receivable, temporary investments, notes receivable), or nonmonetary. Nonmonetary assets consumed in the creation of goods and services have limited lives, while others, such as land, have unlimited lives. CAPITAL ASSETs are long-term assets that are not bought or sold in the normal course of business. Such assets may be further classified as TANGIBLE CAPITAL ASSETs and INTANGIBLE CAPITAL ASSETs.

ASSET ACCOUNTABILITY UNIT A TANGIBLE CAPITAL ASSET that is a component of plant and equipment that is capitalized (see CAPITALIZATION) when acquired or whose replacement is capitalized when the unit is removed, transferred, sold, abandoned, demolished, or otherwise disposed of. CAS 404, 48 C.F.R. § 9904.404-30. A contractor's capitalization policy must provide for identification of asset accountability units to the maximum extent practical. 48 C.F.R. § 9904.404-40(b)(3).

ASSIGNEE A person or entity to whom all or part of one's property, interest, or rights are transferred. *Black's Law Dictionary* 118–19 (6th ed. 1990). In most cases, the assignee of a contract or a claim is an organization to which a contractor transfers its rights and/or obligations. See ASSIGNMENT OF CONTRACT and ASSIGNMENT OF CLAIMS; FAR Subpart 32.8. See Schooner & Schooner, *Look Before*

You Lend: A Lender's Guide to Financing Government Contracts Pursuant to the Assignment of Claims Act, 48 Bus. Law. 535 (1993).

ASSIGNMENT OF CLAIMS A contractor's transfer or making over to a bank, trust company, or other financing institution, as security for a loan to the contractor, of the contractor's right to be paid by the Government for contract performance. FAR 32.801. Under the Assignment of Claims Act, 31 U.S.C. § 3727a, a contractor may assign moneys due—or to become due—under a contract, if (1) the contract specifies payments aggregating $1,000 or more; (2) the assignment is made to a bank, trust company, or other financing institution, including any federal lending agency; (3) the contract does not prohibit the assignment; (4) the assignment covers all unpaid amounts payable under the contract, is made to only one party, and is not subject to further assignment; and (5) the ASSIGNEE sends a written notice of the assignment to the contracting officer, to the SURETY on any BOND applicable to the contract, and to the DISBURSING OFFICER designated in the contract to make payment. FAR 32.802. Once a proper assignment of claims has occurred, the Government will be liable to the financing institution if it pays the contractor. See Schooner, *Costly Noncompliance with the Assignment of Claims Act: A Reminder for Counsel and Disbursing Officers*, Army Law. 50 (July 1994); Schooner & Schooner, *Look Before You Lend: A Lender's Guide to Financing Government Contracts Pursuant to the Assignment of Claims Act*, 48 Bus. Law. 535 (1993); Vickery & Paalborg, *Assignment of Claims Act*, 87-3 Briefing Papers (Feb. 1987).

ASSIGNMENT OF CONTRACT Transfer of the rights and obligations under a contract to another party. When such assignment occurs, the ASSIGNOR (the original contractor) remains liable to the Government if the ASSIGNEE fails to complete performance of the contract. 31 U.S.C. § 3727 and 41 U.S.C. § 15 prohibit contractors from assigning contracts; however, assignment of contracts may be made with the consent of the contracting officer. *Tuftco Corp. v. United States*, 222 Ct. Cl. 277, 614 F.2d 740 (1980). Such assignments are called NOVATIONs in FAR Subpart 42.12, which contains procedures for entering into such agreements. See Nash, *Assignment of Contracts in the Rights of Performance Bond Securities: It Depends on the Circumstances*, 6 N&CR ¶ 57 (Oct. 1992); Mullin, *Novation Agreements in Response to Merger and Consolidation in the Aerospace Industry*, 29 A.F. L. Rev. 69 (1988); Victorino et al., *Acquisitions & Mergers*, 85-9 Briefing Papers (Sept. 1985); Nash & Cibinic, *Federal Procurement Law,* vol. II, 1958–70 (3d ed. 1980).

ASSIGNMENT OF COST TO COST ACCOUNTING PERIODS A method or technique used in determining the amount of cost to be assigned to individual cost accounting periods. 48 C.F.R. § 9903.302-1. Examples of COST ACCOUNTING PRACTICEs that involve the assignment of cost to cost accounting periods are requirements for the use of specified ACCRUAL BASIS ACCOUNTING or CASH BASIS ACCOUNTING for a cost element.

ASSIGNOR A person or entity "who assigns or transfers property to an ASSIGNEE." *Black's Law Dictionary* 119 (6th ed. 1990). In most cases, the assignor of a contract or a claim is a contractor. See ASSIGNMENT OF CONTRACT and ASSIGNMENT OF CLAIMS; FAR Subpart 32.8.

ASSIST AUDIT An AUDIT performed by one audit office at the request of another. The assist audit is usually an adjunct to or an integral part of an audit being performed by the requesting audit office. The DEFENSE CONTRACT AUDIT AGENCY (DCAA) CONTRACT AUDIT MANUAL explains that the prime contractor is primarily responsible for awarding subcontracts, monitoring their performance, and paying each subcontractor for the work accomplished under the subcontracts' terms. Accordingly, the prime contractor is also responsible for audits of its subcontractors. However, it is DCAA's policy to perform assist audits of incurred costs whenever such audits are determined to be of potential benefit to the Government and necessary to ensure adequate and effective review of a contractor's operations or cost representations. *DCAA Contract Audit Manual* 6-801.1.

ASSISTANCE SERVICES See ADVISORY AND ASSISTANCE SERVICES.

ASSOCIATED GENERAL CONTRACTORS OF AMERICA (AGC) A national trade association, founded in 1918, whose members include general contractors, subcontractors, industry suppliers, and service firms. AGC conducts seminars and conferences, provides tax services, compiles statistics on job accidents, and bestows safety and outstanding achievement awards. It maintains 65 committees, including liaison committees with federal agencies, and it publishes manuals, studies, and model contract documents. [AGC, 1957 E Street, N.W., Washington, DC 20006; (202) 393-2040]

ATTEMPTING TO INFLUENCE See INFLUENCING OR ATTEMPTING TO INFLUENCE.

ATTORNEY WORK-PRODUCT PRIVILEGE An exemption under the FREEDOM OF INFORMATION ACT which protects documents prepared by an agency's attorney which reveal the theory of a case or proposed litigation from release. 5 U.S.C. § 552(b)(5). This privilege does not extend to routine reports in the ordinary course of business but is limited to documents prepared in anticipation of a particular litigation or related to a specific claim which is likely to lead to litigation. See Nash & Rawicz, *Intellectual Property Series*, vol 3, 205 (3d ed. 1997). See also PRIVILEGED INFORMATION.

ATTORNEY'S FEES Compensation, at an hourly rate, fixed rate, or CONTINGENT FEE, for the performance of professional legal services. Most attorney's fees in Government contract litigation are paid at an hourly rate for time reasonably expended. In Government contracts, contractors generally cannot recover their attorney's fees for litigation against the Government. Under the EQUAL ACCESS TO JUSTICE ACT, however, small contractors that meet prescribed standards can recover their attorney's fees and expenses in litigation before the U.S. COURT OF FEDERAL CLAIMS and the BOARDs OF CONTRACT APPEALS under the CONTRACT DISPUTES ACT OF 1978. Costs related to legal proceedings are unallowable if the proceedings result in a criminal conviction, a finding of contractor liability where there are allegations of FRAUD or similar misconduct, imposition of a monetary penalty, DEBARMENT or SUSPENSION, or termination or voiding of the contract. FAR 31.205-47(b). Costs related to legal proceedings are also unallowable if they are incurred in connection with (1) prosecution or defense of claims or appeals against the Government; (2) organization, reorganization (including mergers and acquisitions), or resisting mergers and acquisitions; (3) defense of antitrust suits; (4) defense of QUI TAM PROCEEDINGS when the contractor is found liable or settled; (5) prosecution or defense of lawsuits or appeals between contractors concerning arrangements of shared interest such as JOINT VENTUREs or teaming agreements unless agreed to by the contracting officer; (6) PATENT INFRINGEMENT; and (7) representation of individuals, groups or legal entities, which the contractor is not legally obligated to provide, where the participant was convicted or found civilly liable for a violation of law or regulation. FAR 31.205-47(f). See Strasavich, *Court-Ordered Attorney's Fees in Contract Actions: What Is Reasonable*, 19 J. Legal Prof. 301 (1994/1995); Elling, *Contesting Applications for Attorney's Fees and Costs in Government Contract Litigation*, Army Law. 21 (July 1994); Smith, *Federal Statutory Attorney Fees: Common Issues & Recent Cases*, 28 Clearinghouse Rev. 744 (Nov. 1994); Connelly &

Schooner, *Recovery of Costs for Defense Against the Government's Charge of Illegality*, 16 Pub. Cont. L.J. 94 (1986).

AUCTION A buying or selling technique whereby open bidding is continued until no competitor is willing to submit a better bid. Prior to FAC 97-02, September 30, 1997, FAR Part 15 prohibited such auction techniques as (1) indicating to an offeror a cost or price that it must meet to obtain further consideration, or (2) advising an offeror of its price standing relative to another offeror. FAR 15.306(e) now provides only that the Government may not reveal an offeror's price without that offeror's permission. However, the contracting officer may inform an offeror that its price is too high or too low, and reveal the results of the analysis supporting that conclusion. It is also permissible to indicate to all offerors the cost or price that the Government's PRICE ANALYSIS, MARKET RESEARCH, and other reviews have identified as reasonable.

AUDIT The systematic examination of records and other documents and the securing of evidence—by confirmation, physical inspection, or otherwise—for one or more of the following purposes: determining the propriety or legality of proposed or consummated transactions; ascertaining whether all transactions have been recorded and are reflected accurately in accounts; determining the existence of recorded assets and the inclusiveness of recorded liabilities; determining the accuracy of financial or statistical statements or reports and the fairness of the facts they present; determining the degree of compliance with established policies and procedures of financial transactions and business management; and appraising an accounting system and making recommendations concerning it. Contract audit is an integral part of procurement by NEGOTIATION. Its purpose is to assist in achieving prudent contracting by having Government AUDITORs provide Government procurement personnel with financial information and advice on contractual matters and the effectiveness, efficiency, and economy of the contractor's operations. *DCAA Contract Audit Manual* 1-104.2. On COST-REIMBURSEMENT CONTRACTS, audit ensures that a contractor has incurred all costs claimed for reimbursement. In conducting a contract audit before award of a contract or negotiation of a CLAIM, the auditor must examine or develop sufficient evidence to support a valid opinion of the extent to which costs or estimates contained in a contractor's claim or PROPOSAL are (1) reasonable as to nature and amount, (2) allocable, (3) measurable by the application of duly promulgated COST ACCOUNTING STANDARDS (CAS) and GENERALLY ACCEPTED ACCOUNTING PRINCIPLES (GAAP) and practices appropriate to the particular circumstances, and (4) in accordance with applicable cost limitations or exclusions as stated in the contract or in the FAR. Although the detection of FRAUD or similar unlawful activity is not a primary function of contract audit, the auditor must constantly be alert to situations or transactions that may indicate such activity. *DCAA Contract Audit Manual* 1-102. See Murphy & Wilkins, *Defense Contract Audit Agency Access to Contractor "Reserves" Used for Financial Statements Revenue Recognition Purposes*, 23 Pub. Cont. L.J. 607 (1994); Cibinic & Nash, chap. 7, *Cost-Reimbursement Contracting* (2d ed. 1993); Cibinic, *Audit of Contractors' Records: "Everything I've Got Belongs to You,"* 5 N&CR ¶ 5 (Jan. 1991); Cibinic, *Keeping Audit Reports Away from the Auditee: What You Don't Know Can Hurt You*, 4 N&CR ¶ 21 (Apr. 1990); Millspaugh, *The Courts Deny Defense Auditors Access to Contractor Records: Issues and Implications*, 18 Pub. Cont. L.J. 320 (1989).

AUDITOR A person conducting AUDIT activities. Broad authority to audit Government programs is vested in the Comptroller General of the United States (see GENERAL ACCOUNTING OFFICE). The Comptroller General also has authority under the EXAMINATION OF RECORDS clause to audit Government contractors. Most contract audit is performed by agency auditors, who are generally assigned to the agency INSPECTOR GENERAL, except in DOD where they are assigned to the DEFENSE CONTRACT AUDIT AGENCY. Auditors perform work for other agencies through cross-servicing arrangements. See FAR Subpart 42.1. See also Cibinic, *Auditor Interviews of Contractor Employees: Dropped From Estimating System Regulations*, 2 N&CR ¶ 28 (May 1988); Cibinic, *Auditor Interviews of Contractor Employees: Wolf in Sheep's Clothing*, 1 N&CR ¶ 92 (Dec. 1987); Cibinic, *Role of the Auditor: Any Room Left for the Contracting Officer?*, 1 N&CR ¶ 66 (Aug. 1987).

AUTHORITY FOR SYSTEMS ACQUISITION An umbrella term used by DOD to describe the framework granting authority for it to develop, produce, and field weapon systems. This authority emanates from four sources: the law (legal basis), executive direction (orders), Office of Management and Budget Circular No. A-109, and the FEDERAL ACQUISITION REGULATION. The framework guides and grants authority, enables DOD to conduct business, and is the apparatus for decisionmaking and execution. Jones, *Glossary: Defense Acquisition Acronyms and Terms* (8th ed., Defense Systems Management College).

AUTHORIZATION Legal authority to carry out a program. Statutes granting authorization are initiated in the legislative committees of Congress having cognizance over the agency involved. Generally, they are a prerequisite to an APPROPRIATION for that program or agency. The purpose of the authorization process is to ensure that the legislative committees have reviewed and approved the current programs of their respective agencies before the appropriations committees make the final decisions on the amount of funds that should be provided to carry out agency missions. See Cibinic & Nash, chap. 1, Sec. II., *Formation of Government Contracts* (3d ed. 1998).

AUTHORIZATION AND CONSENT Authorization by the Government for a contractor to use an invention that has been patented but to which the Government has no rights. Under 28 U.S.C. § 1498(a), when such authorization and consent has been granted, the owner of the PATENT can sue only the Government in the U.S. COURT OF FEDERAL CLAIMS (it cannot sue the contractor for damages or obtain an injunction against the contractor to block use of the patent). The Government grants such authorization and consent in order to further the progress of work on its contracts—to obtain the performance of the work in the most effective manner without the need to create new technology. FAR 27.201-2 provides for the use of two different Authorization and Consent clauses. The clause in FAR 52.227-1 is used in supply and service contracts (including CONSTRUCTION contracts) and gives authorization and consent to use all patents necessary to perform the specified work or required to be used by the contracting officer. The Alternate I clause in FAR 52.227-1 is used in RESEARCH AND DEVELOPMENT contracts and gives blanket authorization and consent to use any invention.

AUTHORIZED REPRESENTATIVE An employee of a CONTRACTING ACTIVITY with the authority to perform CONTRACT ADMINISTRATION activities. Both FAR 2.101 and the Definitions clause in FAR 52.202-1 state that authorized representatives are CONTRACTING OFFICERs. However, it is generally recognized that they do not have the authority to enter into agreements or MODIFICATIONs that alter the terms of existing contracts. When authorized representatives act within the scope of their authority, the Government agency runs the risk that it will be bound by their actions under the doctrine of IMPLIED AUTHORITY. See Cibinic & Nash, *Administration of Government Contracts* 29–67 (3d ed. 1995); Reifel & Bastianelli, *Contracting Officer Authority*, 86-4 Briefing Papers (Mar.

1986); Tepfer, *Authority and the Contracting Officer's Representatives*, 24 A.F. L. Rev. 1 (1984).

AUTOMATIC DATA PROCESSING EQUIPMENT (ADPE) Defined by the BROOKS ACT (AUTOMATIC DATA PROCESSING PROCUREMENT) (repealed by Pub. L. No. 104-106) as any equipment or interconnected systems or subsystems of equipment used in the automatic acquisition, storage, manipulation, management, movement, control, display, switching, interchange, transmission, or reception of data or information by a federal agency or under a contract with a federal agency. These systems include computers, ancillary equipment, software, and related services. National Communications System Technology and Standards Division, *Telecommunications: Glossary of Telecommunication Terms*, Federal Standard 1037C (Aug. 1996).

AUTOMATIC DATA PROCESSING EQUIPMENT/DATA SYSTEM (ADPE/DS) Any equipment or interconnected systems or subsystems of equipment is used in the automatic acquisition, storage, manipulation, management, movement, control, display, switching, interchange, transmission, or reception of data or information by a federal agency or under a contract with a federal agency that (1) requires the use of such equipment, or (2) requires the performance of a service or the furnishing of a product that is performed or produced making a significant use of such equipment. National Communications System Technology and Standards Division, *Telecommunications: Glossary of Telecommunication Terms*, Federal Standard 1037C (Aug. 1996).

AUTOMATIC DATA PROCESSING FUND See INFORMATION TECHNOLOGY FUND.

AUTOMATIC STAY (BANKRUPTCY) A temporary restraining order against any party attempting to bring an action against a bankrupt individual or organization. At the time bankruptcy proceedings commence, the Bankruptcy Code basically freezes the status quo for business transactions involving the bankrupt contractor. The automatic stay, for example, might impede a Contract Disputes Act CLAIM against a bankrupt contractor or prohibit the Government from terminating for default a contract with a bankrupt contractor. Permission of the Bankruptcy Court generally is required to avoid the stay. 11 U.S.C. § 362; Maizel & Whitaker, *The Government's Contractual Rights and Bankruptcy's Automatic Stay; Irreconcilable Difference?*, 25 Pub. Cont. L.J. 711 (1996).

AUTOMATIC STAY (GAO PROTEST FILING) A mechanism by which contract AWARD is withheld or further performance of a contract is suspended when a disappointed bidder or offeror files a timely PROTEST with the COMPTROLLER GENERAL. This authority derives from the COMPETITION IN CONTRACTING ACT. 31 U.S.C. § 3553(c) and (d). It is implemented in FAR 33.104 and 4 C.F.R. § 21.4. When an agency is notified that a protest has been filed prior to contract award, the agency is required by law not to make award before the protest is resolved, unless the HEAD OF THE CONTRACTING ACTIVITY decides that urgent and compelling circumstances significantly affecting the interests of the United States will not permit waiting for the decision. Similarly, when an agency is notified of a protest within 10 calendar days after award has been made, the law requires the agency to direct the contractor to suspend performance until the protest is resolved. Because little more than a postage stamp and a letter of protest is required to stop the procurement process, the stay is often referred to as the "thirty-two-cent injunction." See Saviano, *Overriding a CICA Stay*, The Geo. Univ. L. School, Government Contracts Program (1994); Dempsey & Fioravanti, *The Automatic Suspension Provision for GAO Bid Protests: When 10 Days May Not Be 10 Days*, 30 Cont. Mgmt. 9 (Mar. 1990).

AUTOMATIC SUSPENSION See AUTOMATIC STAY.

AUXILIARY ITEM An item without which the basic unit of PLANT EQUIPMENT cannot operate. FAR 45.501. FAR 45.505-5 requires that records of such items be maintained as a part of the record of the associated item of plant equipment.

AVAILABILITY OF APPROPRIATIONS Appropriations are available for obligation only in that budget year, unless the language in the appropriation act specifies a longer period. If the language specifies that the funds are to remain available until the end of a certain year beyond the budget year, the availability is said to be multiyear. If the language specifies that the funds are to remain available until expended, the availability is said to be no-year. Appropriations for major procurements and construction projects are typically made available for multiple years or until expended. GAO, *Principles of Budgeting for Capital Asset Acquisitions*, 8 Budget of the United States Government, Fiscal Year 1998 (1997).

AVERAGE UNIT PROCUREMENT COST (AUPC) OBJECTIVES A DOD projected all-encompassing measure of per-item cost. AUPC includes recurring flyaway (e.g., for an aircraft program), rollaway, sailaway costs (including nonrecurring production costs) adjusted for data, training, support equipment, and initial spares costs. Design to average unit procurement COST OBJECTIVEs, expressed in constant dollars, are established within DOD as part of obtaining approval to begin a new ACQUISITION PROGRAM. Jones, *Glossary: Defense Acquisition Acronyms and Terms* (8th ed., Defense Systems Management College).

AVOIDABLE COST A term used by the DOE in its MANAGEMENT AND OPERATING CONTRACTs to identify costs that are unreasonable. It is any cost incurred by the contractor and/or its subcontractors, in carrying out the terms and conditions of the contract when: (1) the work is clearly within the sole and exclusive control of the contractor or subcontractor personnel at any tier or level; and (2) the increased costs or expenses result from the negligence or wilful misconduct of the contractor or subcontractor personnel at any tier or level; and (3) DOE is not responsible in any way for the act or omission that resulted in the additional costs. DEAR 970.5204-56(a). Avoidable costs shall not include the cost of losses or damages incurred by the contractor as a result of the acts or omissions of employees who, during the phase-in period of a new contract, the contractor is required to employ as a result of assuming the management of a DOE facility. DEAR 970.5204-56(c). For guidance on determining avoidable costs for profit-making contractors, see DEAR 970.3102-22.

AVOIDANCE OF CONTRACT The withdrawal by one party from a contract or contract MODIFICATION without performance because of a defect in the process of entering into the contract or contract modification. The most common grounds for avoidance are ECONOMIC DURESS, FRAUD, illegality, MUTUAL MISTAKE, and UNCONSCIONABILITY. When one party to a contract finds that any of these things has occurred in the formation of a contract, it has the right of avoidance without recourse by the other party.

AWARD The notification by the Government that it is entering into a contract with a private party. The award of a contract is usually made by ACCEPTANCE OF an OFFER that has been made by an offeror. In procurement by SEALED BIDDING, the contracting officer makes a contract award by written notice, within the time for acceptance specified in the bid or the extension, to the responsible bidder whose bid, conforming to the SOLICITATION, is the most advantageous to the Government, considering only price and the price-related factors included in the solicitation. FAR 14.407-1. In procurement by NEGOTIATION, the contracting officer awards a contract with reasonable promptness by transmitting a written NOTICE OF AWARD to the successful offeror (the source whose offer is most advantageous to the Government, considering price and other factors included in the solicitation. FAR 15.504. Award is frequently made by signing one of the standard forms provided by the FAR. See Standard Form 26, Award/Contract, FAR 53.301-26; Standard Form 33, Solicitation, Offer and Award, FAR 53.301-33.

AWARD FEE The FEE that a contractor receives above the BASE FEE in a COST-PLUS-AWARD-FEE CONTRACT. The total amount of fee available to be awarded is set forth in the original contract and should be an amount that is sufficient to provide motivation for excellence in such areas as quality, timeliness, technical ingenuity, and cost-effective management. FAR 16.305; FAR 16.404-2. The amount of the award fee that is actually paid is determined by the Government's evaluation of the contractor's performance in terms of criteria stated in the contract. This determination is made unilaterally by the Government and is not subject to the DISPUTEs clause. FAR 16.404-2. The award fee is usually paid in increments of 3, 4, or 6 months based on the contractor's performance during that period. DFARS 216.404-2 and NFS 18-16.405-270 permit the award fee feature to be used in appropriate circumstances in fixed-price contracts as well. See Cibinic & Nash, chap. 9, Sec. V., *Formation of Government Contracts* (3d ed. 1998); Cibinic & Nash, *Cost-Reimbursement Contracting* 101–21 (2d ed. 1993).

AWARD FEE DETERMINATION OFFICIAL (FDO) An official who determines the amount of fee to be earned in a COST-PLUS-AWARD-FEE CONTRACT. In major procurements the FDO should be at the management level of the procuring agency. The findings of the FDO concerning the amount of fee earned is binding on both parties and are not subject to appeal under the DISPUTEs clause or to any other appeal. See Cibinic & Nash, *Cost-Reimbursement Contracting* 119–21 (2d ed. 1993).

AWARD ON INITIAL PROPOSALS Award of a competitively negotiated contract (see NEGOTIATION) on the basis of the initial proposals received, without conducting DISCUSSION with the OFFERORs in the COMPETITIVE RANGE. Under the COMPETITION IN CONTRACTING ACT, such award could be made only if it could be clearly demonstrated from the existence of FULL AND

OPEN COMPETITION or accurate prior cost experience that it would result in "the lowest overall cost to the Government." Because this standard prevented award on initial proposals unless the selected proposal contained the lowest cost to the Government offered by any contractor submitting a technically acceptable proposal, it was changed in 1990 by amendment of the ARMED SERVICES PROCUREMENT ACT at 10 U.S.C. § 2305(b)(4). The FEDERAL ACQUISITION STREAMLINING ACT OF 1994 made the same change to the FEDERAL PROPERTY AND ADMINISTRATIVE SERVICES ACT OF 1949 at 41 U.S.C. § 253b(2)(B). The change permits award on initial proposals whenever the contracting officer determines that discussions are not necessary and the solicitation contains a clause stating that the agency intends to award without discussions. FAR 15.306(a)(2). FAR 52.215-1 contains two clauses to be used depending on whether the contracting officer decides that discussions will be necessary or that award without discussions will probably be possible. See Cibinic & Nash, chap. 6, *Formation of Government Contracts* (3d ed. 1998); Nash, *Pre-"Competitive Range" Communications During Best Value Procurement: The New Proposed Rule*, 11 N&CR ¶ 43 (Aug. 1997); Nash, *Postscript: Award Without Discussions*, 5 N&CR ¶ 1 (Jan. 1991); Mark, *Contract Award on Initial Proposals*, 19 Pub. Cont. L.J. 252 (1990); Cibinic, *Award on Initial Proposals: Love at First Sight*, 1 N&CR ¶ 81 (Nov. 1987).

AWARD WITHOUT DISCUSSIONS See AWARD ON INITIAL PROPOSALS.

B

BACK PAY Payment to employees of previously earned compensation. Back pay may result from a negotiated settlement, order, or court decree that resolves a violation of federal labor laws or the Civil Rights Act of 1964. It falls into two categories: (1) payment of additional compensation to employees for work performed for which they were underpaid, and (2) payment resulting from such violations as improper discharge or discrimination. Back pay resulting from underpaid work is compensation for the work performed and is an ALLOWABLE COST; all other back pay resulting from violation of federal labor laws or the Civil Rights Act is unallowable. FAR 31.205-6(h). See Cibinic & Nash, *Cost-Reimbursement Contracting* 807–9 (2d ed. 1993). See also Walterscheid, *Back Pay as a Remedy under Executive Order 11246: A Study in Administrative Activism*, 18 Pub. Cont. L.J. 559 (1989).

BAD DEBTS Losses arising from uncollectible accounts receivable due from customers. FAR 31.205-3 makes such losses, whether actual or estimated, UNALLOWABLE COSTs. See Cibinic & Nash, *Cost-Reimbursement Contracting* 865–66 (2d ed. 1993).

BALANCE OF PAYMENTS PROGRAM A nonstatutory program giving preference to American products over foreign products. See FAR Subpart 25.3. The program applies to acquisitions of work to be performed outside of the United States. It provides that, unless one of nine exceptions applies, the foreign offer must be increased for evaluation purposes by a factor of 50 percent (excluding duty). FAR 25.302. In its implementation of the BUY AMERICAN ACT, DOD uses the balance of payments evaluation factor (50 percent of the price excluding duty) as an alternate evaluation factor. DFARS 225.105. See Cibinic & Nash, chap. 10, Sec. IV., *Formation of Government Contracts* (3d ed. 1998); Stamps, *The Department of Defense Balance of Payments Program: A Brief History and Critique*, 18 Pub. Cont. L.J. 528 (1989).

BALANCE SHEET A financial statement of a contractor setting forth its ASSETs, LIABILITIES, and NET WORTH. Contracting officers review prospective contractors' financial statements, including balance sheets, to determine if they have, or are able to obtain, adequate financial resources to perform the contract (see RESPONSIBILITY).

BARGAINING NEGOTIATIONs with an offeror including persuasion, alteration of assumptions and positions, give-and-take, that apply to price, schedule, technical requirements, type of contract, or other terms and conditions. FAR 15.306(d). Bargaining may occur in sole source procurements or during competitive negotiations. When it occurs in the competitive negotiation process after establishment of the COMPETITIVE RANGE, it is called DISCUSSIONs. FAR 15.306(d)(3) indicates that, in this situation, bargaining may include negotiation with an offeror to increase performance beyond mandatory minimums or suggesting to an offeror that they have exceeded mandatory minimums in a way that makes their offer noncompetitive.

BASE The numerical measure, such as costs, hours of LABOR, or hours of machine usage, to which INDIRECT COSTs are allocated (see ALLOCATION OF COST). The base must be selected to permit allocation of indirect costs on the basis of the benefits accruing to all COST OBJECTIVEs within the base. FAR 31.203(b). Once an appropriate base has been selected, individual elements may not be removed; thus, all items within these should bear their pro rata share of indirect costs. FAR 31.203(c). See Cibinic & Nash, *Cost-Reimbursement Contracting* 684–94 (2d ed. 1993).

BASE FEE A fixed dollar amount established at the inception of a COST-PLUS-AWARD-FEE (CPAF) CONTRACT as the amount of PROFIT the contractor will receive under the contract, regardless of the quality of performance. In addition to this base fee, the contractor receives an AWARD FEE in an amount that reflects the Government's periodic judgmental evaluation of contractor performance. The base fee is established, administered, and paid like a fixed fee under a COST-PLUS-FIXED-FEE (CPFF) CONTRACT. See Cibinic & Nash, *Cost-Reimbursement Contracting* 571–607 (2d ed. 1993).

BASE PERIOD The cost accounting period during which INDIRECT COSTs are incurred and accumulated for distribution to work performed in that period. FAR 31.203(e). For contracts subject to the COST ACCOUNTING STANDARDS, CAS 406, 48 C.F.R. § 9904.406, entitled "cost accounting period," provides guidance for selecting the base period. CAS 406 requires that contractors use the same fiscal year for cost accounting purposes, subject to several limited exceptions.

48 C.F.R. § 9904-406.40(2). For contracts not subject to the Cost Accounting Standards, the COST PRINCIPLES indicate that the contractor's fiscal year is normally the appropriate base period, but the use of a shorter period is permitted (1) for contracts in which performance involves only a minor portion of the fiscal year, or (2) when it is general practice in the industry to use a shorter period. FAR 31.203(e). Cibinic & Nash, *Cost-Reimbursement Contracting* 80 (2d ed. 1993).

"BASED ON" PRICE A price that was comparable to a previous price that was an ESTABLISHED CATALOG OR MARKET PRICE or a price established through ADEQUATE PRICE COMPETITION. When a "based on" price was submitted in a negotiated procurement, the contracting officer did not need to obtain COST OR PRICING DATA. With the new policies on cost or pricing data adopted in 1995 and 1996, this concept is no longer stated in the FAR.

BASIC AGREEMENT A written instrument of understanding (not a CONTRACT) negotiated between a procuring activity and a contractor. FAR 16.702. It sets forth the contract clauses that will apply to future procurement. Basic agreements are used to expedite future procurement when there is a likelihood that a substantial number of future contracts will be issued. Basic agreements must be revised annually to incorporate contract clauses that are currently applicable. FAR 16.702(b)(3).

BASIC ASSUMPTION A matter that is a significant part of the bargaining process in the formation of a contract. To be a basic assumption, the facts on which the assumption is based must have been knowable at the time the contract was formed; events that could not be foreseen cannot be considered a basic assumption. If there is a MUTUAL MISTAKE as to a basic assumption in a contract, relief may be granted where, had the parties known the correct information at the time the contract was formed, they would have altered the contract. Cibinic & Nash, *Administration of Government Contracts* 322–23 (3d ed. 1995).

BASIC ORDERING AGREEMENT (BOA) A written instrument of understanding (not a CONTRACT) negotiated between a procuring activity and a contractor. FAR 16.703. A BOA contains (1) terms and clauses that will apply to any future orders placed during the BOA's term; (2) a description, as specific as practicable, of supplies or services to be provided; and (3) methods for pricing, issuing, and delivering future orders. BOAs may be used to expedite contracting for supplies or services when specific items, quantities, and prices are not known but a substantial number of requirements are anticipated. They are frequently issued to multiple contractors and may not be used to avoid the requirements for competition. FAR 16.703(d). See Raleigh, *The Basic Ordering Agreement: Basically*, 22 Cont. Mgmt. 12 (Dec. 1982).

BASIC RESEARCH Research that is directed toward increase of knowledge in science. FAR 35.001; FAR 31.205-18. The primary aim of basic research is a fuller knowledge or understanding of the subject under study, rather than any practical application thereof. It is the first stage of the RESEARCH AND DEVELOPMENT process and is followed by APPLIED RESEARCH. Most basic research is acquired through the BROAD AGENCY ANNOUNCEMENT process. See Cibinic & Nash, chap. 7, Sec. V., *Formation of Government Contracts* (3d ed. 1998).

BENCHMARK Any test conducted on computer hardware, software, or telecommunications equipment to determine (1) that the configuration performs in accordance with vendor-published PERFORMANCE SPECIFICATIONS; (2) that the configuration satisfies certain functional requirements that cannot be measured in terms of performance and/or design criteria; (3) the estimated annual costs to an agency for teleprocessing services; and (4) the size system that must be purchased (e.g., how many components are needed to process the anticipated workload). The term has been broadly interpreted to include evaluation exercises of varying degrees of complexity. In general, there are two types of benchmarks: operational capability demonstrations (OCDs) and live test demonstrations (LTDs), the latter being the more rigorous. See CAPABILITY VALIDATION.

BEST AND FINAL OFFER (BAFO) An OFFER submitted to the Government in a competitive negotiated procurement (see NEGOTIATION) after written or oral DISCUSSIONs have been conducted. FAC 97-02, September 30, 1997, changed this term to FINAL PROPOSAL REVISION. Under the prior FAR, the contracting officer would issue a request for BAFOs to all offerors still within the COMPETITIVE RANGE. The request included (1) notice that discussions are concluded, (2) notice that the offeror has the opportunity to submit a BAFO, (3) a common cutoff date and time allowing a reasonable opportunity for submission of BAFOs, and (4) notice of the ramifications of late submission. Once the contracting officer received the BAFOs, the contracting officer could not reopen discussions unless it was clearly in the Government's interest to do so. If the contracting officer did reopen discussions, the contracting officer had to issue an additional request for BAFOs to all offerors still within the competitive range. Following evaluation of the BAFOs, the contracting officer selected the source whose offer was most advantageous to the Government, considering price and the other factors included in the solicitation. See Cibinic, *BAFO's and Common Cutoff Dates: Paul Shnitzer Responds*, 9 N&CR ¶ 41 (July 1995); Cibinic, *BAFO's and Common Cutoff Dates: Costly and Unnecessary Relics*, 9 N&CR ¶ 25 (Apr. 1995); Nash, *Limiting Multiple Best and Finals: Cure or Disease?*, 2 N&CR ¶ 60 (Oct. 1988); Feldman, *Traversing the Tightrope Between Meaningful Discussions and Improper Practices in Negotiated Federal Acquisitions: Technical Transfusion, Technical Leveling, and Auction Techniques*, 17 Pub. Cont. L.J. 211, 246 (1987).

BEST EFFORTS A contractual obligation to *attempt* to meet a goal—as, for example, under the LIMITATION OF COST CLAUSE, which requires contractors to use their best efforts to perform the work within the estimated cost of the contract. Under the Utilization of Indian Organizations and Indian-Owned Economic Enterprises clause at FAR 52.226.1, the contractor must agree to use its best efforts to give Indian organizations and Indian-owned economic enterprises the maximum practicable opportunity to participate in the subcontracts it awards to the fullest extent consistent with efficient performance of its contract. FAR 26.104.

BEST PRACTICES GUIDES A series of guidebooks on best practices developed by the OFFICE OF FEDERAL PROCUREMENT POLICY. (As Government agencies implement reinvention policies, they may develop promising practices that may be applied by other organizations, thus becoming best practices.) Guides are currently (or will soon be) available addressing: PAST PERFORMANCE; PERFORMANCE BASED SERVICE CONTRACTING; CONTRACT ADMINISTRATION; and TASK ORDER and DELIVERY ORDER contracting. Copies may be obtained from the Executive Office of the President's Publications Office by calling (202) 395-7332 or by writing Office of Publications, 725 17th Street, N.W., Room 2200, New Executive Office Building, Washington, DC 20503. The ARNet also provides a best practices site, which contains numerous success stories from various federal agencies. These best practices illustrate increased efficiencies and savings in time and costs that agencies have experienced as they adopt innovative measures to communicate their acquisition needs.

BEST VALUE The expected outcome of an acquisition that, in the Government's estimation, provides the greatest overall benefit in response to the requirement. FAR 2.101. This term was added to the FAR by FAC 97-02, September 30, 1997, as part of the rewrite of FAR Part 15. It pertains to procurements using the competitive negotiation process and describes the outcome that should be achieved by that process. See BEST VALUE PROCUREMENT.

BEST VALUE PROCUREMENT Any competitive procurement conducted in accordance with the procedures in FAR Part 15. FAR 15.101 describes the "best value continuum" as any one or a combination of source selection approaches that are used to obtain BEST VALUE. Two specific techniques are described: (1) the TRADEOFF PROCESS, and (2) the LOWEST PRICE TECHNICALLY ACCEPTABLE source selection process. Prior to FAC 97-02, September 30, 1997, the term best value procurement was not included in the FAR but was widely used to describe the competitive negotiation process where the Government evaluated both price and non-price factors and awarded the contract to the offeror that was perceived to have the best value considering all of the factors. This technique is now called the tradeoff process. See Nash, *Best Value Procurement: Random Musings on the Current State of the Art*, 11 N&CR ¶ 44 (Sept. 1997); Nash, *Best Value: The Gap Between the Intent and the Act*, 11 N&CR ¶ 3 (Jan. 1997); Nash, *Selecting the Evaluation Factors in Best Value Procurement*, 10 N&CR ¶ 32 (June 1996); Cibinic, *Postscript VI: Best Value Procurement*, 10 N&CR ¶ 15 (Apr. 1996); Nash, *Postscript V: Best Value Procurement*, 9 N&CR ¶ 6 (Jan. 1995); Edwards, with commentary and analysis by Nash, *Questions and Answers About Best-Value Source Selection*, The Geo. Wash. Univ. Nat'l Law Center, Government Contracts Program (1994); Koch, *Best Value Procurement: Disclose the Price/Technical Tradeoff!*, 34 Cont. Mgmt. 10 (May 1994); Kitchenman, *Why Best Value? A Business Perspective*, 34 Cont. Mgmt. 11 (Mar. 1994); Nash, *Postscript IV: Best Value Procurement*, 8 N&CR ¶ 61 (Nov. 1994); Nash, *Postscript III: Best Value Procurement*, 8 N&CR ¶ 34 (June 1994); Nash, *Postscript II: Best Value Procurement*, 8 N&CR ¶ 26 (May 1994); Kenney & Sweeney, *Best Value Procurement*, 93-4 Briefing Papers (1993); Bail, *"Best Value" Procurement for Hazardous Waste and Remediation Services*, 33 Cont. Mgmt. 22 (Apr. 1993); Peckinpaugh & Goldstein, *Best Value Source Selection: Contracting for Value, or Unfettered Agency Discretion?*, 22 Pub. Cont. L.J. 275 (1993); Nash, *Postscript: Best Value Procurement*, 7 N&CR ¶ 10 (Feb. 1993); The Geo. Wash. Univ. Nat'l Law Center, Government Contracts Program, Symposium Proceedings, *Best-Value Procurement*

(Feb. 10–11, 1993); Cibinic, *Best Value Procurement: Two More Views*, 6 N&CR ¶ 59 (Oct. 1992); Cibinic, *In Defense of Best Value Procurement*, 6 N&CR ¶ 45 (Aug. 1992).

BID An OFFER submitted to the Government in response to an INVITATION FOR BIDS (IFB). BIDDERs must be given a reasonable time (generally at least 30 days) to prepare and submit bids, consistent with the needs of the Government. FAR 14.202-1. Bids must conform in all material respects to the IFB in order to be responsive (see RESPONSIVENESS) and thus eligible for award. See Cibinic & Nash, chap. 5, Sec. I., *Formation of Government Contracts* (3d ed. 1998); Shnitzer, chap. 11, *Government Contract Bidding* (3d ed. 1987 & Supp. 1991).

BID AND PROPOSAL (B&P) COSTS Costs incurred by a contractor in preparing, submitting, and supporting BIDs and PROPOSALs (whether or not solicited) on potential contracts. B&P costs do not include the costs of efforts sponsored by a GRANT or COOPERATIVE AGREEMENT or required in contract performance. FAR 31.205-18. Generally discussed in conjunction with INDEPENDENT RESEARCH AND DEVELOPMENT (IR&D) costs, B&P costs receive extensive treatment as a SELECTED COST under FAR 31.205-18 and under CAS 420, FAR 30.420. See Cibinic & Nash, *Cost-Reimbursement Contracting* 765–70 (2d ed. 1993). Instructions for negotiating ADVANCE AGREEMENTs for IR&D/B&P costs are given in FAR Subpart 42.10. See Cibinic, *Independent Research and Development, Bid and Proposal, and Precontract Costs: The Troublesome Troika*, 6 N&CR ¶ 42 (July 1992); Shnitzer, *Bid or Proposal & Protest Costs Under CICA*, 88-12 Briefing Papers (Nov. 1988); Victorino & Briggerman, *The IR&D/B&P/Selling Costs Dilemma*, 87-10 Briefing Papers (Sept. 1987). Recovery of bid or proposal costs represents a potential monetary remedy for a successful protester before the GENERAL ACCOUNTING OFFICE (GAO), the U.S. COURT OF FEDERAL CLAIMS, or a district court. See 31 U.S.C. § 3554(c)(1)(B) for the authority of the GAO to award such costs. If the protester prevails in the protest action and had a substantial chance for award of the contract but does not receive the award, the protester may recover the costs of preparing the bid or proposal. Typically, however, the protest forums will not award bid or proposal costs if the successful protester gains the opportunity to compete for the procurement.

BID BOND A BOND that serves as a BID GUARANTEE. Such bonds are used frequently in public construction projects and sometimes, but rarely, in nonconstruction contracts. See Shnitzer, chaps. 7 & 14, *Government Contract Bidding* (3d ed. 1987 & Supp. 1991); Patin, chap. 17, *Construction Contracting* 1209–22 (1991); Cibinic, *Bid Bonds and Bid Guarantees: Is the Tail Wagging the Dog?,* 2 N&CR ¶ 16 (Mar. 1988).

BID GUARANTEE A form of security assuring that the BIDDER (1) will not withdraw a BID within the period specified for acceptance and (2) will execute a written contract and furnish required BONDs, including any necessary coinsurance or reinsurance agreements, within the time specified in the bid. FAR 28.001. FAR 28.101-1(a) permits the use of bid guarantees *only* when a PERFORMANCE BOND or a PAYMENT BOND is required. Such guarantees must be in an amount adequate to protect the Government from loss and must be at least 20 percent of the bid price, but not more than $3 million. FAR 28.101-2. The Bid Guarantee solicitation provision at FAR 52.228-1 states that bid guarantees must be "in the form of a firm commitment, such as a bid bond, postal money order, certified check, or, under Treasury Department regulations, certain bonds or notes of the United States." See Cibinic, *Return of Bid Guarantees to Bidders*, 7 N&CR ¶ 21 (Apr. 1993); Cibinic, *Bid Guarantees: The Tail's Still Wagging!,* 6 N&CR ¶ 36 (June 1992); Cibinic, *Bid Bonds and Bid Guarantees: Is the Tail Wagging the Dog?*, 2 N&CR ¶ 16 (Mar. 1988).

BID OPENING The public opening of BIDs submitted to the Government in a sealed bid procurement (see SEALED BIDDING). The INVITATION FOR BIDS specifies an exact date and time for opening of bids. When the set time arrives, the bid opening officer informs those present of that fact and then (1) personally and publicly opens all bids received before the set time, (2) if practical, reads the bids aloud to the persons present, and (3) has the bids recorded. FAR 14.402-1. However, the general public may not have access to the opening of classified bids (see CLASSIFIED ACQUISITION). FAR 14.402-2. Bid openings may be postponed if the CONTRACTING OFFICER has reason to believe that the bids of an important segment of bidders have been delayed for causes beyond the bidders' control, or in the case of an emergency or unanticipated event that interrupts normal Government processes. FAR 14.402-3. Bids are recorded on an ABSTRACT OF OFFERS. See Schnitzer, chap. 18, *Government Contract Bidding* (3d ed. 1987 & Supp. 1991).

BID PROTEST See PROTEST.

BID SAMPLE A sample to be furnished by a BIDDER to show the characteristics of the product offered in a BID. FAR 14.202-4. Such a sample may be required only when the product has characteristics that cannot be described adequately in the SPECIFICATION or PURCHASE DESCRIPTION. Bid samples are used only to determine the RESPONSIVENESS of the bid, not to determine a bidder's ability to produce the required items. They provide the Government extra assurance that a bidder has submitted a bid that is responsive on its face can actually provide a product that meets the Government's requirements. FAR 14.202-4(c) provides that the use of bid samples is appropriate for products that must be suitable from the standpoint of balance, facility of use, general feel, color, pattern, or other characteristic that cannot be described adequately in the specification. A standard solicitation provision to be used when bid samples are required is provided in FAR 52.214-20.

BIDDER One who submits a BID. While this term technically refers only to an OFFEROR on a sealed bid procurement (see SEALED BIDDING), it is frequently used to refer to any offeror on a Government procurement—whether sealed bid, competitive negotiation, or otherwise. See Schnitzer, chap. 3, *Government Contract Bidding* (3d ed. 1987 & Supp. 1991).

BIDDERS' CONFERENCE See PRE-BID CONFERENCE and PRE-PROPOSAL CONFERENCE.

BIDDERS MAILING LIST See SOLICITATION MAILING LIST.

BIDDING TIME The time allowed prospective BIDDERs to prepare and submit their BIDs—the time between SOLICITATION issuance and BID OPENING. All INVITATION FOR BIDS (IFBs) must allow a reasonable bidding time, consistent with the needs of the Government; bidding time of at least 30 calendar days must be provided when SYNOPSIS in the COMMERCE BUSINESS DAILY is required by the SMALL BUSINESS ACT, 15 U.S.C. § 631, and the OFFICE OF FEDERAL PROCUREMENT POLICY ACT, 41 U.S.C. § 401. If bidding time were unduly limited, some potential sources might be precluded from bidding, and others might be forced to raise their bids by including amounts to cover contingencies. Thus, to avoid unduly restricting competition or paying higher than necessary prices, consideration must be given to the following factors in establishing a reasonable bidding time: (1) the degree of urgency, (2) the complexity of the requirement, (3) the anticipated extent of subcontracting, (4) whether a

PRE-SOLICITATION NOTICE was issued, (5) the geographic distribution of bidders, and (6) normal mailing time for both IFBs and bids. FAR 14.202-1; FAR 36.303(a) (construction contracts). See Schnitzer, chap. 5, *Government Contract Bidding* (3d ed. 1987 & Supp. 1991).

BIFURCATION OF ENTITLEMENT AND QUANTUM A distinction between the *right* to recover additional compensation under a contract and the *amount* of compensation to be recovered; the separation of issues of entitlement (referring to whether a party prevails) and quantum (referring to the amount a party recovers) in the hearing of a DISPUTE before a BOARD OF CONTRACT APPEALS (BCA). (The U.S. COURT OF FEDERAL CLAIMS does not follow this procedure.) BCAs generally prefer to hear only entitlement issues initially, assuming that, in most cases, the parties will be able to negotiate quantum successfully if the contractor is held to be entitled to compensation. The facts relating to entitlement are often simple, whereas the quantum issues may be complex; if the contractor fails to establish a right to recover, the BCA and the parties need not invest time and energy in calculating how much the contractor will *not* recover. Thus, prehearing instructions often explain that quantum will not be heard unless the BCA has expressly agreed to hear it, full cost schedule and supporting information have been furnished, and the Government has had an opportunity to conduct an AUDIT. When a case has been bifurcated and a contractor's claim to entitlement is sustained, the BCA remands the negotiation of quantum to the contracting officer and closes the file. If the parties fail to agree, the contractor must request a DECISION OF THE CONTRACTING OFFICER on quantum. Upon receipt of this decision, or after sufficient time passes for DEEMED DENIAL jurisdiction, the contractor can file a new notice of appeal with the BCA. See Nash, *Bifurcation: A Good Appeals Board Procedure That Is in Jeopardy*, 4 N&CR ¶ 71 (Dec. 1990).

BILATERAL CONTRACT A contract in which parties exchange promises to perform reciprocal obligations in the future. Except for contracts using SIMPLIFIED ACQUISITION PROCEDURES, where the contracting officer must decide whether to use a bilateral PURCHASE ORDER (see FAR 13.302), virtually all Government contracts are bilateral contracts. Bilateral contracts are contrasted with UNILATERAL CONTRACTs.

BILATERAL MODIFICATION See MODIFICATION.

BILL OF LADING A document evidencing receipt of goods for shipment, issued by a person engaged in the business of transporting or forwarding goods (including air bills). U.C.C. § 1-201(6). A bill of lading is the standard form of contract between a COMMON CARRIER and a party shipping goods. In Government contracting this form of contract can be used by the Government (a Government bill of lading) or a contractor (a commercial bill of lading). Guidance on the use of bills of lading is found in FAR Part 47. FAR 9.403 provides that firms shipping goods for the Government on either Government or commercial bills of lading are contractors subject to DEBARMENT and SUSPENSION.

BILL OF MATERIALS A report by a supplier that specifies the quantities of various materials required to produce a designated quantity of supplies of a particular kind. DFARS 210.001. A bill of materials is a descriptive and quantitative listing of materials, supplies, parts, and components required to produce a designated complete end item of material or assembly or subassembly. It may also show estimated costs or fixed prices. A bill of materials is the normal format used to summarize the material costs a contractor has included in its estimate of the contract price. See Cibinic & Nash, chap. 9, Sec. IV., *Formation of Government Contracts* (3d ed 1998); Cibinic & Nash, *Cost-Reimbursement Contracting* 540–44 (2d ed. 1993).

BILLING RATE An INDIRECT COST rate established temporarily for interim reimbursement of incurred indirect costs and adjusted as necessary pending establishment of a FINAL INDIRECT COST RATE. FAR 42.701. The contracting officer establishes a billing rate on the basis of information resulting from recent review, previous AUDITs or experience, or similar reliable data or experience of other contracting activities. Once established, billing rates may be prospectively or retroactively revised by mutual agreement of the contracting officer or AUDITOR and the contractor, at either party's request, to prevent substantial overpayment or underpayment. The elements of indirect cost and the base used in computing billing rates must not be construed as determining either the indirect costs to be distributed or the bases for distribution in the final settlement. FAR 42.704.

BLANKET PURCHASE AGREEMENT (BPA) A simplified method of filling the Government's anticipated repetitive needs for supplies or services by establishing charge accounts with qualified sources of supply. FAR 13.303. BPAs are designed to reduce administrative costs in accomplishing simplified acquisitions by eliminating the need for individual purchase documents. BPAs must contain the following terms and conditions: (1) a description of the agreement, (2) the extent of obligation, (3) pricing, (4) a purchase limitation, (5) notice of individuals authorized to purchase under the BPA, and dollar limitations by title of position and name, (6) delivery tickets, and (7) INVOICEs. FAR 13.303-3. Individual purchases under BPAs may not exceed the dollar limitation for simplified acquisitions, and the existence of a BPA does not justify sole source purchasing (see SOLE SOURCE). FAR 13.303-5. BPAs are also being used with vendors that have products or services on a FEDERAL SUPPLY SCHEDULE. FAR 8.404(b)(4). Within DOD, BPAs are issued on DD Form 1155, DFARS 213.203-1.

BLIND OR SEVERELY DISABLED **BLIND**—An individual or class of individuals whose central visual acuity does not exceed 20/200 in the better eye with correcting lenses; or, where the acuity is better than that, it is accompanied by a limit to the field of vision in the better eye that subtends an angle of no greater than 20 degrees at its largest diameter. **SEVERELY DISABLED**—An individual or class of individuals with a physical or mental disability that constitutes a substantial handicap to employment and is of such a nature as to prevent the individual from currently engaging in normal competitive employment. 41 U.S.C. § 48b. The JAVITS-WAGNER-O'DAY ACT ("the JWOD Act"), 41 U.S.C. §§ 46–48c, requires Government entities to purchase certain supplies and services from JWOD PARTICIPATING NONPROFIT AGENCIES for people who are blind or severely disabled, if the supplies or services are available when required. FAR Subpart 8.7 prescribes policies and procedures for implementing the Act and the rules of the Committee for Purchase from People Who Are Blind or Severely Disabled.

BOARD OF CONTRACT APPEALS (BCA) An administrative board established in a procuring agency to hear and decide DISPUTEs under the CONTRACT DISPUTES ACT (CDA) OF 1978. There are presently 11 BCAs. The CDA established the BCAs at 41 U.S.C. § 607(a) and defined their jurisdiction over federal contract performance disputes at 41 U.S.C. § 607(d). The BCAs resolve disputes, as distinguished from PROTEST actions, between the Federal Government and contractors. However, BCAs have on occasion been granted jurisdiction by specific statute or agency delegation to process protests as well; the primary example was the GENERAL SERVICES ADMINISTRATION BOARD OF CONTRACT APPEALS, which, pursuant to the COMPETITION IN CONTRACTING ACT and the BROOKS ACT (AUTOMATIC DATA PROCESSING PROCUREMENT), handled protests relating to FEDERAL INFORMATION PROCESSING RESOURCES from 1984 to 1996. The ARMED SERVICES BOARD OF CONTRACT APPEALS is the largest BCA with 28 ADMINISTRATIVE JUDGEs. The second largest, the GSBCA, has 11 administrative judges. The other BCAs have from three to seven administrative judges. The personnel, rules of procedure, and decisions of the BCAs are published in the *Contract Appeals Decisions Reporter*, Commerce Clearing House, Inc., 4025 Peterson Ave., Chicago, IL 60646. See Cibinic & Nash, *Administration of Government Contracts* 1311–13 (3d ed. 1995); Foss, *U.S. Government Printing Office Board of Contract Appeals: The First Decade*, 24 Pub. Cont. L.J. 579 (1995); Lee, *Hiring the Cheapest Piper: Arbitration of Subcontract Disputes by Boards of Contract Appeals*, 23 Pub. Cont. L.J. 105 (1993); Hordell & Lipman, *The Rise and Use of Protective Orders at the General Services Board of Contract Appeals*, 20 Pub. Cont. L.J. 22 (1990). See also APPEAL FROM A CONTRACTING OFFICER'S DECISION and APPEAL FROM THE RULING OF A COURT OR BOARD.

BOILERPLATE Standard contract language that is used by a party on all contracts of a certain type. In Government procurement this term is generally used to describe the GENERAL PROVISIONS that are included in contracts pursuant to FAR Part 52.

BONA FIDE AGENCY An established commercial or selling agency, maintained by a contractor for the purpose of securing business, that neither exerts nor proposes to exert IMPROPER INFLUENCE to solicit or obtain Government contracts, nor holds itself out as being able to obtain any Government contract or contracts through improper influence. FAR 3.401. Payments to such an agency are not improper under the contract provisions barring CONTINGENT FEEs. See Cibinic & Nash, chap. 1, Sec. VII., *Formation of Government Contracts* (3d ed. 1998).

BONA FIDE EMPLOYEE A person, employed by a contractor and subject to the contractor's supervision and control as to time, place, and manner of performance, who neither exerts nor proposes to exert improper influence to solicit or obtain Government contracts, nor holds out as being able to obtain any Government contract or contracts through improper influence. FAR 3.401. Payments to such employees are not improper under the contract provisions barring CONTINGENT FEEs. See Cibinic & Nash, chap. 1, Sec. VII., *Formation of Government Contracts* (3d ed. 1998).

BOND A written instrument executed by an offeror or contractor (the principal) and a second party (the SURETY or sureties) to ensure fulfillment of the principal's obligations to a third party (the obligee or the Government) identified in the bond. If the principal's obligations are not met, the bond ensures payment, to the extent stipulated, of any loss sustained by the obligee. Types of bonds discussed in the FAR include: (1) ADVANCE PAYMENT bonds, which secure fulfillment of the contractor's obligations under an advance payment provision; (2) BID BONDs, a form of BID GUARANTEE ensuring that the bidder will not withdraw a bid within the period specified and will execute a written contract within the time specified in the bid; (3) PERFORMANCE BONDs, which secure performance and fulfillment of the contractor's obligations under the contract; (4) PAYMENT BONDs, which ensure payments as required by law to all persons supplying LABOR or material in the prosecution of the work required by the contract; and (5) PATENT INFRINGEMENT bonds, which secure fulfillment of the contractor's obligations under a PATENT provision. FAR 28.001. Mentioned but not discussed in the FAR are fidelity bonds, used for ensuring the faithful performance of employees to their employers and their employers' clients (e.g., to cover losses by theft or embezzlement). See Patin, chap. 17, *Construction Contracting* 1209–1320 (1991); Cibinic, *Bid Bonds and Bid Guarantees: Is the Tail Wagging the Dog?,* 2 N&CR ¶ 16 (Mar. 1988).

BONDING COSTS The cost incurred by a contractor when the Government requires assurance against financial loss to itself or others stemming from an act or default of the contractor, or when the contractor requires similar assurance. Included are the costs of such BONDs as bid, performance, payment, ADVANCE PAYMENT, PATENT INFRINGEMENT, and fidelity bonds. Costs of bonding required by the terms of the contract are ALLOWABLE COSTs. FAR 31.205-4. Costs of bonding required by the contractor in the general conduct of its business are allowable to the extent that (1) such bonding is in accordance with sound business practice and (2) the rates and premiums are reasonable under the circumstances. See Cibinic & Nash, *Cost-Reimbursement Contracting* 867 (2d ed. 1993).

BONUS A payment of extra compensation to an employee. FAR 31.205-6(f) specifies when the costs of such payments by contractors may be treated as ALLOWABLE COSTs. See Cibinic & Nash, *Cost-Reimbursement Contracting* 801–2 (2d ed. 1993).

BORROWER The recipient of a loan. FAR 32.301 defines the term narrowly to include only a contractor, subcontractor (at any tier), or other supplier who receives a GUARANTEED LOAN.

BRAND-NAME-OR-EQUAL DESCRIPTION A PURCHASE DESCRIPTION that identifies a product by its brand name and model or part number or other appropriate nomenclature by which it is offered for sale and permits offers on products essentially equal to the specified brand name product. A brand-name-or-equal description is generally the minimum acceptable description in Government contracting; prospective contractors must be allowed to offer products other than those named by brand if those other products will meet the needs of the Government in essentially the same manner. FAR 11.104. This policy is incorporated in all construction contracts in paragraph (a) of the Material and Workmanship clause at FAR 52.236-5, which permits contractors to furnish equal items whenever an item is specified by trade name, make, or catalog number. Traditionally, this type of purchase description was required to set forth those salient physical, functional, or other characteristics of the brand name product that were deemed essential in meeting the Government's needs. However, the FAR contains no such requirement; it leaves this issue to agency policy. See DFARS 211.270-1, requiring the inclusion of SALIENT CHARACTERISTICS in DOD procurements using this type of purchase description. See Cibinic & Nash, *Administration of Government Contracts* 836–39 (3d ed. 1995); Nash, *"Brand Name or Equal": The Contractor's Rights*, 8 N&CR ¶ 39 (July 1994).

BREACH OF CONTRACT Failure, without legal excuse, to perform any promise that forms the whole or part of a contract. Breach can be found of both express promises in a contract and IMPLIED PROMISEs that are inherent in the transaction. "Breach" also means the unequivocal, distinct, and absolute refusal to perform under the agreement. It may also entail the prevention or hindrance by a party to the contract of any occurrence or performance required under the contract for the creation or continuance of a right in favor of the other party or for the discharge of a duty by that party. Constructive breach, which entails the concept of REPUDIATION, takes place when a party disables itself from performance by some act or declares, before the time of performance comes, that it does not intend to perform. *Black's Law Dictionary* 188–89 (6th ed. 1990). Traditionally, in Government contract law, breach of contract by the Government meant the Government's failure to perform one of its contractual obligations that was not redressable under a contract clause (thus not a CONSTRUCTIVE

CHANGE). Prior to the CONTRACT DISPUTES ACT OF 1978, appeals boards could not award damages for such breaches of contract. However, under the Act they now have the authority to award such damages. See Cibinic & Nash, *Administration of Government Contracts* 1244–46 (3d ed. 1995); Levey, *Tortious Government Conduct and the Government Contract: Tort, Breach of Contract, or Both?*, 22 Pub. Cont. L.J. 706 (1993); Braude, chap. 15, *Construction Contracting* 1086–1101 (1991); Toomey et al., *Good Faith and Fair Dealings: The Well-Nigh Irrefragable Need for a New Standard in Public Contract Law*, 20 Pub. Cont. L.J. 87 (1990).

BREAK-EVEN ANALYSIS The study of cost-volume-profit (C-V-P) relationships, or the analysis of proposed procurement and facilitization to compare potential costs of establishing a second source with potential savings due to competitive pressure from the second source. Jones, *Glossary: Defense Acquisition Acronyms and Terms* (8th ed., Defense Systems Management College). See BREAK-EVEN POINT.

BREAK-EVEN POINT In a business enterprise, the point at which revenues from sales exactly equal total INCURRED COST (revenues = variable costs + fixed costs). In decisionmaking (such as MAKE OR BUY), the point of indifference; that level of activity where either method results in exactly the same cost. These type of break-even decisions often involve making assumptions about levels of activity such as the number of units needed. Jones, *Glossary: Defense Acquisition Acronyms and Terms* (8th ed., Defense Systems Management College). See BREAK-EVEN ANALYSIS.

BREAKOUT A Government decision to procure a component or part directly from its manufacturer rather than from a systems contractor. DFARS appendix D contains guidance on breakout during the manufacturing process (involving furnishing the components to the systems contractor as GOVERNMENT-FURNISHED MATERIAL); DFARS appendix E addresses breakout during the procurement of replenishment parts. The purpose of breakout is to acquire the components or parts at a reduced price by avoiding the need to pay a systems contractor's overhead and PROFIT. See Payson & Hernaez, *Systems Breakout: An Alternative Acquisition Strategy*, 29 Cont. Mgmt. 8 (Aug. 1989); Young, *Breakout—The Mystery Unveiled*, 19 Nat'l Cont. Mgmt. J., Issue No. 1, p. 33 (1985). Breakout is also loosely used to mean obtaining additional competition, especially from small businesses. See BREAKOUT ADVOCATE.

BREAKOUT ADVOCATE An employee of a CONTRACTING ACTIVITY specifically assigned the task of seeking opportunities to reduce Government expenditures by using BREAKOUT. 10 U.S.C. § 2452 requires the Secretary of Defense to have breakout advocates. See also 15 U.S.C. § 644. These advocates are frequently called breakout procurement center representatives (PRCs) when they participate in the activities of the SMALL BUSINESS ADMINISTRATION procurement center representatives. PCRs are advocates for increasing SMALL BUSINESS CONCERN participation in federal procurement through traditional SET-ASIDEs. Breakout PCRs further that objective by advocating COMPETITION; they identify items being procured on a sole source basis (see SOLE SOURCE) and then identify and overcome factors that prevent competitive procurement of those items. In other words, breakout PCRs break the item out for competition and encourage small business concerns to participate in future competitive procurements for those items. Breakout PCRs assert that small business concerns can frequently provide breakout items at prices substantially lower than the sole source price being paid to the prime contractor for a major system.

BRIBERY The crime of offering, giving, receiving, or soliciting anything of value to influence action as an official or in discharge of a public duty. 18 U.S.C. § 201 proscribes such behavior on the part of "any officer or employee or person acting for or on behalf of the United States, or any department or agency or branch of government thereof, . . . in any official function." Giving or receiving GIFTs DURING THE CONDUCT OF A PROCUREMENT was also proscribed by the PROCUREMENT INTEGRITY provisions of 41 U.S.C. § 423 in effect prior to 1997. However, these provisions were repealed by the 1996 revisions of that act. See Cibinic & Nash, chap. 1, Sec. VII., *Formation of Government Contracts* (3d ed. 1998).

BRIDGE CONTRACT An extension, typically through a CHANGE ORDER or MODIFICATION, of an existing contract. A bridge contract with the incumbent contractor is often required when, for example, a BID PROTEST or disappointed-offeror suit results in a stay of the award or performance of the follow-on contract. Bridge contracts may be awarded noncompetitively in certain circumstances, particularly when they fall between two competitively awarded contracts, when the bridge contract is necessary to avoid disruption of necessary services, and the bridge contract is not necessary due to the lack of advance planning. See Jackson & Alerding, *Expanding Contracting Opportunities Without Competition*, 27 Pub. Cont. L.J. 205, 214–16 (1997).

BROAD AGENCY ANNOUNCEMENT (BAA) An announcement by a procuring agency of areas of RESEARCH interest, including criteria for selecting proposals and soliciting the participation of all offerors capable of satisfying the agency's needs. FAR 6.102(d)(2)(i). Under 10 U.S.C. § 2302(2) and 41 U.S.C. § 259(b), the solicitation of research proposals by BAAs is one of the COMPETITIVE PROCEDURES meeting the statutory requirement for FULL AND OPEN COMPETITION. However, BAAs may be used only when meaningful proposals with varying scientific or technical approaches can reasonably be expected. BAAs should (1) describe the agency's research interest; (2) describe the criteria for selecting the proposals, their RELATIVE IMPORTANCE, and the method of evaluation; (3) specify the period of time during which proposals will be accepted; and (4) contain instructions for the preparation and submission of proposals. Proposals are evaluated by PEER OR SCIENTIFIC REVIEW. The primary bases for award are technical excellence, importance to agency programs, and fund availability. FAR 35.016. Contracts are awarded until the agency has utilized its research funds in the area of interest. See Cibinic & Nash, chap. 7, Sec. V., *Formation of Government Contracts* (3d ed. 1998); Bolos, *Innovative Procurement Concepts—The Broad Agency Announcement*, 31 Cont. Mgmt. 4 (Feb. 1991). See also RESEARCH AND DEVELOPMENT.

BROOKS ACT (ARCHITECT-ENGINEER PROCUREMENTS) A 1972 Act, Pub. L. No. 92-582 as amended, 40 U.S.C. § 541 et seq., requiring the use of special procedures to procure ARCHITECT-ENGINEER (A-E) SERVICES. The procedures to be followed are set forth in FAR Subpart 36.6. They call for the selection of A-Es based on qualifications (as stated in Standard Form 254, Architect-Engineer and Related Services Questionnaire, FAR 53.301-254, or in Standard Form 255, Architect-Engineer and Related Services Questionnaire for Specific Project, FAR 53.301-255, and assessed during discussions) without evaluation of the proposed price for the work to be accomplished. Contract negotiations must be conducted with the highest-ranked offeror, and award must be made to that firm unless a reasonable price cannot be agreed upon. See Cibinic & Nash, chap. 7, Sec. III., *Formation of Government Contracts* (3d ed. 1998).

BROOKS ACT (AUTOMATIC DATA PROCESSING PROCUREMENTS) A 1965 Act, Pub. L. No. 89-306 as amended, repealed by Pub. L. No. 104-106, that required the use of special procedures to procure FEDERAL INFORMATION PROCESSING (FIP) RESOURCES. Under the Act, the GENERAL SERVICES

ADMINISTRATION (GSA) had exclusive authority to procure FIP resources for Government agencies; but it could delegate to agencies, by means of DELEGATIONs OF PROCUREMENT AUTHORITY, procurement authority to lease, purchase, or maintain FIP resources. GSA could also transfer FIP resources between federal agencies and create equipment pools and data processing centers. Through subsequent amendments to the Brooks Act, including the COMPETITION IN CONTRACTING ACT (CICA), the GENERAL SERVICES ADMINISTRATION BOARD OF CONTRACT APPEALS had jurisdiction over PROTESTs regarding FIP resources procurements, 40 U.S.C. § 759(f). Implementing regulations were found in the FEDERAL INFORMATION RESOURCES MANAGEMENT REGULATION, 41 C.F.R. § 201, and the Rules of the General Services Board of Contract Appeals. See McDonnell, *The Process of Procuring Information Technology*, 25 Pub. Cont. L.J. 379 (1996); Gabig, *A Primer on Federal Information Systems Acquisitions: Part Two of a Two-Part Article*, 17 Pub. Cont. L.J. 553 (1988); Gabig, *A Primer on Federal Information Systems Acquisitions: First Part of a Two-Part Article*, 17 Pub. Cont. L.J. 31 (1987).

BUDGET AUTHORITY Authority provided by law to enter into OBLIGATIONs that will result in immediate or future outlays involving Government funds. 2 U.S.C. § 622(2). Budget authority is that authority required to enter into a binding obligation in accordance with the ANTI-DEFICIENCY ACT. Budget authority is conferred by the enactment of (1) an APPROPRIATION act or (2) a statute conferring contracting authority.

BUDGET ENFORCEMENT ACT OF 1990 (BEA) A law designed to limit discretionary spending while ensuring that any new entitlement program or tax cuts did not make the federal budget deficit (when spending exceeds revenues) worse. The law sets annual limits on total discretionary spending and created pay-as-you-go rules for any changes, such as increases in entitlements or decreases in taxes. The pay-as-you-go rules require that new spending proposals or suggested tax reductions must be offset by cuts in other entitlements or by other tax increases. GAO, *A Citizen's Guide to the Federal Budget*, 35–37 Budget of the United States Government, Fiscal Year 1998 (1997).

BUDGETING AND FUNDING A required element of the Plan of Action in the written ACQUISITION PLAN where the contracting officer describes how budget estimates for the procurement were derived and discusses the schedule for obtaining adequate funds at the time they are required. FAR 7.105(b)(5). Generally, the ANTI-DEFICIENCY ACT, 31 U.S.C. § 1341, requires that contracts be fully funded. Under MULTIPLE YEAR CONTRACTs, INCREMENTALLY FUNDED CONTRACTs, and contracts conditioned on the availability of funds, however, contracts can be awarded without full funds. See Cibinic & Nash, chap. 3, Sec. I., *Formation of Government Contracts* (3d ed. 1998); Nash & Cibinic, *Competitive Negotiation: The Source Selection Process* 93–97 (1993).

BUILDING CONSTRUCTION An activity as distinguished from manufacturing, furnishing materials, or servicing and maintenance work. FAR 22.401. The term refers to work on buildings, structures, and improvements of all types, such as bridges, dams, plants, highways, parkways, streets, subways, tunnels, sewers, mains, power lines, pumping stations, heavy generators, railways, airports, terminals, docks, piers, wharves, ways, lighthouses, buoys, jetties, breakwaters, levees, canals, dredging, shoring, rehabilitation and reactivation of plants, scaffolding, drilling, blasting, excavating, clearing, and landscaping. Manufacturing or furnishing materials, articles, supplies, or equipment is not "building" unless conducted in connection with, and at the site of, construction activity as described above. Contracting for building-type work is subject to the DAVIS-BACON ACT and the procedures in FAR Part 36. See Patin, chap. 18, *Construction Contracting* 1395–1439 (1991).

BULK FUNDING A system whereby a contracting officer receives authorization from a fiscal and accounting officer to obligate funds on purchase documents, against a specified lump sum of funds reserved for the purpose, for a specified period of time, rather than obtaining individual obligational authority on each purchase document. FAR 13.101(b)(4). Agencies are required to use bulk funding to the maximum extent practicable to increase the efficiency of SIMPLIFIED ACQUISITION PROCEDURES. FAR 13.101(b)(4).

BUNDLING The practice of pooling potentially smaller purchases to leverage the Government's purchasing power and obtain the benefits of ECONOMIES OF SCALE or reduce the Government's administrative costs. Also known as aggregation or packaging, the term refers to the practice of consolidating into a single larger contract solicitation multiple procurement requirements. The term "bundling" typically carries the connotation that the consolidation achieves a magnitude that denies small businesses the opportunity to compete for the award of the contract. Section 412 of the Small Business Reauthorization Act of

1997, Pub. L. No. 105-137 requires the head of the agency to conduct MARKET RESEARCH before proceeding with an ACQUISITION STRATEGY that could lead to bundling of contract requirements. Section 414 of the Act requires the Federal Procurement Data System to be modified in order to collect data regarding contract bundling. See National Defense Authorization Act for FY94, Pub. L. No. 103-160; Small Business Credit and Business Opportunity Act, Pub. L. No. 102-366. See also Pangburn, *The Impact of Contract Bundling and Variable-Quantity Contracts on Competition and Small Business,* 25 Pub. Cont. L.J. 69 (1995); Nash, *Packaging the Work; An Anti-competitive Device?,* 7 N&CR ¶ 27 (May 1993).

BUREAU HELIUM DISTRIBUTOR A private helium distributor that has established and maintains eligibility to distribute helium purchased from the Bureau of Mines, as specified in 30 C.F.R. Part 602. See FAR 8.501, implementing the HELIUM ACT, 50 U.S.C. § 167a et seq., which concerns the acquisition of liquid or gaseous helium by federal agencies or by Government contractors or subcontractors for use in the performance of a Government contract. See also FAR 52.208-8, Helium Requirement Forecast and Required Sources for Helium.

BUREAU OF STANDARDS See NATIONAL INSTITUTE OF STANDARDS AND TECHNOLOGY.

BUSINESS AND FINANCIAL MANAGEMENT Within DOD, business and financial functions, including the management of acquisition funds and contracting activities, typically includes: the ACQUISITION PLAN or checklist; ACQUISITION STRATEGY or road map; contract types, contract award, and contract monitoring; cost estimating; formulation of input for the program objectives memorandum, the budget, and other programmatic or financial documentation of the PLANNING, PROGRAMMING, AND BUDGETING SYSTEM; REQUEST FOR PROPOSALS preparation; SOURCE SELECTION; contractor surveillance; and budget execution or paying bills. Jones, *Glossary: Defense Acquisition Acronyms and Terms* (8th ed., Defense Systems Management College).

BUSINESS CLEARANCE MEMORANDUM (BDM) A document produced by DOD agencies that describes the prenegotiation objectives for a procurement to be made using a COST-REIMBURSEMENT CONTRACT. The purpose of the BCM is to illustrate that a proposed contractual action represents good business judgment, conforms to federal, DOD, or other agency acquisition policies, and establishes a fair and reasonable price. NASA documents its prenegotiation findings in a prenegotiation position memorandum, which is similar to a BCM. Cibinic & Nash, *Cost-Reimbursement Contracting* 496 (2d ed. 1993). The process for determining prenegotiation objectives is outlined in FAR 15.406-1.

BUSINESS COMBINATION The legal bringing together under common control of a corporation and one or more incorporated or unincorporated firms, generally into a single organization. The single organization carries on the activities of the previously separate, independent enterprises. There are two basic approaches to obtaining control over assets owned and used by other firms. The acquiring firm may buy the desired assets and thereby obtain title to their use directly, or it may obtain an ownership interest in the common stock of another company, enabling the acquiring firm to exercise indirect control over the other firm's assets. The two basic approaches can be adopted in various forms: (1) acquisition of assets, (2) acquisition of stock, (3) statutory merger, (4) statutory consolidation. There are two methods of accounting for a business combination: the purchase method and the pooling-of-interest method. *DCAA Contract Audit Manual* 7-1700. FAR 31.205-52 limits the allowability of AMORTIZATION, cost of money (see COST OF MONEY FACTORS), and DEPRECIATION when the purchase method is used. FAR Subpart 42.12 contains procedures for recognizing business combinations by processing CHANGE OF NAME AGREEMENTs or NOVATIONs. See Burton, *Business Combinations: Treatment of Costs on Defense Contracts*, 24 Pub. Cont. L.J. 217 (1995); Chierichella & Perry, *Mergers and Acquisitions of Government Contractors: Special Considerations and Due Diligence Concerns*, 23 Pub. Cont. L.J. 471 (1994); Yao & DeSanti, *Antitrust Analysis of Defense Industry Mergers*, 23 Pub. Cont. L.J. 379 (1994); Wilkinson & Bernstein, *Mergers in the Defense Industry: Application of the 1992 Horizontal Merger Guidelines*, 23 Pub. Cont. L.J. 1 (1993); Murphy, *Business Combinations Mergers and Acquisitions*, 19 Pub. Cont. L.J. 581 (1990).

BUSINESS UNIT Any part of an organization, or an entire business organization, that is not divided into SEGMENTs. FAR 31.001. To ensure consistency and efficiency, single OVERHEAD RATEs must be established for all contracts held by a contractor business unit. FAR 42.703. This is accomplished by designating a single contracting agency to negotiate or determine such rates. CAS 410, FAR 30.410, provides criteria for the process of allocating a business unit's

GENERAL AND ADMINISTRATIVE EXPENSE to its final COST OBJECTIVEs.

BUY AMERICAN ACT An Act, 41 U.S.C. §§ 10a–10d, originally enacted in 1933, that generally requires that only DOMESTIC END PRODUCTs may be procured in purchasing supplies and CONSTRUCTION MATERIALS for public use, unless the items (1) are for use outside the United States, (2) would be unreasonable in cost, or (3) are not mined, produced, or manufactured domestically in sufficient and reasonably available commercial quantities of satisfactory quality. Also exempt are items purchased for commissary resale and items for which the HEAD OF THE AGENCY determines that domestic preference would be inconsistent with the public interest. FAR 25.102(a). The FAR contains separate regulations for supplies (FAR Subpart 25.1) and construction materials (FAR Subpart 25.2). With regard to supplies, it provides a preference evaluation system for domestic end products over foreign end products as defined in FAR 25.101. Foreign offers are evaluated by including duty, whether or not actually paid, and adding 6 percent to the total (or 12 percent if the domestic offeror is a SMALL BUSINESS CONCERN). When they exceed these margins, domestic prices are deemed unreasonable and competing foreign offers may be accepted. FAR 25.105. FAR 25.108 lists approximately 100 articles, materials, and supplies excepted from application of the Buy American Act. DOD and NASA have also created exceptions to the Act by negotiating memoranda of understanding with foreign governments. FAR 25.103; DFARS 225.103. The Buy American Act does not apply to products covered by the TRADE AGREEMENTS ACT or the NORTH AMERICAN FREE TRADE AGREEMENTS ACT. FAR 25.402. See Nash, *Postscript: Postaward Exceptions to the Buy American Act*, 11 N&CR ¶ 11 (Mar. 1997); Nash, *Buy American Act: Exceptions After Contract Award*, 8 N&CR ¶ 59 (Oct. 1994); Kenney et al., *Domestic Preference Provisions/Ed. II*, 94-3 Briefing Papers (Feb. 1994); Szurgot, *The Buy American Act: Reverse Discrimination Against Domestic Manufacturers; Implications of the Trade Agreements Act of 1979 On the Rule of Origin Test*, 7 Admin. L.J. Am. U. 737 (Fall 1993/Win. 1994); Nash, *The Buy American Act: Does it Control Content of a Product?*, 6 N&CR ¶ 63 (Nov. 1992); Kenney & Duberstein, *Domestic Preference Provisions*, 89-3 Briefing Papers (Feb. 1989); Golub & Fenske, *U.S. Government Procurement: Opportunities and Obstacles for Foreign Contractors*, 20 Geo. Wash. J. Int'l L. & Econ. 567 (1987).

BUY INDIAN ACT An Act, 25 U.S.C. § 47, authorizing the Secretary of the Interior to SET ASIDE procurements for Indian-owned and -controlled enterprises. In 1976, the Bureau of Indian Affairs formally adopted the policy that purchases and contracts be made with qualified Indian contractors to the maximum practicable extent. Buy Indian procurements are conducted in much the same way as other procurements, the primary difference being that only Indian-owned or -controlled enterprises are eligible for award.

BUY ITEM An item or work effort to be produced or performed by a SUBCONTRACTOR. FAR 15.407-2. Such items are reviewed by the contracting officer when FAR 15.407-2 requires review of a contractor's MAKE-OR-BUY PROGRAM. See also MAKE ITEM.

BUYING-IN Submitting an OFFER below anticipated costs in the expectation of increasing the contract amount after award (for example, through unnecessary or excessively priced contract MODIFICATIONs or receiving FOLLOW-ON CONTRACTs at artificially high prices) to recover LOSSes incurred on the buy-in contract. FAR 3.501-1. Buying-in may decrease competition or result in poor contract performance. The Government should minimize the opportunity for buying-in. It can seek a price commitment covering as much of the program as is practical by using MULTIYEAR CONTRACTING or priced OPTIONs for additional quantities that, together with the firm contract quantity, equal the program requirements. It can also employ other safeguards, such as amortizing NONRECURRING COSTS or determining that the offered price is unreasonable. When a buy-in is suspected, the contracting officer generally has the discretion to award a contract at the buy-in price but is directed to take appropriate action to ensure that buying-in losses are not recovered by the contractor through contract modifications or follow-on contracts. FAR 3.501-2. See Cibinic & Nash, chap. 5, Sec. III., *Formation of Government Contracts* (3d ed. 1998); Nash, *Dealing With "Significantly" Low Bids: When It's Too Good to Be True*, 8 N&CR ¶ 23 (Apr. 1994); Virdin & Gallatin, *Buying In*, 84-3 Briefing Papers (Mar. 1984).

BYRD AMENDMENT A provision in the Department of the Interior Appropriations Act for FY90, Pub. L. No. 101-121, 31 U.S.C. § 1352, that imposes lobbying restrictions on all Government contractors. These restrictions, which became effective in December 1989, prohibit recipients of federal funds (that is, recipients of contracts, GRANTs, loans, or COOPERATIVE AGREEMENTs) from using those funds to pay persons to attempt to influence members of Congress or their staffs or members of the executive branch in connection with the award, extension, or MODIFICATION of a contract, grant, or other funding instrument. The provisions, which flow down to subcontracts exceeding $100,000 regardless of tier, carry civil penalties of $10,000 to $100,000. This act is implemented by FAR Subpart 3.8, which requires the use of the solicitation provision Certification and Disclosure Regarding Payments to Influence Certain Federal Transactions (FAR 52.203-11) in all solicitations for contracts exceeding $100,000.

C

CABLE TELEVISION FRANCHISE AGREEMENTS See FRANCHISE AGREEMENTS.

CANCELLATION CEILING The maximum amount that the Government is obligated to pay a contractor when there is a CANCELLATION OF a MULTIYEAR CONTRACT. FAR 17.101. Under 10 U.S.C. § 2306b(c), both RECURRING COSTS and NONRECURRING COSTS may be included in this ceiling. 41 U.S.C. § 254c permits the civilian agencies to use multiyear contracts but contains no guidance on the costs to be included in cancellation ceilings. FAR 17.103(d) provides that the contracting officer will establish a cancellation ceiling, in diminishing amounts, for each program year and that it will include a reasonable estimate of the nonrecurring costs that will not have been recovered if the contract is canceled. See also DFARS 217.103(d). The amount that is actually paid to the contractor upon settlement for unrecovered costs (which cannot exceed the ceiling) is referred to as the cancellation charge. See Cibinic & Nash, chap. 8, Sec. VI., *Formation of Government Contracts* (3d ed. 1998); Nash, *Multiyear Procurement: The Different Faces of Congress*, 9 N&CR ¶ 40 (July 1995).

CANCELLATION OF CONTRACT Notification to a contractor that the Government considers the contract null and void and will not be bound by its terms. Cancellation is generally proper only when the contractor has violated a criminal statute or committed some other gross impropriety. *United States v. Mississippi Valley Generating Company*, 364 U.S. 520 (1961). Cancellation for BRIBERY, gratuities (see GRATUITY), or CONFLICT OF INTEREST is permitted by 18 U.S.C. § 218. See FAR Subpart 3.7.

CANCELLATION OF MULTIYEAR CONTRACT Notification to a contractor that the Government will not make funds available for contract performance for the total requirement of any future year of a multiyear contract, or failure to notify the contractor that funds are available for performance of the succeeding program-year requirement.

FAR 17.101. Such cancellation permits the contractor to recover costs in accordance with the Cancellation of Items clause in FAR 52.217-2, up to the amount of the CANCELLATION CEILING.

CANCELLATION OF SOLICITATION Notification to potential offerors, before AWARD, that a procurement will be permanently or temporarily stopped. Cancellation of an INVITATION FOR BIDS (IFB) involves a loss of time, effort, and money spent by the Government and bidders. Therefore, IFBs should not be canceled unless cancellation is clearly in the public interest (for instance, when the supplies or services are no longer required or when amendments to the IFB would be of such magnitude that a new IFB is desirable). FAR 14.209. When an IFB is canceled, bids that have been received must be returned unopened to the bidders and a notice of cancellation must be sent to all prospective bidders to which IFBs were issued. For bids received electronically, the data received must not be viewed and must be purged from primary and backup storage systems. Cancellation of IFBs after BID OPENING is to be avoided even more than cancellation before bid opening because at that time all of the bids have been exposed. Therefore, FAR 14.404-1 prohibits cancellation after bid opening unless there is a compelling reason to reject all bids and cancel the invitation. See Cibinic & Nash, chap. 5, Sec. III, *Formation of Government Contracts* (3d ed. 1998). With regard to competitive proposals solicited in contracting by NEGOTIATION, the contracting officer is to cancel the original REQUEST FOR PROPOSALS (RFPs) and issue a new one, regardless of the stage of the acquisition, if a change is so substantial that it warrants complete revision of the RFP. FAR 15.206(e). See Cibinic, *Cancellation of Solicitations: Are Bids and Proposals Sweeter the Second Time Around?,* 7 N&CR ¶ 36 (July 1993); Ginsburg & Patin, chap. 2, *Construction Contracting* 169–80 (1991).

CAPABILITY The ability of a prospective contractor to perform a contract. In procurement using SEALED BIDDING, capability is assessed by making a RESPONSIBILITY determination. In procurement using COMPETITIVE NEGOTIATION, capability is assessed by using one or more capability EVALUATION FACTORs.

CAPABILITY OR PERFORMANCE One of eight required elements of the Acquisition Background and Objectives in the written ACQUISITION PLAN prepared by the contracting agency. FAR 7.105(a)(4) provides that the acquisition should specify the required capabilities or performance characteristics of the supplies or services being acquired and state how they are related to the need. The requirement for a specific statement of the key performance characteristics of the proposed acquisition should assist the agency in identifying restrictive provisions in the STATEMENT OF WORK that may preclude potential contractors from participating in the procurement. When such provisions are identified, an agency can address options to eliminate them. Nash & Cibinic, *Competitive Negotiation: The Source Selection Process* 30 (1993).

CAPABILITY VALIDATION Technical verification of the ability of a proposed ADP system configuration or replacement component, or the features or functions of its software, to satisfy functional requirements. The intent of the capability validation is to ensure that the proposed FEDERAL INFORMATION PROCESSING (FIP) RESOURCEs can provide the functions required by the Government. FIP performance requirements are not implied or measured in the validation. Examples of capability validation include operational capability demonstrations, verification of conformance with information processing standards, expert examination of the technical literature supplied with the offer, contacts with other users of the proposed resource, and vendor certification of conformance with the functional requirements. See also BENCHMARK.

CAPITAL ASSET An ASSET of a contractor that has been capitalized. See CAPITALIZATION. With regard to Government assets, this term means land, structures, equipment, and intellectual property (including software) that are used by the Federal Government and have an estimated useful life of two years or more. Capital assets include leasehold improvements and lease rights, assets owned by the Federal Government but located in a foreign country, and assets whose ownership is shared by the Federal Government with other entities. Capital assets include all additions, improvements, replacements, rearrangements, reinstallations, and major repairs made to the asset. The cost of a capital asset includes both its purchase price and all other costs incurred to bring it to a form and location suitable for its intended use. GAO, *Principles of Budgeting for Capital Asset Acquisitions*, 8–9 Budget of the United States Government, Fiscal Year 1998 (1997). See also TANGIBLE CAPITAL ASSET.

CAPITAL INVESTMENTS The amount of funds a contractor has invested in FACILITIES and equipment that contributes to efficient and economic contract performance. Capital investments are one of the six factors agencies must consider in developing their PROFIT

OBJECTIVE when they use the structured approach to profit determination, and contracting officers must also consider them in analyzing profit whether or not they are using a structured approach. FAR 15.404-4(d). The agencies have developed various systems for determining the amount of profit that should be attributed to capital investments. See NFS 18-15.970-2 and GSAR 515.905-1(c)(4). DOD has a rather precise mathematical method which gives far greater weight to this segment of the profit objective. See DFARS 215.971-4(c). See Cibinic & Nash, chap. 9, Sec. V., *Formation of Government Contracts* (3d ed. 1998).

CAPITALIZATION Setting up expenditures as ASSETs rather than treating them as current expenses. General accounting practices require contractors to capitalize the costs of tangible assets when they exceed predetermined amounts. CAS 404, 48 C.F.R. § 9904.404, sets forth principles governing such capitalization. Once assets are capitalized, their cost is charged to contracts through DEPRECIATION.

CARDINAL CHANGE A CHANGE that is beyond the SCOPE OF THE CONTRACT and, thus, cannot be ordered by the contracting officer under the contract's Changes clause. Cardinal changes are BREACHes OF CONTRACT. In determining whether a change is beyond the scope of the contract, courts and boards compare the total work performed by the contractor with the work called for by the original contract. Work lies within the scope of contract if it can fairly and reasonably be regarded as within the contemplation of the parties when the contract was entered into or if it is essentially the same work that the parties bargained for when the contract was awarded. See Cibinic & Nash, chap. 3, Sec. II., *Formation of Government Contracts* (3d ed. 1998); Cibinic & Nash, *Administration of Government Contracts* 286–96 (3d ed. 1995); Powell, *The Cardinal Change Doctrine and its Application to Government Construction Contracts*, 24 Pub. Cont. L.J. 377 (1995); Nash, chap. 6, *Construction Contracting* 504–6 (1991).

CARGO PREFERENCE ACTS Acts giving preference to U.S.-owned vessels in the shipment of work under Government contracts. See FAR Subpart 47.5. The Cargo Preference Act of 1904, 10 U.S.C. § 2631, requires that DOD use only U.S.-FLAG VESSELs for ocean transportation of supplies for the Army, Navy, Air Force, or Marine Corps, unless those vessels are not available at fair and reasonable rates. Under the Cargo Preference Act of 1954, 46 U.S.C. § 1241(b), Government agencies acquiring supplies that require ocean transportation must ensure that at least 50 percent of the gross tonnage of the supplies is transported in privately-owned U.S.-flag commercial vessels, to the extent that such vessels are available at fair and reasonable rates. The Cargo Preference Act of 1954 may be temporarily waived when the Congress, the President, or the Secretary of Defense declares the existence of an emergency that justifies a temporary waiver. 46 U.S.C. § 1241(c)(1). When this Act is applicable, the clause at FAR 52.247-64 is used. See Cibinic, *Correction: Cargo Preference*, 5 N&CR ¶ 64 (Nov. 1991); Cibinic, *Postscript: Cargo Preference*, 5 N&CR ¶ 29 (May 1991); Cibinic, *Transportation of Supplies: Up With American Bottoms*, 4 N&CR ¶ 34 (May 1990).

CARIBBEAN BASIN COUNTRY END PRODUCT A product produced or manufactured in a country designated by the President as a beneficiary under the CARIBBEAN BASIN ECONOMIC RECOVERY ACT. Such an end product must be an article (1) that is wholly the growth, product, or manufacture of a Caribbean Basin country, or (2) that, in the case of an article consisting in whole or in part of materials from another country or instrumentality, has been substantially transformed in a Caribbean Basin country into a new and different article of commerce with a name, character, or use distinct from that of the article or articles from which it was transformed. The term does not, however, embrace products excluded from duty-free treatment for Caribbean countries under 19 U.S.C. § 2703(b) (certain textiles, footwear, luggage, leather products, tuna, petroleum, watches, and watch parts). FAR 25.401. See Kenney et al., *Domestic Preference Provisions/Edition II*, 94-3 Briefing Papers (Feb. 1994); Kenney & Duberstein, *Domestic Preference Provisions*, 89-3 Briefing Papers (Feb. 1989).

CARIBBEAN BASIN ECONOMIC RECOVERY ACT A 1983 Act, 19 U.S.C. § 2701 et seq., making certain countries eligible for the TRADE AGREEMENTS ACT OF 1979 exceptions to the BUY AMERICAN ACT. These countries are in addition to those designated in the Trade Agreements Act itself. FAR 25.401 makes these countries, which the President designated as beneficiaries under the Act, eligible for this preference. The list currently includes Antigua and Barbuda, Aruba, Bahamas, Barbados, Belize, British Virgin Islands, Costa Rica, Dominica, Dominican Republic, El Salvador, Grenada, Guatemala, Guyana, Haiti, Honduras, Jamaica, Monserrat, Netherlands Antilles, Nicaragua, Panama, St. Kitts and Nevis, St. Lucia, St. Vincent and the Grenadines, and Trinadad and Tobago. The U.S. Trade Representative has determined that these countries provide appropriate reciprocal, competitive Government procurement opportunities for U.S. products and suppliers. The FAR contains a list of products excluded from duty-free treatment for Caribbean countries, such as (1) certain textiles and apparel, (2) leather wearing apparel (footwear, gloves, luggage), (3) tuna (in airtight containers), (4) petroleum goods, and (5) watches and watch parts. FAR 25.401. See Kenney et al., *Domestic Preference Provisions/Edition II*, 94-3 Briefing Papers (Feb. 1994); Kenney & Duberstein, *Domestic Preference Provisions*, 89-3 Briefing Papers (Feb. 1989).

CARRIER (TELECOMMUNICATIONS) A COMMON CARRIER, foreign carrier, or noncommon carrier engaged in providing TELECOMMUNICATIONS SERVICES. "Common carrier" means any entity engaged in the business of providing telecommunications services that are regulated by the Federal Communications Commission or other Governmental body. "Noncommon carrier" means any entity other than a common carrier offering telecommunications facilities, services, or equipment for lease. "Foreign carrier" means any person, partnership, association, joint-stock company, trust, Governmental body, or corporation not subject to regulation by a U.S. Governmental body and not doing business as a citizen of the United States, providing telecommunications services outside the territorial limits of the United States. DFARS 239.7401. DFARS Subpart 239.74 states DOD policy on acquiring telecommunications services from common, noncommon, and foreign carriers.

CARRIER (TRANSPORTATION) A COMMON CARRIER or a contract carrier. FAR 47.001. "Common carrier" means an entity holding itself out to the general public to provide transportation for compensation. "Contract carrier" means an entity providing transportation for compensation under a continuing agreement with one party or a number of parties. FAR 47.001. Guidance on contracts for transportation is contained in FAR Subpart 47.2.

CAS-COVERED CONTRACT Any negotiated contract or subcontract that is subject to the COST ACCOUNTING STANDARDS (CAS). 48 C.F.R. § 9903.201-2 provides that such contracts are subject to either full or modified coverage of the Cost Accounting Standards requirements in accordance with the rules in FAR 30.301(b), which provide 15 exemptions from those requirements.

CASH BASIS ACCOUNTING An accounting method in which revenue, expense, and BALANCE SHEET items are recorded when cash is paid or received. Although there is no specific prohibition against the use of the cash basis in Government contract accounting, most Government contractors use the ACCRUAL BASIS. See Cibinic & Nash, *Cost-Reimbursement Contracting* 638 (2d ed. 1993).

CATALOG OR MARKET PRICE See ESTABLISHED CATALOG OR MARKET PRICE.

CATEGORY OF MATERIAL A particular kind of goods, comprised of identical or interchangeable units, acquired or produced by a contractor, that are intended to be sold or consumed or used in the performance of either direct or indirect functions. 48 C.F.R. § 9904.411-30(a)(3). Under CAS 411, 48 C.F.R. § 9904.411-50(a), contractors must adjust the purchase price of a category of material by extra charges incurred, or discounts and credits earned, when accounting for the acquisition costs of material.

CATEGORY I CONDITION A DIFFERING SITE CONDITION that FAR 52.236-2(a)(1) defines as "subsurface or latent physical conditions at the site which differ materially from those indicated in [the] contract." A successful Category I claim must contain six elements: (1) the contract documents must have affirmatively indicated or represented the subsurface conditions that form the basis of the claim; (2) the contractor must have acted with reasonable prudence in interpreting the contract documents; (3) the contractor must have reasonably relied on the indications of subsurface conditions in the contract; (4) the subsurface conditions actually encountered, within the contract site area, must have differed materially from the subsurface conditions indicated in the same contract area; (5) the actual subsurface conditions encountered must have been reasonably unforeseeable; and (6) the contractor's claimed excess costs must be shown to be solely attributable to the materially different subsurface conditions within the contract site. *Weeks Dredging & Contracting, Inc. v. United States*, 13 Cl. Ct. 193 (1987), *aff'd*, 861 F.2d 728 (Fed. Cir. 1988). See Cibinic & Nash, chap. 5, *Administration of Government Contracts* (3d ed. 1995); Braude, chap. 7, *Construction Contracting* 557–615 (1991); McClure, *Differing Site Conditions: Evaluating the Material Difference*, 15 Pub. Cont. L.J. 138 (1984).

CATEGORY II CONDITION A DIFFERING SITE CONDITION of an unusual nature that differs materially from those ordinarily encountered and generally recognized as inherent in the work of the character provided for in the contract. FAR 52.236-2(a)(2). A Category

II claim requires that the contractor demonstrate that the condition was unknown, unforeseeable, and unusual. *Lathan Co. v. United States*, 20 Cl. Ct. 122 (1990). In asserting a Category II claim, the contractor faces a relatively heavy burden of proof, and the court has stated that "[a]s a general matter, it is more difficult to establish a Type II differing site condition", *CCI Contractors, Inc.*, AGBCA 84-314-1, 91-3 BCA ¶ 24,225, *aff'd*, 979 F.2d 216 (Fed. Cir. 1992). See Cibinic & Nash, chap. 5, *Administration of Government Contracts* (3d ed. 1995); Braude, chap. 7, *Construction Contracting* 557–615 (1991); McClure, *Differing Site Conditions: Evaluating the Material Difference*, 15 Pub. Cont. L.J. 138 (1984).

CBDNET The official online listing of Government contracting opportunities that is published in the COMMERCE BUSINESS DAILY (CBD). The CBD lists notices of proposed Government procurement actions, contract awards, sales of Government property, and other procurement information. A new edition of the CBD is issued every business day. Although there is a charge for a subscription to the paper version of the CBD, CBDNet is free to all users. CBDNet is provided through an alliance of the United States Department of Commerce and the United States Government Printing Office and can be found on the Internet at <http://cbdnet.gpo.gov/>.

CEILING PRICE A price established by the parties that is the maximum price that the Government will pay regardless of the cost of performance. Ceiling prices are included in all FIXED-PRICE-INCENTIVE CONTRACTs (FAR 16.403(a)) and FIXED-PRICE REDETERMINATION—RETROACTIVE CONTRACTs (see FAR 16.206) and may be used in FIXED-PRICE REDETERMINATION—PROSPECTIVE CONTRACTs (see FAR 16.205). They are also included in COST-REIMBURSEMENT CONTRACTs on occasion. See Cibinic & Nash, *Cost-Reimbursement Contracting* 24–27 (2d ed. 1993). Ceiling prices are subject to revision under all contract clauses calling for EQUITABLE ADJUSTMENT or PRICE ADJUSTMENT.

CENTRAL CONTRACTOR REGISTRATION (CCR) Operated by DOD, CCR is a method for the Government to have one master registration database of all contractors wishing to contract with any agency of the Government. FAR 4.503(a) provides that in order for a contractor to conduct electronic commerce with the Government, the contractor must provide information to the CCR. There are three methods of registration: (1) obtaining a registration kit and mailing in registration; (2) using the electronic bulletin board; and (3) registering on the internet. See Cibinic, *Central Contractor Registration: Ready or Not, Here They Come*, 11 N&CR ¶ 26 (June 1997).

CERTIFICATE OF APPOINTMENT See WARRANT.

CERTIFICATE OF COMMERCIAL PRICING See COMMERCIAL PRICING CERTIFICATE.

CERTIFICATE OF COMPETENCY (COC) Certification by the SMALL BUSINESS ADMINISTRATION (SBA) under the Small Business Act, 15 U.S.C. § 637(b)(7), that a SMALL BUSINESS CONCERN meets the standard of RESPONSIBILITY with regard to performing a particular Government contract. The issuance of a COC overrides a determination of nonresponsibility made by a contracting officer. When a contracting officer determines that a small business concern is nonresponsible, the concern must be given the opportunity to refer the matter to the SBA, which will decide whether or not to issue a COC. An SBA decision to issue a COC can be appealed by the contracting officer to the SBA Central Office. See FAR Subpart 19.6. Application for a COC consists of two forms to be completed by the small business contractor: SBA Form 74, Application for Certificate of Competency, and SBA Form 355, Application for Small Business Size Determination. See Efron & Muchmore, *Certificates of Competency*, 87-11 Briefing Papers (Oct. 1987).

CERTIFICATE OF CONFORMANCE A certification of a contractor that contractual supplies or services are of the quality specified and conform in all respects to the contract requirements. FAR 52.246-15. This certificate may be required of contractors and is used as a substitute for full inspection by the Government. FAR 46.504. A certificate of conformance may increase a contractor's liability for defective work. See Cibinic & Nash, *Administration of Government Contracts* 876–79 (3d ed. 1995); Nash, *Unbalanced Bidding in Long-Term Contracts: The Comptroller General's Accounting Lapse*, 9 N&CR ¶ 54 (Oct. 1995).

CERTIFICATE OF CURRENT COST OR PRICING DATA Certification by a successful offeror on a negotiated procurement that the COST OR PRICING DATA submitted to the Government was, to the best of its knowledge and belief, ACCURATE, COMPLETE, AND CURRENT as of the date when price agreement was reached or a cutoff date agreed to by the parties. FAR 15.406-2 contains a copy of the certificate and requires that it be submitted as soon as practicable after price agreement is reached. See Cibinic & Nash, chap. 9, Sec. IV., *Formation of Government Contracts* (3d ed. 1998); Seyfarth et al., *The*

Government Contract Compliance Handbook 10-8 (1996 Supp.); Pettit & Meagher, *Certification*, 87-7 Briefing Papers (June 1987).

CERTIFICATION A signed representation that certain facts are accurate. A certification can entail either (1) an explicit representation of fact requiring the inclusion of data and signature by the contractor ("The contractor hereby certifies that . . ." or "This is to certify that . . ."), or (2) a deemed representation of a particular fact without execution of a specific certification document or use of specific certification language. All certifications required by solicitations are included in Section K of the UNIFORM CONTRACT FORMAT. FAR 14.201-5, FAR 15.204-5. The Government has traditionally used certifications in such matters as contractor status; truth of a matter; origin of a component; compliance with specifications; compliance with applicable laws; accuracy, currency, and completeness of cost or pricing data (see CERTIFIED COST OR PRICING DATA); and good faith, accuracy, and completeness in reflecting the amount owed with regard to claims, past contractual performance, and other matters. The CLINGER-COHEN ACT OF 1996 required the Government to reduce the number of certifications in its contracts, and this was accomplished by 62 Fed. Reg. 233 (Jan. 2, 1997) and 62 Fed. Reg. 2612 (Jan. 17, 1997). See Allen & Davis, *Government Contract Certifications*, 28 Cont. Mgmt. 5 (June 1988); Pettit & Meagher, *Certification*, 87-7 Briefing Papers (June 1987); Lovitky, *Frequently Encountered Problems with Certification of Claims under the Contract Disputes Act*, 16 Pub. Cont. L.J. 511 (1987).

CERTIFICATION OF CLAIM A certification by a contractor under the CONTRACT DISPUTES ACT (CDA) that (1) a claim is made in good faith, (2) the supporting data are accurate and complete to the best of the certifier's knowledge and belief, and (3) the amount requested accurately reflects the contract adjustment for which the contractor believes the Government is liable. This certification is required by 41 U.S.C. § 605(c)(1) for all claims over $100,000. FAR 33.207 requires that this certification be executed by any person duly authorized to bind the contractor with respect to the claim. This certification was required by the courts and BOARDs OF CONTRACT APPEALS to be signed by very high-level officials until the CDA was amended in 1992 by Pub. L. No. 102-572 to relax this requirement and permit defective certificates to be corrected during the litigation. See Cibinic & Nash, *Administration of Government Contracts* 1269–73 (3d ed. 1995); Nash, *Contract Disputes Act Claims: Improvements in the Rules*, 7 N&CR ¶ 1 (Jan. 1993); Ivey, *Claim Certification*, 91-11 Briefing Papers

(Oct. 1991); Cibinic, *Contractor Certification of Claims: Looking for "Mr./Ms. Right,"* 5 N&CR ¶ 27 (May 1991); Nash, *The Contract Disputes Act: A Prescription for Wheelspinning*, 4 N&CR ¶ 29 (May 1990).

CERTIFIED COST OR PRICING DATA COST OR PRICING DATA submitted by an offeror on a negotiated procurement as required by the TRUTH IN NEGOTIATIONS ACT. Unless an exemption applies, the Act requires such submission for negotiated procurement actions (see NEGOTIATION) expected to exceed $500,000. FAR 15.403-4. Exempt are actions whose prices are (1) based on ADEQUATE PRICE COMPETITION, (2) for COMMERCIAL ITEMs, or (3) set by law or regulation. FAR 15.403-1(b). The contracting officer may require submission of cost or pricing data in the format indicated at Table 15-2 of 15.408, specify an alternative format, or permit submission in the contractor's format. FAR 15.408. After price agreement is reached on a contract that requires submission of certified cost or pricing data, the contractor must submit a CERTIFICATE OF CURRENT COST OR PRICING DATA. See also DEFECTIVE COST OR PRICING DATA. See Cibinic & Nash, chap. 9, Sec. I., *Formation of Government Contracts* (3d ed. 1998).

CERTIFIED PROFESSIONAL CONTRACTS MANAGER (CPCM) An individual who has attained certain levels of education, experience, and knowledge pertaining to contracts management. To be eligible, candidates must have two years of relevant procurement or contracting experience, hold a bachelor's degree, and have taken two procurement and contracting classes, one legal class, one financial management class, and four procurement-related classes. Candidates must pass a two-part, six-hour written examination administered by the NATIONAL CONTRACT MANAGEMENT ASSOCIATION (NCMA). The first part includes two required questions and a number of general questions. The second part concentrates on specific areas of contracts management: legal, finance, economics, and accounting; production; contracting; logistics of management; commercial purchasing; and state and local government procurement. Many NCMA chapters have created study groups to help candidates prepare for the examination. CPCM recertification is required every five years. See 27 Cont. Mgmt. (Special Education Issue, Nov. 1987).

CHANGE-OF-NAME AGREEMENT A legal instrument executed by the contractor and the Government that recognizes the legal change of name of the contractor without disturbing the original contractual rights and obligations of the parties. FAR 42.1201. FAR 42.1205 contains guidance on when such an agreement should be used and provides a model agreement. See also NOVATION.

CHANGE Any alteration to a contract permitted by a contract clause. Most changes are issued under the Changes clause of a contract. Contract changes may be bilateral (signed by both the contractor and the contracting officer) or unilateral (signed only by the contracting officer). A bilateral change is issued by a bilateral MODIFICATION and is often referred to as a supplemental agreement. A UNILATERAL CHANGE is issued by a UNILATERAL MODIFICATION and is generally called a CHANGE ORDER. FAR 43.103. See also CONSTRUCTIVE CHANGE. See Jackson & Alerding, *Expanding Contracting Opportunities Without Competition*, 27 Pub. Cont. L.J. 205 (1997); Cibinic & Nash, chap. 4, *Administration of Government Contracts* (3d ed. 1995); Nash, *Government Contract Changes* (2d ed. 1989 & Supp. 1993).

CHANGE ORDER A written order signed by the contracting officer, directing the contractor to make a CHANGE without the contractor's consent, as authorized by the contract's Changes clause. FAR 43.101. Generally, Government contracts contain one of the Changes clauses in FAR 52.243-1 through -6 permitting the contracting officer to make unilateral changes, in designated areas, within the general SCOPE OF THE CONTRACT. These changes are accomplished by issuing written orders on Standard Form 30, Amendment of Solicitation/Modification of Contract, FAR 53.301-30. Change orders must be issued by the contracting officer, except when authority to issue such orders is delegated to an administrative contracting officer. FAR 43.202. Upon receipt of a change order, the contractor must continue performance of the contract as changed, except that, in cost-reimbursement or incrementally funded contracts, the contractor is not obligated to continue performance or incur costs beyond the established funding limits. FAR 43.201 and 52.243-1 through -6. See Nash, chap. 7, *Government Contract Changes* (2d ed. 1989 & Supp. 1993).

CHANGE TO COST ACCOUNTING PRACTICE Any alteration in a COST ACCOUNTING PRACTICE, whether or not the practice is covered by a DISCLOSURE STATEMENT, except the following: (1) the initial adoption of a cost accounting practice when a cost is first incurred or a function is first created, (2) the partial or total elimination of a cost or the cost of a function, or (3) the revision of a cost accounting practice for a cost that previously had been immaterial. 48 C.F.R. § 9903.302-2. 48 C.F.R. § 9903.302-3 contains illustrations of changes that meet this definition and 48 C.F.R. § 9903.302-4 describes changes that do not. The COST ACCOUNTING STANDARDS clause in FAR 52.230-3 requires that the parties negotiate an EQUITABLE ADJUSTMENT if the price is affected by a change to the contractor's cost accounting practice. See Cibinic, *Restructuring Costs Update*, 9 N&CR ¶ 18 (Mar. 1995); Davis, *Changes in Cost Accounting Practice*, 1989 (unpublished L.L.M. thesis, The Geo. Wash. Univ. Nat'l Law Center, Government Contracts Program).

CHANGED CONDITIONS Conditions at the site of a CONSTRUCTION project that the Government agreed were subject to price adjustment. In 1969 this term was changed to DIFFERING SITE CONDITIONS.

CHARTER Authorization to establish an organization, frequently containing limitations on the authority of the organizations. In DOD program management, the program manager's (PM's) charter provides the authority to conduct the program within cost, schedule, and performance constraints approved by the decision authority. The charter establishes human resources for the program office and includes assignment of personnel to perform the functions of technical management/systems engineering, logistics, business and financial management, as well as the designation of a contracting officer. The charter also defines the PM's line of authority and reporting channels. The Joint Program Manager's Charter is a formal document, prepared by the lead service (e.g., Army, Navy, or Air Force) with approval of the participating services that delineates the PM's responsibility, authority, and major functions, and describes relationships with other organizations that will use and/or support the program. The charter also describes and assigns responsibility for satisfying unique management requirements of participating services. Jones, *Glossary: Defense Acquisition Acronyms and Terms* (8th ed., Defense Systems Management College).

CHIEF INFORMATION OFFICERS (CIO) COUNCIL The principal interagency forum to improve agency practices on such matters as the design, modernization, use, sharing, and performance of agency information resources. Clinger-Cohen Act of 1996, Pub. L. No. 104-106, § 5124. The Council is expected to: (1) develop recommendations for overall federal INFORMATION TECHNOLOGY management policy, procedures, and standards; (2) share experiences, ideas, and promising practices to improve the management of information resources; (3) identify opportunities, make recommendations for, and sponsor cooperation in using information resources; (4) assess and address the hiring, training, classification, and professional development needs of the Federal Government with respect to information resources management; and (5) make recommendations and provide advice to appropriate executive agencies, organizations and OMB. The CIO Council is composed of the CIOs and Deputy CIOs of the Departments of State, Treasury, Defense (and the Army, Navy, and Air Force), Justice, Interior, Agriculture, Commerce, Labor, Health and Human Services, Housing and Urban Development, Transportation, Energy, Education, Veterans Affairs, the Environmental Protection Agency, Federal Emergency Management Agency, Central Intelligence Agency, Small Business Administration, Social Security Administration, National Aeronautics and Space Administration, Agency for International Development, General Services Administration, National Science Foundation, Nuclear Regulatory Commission, and Office of Personnel Management. Other members include the Administrators of the OFFICE OF INFORMATION AND REGULATORY AFFAIRS and OFFICE OF FEDERAL PROCUREMENT POLICY, the controller of the Office of Management and Budget's Office of Federal Financial Management, a senior representative of the Office of Science and Technology Policy, and the chairs of the GOVERNMENT INFORMATION TECHNOLOGY SERVICES BOARD and INFORMATION TECHNOLOGY RESOURCES BOARD. Exec. Order No. 13011, 61 Fed. Reg. 37657 (July 16, 1996).

CHILD CARE SERVICES Services to include child protective services, including the investigation of child abuse and neglect reports; social services; health and mental health care; day care; education; foster care; residential care; recreational and rehabilitative programs; as well as detention, correctional, or treatment services. FAR 37.101.

CHRISTIAN DOCTRINE A legal rule providing that clauses required by regulation to be included in Government contracts will be read into a contract whether or not physically included in the contract, unless a proper DEVIATION from the regulations has been obtained. The doctrine derives from the case of *G. L. Christian & Assoc. v. United States*, 160 Ct. Cl. 1, 312 F.2d 418, 160 Ct. Cl. 58, 320 F.2d 345, *cert. denied*, 375 U.S. 954 (1963), 170 Ct. Cl. 902, *cert. denied*, 382 U.S. 821 (1965), in which it was held that the TERMINATION FOR CONVENIENCE clause applied even though it had been omitted from the contract, since the procurement regulations required its inclusion. The Christian doctrine should not, however, be read to mean that *all* procurement regulations have the force and effect of law; it applies only to those regulations that implement fundamental procurement policy. See Nash, *The "Christian Doctrine": What is the Rule?*, 10 N&CR ¶ 48 (Sept. 1996); Wyatt, *The Christian Doctrine: Born Again but Sinfully Confusing*, 33 Cont. Mgmt. 22 (Nov. 1993); Nash, *Mandatory Clauses: The Regulations Override the Contract*, 4 N&CR ¶ 13 (Feb. 1990).

CIVIL DEFENSE COSTS Costs incurred by a contractor in planning for, and protecting life and property against, the possible effects of enemy attack. FAR 31.205-5. Costs of civil defense measures (including costs in excess of normal plant protection costs, first-aid training and supplies, fire-fighting training and equipment, posting of additional exit notices and directions, and other approved civil defense measures) undertaken on the contractor's premises pursuant to suggestions or requirements of civil defense authorities are allowable (see ALLOWABLE COST) when allocated to all work of the contractor. Costs of capital ASSETs acquired for civil defense purposes are allowable through depreciation. Contributions to local civil defense funds and projects are unallowable.

CIVIL FALSE CLAIMS ACT See FALSE CLAIMS ACT.

CIVIL INVESTIGATIVE DEMAND A demand by the DOJ that a person (1) produce any documentary material for inspection and copying, (2) answer any written INTERROGATORY with respect to such material, or (3) give oral testimony concerning such material. Such demands may be made in the course of any false claims investigation (See FALSE CLAIMS ACT). 31 U.S.C. § 3733.

CIVILIAN AGENCY ACQUISITION COUNCIL (CAAC) The Government body that, with the DEFENSE ACQUISITION REGULATORY COUNCIL, prepares and issues revisions to the FEDERAL ACQUISITION REGULATION (FAR) through coordinated action. FAR 1.201-1. Each council maintains cognizance over specified portions of the FAR and is responsible for (1) agreeing with the other council on all revisions, (2) submitting to the FAR Secretariat information required for publishing a FEDERAL REGISTER notice soliciting comments, (3) considering all comments received, (4) arranging for public meetings, (5) preparing any final revision in the appropriate FAR format and language, and (6) submitting any final revision to the FAR Secretariat for publication in the Federal Register and printing. Members of the CAAC (1) represent their agencies on a full-time basis, (2) are selected for their superior qualifications in terms of acquisition experience and demonstrated professional expertise, and

(3) are funded by their respective agencies. The chairperson of the CAAC is the representative of the Administrator of General Services Administration; the other members represent the Departments of Agriculture, Commerce, Energy, Health and Human Services, the Interior, Labor, State, Transportation, the Treasury, and Veterans Affairs, as well as the Environmental Protection Agency and the Small Business Administration.

CLAIM A written demand or assertion by one of the contracting parties seeking, as a matter of right, the payment of money, the adjustment or interpretation of contract terms, or other relief arising under, or relating to, the contract. FAR 33.201. A claim ARISING UNDER THE CONTRACT is a claim that can be resolved under a contract CLAUSE providing for relief sought by the claimant; a claim RELATING TO THE CONTRACT is one for which no specific contract clause provides such relief. A written demand or assertion by the contractor seeking the payment of money exceeding $100,000 is subject to the CERTIFICATION OF CLAIM requirement of the CONTRACT DISPUTES ACT OF 1978 and FAR 33.207. A VOUCHER, INVOICE, or other routine request for payment that is not in DISPUTE when submitted is not a claim. See Cibinic, *The Ellett Case: What's All The Fuss About?*, 11 N&CR ¶ 8 (Feb. 1997); McWhorther & Hahn, *Virtual Final Decisions on Government Claims*, 26 Pub. Cont. L.J. 157 (1997); Fish, *When A Termination for Convenience Settlement Proposal Constitutes A Claim Under the Contract Disputes Act*, 26 Pub. Cont. L.J. 423 (1977); Cibinic & Nash, *Administration of Government Contracts* 1257–81 (3d ed. 1995); Zupa, *Reflectone v. Dalton: A Victory for Government Contractors*, 42 Fed. Lawyer 28 (Nov./Dec. 1995); Nash, *Postscript: Further Reflections on Reflectone*, 9 N&CR ¶ 59 (Nov. 1995); Cibinic, *Reflections on Reflectone: Narrowing the "In Dispute" Requirement*, 9 N&CR ¶ 55 (Oct. 1995); Wyatt, *When a Claim Is a Claim*, 25 Nat'l Cont. Mgmt. J., Issue No. 2, p. 7 (1994); Arnavas, *To Claim or Not to Claim*, 8 N&CR ¶ 63 (Nov. 1994); McWhorter & Hahn, *Disputing the Meaning of a Claim: The Fallout from Dawco Construction*, 23 Pub. Cont. L.J. 451 (1994); Nash, *Contract Disputes Act Claims: Improvements in the Rules*, 7 N&CR ¶ 1 (Jan. 1993); Zupa, *When Is a Claim Not a Claim?*, 22 Pub. Cont. L.J. 654 (1993); Cibinic, *Unallowable Claims Costs: When Is A Claim A Claim?*, 7 N&CR ¶ 48 (Sept. 1993); Nash, chap. 6, *Construction Contracting* 531–56 (1991); Patin & Ginsburg, chap. 16, *Construction Contracting* 1186–1207 (1991); Seyfarth et al., chap. 17, *The Government Contract Compliance Handbook* (2d ed. 1991 & 1996 Supp.); Nash, *The Contract Disputes Act: No Claim, No Jurisdiction*, 5 N&CR ¶ 66 (Dec. 1991); Cibinic,

What's a "Claim": Is Prior Disagreement Necessary?, 2 N&CR ¶ 25 (May 1988); Hoover, *Recognizing Government Contractors' Claims and Contracting Officers' Final Decisions*, 29 A.F. L. Rev. 85 (1988).

CLAIMS COURT See COURT OF FEDERAL CLAIMS.

CLARIFICATION A Government communication with an offeror on a competitively negotiated procurement (see NEGOTIATION) which is a limited exchange, between the Government and an offeror, that occurs when AWARD ON INITIAL PROPOSALS is contemplated. FAR 15.306(a). Clarification may be used to resolve minor or clerical errors or "certain aspects of proposals." FAR 15.306(a)(2). Prior to FAC 97-02, September 30, 1997, clarification was defined as communication with an offeror for the sole purpose of eliminating minor irregularities, informalities, or apparent CLERICAL MISTAKEs in a proposal. Under that definition, clarification was accomplished by explanation or substantiation, either in response to Government inquiry or as initiated by the offeror, and unlike DISCUSSION, clarification did not give the offeror an opportunity to revise or modify its proposal, except to the extent that correction of apparent clerical mistakes resulted in a revision. The term "clarification" is also used to describe an inquiry by a contractor regarding ambiguous specifications. See DUTY TO SEEK CLARIFICATION. See Nash, *Pre-"Competitive Range" Communications During Best Value Procurement: The New Proposed Rule*, 11 N&CR ¶ 43 (Aug. 1997).

CLASS DETERMINATIONS AND FINDINGS (D&Fs) Provides authority for a class of contracting actions. A class of contracting actions typically entails the same or related supplies or services or other contracting actions that require essentially identical justification. FAR 1.703.

CLASS DEVIATION A DEVIATION from the FAR that affects more than one contracting action. FAR 1.404. See also DFARS 20-1.402; GSAR 501.404. The authority to approve class deviations is limited to higher-level officials in accordance with the FAR Supplements of each agency. FAR 1.405 contains special rules for class deviations that pertain to treaties and executive agreements.

CLASSIFIED ACQUISITION An ACQUISITION that consists of one or more contracts in which offerors are required to have access to CLASSIFIED INFORMATION in order to properly submit an OFFER or QUOTATION, to understand the performance requirements of a CLASSIFIED CONTRACT under the acquisition, or to perform the contract. FAR 4.401. FAR Subpart 4.4 provides guidance on such acquisitions. See also DFARS Subpart 204.4; DEAR Subpart 904.4; NFS Subpart 18.4-4.

CLASSIFIED CONTRACT Any contract whose performance requires, or will require, access to CLASSIFIED INFORMATION by the contractor or its employees. A contract may be a classified contract even though the contract document is not classified. FAR 4.401. Such contracts may be awarded only to contractors that have complied with the security requirements of DOD or any other agency that has classified necessary information.

CLASSIFIED INFORMATION Any information or material, regardless of its physical form or characteristics, that is owned by, produced by or for, or under the control of the U.S. Government; is determined, pursuant to Exec. Order No. 12356, 47 Fed. Reg. 14874 (Apr. 2, 1982), to require protection against unauthorized disclosure; and is so designated. FAR 4.401. Such information is classified Confidential, Secret, or Top Secret. National Security Act, 50 U.S.C. § 401 et seq. See DEAR 904.401; Exec. Order No. 12333, 46 Fed. Reg. 59941 (Dec. 4, 1981); Exec. Order No. 12969, 60 Fed. Reg. 40989 (Aug. 2, 1995), "Access to Classified Information," Exec. Order No. 12829, 58 Fed. Reg. 3479 (Jan. 6, 1993), which established the National Industrial Security Program.

CLAUSE A term or condition used in CONTRACTs—or in both SOLICITATIONs and contracts—and applying after contract award, or both before and after award. FAR 52.101. A term used only in solicitations is called a PROVISION. FAR Subpart 52.2 sets forth the texts of all standard FAR clauses (as does DFARS Subpart 252.2 for DFARS clauses), each in its own separate subsection. The subpart is arranged by subject matter in the same order as, and keyed to, the parts of the FAR. All FAR clause numbers begin with "52.2." The next two digits correspond to the number of the FAR part in which the clause is prescribed. The number is completed by a hyphen and a sequential number assigned within each section of FAR Subpart 52.2. The FAR clause number will be followed by the clause's title and—in contracts—by its effective date (e.g., FAR 52.203-3, Gratuities (Apr. 1984)). FAR Subpart 52.1 contains instructions for using clauses, and FAR Subpart 52.3 contains an extensive PROVISION AND CLAUSE MATRIX. See Farrell & Pankowski, *FAR Contract Clauses—First Impressions*, 24 Cont. Mgmt. 21 (Feb. 1984).

CLAUSE MATRIX See PROVISION AND CLAUSE MATRIX.

CLAYTON ACT An antitrust statute, 15 U.S.C. § 12 et seq., first enacted in 1914, that, among other things, prohibits mergers or acquisitions that may substantially lessen competition or tend to create a monopoly. 15 U.S.C. § 18. Mergers and acquisitions are subject to antitrust review by the DEPARTMENT OF JUSTICE and the Federal Trade Commission. The reviewer's goal is to prevent mergers or acquisitions that would hinder or terminate price competition in an industry over a long period of time. The Clayton Act plays a role in the debate over federal intrusion in defense industry mergers. See Kovacic, *Expanded Antitrust Scrutiny Requires Greater Caution*, 30 Procurement Law. 23 (Spr. 1995); Spratling, *Will Teaming Be a Problem?,* 30 Procurement Law. 23 (Spr. 1995); Chierchella, *Mergers and Acquisitions of Government Contractors: Special Considerations and Due Diligence Concerns*, 23 Pub. Cont. L.J. 471 (1994); Yao & DeSanti, *Antitrust Analysis of Defense Industry Mergers*, 23 Pub. Cont. L.J. 379 (1994); Hershey, *Avoiding Antitrust Problems: A Guide for Government Contractors*, 34 Cont. Mgmt. 4 (Jan. 1994); Kattan, *The Declining Defense Sector and Federal Antitrust Enforcement*, 23 Pub. Cont. L.J. 21 (1993); Victorino et al., *Antitrust Implications of Defense Industry Business Combinations*, 93-7 Briefing Papers (June 1993 and 1995 Revision Note); Nash, *Postscript: Antitrust Violations in Government Contracting*, 7 N&CR ¶ 4 (Jan. 1993); Elwell, *Teaming and Antitrust for Government Contracts in Aerospace*, 32 Cont. Mgmt. 4 (Feb. 1992); Nash, *Antitrust Violations in Government Contracting*, 3 N&CR ¶ 66 (Sept. 1989).

CLERICAL MISTAKE A mistake of a contractor in a BID or PROPOSAL that results from a clerical error. When such mistakes are apparent on the face of a bid, they may be routinely corrected by contracting officers in accordance with the procedures set forth in FAR 14.407-2. Other mistakes in bids alleged before contract award are dealt with under more elaborate procedures in accordance with FAR 14.407-3. See FAR 15.306 for limited guidance on mistakes in negotiated procurements, including authority to resolve clerical errors prior to AWARD ON INITIAL PROPOSALS. Examples of such apparent clerical mistakes are obvious misplacement of decimal points, incorrect discounts, reversal of prices and misdesignation of units. See Cibinic & Nash, chaps. 5, Sec. IV. & chap. 6, *Formation of Government Contracts* (3d ed. 1998).

CLINGER-COHEN ACT OF 1996 Division D, formerly known as the FEDERAL ACQUISITION REFORM ACT OF 1996 (FARA), and Division E, formerly known as the Information Technology Reform Act (ITMRA) of the National Defense Authorization Act. Pub. L. No. 104-208, section 808 of the Omnibus Consolidated Appropriations Act, renamed these divisions to honor retiring members of Congress who had played a large part in the statutory reform of the ACQUISITION PROCESS: Representative William Clinger and Senator William Cohen.

CLOSEOUT The process of settling all outstanding contractual issues to ensure that each party has met all of its obligations, and documenting the contract file accordingly. The primary objectives of contract closeout are (1) to identify and resolve, before memories fade, any uncompleted obligations or pending liabilities on the part of either the Government or the contractor; and (2) to ensure that contract-related decisions and actions have been properly documented. FAR 4.804-1 through -5 provides instructions for the closeout of contract files. FAR 42.708 contains "quick closeout procedures" for contracts where the amount of unsettled INDIRECT COSTs are relatively insignificant.

CODE OF ETHICS A written code, adopted by a Government contractor, setting forth the basic ethical rules that the contractor follows. DOD has strongly encouraged its contractors to adopt such codes to ensure that they conduct themselves with only the highest degree of integrity (see PROCUREMENT INTEGRITY) and honesty. Thus, DFARS 203.7001 states that contractor systems of management controls should provide for a written code of business ethics. A code of ethics serves as a mechanism by which questionable activities can be brought to the attention of management and places the contractor's corporate seal on compliance with Government antifraud initiatives. The code of ethics gains effectiveness if (1) the policy is communicated to employees in writing, (2) employees certify that they have read the code and understand it, and (3) individuals found violating the code are disciplined. See Seyfarth et al., *The Government Contract Compliance Handbook* 2-2 (1996 Supp.); Mur, *Ethics in Government Contracting: Putting Your House in Order*, 20 Nat'l Cont. Mgmt. J., Issue. No. 2, p. 15 (1987) (see appendices for sample codes, including the Grumman Code of Business Conduct).

CODE OF FEDERAL REGULATIONS (C.F.R.) A Government codification of the general and permanent rules published in the FEDERAL REGISTER by the executive departments and agencies of the Federal Government. The Code is divided into 50 titles, each representing a broad area subject to federal regulation. Each title is subdivided into chapters, which usually bear the name of the issuing agency. Each chapter is further subdivided into parts covering specific regulatory areas. For example, Title 48 contains the Federal Acquisition Regulations System (Chapter 1 contains the FAR, Chapter 2 contains the DFARS, and following chapters include other supplemental regulations). The C.F.R. is published annually and is available from the U.S. Government Printing Office, Washington, DC 20402.

COLLATERAL COSTS Agency costs of operation, maintenance, logistic support, or GOVERNMENT-FURNISHED PROPERTY. FAR 48.001. If these costs are reduced as a result of a VALUE ENGINEERING CHANGE PROPOSAL, the contractor is entitled to a share of the resulting COLLATERAL SAVINGS.

COLLATERAL SAVINGS Measurable net reductions in an agency's overall projected COLLATERAL COSTS, resulting from a VALUE ENGINEERING CHANGE PROPOSAL. Such savings are exclusive of ACQUISITION SAVINGS; they result without regard to changes in the ACQUISITION COST. FAR 48.104-2 and the Value Engineering clauses in FAR 52.248-1, -2, and -3 provide that such savings are calculated solely by the CONTRACTING OFFICER and may not exceed $100,000 or the contract price or cost, whichever is greater. See Cibinic & Nash, *Administration of Government Contracts* 310–11 (3d ed. 1995).

COLLUSIVE BIDDING A fraudulent agreement between OFFERORs to eliminate competition or restrain trade. FAR 3.301(a). Generally, such bidding involves exchanging information before bidding or agreeing which offeror will submit the low bid. Collusive bidding violates antitrust laws and must be reported to the Attorney General by the procuring agency. FAR 3.303. See Seyfarth et al., *The Government Contract Compliance Handbook* 8-8 through 8-11 (1996 Supp.); Coate, *Techniques for Protecting Against Collusion in Sealed Bid Markets*, 30 Antitrust Bull. 897 (Win. 1985).

COLOR CODING A NOTATIONAL SCORING SYSTEM in which colors are used to describe the quality of elements of an offeror's proposal. See paragraph 304 of AFFARS appendix AA, which sets forth a description of a color coding system. See Nash & Cibinic, *Competitive Negotiation: The Source Selection Process* 158–59 (1993). See also ADJECTIVAL RATINGS.

COMBINED SYNOPSIS/SOLICITATION A procedure which combines the COMMERCE BUSINESS DAILY synopsis required by FAR 5.203 and the issuance of the SOLICITATION into a single document with a response time no longer than is necessary to give potential offerors a reasonable opportunity to respond to the solicitation. This allows greatly shortening the statutory requirements for standard procurement that require a 15-day synopsis period and a 30-day offer period. This combined synopsis/solicitation is only appropriate where the solicitation is relatively simple. See Cibinic & Nash, chap. 7, Sec. I, *Formation of Government Contracts* (3d ed. 1998).

COMMERCE BUSINESS DAILY (CBD) A daily publication of the DEPARTMENT OF COMMERCE listing U.S. Government SOLICITATIONs, contract AWARDs, subcontracting leads, sales of surplus property, and foreign business opportunities. 15 U.S.C. § 637(e) and 41 U.S.C. § 416 require that agencies publish a SYNOPSIS of proposed contract actions in the CBD at least 15 days before issuing an INVITATION FOR BIDS or REQUEST FOR PROPOSALS. See FAR Subpart 5.2. The primary purposes of the CBD notice are to improve small business access to acquisition information and to enhance competition by publicizing contracting and subcontracting opportunities. Subscriptions to the CBD are available from the U.S. Government Printing Office, Washington, DC 20402. The CBD is also available on the Internet at <http://cbdnet.gpo.gov>. See CBDNet. Extensive discussion of the preparation and transmittal of CBD notices can be found at FAR 5.207.

COMMERCIAL BILL OF LADING See BILL OF LADING.

COMMERCIAL COMPUTER SOFTWARE Computer software developed or regularly used for non-Governmental purposes that (1) has been sold, leased, or licensed to the public; (2) has been offered for sale, lease, or license to the public; (3) has not been offered, sold, leased, or licensed to the public but will be available for commercial sale, lease, or license in time to satisfy the delivery requirements of the contract; or (4) requires only minor modifications to the above categories. DFARS 252.227-7014. Under 1995 DOD policy, such software should be acquired under licenses customarily provided to the public unless they are inconsistent with federal procurement law. DFARS 227.7202-1(a). Under pre-1995 DOD policy, commercial computer software was software used regularly for other than Government purposes and sold, licensed, or leased in significant quantities to the general public at established market or catalog prices. DFARS 227.471

(pre-1995 version). It was governed by special rights provisions in the Rights in Technical Data and Computer Software (Oct. 1988) clause in DFARS 252.227-7013, or it could be acquired separately (after May 1991) using the procedures in DFARS Subpart 211.70. Under the FAR policy, commercial computer software is existing computer software. FAR 27.409(k). It is to be acquired using the Commercial Computer Software—Restricted Rights clause in FAR 52.227-19, which specifies the RESTRICTED RIGHTS that pertain to such software. See Nash & Rawicz, *Intellectual Property Series*, vol 3 (3d ed. 1997); Vogel & Simchak, *What a Commercial Software License Should Say About Purchases by the Federal Government*, 26 Pub. Cont. L.J. 241 (1997); Nash, *The New DOD "Rights in Software" Policy: Half a Loaf*, 10 N&CR ¶ 12 (Mar. 1996).

COMMERCIAL IMPRACTICABILITY See IMPRACTICABILITY OF PERFORMANCE.

COMMERCIAL ITEM (1) Any item, other than real property, that is of a type customarily used for non-Governmental purposes and that has been sold, leased, or licensed to the general public or has been offered for sale, lease, or license to the general public; (2) any item that evolved from an item that has been sold, leased, or licensed to the general public through advances in technology or performance and that is not yet available in the commercial marketplace but will be available in the commercial marketplace in time to satisfy the delivery requirements under a Government solicitation; (3) any item that would satisfy the above criterion but for modifications of a type customarily available in the commercial marketplace or minor modifications of a type not customarily available in the commercial marketplace made to meet Federal Government requirements; (4) installation services, maintenance services, repair services, training services, and other services, if such services are procured for support of an item referred to above and if the source of such services offers such services to the general public and the Federal Government contemporaneously and under similar terms and conditions and offers to use the same work force for providing the Federal Government with such services as the source uses for providing such services to the general public; (5) services of a type offered and sold competitively in substantial quantities in the commercial marketplace based on established catalog or market prices for specific tasks performed under standard commercial terms and conditions, not including services that are sold based on hourly rates without an established catalog or market price for a specific service performed; (6) any item, combination of items, or service referred to above, notwithstanding the fact that the item, combination of items, or service is transferred between or among separate divisions, subsidiaries, or affiliates of a contractor; and (7) a nondevelopmental item is a commercial item if the procuring agency determines the item was developed exclusively at private expense and sold in substantial quantities on a competitive basis to multiple state and local governments. FAR 2.101. Title VIII of the FEDERAL ACQUISITION STREAMLINING ACT OF 1994, Pub. L. No. 103-355, contains detailed provisions stating a preference for commercial items and establishing acquisition policies for commercial items more closely resembling those of the commercial marketplace. These policies are set forth in FAR Part 12. See Nash, *Postscript II: Defining Commercial Services*, 11 N&CR ¶ 62 (Dec. 1997); O'Sullivan & Perry, *Commercial Item Acquisitions*, 97-5 Briefing Papers (Apr. 1997); Nash, *Postscript: Defining Commercial Services*, 11 N&CR ¶ 34 (July 1997);Cibinic, *Commercial Item Terms and Conditions: Neither Fish Nor Fowl*, 10 N&CR ¶ 61 (Dec. 1996); Cibinic, *Defining Commercial Services: An Exercise in Obfuscation*, 10 N&CR ¶ 18 (Apr. 1996); Pavilick & Madden, *Procurement Reforms of the FY 1996 Defense Authorization Act*, 96-6 Briefing Papers (May 1996); Seyfarth et al., chap. 11, *The Government Contract Compliance Handbook* (1996 Supp.); Wall & Sherry, *Pricing Commercial Items*, 95-13 Briefing Papers (Dec. 1995); Nash, *Truth in Negotiations: The FAR Implementation of FASA*, 9 N&CR ¶ 57 (Nov. 1995); Gaudio & Trowel, *New Government Contracting Rules for Commercial Items*, 35 Cont. Mgmt. 11 (Nov. 1995); Heberling, *What Is and What Is Not a Commercial Item*, 35 Cont. Mgmt. 10 (Aug. 1995).

COMMERCIAL ITEM DESCRIPTION (CID) A type of PURCHASE DESCRIPTION prepared by private industry to describe COMMERCIAL ITEMs that are available in the commercial marketplace. DOD policy contains a preference for the use of CIDs over MILITARY SPECIFICATIONS AND STANDARDS. Memorandum for Secretaries of the Military Departments (June 29, 1994). CIDs for items bought by the Government are listed in the General Services Administration (GSA) Index of Federal Specifications, Standards and Commercial Item Descriptions, FAR 11.201, and the DOD Index of Specifications and Standards, DFARS 211.201. Agencies are permitted to tailor CIDs to meet specific agency requirements. The guidance for CIDs is in the *GSA Federal Standardization Manual* and the *Defense Standardization Manual*, DOD 4120.3-M.

COMMERCIAL ITEM EXEMPTION An exception to the requirement for the submission of COST OR PRICING DATA under the TRUTH IN NEGOTIATIONS ACT. This exception was added to 10 U.S.C. § 2306a(d) and 41 U.S.C. § 254b(d) by the FEDERAL ACQUISITION STREAMLINING ACT OF 1994, Pub. L. No. 103-355. It became the sole exception for commercial items when the standard catalog or market price exception was repealed in 1996 by the CLINGER-COHEN ACT OF 1996, Pub. L. No. 104-106. It is implemented in FAR 15.403-1. Under this exception a contracting officer may not require the submission of cost or pricing data for an acquisition of any item that meets the definition in FAR 2.101.

COMMERCIAL, OFF-THE-SHELF (COTS) Typically refers to COMMERCIAL ITEMS that require no unique Government modifications or maintenance over the life cycle of the product to meet the needs of the procuring agency. Also stated as "commercially available off-the-shelf." COTS items generally are customarily used by the general public for non-Governmental purposes, sold in substantial quantities in the commercial marketplace, and procured by the Government in the same form in which they appear in the commercial marketplace. Clinger-Cohen Act, Pub. L. No. 104-106, § 4203.

COMMERCIAL PRODUCT A product—such as an item, material, component, subsystem, or system—that was regularly used for other than Government purposes and that was sold or traded to the general public in the course of normal business operations at prices based on ESTABLISHED CATALOG OR MARKET PRICEs. This term was used prior to the enactment of the FEDERAL ACQUISITION STREAMLINING ACT OF 1994, Pub. L. No. 103-355, which substituted the term COMMERCIAL ITEM. See Kirby & Ursini, *Commercial Products Procurement*, 91-3 Briefing Papers (Feb. 1991); Nash, *Buying Commercial Products: Can the Government Benefit by Adopting Commercial Practices?,* 4 N&CR ¶ 30 (May 1990).

COMMISSION ON GOVERNMENT PROCUREMENT (COGP) Commission that studied federal procurement and recommended to Congress methods to promote the economy, efficiency, and effectiveness of procurement by the executive branch. Created by Pub. L. No. 91-129 in 1969, the Commission, made up of 12 members (two congressmen, two senators, the Comptroller General, two executive branch officials, and five non-Government persons), submitted its findings and recommendations in 1972. The Commission's four-volume report included a Blueprint for Action that outlined an integrated system for the federal procurement process, addressing policy control, the statutory framework, the workforce, funding, contracting officer authority, contract administration and AUDIT, disputes and protests, and the uses of commercial products and services. The recommendations of the Commission led to significant statutory changes including the creation of the OFFICE OF FEDERAL PROCUREMENT POLICY in 1974 (Pub. L. No. 93-400), the enactment of the CONTRACT DISPUTES ACT of 1978, (Pub. L. No. 95-563), and the enactment of the COMPETITION IN CONTRACTING ACT in 1984 (Div. B., Title VII, Pub. L. No. 98-369). See the Procurement Round Table Report, *Reforming Federal Procurement: What the Commission on Government Procurement Recommended and What Has Happened*, 31 Cont. Mgmt. 16 (Feb. 1991).

COMMON CARRIER An entity that, without right of refusal, provides services to the general public as required by law. *Black's Law Dictionary* 275 (6th ed. 1990). See also CARRIER (TELECOMMUNICATIONS) and CARRIER (TRANSPORTATION).

COMMON ITEMS Material that is common to the applicable Government contract and to the contractor's other work. FAR 45.601. In contract terminations, the costs of common items reasonably usable on the contractor's other work are not allowable unless the contractor submits evidence that the items could not be retained at cost without sustaining a loss. FAR 31.205-42.

COMMUNICATIONS SECURITY (COMSEC) The communications security systems, services, and concepts that constitute protective measures taken to deny unauthorized persons information derived from telecommunications of the U.S. Government related to national security and to ensure the authenticity of any such communications. National Communications System Technology and Standards Division, *Telecommunications: Glossary of Telecommunication Terms*, Federal Standard 1037C (Aug. 1996).

COMPARABILITY The condition that exists when an offered price can be compared with some other price in the process of PRICE ANALYSIS. This condition, necessary for effective price comparison, exists when all price-related differences have been identified and accounted for so that the prices being compared are based on relatively equal assumptions. A practical definition of "comparable" is "having enough similar characteristics or qualities to make comparison useful." The Government has two choices if it cannot establish comparability in price analysis: it can disregard the data, or it can discount them. See Federal Acquisition Institute and Air Force Institute of Technology, *Price Analysis, Contract Pricing Reference Guide*, vol. I, chap. 6 (Dec. 1996).

COMPENSABLE DELAY A DELAY, incurred by a contractor in contract performance, for which the Government is required to give compensation. There are two standard clauses providing for such compensation: (1) the Suspension of Work clause in FAR 52.242-14, which must be used in all fixed-price construction and architect-engineer contracts; and (2) the Government Delay of Work clause in FAR 52.242-17, which must be used in all fixed-price supply contracts except those for commercial or modified-commercial items. These clauses give a PRICE ADJUSTMENT (excluding PROFIT) when an unreasonable delay is caused by an act (or failure to act) of the contracting officer in the administration of the contract. If a clause of this nature is not included in the contract, the contractor may obtain compensation for a delay caused by the Government under a BREACH OF CONTRACT theory. See Cibinic & Nash, *Administration of Government Contracts* 450–78 (3d ed. 1995); McGovern, *Compensating Contractors for Delay Related Costs*, 24 Cont. Mgmt. 12 (Oct. 1984).

COMPENSATED PERSONAL ABSENCE The cost of vacations, sick leave, holidays, and other compensated absences of employees from work. CAS 408, 48 C.F.R. § 9904.408-30(a)(1) requires that such costs be assigned to the accounting period in which the entitlement was earned and provides guidance on the interpretation of this requirement. FAR 31.205-6(m) provides that such costs incurred by a contractor are allowable (see ALLOWABLE COST) to the extent that they are reasonable.

COMPENSATION FOR PERSONAL SERVICES All remuneration paid by a contractor currently or accrued, in whatever form and whether paid immediately or deferred, for services rendered by employees to the contractor during the period of contract performance (with some exceptions with regard to severance pay costs and pension costs). FAR 31.205-6. Such compensation is generally an ALLOWABLE COST subject to the detailed guidance in FAR 31.205-6. See Cibinic & Nash, *Cost-Reimbursement Contracting* 784–817 (2d ed. 1993). Compensation for personal services includes, but is not limited to, salaries; wages; directors' and executive committee members' fees; bonuses (including stock bonuses); incentive awards; employee stock options, stock appreciation rights and stock ownership plans; employee insurance; fringe benefits; contributions to pension, annuity, and management-employee incentive compensation plans; and allowances for off-site pay, incentive pay, location allowances, hardship pay, severance pay, and cost-of-living differentials. Congress has enacted ceilings on executive compensation ($200,000 in FY96 and $250,000 in FY97). These are implemented in FAR 31.205-6(p) (interim rule); DFARS 231.205-6 (interim rule). See also § 808 of the DOD Authorization Act for FY 1998. See Chierchella & Weitzel, *Complying With the New Limits on Personal Compensation Under FY 1995 DOD Contracts*, 95-1 CP&A Rep. 3 (Jan. 1995); Albertson et al., *Proposed FAR Amendments on Compensation Costs & Systems—A Critique*, 95-2 CP&A Rep. 3 (Feb. 1995); Petit & Victorino, *Personal Compensation Costs*, 84-6 Briefing Papers (June 1984).

COMPENSATORY DAMAGES See DAMAGES.

COMPETING CONTRACTOR Any entity that is, or is reasonably likely to become, a competitor for or recipient of a contract or subcontract under any procurement of property or services; or any person acting on behalf of such an entity. Competing contractors were subject to many of the provisions governing PROCUREMENT INTEGRITY until the law was changed in 1996. Contracts signed before Jan. 1, 1997, will impose these rules on competing contractors. FAR 3.104-4(b), prior to its revision on Jan. 2, 1997, contained additional guidance on the meaning of "competing contractor."

COMPETITION The effort of sellers of products or services to secure the business of the buyer by proposing the most attractive contract terms. In Government procurement, competition involves the attempt by more than one offeror to obtain a contract, with the winner being selected on the basis of criteria established in a SOLICITATION issued by the purchasing activity. The COMPETITION IN CONTRACTING ACT of 1984 established FULL AND OPEN COMPETITION as the primary goal of Government procurement. FAR Part 6 sets forth the competition requirements that derive from this act. When the Government obtains ADEQUATE PRICE COMPETITION in a negotiated procurement, the contracting officer may not require the submission of CERTIFIED COST OR PRICING DATA. See Cibinic & Nash, chap. 3, Sec. II., *Formation of Government Contracts* (3d ed. 1998); Doke, *Competition Requirements in Public Contracting: The Myth of Full and Open Competition*, 64 Fed. Cont. Rep. Spl. Supp. (July 17, 1995).

COMPETITION ADVOCATE An employee of a CONTRACTING ACTIVITY specifically assigned the task of challenging barriers to competition and promoting FULL AND OPEN COMPETITION. 41 U.S.C. § 418 requires that each executive agency and each contracting activity appoint a competition advocate. Such advocates are generally high-ranking employees reporting directly to the heads of their agency or activity. 41 U.S.C. § 418 requires that they report their activities and remaining barriers to the senior procurement executive of the agency on an annual basis. FAR 6.501 requires that they must be in a position other than that of the agency SENIOR PROCUREMENT EXECUTIVE, must not be assigned any duties inconsistent with those of competition advocate, and must be provided with necessary staff or assistance. Competition advocates are charged with (1) promoting full and open competition and challenging barriers to it; (2) reviewing contracting operations to identify (a) opportunities and actions necessary to achieve full and open competition and (b) the conditions that unnecessarily restrict it; (3) preparing annual reports; (4) recommending goals and plans for increasing competition; and (5) recommending a system of personal and organizational accountability—one that motivates individuals to promote competition and recognizes those who do. FAR 6.502.

COMPETITION IN CONTRACTING ACT (CICA) A 1984 Act, 41 U.S.C. § 251 et seq. and 10 U.S.C. § 2304 et seq., that amended the two basic procurement statutes (the ARMED SERVICES PROCUREMENT ACT and the FEDERAL PROPERTY AND ADMINISTRATION SERVICES ACT OF 1949) to enhance competition, granted statutory authorization for the General Accounting Office's PROTEST function, created protest jurisdiction for federal information processing resources procurement at the GENERAL SERVICES ADMINISTRATION BOARD OF CONTRACT APPEALS, and revised protest procedures. CICA was the first major revision to the procurement statutes since the 1940s. It introduced the phrase FULL AND OPEN COMPETITION, replaced the familiar non-negotiated procurement label "formal advertising" with "SEALED BIDDING," and placed the COMPETITIVE PROPOSALS (competitive NEGOTIATION) method on a par with sealed bidding. Recognizing that negotiation could be as competitive as sealed bidding, CICA did away with the requirement to execute a DETERMINATION AND FINDINGS to justify use of negotiation instead of formal advertising. Instead, it established a requirement to execute a justification—and obtain approval of it—for any procurement in which full and open competition would not be obtained. See FAR Parts 6, 14, 15, and 33; Callahan & Vest, *The*

Competition in Contracting Act—A Marketing Tool, 20 Nat'l Cont. Mgmt. J., Issue No. 2, p. 67 (1987); Cohen, *The Competition in Contracting Act*, 14 Pub. Cont. L.J. 1 (1983).

COMPETITIVE ADVANTAGE An advantage of one competitor over another. Normally, the Government is not concerned with competitive advantages held by one competitor in the procurement process because many advantages are inherent in a free economy. For example, a competitor may have an advantage because of its superior design capabilities, its geographic location (resulting in lower transportation costs), its lower taxes (because its state has low tax rates), or its more productive employees. However, it is the policy of the Government to attempt to overcome UNFAIR COMPETITIVE ADVANTAGEs. The Government also attempts to compensate for the advantage gained by manufacturing materials and products in a foreign country. See BUY AMERICAN ACT; Tomanelli, *Competitive Advantage Arising from Contractor Possession of Government-Furnished Property*, 23 Pub. Cont. L.J. 243 (1994); Tomanelli, *The Duty to Eliminate Competitive Advantage Arising from Contractor Possession of Government-Furnished Property*, 142 Mil. L. Rev. 141 (Fall 1994).

COMPETITIVE ALTERNATIVE SOURCE See DUAL SOURCE.

COMPETITIVE NEGOTIATION See COMPETITIVE PROPOSALS.

COMPETITIVE PROCEDURES Contracting procedures that meet the statutory requirement for FULL AND OPEN COMPETITION in Government procurement. 10 U.S.C. § 2304(a)(2) and 41 U.S.C. § 253(a)(2) cite two major types of competitive procedures: SEALED BIDDING and COMPETITIVE PROPOSALS. 10 U.S.C. § 2302(2) and 41 U.S.C. § 259(b) list five additional types of competitive procedures: (1) BROOKS ACT (ARCHITECT-ENGINEER (A-E) PROCUREMENT) procedures, (2) BROAD AGENCY ANNOUNCEMENT, (3) MULTIPLE-AWARD SCHEDULE contracting, (4) procurement under 15 U.S.C. § 644 (small business SET-ASIDE), and (5) SMALL BUSINESS INNOVATIVE RESEARCH contracting. See Cibinic & Nash, chap. 3, Sec. II., *Formation of Government Contracts* (3d ed 1998).

COMPETITIVE PROPOSALS A procedure used in negotiated procurement (see NEGOTIATION) that (1) is initiated by a REQUEST FOR PROPOSALS setting out the Government's requirements and the criteria for evaluation of offers, (2) contemplates the submission of timely proposals by the maximum number of known qualified offerors,

(3) usually provides for DISCUSSION or negotiation with those offerors found to be within the COMPETITIVE RANGE, and (4) concludes with the award of a contract to the offeror whose offer is most advantageous to the Government, considering price and the other factors included in the solicitation. Guidance on this procedure is contained in FAR Parts 6 and 15. This procedure is one of the major COMPETITIVE PROCEDURES that meets the requirement for FULL AND OPEN COMPETITION. See Cibinic & Nash, chap. 6, *Formation of Government Contracts* (3d ed. 1998); Shnitzer, *How to Recognize a Protestable Issue*, 93-3 Briefing Papers (Feb. 1993).

COMPETITIVE RANGE The range of proposals that are most highly rated, unless the range is further reduced for purposes of efficiency. FAR 15.306(c). FAR 15.306 requires that this range be determined by the contracting officer on the basis of the ratings of each proposal against all evaluation criteria. After evaluating all proposals the contracting officer may determine that the number of most highly rated proposals that might otherwise be included in the competitive range exceeds the number at which an efficient competition can be conducted. In this case, provided the SOLICITATION notifies offerors that the competitive range can be limited for efficiency, the contracting officer may limit the number of proposals in the competitive range to the greatest number that will permit an efficient competition among the most highly rated proposals. FAR 15.306(c)(2). The contracting officer must then indicate to, or discuss with, each offeror still being considered for award, significant weaknesses, deficiencies, and other aspects of its proposal that could be altered to enhance materially the proposal's potential for award. FAR 15.306(d)(3). See BARGAINING. If, after these communications, the contracting officer decides that an offeror's proposal should no longer be included in the competitive range, the proposal is eliminated from consideration for award. FAR 15.306(c)(3). Written notice is provided to unsuccessful offerors in accordance with FAR 15.503. Offerors excluded or otherwise eliminated from the competitive range may request a DEBRIEFING (see FAR 15.505 and FAR 15.506). FAR 15.306(c)(4). See Nash, *The FAR Part 15 Rewrite: A final Scorecard*, 11 N&CR ¶ 63 (Dec. 1997).

COMPLAINT In a contract DISPUTE, a written statement in which a PLAINTIFF before the U.S. COURT OF FEDERAL CLAIMS or an APPELLANT BEFORE a BOARD OF CONTRACT APPEALS gives a direct statement of each of its claims, the bases for these claims, and the dollar amount claimed to the extent known.

COMPLETION BOND See PERFORMANCE BOND.

COMPLETION FORM CONTRACT A COST-PLUS-FIXED-FEE CONTRACT that describes the work by stating a definite goal or target and specifying an end product. FAR 16.306(d). This is contrasted with a TERM CONTRACT where the contractor's obligation is stated in terms of a specified level of effort for a stated period of time. In the completion form contract, the contractor does not earn the full FIXED FEE until the work, as specified, has been satisfactorily completed. See Cibinic & Nash, *Cost-Reimbursement Contracting* 71–74, 1106–08 (2d ed. 1993).

COMPONENT An assembly, or part thereof, that is essential to the operation of some larger assembly and is an immediate subdivision of the assembly to which it belongs. National Communications System Technology and Standards Division, *Telecommunications: Glossary of Telecommunication Terms*, Federal Standard 1037C (Aug. 1996); FAR 2.101.

COMPTROLLER GENERAL (COMP. GEN.) The Government officer, appointed by the President of the United States to serve a 15-year term as head of the GENERAL ACCOUNTING OFFICE (GAO). The GAO is part of the legislative branch of the Government. Title 31 of the United States Code requires the Comptroller General to investigate all matters relating to the receipt, disbursement, and application of public funds. The Comptroller General also has the power to examine the records of contractors doing business with the Government (see EXAMINATION OF RECORDS CLAUSE), evaluate and assess the results of Government programs (and typically issue reports), and evaluate and issue recommendations on PROTESTs pursuant to the COMPETITION IN CONTRACTING ACT. FAR 33.104. See also Hordell, *Everyone Has Heard of the United States General Accounting Office—But What Does It Do?,* 36 Fed. B. News & J. 328 (1989).

COMPUTER A data processing device capable of accepting data, performing prescribed operations on the data, and supplying the results of these operations (for example, a device that operates on discrete data by performing arithmetic and logic processes on the data, or a device that operates on analog data by performing physical processes on the data). This definition was included in the 1988 DOD policy on TECHNICAL DATA at DFARS 227.471 but was omitted from the 1995 policy.

COMPUTER DATABASE A collection of data recorded in a form capable of being processed and operated on by a COMPUTER. DFARS 252.227-7013. Under the 1995 DOD policy on TECHNICAL DATA and COMPUTER SOFTWARE, computer databases are considered to be technical data not computer software. Under the 1988 DOD policy (see DFARS 227.471 (pre-1995 version)) and the FAR policy (see FAR Subpart 27.4) on technical data and computer software, computer databases are considered to be computer software.

COMPUTER PROGRAM A set of instructions, rules, or routines recorded in a form that is capable of causing a computer to perform a specific operation or series of operations. DFARS 252.227-7013. The 1988 DOD policy on COMPUTER SOFTWARE contained a more complete definition stating that computer programs include operating systems, assemblers, compilers, interpreters, data management systems, utility programs, sort-merge programs, and ADPE maintenance/diagnostic programs, as well as applications programs such as payroll, inventory control, and engineering analysis programs; and that they may be either machine-dependent or machine-independent and may be general-purpose in nature or designed to satisfy the requirements of a particular user. DFARS 227.471 (pre-1995 version). Computer programs are one type of computer software. These DOD definitions appear to include only OBJECT CODE. Under the FAR policy (see FAR Subpart 27.4) on TECHNICAL DATA and computer software, the term "computer program" appears to include not only the object code but the SOURCE CODE and all documentation of the program's requirements and design. The Copyright Act, 17 U.S.C. § 101, defines a computer program as a set of statements or instructions to be used directly or indirectly in a computer in order to bring about a certain result. This would appear to include both object code and source code, at a minimum. See Nash, *Patentability of Computer Programs: The Wave of the Future?,* 8 N&CR ¶ 69 (Dec. 1994); Nash, *Copyright of Computer Programs*, 6 N&CR ¶ 65 (Nov. 1992).

COMPUTER SOFTWARE This term has a different meaning in each of the three policies on TECHNICAL DATA and computer software. In the FAR policy, it means COMPUTER PROGRAMs, COMPUTER DATABASEs, and COMPUTER SOFTWARE DOCUMENTATION, FAR 27.401. In the 1995 DOD policy, it means computer programs, SOURCE CODE, source code listings, object code listings, design details, algorithms, processes, flowcharts, formulae, and related material that would enable the software to be reproduced, recreated, or recompiled; but not computer databases and computer software documentation, DFARS 252.227-7013. In the 1988 DOD policy, it means computer programs and computer databases but not computer software documentation. DFARS 227.471 (pre-1995 version). In general, both the FAR and the DFARS regulations permit the contractor to claim RESTRICTED RIGHTS to software that is DEVELOPED AT PRIVATE EXPENSE. See Vogel & Simchak, *What a Commercial Software License Should Say About Purchases by the Federal Government*, 26 Pub. Cont. L.J. 241 (1997); Nash, *The New DOD 'Rights in Software' Policy*, 10 N&CR ¶ 12 (Mar. 1996); Burgett et al., *Government Rights in Data and Software/Edition II*, 95-11 Briefing Papers (Oct. 1995); Nash, *The New DOD Policy on Technical Data and Computer Software*, 8 N&CR ¶ 22 (Apr. 1994); Nash, *Rights in Computer Software: Something Worth Fighting For*, 4 N&CR ¶ 16 (Mar. 1990); Davis, *Acquisition of Rights in Computer Software by the Department of Defense*, 17 Pub. Cont. L.J. 77 (1987); Samuelson, *Understanding the Implications of Selling Rights in Software to the Defense Department: A Journey Through the Regulatory Maze*, 13 Rutgers Computer Tech. L.J. 33 (1987).

COMPUTER SOFTWARE DOCUMENTATION This term has a different meaning in each of the three policies on TECHNICAL DATA and COMPUTER SOFTWARE. In the 1995 DOD policy, it means the owner's manuals, user's manuals, installation instructions, operating instructions, and other similar items, regardless of storage medium, that explain the capabilities of the computer software and provides instructions for using the software. DFARS 252.227-7013. Such documentation must be in human-readable form (as distinguished from machine-readable). See DFARS 227.403-77. In the 1988 DOD policy, it means TECHNICAL DATA, including computer listings and printouts, in human-readable form which (a) documents the design or details of computer software, (b) explains the capabilities of the software, or (c) provides operating instructions for using the software to obtain desired results from a computer. DFARS 227.471 (pre-1995 version). This appears to include the SOURCE CODE. For the purposes of allocating the rights of the contracting parties to the information, this documentation is technical data under DOD policies and computer software under FAR Subpart 27.4. See Vogel & Simchak, *What a Commercial Software License Should Say About Purchases by the Federal Government*, 26 Pub. Cont. L.J. 241 (1997); Samuelson, *Understanding the Implications of Selling Rights in Software to the Defense Department: A Journey Through the Regulatory Maze*, 13 Rutgers Computer Tech. L.J. 33 (1987).

CONCEPT EXPLORATION The process, conducted at the beginning of a MAJOR SYSTEM ACQUISITION, of refining the proposed concept and reducing the concept's technical uncertainties. FAR 34.005-3. This is designated as "Phase 0" of the DOD acquisition process. See Part 1.4.2 of DOD Regulation 5000.2-R, *Mandatory Procedures for Major Defense Acquisition Programs (MDAPs) and Major Automated Information System (MAIS) Acquisition Programs*, Mar. 15, 1996. The process has also been called "concept formulation." Agencies have generally awarded two or more firm-fixed-price contracts to competing contractors to perform this task.

CONCEPTION The formation in the mind of an inventor of a definite idea of a complete and operative invention as it is thereafter to be reduced to practice. Conception of a patentable idea is the act of invention that entitles an inventor to a PATENT. If the conception of an invention occurs during the performance of a Government contract containing a Patent Rights clause, the invention will be classified as a SUBJECT INVENTION and the Government will obtain rights (at least a royalty-free license) in any patent that issues on that invention. See Nash & Rawicz, *Intellectual Property in Government Contracts*, vol. 1 (3d ed. 1997).

CONCEPTUAL DESIGN The initial stage of a contract for ARCHITECT-ENGINEER (A-E) SERVICES. In contracts with DOE, conceptual design requires the A-E to provide preliminary studies to (1) develop a project scope that satisfies a program need or statutory requirements; (2) validate feasibility and attainable performance levels; (3) identify and quantify risks; (4) develop a reliable budget estimate and a realistic performance schedule; (5) develop project criteria and design parameters for all engineering disciplines; and (6) identify applicable codes and standards, quality assurance requirements, environmental studies, construction materials, space allowances, energy conservation features, health and safety safeguards, security requirements, and any other features or requirements necessary to describe the project. DEAR 936.605(c)(1). See also TITLE I, TITLE II, TITLE III SERVICES.

CONCERN Any business entity organized for PROFIT (even if its ownership is in the hands of a nonprofit entity) that has a place of business located in the United States and that makes a significant contribution to the U.S. economy through payment of taxes or use of American products, material or LABOR, etc. "Concern" includes, but is not limited to, an individual, partnership, corporation, JOINT

VENTURE, association, or cooperative. FAR 19.001. This term is used in the FAR Part 19 guidance on determining whether potential contractors are eligible for the benefits of the SMALL BUSINESS ACT.

CONCURRENT CONTRACT SAVINGS Net reductions in the prices of other contracts that are definitized and ongoing at the time a VALUE ENGINEERING CHANGE PROPOSAL is accepted. FAR 48.001. FAR 48.104-1 contains guidance on Government-contractor sharing arrangements for such savings. Under the Value Engineering clause in FAR 52.248-1, these savings are shared with the contractor only if they pertain to contracts issued by the same contracting office or its successor for essentially the same unit. See Cibinic & Nash, *Administration of Government Contracts* 415 (3d ed. 1995); Nash, *"Value Engineering" Clauses: Read Them Carefully!*, 8 N&CR ¶ 18 (Mar. 1994).

CONFIDENTIALITY CLAUSE A stipulation commonly attached to research grants or contracts with the Government that seeks to restrict the researcher's ability to publish or otherwise disseminate research results. See the Rights in Data—Special Works clause at FAR 52.227-17(d) where the contractor may not release, reproduce, distribute, or publish any data first produced in the performance of the contract without written permission of the contracting officer. The Department of Health and Human Services Regulation Subpart 324.70 and the Confidentiality of Information clause at HHSAR 352.224-70 require contractors to handle disclosure of certain types of information prudently and address the kinds of data that are considered confidential and how they should be treated. HHSAR 324.7001.

CONFIGURATION A collection of an item's descriptive and governing characteristics. These characteristics can be expressed in functional terms, such as describing the performance the item is expected to achieve, or in physical terms, such as describing what the item should look like and consist of when it is built. Jones, *Glossary: Defense Acquisition Acronyms and Terms* (8th ed., Defense Systems Management College). See CONFIGURATION IDENTIFICATION; CONFIGURATION ITEM.

CONFIGURATION IDENTIFICATION The process of establishing and describing the contractual baselines (for example, identification of configuration items). Jones, *Glossary: Defense Acquisition Acronyms* *and Terms* (8th ed., Defense Systems Management College). See CONFIGURATION; CONFIGURATION ITEM.

CONFIGURATION ITEM An aggregation of hardware, firmware, COMPUTER SOFTWARE, or any of their discrete portions, that satisfies an end use function and is designated by the Government for separate configuration management. Configuration items may vary widely in complexity, size, and type, from an aircraft, electronic, or ship system to a test meter or round of ammunition. Any item required for logistic support and designated for separate procurement is a configuration item. Jones, *Glossary: Defense Acquisition Acronyms and Terms* (8th ed., Defense Systems Management College). See CONFIGURATION; CONFIGURATION IDENTIFICATION.

CONFIGURATION MANAGEMENT A procedure for applying technical and administrative direction and surveillance to identify and document the functional and physical characteristics of an item or SYSTEM, control any changes to those characteristics, and record and report the change process and implementation status. The goal of configuration management is to ensure that continuous changes to a product do not result in unacceptable cost growth. The configuration management process must be carefully tailored to the capacity, size, scope, nature, complexity, and phase of the life cycle of the system involved. Brechtel, *Subcontracts: Government and Industry Issues* (NCMA 1989). In DOD configuration management, procedures are contained in Military Standard 480B, July 15, 1988 (major systems), and Military Standard 481B, July 15, 1988 (other items). See Gregory, *The Role of Configuration Management in the Acquisition Process*, 26 Nat'l Cont. Mgmt. J., Issue No. 1, p. 23 (1995); Collins et al., *Configuration Management and Complex Weapon Systems: Challenges in the Competitive Environment*, 27 Cont. Mgmt. 20 (Sept. 1987).

CONFLICT OF INTEREST A clash between the public interest and the private pecuniary interest of the individual concerned. *Black's Law Dictionary* 299 (6th ed. 1990). The term is typically used in regard to public officials and their relationship to matters of private interest or private gain; see PERSONAL CONFLICT OF INTEREST. It is also used in regard to persons who have left Government employment; see REVOLVING DOOR. The term also identifies those situations in which contractors or prospective contractors have some bias relating to a procurement or would gain a competitive advantage from a procurement; see ORGANIZATIONAL CONFLICT OF INTEREST. The term is also used in the context of prohibiting contracting officers from knowingly awarding contracts to Government employees or to business concerns owned or controlled by Government employees. FAR 3.601. This policy seeks to avoid any conflict of interest that might arise between the employees' interest and their Government duties, and any appearance of favoritism or preferential treatment. See Sutton, *Conflicts of Interest in the Acquisition Process*, 29 A.F. L. Rev. 165 (1988). See also PROCUREMENT INTEGRITY; Seyfarth et al., chap. 9, *The Government Contract Compliance Handbook* (2d ed. 1991 & 1996 Supp.); Darley, *Personal Conflicts of Interest Digest*, 20 Pub. Cont. L.J. 302 (1991); Darley, *Conflict of Interest Restrictions Applicable to Separating and Former Department of Defense Personnel*, 17 Pub. Cont. L.J. (1988); Woehr, *Agency Cancellation of Federal Contracts for Fraud and Conflicts of Interest*, 16 Pub. Cont. L.J. 386 (1987).

CONSEQUENTIAL DAMAGES Those losses, injuries, or damages that do not flow directly and immediately from the act of a party but flow instead from some of the consequences or results of that party's act. Consequential damages resulting from a seller's BREACH OF CONTRACT, for example, include (1) any loss resulting from general or particular requirements and needs that the seller at the time of contracting had reason to know of and that could not reasonably be prevented by COVER or otherwise, and (2) any injury to persons or property proximately resulting from any breach of warranty. *Black's Law Dictionary* 390 (6th ed. 1990); U.C.C. § 2-715(2). Contractors generally cannot recover consequential damages from the Government, and FAR Subpart 46.8 provides that it is the policy of the Government to relieve contractors from liability for Government property that is damaged after acceptance of items delivered on contracts. See the Limitation of Liability clauses in FAR 52.246-23 through -25. See Nash, *Implied Promises by the Government: The Supreme Court Speaks in Hercules*, 10 N&CR ¶ 21 (May 1996); Nash, *Pricing Defective Specification Claims: Does the Theory Matter?*, 8 N&CR ¶ 1 (Jan. 1994); Nash, *Recovering Consequential Damages From the Government: An Impossible Dream?*, 5 N&CR ¶ 20 (Apr. 1991).

CONSIDERATION A performance or return promise that is the inducement to a contract because it is sought by the promisor in exchange for his promise and is given by the promisee in exchange for that promise. *Restatement (Second) Contracts* § 71 (1981). A binding contract requires an OFFER, ACCEPTANCE of the offer, and consideration. Consideration generally requires two elements: (1) something must be given that the law regards as of sufficient legal value for the purpose—either a benefit to the seller or a detriment to the buyer, and

(2) that benefit or detriment of legal value must be dealt with by the parties as the agreed-upon price or exchange for the promise—there must be a "bargained-for exchange." The requirement for consideration does not require that what is relied upon for consideration be equivalent in value to the promise; the consideration need only have "some value." *Murray On Contracts* § 55 (3d ed. 1990). See Cibinic & Nash, chap. 2, Sec. II., *Formation of Government Contracts* (3d ed. 1998).

CONSISTENCY IN ALLOCATING COSTS The allocation of each type of contract cost on the same basis. CAS 402, 48 C.F.R. § 904.402, requires such consistency and gives detailed guidance on the interpretation of this rule. See COST ACCOUNTING STANDARDS.

CONSISTENCY IN ESTIMATING, ACCUMULATING, AND REPORTING COSTS The treating of comparable transactions in the same manner for cost accounting purposes whether a contractor is estimating costs or accumulating and reporting costs. CAS 401, 48 C.F.R. § 9904.401, requires such consistency and gives detailed guidance on the interpretation of this rule. See COST ACCOUNTING STANDARDS.

CONSOLIDATED LOCAL TELECOMMUNICATIONS (CLT) SERVICE The local communications service to all federal agencies located in a building, complex, or geographical area. 41 C.F.R. § 101-35.5. Consolidated local telecommunications service is available in most buildings occupied by concentrations of federal employees. Local telecommunications includes any access services that provide, for a monthly fee, electronic connectivity to a larger telecommunications network and those support services that provide for the acquisition, operation, and management of attached systems. 41 C.F.R. § 101-35.401. Information on the use of consolidated local telecommunications services may be obtained from General Services Administration Federal Telecommunications Service, Office of Regional Services (TR), 1730 M St., N.W., Washington, DC 20036.

CONSTANT DOLLARS A method of relating dollars in several years by removing the effects of inflation and showing all dollars at the value they would have in a selected base year. When used in the procurement process, this method is generally called the PRESENT VALLUE method. Constant dollar series are derived by dividing current dollar estimates by appropriate price indices, a process generally known as deflating. The result is a time series as it would presumably exist if prices were the same throughout as in the base year. In other words, constant dollars reflect what a present cost would be if the dollar had constant purchasing power. Any changes in such a series would reflect only changes in the real (physical) volume of output. Constant dollar figures are commonly used for gross domestic product and its components. Jones, *Glossary: Defense Acquisition Acronyms and Terms* (8th ed., Defense Systems Management College).

CONSTANT YEAR DOLLARS See CONSTANT DOLLARS.

CONSTRUCTION Construction, alteration, or repair (including dredging, excavating, and painting) of buildings, structures, or other REAL PROPERTY. FAR 36.102. For purposes of the FAR definition, the terms "buildings, structures, or other real property" include, but are not limited to, improvements of all types, such as improvements to bridges, dams, plants, highways, parkways, streets, subways, tunnels, sewers, mains, power lines, cemeteries, pumping stations, railways, airport facilities, terminals, docks, piers, wharves, ways, lighthouses, buoys, jetties, breakwaters, levees, canals, and channels. Construction does not include the manufacture, production, furnishing, construction, alteration, repair, processing, or assembling of vessels, aircraft, or other kinds of PERSONAL PROPERTY. FAR Part 36 contains guidance on the procedures to be followed in buying construction, and FAR Subpart 22.4 covers the procedures required by the DAVIS-BACON ACT. The FAR contains special clauses for construction contracts. See the PROVISION AND CLAUSE MATRIX in FAR Subpart 52.3. And see Bednar et al., chaps. 1–18, *Construction Contracting* (1991).

CONSTRUCTION ACTIVITY An activity at any organizational level of DOD that (1) is responsible for the architectural, engineering, and related technical aspects of the planning, design, and CONSTRUCTION of FACILITIES; and (2) receives its technical guidance from the Army Office of the Chief of Engineers, Naval Facilities Engineering Command, or Air Force Directorate of Civil Engineering. DFARS 236.102.

CONSTRUCTION, ALTERATION, OR REPAIR See CONSTRUCTION.

CONSTRUCTION MANAGEMENT A method of acquiring CONSTRUCTION in which the Government contracts with a construction manager to assist in project design and construction. During the design phase the construction manager monitors the design for constructability and conformance with the project budget. During construction the construction manager acts as the agent of the Government in assisting in the award of contracts for elements of the project and as a GENERAL CONTRACTOR to coordinate the construction process. See Douthwaite, *Why Procure Construction by Negotiation?,* 25 Pub. Cont. L.J. 423 (1996); Nash, chap. 1, *Construction Contracting* 5–7 (1991).

CONSTRUCTION MANAGEMENT ASSOCIATION OF AMERICA (CMAA) A national trade association, founded in 1918, that encourages the growth of construction management as a professional service and promotes ethical standards. CMAA presents seminars, forums, and awards, and it publishes a Standards of Practice manual and model contract documents. The organization also provides telephone referral services on technical and legal issues. [CMAA, 7918 Jones Branch Drive, Suite 540, McLean, VA 22102; (703) 356-2622]

CONSTRUCTION MATERIALS Articles, materials, and supplies brought to the construction site for incorporation into the building or work. FAR 25.201. Under the provisions of the BUY AMERICAN ACT, such materials must be of domestic origin unless their cost is unreasonable or they are not reasonably available in commercial quantities. FAR 25.202.

CONSTRUCTIVE CHANGE An oral or written act or omission by the contracting officer or other authorized Government official that is construed as having the same effect as a written CHANGE ORDER. A constructive change consists of two elements: (1) a change element, which calls for examination of the actual performance to see whether it went beyond the minimum standards demanded by the contract; and (2) an order element, in which the Government's representative, by word or deed, requires the contractor to perform work that is not a necessary part of its contract. The order element is also satisfied if the Government is at fault in issuing the contract, such as by using defective specifications (see IMPLIED WARRANTY OF SPECIFICATIONS) or failing to disclose vital information (see SUPERIOR KNOWLEDGE). Claims for constructive changes are the primary means used by contractors to obtain additional compensation for performing fixed-price contracts. Included are claims concerning CONTRACT INTERPRETATION, defective specifications, nondisclosure of information, IMPRACTICABILITY OF PERFORMANCE, breach of the DUTY TO COOPERATE, and ACCELERATION. See Cibinic & Nash, *Administration of Government Contracts* 429–75 (3d ed. 1995); Nash, chaps. 10 through 15, *Government Contract Changes* (2d ed. 1989 & Supp. 1993).

CONSULTANTS See ADVISORY AND ASSISTANCE SERVICES; EXPERTS; PROFESSIONAL AND CONSULTANT SERVICES.

CONSUMER PRODUCT For the purposes of energy conservation regulations, any article (other than an automobile) that consumes energy and is distributed in commerce for personal use or consumption by individuals. FAR 23.202. See also 42 U.S.C. §§ 6361(a)(1), 6901 et. seq., 8253, and 8262g.

CONTINGENCY A possible future event or condition arising from presently known or unknown causes, the cost outcome of which is indeterminable at the present time. FAR 31.205-7(a). Costs of allowances for contingencies are generally considered UNALLOWABLE COSTs for historical costing purposes because historical costing deals with costs incurred and recorded on the contractor's books. FAR 31.205-7. However, in some cases (for example, contract terminations), a contingency factor applicable to a past period may be recognized in the interest of expediting settlement. FAR 49.201(c). In connection with estimates of future costs, contingencies fall into two categories: (1) those that may arise from presently known and existing conditions, the effects of which are foreseeable within reasonable limits of accuracy (for example, anticipated costs of rejects and defective work); and (2) those that may arise from presently known or unknown conditions, the effects of which cannot be anticipated so precisely (the results of pending litigation, for example). In negotiating contract prices, contracting officers generally are willing to include the first category but attempt to exclude the second category from the price.

CONTINGENT FEE Any commission, percentage, brokerage, or other fee that is contingent upon the success that a person or concern has in securing a Government contract. FAR 3.401. Such fees are prohibited by 10 U.S.C. § 2306(b) and 41 U.S.C. § 254(a). Contractors' arrangements to pay contingent fees for soliciting or obtaining Government contracts have long been considered contrary to public policy because such arrangements may lead to attempted or actual exercise of improper influence (which is *any* influence that induces or tends to induce a Government employee or officer to give consideration or to act regarding a Government contract on any basis other than the merits of the matter). Negotiated solicitations and contracts must contain a warranty by the contractor against contingent fees. FAR 52.203-5, Covenant Against Contingent Fees. As an exception to the warranty, contingent fee arrangements between a contractor and a BONA FIDE EMPLOYEE or a BONA FIDE AGENCY are permitted. For breach of the contractor's warranty, the Government may annul the contract or recover the full amount of the contingent fee. FAR 3.402. FAR 31.205-33(b) also precludes the allowability of the cost of consultants when they are contingent on the recovery of costs.

CONTINUING RESOLUTION AUTHORITY (CRA) Legislation enacted by Congress to provide BUDGET AUTHORITY for specific ongoing activities in cases where the regular FISCAL YEAR appropriation has not been enacted by the beginning of the fiscal year. For example, a CRA permits avoidance of ANTI-DEFICIENCY ACT violations and provides for some amount of necessary services when Congress and the President cannot agree on the budget. A CRA usually specifies a designated period and maximum rate at which the agency may incur obligations, based on the rate of the prior year, the President's budget request, or an appropriation bill passed by either or both Houses of Congress. Normally, new programs cannot be started under a CRA. Jones, *Glossary: Acquisition Acronyms and Terms* (8th ed., Defense Systems Management College). See Tomanelli, *The Law of Funding Gaps & Continuing Resolutions*, 96-5 CP&A Rep. 3 (May 1996).

CONTINUOUS ACQUISITION AND LIFE-CYCLE SUPPORT (CALS) A strategy of DOD and the defense industry "to enable more effective generation exchange, management and use of digital data supporting defense systems. The primary goal of the CALS strategy is to migrate from manual, paper-intensive defense system operations to integrated, highly automated acquisition and support processes." *What is CALS?* (visited Jan. 8, 1997) <http://150.149.1.11/what-is-cals.html>.

CONTRA PROFERENTEM A rule of contract interpretation meaning "against the party who proffers or puts forward a thing." The rule is applied to construe ambiguous provisions or clauses (see AMBIGUITY) most strongly against the party who selected the language or drafted the clause or provision. *Black's Law Dictionary* 327 (6th ed. 1990). In most cases, the rule applies against the Government; as the customary drafter, the Government bears the responsibility for using language that permits only one reasonable interpretation. The rule is not applied against the Government, however, if the contractor has failed to meet its DUTY TO SEEK CLARIFICATION. The rule also does not apply when the language is drafted by both parties. See Cibinic & Nash, *Administration of Government Contracts* 220–37 (3d ed. 1995); Beran, *Specifications: The Duty Trilogy—Government and Contractor Responsibilities, Part One—The Drafter's Duty to Convey Unambiguous Infor-*

mation and the Other's Duty to Seek Clarification, 27 Cont. Mgmt. 4 (Aug. 1987), 12 (Sept. 1987), and 11 (Oct. 1987); Flynn, *The Rule Contra Proferentem in the Government Contract Interpretation Process*, 11 Pub. Cont. L.J. 2 (1980).

CONTRACT An agreement, enforceable by law, between two or more competent parties, to do or not to do something not prohibited by law, for a legal CONSIDERATION. FAR 2.101 defines a contract as a mutually binding legal relationship that obligates the seller to furnish supplies or services (including construction) and the buyer to pay for them. This is actually a definition of a PROCUREMENT CONTRACT as distinguished from a contract for employment or for sale of property. The definition encompasses all types of commitments that obligate the Government to an expenditure of appropriated funds and that, except as otherwise authorized, are in writing. The FAR states that, in addition to the standard bilateral instruments, Government contracts take the form of awards and NOTICEs OF AWARD; job orders or task letters issued under BASIC ORDERING AGREEMENTs; LETTER CONTRACTs; orders, such as PURCHASE ORDERs, under which the contract becomes effective upon written acceptance or actual performance; bilateral contract modifications (see MODIFICATIONS); and other written instruments. See Nash, *Postscript: Identifying What's in a Contract*, 11 N&CR ¶ 42 (Aug. 1997); Nash, *Identifying What's in a Contract*, 11 N&CR ¶ 31 (June 1997).

CONTRACT ADMINISTRATION Any administrative activity undertaken by either the Government or the contractor during the time from contract AWARD to contract CLOSEOUT. More specifically, the term refers to steps taken by the Government representatives responsible for ensuring Government and contractor compliance with the TERMS AND CONDITIONS of the contract. Such steps include routine tasks such as monitoring contractor progress, reviewing INVOICEs, processing payments, inspecting deliverables, and closing out the contract file; they also include problem-solving activities that are necessitated by unforeseeable circumstances—changes, problems, and disagreements—that arise following contract award. FAR Part 42 contains general guidance on these activities, including a long list of functions that are generally considered to be part of the contract administration process. See Cibinic & Nash, chap. 1, *Administration of Government Contracts* (3d ed. 1995); Nash, *Contract Administration: What's It All About?,* 9 N&CR ¶ 1 (Jan. 1995).

CONTRACT ADMINISTRATION OFFICE An office within a contracting activity that performs assigned postaward functions related to CONTRACT ADMINISTRATION and also handles certain assigned preaward functions. FAR 2.101.

CONTRACT AUDIT MANUAL See DCAA CONTRACT AUDIT MANUAL.

CONTRACT AUTHORITY A form of BUDGET AUTHORITY under which contracts or other obligations may be entered into in advance of an APPROPRIATION or in excess of amounts otherwise available in a revolving fund. Legislation providing new contract authority must also provide that it will be effective for any fiscal year only to such extent or in such amounts as provided in appropriations acts. 2 U.S.C. § 651(a). When an agency has contract authority, it may enter into contracts without an appropriation without violating the ANTI-DEFICIENCY ACT. Since contract authority itself is not an appropriation—it provides authority to enter into binding contracts rather than the funds to make payments under them—a contractor cannot be paid until the obligation is funded by a subsequent appropriation or by the use of a revolving fund. See GAO, *Principles of Federal Procurement Law*, vol. I, chap. 2 (2d ed. 1991); Cibinic & Nash, chap. 1, Sec. II., *Formation of Government Contracts* (3d ed. 1998).

CONTRACT AWARD See AWARD.

CONTRACT BUNDLING See BUNDLING.

CONTRACT CARRIER See CARRIER (TRANSPORTATION).

CONTRACT CLAUSE See CLAUSE.

CONTRACT COST PRINCIPLES See COST PRINCIPLES.

CONTRACT DATA REQUIREMENTS LIST (CDRL) A list of all technical data to be delivered on a contract with DOD, prepared using DD Form 1423, DFARS 253.303-1423. The purpose of this list is to identify, in a single document, all technical data ordered under a contract in order to permit the management of such data. Detailed guidance on the preparation and use of this form is contained in DOD Instruction 5010.12-M. DFARS 215.873 provides that when data are required be delivered under a contract, the solicitation must include DD Form 1423. See Nash & Rawicz, *Intellectual Property in Government Contracts*, vol. 2, 87–89 (3d ed. 1997).

CONTRACT DEBT An amount of money owed to the Government by a contractor because of one or more occurrences in the performance of a contract. FAR 32.602 gives the following examples of causes of contract debts: (1) default termination, (2) BREACH OF CONTRACT, (3) defective goods or services, (4) overpayment, (5) price redetermination, (6) delinquency in contractor payments, and (7) misrepresentation. FAR Subpart 32.6 provides guidance on collection of contract debts through techniques such as WITHHOLDING and SETOFF. See Cibinic & Nash, *Administration of Government Contracts* 1172–91 (3d ed. 1995).

CONTRACT DISPUTES ACT (CDA) OF 1978 An Act, Pub. L. No. 95-563, 41 U.S.C. §§ 601–613, that establishes the procedures to be used by contractors and contracting officers in resolving DISPUTEs arising out of and relating to contracts. The Act contains detailed provisions for handling contract CLAIMs by and against the Government, including (1) certification of contractor claims of $100,000 or more (see CERTIFICATION OF CLAIM), (2) contractor and Government claims as the subject of a DECISION OF THE CONTRACTING OFFICER, (3) APPEAL FROM A CONTRACTING OFFICER'S DECISION to a BOARD OF CONTRACT APPEALS (BCA) within 90 days or to the U.S. COURT OF FEDERAL CLAIMS within 12 months of becoming final, (4) appeals from either the BCAs or the Court of Federal Claims to the COURT OF APPEALS FOR THE FEDERAL CIRCUIT, (5) establishment of the BCAs and ADMINISTRATIVE JUDGEs (members of BCAs), (6) SMALL CLAIMS PROCEDUREs and ACCELERATED PROCEDUREs before the BCAs, (7) payment of INTEREST on claims to contractors, (8) BCA subpoena power, (9) penalties for submission of fraudulent claims, and (10) payment of claims. The Act is implemented by FAR Subpart 33.2 and the Disputes clause at FAR 52.233-1. See Cibinic & Nash, chap. 13, *Administration of Government Contracts* (3d ed. 1995); Bednar, chap. 13, *Construction Contracting* 960–77, 1009–18 (1991); Zupa & Siebel, *Reflectone, Inc. v. Dalton: Changing the Rules for CDA Claims*, 35 Cont. Mgmt. 13 (Dec. 1995); Gardner, *Practitioner's Viewpoint—Quality Tooling for the Contract Disputes Act?*, 25 Pub. Cont. L.J. 129 (1995); Nash, *Fixing the Contract Disputes Act: The Inadequate Documentation Problem*, 9 N&CR ¶ 38 (June 1995); Nash, *Contract Disputes Act Claims: Improvements in the Rules*, 7 N&CR ¶ 1 (Jan. 1993); Dover & Pollack, *Invoking the Contract Disputes Act: Potential Pitfalls*, 90-8 Briefing Papers (July 1990).

CONTRACT FINANCING See FINANCING.

CONTRACT FINANCING PAYMENT See FINANCING PAYMENT.

CONTRACT INSURANCE/PENSION REVIEW (CPIR) An in-depth evaluation of a contractor's insurance program, pension plans, other deferred compensation plans, and related policies, procedures, practices, and costs. The Defense Logistics Agency (DLA) is the designated DOD executive agency for CIPRs. DFARS 242.7301. ADMINISTRATIVE CONTRACTING OFFICERs (ACOs) are responsible for determining the reasonableness of Government contractors' insurance/pension costs. Insurance/pension specialists assigned to certain DLA defense contract administration services regions conduct CIPRs to help ACOs make these determinations. A CIPR should be the only formal review of a contractor's insurance/pension program, except for (1) periodic tests of the system performed by contract administration personnel and by the DEFENSE CONTRACT AUDIT AGENCY, or (2) any special reviews the ACO may initiate. If any organization believes that additional reviews of the contractor's insurance/pension program should be performed, that request should be conveyed to the ACO. DFARS 242.7301. See also INSURANCE and PENSION PLAN.

CONTRACT INTERPRETATION The process of determining what the parties agreed to in their bargain. Contract interpretation involves determining the meaning of words, supplying missing terms and filling in gaps, resolving ambiguities, and, at times, finding that the parties must perform in a manner that appears contrary to the words of the contractual document. The basic objective of contract interpretation is to determine the intent of the parties. Various rules of interpretation define contract terms, determine ORDER OF PRECEDENCE among the various parts of the contract, or seek to read the contract as a whole, interpreting it so as to (1) avoid rendering its terms meaningless, (2) avoid conflict, and (3) fulfill the principal purpose of the parties. See Nash, *Following a Reasonable Interpretation of a Contract*, 10 N&CR ¶ 9 (Feb. 1996); Cibinic & Nash, chap. 2, *Administration of Government Contracts* (3d ed. 1995); Nash, *The "Plain Meaning" Rule: Does It Help or Hinder Interpretation?*, 8 N&CR ¶ 37 (June 1994); Nash, *Ambiguities: They Can't Be Proved By Subsequent Clarification of the Language*, 5 N&CR ¶ 25 (May 1991).

CONTRACT LINE ITEM See LINE ITEM.

CONTRACT MODIFICATION See MODIFICATION.

CONTRACT NUMBER A number assigned by a contracting agency to identify a procurement action and provide the most efficient point of reference in correspondence dealing with the action. In DOD contracting actions, uniform PROCUREMENT INSTRUMENT IDENTIFICATION NUMBERS are assigned to all contracts and related instruments. DFARS 204.7000. NASA has a uniform ACQUISITION INSTRUMENT IDENTIFICATION system covering solicitations and contracts. NFS Subpart 18-4.71.

CONTRACT PRICING The function that gathers, assimilates, evaluates, and, in establishing objectives, brings to bear all the skills and techniques needed to shape a specific PRICING ARRANGEMENT. Those skills and techniques include PRICE ANALYSIS, COST ANALYSIS, and use of accounting and technical evaluations and systems analysis techniques to facilitate the negotiation of realistic pricing arrangements. Federal Acquisition Institute and Air Force Institute of Technology *Price Analysis, Contract Pricing Reference Guide*, vol. I (Dec. 1996). See Cibinic & Nash, chap. 9, *Formation of Government Contracts* (3d ed. 1998).

CONTRACT PRICING PROPOSAL COVER SHEET A document (Standard Form 1411) formerly prescribed by FAR 15.804-6(b) for contractors' use in submitting pricing proposals for negotiated procurements when COST OR PRICING DATA is required. This form is no longer used. Contracting officers may now require submission of cost or pricing data in the format indicated at Table 15-2 of FAR 15.408, specify an alternative format, or permit submission in the contractor's format. FAR 15.403-5.

CONTRACT QUALITY REQUIREMENTS The technical requirements in the contract relating to the quality of the product or service and those contract clauses prescribing inspection, and other quality controls incumbent on the contractor, to assure that the product or service conforms to the contractual requirements. FAR 46.101. Contract quality requirements fall into four general categories, depending on the extent of quality assurance needed by the Government for the acquisition involved: (1) reliance on contractors' existing quality assurance systems on contracts for commercial items, (2) Government reliance on inspection by the contractor, (3) standard inspection requirements, and (4) higher-level contract quality requirements. FAR 46.202-1 through -4. The extent of contract quality requirements, including contractor inspection, required under a contract is usually based on the classification of the contract item (supply or service) as determined by its technical description, its complexity, and the criticality of its application. FAR 46.203. See Cibinic & Nash, chap. 9, *Administration of Government Contracts* (3d ed. 1995).

CONTRACT SCOPE See SCOPE OF THE CONTRACT.

CONTRACT SPECIALIST An employee of a CONTRACTING ACTIVITY in the GS 1102 personnel series. This series also includes procurement analysts, contract negotiators, cost/price analysts, and contract administrators. This series of employees forms the pool that is the main source of CONTRACTING OFFICERs.

CONTRACT TYPE See TYPE OF CONTRACT.

CONTRACT WORK HOURS AND SAFETY STANDARDS ACT (CWHSSA) A 1962 Act, 40 U.S.C. §§ 327–333, that regulates the wages and working conditions of LABORERS OR MECHANICS performing work under certain Government contracts. The Act requires that at least time-and-a-half overtime be paid to any such laborer or mechanic who works more than 8 hours in a day or 40 hours in a week. Any contractor or subcontractor who violates these requirements is liable to the employee for unpaid wages and to the Government for liquidated damages of $10 for each calendar day in violation. FAR Subpart 22.3 implements the CWHSSA requirements. See Stephenson, chap. 3, *Construction Contracting* 230–33 (1991).

CONTRACTED ADVISORY AND ASSISTANCE SERVICES (CAAS) See ADVISORY AND ASSISTANCE SERVICES.

CONTRACTING Purchasing, renting, leasing, or otherwise obtaining supplies or services from non-federal sources. FAR 2.101. Contracting includes description (but not determination) of supplies and services required, selection and solicitation of sources, preparation and award of contracts, and all phases of contract administration. It does not include making GRANTs or COOPERATIVE AGREEMENTs. Contracting is a subset of ACQUISITION and PROCUREMENT.

CONTRACTING ACTIVITY An element of an agency so designated by the agency head and delegated broad authority for acquisition functions. FAR 2.101. In NASA regulations, the term is synonymous with "NASA Headquarters," "installation," and "field installation." NFS 1802.101. DOD contracting activities are listed at DFARS 202.101.

CONTRACTING METHODS See METHODS OF PROCUREMENT.

CONTRACTING OFFICE An office that awards or executes a CONTRACT for supplies or services and performs postaward functions not assigned to a CONTRACT ADMINISTRATION OFFICE. FAR 2.101.

CONTRACTING OFFICER (CO) An employee of the Government with the authority to bind the Government legally by signing a contractual instrument. FAR 1.601(a). FAR 2.101 defines a contracting officer as a person with the authority to enter into, administer, and/or terminate contracts and make related DETERMINATIONs AND FINDINGS. It then states: "The term includes certain AUTHORIZED REPRESENTATIVEs of the contracting officer acting within the limits of their authority as delegated by the contracting officer." In some agencies, such as DOD, there are three types of contracting officers, each with different responsibilities in contract procurement, management, and execution. A purchasing or PROCURING CONTRACTING OFFICER has authority to enter into a contract; an ADMINISTRATIVE CONTRACTING OFFICER administers the performance of the contract; and a TERMINATION CONTRACTING OFFICER is responsible for contract termination. Contracting officers are responsible for ensuring performance of all necessary actions for effective contracting, for ensuring compliance with the terms of the contract, and for safeguarding the interest of the Government in its contractual relationships. FAR 1.602-2. Contracting officers are appointed in writing, on Standard Form 1402, Certificate of Appointment (see WARRANT). FAR 53.301-1402. In selecting contracting officers, the appointing official must consider the complexity and dollar value of the acquisitions to be assigned and the candidates' training, education, business acumen, judgment, character, and reputation. FAR 1.603-2. See Nash, *The Contracting Officer: Defining the Role*, 10 N&CR ¶ 58 (Nov. 1996); Cibinic, *Can Procurement Be Both Fair and Efficient?*, 9 N&CR ¶ 2 (Jan. 1995); Reifel & Bastianelli, *Contracting Officer Authority*, 86-4 Briefing Papers (Mar. 1986).

CONTRACTING OFFICER REPRESENTATIVE (COR) An employee of a CONTRACTING ACTIVITY designated by a CONTRACTING OFFICER to perform certain CONTRACT ADMINISTRATION activities. A COR is an AUTHORIZED REPRESENTATIVE of a contracting officer within the scope of his or her authority but is rarely given the authority to enter into contractual agreements or MODIFICATIONs. Not all agencies use the term COR, but some of their regulations contain guidance on the functions of such employees. See GSARS Subpart 542.2 and AFARS Subpart 42.90. See also Cibinic & Nash, *Administration of Government Contracts* 28–47 (3d ed. 1995); Reifel & Bastianelli, *Contracting Officer Authority*, 86-4 Briefing Papers (Mar. 1986).

CONTRACTING OFFICER TECHNICAL REPRESENTATIVE (COTR) An employee of a CONTRACTING ACTIVITY designated by a CONTRACTING OFFICER to perform CONTRACT ADMINISTRATION activities in regard to technical issues. A COTR is an AUTHORIZED REPRESENTATIVE of a contracting officer but is rarely given the authority to enter into contractual agreements or MODIFICATIONs. Frequently the authority of COTRs is delineated by TECHNICAL DIRECTION clauses. Not all of the agencies use the term COTR, but some of their regulations contain guidance on the functions of such employees. See, for example, NFS 18-42.270 and 18-53.242-70. See also Reifel & Bastianelli, *Contracting Officer Authority*, 86-4 Briefing Papers (Mar. 1986).

CONTRACTING OFFICER'S DECISION See DECISION OF THE CONTRACTING OFFICER.

CONTRACTING OUT See A-76 POLICY.

CONTRACTOR Usually denotes a party that enters into a CONTRACT with the Government. However, the term may be applied to any individual or other legal entity that directly or indirectly (through an affiliate) submits offers for or receives a Government contract, that may reasonably be expected to submit offers for or receive a Government contract, or that conducts business (or may reasonably be expected to conduct business) with the Government as an agent or representative of another contractor. ("Government contract," as used here, includes a contract for carriage under Government or commercial bills of lading, or a subcontract under a Government contract.) FAR 9.403. With regard to subcontracting, "contractor" (i.e., PRIME CONTRACTOR) means the total contractor organization or a separate entity of it (such as an affiliate, division, or plant) that performs its own purchasing. FAR 44.101. Both the prime contractor and any SUBCONTRACTOR are defined as contractors for the purposes of equal employment opportunity (FAR 22.801) and Service Contract Act (FAR 22.1001) compliance.

CONTRACTOR-ACQUIRED PROPERTY Property acquired or otherwise provided by a contractor for performing a contract and to which the Government has title. FAR 45.101. Contractor-acquired property is treated as GOVERNMENT PROPERTY for the purpose of management and control under the provisions of FAR Subpart 45.5.

CONTRACTOR BID OR PROPOSAL INFORMATION Information of the following types submitted to a federal agency as part of or in connection with a BID or PROPOSAL to enter into a FEDERAL AGENCY PROCUREMENT CONTRACT and not previously made available to the public or disclosed publicly: (1) COST OR PRICING DATA; (2) INDIRECT COSTs and direct labor rates; (3) proprietary information about manufacturing processes, operations, or techniques marked by a contractor as proprietary; (4) information marked as "contractor bid or proposal information" in accordance with applicable law or regulation; and (5) information marked in accordance with the Instructions to Offerors—Competitive Acquisition clause in FAR 52.215-1. FAR 3.104-3. This class of information may not be disclosed or obtained under the new PROCUREMENT INTEGRITY rules. The synonymous term under the old rules was PROPRIETARY INFORMATION. Guidance on the treatment of information is contained in FAR 3.104-5.

CONTRACTOR COST DATA REPORTING (CCDR) A system through which contractors report projected and ACTUAL COSTs and related data to DOD for selected procurements, typically MAJOR SYSTEM ACQUISITION programs. The CCDR provides the procuring activity with an "independent" cost estimate of all of the activity's major acquisitions as well as the means to compare a system with other related systems. Part 6.4.1. of DOD Regulation 5000.2-R, *Mandatory Procedures for Defense Acquisition Programs (MDAPs) and Major Automated Information System (MAIS) Acquisition Programs*, Mar. 15, 1996 requires CCDR on all systems except commercial systems and noncommercial systems bought under firm-fixed-price contracts that are competitively awarded. Reports are submitted on DD Form 1921, Cost Data Summary Report, DFARS 253.303-1921. See Grskovich, *What Is C/SCSC?—In English, Please!,* 23 Nat'l Cont. Mgmt. J., Issue No. 2, p. 25 (1990). See also COST/SCHEDULE CONTROL SYSTEMS CRITERIA and WORK BREAKDOWN STRUCTURE.

CONTRACTOR DATA REPOSITORY See DATA REPOSITORY.

CONTRACTOR INVENTORY See INVENTORY.

CONTRACTOR PAST PERFORMANCE See PAST PERFORMANCE.

CONTRACTOR PERFORMANCE ASSESSMENT REPORT (CPAR) A method used by the Air Force Materiel Command for systematically assessing contractor performance on current systems acquisitions greater than $5 million. It is an assessment of a contractor's performance, both positive and negative, on a given contract during a specific period of time. Such assessments must be based on objective facts and be supportable by program and contract management data, such as cost performance reports, customer complaints, quality reviews, technical interchange meetings, financial solvency assessments, production management reviews, contractor operations reviews, functional performance evaluations, and earned contract incentives. Subjective assessments concerning the cause or implications of the contractor's performance are also included. The purpose of the CPARS is to ensure a current, command-wide database of contractor performance information available for use in responsibility determinations and in formal and informal source selections. See AFMC Instruction 64–107, Contractor Performance Assessment Reporting System (CPARS) (July 15, 1996). See PAST PERFORMANCE INFORMATION.

CONTRACTOR PURCHASING SYSTEM REVIEW (CPSR) The complete evaluation by the Government of a contractor's purchasing of material and services, subcontracting, and subcontract management, from development of the requirement through completion of subcontract performance. FAR 44.101. The objective of a CPSR is to evaluate the efficiency and effectiveness with which the contractor spends Government funds and complies with Government policy when subcontracting. The review provides the administrative contracting officer with a basis for granting, withholding, or withdrawing approval of the contractor's purchasing system. FAR 44.301. Contractors are subject to a CPSR if their expected sales to the Government under other than sealed bid procedures are expected to exceed $25 million during the next 12 months. FAR 44.302. The review specifically focuses on (1) the degree of price competition obtained, (2) pricing policies and techniques, (3) methods of evaluating subcontractors' responsibility, (4) treatment accorded affiliates, (5) policies and procedures regarding small business concerns, (6) planning, award, and postaward management of major subcontract programs, (7) compliance with Cost Accounting Standards in awarding subcontracts, (8) appropriateness of types of contracts used, and (9) management control systems to administer progress payments to subcontractors. FAR 44.303. See DFARS Subpart 244.3 and appendix C; Beckman & Martens, *Subcontracting: Creative CPSR Oversight*, 35 Cont. Mgmt. 23 (June 1995); Prokopy, *Contractor Purchasing System Review: What Is It?,* 28 Cont. Mgmt. 20 (Oct. 1988).

CONTRACTOR RISK ASSESSMENT GUIDE (CRAG) A DOD initiative providing for reduced oversight of contractors that meet certain specified standards of internal AUDIT and control. The purpose is to launch a cooperative effort by DOD and private industry to (1) encourage contractors to develop more effective internal control systems and (2) improve the effectiveness and efficiency of DOD oversight. CRAG is a voluntary endeavor under which a contractor can seek administrative contracting officer review and approval of its program. Two guides available through industry associations, *DOD Contractor Risk Assessment Guide* (Oct. 1988) and *DOD Contractor Risk Assessment Guide Program* (Nov. 1988), identify control objectives for the five areas that the Government considers of highest risk in relation to cost or pricing: INDIRCT COST submissions, LABOR charging, MATERIAL MANAGEMENT AND ACCOUNTING SYSTEMs, estimating systems, and purchasing. See SELF-GOVERNANCE. See also Carren & Seal, *The Challenges of CRAG*, 89-6 CP&A Rep. 3 (June 1989); Menestrina, *CRAG: Just Another Four-Letter Word?,* 29 Cont. Mgmt. 8 (Apr. 1989); *DOD Unveils Contractor Risk Assessment Guide Program to Reduce Oversight*, 50 Fed. Cont. Rep. 913, 933 (Dec. 5, 1988).

CONTRACTOR TEAM ARRANGEMENT See TEAM AGREEMENT.

CONTRACTOR VERSUS GOVERNMENT PERFORMANCE See A-76 POLICY.

CONTRACTOR WEIGHTED AVERAGE SHARE (CWA) A DOD system, used in the late 1960s and 1970s, for reduced Government oversight when a contractor's business was predominantly commercial or competitive fixed-priced work. DOD considered it desirable (1) to measure the cost-risk motivation imposed on individual contractors (as evidenced by the nature and type of the contracts), and (2) whenever practicable, to eliminate administrative controls and overhead AUDITs on those contractors that attained a verifiable "weighted average share" or risk that met a prescribed threshold. The CWAS concept was based on the premise that companies would exercise good management to be cost-conscious under contracts for commercial work or entered into on a competitive fixed-price basis—with the result that detailed review, control, and overhead audit by Government personnel was not necessary. ASPR 3-1001. DOD eliminated the program in 1983.

CONTRACTUAL RELIEF See EXTRAORDINARY CONTRACTUAL ACTION.

CONTRIBUTION See DONATION.

CONTROLLED MATERIALS The various shapes and forms of steel, copper, aluminum, and nickel alloys specified in Schedule II and defined in Schedule III of the DEFENSE PRIORITIES AND ALLOCATION SYSTEM. FAR 11.601. The use of these materials on defense contracts is given priority by their designation as RATED ORDERs in contracts and subcontracts. See FAR Subpart 11.6. The basic premise of this system is that the industrial production of the United States can be controlled, in emergency circumstances, if the use of these four materials is controlled.

CONUS The continental United States: the 48 contiguous states and the District of Columbia. FAR 47.001. The policies in FAR Subpart 47.3 for the transportation of supplies are different for transportation within the continental United States and outside the continental United States.

CONVENIENCE TERMINATION See TERMINATION FOR CONVENIENCE.

CONVERSION DIRECT LABOR A PROFIT analysis subfactor that measures the contribution of direct engineering, manufacturing, and other LABOR to converting the raw materials, data, and subcontracted items into the contract items using the theory that such labor should yield the highest rates of profit. Considerations include the diversity of engineering, scientific, and manufacturing labor skills required and the amount and quality of supervision and coordination needed to perform the contract task. FAR 15.404-4(d)(1)(i)(B).

CONVERSION-RELATED INDIRECT COSTS A PROFIT analysis subfactor that measures how much the INDIRECT COSTs contribute to contract performance. The LABOR elements in the allocable indirect costs should be given the profit consideration they would receive if treated as direct labor. The other elements of indirect costs should be evaluated to determine whether they merit only limited profit consideration because of their routine nature, or are elements that contribute significantly to the proposed contract. FAR 15.404-4(d)(1)(i)(C).

COOPERATIVE AGREEMENT A legal instrument used principally for transferring money, property, or services to a state or local government or to another recipient in order to accomplish a public purpose of support or stimulation where substantial involvement is expected between the Government agency and the recipient. 31 U.S.C. § 6305. See Riley, *III Federal Contracts, Grants and Assistance* 85 (1984). A cooperative agreement is frequently similar to a COST-SHARING CONTRACT. However, a cost-sharing contract is subject to the FEDERAL ACQUISITION REGULATION, whereas a cooperative agreement is not. Thus, agencies entering into cooperative agreements generally have substantial freedom to structure the terms and conditions of the agreement. Regulatory guidance is issued by agencies in the form of assistance regulations, in cooperation with the OFFICE OF MANAGEMENT AND BUDGET. However, statutes establishing specific programs, as well as certain other regulations, may contain requirements for cooperative agreements that differ from the usual assistance regulations or even resemble ACQUISITION approaches. For example, the Cooperative Agreement with Canada is a MEMORANDUM OF UNDERSTANDING that does not fall within the scope of 31 U.S.C. § 6305. See Cibinic & Nash, chap. 1, Sec. I., *Formation of Government Contracts* (3d ed 1998); Walker, *Enforcing Grants and Cooperative Agreements as Contracts Under the Tucker Act*, 26 Pub. Cont. L.J. 683 (1997); Cibinic, *Cooperative Agreements: Many Things to Many People*, 9 N&CR ¶ 39 (July 1995); Cushman, *Cooperative Agreements: A Different Kind of Grant*, 35 Cont. Mgmt. 23 (Apr. 1995); Brown, *A Federal Agency's Authority to Use a Cooperative Agreement for a Particular Project*, 18 Pub. Cont. L.J. 188 (1988).

COOPERATIVE PROGRAMS Programs that comprise one or more specific cooperative projects conducted under an international agreement and that are implemented under the ARMS EXPORT CONTROL ACT, including specific provisions of 22 U.S.C. § 2767, regarding cooperative projects with friendly foreign countries, or 10 U.S.C. § 2350a, regarding cooperative RESEARCH AND DEVELOPMENT programs with allied countries. Cooperative programs exclude programs that entail acquisition for solely foreign military requirements, as distinct from joint U.S.-foreign military requirements. (Acquisition for solely foreign military requirements will be satisfied through either FOREIGN MILITARY SALES or direct commercial transactions with U.S. contractors.) Cooperative programs may also comprise one or more specific cooperative projects whose arrangements are defined in a written agreement between the parties and that involve: (1) research, development, testing, and evaluation (RDT&E) of defense articles, joint production of a defense article that was developed by one or more of the participants, and procurement by the United States of a foreign defense article, technology, or service that are implemented under 22 U.S.C. § 2767, to promote the rationalization, standardization, and interoperability of NATO armed forces or to enhance the ongoing efforts of non-NATO countries to improve their conventional defense capabilities; (2) cooperative research and development with NATO and major non-NATO allies implemented under 10 U.S.C. § 2350a, to improve the conventional defense capabilities of NATO and enhance rationalization, standardization, and interoperability; (3) data, information, and personnel exchange activities conducted under approved DOD programs; or (4) testing and evaluation of conventional defense equipment, munitions, and technologies developed by allied and friendly nations to meet valid existing U.S. military requirements. Jones, *Glossary: Defense Acquisition Acronyms and Terms* (8th ed., Defense Systems Management College).

COOPERATIVE PURCHASING Two or more organizations purchasing under the same contract; the organizations can be a mixture of state or local government agencies, or a combination of federal agencies. In addition to the advantage of achieving better prices, organizations may participate in cooperative purchasing arrangements to reduce possible duplication of effort, attract a larger number of bidders, or share information regarding specific items. See INTERAGENCY ACQUISITION.

COOPERATIVE RESEARCH AND DEVELOPMENT AGREEMENT (CRADA) Agreement between a Government laboratory or Government-owned, contractor-operated laboratory and a private organization to conduct RESEARCH AND DEVELOPMENT jointly. Such an agreement combines the resources of the private sector, state and local governments, universities, or consortia with those of the Federal Government. CRADAs are authorized by 15 U.S.C. § 3701 et seq. They are a means of FEDERAL TECHNOLOGY TRANSFER whereby the Government may share its research resources but may not use appropriated funds to conduct joint research projects. See generally Nash & Rawicz, *Intellectual Property in Government Contracts*, vol. 1, chap. 2 (3d ed. 1997). See Cibinic, *Postscript: Cooperative Agreements*, 9 N&CR ¶ 53 (Oct. 1995); Cibinic, *Cooperative Agreements: Many Things To Many People*, 9 N&CR ¶ 39 (July 1995); Duncombe,

Federal Technology Transfer: A Look at the Benefits and Pitfalls of One of the Country's Best Kept Secrets, 37 Fed. B. News & J. 608 (1990).

COPELAND ANTI-KICKBACK ACT A 1934 Act, 18 U.S.C. § 874, 40 U.S.C. § 276c, that contains provisions to prevent KICKBACKs by construction workers to contractors or subcontractors on projects financed in whole or in part by the Government. This act is implemented by FAR 22.403-2 and the clause at FAR 52.222-10.

COPYRIGHT The exclusive rights of an author in works (literary, musical, dramatic, choreographic, pictorial, graphic, sculptural, audiovisual or sound recordings) that he or she has created. The key rights are (1) reproduction, (2) preparation of DERIVATIVE WORKs, (3) distribution by sale or leasing, (4) performance, and (5) public display. Title 17 of the United States Code governs these rights. Authors obtain the rights at the time the work is first created (without regard to publication) and may register their works in the Copyright Office of the Library of Congress. Copyright has become an important facet of Government contracting because most SOFTWARE is copyrighted by its creators. Contractual provisions governing the ownership and use of copyrights are contained in the Rights in Data—General clause in FAR 52.227-14, the Rights in Technical Data clause in DFARS 252.227-7013 and the Rights in Computer Software clause in DFARS 252.227-7014. See Nash & Rawicz, *Intellectual Property in Government Contracts*, vol. 2, chap.1.II; vol. 3, chaps. 1.I.B (3d ed. 1997); Thibodeaux, *What Everyone Should Know About Copyright, Patents and Trademarks*, 36 Cont. Mgmt. 12 (Mar. 1996); Nash, *The New DOD "Rights in Software" Policy: Half a Loaf*, 10 N&CR ¶ 12 (Mar. 1996); Nash, *The New DOD Policy on Technical Data and Computer Software*, 8 N&CR ¶ 22 (Apr. 1994); Nash, *Copyright of Computer Programs: How Much Protection Is Possible?*, 6 N&CR ¶ 65 (Nov. 1992).

CORPORATE ADMINISTRATIVE CONTRACTING OFFICER (CACO) An ADMINISTRATIVE CONTRACTING OFFICER (ACO) assigned to a corporation that has more than one location with resident ACOs. CACOs deal with corporate management and perform Government review and approval of corporate-wide policies, procedures, and activities in order to ensure uniform treatment. FAR 42.601. Typical CACO functions include (1) determining final INDIRECT COST rates for cost-reimbursement contracts, (2) establishing ADVANCE AGREEMENTs or recommendations on corporate/ HOME OFFICE expense allocations, and (3) administering COST ACCOUNT-

ING STANDARDS applicable to corporate-level and corporate-directed accounting practices. FAR 42.603.

COST The sum or equivalent expended, paid, or charged for something. *Black's Law Dictionary* 345 (6th ed. 1990). The Government recognizes only ALLOWABLE COSTs in computing the costs that it will reimburse under COST-REIMBURSEMENT CONTRACTs and in pricing actions under FIXED-PRICE CONTRACTs. See Generally, Cibinic & Nash, chap. 5, *Cost-Reimbursement Contracting* (2d ed. 1993).

COST ACCOUNTING The area of accounting that focuses on the method and system used to compile and analyze the costs of selling and manufacturing products and services. It includes the method for classifying, summarizing, recording, and allocating the ACTUAL COSTs incurred and comparing them with the estimated or standard costs that have been established by a contractor. *Black's Law Dictionary* 345 (6th ed. 1990). See Mizoguchi, *Post-Retirement Benefits: Accounting for and Recovering the Cost of Health Care for Retirees*, 24 Pub. Cont. L.J. 357 (1995); Cibinic, *Accounting for Price Adjustments*, 8 N&CR ¶ 30 (May 1994); Lynch, *Allocation of Home Office Expenses to Segments and Business Unit G&A Expenses to Final Cost Objectives*, 22 Pub. Cont. L.J. 339 (1993); Hertling, *Activity Based Costing and Cost Estimating*, 33 Cont. Mgmt. 4 (Aug. 1993); Lemmer & Davis, *Generally Accepted Accounting Principles and Government Contract Cost Accounting: A Survey of Theory and Practice*, 92-11 CP&A Rep. 3 (Nov. 1992); Avery, *Accounting for Corporate Home Office Expenses*, 32 Cont. Mgmt. 20 (Sept. 1992); Sourwine, *Contracting = Law + Accounting*, 32 Cont. Mgmt. 10 (May 1992). See generally Cibinic & Nash, *Cost-Reimbursement Contracting* 616–27 (2d ed. 1993).

COST ACCOUNTING PERIOD See BASE PERIOD.

COST ACCOUNTING PRACTICE Any disclosed or established accounting method or technique that is used for (1) measuring cost (defining the components of cost, determining the basis for cost measurement, and establishing criteria for the use of alternative cost management techniques); (2) determining the amount of cost to be assigned to individual cost accounting periods; and (3) allocating costs to COST OBJECTIVEs, both directly and indirectly. 48 C.F.R. § 9904.302-1. The determination of the amount paid or a change in the amount paid for a unit of goods and services is not a cost accounting practice. CAS 402, 48 C.F.R. § 9904.402, requires that contractors follow consistent cost accounting practices. Contractors subject to the COST ACCOUNTING STANDARDS must disclose their cost accounting practices on DISCLOSURE STATEMENTs. See Cibinic & Nash, *Cost-Reimbursement Contacting* 616–27 (2d ed. 1993).

COST ACCOUNTING STANDARDS (CAS) A series of accounting standards originally issued by the COST ACCOUNTING STANDARDS BOARD under Pub. L. No. 91-379, 50 U.S.C. app. § 2168, to achieve uniformity and consistency in measuring, assigning, and allocating costs to contracts with the Federal Government. The 19 standards that were issued between 1970 and 1980 are now incorporated in FAR appendix B, 48 C.F.R. Part 9904. Under Pub. L. No. 91-379, only contractors and subcontractors awarded negotiated contracts by DOD and NASA were subject to the standards. However, under Pub. L. No. 100-679, 41 U.S.C. § 422, which reestablished the CAS Board after it had been abolished in 1980, the standards promulgated by the new Board apply to contracts issued by all agencies of the Government. The standards do not apply to sealed bid contracts or contracts with SMALL BUSINESS CONCERNs. FAR 30.000. In 1996, Pub. L. No. 104-106 made the CAS inapplicable to contracts and subcontracts for commercial items. Each of the 19 standards consists of 6 parts: purpose, fundamental requirement, technique for application, illustration, interpretation, and exemption. The standards deal with consistency in estimating, accumulating, and reporting costs (CAS 401); consistency in allocating costs incurred for the same purpose (CAS 402); allocation of HOME OFFICE expenses (CAS 403); capitalization of tangible assets (CAS 404); accounting for unallowable costs (CAS 405); selection of cost accounting periods (CAS 406); use of standard costs for direct material and direct labor (CAS 407); accounting for costs of compensated personal absence (CAS 408); depreciation of TANGIBLE CAPITAL ASSETs (CAS 409); allocation of BUSINESS UNIT general and administrative expenses to final cost objectives (CAS 410); accounting for acquisition costs of material (CAS 411); composition and measurement of pension cost (CAS 412); adjustment and allocation of pension cost (CAS 413); cost of money as an element of the cost of facilities capital (CAS 414); accounting for the cost of deferred compensation (CAS 415); accounting for insurance costs (CAS 416); cost of money as an element of the cost of capital assets under construction (CAS 417); allocation of direct and indirect costs (CAS 418); and accounting for independent research and development and bid and proposal costs (CAS 420). See Boyd & Villet, *Cost Accounting Standards Fundamentals*, 96-12 (Nov. 1996); Sourwine, *CAS Applicability, Coverage & Disclosure Revisited*, 36 Cont. Mgmt. 16 (Apr.

1996); Cibinic, *CAS: Do They Permit Contract Repricing?,* 10 N&CR ¶ 14 (Mar. 1996); Seyfarth et al., chap. 16, *The Government Contract Compliance Handbook* (2d ed. 1991 & 1996 Supp.); Carlton & Manos, *Voluntary Accounting Changes Under the CAS: A Windfall for the Government?,* 25 Pub. Cont. L.J. 457 (1996); Cibinic, *Applicability of Cost Accounting Standards*, 9 N&CR ¶ 62 (Dec. 1995); Bruce, *Cost Accounting Standards for Colleges and Universities*, 35 Cont. Mgmt. 4 (Sept. 1995); Sourwine, *Untangling the Web of CAS Requirements*, 34 Cont. Mgmt. 4 (July 1994); Cibinic, *Cost Accounting Standards Compliance and Cost Allocability: Who's In Charge?,* 7 N&CR ¶ 43 (Aug. 1993); Sourwine, *Demystifying CAS Applicability, Coverage and Disclosure*, 33 Cont. Mgmt. 3 (Mar. 1993); Cibinic & Nash, *Cost-Reimbursement Contracting* 616–27 (2d ed. 1993); Gallagher & Chadick, *Cost Accounting Standards: New Developments*, 89-6 Briefing Papers (May 1989).

COST ACCOUNTING STANDARDS (CAS) BOARD The Governmental entity with the exclusive authority to make, promulgate, amend, and rescind COST ACCOUNTING STANDARDS and interpretations of them. The CAS Board was originally established in 1970 by Pub. L. No. 91-379, 50 U.S.C. app. § 2168. That Board, which promulgated the current 19 standards, was part of the legislative branch and was chaired by the Comptroller General. Its jurisdiction was limited to national defense contracts, and it was abolished in 1980 after Congress failed to provide an appropriation. Section 5 of Pub. L. No. 100-679, 41 U.S.C. § 422, the Office of Federal Procurement Policy Act Amendments of 1988, reestablished the CAS Board as an independent board within the Office of Management and Budget's OFFICE OF FEDERAL PROCUREMENT POLICY (OFPP). By law, the Board consists of five members. The Administrator of OFPP chairs the Board. The other four members, each experienced in Government contract cost accounting, are as follows: two representatives of the Federal Government, one representing DOD and the other representing GSA; and two individuals from the private sector (both appointed by the Administrator of OFPP), one representing industry and one who is particularly knowledgeable about cost accounting problems and systems. 41 U.S.C. § 422(a). Rules and regulations promulgated by the CAS Board are presently incorporated into FAR Part 30 and at 48 C.F.R. chap. 99 in a supplementary chapter of the FAR; appendix B, FAR loose-leaf edition. See Bossalona & Kaplan, *The New CASB DS-1—Potential Pitfalls & Opportunities*, 96-3 CP&A Rep. 3 (Mar. 1996); Sourwine, *Cost Accounting Standards Board—It's Back*, 25 Nat'l Cont. Mgmt. J., Issue No. 2, p 41 (1993); Lemmer & Hildebrandt, *Latest Developments from* *the CAS Board*, 32 Cont. Mgmt. 15 (Oct. 1992); Lemmer & Hildebrandt, *The New CAS Board: Whose Wish Has Come True?*, 31 Cont. Mgmt. 22 (Dec. 1991); Cibinic, *Postscript: Cost Accounting Standards Board*, 3 N&CR ¶ 85 (Dec. 1989); Cibinic, *Cost Accounting Standards Board*, 3 N&CR ¶ 50 (July 1989); Cibinic, *The Reincarnation of the Cost Accounting Standards Board*, 2 N&CR ¶ 74 (Dec. 1988).

COST ANALYSIS Review and evaluation of the separate cost elements and proposed profit contained in an offeror's or contractor's proposal (including COST OR PRICING DATA or INFORMATION OTHER THAN COST OR PRICING DATA) and the application of judgment to determine how well the proposed costs represent what the cost of the contract should be, assuming reasonable economy and efficiency. FAR 15.404-1(c). Cost analysis is used to establish the basis for negotiating contract prices when PRICE COMPETITION is inadequate or lacking altogether and when PRICE ANALYSIS, by itself, does not ensure price reasonableness (see FAIR AND REASONABLE PRICE). See Federal Acquisition Institute and Air Force Institute of Technology, *Cost Analysis, Contract Pricing Reference Guide*, vol. III (Dec. 1993). The contracting officer uses the following techniques and procedures, as appropriate, to perform cost analysis: (1) verification of cost or pricing data and evaluation of cost elements; (2) evaluation of the effect of current practices on future costs; (3) comparison of costs proposed for individual cost elements with previously incurred ACTUAL COSTs, previous cost estimates, independent Government estimates, and forecasts; (4) verification of compliance with the FAR COST PRINCIPLES and applicable COST ACCOUNTING STANDARDS; (5) identification of any COST OR PRICING DATA needed to make the proposal ACCURATE, COMPLETE, AND CURRENT; and (6) analysis of the results of MAKE-OR-BUY PROGRAM reviews. FAR 15.404-1(c)(2). The contracting officer should also perform cost analysis in selecting and negotiating a contract type in the absence of effective price competition and when price analysis is insufficient. FAR 16.104(c). See Cibinic & Nash, chap. 9, Sec. IV., *Formation of Government Contracts* (3d ed. 1998).

COST AS AN INDEPENDENT VARIABLE Treating the ultimate cost of a system as a variable that has the same importance as performance goals and completion requirements during the development process. Paragraph 3.3.3 of DOD Regulation 5000.2-R, *Mandatory Procedures for Major Defense Acquisition Programs (MDAPs) and*

Major Automated Information System (MAIS) Acquisition Programs, Mar. 15, 1996, requires that acquisition strategies establish aggressive, achievable cost objectives and that acquisition programs be managed to maximize the possibility that these objectives be met. This is accomplished by continually trading off cost with performance requirements and completion schedules. See Nash, *Cost As An Independent Variable: A New Technique?*, 11 N&CR ¶ 35 (July 1997).

COST BASE See BASE.

COST CONTRACT A COST-REIMBURSEMENT CONTRACT in which the contractor receives no fee. FAR 16.302. Such a contract may be appropriate for RESEARCH AND DEVELOPMENT work, particularly with nonprofit educational institutions or other nonprofit organizations, and for FACILITIES CONTRACTs. See Cibinic & Nash, *Cost-Reimbursement Contracting* 134–39 (2d ed. 1993).

COST IMPACT PROPOSAL The documentation of a contract price adjustment if increased costs result from a contractor's failure either to comply with a cost accounting standard or to follow a cost accounting practice consistently. Whenever a contractor makes a change to disclosed or established accounting practices or is determined to be in noncompliance. The Administration of Cost Accounting Standards clause at FAR 52.230-6 requires the submission of a cost impact proposal within 60 days (or other mutually agreed-upon date) after the proposed change is determined adequate and compliant. *DCAA Contract Audit Manual* 8 502.2. An integral part of the cost proposal is the list of CAS-covered contracts and subcontracts which will be affected by the change or noncompliance. In evaluating cost impact proposals, the auditor will perform essentially two types of reviews: (1) an evaluation of the contractor's estimate of the cost impact on covered contracts caused by changes in cost accounting practices; and (2) a review of proposed cost increases to the Government caused by the contractor's failure to follow consistently its disclosed or established practices or to comply with applicable cost accounting standards. The amount of the adjustment is the increase in cost to the Government over what the cost would have been had the contractor complied with the standards and/or followed consistently its disclosed or established practices. *DCAA Contract Audit Manual* 8-503.1. See Cibinic & Nash, *Cost-Reimbursement Contracting* 1064–65 (2d ed. 1993).

COST INCURRED See INCURRED COST.

COST INPUT The cost, except GENERAL AND ADMINISTRATIVE (G&A) EXPENSEs, that for contract costing purposes is allocable (see ALLOCABLE COST) to the production of goods and services during a cost accounting period. FAR 31.001. The cost input is usually the COST BASE to which G&A expenses are allocated.

COST OBJECTIVE A function, organizational subdivision, contract, or other work unit for which cost data are desired and for which provision is made to accumulate and measure the cost of processes, products, jobs, capitalized projects, and so forth. FAR 31.001. A final cost objective is a cost objective that has allocated to it both DIRECT COSTs and INDIRECT COSTs and, in the contractor's accumulation system, is one of the final accumulation points. See Cibinic & Nash, *Cost-Reimbursement Contracting* 658–68 (2d ed. 1993).

COST OF CAPITAL COMMITTED TO FACILITIES An imputed cost of the capital a contractor has committed to its FACILITIES, determined by applying a cost of money rate to facilities capital. FAR 31.001. Also called "facilities capital cost of money." This cost is computed in accordance with CAS 414, 48 C.F.R. § 9904.414 and, in effect, is the imputed INTEREST the contractor would have to pay if it had borrowed funds to finance the purchase of the facilities. The computation derives the cost by multiplying the NET BOOK VALUE of facilities allocated to a contract by the TREASURY INTEREST RATE. The amount is imputed because it does not depend on whether a contractor has financed the purchase of the facilities by borrowed capital or equity financing. FAR 31.205-10 provides that such cost is allowable (see ALLOWABLE COST) when it is "specifically identified or proposed in cost proposals." NFS Subpart 18-30.70 governs facilities capital employed for facilities by NASA. See also COST OF MONEY AS A COST OF CAPITAL ASSETS UNDER CONSTRUCTION and COST OF MONEY FACTORS.

COST OF MONEY AS A COST OF CAPITAL ASSETS UNDER CONSTRUCTION An imputed cost of the capital a contractor has used to construct, fabricate, or develop new FACILITIES. 48 C.F.R. § 9904.417-40. This cost is computed in accordance with CAS 417, 48 C.F.R. § 9904.417. It is added to the capitalized acquisition cost of the facilities when they are placed on the contractor's BALANCE SHEET as an ASSET.

COST OF MONEY FACTORS (CMF) Factors developed by overhead pools at contractors' BUSINESS UNITs, using Form CASB CMF

(48 C.F.R. § 9904.414, Appendix A, Facilities Capital Cost of Money Factors Computation), to measure a contractor's COST OF CAPITAL COMMITTED TO FACILITIES. Three elements are required: (1) business unit facilities capital data (the NET BOOK VALUE for each cost accounting period), (2) overhead allocation bases (the same as the bases used to compute the proposed overhead rates), and (3) the TREASURY INTEREST RATE. Cost of money factors are also used to develop the "facilities capital employed" base used in prenegotiation profit objectives under the DOD WEIGHTED GUIDELINES METHOD. DFARS 215.970. Actual CFMs are required when it is necessary to determine final allowable costs for cost settlement or repricing in accordance with CAS 414, Cost of Money as an Element of the Cost of Facilities Capital, and with FAR 31.205-10. See DFARS 230.7003-1.

COST OF REPROCUREMENT See EXCESS COST OF REPROCUREMENT.

COST OR PRICING DATA All facts that, as of the date of agreement on the price of a contract (or the price of a contract modification), a prudent buyer or seller would reasonably expect to affect price negotiations significantly. The term does not include judgments but does include the factual information from which a judgment was derived (see FACT and JUDGMENT IN PRICING). 10 U.S.C. § 2306a(h)(1); 41 U.S.C. § 254b(i)(1). A more elaborate definition is included in FAR 15.401. It states that cost or pricing data are all facts that can reasonably be expected to contribute to the soundness of estimates of future costs and to the validity of determinations of costs already incurred. They include such factors as vendor quotations, NONRECURRING COSTS, information on changes in production methods and changes in production or purchasing volume, data supporting projections of business prospects and objectives and related operations costs, unit-cost trends such as those associated with labor efficiency, make-or-buy decisions, estimated resources needed to attain business goals, and information on management decisions that could have a significant bearing on costs. See Cibinic & Nash, chap. 9, Sec. I., *Formation of Government Contracts* (3d ed. 1998); Seyfarth et al., chap. 10, *The Government Contract Compliance Handbook* (2d ed. 1991 & 1996 Supp.); Nash, *Truth in Negotiations: The FAR Implementation of FASA*, 9 N&CR ¶ 57 (Nov. 1995); Cibinic, *Cost or Pricing Data: Defining and Furnishing Data*, 9 N&CR ¶ 45 (Aug. 1995); Lovitky, *Cost and Pricing Data Defined: An Analysis of the Scope of Contractor Disclosure Requirements Pursuant to the Truth in*

Negotiations Act, 20 Nat'l Cont. Mgmt. J., Issue No. 2, p. 79 (1987). See also CERTIFIED COST OR PRICING DATA.

COST OVERRUN The excess of ALLOWABLE COSTs incurred by a contractor on a COST-REIMBURSEMENT CONTRACT over the ESTIMATED COST of the contract. Under the LIMITATION OF COST CLAUSE, contractors are not obligated to incur such overruns and the Government is not obligated to reimburse such costs. This term is also used, on occasion, to refer to the incurrence of more costs than predicted in the performance of FIXED-PRICE CONTRACTs. See CAS 405, 48 C.F.R. § 9904.405-40, which requires that unallowable cost overruns be allocated to the contract on which they were incurred rather than to some other account. See also Christensen, *Cost Overrun Optimism: Fact or Fiction?,* 1 Acquisition Rev. Q. 19 (Win. 1994); Cibinic, *Notice of Cost Overruns: Tell It Like It Is*, 7 N&CR ¶ 5 (Jan. 1993).

COST PERFORMANCE INDEX (CPI) A key indicator used to analyze cost and schedule performance data reported by defense contractors. This figure informs the agency of the contractor's efficiency and whether the contractor is above or below cost. See Christensen & Heise, *Cost Performance Index Stability*, 25 Nat'l Cont. Mgmt. J., Issue No. 1, p. 7 (1993).

COST PERFORMANCE REPORT (CPR) A primary means of communication between the contractor and the procuring agency to report cost and schedule performance and trends. The CPR serves to alert the agency of any problems arising with cost or schedule and demonstrates the results of any corrective action taken to address earlier deficiencies. CPRs are required on all contracts that require compliance with Cost/Schedule Control Systems Criteria but agencies are encouraged to permit contractors to use their own systems if they provide accurate and timely information. DOD Regulation 5000.2-R, *Mandatory Procedures for Major Defense Acquisition Programs (MDAPs) and Major Automated Information System (MAIS) Acquisition Programs*, Part 6.4.2, Mar. 15, 1996. See Steiger, *Federal Contract Management: A Manual for the Contract Professional* ¶ 16.02[2][d][vii] (Matthew Bendar 1982).

COST-PLUS-A-PERCENTAGE-OF-COST (CPPC) CONTRACT A type of contract containing some element that obligates the Government to pay the contractor an amount (in the form of either profit or cost) undetermined at the time the contract was made and to be incurred in the future, based on a percentage of future costs. *Muschany v. United States*, 324 U.S. 49, 61–62 (1944). A cost-plus-a-percentage-of-cost system of contracting is prohibited by 10 U.S.C. § 2306(a) and 41 U.S.C. § 254(b). This prohibition can apply to either a COST-REIMBURSEMENT CONTRACT or a FIXED-PRICE CONTRACT if either contains any element that is paid as a percentage of another cost thus permitting payment to increase if the contractor incurs greater costs. The purpose of the prohibition is to prevent contracts that motivate a contractor to increase its profits by increasing costs of performance. See Cibinic & Nash, *Cost-Reimbursement Contracting* 44–52 (2d ed. 1993).

COST-PLUS-AWARD-FEE (CPAF) CONTRACT A COST-REIMBURSEMENT CONTRACT that provides for a fee consisting of (1) a BASE FEE (which may be zero) fixed at inception of the contract and (2) an AWARD FEE, based upon a periodic judgmental evaluation by the Government, sufficient to provide motivation for excellence in such areas as quality, timeliness, technical ingenuity, and cost-effective management during contract performance. FAR 16.305. The contractor may earn the award amount in whole or in part. FAR 16.404-2 states that the determination of the award fee is made unilaterally by the Government and is not subject to the DISPUTEs clause. However, in *Burnside-Ott Aviation Training Center v. Dalton*, 107 F.3d 854 (Fed. Cir. 1997), it was held that award for determinations are reviewable under the CONTRACT DISPUTES ACT. CPAF contracts have been widely used to contract for services. One of their major features is that they require the Government to give contractors regular evaluations of their performance (usually every three to six months). See Cibinic & Nash, chap. 8, Sec. IV., *Formation of Government Contracts* (3d ed. 1998); Cibinic & Nash, *Cost-Reimbursement Contracting* 101–25 (2d ed. 1993); Kannan, *Challenging Award Fee Determinations under Federal Government Contracts*, 20 Pub. Cont. L.J. 197 (1991).

COST-PLUS-FIXED-FEE (CPFF) CONTRACT A COST-REIMBURSEMENT CONTRACT that provides for payment to the contractor of a negotiated FEE (profit) that is fixed at the inception of the contract. FAR 16.306(a). This fixed fee does not vary with ACTUAL COST but may be adjusted as a result of changes in the work to be performed under the contract. The CPFF type of contract permits contracting for efforts that might otherwise present too great a risk to contractors, but it is thought to give the contractor less incentive to control costs than does a FIXED-PRICE CONTRACT. FAR 16.306(b) limits its use to those situations where the Government has not established reasonably firm objectives (such as contracts for research). There are two forms of CPFF contracts: (1) the COMPLETION FORM CONTRACT, in which the work is described by stating a definite goal or target and an end product (frequently a report); and (2) the term form, in which the contract calls for a stated level of effort (usually hours or days of specified classes of LABOR) over a given period of time (see TERM CONTRACT). FAR 16.306(d). See Cibinic & Nash, chap. 8, Sec. III., *Formation of Government Contracts* (3d ed. 1998); Cibinic & Nash, *Cost-Reimbursement Contracting* 75–77 (2d ed. 1993).

COST-PLUS-INCENTIVE-FEE (CPIF) CONTRACT A COST-REIMBURSEMENT CONTRACT that provides for the initially negotiated TARGET FEE to be adjusted later by a formula based on the relationship of total ALLOWABLE COSTs to total TARGET COSTs. FAR 16.304. This contract type specifies a target cost, a target fee, a MINIMUM FEE, a MAXIMUM FEE, and a fee adjustment formula. After contract performance, the fee payable to the contractor is determined in accordance with the formula. FAR 16.404-1. To encourage the contractor to manage the contract effectively, the formula provides, within limits, for increases in fee above target fee, when total ALLOWABLE COSTs are less than target costs, and decreases in fee below target fee, when total allowable costs exceed target costs. When the total allowable cost is greater or less than the range of costs (the RANGE OF INCENTIVE EFFECTIVENESS) within which the fee adjustment formula operates, the contractor is paid total allowable costs plus the minimum or maximum fee. See the Incentive Fee clause at FAR 52.216-10. See also Cibinic & Nash, chap. 8, Sec. III., *Formation of Government Contracts* (3d ed. 1998); Cibinic & Nash, *Cost-Reimbursement Contracting* 77–101 (2d ed. 1993).

COST POOL See INDIRECT COST POOL.

COST PRINCIPLES The rules promulgated by the Government in FAR Part 31 that define which costs are allowable (see ALLOWABLE COST) in the negotiation and administration of Government contracts. This part of the FAR contains contract cost principles and procedures for (1) the pricing of contracts, subcontracts, and contract modifications whenever cost analysis is performed and (2) the determination, negotiation, or allowance of costs when required by a contract clause. These principles are made a part of all COST-REIMBURSEMENT CONTRACTs by incorporation by reference in the Allowable Cost and Payment clause at FAR 52.216-7. See Cibinic, *Cost Principles Changes Chart: FAR 1990 Edition*, 11 N&CR ¶ 7 (Feb. 1997); Cibinic

& Nash, *Cost-Reimbursement Contracting* 747–927 (2d ed. 1993); Cibinic, *Cost Principles Changes Chart: FAR 1990 Edition*, 7 N&CR ¶ 9 (Feb. 1993).

COST-REALISM ANALYSIS The process of independently reviewing and evaluating specific elements of each offeror's proposed cost estimate to determine whether the estimated proposed cost elements are realistic for the work to be performed; reflect a clear understanding of the requirements; and are consistent with the unique methods of performance and materials described in the offeror's technical proposal. FAR 15.404-1(d)(1). Cost realism analysis is required on COST-REIMBURSEMENT CONTRACTs to determine the PROBABLE COST of performance of the contract, which is used as the evaluation factor in selecting the winning contractor. FAR 15.305(a)(1), FAR 15.404-1(d)(2). A cost realism analysis may also be made in limited circumstances on FIXED-PRICE CONTRACTs for purposes of determining whether a contractor understands the work or is a responsible contractor (see RESPONSIBILITY). FAR 15.404-1(d)(3). In such cases, the proposed prices are not adjusted for purposes of evaluation. See Bleiweis, *Cost Realism Analysis—Selected Issues*, 96-1 CP&A Rep. 3 (Jan. 1996); Cibinic & Nash, *Cost-Reimbursement Contracting* 552–67 (2d ed. 1993); Lieg, *Cost Realism—A Critical Factor in the Procurement of Professional and Technical Services*, 33 Cont. Mgmt. 4 (July 1993); Nash, *Cost Realism Analysis in Cost Reimbursement Contracts: What Are the Rules of the Game?*, 5 N&CR ¶ 40 (July 1991); Cibinic, *Cost Realism Analysis in Negotiated Fixed Price Contracts: Confusion at the GAO or a New Limitation on Buy-ins?*, 4 N&CR ¶ 61 (Oct. 1990).

COST-REIMBURSEMENT CONTRACT A contract that provides for payment to the contractor of ALLOWABLE incurred COSTs to the extent provided in the contract. FAR 16.301-1. Cost-reimbursement contracts are distinguished from FIXED-PRICE CONTRACTs, under which payment is made to the contractor on the basis of pre-established prices. Cost-reimbursement contracts are suitable for use only when the uncertainties involved in contract performance do not permit costs to be estimated with sufficient accuracy to use any type of fixed-price contract. FAR 16.301-2. They may be used only when (1) the contractor's accounting system is adequate for determining applicable costs, and (2) Government surveillance during performance will provide reasonable assurance that efficient methods and effective cost controls are used. FAR 16.301-3(a). The use of cost-reimbursement contracts is prohibited for the acquisition of commercial items. FAR 12.207. In order to avoid violation of the ANTI-DEFICIENCY ACT, all cost-reimbursement contracts must contain the LIMITATION OF COST (LOC) CLAUSE. This clause limits the Government's obligation by stipulating that it will pay only the amount contained in the contract's ESTIMATED COST or TARGET COST cost (plus any prescribed FEE). Cost-reimbursement pricing arrangements include COST CONTRACTs, COST-SHARING CONTRACTs, COST-PLUS-INCENTIVE-FEE CONTRACTs, COST-PLUS-AWARD-FEE CONTRACTs, and COST-PLUS-FIXED-FEE CONTRACTs. COST-PLUS-A-PERCENTAGE-OF-COST CONTRACTs are prohibited. See Nash, *Increasing the Fixed Fee in Equitable Adjustments to Cost-Reimbursement Contracts*, 9 N&CR ¶ 49 (Sept. 1995); Cibinic & Nash, chap. 2, *Cost-Reimbursement Contracting* (2d ed. 1993).

COST RISK An assessment of possible monetary loss or gain in light of the work to be done under a contract. It is one of the elements to be considered in negotiating a FAIR AND REASONABLE PRICE, as well as in determining the TYPE OF CONTRACT to be used. See FAR 16.104. Cost risk is assessed in order that the contractor can be compensated commensurately with the extent of risk assumed. Factors included in a cost risk assessment are the reliability of the contractor's proposed costs; the extent of contingency factors included in the proposed costs; the relative firmness or uncertainty of the estimated costs for major components, subcontracts, etc.; and the contractor's prior profit experience with the same or similar supplies or systems. *DCAA Contract Audit Manual* 9-906.2.

COST/SCHEDULE CONTROL SYSTEM A management system requiring the contractor to establish a WORK BREAKDOWN STRUCTURE for all work to be performed on the contract and to record performance and costs for each element of that structure as the work progresses. The purpose of such systems is to track the contractor's performance at a level of detail that will provide early information if a contractor is not performing on schedule or at the predicted costs. Guidance on such systems is contained in DOD Regulation 5000.2-R, *Mandatory Procedures for Major Defense Acquisition Programs (MDAPs) and Major Automated Information System (MAIS) Acquisition Programs*, Part 5, Mar. 15, 1996.

COST/SCHEDULE CONTROL SYSTEMS CRITERIA (C/SCSC) A set of criteria that specify the minimum requirements a contractor's management control system must satisfy in order to meet the COST/SCHEDULE CONTROL SYSTEM requirement in certain contracts with DOD. Typically, the criteria apply to major system acquisition programs and subcontracts within those programs. The criteria are broken down into five groups: (1) organization (five criteria), (2) planning and budgeting (eleven criteria), (3) accounting (seven criteria), (4) analysis (six criteria), and (5) revisions and access to data (six criteria). C/SCSC basically entails four steps: establishing a baseline with the development of a WORK BREAKDOWN STRUCTURE and an applicable budget down to the lowest work element possible, managing the base line, measuring performance as the work is accomplished, and assessing what is left to be accomplished from the plan and making a projection of the estimate to complete the work. These steps should produce a reliable estimate of the TOTAL COST of a given contract. See Grskovich, *What Is C/SCSC?—In English, Please!,* 23 Nat'l Cont. Mgmt. J., Issue No. 2, p. 25 (1990); DOD Regulation 5000.2-R, *Mandatory Procedures for Major Defense Acquisition Programs (MDAPs) and Major Automated Information System (MAIS) Acquisition Programs*, Mar. 15, 1996, appendix VI.; Mauldin, *Innovative Incentive-Fee Plan Reflects Government Reform Initiatives: Project Management, Acquisition, and C/SCSC Performance Measurement*, 36 Cont. Mgmt. 13 (Feb. 1996); Chambers, *Variance Analysis Within C/SCSC*, 1 Acquisition Rev. Q. 61 (Win. 1994). See also COST/ SCHEDULE STATUS REPORT.

COST/SCHEDULE STATUS REPORT (C/SSR) A report submitted by a contractor that provides summarized cost and schedule performance status for use by the PROGRAM MANAGER in decisionmaking. The C/SSR is intended to provide the program manager with a clear description of the contract cost and schedule status at a given point in time. If the Government desires the contractor to submit these reports, the requirement for submission must be included in the solicitation document and the contract as a CONTRACT DATA REQUIREMENTS LIST requirement on DD Form 1423 (DFARS 253.303-1423). See Dominic, *Understanding the C/SSR*, 30 Cont. Mgmt. 8 (Nov. 1990).

COST-SHARING CONTRACT An explicit arrangement under which the contractor bears some of the burden of reasonable, allocable, and allowable contract cost. FAR 35.001. A cost-sharing contract is a COST-REIMBURSEMENT CONTRACT under which the contractor receives no FEE and is reimbursed only for an agreed-upon portion of its ALLOWABLE COSTs. Such a contract may be used only when the contractor agrees to absorb a portion of the costs in the expectation of substantial compensating benefits. FAR 16.303. Cost-sharing arrangements may call for the contractor to participate in the costs of the contract by accepting INDIRECT COST rates lower than the anticipated actual rates. In such cases, a negotiated indirect cost rate ceiling may be incorporated into the contract for prospective application. FAR 42.707. Another common form of cost sharing is the award of a FIXED-PRICE CONTRACT at less than the contractor's estimated costs of performance. See Cibinic & Nash, *Cost-Reimbursement Contracting* 134–41 (2d ed. 1993).

COST TO THE GOVERNMENT The amount to be paid to the contractor and other costs that the Government incurs in procuring and using articles or services. In cost reimbursement contracts, the amount to be paid to the contractor is the estimated or TARGET COST plus the fee. In fixed-price contracts, this amount is the contract price. Cost to the Government is a mandatory EVALUATION FACTOR. See 10 U.S.C. § 2305(a)(2)(A); 41 U.S.C. § 253. See also Nash & Cibinic, *Competitive Negotiation: The Source Selection Process* 149–54 (1993).

COST UNDERRUN The incurrence of costs less than those in the contract's TARGET COST (in a FIXED-PRICE-INCENTIVE CONTRACT or a COST-PLUS-INCENTIVE-FEE CONTRACT), ESTIMATED COST (in any other COST-REIMBURSEMENT CONTRACT), or a redeterminable price (in a FIXED-PRICE REDETERMINATION—PROSPECTIVE CONTRACT or FIXED-PRICE REDETERMINATION—RETROACTIVE CONTRACT). An underrun is caused by the contractor's ACTUAL COSTs being under target or under anticipated contract cost, but not for reasons such as quantity changes, engineering changes, or economic changes. See *DCAA Contract Audit Manual* 3-S102.1.

COSTS CONTINUING AFTER TERMINATION Costs that cannot be discontinued immediately after the effective date of TERMINATION FOR CONVENIENCE. These costs are generally allowable; however, any costs that continue after the effective date of the termination due to the negligent or wilful failure of the contractor to discontinue the costs are unallowable. FAR 31.205-42(b). Costs continuing after termination are often associated with a contractor's facilities, such as contractor-owned and contractor-leased buildings, machinery, and equipment. Recovery for the loss of useful value of facilities is covered under FAR 31.205(d) and rental costs under unexpired leases is dealt with under FAR 31.205-42(e). Costs of UNABSORBED OVERHEAD are not includable in these costs. See Cibinic & Nash, *Administration of*

Government Contracts 1106–108 (3d ed. 1995); Cibinic & Nash, *Cost-Reimbursement Contracting* 909–11 (2d ed. 1993).

COUNCIL OF DEFENSE AND SPACE INDUSTRY ASSOCIATIONS (CODSIA) An association formed in 1964 by industry associations with common interests in the defense and space fields. DOD encouraged formation of this organization to provide a vehicle to obtain broad industry reactions to procurement regulations, policies, and procedures. CODSIA currently is composed of nine associations, including the AEROSPACE INDUSTRY ASSOCIATION, the Contract Services Association, the ELECTRONIC INDUSTRIES ASSOCIATION, the American Electronics Association, the Manufacturers Alliance for Productivity and Innovation, the Professional Services Council, the Shipbuilders Council of America, the National Defense Industrial Association (representing the merger of the American Defense Preparedness Association and the National Security Industrial Association), and the American Shipbuilding Association. [CODSIA, 1250 Eye Street, N.W., Suite 1200, Washington, DC 20005; (202) 371-8414]

COURSE OF DEALING See PRIOR COURSE OF DEALING.

COURT OF APPEALS FOR THE FEDERAL CIRCUIT (CAFC OR FED. CIR.) The appellate (reviewing) court for both the U.S. COURT OF FEDERAL CLAIMS and the various agency BOARDs OF CONTRACT APPEALS. 28 U.S.C. § 1295(a)(3), (a)(10); 41 U.S.C. § 607(g). Because the Supreme Court rarely considers decisions regarding Government contract disputes, the Court of Appeals for the Federal Circuit typically provides the last opportunity for their review. The Federal Courts Improvement Act of 1982 created the U.S. Court of Appeals for the Federal Circuit from the Appellate Division of the Court of Claims and the Court of Customs and Patent Appeals. See Cibinic, *Federal Circuit Review of ADPE Protest Decisions*, 6 N&CR ¶ 31 (May 1992); Shea & Schaengold, *A Guide to the Court of Appeals for the Federal Circuit*, 90-13 Briefing Papers (Dec. 1990); Latham, chap. 18, *Government Contract Disputes* (2d ed. 1986); White, *The New Government Contract Courts*, 83-11 Briefing Papers (Nov. 1983); Anthony & Smith, *The Federal Courts Improvement Act of 1982: Its Impact on the Resolution of Federal Contract Disputes*, 13 Pub. Cont. L.J. 201 (1983).

COURT OF CLAIMS The original court, established in 1855, to hear and decide claims against the Government. The court was divided into a trial division and an appellate division with the result that most cases were subject to decision by two sets of judges. The court was split in 1982, by the Federal Courts Improvement Act, into the COURT OF APPEALS FOR THE FEDERAL CIRCUITT and the CLAIMS COURT (subsequently named the COURT OF FEDERAL CLAIMS). The Court of Claims frequently took a board view of the obligations of the Government—regarding itself as the "conscience of the nation." See Nash, *Government Liability for Nondisclosure of Vital Information: Where Are Its Roots?*, 8 N&CR ¶ 52 (Sept. 1994).

COURT OF FEDERAL CLAIMS (FED. CL.) A court of the United States established especially to hear and decide legal claims against the Government. It is an Article I court with judges appointed for 15-year terms. Its basic jurisdiction is conferred by 28 U.S.C. § 1491(a), but it has a variety of additional jurisdictional statutes. Under the CONTRACT DISPUTES ACT OF 1978, 41 U.S.C. §§ 601–613, as amended, this court shares concurrent jurisdiction with the BOARDs OF CONTRACT APPEALS (BCAs) over Government contract DISPUTEs (each contractor appealing a DECISION OF THE CONTRACTING OFFICER must elect either the agency BCA or the Court of Federal Claims). The other jurisdiction of the Court of Federal Claims most relevant to Government procurement concerns PROTESTs, 28 U.S.C. § 1491(b), disputes concerning fraud or forfeiture, 41 U.S.C. § 604, and PATENT and COPYRIGHT disputes, 28 U.S.C. § 1498. The Federal Courts Improvement Act of 1982 created this court (called the Claims Court until 1992) from the Trial Division of the Court of Claims. See Churchill et at., *The Court of Federal Claims Should Adopt the New Mandatory Disclosure Requirements of Rule 26*, 24 Pub. Cont. L.J. 131 (1994); England, *Constitutionality of Article I Court Adjudication of Contract Disputes Act Claims*, 16 Pub. Cont. L.J. 338 (1987); White, *The New Government Contract Courts*, 83-11 Briefing Papers (Nov. 1983); Anthony & Smith, *The Federal Courts Improvement Act of 1982: Its Impact on the Resolution of Federal Contract Disputes*, 13 Pub. Cont. L.J. 201 (1983).

COVER The common-law right of a buyer, after BREACH OF CONTRACT by a seller, to purchase goods in substitution for those due from the seller if such purchase is made in good faith and without unreasonable delay. The buyer may then recover as DAMAGES the difference between the cost of such cover and the contract price, plus any incidental and CONSEQUENTIAL DAMAGES but less expenses saved. U.C.C. § 2-712(1), (2). The DEFAULT clause in Government contracts gives the Government the equivalent right to recover the EXCESSS COST OF REPROCUREMENT after a TERMINATION FOR DEFAULT.

CRADLE-TO-GRAVE A representation of the life cycle of a given system, from concept through development, acquisition, operations phases, and final disposition. Also called womb-to-tomb. Jones, *Glossary: Defense Acquisition Acronyms and Terms* (8th ed., Defense Systems Management College).

CREDIT CARD See GOVERNMENT-WIDE COMMERCIAL PURCHASE CARD.

CRITICAL ISSUE An aspect of a SYSTEM's capability—operational, technical, or other—that must be questioned before the system's overall suitability can be known. This aspect is of primary importance in reaching a decision to allow the system to advance to the next phase of DEVELOPMENT. Jones, *Glossary: Defense Acquisition Acronyms and Terms* (8th ed., Defense Systems Management College).

CRITICAL ITEM A subsystem, component, material, or other item whose nonavailability when required could seriously jeopardize the successful completion of program requirements. A critical item is also an item that could have an adverse impact on cost, schedule, quality, or technical performance. Brechtel, *Subcontracts: Government and Industry Issues* (NCMA 1989).

CRITICAL PATH METHOD (CPM) A network scheduling technique used by contractors to plan, coordinate, and control work activities so as to complete contract work as quickly and economically as possible. The Schedules for Construction Contracts clause in FAR 52.236-15 requires construction contractors to provide a schedule of anticipated performance to the contracting officer shortly after award of the contract. CPM has become an accepted means of substantiating delay CLAIMs before the courts and boards of contract appeals. The critical path represents the longest chain of interrelated activities in the project schedule diagram. A delay in completing an item on this path delays the entire project. Proving delay typically entails comparing AS-PLANNED DRAWINGS or CPM diagrams with RECORD (as-built) DRAWINGS or CPM diagrams. See Margulies, chap. 8, *Construction Contracting* 662–67 (1991); Wickwire et al., *Use of Critical Path Method Techniques in Contract Claims: Issues and Developments 1974 to 1988*, 18 Pub. Cont. L.J. 338 (1989); Wickwire & Smith, *The Use of*

Critical Path Method Techniques in Contract Claims, 7 Pub. Cont. L.J. 1 (1974).

CRITICALITY One of three criteria used in determining the extent of contract quality requirements to be used in the quality assurance and inspection sections of the REQUEST FOR PROPOSALS and the contract. FAR 46.203 states that a critical application of an item is one in which the failure of the item could injure personnel or jeopardize a vital agency mission. A critical item may be either peculiar, meaning it has only one application, or common, meaning it has multiple applications. The remaining two criteria are technical description and complexity.

CROSS-SERVICING An arrangement between federal agencies where one agency will make or oversee an AUDIT for another agency that is unable to perform the audit needed by a contracting officer or other official. federal regulatory policy strongly encourages the use of cross-servicing to conserve staff resources, promote efficiency, and minimize the impact of audits on the operations of the organizations subject to audit. See OMB Circular No. A-73, *Audit of Federal Operations and Programs;* OFPP Policy Letter No. 78-4, *Field Contract Support Cross-Servicing Program,* Aug. 8, 1978; and FAR Subpart 42.1. Because of its greater resources, the DEFENSE CONTRACT AUDIT AGENCY (DCAA) performs most of the work done under cross-servicing arrangements. *DCAA Contract Audit Manual* 1-303 contains guidance on when DCAA will perform an audit under a cross-servicing agreement.

CURE NOTICE A delinquency notice that must be issued by the Government prior to TERMINATION FOR DEFAULT of a supply or service contract before the contract's delivery date. See paragraph (a)(2) of the Default (Fixed-Price Supply and Service) clause in FAR 52.249-8. FAR 49.607(a) contains a suggested form of the notice. FAR 49.402-3 contains the procedures that must be followed by contracting officers in determining whether to terminate for default. FAR 49.402-3(d) provides that, if the time remaining does not permit a "cure" period of 10 days or more, the cure notice should not be issued. Failure to issue a cure notice when required will result in an invalid termination for default, with the result that the termination will be converted to a TERMINATION FOR CONVENIENCE. See also SHOW CAUSE NOTICE. See Cibinic & Nash, *Administration of Government Contracts* 988–93 (3d ed. 1995).

CUSTODIAL RECORDS Written memoranda of any kind, such as requisitions, issue hand receipts, tool checks, and stock record books, used to control items from tool cribs, tool rooms, and stockrooms. FAR 45.501. FAR 45.505-3(c) requires that the contractor maintain such records of tool crib items, guard force items, protective clothing, and other items issued to employees when these items are GOVERNMENT-FURNISHED MATERIAL or material to which the Government has title.

CUSTOMARY PROGRESS PAYMENT A PROGRESS PAYMENT made under general FAR guidance, using the customary progress payment rate (which is adjusted from time to time in accordance with economic conditions and is currently 80 percent for large businesses and 85 percent for small businesses), the cost base, and the frequency of payment established in the Progress Payments clause in FAR 52.232-16, and either the ordinary LIQUIDATION method (see FAR 32.503-8) or the alternate method (see FAR 32.503-9). FAR 32.501. Any other progress payment based on cost is considered an UNUSUAL PROGRESS PAYMENT. Criteria for the use of customary progress payments are contained in FAR 32.502-1, which generally provides that they may be used for contracts of $1 million or more where the initial billing will not be made for six months (with lesser requirements for contracts with a small business). See Cibinic & Nash, *Administration of Government Contracts* 1138–43 (3d ed. 1995).

CUSTOMER SERVICE PLAN A document mandated by Exec. Order No. 12862, 58 Fed. Reg. 48257 (Sept. 1993) *Setting Customer Service Standards*, that all agencies subject to the Order must prepare for any individual or entity that is directly served by the agency. It must be comprehensible, include CUSTOMER SERVICE STANDARDS, and describe future plans for customer surveys. It must also identify the private- and public-sector standards that the agency used to set its performance in customer service against the best in business. The plans must have been completed by September 1994.

CUSTOMER SERVICE STANDARDS Federal standards for executive agencies' management practices and policies mandated by Exec. Order No. 12862, 58 Fed. Reg. 48257 (Sept. 1993) *Setting Customer Service Standards*. The Order's goal is for federal agencies to provide a heightened quality of service to any individual or entity that is directly served by an executive agency. The guidepost for agencies to construct their standards is to provide customer service equal to the best in business. The term "best in business" means the highest quality of service delivered to customers by private organizations providing a comparable or analogous service. The Order directed agencies to (1) identify the customers who are served by the agency, (2) survey customers to determine the kind and quality of services they want, (3) post service standards, (4) compare agency customer service with the best in business, (5) survey front-line employees for ideas to match the best in business, (6) provide customers with choices in sources of service and means of delivery, (7) make information and services easily accessible, and (8) provide means to address customer complaints. See Section 1 of the Order.

D

DAMAGES Pecuniary compensation or indemnity, which may be recovered in a judicial or quasi judicial forum (e.g., the U.S. COURT OF FEDERAL CLAIMS or the BOARDs OF CONTRACT APPEALS) by one who suffers loss, detriment, or injury through BREACH OF CONTRACT by the act, omission, or negligence of another. Compensatory damages compensate the injured party for the injury sustained and for nothing more. CONSEQUENTIAL DAMAGES do not flow directly and immediately from the act of the other party but, rather, from the consequences or results of the act. PUNITIVE (or exemplary) DAMAGES are generally not included in contract damages. *Black's Law Dictionary* 389–93 (6th ed. 1990). Damages are infrequently awarded in Government contracts because of the large number of contract clauses giving EQUITABLE ADJUSTMENTs and PRICE ADJUSTMENTs. See Cibinic & Nash, *Administration of Government Contracts* 692–97 (3d ed. 1995).

DATA Recorded information, regardless of form or the media on which the information is recorded. FAR 27.401. The term includes TECHNICAL DATA and COMPUTER SOFTWARE. The term does not include information incidental to contract administration, such as financial, administrative, cost, pricing, or management information. When this type of information is created by contractors in the performance of contracts, it is subject to LIMITED RIGHTS, RESTRICTED RIGHTS, or UNLIMITED RIGHTS as specified in contract clauses. This term is not used in the 1995 DOD policy on technical data and computer software. It was used in the 1988 DOD policy with essentially the same meaning as in the FAR.

DATA ITEM DESCRIPTION (DID) A description of a TECHNICAL DATA item to be provided under a contract with DOD. The form used for this description is DD Form 1664, DFARS 253.303-1664. DIDs are listed on the CONTRACT DATA REQUIREMENTS LIST that is incorporated into contracts.

DATA PROCESSING EQUIPMENT See AUTOMATIC DATA PROCESSING EQUIPMENT.

DATA REPOSITORY An office with the responsibility for the storage and maintenance of TECHNICAL DATA necessary to support Government programs. DOD agencies and contracting activities generally maintain data repositories and this function has, on occasion, been given to contractors. DFARS 227.7108 provides guidance on the contractual provisions that should be used when establishing contractor data repositories. DFARS 227.7207 states that this guidance is applicable when the Government establishes a contractor COMPUTER SOFTWARE repository.

DATA UNIVERSAL NUMBERING SYSTEM A nine-digit number, assigned by Dun and Bradstreet Information Services, used to identify contractors. FAR 52.204-6.

DAVIS-BACON ACT An Act, 40 U.S.C. § 276a, passed in 1931, requiring payment of not less than PREVAILING WAGE RATEs to workers on federal or federally funded CONSTRUCTION projects of over $2,000. FAR 22.403-1. WAGE DETERMINATIONs, issued by the DOL, must be included in construction contracts for such projects. See Pendolino, *The Davis-Bacon & Service Contracts Acts: Laws Whose Time has Passed?*, 147 Mil. L. Rev. 218 (Win. 1995); Bernstein, *The Davis-Bacon Act: Vestige of Jim Crow*, 13 Natl. Black L.J. 276 (Fall 1994); Stephenson, chap. 3, *Construction Contracting* 225–30 (1991); Schooner, *The Davis-Bacon Act: Controversial Implementation of the 50% Rule*, 10 Employee Rel. L.J. 702 (1985).

DCAA CONTRACT AUDIT MANUAL (CAM) A publication of the DEFENSE CONTRACT AUDIT AGENCY (DCAA) (sometimes referred to as the *Defense Contract Audit Manual*, or DCAM) containing detailed guidance on auditing policies and procedures followed by DCAA AUDITORs. The manual is instructive rather than directive in nature, and its contents apply to the AUDIT of all types of contracts. The manual is available from the U.S. Government Printing Office, Washington, DC 20402.

DE FACTO DEBARMENT A refusal of the Government to deal with a contractor that is construed by a court to constitute a DEBARMENT, even though formal debarment procedures are not used. Generally, de facto debarment has been found in cases where a Government agency refuses to award one or more contracts on the basis that the OFFEROR does not meet the requisite standards of RESPONSIBILITY. See *Old*

Dominion Dairy Prod., Inc. v. Secretary of Defense, 631 F.2d 953 (D.C. Cir. 1980), where de facto debarment was found when the agency refused to award a contract because of a perceived lack of integrity. The court held the contractor was entitled to the DUE PROCESS OF LAW accorded by the debarment procedures to protect its constitutional liberty interest. De facto debarments will also be found when an agency declares an offeror nonresponsible on repeated occasions without instituting formal debarment procedures. The FAR contains no guidance on de facto debarments. See Cibinic & Nash, chap. 4, Sec. II., *Formation of Government Contracts* (3d ed. 1998).

DE NOVO Considering a matter without regard to prior procedures. When a contractor files an APPEAL FROM A CONTRACTING OFFICER'S DECISION under the CONTRACT DISPUTES ACT OF 1978, the BOARD OF CONTRACT APPEALS (BCA) or the U.S. COURT OF FEDERAL CLAIMS will rehear the case completely and decide it on the basis of the evidence heard. Thus, the prior decision of the contracting officer is not binding on the BCA or U.S. Court of Federal Claims in any way, and the proceeding before the BCA or U.S. Court of Federal Claims is in the nature of a new trial, not a review of the record made by the contracting officer. See Cibinic & Nash, *Administration of Government Contracts* 1305 (3d ed. 1995); Coburn, *The Importance of De Novo Review to an Adequate Bid Protest Remedy*, 9 N&CR ¶ 26 (Apr. 1995).

DEBARMENT Action taken by a debarring official—the head of the agency or a designee authorized by the agency head to impose debarment—to exclude a contractor from Government contracting and Government-approved subcontracting for a reasonable, specified period. FAR 9.403. FAR Subpart 9.4 contains the policies and procedures governing debarment of contractors. When a contractor is proposed for debarment, it is excluded from the award of contracts by being placed on the LIST OF PARTIES EXCLUDED FROM FEDERAL PROCUREMENT AND NONPROCUREMENT PROGRAMS. FAR 9.404. Causes for debarment include (1) conviction of or civil judgment for (a) commission of a FRAUD or criminal offense related to obtaining or performing a public contract, (b) ANTITRUST VIOLATION, (c) commission of embezzlement, theft, forgery, BRIBERY, making FALSE STATEMENTs, or the like, (d) commission of any other offense indicating a lack of business integrity or business honesty that seriously and directly affects the contractor's present RESPONSIBILITY, or (e) intentionally affixing a label bearing a "Made in America" inscription to a product sold in or shipped to the United

States, when the product was not made in the United States; (2) violation of the terms of a Government contract so serious as to justify debarment, such as (a) willful failure to perform or (b) a history of failure to perform or unsatisfactory performance; (3) violations of the Drug-Free Workplace Act of 1988 (see DRUG-FREE WORKPLACE); (4) commission of an unfair trade practice as defined in FAR 9.403; and (5) any other cause of so serious or compelling a nature that it affects the present responsibility of a Government contractor or subcontractor. FAR 9.406-2. Remedial measures and mitigating factors for debarring officials to consider in making debarment decisions are set forth at FAR 9.406-1(a). See Cibinic & Nash, chap. 4, Sec. II., *Formation of Government Contracts* (3d ed. 1998); Nash, *Suspension and Debarment: Can They Be Punitive?*, 11 N&CR ¶ 29 (June 1997); Gordon, *Suspension and Debarment From Federal Programs*, 23 Pub. Cont. L.J. 573 (1994); Nash, *The Impact of Debarment*, 7 N&CR ¶ 33 (June 1993); Shannon, *The Government-Wide Debarment and Suspension Regulations After a Decade—A Constitutional Framework—Yet, Some Issues Remain in Transition*, 21 Pub. Cont, L.J. 370 (1992); Toomey et al., *Debarment & Suspension/Edition III*, 89-4 Briefing Papers (Mar. 1989); Nadler, *Suspension and Debarment of Government Contractors: The Current Climate*, 22 Nat'l Cont. Mgmt. J., Issue No. 2, p. 9 (1989); Norton, *The Questionable Constitutionality of the Suspension and Debarment Provisions of the Federal Acquisition Regulations: What Does Due Process Require?,* 18 Pub. Cont. L.J. 633 (1989).

DEBARRING OFFICIAL An agency head or a designee authorized by the agency head to impose DEBARMENT. FAR 9.403.

DEBRIEFING Explanation by a procuring agency of why an offeror did not win a competition for a negotiated contract (see NEGOTIATION). Offerors excluded from the COMPETITIVE RANGE or otherwise excluded from the competition before award may request a debriefing. 10 U.S.C. § 2305(b)(6); 41 U.S.C. § 253(f)(1); FAR 15.605. For pre-award debriefings, requests must be received within three days after the offeror receives notice of exclusion from competition. FAR 15.505(a). The debriefing must include (1) the agency's evaluation of significant elements in the offeror' proposal; (2) a summary of the rationale for elimination from the competition; (3) and reasonable responses to relevant questions about whether source selection procedures contained in the solicitation, applicable regulations, and other applicable authorities were followed. FAR 15.505(e). For postaward debriefings, requests must be received within three days after the offeror receives notice of contract award. FAR 15.506(a). At a minimum, the debriefing information must include: (1) the Government's evaluation of the significant weaknesses or deficiencies in the offeror's proposal; (2) the overall evaluated cost or price and technical ratings of successful and debriefed offerors; (3) the overall ranking of all offerors; (4) a summary of the rationale for award; (5) for acquisitions of commercial end items, the make and model of the selected item; and (6) reasonable responses to relevant questions about whether source selection procedures, regulations, and authorities were followed. FAR 15.506(d). The debriefing shall not include point-by-point comparisons or any information exempt from release under the FREEDOM OF INFORMATION ACT, including: TRADE SECRETs; privileged or confidential manufacturing processes and techniques, privileged or confidential commercial and financial information, and the names of individuals providing reference information on PAST PERFORMANCE. The contracting officer shall include an official summary of the debriefing in the contract file. See Cibinic & Nash, chap. 6, *Formation of Government Contracts* (3d ed. 1998); Nash, *Protests & Debriefings: A Tangled Web*, 11 N&CR ¶ 47 (Sept. 1997); Corrao, *Changes in the Notice of Award, Debriefing and Protest Rules After FASA*, 95-10 Briefing Papers (Sept. 1995); Nash, *Debriefing: Congress Has Now Spoken*, 9 N&CR ¶ 3 (Jan. 1995); Cibinic, *Debriefing: Tell It Like It Is*, 4 N&CR ¶ 43 (July 1990).

DEBT COLLECTION ACT A 1982 Act, 5 U.S.C. § 5514, prescribing procedures for the collection of debts owed to the United States. The Debt Collection Act is part of a complex of statutes and regulations making up the process by means of which the Government collects debts. The complex also includes the FEDERAL CLAIMS COLLECTION ACT of 1966, the CONTRACT DISPUTES ACT OF 1978, and the Federal Claims Collection Standards. Of particular note are the procedures agencies must follow in undertaking debt collection through administrative SETOFF. The Government must give the debtor written notice of the type and amount of the CLAIM and an opportunity to (1) inspect and copy the agency's records relating to the claim, (2) request agency review of the agency's decision related to the claim, and (3) enter into a written agreement with the Government to repay the claim. The Debt Collection Act is partially implemented in FAR Subpart 32.6. See Stafford & Farley, *Contract Debts—Navigating the Determination and Collection Process*, 96-4 CP&A Rep. 3 (Apr. 1996); Cibinic & Nash, *Administration of Government Contracts* 1188–90 (3d ed. 1995); Cibinic, *Withholding, Offset, and Debt Collection: A Double Whammy for the Debt Collection Act,* 7 N&CR ¶ 44 (Aug.

1993); Thrasher, *Application of the Debt Collection Act of 1982 to Government Contracts*, 29 A.F. L. Rev. 133 (1988).

DECISION OF THE CONTRACTING OFFICER A written document signed by a CONTRACTING OFFICER ruling on a CLAIM by or against the Government. Under the CONTRACT DISPUTES ACT OF 1978, all claims by a contractor against the Government relating to a contract must be in writing and must be submitted to the contracting officer for a decision. All claims by the Government against a contractor relating to a contract must also be the subject of a decision by the contracting officer. 41 U.S.C. § 605(a). This decision describes the claim, references pertinent contract terms, states areas of factual agreement and disagreement, states the reasons for the decision reached, and informs the contractor of its rights to challenge the decision through an APPEAL FROM A CONTRACTING OFFICER'S DECISION. FAR 33.211(a)(4). Contracting officers' decisions, often called "final decisions," must inform the contractor that it may either appeal the decision to a BOARD OF CONTRACT APPEALS (BCA) within 90 days or bring an action directly in the U.S. COURT OF FEDERAL CLAIMS within 12 months. If the contracting officer fails to render a decision, the BCAs and U.S. Court of Federal Claims may deem the claim denied (see DEEMED DENIAL) 60 days after its submission. Procedures for issuing decisions are contained in FAR 33.211 and the Disputes clause at FAR 52.233-1. See McWhorther & Hahn, *Virtual Final Decisions on Government Claims*, 26 Pub. Cont. L.J. 157 (1997); Cibinic & Nash, *Administration of Government Contracts* 1267–69 (3d ed. 1995).

DECISIONAL RULE The section of the source selection plan that outlines the fundamental basis that will be used to make the source selection decision in a procurement using competitive negotiation. There are two fundamental decisional rules: (1) discretionary tradeoff analysis (see TRADEOFF PROCESS) and (2) LOWEST PRICE TECHNICALLY ACCEPTABLE proposal. When the tradeoff analysis decisional rule is used, the agency makes the award decision by comparing the marginal differences in price with the marginal differences in the other EVALUATION FACTORs. See Cibinic & Nash, chap. 6, *Formation of Government Contracts* (3d ed. 1998).

DECREMENT The amount of a reduction or price reduction. A decrement factor may represent a percentage by which a subcontractor has agreed to reductions in past quoted prices or has agreed to if the prime contractor purchases more than a specified amount of supplies.

Subcontractors may also use a decrement to compensate for the amount of profit generated in an INTER-ORGANIZATIONAL TRANSFER. See *Grumman Aerospace Corp.*, ASBCA 35188, 35189, 90-2 BCA ¶ 22,842. The *DCAA Contract Audit Manual* directs AUDITORs to review the methodologies used by contractors in arriving at subcontractor price reductions, to ensure that the data used for decrements were reasonably accurate, current, and representative. The manual explains that information concerning patterns of reductions from quotes to actual prices paid may be useful in evaluating a cost estimate. *DCAA Contract Audit Manual* 9-404.6.

DECREMENT FACTOR See DECREMENT.

DEDUCTIVE CHANGE A unilateral action by the contracting officer or other procurement official that reduces the amount of work demanded or the quantity of products procured by the contract. Deductive changes entitle the Government to an EQUITABLE ADJUSTMENT reducing the contract price by the amount the reduced work would have cost plus a reasonable profit on that amount. See Cibinic & Nash, *Administration of Government Contracts* 673–77 (3d ed. 1995); Gabig, *Partial "T4C" Versus Deductive Change: The Amount of the Decrease Is Not Always the Same*, 25 Nat'l Cont. Mgmt. J., Issue No. 2, p. 25 (1994).

DEEMED DENIAL A legal rule under the CONTRACT DISPUTES ACT (CDA) OF 1978 permitting a contractor to appeal (see APPEAL FROM THE CONTRACTING OFFICER'S DECISION) the failure of a contracting officer to issue a decision (see DECISION OF THE CONTRACTING OFFICER). 41 U.S.C. § 605(c)(5). If the contractor submits a CLAIM and the contracting officer fails to render a decision within 60 days of receiving the claim (or within a reasonable time for claims over $100,000), the Act provides that this failure will be deemed a decision of the contracting officer to deny the claim and will authorize the commencement of an appeal or suit on the claim. This "deemed denial" jurisdiction confers upon the contractor all rights that flow from receipt of a contracting officer's decision. Although the CDA provides a STATUTE OF LIMITATIONS for appeals (90 days to an agency BOARD OF CONTRACT APPEALS or one year to the U.S. COURT OF FEDERAL CLAIMS) when the contractor has received a decision of the contracting officer, no similar provision exists when the contracting officer fails to render a decision on a valid claim and thereby prompts "deemed denial" jurisdiction. See *Pathman Constr. Co. v. United States*, 817 F.2d 1573 (Fed. Cir. 1987). Thus, the contractor will not lose any appeal rights if it takes no action when a contracting officer fails to render a decision.

DEFAULT The omission or failure to perform a legal or contractual duty, to observe a promise or discharge an obligation, or to perform an agreement. *Black's Law Dictionary* 417 (6th ed. 1990). The Government has the right to terminate the contract when a contractor is found to be in default in the performance of a contract. See TERMINATION FOR DEFAULT. And see Cibinic & Nash, chap. 10, *Administration of Government Contracts* (3d ed. 1995); Williamson & Medill-Jones, *Government Damages for Default*, 89-7 Briefing Papers (June 1989).

DEFAULT TERMINATION See TERMINATION FOR DEFAULT.

DEFECT The absence of something that is necessary for completeness or perfection; or a deficiency in something essential to a thing's intended, proper use. A product is defective if it is not fit for the ordinary purposes for which it is sold and used. A LATENT DEFECT is a defect that is not apparent to the buyer by reasonable observation or INSPECTION. A PATENT DEFECT, in contrast, means a defect that is apparent to the buyer on normal inspection. *Black's Law Dictionary* 1126 (6th ed. 1990). A defect is of concern in the context of both contract formation and contract performance. Defective Government SPECIFICATIONs or plans may result in a contractor's entitlement to a price increase. Defective performance by a contractor may result in the Government's rejection of a contractor's supplies or services or in a contract's TERMINATION FOR DEFAULT.

DEFECTIVE COST OR PRICING DATA COST OR PRICING DATA subsequently found to have been inaccurate, incomplete, or noncurrent. Under the TRUTH IN NEGOTIATIONS ACT, the Government is entitled to an adjustment of the negotiated price, including PROFIT or FEE, to exclude any significant sum by which the price was increased because of defective data, provided the Government had relied on the data. See FAR 15.407-1 for guidance on the computation of the adjustment. The Government's entitlement to a reduction in price is ensured by the inclusion in the contract of one of the clauses prescribed in FAR 15.408(b) and (c), such as Price Reduction for Defective Cost or Pricing Data in FAR 52.215-10 and Price Reduction for Defective Cost or Pricing Data—Modifications in FAR 52.215-11. These clauses give the Government the right to a PRICE ADJUSTMENT for defects in cost or pricing data submitted by the contractor or by a prospective or actual subcontractor. See Cibinic

& Nash, *Administration of Government Contracts* 762–70 (3d ed. 1995); Mateer, *Defective Pricing—The Government's Burden of Proof,* 93-9 CP&A Rep. 3 (Sept. 1993); Shields and Hott, *Arriving at Fair and Reasonable Prices: Defective Pricing Provisions Cannot Replace Cost Analysis*, 32 Cont. Mgmt. 8 (Aug. 1992); Loving, *Defective Pricing Allegations: An Auditor's Perspective,* 32 Cont. Mgmt. 14 (Mar. 1992).

DEFECTIVE PRICING See DEFECTIVE COST OR PRICING DATA.

DEFECTIVE SPECIFICATIONS See IMPLIED WARRANTY OF SPECIFICATIONS.

DEFENDANT The party against whom a suit is filed in court. In the U.S. COURT OF FEDERAL CLAIMS, the Government is always the defendant even though the suit may be based on a Government CLAIM under the CONTRACT DISPUTES ACT OF 1978. In such cases the contractor is referred to as the PLAINTIFF. If such cases are appealed to a BOARD OF CONTRACT APPEALS, the contractor is referred to as the appellant (see APPELLANT BEFORE BOARD OF CONTRACT APPEALS) and the Government is called the RESPONDENT.

DEFENSE ACQUISITION BOARD (DAB) The senior DOD acquisition review board, which controls the initiation and continuation of major acquisition programs. This board is chaired by the Defense Acquisition Executive (DAE); the vice chairman of the Joint Chiefs of Staff serves as the vice chair. The DAB assists the DAE with milestone and program reviews, policy formation, and acquisition resource recommendations. It is the primary forum in which DOD components provide advice and assistance concerning acquisition matters to the Secretary of Defense. The DAB operates under procedures set forth in DOD Directive 5000.1, *Defense Acquisition*, Mar. 15, 1996, and DOD Regulation 5000.2-R, *Mandatory Procedures for Major Defense Acquisition Programs (MDAPs) and Major Automated Information System (MAIS) Acquisition Programs*, Mar. 15, 1996.

DEFENSE ACQUISITION CIRCULARS (DAC) Government publications that revise, amend, and supplement the DEFENSE FAR SUPPLEMENT. DACs are approved and issued by the DEFENSE ACQUISITION REGULATORY (DAR) COUNCIL—in most cases, after a period of public notice and comment that begins with publication in the FEDERAL REGISTER. See DFARS 201.304. DACs are numbered sequentially by edition (for example, 91-1, 91-2).

DEFENSE ACQUISITION DESKBOOK An automated acquisition information system available on CD or via the Internet at <http://deskbook.osd.mil/deskbook.html>. The Defense Acquisition Deskbook provides current information on changes in the acquisition process. By organizing the information in the Deskbook's Reference Information System into Mandatory Direction, Discretionary Practices, and Advice categories, the Deskbook is intended to send a clear message to the acquisition community that discretion and the use of judgment are mainstream elements of the business process. The Deskbook provides an easy-to-use, automated information retrieval system and real-time access to the most current acquisition information. The Deskbook is the primary acquisition reference tool for the entire DOD acquisition workforce, a means to integrate disciplines, and a vehicle to communicate Acquisition Reform. The system includes DOD directives appropriate to the Air Force, Army, Navy, Marine Corps, Defense Logistics Agency, and Special Operations Command (SOCOM). See Harwood & Sylvester, *Reinventing Acquisition: The Defense Acquisition Deskbook*, 36 Cont. Mgmt. 25 (Oct. 1996).

DEFENSE ACQUISITION EXECUTIVE SUMMARY (DAES) Reports mandated by DOD Regulation 5000.2-R, *Mandatory Procedures for Major Defense Acquisition Programs (MDAPs) and Major Automated Information System (MAIS) Acquisition Programs*, Mar. 15, 1996, ¶ 6.2.2, which provide standard, comprehensive summary reporting of defense acquisition programs to the Under Secretary of Defense for Acquisition from the various PROGRAM MANAGERs. The goal of the summaries is to provide advance warnings of potential and actual problems within an ACQUISITION PROGRAM. A DAES may be tailored for each program but must contain, at a minimum, program assessments, unit cost data, current estimates of approved program data, status reporting of exit criteria and vulnerability assessments. In the past, this data could be used to compute the cost performance index. See Christensen & Heise, *Cost Performance Index Stability*, 25 Nat'l Cont. Mgmt. J., Issue No. 1, p. 7 (1993).

DEFENSE ACQUISITION REGULATION (DAR) The regulation that controlled DOD from 1978 until early 1984. Prior to 1978 it was known as the Armed Services Procurement Regulation (ASPR). In 1984, the DAR and the Federal Procurement Regulations were replaced by the current regulatory system, based on the FEDERAL ACQUISITION REGULATION (FAR). Many of the DAR/ASPR clauses, provisions, and textual explanations survived and were incorporated into the FAR in simplified form. Many of the DAR/ASPR remnants that were not incorporated in the FAR were retained in the DOD FAR SUPPLEMENT (DFARS). The DFARS, DAR, and ASPR applied or now apply specifically to procurement involving the Office of the Secretary of Defense; the Departments of the Army, Navy, and Air Force; the Defense Logistics Agency; and other defense agencies.

DEFENSE ACQUISITION REGULATORY (DAR) COUNCIL The organization in DOD responsible for issuing procurement regulations. The DAR Council and the CIVILIAN AGENCY ACQUISITION COUNCIL prepare and issue revisions to the FAR through coordinated action. See FAR 1.201-1. The DAR Council also maintains the DOD FAR SUPPLEMENT. See DFARS 201.201-1. Each council maintains cognizance over specified portions of the FAR and is responsible for (1) agreeing on all revisions with the other council, (2) submitting to the FAR SECRETARIAT information required for publishing a FEDERAL REGISTER notice soliciting comments, (3) considering all comments received, (4) arranging for public meetings, (5) preparing any final revision in the appropriate FAR format and language, and (6) submitting any final revision to the FAR Secretariat for publication in the Federal Register and for printing and distribution. The Director of the DAR Council represents the Secretary of Defense. The Council's membership includes representatives of the military departments, the Defense Logistics Agency, and NASA. See DOD Directive 5000.35, *Defense Acquisition Regulatory System*, Mar. 8, 1978.

DEFENSE ACQUISITION UNIVERSITY (DAU) An organization established by Congress in 1990 to consolidate and integrate education and training for the Defense Acquisition Workforce. DAU's consortium member schools provide more than 85 acquisition courses to entry-, intermediate-, and senior-level civilian and uniformed personnel to allow them to attain certification in any of the 11 defense acquisition career fields. Courses are developed and delivered by 12 DOD educational institutions and by contractors to DAU. The DAU institutions include the: Air Force Institute of Technology (AFIT), Army Logistics Management College (ALMC), Defense Contract Audit Institute (DCAI), Defense Logistics Agency Civilian Personnel Support Office (DCPSO), DEFENSE SYSTEMS MANAGEMENT COLLEGE (DSMC), Industrial College of the Armed Forces (ICAF); Information Resources Management College (IRMC), Lackland Training Facility (LTF), Naval Center for Acquisition Training (NCAT), Naval Facilities Contracts Training Center (NFCTC), Naval Postgraduate School (NPS), and Naval Warfare Assessment Division (NWAD). In addition, the

Office of the Assistant Secretary of the Navy (Research, Development, and Acquisition) (OASN/RDA) sponsors the DAU's contracting executive seminar. See also DEFENSE ACQUISITION WORKFORCE IMPROVEMENT ACT (DAWIA).

DEFENSE ACQUISITION WORKFORCE IMPROVEMENT ACT (DAWIA) A statute that requires the Secretary of Defense to establish policies and procedures for effective management of persons serving in acquisition positions in DOD. The legislation provides for establishment of certain minimum education, training, and experience requirements for individuals filling acquisition positions. The legislation concentrates on the professionalism of the workforce rather than on organizational structure or process. The legislation addresses acquisition positions rather than acquisition personnel in recognition of the fact that acquisition is a multi-disciplinary or multi-functional career field. For the purposes of this statute, the acquisition discipline includes such functions as: program management; systems planning, research, development, engineering, and testing; procurement, including contracting; industrial property management; logistics; quality control and assurance; manufacturing and production; business, cost estimating, financial management and auditing; education, training, and career development; construction; and joint development and production with other government agencies and foreign countries. DAWIA requires that each military department have an acquisition career program board to advise the service acquisition executive on acquisition workforce issues. The Act also identifies education and training requirements, education assistance, increasing other acquisition training opportunities, and establishing a DEFENSE ACQUISITION UNIVERSITY structure. See 10 U.S.C. § 87, 1701 et seq.

DEFENSE ADVANCED RESEARCH PROJECTS AGENCY (DARPA) The central research and development organization for DOD. It manages and directs selected basic, advanced, and applied research and development projects for DOD. Its prime responsibility is to enter into and administer contracts, grants, and cooperative agreements, directly or through a military department, in pursuit of its research and development mission. 10 U.S.C. § 2358. Further, 10 U.S.C. § 2371 authorizes DARPA to enter into OTHER TRANSACTIONS, which are not procurement contracts, grants or cooperative agreements, when such innovative arrangements are in the best interests of the Government. Primarily, DARPA solicits research and development work through advertising in the COMMERCE BUSINESS DAILY and the SMALL BUSINESS INNOVATION RESEARCH

PROGRAM solicitation. CBD solicitations may be BROAD AGENCY ANNOUNCEMENTS, REQUESTS FOR PROPOSALS, Sources-Sought Announcements, or Special Research Announcements. DARPA's SBIR Program has an estimated annual budget of $40 million. [Internet site at <http://www.arpa.mil/>]

DEFENSE CONTRACT ADMINISTRATIVE SERVICE (DCAS) An organization within the Defense Logistics Agency that performed CONTRACT ADMINISTRATION on assigned contracts at contractor plants. It has been renamed the DEFENSE CONTRACT MANAGEMENT COMMAND.

DEFENSE CONTRACT AUDIT AGENCY (DCAA) A DOD agency responsible for performing contract AUDIT services for the department. The DCAA was established by DOD Directive 5105.36, *Defense Contract Audit Agency*, June 8, 1978, to perform all contract auditing for DOD and to provide all DOD procurement and contract administration activities with accounting and financial advisory services in connection with negotiating, administering, and settling contracts and subcontracts. DCAA also furnishes contract audit services to other Government agencies. *DCAA Contract Audit Manual* 1-102. DCAA is a separate DOD agency under the direction, authority, and control of the Assistant Secretary of Defense (Comptroller). *DCAA Contract Audit Manual* 1-103. See Arnavas et al., *DCAA Audits*, 94-9 Briefing Papers (Aug. 1994).

DEFENSE CONTRACT AUDIT MANUAL (DCAM) See DCAA CONTRACT AUDIT MANUAL.

DEFENSE CONTRACT MANAGEMENT COMMAND (DCMC) An organization within the Defense Logistics Agency that performs CONTRACT ADMINISTRATION services for all parts of DOD and other agencies. It was established under Defense Management Review recommendation DMR 916, effective February 1990, to replace Defense Contract Administrative Services, and it performs the services described at FAR 42.302 and DFARS 242.302. Contract administration services include all actions accomplished in or near a contractor's plant for the Government's benefit that are necessary to the performance of a contract or in support of the buying offices, system and project managers, and other organizations.

DEFENSE CONTRACTOR An entity (including affiliates and subsidiaries) that contracts directly with DOD to supply goods or services. It does not include a state or local government or any person who contracts to supply commercial items to DOD. DFARS 252.203-7000. A defense contractor is an employer that, under a contract with the United States or any other contract that the President, Secretary of the Army, Secretary of the Air Force, Secretary of the Navy, or Secretary of Transportation certifies to be necessary to the national defense, either (1) produces, maintains, or stores arms, armaments, ammunition, implements of war, munitions, machinery, tools, clothing, food, fuel, or other articles or supplies (or parts or ingredients of articles or supplies) or (2) constructs, reconstructs, repairs, or installs a building, plant, structure, or facility. 41 U.S.C. § 50. See Davidson, *10 U.S.C. § 2408: An Unused Weapon in the Procurement Fraud Wars*, 26 Pub. Cont. L.J. 181, 185-88 (1997).

DEFENSE COOPERATION A generic term for the range of activity undertaken by DOD with its allies and other friendly nations to promote international security. Such activity includes, but need not be confined to, security assistance, industrial cooperation, armaments cooperation, FOREIGN MILITARY SALES, training, logistics cooperation, cooperative RESEARCH AND DEVELOPMENT, Foreign Comparative Testing, and host nation support. A defense cooperation country is a "qualifying country" that has a defense cooperation agreement with the United States and for which a DETERMINATION AND FINDINGS has been made by the Secretary of Defense waiving the BUY AMERICAN ACT restrictions for a list of mutually agreed-upon items (see DFARS Subpart 225.75). Jones, *Glossary: Defense Acquisition Acronyms and Terms* (8th ed., Defense Systems Management College).

DEFENSE INDUSTRIAL SUPPLY CENTER (DISC) Established in 1962 as a field activity of the Defense Logistics Agency, DISC is responsible for the wholesale support of the military services with industrial type items. It manages over one million commodity items that include basic industrial-type hardware for everyday repairs, complex weapon system items such as rocket engine components, and general items such as lumber and plumbing and food preparation equipment. [DISC, 700 Robbins Avenue, Philadelphia, PA 19111-5096; (215) 697-2301; <http://www.disc.dla.mil/>]

DEFENSE PERSONNEL SUPPORT CENTER (DPSC) Provider of over $3.4 billion of food, clothing, textiles, medicines, and medical supplies to the U.S. military worldwide. Located in Philadelphia, PA, the DPSC is one of the largest activities within the Defense Logistics

Agency. [DPSC, 2800 South 20th Street, Philadelphia, PA 19145; <http://www.dpsc.dla.mil/>]

DEFENSE PRIORITIES AND ALLOCATIONS SYSTEM (DPAS) A system controlling the usage of critical materials and facilities to ensure that they would be used for national defense in the event of an emergency. See FAR Subpart 11.6. Certain contracts and orders are accorded preferential treatment by being designated as RATED ORDERs under the Defense Priorities and Allocations System regulation, which guides the Department of Commerce's Office of Industrial Resource Administration in developing, coordinating, and administering a system of priorities and allocations with respect to industrial resources, pursuant to Title I of the Defense Production Act of 1950, 50 U.S.C. app. § 2061 et seq. The DPAS legislation also provides that programs that maximize domestic energy supplies are eligible for priorities and allocations support. Rated orders placed in support of authorized energy programs are equivalent to orders placed in support of authorized defense programs under the DPAS; they receive the same preferential treatment throughout the industrial supply chain. DEAR 911.602(d). The Federal Emergency Management Agency authorizes certain national defense programs for priorities and allocations support. 15 C.F.R. § 700.2.

DEFENSE PRODUCTION POOL A pool of SMALL BUSINESS CONCERNs that have joined together to submit offers on one or more defense production contracts; that have entered into an agreement governing their organization, relationship, and procedures; and that have gained appropriate approvals. FAR 9.701. FAR 9.702 provides that Government agencies must treat such pools as they treat any other Government contractor.

DEFENSE RESEARCH AND DEVELOPMENT POOL A pool of SMALL BUSINESS CONCERNs that have joined together to submit offers on one or more defense RESEARCH AND DEVELOPMENT contracts; that have entered into an agreement governing their organization, relationship, and procedures; and that have gained appropriate approvals. FAR 9.701. FAR 9.702 provides that Government agencies must treat such pools as they treat any other Government contractor.

DEFENSE SYSTEMS MANAGEMENT COLLEGE (DSMC) A joint Military Service and Office of the Secretary of Defense professional institution that operates under the direction of a policy guidance council chaired by the Under Secretary of Defense (Acquisition & Technology) to support acquisition management and fulfill education and training requirements. The DSMC's mission entails conducting advanced courses of study in managing the acquisition of defense systems; conducting research and special studies in defense acquisition management; assembling and disseminating information about new policies, methods, and practices in defense acquisition management; and providing oversight for DOD's education and training program for the acquisition work force. DSMC, *Program Manager's Notebook* (1995).

DEFERMENT AGREEMENT A debt collection procedure where the Government agrees to delayed payments from a contractor if it is unable to pay or if the amount is in dispute. FAR 32.613 contains detailed guidance for deferment of collection actions. At a minimum, a deferment agreement must contain the following: (1) a description of the debt, (2) the date of first demand for payment, (3) a notice of an interest charge, (4) identification of the office to which the contractor is to send debt payments, (5) a requirement for the contractor to submit financial information requested by the Government and for reasonable access to the contractor's records and property, (6) provision for the Government to terminate the deferment agreement and accelerate the maturity of the debt if the contractor defaults or if bankruptcy or insolvency proceedings are instituted, and (7) protective requirements that are considered by the Government to be prudent and feasible in the specific circumstances. FAR 32.613(h). See Cibinic & Nash, *Administration of Government Contracts* 1184–85 (3d ed. 1995); Cibinic & Nash, *Cost-Reim-bursement Contracting* 1136–37 (2d ed. 1993).

DEFERRAL OF BUDGET AUTHORITY The temporary withholding or delaying the obligation or expenditure of BUDGET AUTHORITY or any type of executive action that effectively precludes the obligation or expenditure of budget authority. 2 U.S.C. § 684. Budget authority may be deferred to provide for contingencies, to achieve savings or greater efficiency in the operations of Government, or as otherwise specified by law. Budget authority may not be deferred in order to effect a policy in lieu of one established by law or for any other reason. Deferrals must be communicated to the Congress by the President in a special message. The special message must state (1) the amount of the budget authority proposed to be deferred; (2) any account, department, or establishment which such budget authority is available for obligation; (3) the period of time during which the budget authority is proposed to be deferred; (4) the reasons for the proposed deferral; (5) the estimated fiscal, economic, and budgetary effect of the proposed deferral; and (6) all facts bearing on the proposed deferral. A deferral may not be proposed for any period of time extending beyond the end of the fiscal year in which the message proposing the deferral is transmitted to Congress. 2 U.S.C. § 684. Jones, *Glossary: Defense Acquisition Acronyms and Terms* (8th ed., Defense Systems Management College). See IMPOUNDMENT; RESCISSION OF BUDGET AUTHORITY.

DEFERRED COMPENSATION An award an employer makes to compensate an employee for services rendered one or more cost accounting periods before the date when the employee receives the compensation. FAR 31.001. This definition does not include the amount of year-end accruals for salaries, wages, or bonuses that are to be paid within a reasonable period of time after the end of a cost accounting period. The costs of such compensation are generally considered to be ALLOWABLE COSTs pursuant to FAR 31.205-6(k), if the costs are accounted for in accordance with CAS 415, 48 C.F.R. § 9904-415.

DEFICIENCY A material failure of a proposal to meet a Government requirement or a combination of significant weaknesses in a proposal that increases the risk of unsuccessful contract performance to an unacceptable level. FAR 15.301. When an agency conducts DISCUSSIONs after establishing a COMPETITIVE RANGE in a competitively negotiated procurement, all deficiencies must be identified. FAR 15.306(d)(3). This permits each offeror to submit FINAL PROPOSAL REVISIONs that maximize the Government's ability to obtain the BEST VALUE. See Cibinic & Nash, chap. 6, *Formation of Government Contracts* (3d ed. 1998).

DEFINITE-QUANTITY CONTRACT A type of contract providing for delivery of a definite quantity of specific supplies or services for a fixed period, with deliveries at designated locations to be scheduled upon order. FAR 16.502. Definite-quantity contracts are one of the three types of INDEFINITE-DELIVERY CONTRACTs. They may be used when it can be determined in advance that (1) a definite quantity of supplies or services will be required during the contract period, and (2) the supplies or services are regularly available or will be available after a short lead-time. By buying a stated quantity for delivery on a deferred basis, the Government seeks to induce contractors to submit low prices and to reduce its costs of maintaining high levels of inventory.

DEFINITIZATION Agreement between a Government agency and a contractor on definitive terms, specifications, and price to replace an UNDEFINITIZED CONTRACTUAL ACTION. DFARS 217.7401. 10 U.S.C. § 2326 places strict requirements on the definitization of such actions. This term is generally used with regard to LETTER CONTRACTs.

DELAY An event that slows the performance of the work by a Government contractor. In Government contracts, the contractor generally bears the RISK of both time and cost for delays caused by the contractor or within the contractor's control. However, the contractor is generally entitled to a time extension if there is an EXCUSABLE DELAY and to additional compensation if there is a COMPENSABLE DELAY. See Kenyon, *Fixed Costs and Contract Delay*, 27 Nat'l Cont. Mgmt. J., Issue No. 2, p. 1 (1996); Cibinic & Nash, chap. 6, *Administration of Government Contracts* (3d ed. 1995); Toder & Simpson, *The Delay and Disruption Cost Proposal*, 35 Cont. Mgmt. 12 (July 1995); Toder & Simpson, *What Every Contract Manager Should Know About Delay and Disruption Cost Recovery*, 34 Cont. Mgmt. 18 (Aug. 1994); Finke, *The Burden of Proof in Government Contract Schedule Delay Claims*, 22 Pub. Cont. L.J. 125 (1992); Wiezel, *Refining the Concept of Concurrent Delay*, 21 Pub. Cont. L.J. 161 (1992); Margulies, chap. 8, *Construction Contracting* 617–79 (1991).

DELEGATION OF CONTRACTING OFFICER AUTHORITY The granting of authority to act as a CONTRACTING OFFICER for an EXECUTIVE AGENCY. FAR 1.603-1 requires that each agency establish a system for the selection, appointment, and termination of appointment of contracting officers. Agency procedures for delegating contracting officer authority are found in each agency FAR Supplement. Each contracting officer with delegated authority is given a WARRANT using the Certificate of Appointment in Standard Form 1402, FAR 53.301-1402. See Cibinic & Nash, chap. 1, Sec. III., *Formation of Government Contracts* (3d ed. 1998).

DELEGATION OF PROCUREMENT AUTHORITY (DPA) The granting of authority by the General Services Administration to an agency to procure FEDERAL INFORMATION PROCESSING RESOURCES, or ADPE. Such delegation was necessary under the BROOKS ACT (AUTOMATIC DATA PROCESSING EQUIPMENT) because GSA had the sole authority to procure ADPE. Such delegations are no longer necessary because the Brooks Act was repealed by the INFORMATION TECHNOLOGY MANAGEMENT REFORM

ACT OF 1996, Pub. L. No. 104-106 (which was later renamed the CLINGER-COHEN ACT OF 1996, Pub. L. No. 104-208 § 808).

DELINQUENCY NOTICE A notice from a contracting officer to a contractor asserting that contract performance is delinquent and requesting that the contractor provide information as to the delinquency. FAR 49.607 discusses two types of delinquency notices: (1) CURE NOTICEs and (2) SHOW CAUSE NOTICEs.

DELIVERY OR PERFORMANCE PERIOD REQUIREMENTS One of the eight required elements of the Acquisition Background and Objectives section of the written ACQUISITION PLAN that outlines the timing requirements for contract performance or supply delivery. FAR Subpart 11.4 gives contracting officers a number of factors to consider in establishing the delivery schedule or performance period. Contracting officers must ensure that delivery or performance schedules are realistic and meet the requirements of the acquisition. Schedules that are unreasonably tight or difficult of attainment tend to restrict competition, are inconsistent with small business policies, and may result in higher contract prices. FAR 11.401.

DELIVERY OR PERFORMANCE SCHEDULE The contract provision setting forth the time of delivery or performance. This provision is included in Section F of the UNIFORM CONTRACT FORMAT. FAR 14.201-1; FAR 15.204-1. FAR 11.401 requires that contracting officers ensure that delivery schedules are realistic and meet the requirements of the acquisition. Schedules that are unreasonably tight tend to restrict competition, are inconsistent with small business policies, and may result in higher contract prices. When establishing contract delivery schedules for supply or service contracts, the contracting officer must consider factors such as urgency of the need, production time, market conditions, transportation time, industry practices, capabilities of small business concerns, administrative time for obtaining and evaluating offers and awarding contracts, time for contractors to comply with any conditions precedent to contract performance, and time for the Government to perform its obligations under the contract. Scheduling the completion date for construction contracts requires consideration of the nature and complexity of the project, construction seasons involved, required completion date, availability of materials and equipment, capacity of the contractor to perform, and advisability of multiple completion dates. FAR 11.402.

DELIVERY ORDER An order for supplies or services placed against an established contract or with Government sources of supply. FAR 13.101. FAR 13.307 provides that such orders may be issued using Optional Form 347, Order for Supplies or Services, or Optional Form 348, Order for Supplies or Services Schedule—Continuation, which are set forth at FAR 53.302-347 and -348. Delivery orders placed on DELIVERY ORDER CONTRACTS must be issued in accordance with the procedures in FAR 16.505. Competitors for delivery orders on such contracts may not PROTEST but may refer the matter to an agency OMBUDSMAN. 10 U.S.C. § 2304c and 42 U.S.C. § 253j.

DELIVERY ORDER CONTRACT A contract for supplies that does not procure or specify a firm quantity of supplies (other than a minimum or maximum quantity) and that provides for the issuance of orders for the delivery of supplies during the period of the contract. FAR 16.501-1. Under 10 U.S.C. § 2304a and 41 U.S.C. § 253h, delivery order contracts must contain (1) the period of the contract, including options; (2) the maximum quantity or dollar value of the supplies to be procured; and (3) a statement of work that reasonably describes the general scope, nature, complexity, and purposes of the supplies being procured. 10 U.S.C. § 2304a(d) and 41 U.S.C. § 253h(d) require that such contracts be issued to multiple contractors whenever practicable (see MULTIPLE AWARD PREFERENCE). Delivery order contracts are generally issued as INDEFINITE-QUANTITY CONTRACTs. See Cibinic & Nash, chap. 8, Sec. VI., *Formation of Government Contracts* (3d ed. 1998).

DEMOBILIZATION The effort of a construction contractor in leaving the site after the contract work is completed. In major construction contracts agencies frequently pay for the cost of this effort as a separate pay item. DFARS 236.570(b)(ii) requires the use of the Payment for Mobilization and Demobilization clause in DFARS 252.236-7004 in these circumstances.

DEPARTMENT OF AGRICULTURE (USDA) Government agency created by act of May 15, 1862, 7 U.S.C. § 2201. USDA works to improve and maintain farm income and to develop and expand markets abroad for agricultural products. USDA also helps to curb and cure poverty, hunger, and malnutrition. Through its rural development, credit and conservation programs, it works to enhance the environment and maintain production capacity. Further, it safeguards and ensures standards of quality in the daily food supply through inspection and grading services. USDA contracts fall under the coverage of the FEDERAL ACQUISITION REGULATION and the Agriculture Acquisition Regulation (AGAR), 48 C.F.R. chap. 4. See the U.S. Government Manual. [USDA, 14th Street and Independence Avenue, S.W., Washington, DC 20250; <http://www.usda.gov/>]

DEPARTMENT OF COMMERCE Government agency created by act of February 14, 1903, 15 U.S.C. § 1501. The agency was established to promote American businesses and trade. Its broad range of responsibilities includes expanding U.S. exports, developing innovative technologies, gathering and disseminating statistical data, measuring economic growth, granting patents, registering trademarks, promoting minority entrepreneurship, and predicting the weather. Department of Commerce contracts fall under the coverage of the FEDERAL ACQUISITION REGULATION and the Department of Commerce Acquisition Regulation (CAR), 48 C.F.R. chap. 13. See the U.S. Government Manual. [Department of Commerce, 14th Street and Constitution Avenue, N.W., Wash., DC 20230; <http://www.doc.gov/>]

DEPARTMENT OF DEFENSE (DOD) The Office of the Secretary of Defense, the military departments, and the defense agencies. The military departments include the Departments of the Army, the Navy, and the Air Force (the Marine Corps is a part of the Department of the Navy). The defense agencies are the Defense Advanced Research Projects Agency, the Defense Commissary Agency, the Defense Information Systems Agency, the Defense Intelligence Agency, the Defense Investigative Service, the Defense Logistics Agency, the Defense Mapping Agency, the Defense Nuclear Agency, the National Security Agency, the On-Site Inspection Agency, the Ballistic Missile Defense Organization, and the United States Special Operations Command. DFARS 202.101. DOD contracts fall under the coverage of the FEDERAL ACQUISITION REGULATION (FAR) and the DOD FAR SUPPLEMENT (DFARS), as well as lower-level supplemental regulations for the military services and defense agencies. Before the FAR went into effect in 1984, DOD contracts were governed by the DEFENSE ACQUISITION REGULATION and its predecessor, the ARMED SERVICES PROCUREMENT REGULATION. See the U.S. Government Manual. [DOD, 1000 Defense Pentagon, Washington, DC 20301-1000; <http://www.dtic.dla.mil/defenselink>]

DEPARTMENT OF DEFENSE DIRECTIVES SYSTEM A single, uniform system governing the coordination, publication, dissemination, implementation, and biennial review of issuances maintained within

DOD. The system includes (1) DOD Directives (DODDs), which publish Secretary of Defense decisions on policies, plans, programs, charters, delegations of authority, or other major actions; (2) DOD Instructions (DODIs), which provide supplementary guidance to implement Secretary of Defense decisions; (3) DOD publications, which implement or supplement DODDs and DODIs by providing uniform procedures for management or operational systems and by disseminating administrative information (these publications include handbooks and manuals, designated by the suffixes "H" and "M," respectively); and (4) DOD transmittals, which change or cancel DOD issuances. When directive-type memoranda of continuing application issued by principal staff assistants cannot, because of time constraints, be published in the DOD Directives System at the time of signature, they are to be reissued as DOD issuances within 90 days. Directive-type memoranda of a one-time nature are not issued in the DOD Directives System. DOD Directive 5025.1, *Department of Defense Directives System*, Dec. 23, 1988, and DOD Directive 5025.1-M, *Department of Defense Directives System Procedures*, Dec. 1990. Although all procurement regulations are required to be included in the FAR and the DFARS, the DOD Directives System contains a significant amount of information bearing directly on the procurement process. Instructions for obtaining documents in the DOD Directives System are available from the DOD Directives Division, Room 286, The Pentagon, Washington, DC 20301-1155; (703) 697-4111.

DEPARTMENT OF DEFENSE FAR SUPPLEMENT (DFARS) The procurement regulation applicable to DOD that implements and supplements the FEDERAL ACQUISITION REGULATION (FAR). It applies specifically to procurement involving the Office of the Secretary of Defense; the Departments of the Army, Navy, and Air Force; and the Defense Logistics Agency (DLA) and other defense agencies. The FAR and the DFARS contain guidance and direction to DOD contracting personnel as to (1) which provisions, clauses, cost principles, and Cost Accounting Standards are authorized for DOD contracts; and (2) what other procedures and actions must be followed in awarding and administering DOD contracts. The DFARS is not a stand-alone document; it must be read in conjunction with the FAR. The DFARS is amended through the use of DEFENSE ACQUISITION CIRCULARS, which are issued by the DEFENSE ACQUISITION REGULATORY COUNCIL and resemble FEDERAL ACQUISITION CIRCULARS. DFARS 201.304. Implementing coverage in the DFARS is numbered in the same way as the FAR material it implements, except for the addition of a "2" or "20" prefix (the DFARS is Chapter 2 of Title 48 of the CODE OF FEDERAL REGULATIONS). Thus, DFARS Parts 201 through 253 corresponds to FAR Parts 1 through 53, DFARS Subpart 252.1 parallels FAR Subpart 52.1, and DFARS 201.101 implements FAR 1.101. Supplementary coverage, for which there is no parallel in the FAR, is distinguished by using numbers 70 and above (e.g., Part 270, Subpart 245.73). Supplementary numbering is used only when the DFARS text cannot be integrated intelligibly with counterpart text in the FAR. DFARS 201.303. The DFARS can be purchased in paperback from Commerce Clearing House, Inc., 4025 West Peterson Avenue, Chicago, IL 60646, or as part of the loose-leaf-bound subscription edition of the FEDERAL ACQUISITION REGULATIONS SYSTEM available from the U.S. Government Printing Office, Washington, DC 20402.

DEPARTMENT OF EDUCATION Government agency created by the Department of Education Organization Act of May 4, 1980, 20 U.S.C. § 3411. The agency establishes policy for, administers, and coordinates most federal assistance to education. The Department of Education operates 200 programs that cover every area of education and range from preschool education through postdoctoral research. The Department's contracts fall under the coverage of the FEDERAL ACQUISITION REGULATION and the Department of Education Acquisition Regulation (EDAR), 48 C.F.R. chap. 34. See the U.S. Government Manual. [Department of Education, 600 Independence Avenue, S.W., Washington, DC 20202; <http://www.ed.gov/>]

DEPARTMENT OF ENERGY (DOE) Government agency established by the Department of Energy Organization Act, 42 U.S.C. § 7131, effective Oct. 1, 1977, pursuant to Exec. Order No. 12009, 42 Fed. Reg. 46267 (Sept. 13, 1977). The Act consolidated the major federal energy functions into one cabinet-level department, transferring to the department all the responsibilities of several components of the Department of the Interior, including the Energy Research and Development Administration and the Federal Energy Administration. DOE is responsible for long-term, high-risk research and development of energy technology; the marketing of federal power; energy conservation; the nuclear weapons program; energy regulatory programs; and a central energy data collection and analysis program. DOE contracts fall under the coverage of the FEDERAL ACQUISITION REGULATION (FAR) and the DEPARTMENT OF ENERGY ACQUISITION REGULATION (DEAR), 48 C.F.R. chap. 9. See the U.S. Government Manual. [DOE, 1000 Independence Avenue, S.W., Washington; DC 20585: <http://www.doe.gov/>]

DEPARTMENT OF ENERGY ACQUISITION REGULATION (DEAR) The DOE regulation that implements and supplements the FEDERAL ACQUISITION REGULATION (FAR). The DEAR is not a stand-alone document but must be read in conjunction with the FAR. DEAR 901.101. It is divided into the same parts, subparts, sections, subsections, and paragraphs as the FAR. The implementing passages of the DEAR are numbered the same as the FAR to the extent possible, except that they are preceded with a "9" or a "90" because the DEAR is Chapter 9 of Title 48 of the CODE OF FEDERAL REGULATIONS (CFR). DEAR 901.104-2. The DEAR is revised by acquisition letters issued by the DOE SENIOR PROCUREMENT EXECUTIVE. DEAR 901.301-70. The DEAR is available from the U.S. Government Printing Office, Washington DC 20402, as part of the loose-leaf-bound subscription edition of the FEDERAL ACQUISITION REGULATIONS SYSTEM.

DEPARTMENT OF HEALTH AND HUMAN SERVICES (HHS) Government agency created on April 11, 1953, as the Department of Health, Education, and Welfare. It was redesignated as the Department of Health and Human Services by the Department of Education Organization Act, 20 U.S.C. § 3508, effective May 4, 1980. HHS is the Government's principal agency for protecting the health of all Americans and providing essential human services. It operates more than 300 programs covering a wide spectrum of activities, including: medical and social science research, preventing outbreak of infectious disease, assuring food and drug safety, Medicare and Medicaid, financial assistance for low-income families (AFDC), child-support enforcement, improving maternal and infant health, Head Start, prevention of child abuse and domestic violence, substance abuse treatment and prevention, and services for older Americans. HHS contracts fall under the coverage of the FEDERAL ACQUISITION REGULATION and the Department of Health and Human Services Acquisition Regulation (HHSAR), 48 C.F.R. chap. 3. See the U.S. Government Manual. [HHS, 200 Independence Avenue, S.W., Washington DC 20201; <http://www.os.dhhs.gov/>]

DEPARTMENT OF HOUSING AND URBAN DEVELOPMENT (HUD) Government agency created by the Department of Housing and Urban Development Act, 42 U.S.C. §§ 3532–3537, effective November 9, 1965. HUD is responsible for programs concerned with the Nation's housing needs, fair housing opportunities, and improvement and development of the nation's communities. HUD administers a wide variety of programs, including federal housing administration mortgage insurance programs, rental assistance programs, the Government National Mortgage Association mortgage-backed securities program, programs to combat housing discrimination, programs that aid community and neighborhood development and preservation, and programs to protect the homebuyer in the marketplace. HUD contracts fall under the coverage of the FEDERAL ACQUISITION REGULATION and the Department of Housing and Urban Development Acquisition Regulation (HUDAR), 48 C.F.R. chap. 24. See the U.S. Government Manual. [HUD, 451 Seventh Street, S.W., Washington, DC 20410; <http://www.hud.gov/>]

DEPARTMENT OF JUSTICE (DOJ) Government agency established by act of June 22, 1870, 28 U.S.C. §§ 501, 503, with the Attorney General as its head. DOJ serves as counsel for the nation's citizens, representing them in enforcing the law in the public interest. DOJ's roles include protection against criminals and subversion; ensuring healthy competition in business; safeguarding the consumer; and enforcing drug, immigration, and naturalization laws. It also protects citizens through its efforts for effective law enforcement, crime prevention, crime detection, and prosecution and rehabilitation of offenders. DOJ conducts all suits in the Supreme Court in which the United States is concerned and represents the Government in legal matters generally. DOJ contracts fall under the coverage of the FEDERAL ACQUISITION REGULATION and the Department of Justice Acquisition Regulation (JAR), 48 C.F.R. chap. 28. See the U.S. Government Manual. [DOJ, 10th Street and Constitution Avenue, N.W., Washington, DC 20530; <http://www.usdoj.gov/>]

DEPARTMENT OF LABOR (DOL) Government agency created by act of March 4, 1913, 42 U.S.C. § 551. The Department of Labor administers a variety of federal labor laws; protects workers' pension rights; provides job training programs; helps workers find jobs; works to strengthen free collective bargaining; and keeps track of changes in employment, prices, and other national economic measurements. DOL contracts fall under the coverage of the FEDERAL ACQUISITION REGULATION (FAR) and the Department of Labor Acquisition Regulation (DOLAR), 48 C.F.R. chap. 29. See the U.S. Government Manual. [DOL, 200 Constitution Avenue, N.W., Washington, DC 20210; <http://www.dol.gov/>]

DEPARTMENT OF STATE The senior Government agency created by act of July 27, 1789, 1 Stat. 28, as the Department of Foreign Affairs and renamed Department of State by act of September 15, 1789, 1 Stat.

68. The Department of State advises the President in the formulation and execution of foreign policy. The Department of State determines and analyzes the facts relating to American overseas interests, makes recommendations on policy and future action, and takes the necessary steps to carry out established policy. In doing so, the department engages in consultations with the American public, Congress, other U.S. departments and agencies, and foreign governments; negotiates treaties and agreements with foreign nations; speaks for the United States in the United Nations and in more than 50 international organizations; and represents the United States at more than 800 international conferences annually. The department operates more than 250 diplomatic and consular posts around the world, including embassies, consulates, and delegations and missions to international organizations. Department of State contracts fall under the coverage of the FEDERAL ACQUISITION REGULATION (FAR) and the Department of State Acquisition Regulation (SAR), 48 C.F.R. chap. 6. See the U.S. Government Manual. [Department of State, 2201 C Street, N.W., Washington, DC 20520; <http://www.state.gov/>]

DEPARTMENT OF THE INTERIOR (DOI) Government agency created by act of March 3, 1849, 43 U.S.C. § 1451. As the nation's principal conversation agency, DOI has responsibility for most nationally owned public lands and natural resources. These responsibilities include: fostering sound use of land and water resources; protecting fish, wildlife, and biological diversity; preserving and operating national parks and historical places; and providing for the enjoyment of life through outdoor recreation. DOI also has a major responsibility for American Indian reservation communities and for people who live in island territories under U.S. administration. DOI contracts fall under the coverage of the FEDERAL ACQUISITION REGULATION (FAR) and the Department of the Interior Acquisition Regulation (DIAR), 48 C.F.R. chap. 14. See the U.S. Government Manual. [DOI, 1849 C Street, N.W. Washington, DC 20240; <http://www.doi.gov/>]

DEPARTMENT OF THE TREASURY Government agency created by act of September 2, 1789, 31 U.S.C. § 1001. The Department of the Treasury performs four basic functions: formulating and recommending economic, financial, tax, and fiscal policies; serving as financial agent for the U.S. Government; enforcing the law; and manufacturing coins and currency. Department of the Treasury contracts fall under the coverage of the FEDERAL ACQUISITION REGULATION (FAR) and the Treasury Acquisition/Procurement Regulation (TAPR), 48 C.F.R.

chap. 10. See the U.S. Government Manual. [Department of the Treasury, 1500 Pennsylvania Avenue, N.W., Washington, DC 20220; <http://www.ustreas.gov/>]

DEPARTMENT OF TRANSPORTATION (DOT) Government agency established by act of October 15, 1966, 49 U.S.C. app. § 1651 note. DOT establishes the nation's overall transportation policy. It operates 10 administrations whose jurisdictions include highway planning, development, and construction; urban mass transit; railroads; aviation; and the safety of waterways, ports, highways, and oil and gas pipelines. Except for contracts of the FEDERAL AVIATION ADMINISTRATION, DOT contracts fall under the coverage of the FEDERAL ACQUISITION REGULATION and the Transportation Acquisition Regulation (TAR), 48 C.F.R. chap. 12. See the U.S. Government Manual. [DOT, 400 Seventh Street, S.W., Washington DC 20590; <http://www.dot.gov/>]

DEPARTMENT OF VETERANS AFFAIRS (VA) Government agency established as an executive department by the Department of Veterans Affairs Act, 38 U.S.C. § 201 note. The Department's predecessor, the Veterans Administration, had been established as an independent agency by Exec. Order No. 5398 of July 21, 1930, in accordance with the act of July 3, 1940, 46 Stat. 1016. The Department operates programs to benefit veterans and their families, including: compensation payments for disabilities or death related to military service; pensions; education and rehabilitation; home loan guaranty; and a medical care program incorporating nursing homes, clinics, and medical centers. VA contracts fall under the coverage of the FEDERAL ACQUISITION REGULATION (FAR) and the Veterans Affairs Acquisition Regulation (VAAR), 48 C.F.R. chap. 8. See the U.S. Government Manual. [VA, 810 Vermont Avenue, N.W., Washington, DC 20420; <http://www.va.gov/>]

DEPOSITION The examination of a potential witness in writing or in person with information concerning a pending litigation by a party to the litigation. Rule 27 of the Federal Rules of Civil Procedure permits depositions to be taken for the purpose of gathering evidence (discovery depositions) and requires the other party to a litigation to make its employees and witnesses available for such depositions. Rule 32 of the Federal Rules of Civil Procedure permits depositions to be used for evidentiary purposes. Rule 14 of the UNIFORM RULES (before the BOARDs OF CONTRACT APPEALS) permits the use of depositions for both discovery and evidentiary purposes (if the witness is not present at the hearing).

DEPOT MAINTENANCE Maintenance performed on material requiring overhauling or rebuilding of parts, assemblies, subassemblies, and end items. Depot maintenance operations include manufacture of parts, modifications, testing, and reclamation. It supports base-level technicians by providing technical assistance and performing any repairs beyond their responsibility. Depot maintenance includes all forms of software maintenance. AF Instruction 21-102, *Depot Maintenance Management* (July 19, 1994). Depot maintenance costs include all costs of personnel, material, overhead support, and depot-purchased maintenance required to perform major overhaul and maintenance of a defense system, its components, and support equipment at DOD centralized repair depots, contractor repair facilities, or on site by depot teams. DOD 5000.4M. *Department of Defense Manual: Cost Analysis Guidance and Procedures* (Dec. 1992). Section 357 of the DOD Authorization Act for Fiscal Year 1998 amended 10 U.S.C. § 2466 to require that "not more than 50 percent of the funds made available in a fiscal year to a military department or a Defense Agency for depot-level maintenance and repair workload may be used to contract for the performance by non-Federal Government personnel."

DEPRECIATION A charge to current operations that systematically and logically distributes the cost of a TANGIBLE CAPITAL ASSET, less estimated RESIDUAL VALUE, over the estimated useful life of the ASSET. FAR 31.205-11(a). Depreciation does not involve a process of valuation but is based on the ACQUISITION COST of the asset. Useful life, as distinguished from physical life, is the prospective period of economic usefulness in a particular contractor's operations. CAS 409, 48 C.F.R. § 9904-409, provides guidance on the computation of depreciation and generally requires that the costs be distributed equally over the years of use of the asset. FAR 31.205-11 provides that depreciation is an ALLOWABLE COST. See Cibinic & Nash, *Cost-Reimbursement Contracting* 845–54 (2d ed. 1993).

DERIVATIVE WORK A WORK based on one or more preexisting works, such as a translation, musical arrangement, dramatization, fictionalization, motion picture version, sound recording, art reproduction, abridgment, condensation, or any other form in which a work may be recast, transformed, or adapted. 17 U.S.C. § 101. The owner of a COPYRIGHT has the exclusive right to prepare derivative works of the work covered by the copyright. 17 U.S.C. § 106. Under the Rights in Data—General clause in FAR 52.227-14, the Rights in Technical Data—Noncommercial Items clause in DFARS 252.227- 7013, and the Rights in Noncommercial Computer Software and Noncommercial Computer Software Documentation clause in DFARS 252.227-7014 the Government has the right to make derivative works through its LIMITED RIGHTS or RESTRICTED RIGHTS, which permit modification of the technical data or computer software.

DESCRIPTION OF WORK See STATEMENT OF WORK.

DESCRIPTIVE LITERATURE Information such as cuts, drawings, illustrations, drawings, and brochures showing the characteristics or construction of a product or explaining its operation. FAR 14.202-5(a). When required by the Descriptive Literature solicitation provision in FAR 52.214-21, descriptive literature is furnished by bidders as part of their bids to describe the products offered. The term includes only information required to determine acceptability of the product. Descriptive literature excludes other information, such as that furnished in connection with the qualifications of a bidder or for use in operating or maintaining equipment. FAR 14.202-5(b) states that the Government should not require bidders to furnish descriptive literature unless the contracting office needs it before award to determine whether the products offered meet the SPECIFICATION and to establish exactly what the bidder proposes to furnish. However, requiring descriptive literature is a means that contracting officers use to determine whether bidders actually intend to meet the contract SPECIFICATIONs and to identify bids that are not responsive (see RESPONSIVENESS).

DESIGN (IN CONSTRUCTION CONTRACTING) Defining the construction requirement (including the functional relationships and technical systems to be used, such as architectural, environmental, structural, electrical, mechanical, and fire protection), producing the technical SPECIFICATIONs and DRAWINGS, and preparing the construction cost estimate. FAR 36.102. This work is the major part of ARCHITECT/ENGINEER (A-E) SERVICES. It can be procured under a single ARCHITECT/ENGINEER CONTRACT or as part of a DESIGN-BUILD contract.

DESIGN (IN RESEARCH AND DEVELOPMENT CONTRACTING) The preparation of DRAWINGS and SPECIFICATIONs for a product. Design is one of the major tasks in the DEVELOPMENT process.

DESIGN-BID-BUILD The traditional delivery method for construction projects where design and construction are sequential and contracted for separately with two contracts and two contractors. FAR 36.102. This is contrasted with DESIGN-BUILD contracting where a single contract is used. In design-bid-build contracting the drawings and specifications created under an initial ARCHITECT/ENGINEER CONTRACT are used as the bid documents in the following CONSTRUCTION contract. This permits competition among construction contractors on a project that has quite complete design. However, the Government bears the risk that the drawings and specifications are defective (see IMPLIED WARRANTY OF SPECIFICATIONS). Procedures to be used for design-bid-build contracting are set forth in FAR Subpart 36.2.

DESIGN-BUILD A delivery method for construction projects that combines the architectural, engineering, and construction services required for a project into a single contractual agreement. Under such an agreement, the owner contracts with a single entity; the contractor providing the end product is responsible for both design and construction. Section 4105 of the CLINGER-COHEN ACT OF 1996 adds 10 U.S.C. § 2305a and 41 U.S.C. § 253m to authorize the use of two-phase design-build procedures, limiting the competition in the second phase to five contractors or less. FAR Subpart 36.3 implements this statute by providing guidance on this two-phase procedure. In design-build contracting, the contractor is responsible for any deficiencies or defects in the design, except to the extent that such responsibility is specifically waived or limited by the contract. This format is widely used in the industrial sector. It is sometimes called "turnkey" construction because, at least in theory, the owner presents its requirements to a design/build organization and, at some later date, the designer/builder simply hands over the keys to the building to the owner. See Nash, *Design-Build Contracting: The New Two-Step Procedure*, 11 N&CR ¶ 13 (Mar. 1997); Nash, *Design-Build Contracting: Can the Federal Government Use This Technique Effectively?,* 8 N&CR ¶ 68 (Dec. 1994); Nash, chap. 1, *Construction Contracting* 7–9 (1991).

DESIGN SPECIFICATIONS Specifications that set forth precise measurements, tolerances, materials, in-process and finished-product tests, quality control measures, inspection requirements, and other specific information. The Government uses design specifications in solicitations when the technical requirements are definite and can be communicated clearly to potential offerors. Design specifications permit the Government to award solely on the basis of price and price-related factors, since no flexibility is allowed and all responsive bids are therefore design-identical. Design specifications increase the Government's liability for claims that arise during contract performance regarding design defects, since the Government generally assumes responsibility for the correctness and adequacy of design specifications (see IMPLIED WARRANTY OF SPECIFICATIONS). FAR 11.002 requires that contract requirements be stated in terms of FUNCTIONAL SPECIFICATIONS, PERFORMANCE SPECIFICATIONS, and design specifications; and FAR 11.101 states a preference for performance-oriented requirements documents over design-oriented requirements documents to describe an agency's needs. See Cibinic & Nash, chap. 3, Sec. V., *Formation of Government Contracts* (3d ed. 1998); Golden & Thomas, *The Spearin Doctrine: The False Dichotomy Between Design and Performance Specifications*, 25 Pub. Cont. L.J. 47 (1995); Nash, *Design Defects in Manufacturing Contracts: Is the Contractor Liable?*, 8 N&CR ¶ 5 (Feb. 1994); Nash, *Delegation of Design Responsibility to Construction Contractors: What Are the Risks?,* 7 N&CR ¶ 65 (Nov. 1993); D'Aloisio, *The Design Responsibility and Liability of Government Contractors*, 22 Pub. Cont. L.J. 515 (1993).

DESIGN-TO-COST A management concept in accordance with which (1) rigorous cost goals are established during the development of a system (see ACQUISITION PROCESS), and (2) control of costs (acquisition, operating, and support) is achieved by practical tradeoffs between operational capability, performance, costs, and schedule. Cost, as a key design parameter, is addressed on a continuing basis and as an inherent part of the development and production process. Design-to-cost parameters for operation and support are selected and then expressed in dollars or other measurable factors. Firm goals and thresholds are established before FULL-SCALE DEVELOPMENT begins. Jones, *Glossary: Defense Acquisition Acronyms and Terms* (8th ed., Defense Systems Management College). Procuring agencies are to consider design-to-cost in the ACQUISITION PLANNING process, as appropriate. FAR 7.105. DOD Directive 5000.2, *Defense Acquisition Management Policies and Procedures*, Feb. 23, 1991, part 6K, contained policies and procedures establishing cost as a design constraint early in the acquisition process. See also MIL-STD-337, July 24, 1989, *Design To Cost.* This was replaced by guidance on treating COST AS AN INDEPENDENT VARIABLE in paragraph 3.3.3 of DOD Regulation 5000.2-R, *Mandatory Procedures for Major Defense Acquisition Programs (MDAPs) and Major Automated Information System (MAIS) Acquisition Programs*, Mar. 15, 1996. See Caver & Andrews, *Design to Cost: Achieving Cost Through Product and Process Trade-offs*, 36 Cont. Mgmt. 18 (May 1996).

DESIGNATED BILLING OFFICE The office (or person) designated in a contract as the point to which the contractor submits INVOICEs and contract financing requests. FAR 32.902. This office can be the Government disbursing office, the contract administration office, the office accepting the supplies delivered or services performed, the contract AUDIT office, or even a non-Government agent. In some cases, more than one office may be designated to receive INVOICEs and contract financing requests. When payments are subject to the PROMPT PAYMENT ACT, they must be made within 30 days of the date a proper invoice is received in the designated billing office. FAR 32.905(a).

DESIGNATED PAYMENT OFFICE The place designated in the contract to make invoice payments or contract financing payments. Normally, this will be the Government disbursing office. FAR 32.902. See also DISBURSING OFFICER.

DETERMINATION AND FINDINGS (D&Fs) A written approval by an authorized official that is required by statute or regulation as a prerequisite to certain contracting actions. FAR 1.701. The determination is a conclusion or decision supported by the findings. The findings, which are statements of fact or rationale essential to support the determination, must cover each requirement of the statute or regulation. FAR 1.704 requires that D&Fs set forth enough facts and circumstances to justify the specific determination made clearly and convincingly. As a minimum, a D&F must include (1) identification of the agency and the contracting activity and of the document as a D&F; (2) a description of the contracting action; (3) citation of the appropriate statute and/or regulation; (4) findings that detail the particular circumstances, facts, or reasoning essential to support the determination; (5) a determination based on the findings; (6) the expiration date of the D&F, if required; and (7) the date and signature of the official authorized to sign the D&F. Further requirements may apply in a given situation; for example, FAR 14.407-4 lists specific types of statements that a D&F must contain in documenting the contracting officer's handling of a mistake in bid that the contractor discovers and asks to correct following contract award.

DEVELOPED The condition that applies to an item, component, or process when it exists and is workable. This condition is part of the determination of intellectual property rights in FAR Subpart 27.4 and DFARS Subparts 227.71 and 227.72. The Rights in Technical Data—Noncommercial Items clause at DFARS 252.227-7013 provides that to meet the test of being developed, an item or component must have been constructed or the process practiced. Workability is generally established when the item, component, or process has been analyzed or tested sufficiently to demonstrate to reasonable people skilled in the applicable art that there is a high probability that it will operate as intended. Whether, how much, and what type of analysis or testing is required to establish workability depends on the nature of the item, component, or process, and the state of the art. To be considered developed, the item, component, or process need not be at the stage when it could be offered for sale or sold on the commercial market, nor must the item, component, or process be actually reduced to practice within the meaning of Title 35 of the United States Code. The Rights in Noncommercial Computer Software and Noncommercial Computer Software Documentation clause at DFARS 252.227-7014 provides that to be developed, (1) a COMPUTER PROGRAM must have been successfully operated in a computer and sufficiently tested to demonstrate that it can perform its intended purpose, (2) COMPUTER SOFTWARE other than computer programs must have been sufficiently tested or analyzed to demonstrate that it can perform its intended purpose, and (3) COMPUTER SOFTWARE DOCUMENTATION must have been written in sufficient detail to comply with the requirements of the contract. The FAR contains no definition of this term. See Nash & Rawicz, *Intellectual Property in Government Contracts,* vol. 2 (3d ed. 1997); Nash, *"Developed at Private Expense": Decrypting the Key to Proprietary Rights*, 1 N&CR ¶ 42 (May 1987); DeVecchio, *The Bell Helicopter Textron Decision: Expanding the Government's Rights in Technical Data*, 16 Pub. Cont. L.J. 1 (1986).

DEVELOPED AT PRIVATE EXPENSE A condition of an item, component, or process wherein no part of the cost of development was paid for by the Government. This term is used, without definition, in the policy on rights to TECHNICAL DATA in FAR Subpart 27.4. It is generally believed that private expense includes all costs not charged as DIRECT COSTs to a contract. See Nash & Rawicz, *Intellectual Property in Government Contracts,* vol. 2 (3d ed. 1997); Nash, *"Developed at Private Expense": Decrypting the Key to Proprietary Rights*, 1 N&CR ¶ 42 (May 1987).

DEVELOPED EXCLUSIVELY AT PRIVATE EXPENSE A condition of an item, component, or process where in development was accomplished entirely with costs charged to indirect costs pools, costs not allocated to a Government contract, or any combination thereof. DFARS 252.227-7013 and -7014. This DOD definition pertains to the

1995 data and computer software policy and further provides that private expense determinations should be made at the lowest practicable level and that, under fixed-price contracts where total costs are greater than the fixed price or CEILING PRICE, the additional development costs necessary to complete development shall not be considered in determining whether development was at Government, private, or mixed expense. The term was defined more restrictively in the 1988 DOD data and software policy where it meant that no part of the cost of development was paid for by the Government and the development was not required for the performance of a Government contract or subcontract. DFARS 252.227-7013. Under this definition, INDEPENDENT RESEARCH AND DEVELOPMENT (IR&D) costs and BID AND PROPOSAL COSTS as defined in FAR 31.205-18, whether or not included in a formal IR&D program, were considered to be private expenses, but all other indirect costs of development were considered Government funded when development was required for the performance of a Government contract or subcontract. This definition is important because 10 U.S.C. § 2320(a)(2)(B) provides that, with certain exceptions, TECHNICAL DATA pertaining to items or processes developed exclusively at private expense may be submitted to the Government with markings prohibiting their disclosure. DFARS 227.471 (pre-1995 version). See Nash, *The New DOD Policy on Technical Data and Computer Software*, 8 N&CR ¶ 22 (Apr. 1994); Nash, *"Developed at Private Expense": Decrypting the Key to Proprietary Rights*, 1 N&CR ¶ 42 (May 1987).

DEVELOPMENT The systematic use of scientific and technical knowledge in the design, development, testing, or evaluation of a potential new product or service (or of an improvement in an existing product or service) for the purpose of meeting specific performance requirements or objectives. FAR 35.001. Development includes the functions of design engineering, prototyping, and engineering testing. It generally follows APPLIED RESEARCH in the RESEARCH AND DEVELOPMENT process. In the context of INDEPENDENT RESEARCH AND DEVELOPMENT, FAR 31.205-18 provides that development excludes (1) subcontracted technical effort for the sole purpose of developing an additional source for an existing product; and (2) development effort for manufacturing or production of materials, systems, processes, methods, equipment, tools, and techniques not intended for sale. DFARS 235.001 breaks development into four categories: exploratory development, advanced development, engineering and manufacturing development, and operational system development.

DEVELOPMENTAL TEST AND EVALUATION (DT&E) Testing and evaluation conducted throughout the life cycle of a program to (1) identify potential operational and technological capabilities and limitations of the alternative concepts and design options being pursued; (2) support the identification of cost-performance tradeoffs by providing analyses of the capabilities and limitations of alternatives; (3) support the identification and description of design technical risks; (4) assess progress toward meeting critical operational issues, mitigation of acquisition technical risk, achievement of manufacturing process requirements, and system maturity; (5) assess the validity of assumptions and conclusions from the analysis of alternatives; (6) provide data and analysis in support of the decision to certify the system ready for operational test and evaluation; and (7) in the case of automated information systems, support an information systems security certification prior to processing classified or sensitive data and ensure a standards conformance certification. Jones, *Glossary: Defense Acquisition Acronyms and Terms* (8th ed., Defense Systems Management College).

DEVIATION (FROM REGULATIONS) Noncompliance with a mandatory procurement regulation. FAR Subpart 1.4 sets forth the procedures to be used in obtaining the authority to deviate from the FAR. FAR 1.401 provides that deviation means any one or combination of the following: (1) issuance or use of a policy, procedure, PROVISION, CLAUSE, method, or practice of conducting acquisition actions of any kind, at any stage of the ACQUISITION PROCESS, that is inconsistent with the FAR; (2) omission of any provision or clause when the FAR requires its use; (3) use of any provision or clause with modified or alternate language not authorized by the FAR; (4) use of a provision or clause prescribed by the FAR on a "substantially as follows" or "substantially the same as" basis if such use is inconsistent with the intent, principle, or substance of the prescription or coverage on the subject matter in the FAR; (5) authorization of lesser or greater limitations on the use of any provision, clause, policy, or procedure prescribed by the FAR; and (6) issuance of any policy or procedure that governs the contracting process or otherwise controls contracting relationships that is not incorporated into agency acquisition regulations in accordance with the rules set forth in FAR Subpart 1.3. FAR 52.107 requires contracting officers to use the Authorized Deviation clauses in FAR 52.252-5 and -6 to notify offerors and contractors when a solicitation or contract contains clauses that deviate from the FAR. See DFARS Subpart 201.4 for DOD's policy on deviations. Mandatory clauses that are omitted from a contract without a proper deviation are read into the contract following the CHRISTIAN DOCTRINE. See

Cibinic & Nash, chap. 1, Sec. II., *Formation of Government Contracts* (3d ed. 1998).

DEVIATION (FROM SPECIFICATIONS) A specific written authorization, granted prior to the manufacture of an item, to depart from a particular performance or design requirement of a SPECIFICATION, drawing, or other document for a specific number of units or a specified period of time. MIL-STD-480B, *Configuration Contro—Engineering Changes, Deviations and Waivers*, July 15, 1988. Major or critical deviations may only be approved by contracting officers. If deviations are to become permanent, the specifications or drawings should be changed permanently.

DIFFERING SITE CONDITIONS Conditions at the site of the CONSTRUCTION work for which an EQUITABLE ADJUSTMENT is given under the Differing Site Conditions clause in FAR 52.236-2. This clause provides that differing site conditions are (1) subsurface or LATENT (not discoverable by ordinary inspection) physical conditions at a construction site that differ materially from the conditions indicated in the contract (commonly referred to as "Type I" differing site conditions); or (2) unknown physical conditions at the site, of an unusual nature, that differ materially from conditions ordinarily encountered and generally recognized as inhering in work of the kind provided for in the contract (commonly referred to as "Type II" differing site conditions). See McClure, *Differing Site Conditions: Evaluating the Material Difference*, 15 Pub. Cont. L.J. 138 (1984). The clause serves to take some of the risk out of bidding. For example, bidders do not have to take their own soil borings or consider how large a contingency allowance should be added to the bid price to cover the risk of unanticipated, unfavorable subsurface conditions. The Government benefits from more accurate bidding, without inflation for potentially nonexistent risks, and pays for difficult subsurface work only when such work is found to be necessary but could not reasonably have been anticipated. See Cibinic & Nash, chap. 5, *Administration of Government Contracts* (3d. ed 1995); Braude, chap. 7, *Construction Contracting* (1991); McClure, *Differing Site Conditions: Evaluating the Material Difference*, 15 Pub. Cont. L.J. 138 (1984).

DIRECT ACCESS Litigation of a contract DISPUTE before the U.S. COURT OF FEDERAL CLAIMS. Under the CONTRACT DISPUTES ACT (CDA) OF 1978, the contractor, upon receipt of a DECISION OF THE CONTRACTING OFFICER, may, within 90 days, elect to file an appeal with a BOARD OF CONTRACT APPEALS (BCA). In the alternative, the contractor, within 12 months, may bring an action directly in the U.S. Court of Federal Claims—thus obtaining "direct access" to the court without first going to a BCA. FAR 33.211 mandates that contracting officers explain this election to contractors when rendering a decision on a CLAIM. Whereas litigation before the BCAs is referred to as an "appeal," U.S. Court of Federal Claims litigation is referred to as a "direct access suit." Prior to enactment of the CDA, contractors could obtain direct access to the court only when a BCA had no jurisdiction; that is, only when the claim was not considered "ARISING UNDER THE CONTRACT." The FEDERAL COURTS ADMINISTRATION ACT, Pub. L. No. 102-572, overturned prior case law holding that there was no direct access for appeal of a TERMINATION FOR DEFAULT when no monetary claim is asserted. The U.S. Court of Federal Claims now can determine whether a termination for default was proper, even if no monetary claim is asserted.

DIRECT COST Any cost specifically identified with a particular final COST OBJECTIVE. FAR 31.202. The term is not necessarily limited to items incorporated in the end product as material or LABOR. FAR 31.202(a) provides that no final cost objective may have any cost allocated to it (see ALLOCATION OF COST) as a direct cost if other costs incurred for the same purpose in like circumstances have been included in any INDIRECT COST POOL to be allocated to that or any other final cost objective. Costs identified specifically with the contract are direct costs of the contract and are to be charged directly to the contract. All costs specifically identified with other final cost objectives are direct costs of those cost objectives and are not to be charged to the contract directly or indirectly. FAR 31.202(b) provides that for practical reasons, direct costs of minor dollar amounts may be treated as indirect costs if the accounting treatment is consistently applied and the results achieved are substantially the same as treating them as direct costs. See Cibinic & Nash, *Cost-Reimbursement Contracting* 660–68 (2d ed. 1993); Federal Acquisition Institute and Air Force Institute of Technology, *Cost Analysis, Contract Pricing Reference Guide*, vol. III (Dec. 1993).

DIRECT LABOR Labor specifically identified with a particular final COST OBJECTIVE. Manufacturing direct labor includes fabrication, assembly, inspection, and testing of the end product. Engineering direct labor consists of reliability, quality assurance, test, design, and other engineering work readily identified with the end product. Jones, *Glossary: Defense Acquisition Acronyms and Terms* (8th ed., Defense Systems Management College). Direct labor should be distinguished from indirect labor, which is labor assigned to an INDIRECT COST pool because it is identified with two or more cost objectives but not specifically allocable to any final cost objective. See Loving, *Learning Curves: Uses and Misuses in Direct Labor Hour Projections*, 35 Cont. Mgmt. 15 (Sept. 1995).

DIRECT LICENSE A LICENSE to use TECHNICAL DATA granted by the owner of the rights in that data directly to the party that will use the data. Direct licenses are permitted by DFARS 227.7103-5(d)(2)(ii), but the regulation gives no guidance on their use. They have an advantage over GOVERNMENT PURPOSE RIGHTS in that they establish a direct contractual relationship between the owner of the proprietary right and the user, without interjecting the Government agency between the two parties. DFARS 217.7503(c)(1) states that contracting officers should consider direct licensing as a means of obtaining competition for replenishment parts.

DIRECTIVE A written communication that initiates or governs action, conduct, or procedure. Directives are often issued as circulars, notices, regulations, orders, or handbooks; they include materials usually issued to multiple addresses in multiple copies for insertion in policy, administrative, or operations manuals. News releases, program announcements, catalogs, price lists, training materials, and correspondence are not included. "Directives management" means the effective and efficient development, distribution, maintenance, and use of directives. "External directive" means officially prescribed guidance such as rules, notices, and regulations issued to a primary audience outside the originating agency. "Internal directive" means officially prescribed intra-agency policy or procedure, delegation of authority, or assignment of responsibility. See also DOD DIRECTIVES SYSTEM.

DISALLOWANCE The refusal of the Government to recognize a cost as an ALLOWABLE COST. FAR Subpart 42.8 prescribes policies and procedures for issuing notices of intent to disallow costs and disallowing costs already incurred during the course of performance. DOD has a form for this purpose: DCAA Form 1, Notice of Contract Costs Suspended and/or Disapproved. DFARS 242.803. FAR 42.801 provides that at any time during the performance of a COST-REIMBURSEMENT CONTRACT, FIXED-PRICE INCENTIVE CONTRACT, FIXED-PRICE REDETERMINATION—PROSPECTIVE CONTRACT, or FIXED-PRICE REDETERMINATION—RETROACTIVE CONTRACT, the contracting officer responsible for administering the contract may issue the contractor a written notice of intent to disallow specified costs incurred or planned for incurrence. The purpose of the notice is to inform the contractor of this intent as early as practicable and provide for timely resolution of any resulting disagreement. See the Notice of Intent to Disallow Costs clause in FAR 52.242-1. FAR 42.803 provides that under cost-reimbursement contracts, costs can be disallowed after incurrence and deducted from current payments. If a contractor disagrees with a post-incurrence disallowance, the contractor may request discussions with the contracting officer or file a CLAIM under the Disputes clause at FAR 52.233-1. See Schecter & Maxwell, *Retroactive Cost Disallowances: Looking Backward and Ahead*, 93-7 CP&A Rep. 3 (July 1993).

DISBURSING OFFICER (DO) A Government officer or employee designated to pay out monies and render accounts in accordance with laws and regulations governing the disbursement of public funds. The disbursing officer must (1) disburse monies only upon, and in strict accordance with, VOUCHERs duly certified by the head of the agency or by an officer or employee duly authorized in writing to certify them; (2) examine vouchers as necessary to ascertain whether they are in proper form, duly certified and approved, and correctly computed on the basis of the facts certified; and (3) be held accountable accordingly, except that accountability for the correctness of the computations of certified vouchers lies with the certifying officer and not the disbursing officer. GAO, *Principles of Federal Appropriations Law*, vol. II, chap. 9, Part B (2d ed. 1991). See also 31 U.S.C. § 3322(a) and § 3325(a).

DISCLAIMER See EXCULPATORY CLAUSE.

DISCLOSURE STATEMENT A written description of a contractor's cost accounting practices and procedures that is filed with the cognizant administrative contracting officer, with a copy to the cognizant contract auditor. 48 C.F.R. § 9903.202-1 and -5. In general, a disclosure statement, on Form CASB-DS-1 or DS-2, must be submitted by any company or educational institution receiving CAS-COVERED CONTRACTs or subcontracts totaling more than $25 million in a cost accounting period. (Submission may also be required in certain other circumstances.) The presumed or anticipated presence of a competitive environment does not create an exemption from the requirement to submit a disclosure statement. 48 C.F.R. § 9903.202-1. After submission, disclosure statements are reviewed for adequacy by the cognizant auditor and the ADMINISTRATIVE CONTRACTING OFFICER. FAR 30.202-7. Thereafter, the disclosed cost accounting practices must be followed or a change to the disclosure statement must be requested. See Barsalona & Kaplan, *The New CASB DS-1—Potential Pitfalls & Opportunities*, 96-3 CP&A Rep. 3 (Mar. 1996); Cibinic & Nash, *Cost-Reimbursement Contracting* 633–35 (2d ed. 1993).

DISCOUNT FOR PROMPT PAYMENT An INVOICE PAYMENT reduction voluntarily offered by the contractor, in conjunction with the clause at FAR 52.232-8, Discounts for Prompt Payment, if payment is made by the Government prior to the due date. FAR 32.902. The due date is calculated from the date of the contractor's INVOICE. Prompt payment discounts may be taken only when payment is made within the contractor-specified discount period. FAR 32.903. See also PROMPT PAYMENT ACT.

DISCOVERY The process of gathering and assessing evidence that the other party to a litigation has or intends to use. Generally, discovery is either in the form of a DEPOSITION or INTERROGATORY. When the information to be discovered is privileged, it may be released subject to a PROTECTIVE ORDER. See Fed. R. Civ. P. 26(c). Discovery is permitted in appeals before the BOARDs OF CONTRACT APPEALS. See Uniform Rules 14 and 15. See Peacock, *Discovery before Boards of Contract Appeals*, 13 Pub. Cont. L.J. 1 (1982).

DISCREPANCIES INCIDENT TO SHIPMENT All deficiencies incident to shipment of GOVERNMENT PROPERTY to or from a contractor's facility; differences between the property purported to have been shipped and the property actually received. FAR 45.501. Such discrepancies include loss, damage, destruction, improper status and condition coding, errors in identity or classification, and improper consignment. FAR 45.502-2 requires a contractor to provide a statement of such discrepancy to the PROPERTY ADMINISTRATOR.

DISCRETION A power or right, conferred on Government officers by law, to act officially in certain circumstances, according to the dictates of their own judgment and conscience and uncontrolled by the judgment or conscience of anyone else. *Black's Law Dictionary* 466–67 (6th ed. 1990). To perform the actions necessary for effective contracting, ensuring compliance with the terms of contracts and safeguarding the interests of the United States in its contractual relationships, contracting officers are allowed wide latitude of discretion and business judgment. FAR 1.102, 1.602-2. Situations in which contracting officers are called on to exercise discretion include determining which PROPOSALs are in the COMPETITIVE RANGE (FAR 15.306), selecting the appropriate TYPE OF CONTRACT (FAR 16.104), deciding and settling CLAIMs (FAR 33.210), and determining when TERMINATION FOR DEFAULT or TERMINATION FOR CONVENIENCE is in the best interest of the Government (FAR Part 49). See Schnitzer & Humphrey, *The Scope of the Source Selection Official's Discretion*, 94-5 Briefing Papers (Apr. 1994); Nash, *Source Selection: The Discretion Is Not Unbounded*, 7 N&CR ¶ 28 (May 1993).

DISCRETIONARY FUNCTION Exempts the Federal Government from tort liability under the Federal Tort Claims Act, 28 U.S.C. § 2680a. It provides that the Government is not liable for any claim based upon the execution in due care of a statute or regulation as well as exercise or performance, whether or not in due care, of any discretionary function or duty. See Nash, *Postscript: The Discretionary Function Exemption*, 7 N&CR ¶ 38 (July 1993); Cibinic, *Discretionary Function Exemption: Impenetrable Shield?*, 7 N&CR ¶ 24 (May 1993). See FEDERAL TORT CLAIMS ACT.

DISCUSSION Exchanges between the Government and an offeror in the COMPETITIVE PROPOSALS process undertaken with the intent of allowing the offeror to revise its proposal. Discussions include BARGAINING. FAR 15.306(d). The primary objective of discussions is to maximize the Government's ability to obtain best value, based on the requirements and the evaluation factors set forth in the solicitation. FAR 15.306(d)(2). The contracting officer must discuss with each and every offeror still being considered for award, significant weaknesses, deficiencies, and other aspects of its proposal (such as cost, price, performance, or terms and conditions) that could be altered to enhance materially the proposal's potential for award. FAR 15.306(d)(3). If, after discussions have begun, an offeror in the COMPETITIVE RANGE is no longer considered to be among the most highly rated offerors being considered for award, that offeror may be eliminated from the competitive range whether or not all material aspects of the proposal have been discussed, or the offeror has been afforded an opportunity to submit a PROPOSAL REVISION. FAR 15.307(a). At the conclusion of discussions, each offeror still in the competitive range must be given an opportunity to submit a FINAL PROPOSAL REVISION. FAR 15.307(b). Discussions must not (1) reveal an offeror's technical solution, including technology, innovative and unique uses of COMMERCIAL ITEMs, or any information that would compromise an offeror's intellectual property to another offeror nor (2) reveal an offeror's price without that offeror's permission. FAR 15.306(e). If discussions are held with one offeror, they must be held with all offerors in the COMPETITIVE RANGE. See Cibinic & Nash, chap. 6, *Formation of Government Contracts* (3d ed. 1998); Nash, *Required Discussions: The Cost Realism Trap*, 11 N&CR ¶ 51 (Oct. 1997); Riordan, *Meaningful Discussions—How Much Is Enough?*, 61 Fed. Cont. Rep. 689 (May 23, 1994); Cibinic, *Corrections of Mistakes in Proposals: To Discuss or Not to Discuss?*, 8 N&CR ¶ 4 (Jan. 1994); Nash, *Discussion of "Weaknesses": A Little Knowledge Is a Dangerous Thing*, 7 N&CR ¶ 59 (Oct. 1993); Shnitzer, *Discussions in Negotiated Procurement*, 91-4 Briefing Papers (Mar. 1991); Feldman, *Traversing the Tightrope Between Meaningful Discussions and Improper Practices in Negotiated Federal Acquisitions: Technical Transfusion, Technical Leveling, and Auction Techniques*, 17 Pub. Cont. L.J. 211, 246 (1987).

DISMISSAL WAGES See SEVERANCE PAY.

DISPUTE A disagreement between the contractor and the contracting officer regarding the rights of the parties under a contract. Under the CONTRACT DISPUTES ACT (CDA) OF 1978, 41 U.S.C. §§ 601–613, contractors are permitted to submit CLAIMs (demands for a sum certain) against the Government. Conversely, the Government may make claims against contractors. Prior to 1995, claims could not be adjudicated by a BOARD OF CONTRACT APPEALS or the U.S. COURT OF FEDERAL CLAIMS until there had been a dispute followed by the submission of a claim. However, in *Reflectone, Inc. v. Dalton*, 60 F.3d 1572 (Fed. Cir. 1995), the rule was changed and it was held that there was no requirement that there be a dispute prior to the filing of a proper claim except where the issue was nonpayment of a VOUCHER, INVOICE, or routine request for payment. In normal circumstances, disputes are resolved through negotiation or by the use of ALTERNATIVE DISPUTE RESOLUTION procedures. FAR 33.204. If this is not possible, the dispute must become the subject of a DECISION OF THE CONTRACTING OFFICER with further resolution subject to the CDA. FAR Subpart 33.2 provides guidance to contracting officers on the handling of disputes. A dispute should be distinguished from a PROTEST: a dispute arises between a contractor and the Government during or after the performance of a contract, whereas a protest involves an offeror or prospective contractor and contests the award of the contract or the conduct of the solicitation process itself. See Tomanelli, *Fiscal Implications of Contract Disputes*, 31 Procmt. Law. 1 (Sum. 1996); Cibinic & Nash, chap. 13, *Administration of Government Contracts* (3d ed. 1995); Cibinic, *Reflections on Reflectone: Narrowing the "In Dispute" Requirement*, 9 N&CR ¶ 55

(Oct. 1995); McWhorter & Hahn, *Disputing the Meaning of a Claim: The Fallout from Dawco Construction*, 23 Pub. Cont. L.J. 451 (1994); Cibinic, *No Dispute—No Claim: The Impasse Requirement*, 7 N&CR ¶ 40 (July 1993); Bednar, chap. 13, *Construction Contracting* (1991).

DISQUALIFICATION Exclusion of an offeror from a procurement because of an impropriety in the competitive process. Offerors have been disqualified by contracting officers or by the GENERAL SERVICES ADMINISTRATION BOARD OF CONTRACT APPEALS (GSBCA) or the GENERAL ACCOUNTING OFFICE (GAO) because of a CONFLICT OF INTEREST, improper obtaining of information, or MISREPRESENTATION. See Nash & Cibinic, *Competitive Negotiation: The Source Selection Process* 392–95 (1993); Nash, *Disqualification of Offerors: A New Form of Exclusion from the Procurement Process*, 5 N&CR ¶ 17 (Mar. 1991).

DISTRIBUTION BASE A type of recorded accounting or other data common to all COST OBJECTIVEs to which costs accumulated in indirect cost pools are to be assigned. The most common bases are recorded accounting data such as direct LABOR hours and direct labor dollars. Acceptable distribution bases may also consist of non-accounting data such as floor space or meter readings. See Cibinic & Nash, *Cost-Reimbursement Contracting* 684–94 (2d ed. 1993). FAR 31.203(b) contains guidance for selecting a distribution base. See also BASE.

DOCUMENTATION See COMPUTER SOFTWARE DOCUMENTATION.

DOD See DEPARTMENT OF DEFENSE.

DOD ACQUISITION SYSTEM A single uniform system whereby all equipment, facilities, and services are planned, designed, developed, acquired, maintained, and disposed of within DOD. The system encompasses establishing and enforcing policies and practices that govern acquisitions, to include documenting mission needs and establishing performance goals and baselines; determining and prioritizing resource requirements for ACQUISITION PROGRAMs; planning and executing acquisition programs; directing and controlling the ACQUISITION REVIEW process; developing and assessing logistics implications; contracting; monitoring the execution status of approved programs; and reporting to the Congress. Jones, *Glossary: Defense Acquisition Acronyms and Terms* (8th ed., Defense Systems Management College).

DOD FAR SUPPLEMENT (DFARS) See DEPARTMENT OF DEFENSE FAR SUPPLEMENT.

DOE See DEPARTMENT OF ENERGY.

DOI See DEPARTMENT OF THE INTERIOR.

DOJ See DEPARTMENT OF JUSTICE.

DOL See DEPARTMENT OF LABOR.

DOMESTIC CONSTRUCTION MATERIAL Material that is given preference under the BUY AMERICAN ACT because it is either (1) unmanufactured CONSTRUCTION material mined or produced in the United States; or (2) construction material manufactured in the United States, if the cost of its components mined, produced, or manufactured in the United States exceeds 50 percent of the cost of all its components. FAR 25.201. The cost of each component includes cost of transportation to the place of incorporation into the construction material and any applicable duty (whether or not a duty-free entry certificate is issued). Components of foreign origin are treated as domestic if they are of the same class or kind for which it has been determined that the material is not mined, produced, or manufactured in the United States in sufficient and reasonably available commercial quantities of a satisfactory quality. See Ginsburg & Patin, chap. 2, *Construction Contracting* 116 20 (1991).

DOMESTIC END PRODUCT A product that is given preference under the BUY AMERICAN ACT because it is either (1) an unmanufactured end product mined or produced in the United States; or (2) an end product manufactured in the United States, if the cost of its components mined, produced, or manufactured in the United States exceeds 50 percent of the cost of all its components. FAR 25.101. The cost of each component includes cost of transportation to the place of incorporation into the end product and any applicable duty (whether or not a duty-free certificate is issued). Components of foreign origin are treated as domestic if they are of the same class or kind for which it has been determined either (1) that domestic preference would be inconsistent with the public interest; or (2) that they are not mined, produced, or manufactured in the United States in sufficient and reasonably available commercial quantities of a satisfactory quality. Components of Canadian origin are treated as domestic by NASA and DOD. FAR 25.103; NFS 18-25.103. See Cibinic & Nash, chap. 10, Sec. IV., *Formation of Government Contracts* (3d ed. 1998); Peckinpaugh &

Marcotte, *Confusing, Inconsistent Domestic Preference Rules: Changes can Streamline the Process*, 35 Cont. Mgmt. 10 (June 1995); Kenney et al., *Domestic Preference Provisions/Edition II*, 94-3 Briefing Papers (Feb. 1994).

DOMESTIC PREFERENCE See BALANCE OF PAYMENTS PROGRAM; BUY AMERICAN ACT; CARGO PREFERENCE ACTS; CARIBBEAN BASIN ECONOMIC RECOVERY ACT; DOMESTIC END PRODUCT; TRADE AGREEMENTS ACT OF 1979.

DONATION A gift of cash, property, or services to a charitable organization. FAR 31.205-8 provides that the costs of donations are UNALLOWABLE COSTs. See Cibinic & Nash, *Cost-Reimbursement Contracting* 868–70 (2d ed. 1993).

DOT See DEPARTMENT OF TRANSPORTATION.

DOWN-SELECT A two-step procurement technique where, as a first step, the number of competitors are reduced by preliminary screening, and in the second step, a best value procurement is conducted between the remaining competitors. FAR 15.102 provides for the use of an advisory multi-step source selection when appropriate. In this procedure, the agency must advise those respondents considered not to be viable competitors of the basis for such an opinion, but the respondent may still participate in the resultant acquisition if it so chooses. The FEDERAL AVIATION ADMINISTRATION also uses a SCREENING procedure to make down selects. See also PREQUALIFICATION. See Nash & Cibinic, 10 N&CR Datolino (May 1996).

DRAWINGS A set of documents giving the details of manufacture or construction. Drawings typically contain dimensions and tolerances to be followed, materials or components to be used, testing requirements, and other specific information. They are frequently called DESIGN SPECIFICATIONS.

DRUG-FREE WORKPLACE A site for the performance of work under a specific contract, at which employees of the contractor are prohibited from engaging in the unlawful manufacturing, distribution, dispensing, possession, or use of a controlled substance. FAR 23.503. FAR Subpart 23.5 implements the Drug-Free Workplace Act of 1988, 41 U.S.C. § 701 et seq., and applies to domestic Government contracts of $100,000 or more. To be considered a responsible source (see RESPONSIBILITY), a contractors must certify that it will provide a drug-free workplace, pursuant to the Certification Regarding a Drug-Free Workplace solicitation provision in FAR 52.223-5. Compliance with the certification entails, among other things, posting notices to employees, establishing drug-free awareness programs, requiring notification by employees of related convictions, and making a good-faith effort to maintain a drug-free workplace. Failure to comply may result in suspension of payments, TERMINATION FOR DEFAULT, or SUSPENSION or DEBARMENT of the contractor. See the Drug-Free Workplace clause in FAR 52.223-6. See also Pniewski, *A Drug-Free Transit Workplace*, 33 Cont. Mgmt. 10 (Mar. 1993); Arnavas & Ganther, *The Drug-Free Workplace*, 89-9 Briefing Papers (Aug. 1989).

DRY BULK CARRIER A vessel used primarily for carrying shipload lots of homogeneous, unmarked, nonliquid cargoes such as grain, coal, cement, and lumber. FAR 47.501. This term is used in connection with implementing the policies of the CARGO PREFERENCE ACTS and the Merchant Marine Act of 1936, which give preference to U.S.-FLAG VESSELs when ocean transportation of supplies is required. See the Preference for Privately Owned U.S.-Flag Commercial Vessels clause in FAR 52.247-64, which requires contractors to compute shipments in such vessels separately in determining whether they have met the requirement that at least 50 percent of the gross tonnage shipped be in U.S.-flag vessels.

DRY CARGO LINER A vessel used for the carriage of heterogeneous marked cargoes in parcel lots. However, any cargo may be carried in these vessels, including cargoes of dry bulk items or, when carried in deep tanks, bulk liquids such as petroleum and vegetable oils. FAR 47.501. This term is used in connection with implementing the policies of the CARGO PREFERENCE ACTS and the Merchant Marine Act of 1936, which give preference to U.S.-FLAG VESSELs when ocean transportation of supplies is required. See the Preference for Privately Owned U.S.-Flag Commercial Vessels clause in FAR 52.247-64, which requires contractors to compute shipments in such vessels separately in determining whether they have met the requirement that at least 50 percent of the gross tonnage shipped be in U.S.-flag vessels.

DUAL SOURCE The existence of two or more sources for the same product or service. DFARS 215.804-3 provides that COST OR PRICING DATA need not be obtained because ADEQUATE PRICE COMPETITION normally exists in dual source programs where prices are solicited across a full range of step quantities, normally including a

0-to-100-percent split, between two or more offerors that are individually capable of producing the full quantity.

DUE PROCESS OF LAW A guarantee, found in the Fifth and Fourteenth amendments of the U.S. Constitution, of fundamentally fair treatment by the Government. *Substantive* due process requires that no person be arbitrarily denied life, liberty, or property by Government action. *Procedural* due process includes notice by the Government and an opportunity to be heard by the Government prior to the infringement of a liberty or property interest by the Government. Procedural requirements increase with the importance of the interest taken. *Black's Law Dictionary* 500–01 (6th ed. 1990). In Government contracting, the issue of due process arises whenever a contractor claims that it has been denied a liberty or property right without proper procedures. Such claims may arise in DEBARMENT and SUSPENSION actions, TERMINATION FOR DEFAULT, and nonresponsibility (see RESPONSIBILITY) determinations. See, for example, *Old Dominion Dairy Products, Inc. v. Secretary of Defense*, 631 F.2d 953 (D.C. Cir. 1980), in which the court found that a liberty interest was infringed without due process in a nonresponsibility determination. For a discussion of this case, see Nash, *Postscript: The Due Process Requirement in Responsibility Determinations*, 4 N&CR ¶ 7 (Jan. 1990); Nash, *Integrity-Based Nonresponsibility Determinations: Why Keep the CO in the Dark?*, 1 N&CR ¶ 45 (June 1987).

DURESS A condition in which one party is induced by a wrongful act or threat of another party to enter into a contract under circumstances depriving the first party of the exercise of its free will. Like "undue influence," duress includes conduct that overpowers a party's will and coerces or constrains performance of an act that otherwise would not have been performed. *Black's Law Dictionary* 504 (6th ed. 1990). Duress is also known as business compulsion. The elements of duress in Government contracting are (1) threat of economic harm which is improper as a violation of the contracting officer's DUTY OF GOOD FAITH AND FAIR DEALING; and (2) a showing that the contractor's will was overborne (i.e., that the contractor accepted contract terms because circumstances permitted no alternative). See Cibinic & Nash, *Administration of Government Contracts* 1234–37 (3d ed. 1995); *Williston On Contracts* § 1617 (3d ed. 1967); Nash, *Hard Bargaining or Duress: Walking a Narrow Line*, 3 N&CR ¶ 34 (Apr. 1989). Theoretically, duress, UNCONSCIONABILITY, and undue influence may differ, but all are aimed at unconscionable conduct by one party that may permit the other party to avoid a contract (see AVOIDANCE

OF CONTRACT). See *Murray On Contracts* § 93 (3d ed. 1990); Harley, *Economic Duress and Unconscionability: How Fair Must the Government Be?,* 18 Pub. Cont. L.J. 76 (1988).

DURING THE CONDUCT OF A PROCUREMENT The period that begins on the earliest date on which an identifiable, specific action is taken for a particular procurement and concludes on the AWARD or MODIFICATION of a contract or the cancellation of the procurement. The term included evaluation of OFFERs, SOURCE SELECTION, and conduct of NEGOTIATIONs. It defined the period during which the PROCUREMENT INTEGRITY rules applied before the Procurement Integrity Act was amended in 1996, but it no longer has any relevance. Under that Act, each award or each modification constituted a separate procurement action—that is, a separate period during which the prohibitions and requirements regarding procurement integrity applied. Some agencies promulgated additional guidance on the determination of the beginning date of this period.

DUTY OF GOOD FAITH AND FAIR DEALING An implied obligation of all contracting parties to treat each other fairly during the performance and enforcement of a contract. *Restatement (Second) of Contracts* § 205 (1981). "Good faith" is defined at U.C.C. § 1-201 as "honesty in fact in the conduct or transaction concerned." When this implied duty is discussed in the context of a Government contract dispute, it is usually in reference to the Government's DUTY TO COOPERATE. See Nash, *The Duty of Good Faith and Fair Dealing: An Emerging Concept?,* 3 N&CR ¶ 78 (Nov. 1989).

DUTY OF VERIFICATION The contracting officer's obligation, when a MISTAKE in a BID or PROPOSAL is suspected, to call the mistake or the affected portion of the offer to the offeror's attention, ask for verification that no mistake was made and allow the offeror either to correct the offer before award is made or to withdraw it altogether if a mistake is identified. FAR 14.407 discusses the procedures to be followed for bids. FAR 15.306(b) references FAR 14.407 for the procedures to be followed when a mistake in a proposal is suspected. Requests for verification must inform the offeror of the facts that led the contracting officer to suspect a mistake. If the contracting officer fails to seek verification, the Government may be subject to claims for PRICE ADJUSTMENT or the contractor may use a claimed mistake as a basis for avoiding performance obligations. See Cibinic & Nash, chap. 5, Sec. IV. & chap. 6, *Formation of Government Contracts* (3d ed. 1998).

DUTY TO COOPERATE An implied duty of a contracting party to cooperate with the other party to facilitate the performance of the contract. This duty is most frequently used to hold the Government liable for a CONSTRUCTIVE CHANGE when the Government does not assist the contractor. See Nash, chap. 12, *Government Contract Changes* (2d ed. 1989 & Supp. 1993). Under *Restatement (Second) of Contracts* § 205 (1981), this duty is defined as one aspect of the DUTY OF GOOD FAITH AND FAIR DEALING. See Cibinic & Nash, *Administration of Government Contracts* 297–307 (3d ed. 1995).

DUTY TO DISCLOSE INFORMATION See SUPERIOR KNOWLEDGE.

DUTY TO INQUIRE See DUTY TO SEEK CLARIFICATION.

DUTY TO PROCEED The obligation of a Government contractor to continue to prosecute work under a Government contract or risk TERMINATION FOR DEFAULT (see FAILURE TO MAKE PROGRESS). The Disputes clause in FAR 52.233-1 states that the contractor "shall proceed diligently with performance of this contract, pending final resolution of any request for relief, claim, appeal, or action ARISING UNDER THE CONTRACT, and comply with any decision of the Contracting Officer." Alternate I to that clause, used in MAJOR SYSTEM contracts, requires the contractor to proceed in the face of disputes arising under the contract or RELATING TO THE CONTRACT. With regard to a CHANGE ORDER, the contractor must, except under cost or fund limitations, continue performance of the contract as changed. The Changes—Fixed-Price clause in FAR 52.243-1 (for supply and services contracts) states: "Failure to agree to any adjustment shall be a dispute under the Disputes clause. However, nothing in this clause shall excuse the Contractor from proceeding with the contract as changed." See also the Commencement, Prosecution, and Completion of Work clause in FAR 52.211-10. Exceptions to the duty to proceed are BREACH OF CONTRACT by the Government, CARDINAL CHANGE, and IMPRACTICABILITY. However, it is uncertain whether these exceptions apply to the Alternate I clause. See Cibinic & Nash, *Administration of Government Contracts* 702–17 (3d ed. 1995); Nash, chap. 6, *Government Contract Changes* (2d ed. 1989 & Supp. 1993).

DUTY TO SEEK CLARIFICATION The duty of an offeror to request the guidance of the contracting officer when a patent AMBIGUITY, obvious omission, or drastic conflict is found in the contract language.

The offeror's or contractor's failure to seek clarification in such circumstances is a valid Government defense to a CLAIM for EQUITABLE ADJUSTMENT because of ambiguous specifications. See Cibinic & Nash, *Administration of Government Contracts* 229–37 (3d ed. 1995).

E

EARNED VALUE The budgeted cost of work successfully performed by a contractor. Under cost accounting practice, the computation of earned value is a method used by management to keep track of project status. Recognizing that cost data alone—or schedule data alone—can lead to distorted perceptions of performance, the technique is based on regularly comparing the budgeted cost of work performed with the actual cost of work performed. Thus, if the contractor has earned only one third of the value of the contract (performed only one third of the budgeted work) but has incurred one half of the contract budgeted costs, the computation will show that the contract is in a loss position. See *DCAA Contract Audit Manual* 11-205. This computation is used, in particular to determine if PROGRESS PAYMENTS should be made at the contractual rate or at a reduced rate to reflect the fact that they have not been earned. See OMB Circular No. A-11, Part 3, *Planning, Budgeting and Acquisition of Fixed Assets*, July 1996; GAO, *Principles of Budgeting for Capital Asset Acquisitions* 10 Budget of the United States Government, Fiscal Year 1998 (1997).

ECONOMIC DURESS See DURESS.

ECONOMIC ORDER QUANTITY (EOQ) A quantity of SUPPLIES that will result in a TOTAL COST and unit cost most advantageous to the Government, where practicable, and does not exceed the quantity reasonably expected to be required by the agency. 10 U.S.C. § 2384a and 41 U.S.C. § 253f require agencies to procure economic order quantities and to include a provision in solicitations inviting offerors to state an opinion on whether the quantity of supplies being procured is economically advantageous to the Government. This requirement is implemented by FAR Subpart 7.2, and the Economic Purchase Quantity—Supplies solicitation provision is set forth in FAR 52.207-4. Economic order quantities can also be procured in advance of the procurement of multiyear items under the advance acquisition procedures used in MULTIYEAR CONTRACTING. See FAR 17.101.

ECONOMIC PLANNING COSTS Costs of generalized long-range management planning that addresses the future overall development of the contractor's business and may take into account the eventual possibility of economic dislocations or fundamental alterations in those markets in which the contractor currently does business. FAR 31.205-12. Economic planning costs do not include ORGANIZATION COSTS or reorganization costs. Economic planning costs are allowable (see ALLOWABLE COST) as indirect costs to be properly allocated. RESEARCH AND DEVELOPMENT costs and engineering costs designed to lead to new products for sale to the general public are not allowable under this cost principle. See Cibinic & Nash, *Cost-Reimbursement Contracting* 778–79 (2d ed. 1993).

ECONOMIC PRICE ADJUSTMENT (EPA) See FIXED-PRICE CONTRACT WITH ECONOMIC PRICE ADJUSTMENT.

ECONOMICALLY DISADVANTAGED INDIVIDUALS SOCIALLY DISADVANTAGED INDIVIDUALS whose ability to compete in the free enterprise system is impaired due to diminished opportunities to obtain capital and credit as compared with others in the same line of business who are not socially disadvantaged. FAR 19.001. Individuals who certify that they are members of named groups (Black Americans, Hispanic Americans, NATIVE AMERICANS, ASIAN-PACIFIC AMERICANS, SUBCONTINENT-ASIAN AMERICANS) are to be considered both socially and economically disadvantaged. FAR 19.001. Businesses owned by such individuals are given special preferences in Government procurement. See SMALL DISADVANTAGED BUSINESS CONCERN.

ECONOMIES OF SCALE Reductions in the unit cost of an end product that result from the production of additional units. Economies of scale stem from increased specialization of LABOR as the volume of output increases, decreased unit costs of materials resulting from volume discounts, better utilization of management, acquisition of more efficient equipment, and greater use of by-products. Jones, *Glossary: Defense Acquisition Acronyms and Terms* (8th ed., Defense Systems Management College). Because the costs of contract administration are reduced, the Government may also realize economies of scale when purchasing increased quantities from one contractor.

ECONOMY ACT See INTERAGENCY ACQUISITION.

EDUCATION COSTS Costs of providing education for employees. FAR 31.205-44 specifies that such costs incurred by contractors are

ALLOWABLE COSTs with some limitations. See also TRAINING COSTS. See Cibinic & Nash, *Cost-Reimbursement Contracting* 840–43 (2d ed. 1993).

EFFECTIVE COMPETITION Used in the context of a MAJOR SYSTEMS ACQUISITION, a market condition that exists when two or more contractors, acting independently, actively contend for the Government's business in a manner that ensures that the Government will be offered the lowest cost or price alternative or best technical design meeting its requirements. FAR 34.001. In a major systems acquisition, the program manager is required to both promote FULL AND OPEN COMPETITION and sustain effective competition between alternative major system concepts and sources, as long as it is economically beneficial and practicable to do so. FAR 34.005-1.

EICHLEAY FORMULA The prevalent method for calculating extended and unabsorbed HOME OFFICE overhead when the Government has delayed the work on CONSTRUCTION contracts. In *Eichleay Corp.*, ASBCA 5183, 60-2 BCA ¶ 2688, *mot. for reconsid.*, 61-1 BCA ¶ 2894, the ARMED SERVICES BOARD OF CONTRACT APPEALS found the formula a "realistic method of allocation of continuing home office expenses." Application of the formula entails a three-step process. First, the ratio of contract billings to total billings for the actual contract period is multiplied by the total overhead for the contract period, to arrive at the overhead, or INDIRECT COST, allocable to the contract. Next, the allocable overhead is divided by the number of days of actual performance to determine the daily contract overhead. Finally, the daily contract overhead is multiplied by the number of days of Government caused delay to arrive at the amount claimed for UNABSORBED OVERHEAD. This formula is used in lieu of computing the actual costs incurred. There has been considerable dispute and litigation on the conditions that must be proved to justify recovery of costs using this formula. See Shapiro & Worthington, *Use of the Eichleay Formula to Calculate Unabsorbed Overhead for Government-Caused Delay Under Manufacturing Contracts*, 25 Pub. Cont. L.J. 513 (1996); Nash, *Postscript: The "Eichleay" Formula*, 10 N&CR ¶ 56 (Nov. 1996); McGeehin & Strouss, *Learning from Eichleay: Unabsorbed Overhead Claims in State and Local Jurisdictions*, 25 Pub. Cont. L.J. 351 (1995); Kauffman & Holman, *The Eichleay Formula: A Resilient Means For Recovery of Unabsorbed Overhead*, 24 Pub. Cont. L.J. 319 (1995); Cibinic, *Unabsorbed Overhead on Supply Contracts: An Idea Whose Time Has Come*, 8 N&CR ¶ 45 (Aug. 1994); Schechter & West, *Recovery of*

Home Office Overhead—Resurrection of the Eichleay Formula, 94-3 CP&A Rep. 3 (Mar. 1994); Nash, *The "Eichleay" Formula: Extended vs. Unabsorbed Home Office Overhead*, 6 N&CR ¶ 68 (Dec. 1992); Nash, *The Eichleay Formula: Another Viewpoint*, 6 N&CR ¶ 7 (Jan. 1992); Nash, *The "Eichleay" Formula: Does It Spell Relief?*, 5 N&CR ¶ 62 (Nov. 1991); Cibinic & Braude, chap. 9, *Construction Contracting* 751–64 (1991).

8(A) PROGRAM A program, established by section 8(a) of the SMALL BUSINESS ACT, 15 U.S.C. § 637(a), authorizing the SMALL BUSINESS ADMINISTRATION (SBA) to enter into contracts with procuring agencies and award subcontracts for performing those contracts to firms eligible for program participation. The SBA's subcontractors, which must be SMALL DISADVANTAGED BUSINESS CONCERNs, are referred to as "8(a) contractors." FAR 19.000; FAR 19.801. The program has been in operation since the late 1960s but has met with mixed success. In 1988 Congress sought to make small disadvantaged businesses more competitive and to curb abuse of the 8(a) program. Those reforms, found in Pub. L. No. 100-656, 15 U.S.C. § 631, (1) require competition among 8(a) firms for manufacturing contracts exceeding $5 million; (2) require such competition for service contracts and nonmanufacturing contracts exceeding $3 million; (3) require the SBA to establish business activity targets for businesses that have been in the program for five years; (4) authorize contracting officers to assess "liquidated damages" against prime contractors that fail to meet small disadvantaged business subcontracting goals; and (5) prohibit SBA employees from holding stock in 8(a) firms for two years after leaving the SBA. See Magnotti, *Politics and the SBA's 8(a) Program*, 28 Cont. Mgmt. 8 (June 1988). The Supreme Court in *Adarand Constructors, Inc. v. Pena*, 515 U.S. 200 (1995), however, appears to call this program into question. *Adarand* held that "all racial classifications, imposed by whatever Federal, State, or local Governmental actor, must be analyzed by a reviewing court under strict scrutiny. In other words, such classifications are constitutional only if they are narrowly tailored measures that further compelling governmental interests." All federal agencies have been advised to review their AFFIRMATIVE ACTION PROGRAMs in light of this decision. See Thomas, *Post-Adarand Challenges to Federal Minority Contracting Programs: Why They Are Failing*, 38 Gov't Contractor ¶ 321 (July 10, 1996); Weckstein & Katz, *Adarand Case Prompts Review of Set-Aside Programs*, 35 Cont. Mgmt. 19 (Sept. 1995).

ELECTRONIC DATA INTERCHANGE (EDI) A technique for electronically transferring information between computers. FAR 4.501. EDI is utilized in acquisitions in transmitting solicitations, receiving bids and proposals, and notifying competing contractors of changes to the source selection process. The use of EDI is encouraged for more efficient handling of acquisition procedures. The federal protocol for the structure, format, and content of EDIs was established by the American National Standards Institute (ANSI) and is referred to as ANSI X12. See FAR Subpart 4.5. See also Godes, *Government Contracting on the Internet: Abandoning FACNET as the Government's Network for Electronic Commerce*, 26 Pub. Cont. L.J. 663 (1997); Yukins, *Managing Electronic Commerce on the Federal Acquisition Computer Network (FACNET)*, 27 Nat'l Cont. Mgmt. J., Issue No. 1, p. 35 (1996); Reams et al., *Electronic Contracting Law* (1993–94 ed.).

ELECTRONIC FUNDS TRANSFER (EFT) The direct payment to contractors by the Government through electronic transfer of funds (as opposed to payment by paper check) through either the Automated Clearing House subject to the banking laws of the United States or the Federal Reserve Wire Transfer System. Payment by EFT is now the Government's preferred method of payment in normal contracting situations. 31 U.S.C. § 3332(e) makes payment by EFT mandatory except for contracts that do not have an account at a domestic United States financial institution or an authorized payment agent. This exemption is applicable until January 1, 1999. After January 1, 1999, all federal payments must be made by EFT unless the requirement is waived by the Secretary of the Treasury. See generally FAR Subpart 32.11; FAR 32.1101; FAR 52.232-33 and -34.

ELECTRONIC INDUSTRIES ASSOCIATION (EIA) A national trade organization representing the entire spectrum of electronics manufacturers in the United States. Founded in 1924 as the Radio Manufacturers Association, the EIA is organized along product lines, with groups and divisions providing specialized attention to issues facing the electronics industries. EIA departments provide services in marketing statistics, engineering standards, legislative and regulatory information, and public affairs. [EIA, 2500 Wilson Boulevard, Arlington, VA 22201; (703) 907-7500]

EMERGING SMALL BUSINESS A small business concern whose size is not greater than 50 percent of the numerical size standard for small businesses in the STANDARD INDUSTRIAL CLASSIFICATION code assigned to a contracting opportunity. FAR 19.1002.

Smaller acquisitions in four "designated industry groups" are SET ASIDE for emerging small businesses (FAR 19.1006(c)), and the progress of these firms is being measured as part of the SMALL BUSINESS COMPETITIVENESS DEMONSTRATION PROGRAM. The four designated groups consist of (1) construction, excluding dredging; (2) refuse systems and related services, including portable sanitation services; (3) architectural and engineering services (including surveying and mapping); and (4) nonnuclear ship repair (including overhauls and conversions). FAR 19.1005(a). This program, during calendar years 1989 through 1997, is intended to (1) show the competitive capabilities of small business on certain classes of unrestricted Government contracts, and (2) target for expansion small business set-asides in industries that historically demonstrate low small business involvement. See FAR Subpart 19.10; DFARS Subpart 219.10.

EMPLOYEE, MORALE, HEALTH, WELFARE, FOOD SERVICE, AND DORMITORY COSTS AND CREDITS Aggregate costs incurred on activities designed to improve working conditions, employer-employee relations, employee morale, and employee performance, less the income generated by these activities. FAR 31.205-13(a). These costs are allowable, with the exception of the costs of gifts and the costs of recreation (except for the costs of employees' participation in company-sponsored sports teams or employee organizations designed to improve company loyalty, teamwork, or physical fitness). FAR 31.205-13(b) and (c). Losses from operating food and dormitory services are allowable only if the contractor's objective is to operate them on a break-even basis. FAR 31.205-13(d). See Nibley & Thompson, *The Allowability of Employee Morale & Entertainment Costs After FASA: Questions Remain*, 95-11 CP&A Rep. 3 (Nov. 1995); Cibinic & Nash, *Cost-Reimbursement Contracting* 833–36 (2d ed. 1993).

EMPLOYEE STOCK OWNERSHIP PLAN (ESOP) An individual stock bonus plan designed specifically to invest in the stock of the employer company. FAR 31.205-6(j)(8) specifies when the costs of such plans are ALLOWABLE COSTs. See Cibinic & Nash, *Cost-Reimbursement Contracting* 809–11 (2d ed. 1993).

EMPOWERMENT CONTRACTING A program that grants qualified large and small businesses appropriate incentives to encourage business activity in AREAs OF GENERAL ECONOMIC DISTRESS. These incentives may include a price or evaluation credit when assessing offers for Government contracts in unrestricted competitions. To qualify, businesses must employ a significant number of residents from an area of general economic distress, have a significant physical presence in that area, or have a direct impact on generating significant economic activity in that area. The stated purpose of the program is to strengthen the economy and to improve the efficiency of the federal procurement system by encouraging business development that expands the industrial base and increases competition. This program is premised on the belief that fostering growth of Government contractors in economically distressed communities and ensuring that those contractors become viable businesses for the long term will promote economy and efficiency in federal procurement and help to empower these communities. Exec. Order No. 13005, 61 Fed. Reg. 26069 (May 24, 1996).

ENERGY EFFICIENCY STANDARD For the purposes of energy conservation regulations, a performance standard that prescribes a minimum level of energy efficiency for a covered product (including air conditioners, clothes washers and dryers, dishwashers, refrigerators and freezers, kitchen ranges and ovens, water heaters, humidifiers and dehumidifiers, and televisions) and includes any other requirements that the Secretary of Energy may prescribe under 42 U.S.C. § 6295(c). FAR 23.202. FAR 23.203 provides that agencies should consider using such standards in procuring consumer products covered by this regulation.

ENGINEERING AND MANUFACTURING DEVELOPMENT The third phase of the DOD MAJOR SYSTEM ACQUISITION process in which the SYSTEM is fully designed and tested. Approval must be obtained to enter this phase. See paragraph 1.5.3 of DOD Regulation 5000.2-R, *Mandatory Procedures for Major Defense Acquisition Programs (MDAPs) and Major Automated Information System (MAIS) Acquisition Programs*, Mar. 15, 1996. Its objectives are to (1) translate a promising design approach into a stable, producible, and cost-effective system design, (2) validate the manufacturing or production process, and (3) demonstrate through testing that the system will meet stated requirements. See DFARS 235.001-006.

ENGINEERING CHANGE PROPOSAL (ECP) A proposal initiated by either party to make CHANGEs to the drawings or specifications of a contract. Under the DOD CONFIGURATION MANAGEMENT system prescribed in Military Standards 480B and 481B, both July 15, 1988, contractors must prepare ECPs using either DD Form 1692 or 1693. Both DOD and NASA prescribe an Engineering Change

Proposals clause (DFARS 252.243-7000; NFS 18-52.243-70) that permits the CONTRACTING OFFICER to require the contractor to prepare an ECP documenting the effect of a change being initiated by the Government. See Nash, *Government Contract Changes* 7-3 through 7-13 (2d ed. 1989 & Supp. 1993).

ENGINEERING DATA COMPUTER ASSISTED RETRIEVAL SYSTEM (EDCARS) A program to automate the engineering data repositories at Air Logistics Centers. This program will be replaced by the JOINT ENGINEERING DATA MANAGEMENT INFORMATION AND CONTROL SYSTEM (JEDMICS) in the fiscal year 1996–97 time frame. [<http://wpaftb1.wpafb.af.mil/edcars.html>]

ENTERTAINMENT Amusement, diversion, and social activity such as meals, outings, sporting events, and theatrical performances. FAR 31.205-14 specifies that the costs of entertainment incurred by contractors are UNALLOWABLE COSTs. See also GRATUITY. See Cibinic & Nash, *Cost-Reimbursement Contracting* 776–77 (2d ed. 1993).

ENTITLEMENT The right of a contractor to recover additional compensation from the Government during the performance of a contract. In order to recover such compensation, a contractor must prove that the Government has promised to pay the amount if some event occurred or that the Government is at fault in the administration of the contract (entitlement) and then must prove the amount it has been injured (QUANTUM). In order to conserve resources, BOARDs OF CONTRACT APPEALS frequently permit the parties to litigate only entitlement initially. See BIFURCATION OF ENTITLEMENT AND QUANTUM.

ENTITY OF THE GOVERNMENT Any entity of the legislative or judicial branches, any executive agency, military department, Government corporation, or independent establishment; the U.S. Postal Service; or any NONAPPROPRIATED-FUND INSTRUMENTALITY of the Armed Forces. FAR 8.701. Such entities must purchase supplies and services from nonprofit agencies serving people who are BLIND OR SEVERELY DISABLED under the procedures of FAR Subpart 8.7.

EQUAL ACCESS TO JUSTICE ACT (EAJA) An Act, 5 U.S.C. § 504 and 28 U.S.C. § 2412, permitting small contractors to recover ATTORNEY'S FEES and expenses in litigation against the Government. Under what is called the "American Rule," the parties bear their own litigation expenses; and this rule applies generally when contractors litigate contract disputes. The EAJA is an exception to this rule. It permits small contractors to recover if the contractor prevails in the adjudication (see PREVAILING PARTY), the Government's position is not SUBSTANTIALLY JUSTIFIED, and no special circumstances make an award unjust. See Kinlin, *Equal Access To Justice Act*, 16 Pub. Cont. L.J. 266 (1986). The remedies provided by the BOARDs OF CONTRACT APPEALS are addressed in 5 U.S.C. § 504, whereas the remedies given by courts, including the COURT OF FEDERAL CLAIMS, are covered by 28 U.S.C. § 2412. See Page & Jockisch, *Timeliness for EAJA Application: The Dilemma of a Bifurcated Appeal*, 31 Procmt. Law. 20 (Win. 1996); Richmond, *Eligibility Under the Equal Access to Justice Act in Government Contracts Litigation*, 1995 Army Law. 17 (Mar. 1995); Sisk, *The Essentials of the Equal Access to Justice Act: Court Awards of Attorney's Fees for Unreasonable Government Conduct (Pt. 2)*, 56 La L. Rev. 1 (Fall 1995); Nash, *Postscript III: Equal Access to Justice Act*, 8 N&CR ¶ 61 (Nov. 1994); Nash, *Postscript II: Equal Access to Justice Act*, 8 N&CR ¶ 51 (Sept. 1994); Tiger & Garden, *Attorney Fees and Expenses Under the Equal Access to Justice Act in Government Contract Claims Cases*, 34 Cont. Mgmt. 18 (May 1994); Kinlin, *A Current Guide to Recovery under the Equal Access to Justice Act*, 1989 A.B.A. Sec. Pub. Cont. L.; Nash, *Postscript: Equal Access to Justice Act*, 5 N&CR ¶ 61 (Nov. 1991); Tobin & Stiffler, *Recovering Legal Fees under EAJA/Edition II*, 91-7 Briefing Papers (June 1991); Nash, *Equal Access to Justice Act: A Statute That Is Working Well*, 2 N&CR ¶ 20 (Apr. 1988).

EQUAL EMPLOYMENT OPPORTUNITY (EEO) The treatment of employees and applicants for employment that must be accorded by contractors during the performance of their contracts. The basic requirements are set forth in Exec. Order No. 11246, 30 Fed. Reg. 12319 (Sept. 24, 1965), as amended. See FAR Subpart 22.8 and the Equal Opportunity clause in FAR 52.222-26. During performance of Government contracts, contractors must (1) not discriminate against any employee or applicant for employment because of race, color, religion, sex, or national origin; (2) take AFFIRMATIVE ACTION to ensure that applicants are employed and that employees are treated during employment without regard to their race, color, religion, sex, or national origin; (3) post in conspicuous places available to employees and applicants for employment the notices to be provided by the contracting officer that explain equal opportunity; (4) state that all qualified applicants will receive consideration for employment without regard to race, color, religion, sex, or national origin; (5) send, to each LABOR union or representative of workers with which it has a collective bargaining agreement or other contract or understanding, the notice to be provided by the contracting officer advising the labor union or workers' representative of the contractor's commitments; and (6) comply with Exec. Order No. 11246 and the rules, regulations, and orders of the Secretary of Labor. See Cibinic & Nash, chap. 10, Sec. VI., *Formation of Government Contracts* (3d ed. 1998); Seymour, *A Point of View: Why Executive Order 11246 Should Be Preserved*, 11 Employee Rel. L.J. 568 (1986).

EQUITABLE ADJUSTMENT A fair price adjustment under a contract clause for changed work, including an adjustment in profit, a change in the delivery schedule, if appropriate, and a change in any other affected terms of the contract. Equitable adjustments can result in price increases for the contractor for increased work or price reductions for the Government for reduced work. The major contract clause that calls for equitable adjustments is the Changes clause, FAR 52.243-1 through -5. However, the term is a standard contract term that is used in many other clauses. Equitable adjustments are distinguished from DAMAGES, which are given in the absence of a contract clause calling for an equitable adjustment. See Nash, *Pricing Defective Specification Claims: Does the Theory Matter?,* 8 N&CR ¶ 1 (Jan. 1994). The basic formula for an equitable adjustment is an estimate of the difference between (1) what it would have reasonably cost to perform the work as originally required and (2) what it will reasonably cost to perform the work as changed. See Nash, *Equitable Adjustments for Deleted Work: The Severability Exception to the "Would Have Cost" Rule*, 11 N&CR ¶ 39 (Aug. 1997); Nash, *Postscript: Fixed Overhead in Equitable Adjustments*, 11 N&CR ¶ 27 (June 1997); Nash, *Pricing Equitable Adjustments: How to Deal With Fixed Overhead Costs*, 11 N&C ¶ 15 (Apr. 1997); Farber & Evan, *The Allowability of Costs Incurred in the Preparation of Requests for Equitable Adjustments After Reflectone*, 25 Pub. Cont. L.J. 781 (1996); Nash, *Equitable Adjustments for Deleted Work: The Risk of Unbalanced Bids*, 9 N&CR ¶ 17 (Mar. 1995); McGovern, *Equitably Adjusting Partially Terminated Contracts*, 35 Cont. Mgmt. 24 (Jan. 1995); Nash, chaps. 16–19, *Government Contract Changes* (2d ed. 1989 & Supp. 1993); Cibinic & Nash, *Administration of Government Contracts* 671–92 (3d ed. 1995).

EQUITABLE ALLOCATION A method of allocating INDIRECT COSTs that causes "each product and operation to bear its share of the cost it generates." *Matanuska Valley Farmers Cooperating Ass'n*, ASBCA 7382, 1962 BCA ¶ 3431. Generally, this requires costs to be allocated based on benefits to each element of the work. FAR 31.203(b).

An allocation method that causes the Government to bear a greater portion of the contractor's costs than is attributable to Government work is considered inequitable, and although a contractor has considerable discretion in selecting a method for allocating indirect costs, the method selected will be rejected by the boards or courts if the results are inequitable to the Government. See Cost Accounting Standard 418, 48 C.F.R. 9904.418, Allocation of direct and indirect costs. See Cibinic & Nash, *Cost-Reimbursement Contracting* 676–78 (2d ed. 1993).

ERRORS OR OMISSIONS See OMISSIONS AND MISDESCRIPTIONS.

ESCALATION See FIXED-PRICE CONTRACT WITH ECONOMIC PRICE ADJUSTMENT.

ESTABLISHED CATALOG OR MARKET PRICE A price that established an exemption from the requirements for submission of CERTIFIED COST OR PRICING DATA by an offeror on a negotiated procurement (see NEGOTIATION). This exemption was removed from 10 U.S.C. § 2306a(b) and 41 U.S.C. § 254b(b) by the CLINGER-COHEN ACT OF 1996, Pub. L. No. 104-106. The exemption applied if the prices were, or were based on, established catalog prices or established market prices of commercial items sold in substantial quantities to the general public (see COMMERCIALITY). The exemption was burdensome because the offeror had to claim it by providing detailed sales information on Standard Form 1412, Claim for Exemption from Submission of Certified Cost or Pricing Data, FAR 53.301-1412. The exemption was replaced by the COMMERCIAL ITEM EXEMPTION.

ESTABLISHED MARKET PRICE See ESTABLISHED CATALOG OR MARKET PRICE.

ESTIMATE AT COMPLETION (EAC) The estimated cost, computed by one of many formulas, of the final cost that will be incurred when the contract is completed. It is computed by adding the estimated cost of completing the contract to the INCURRED COSTs. See Christensen, *Determining an Accurate Estimate at Completion*, 25 Nat'l Cont. Mgmt. J., Issue No. 1, p. 17 (1993).

ESTIMATED COST The statement of the anticipated cost of performance of a COST-PLUS-FIXED-FEE CONTRACT, COST-PLUS-AWARD-FEE CONTRACT, or COST CONTRACT. This estimated cost is stated as a separate amount in these types of contracts. It is adjusted for CHANGEs or COST OVERRUNs but, in accordance with the LIMITATION OF COST CLAUSE, is a firm limitation on compensation to the contractor until such adjustment is made by a contract MODIFICATION. The estimated cost is negotiated in accordance with the procedures in FAR Subpart 15.4 or established competitively in accordance with those in FAR Subpart 15.3. See Cibinic & Nash, *Cost-Reimbursement Contracting* 939–43 (2d ed. 1993).

ESTIMATING SYSTEM The system used by a contractor to estimate the cost of performance of work under a contract or contract modification. The accuracy and reliability of proposals are increased through the use of an acceptable estimating system, and the Government policy is to review contractor's estimating systems to verify their reliability. FAR 15.407-5. The Cost Estimating System Requirements clause at DFARS 252.215-7002 defines "estimating system" as contractor policies, procedures, and practices for generating cost estimates and other data included in proposals submitted to customers in the expectation of receiving contract awards. DFARS 215.811-70 states that, to be considered adequate, a contractor's estimating system must be established, maintained, reliable, and consistently applied, and must produce verifiable, supportable, and documented cost estimates. CAS 401, 48 C.F.R. § 9904.401, requires contractors to follow estimating practices that are consistent with their cost accumulation and reporting practices.

ESTIMATING SYSTEM SURVEY REPORT A report containing the results of estimating system reviews. See FAR 15.407-5. See also ESTIMATING SYSTEM; Cibinic & Nash, *Cost-Reimbursement Contracting* 570–71 (2d ed. 1993).

ESTOPPEL A legal doctrine preventing a party from asserting a right to the detriment of the other party, when the first party has acted or made statements contrary to the right asserted and the other party has reasonably relied on such conduct. The Supreme Court has strictly limited the use of estoppel against the Government, *Schweiker v. Hansen*, 450 U.S. 785 (1981), but Government contractors are still permitted to use the doctrine when the action or statement relied on is taken by an officer of the Government with the authority to bind the Government. See Cibinic & Nash, *Administration of Government Contracts* 69–76 (3d ed. 1995); Cibinic, *Equitable Estoppel: Still Hanging In There*, 7 N&CR ¶ 31 (June 1993); Cibinic, *Postscript Estoppel*, 6 N&CR ¶ 10 (Feb. 1992); Nash, *Equitable Estoppel of the Government: An Argument That Is Hanging by a Thread*, 5 N&CR ¶ 7

(Feb. 1991). The most common form of estoppel against the Government occurs when the Government fails within a reasonable period to terminate a contractor for default because of a late delivery and the contractor continues to work in reliance on the Government's actions. See WAIVER. In this situation it is often held that the Government has effectively waived the delivery date and may be estopped from terminating the contract for failure to deliver. *DeVito v. United States*, 188 Ct. Cl. 979, 413 F.2d 1147 (1969); Carberry & Johnstone, *Waiver of the Government's Right to Terminate for Default in Government Contracts*, 17 Pub. Cont. L.J. 470, 478 (1988).

ETHICS The rules of conduct recognized as governing standards of behavior. In the field of Government contracting, Government employees are required to meet specified STANDARDS OF CONDUCT in the performance of their duties. Government contractors and offerors for Government contracts are also required to have a satisfactory record of integrity and business ethics. FAR 9.104-1. Many of the ethical rules are set forth in FAR Part 3. See Bruce, *United States v. Winstar Corp.: A Case Study in Institutional Government Ethics*, 26 Pub. Cont. L.J. 397 (1997); Cibinic & Nash, *Administration of Government Contracts* 80–142 (3d ed. 1995); Nash, *Ethics*, 4 N&CR ¶ 73 (Dec. 1990); Johnson & Alonge, *Ethics in Government Procurement/ Edition II*, 87-8 Briefing Papers (July 1987).

EVALUATION See PROPOSAL EVALUATION.

EVALUATION CRITERIA See EVALUATION FACTORS.

EVALUATION FACTORS The factors used by the Government in a COMPETITIVE PROPOSALS procurement to determine the winning contractor. See FAR 15.304. 10 U.S.C. § 2305(a)(2)(A) and 41 U.S.C. § 253a(b)(1) require that the Government's solicitation (the REQUEST FOR PROPOSALS) clearly state the factors and significant subfactors that will be considered in evaluating proposals and selecting a source and state, in addition, their RELATIVE IMPORTANCE. Evaluation factors should be tailored to each acquisition and should include only the factors that will affect the SOURCE SELECTION decision. The evaluation factors that apply to an acquisition and the relative importance of those factors are within the broad discretion of agency acquisition officials. See Edwards, *The Relative Importance of Source Selection Evaluation Factors*, 10 N&CR ¶ 34 (July 1996); Nash, *Evaluating Competitive Proposals: Relative Importance of the Factors*, 6 N&CR ¶ 17 (Mar. 1992). However, FAR 15.304(d)(1) requires that price or cost to the Government be included as an evaluation factor in every source selection and PAST PERFORMANCE be included in all procurements over stated dollar thresholds. FAR 15.304(d)(2) states that quality (in terms of technical excellence, management, CAPABILITY, personnel qualifications, prior experience, past performance, and schedule compliance) must also be addressed, but this is not interpreted as a firm requirement. See Cibinic & Nash, chap. 6, Sec. II., *Formation of Government Contracts* (3d ed. 1998); Nash, *Best Value Procurement: Random Musings on the Current State of the Art*, 11 N&CR ¶ 44 (Sept. 1997); Nash, *Best Value: The Gap Between the Intent and the Act*, 11 N&CR ¶ 3 (Jan. 1997); Nash, *Selecting the Evaluation Factors in Best Value Procurement*, 10 N&CR ¶ 30 (June 1996); Nash, *Postscript: Streamlining Source Selection by Improving the Quality of Evaluation Factors*, 8 N&CR ¶ 72 (Dec. 1994); Nash, *Source Selection: The "Solicitation-Evaluation-Decision" Linkage*, 1 N&CR ¶ 56 (July 1987).

EVOLUTIONARY ACQUISITION (EA) An acquisition strategy approach in which a core capability is fielded, with a system design that has a modular structure and provisions for future upgrades and changes as requirements are refined. An EA strategy is well suited to high-technology and software-intensive programs where requirements beyond a core capability can generally but not specifically be defined. Jones, *Glossary: Defense Acquisition Acronyms and Terms* (8th ed., Defense Systems Management College). See MODULAR CONTRACTING.

EXAMINATION OF RECORDS The examination by the COMPTROLLER GENERAL or the GENERAL ACCOUNTING OFFICE of a contractor's books, documents, papers, or other records that directly pertain to transactions under the contract. 10 U.S.C. § 2313(c) and 41 U.S.C. § 254d(c) requires that the Government have the right to make such examination in all negotiated contracts, with the exception of contracts for utility services at established rates, contracts or subcontracts for an amount not greater than the SIMPLIFIED ACQUISITION THRESHOLD, and contracts with foreign contractors for which the agency head authorized omission. This authority may be exercised until three years after final payment or for any shorter period specified for a particular type of record in FAR Subpart 4.7, Contractor Records Retention. It also continues until any claim, appeal, or litigation or any GAO exception to a contractor's costs or expenses is disposed of.

EXCESS COSTS OF REPROCUREMENT Costs incurred by the Government in excess of the contract price of a contract that has been terminated for default (see TERMINATION FOR DEFAULT). The standard Default clauses, FAR 52.249-8 through -10, provide that these costs may be recovered from the defaulted contractor if the Government repurchases the supplies or services or completes the work at a price exceeding the price under the terminated contract. FAR 49.402-6 requires the contracting officer, after the default termination, to repurchase against the account of the contractor as soon as practicable and, after payment for the work to complete the contract, make a written demand on the terminated contractor for the total amount of the excess. For the defaulted contractor to be charged for the excess costs of reprocurement (1) the reprocured supplies, services, or work must be the same as or similar to the original; (2) the Government must actually incur the costs; and (3) the Government must reasonably minimize the excess costs (e.g., by obtaining maximum feasible competition). See Cibinic & Nash, *Administration of Government Contracts* 998–1047 (3d ed. 1995); Williamson & Medill-Jones, *Government Damages for Default*, 89-7 Briefing Papers (June 1989).

EXCESS FOREIGN CURRENCY Currencies of certain countries in amounts determined by the Secretary of the Treasury to be excess to the Government's normal requirements. FAR 25.304. These countries are identified in bulletins issued by the OFFICE OF MANAGEMENT AND BUDGET and distributed through agency procedures on an expedited basis. Additional information may be obtained from the DEPARTMENT OF THE TREASURY, Office of the Assistant Secretary for International Affairs, Office of Development Policy. Acquisitions of foreign end products, services, or construction paid for in excess or near-excess foreign currencies are an exception to the BALANCE OF PAYMENTS PROGRAM restrictions. Excess and near-excess foreign currencies are to be used whenever feasible in payment of contracts over $1 million performed wholly or partly in any of the listed countries. In some cases award may be made to an offeror willing to accept payment, in whole or in part, in excess or near-excess foreign currency even though the offer, when compared with offers in U.S. dollars, is not the lowest received. Price differentials may be funded from excess or near-excess foreign currencies available without charge to agency appropriations, subject to OMB Circular No. A-20 (revised), *Systems of Control over the Use of Foreign Currencies*, May 21, 1966.

EXCESS PERSONAL PROPERTY Any personal property under the control of a federal agency that the agency head or a designee determines is not required for that agency's needs and for the discharge of its responsibilities. FAR 8.101. FAR 8.102 provides that it is the policy of the Government to use such property in preference to procuring new property and that such policy also applies to cost-reimbursement contractors. Such property is under the control of the GENERAL SERVICES ADMINISTRATION. See FAR 8.103.

EXCISE TAX A tax on the sale or use of a particular supply or service, levied by the Federal Government and by state and local governments. FAR 31.205-41 specifies the rules governing whether such taxes paid by contractors are ALLOWABLE COSTs. Contractors are frequently not subject to such taxes imposed by the Federal Government. See FAR Subpart 29.2. Contractors bear the risk of determining which excise taxes apply to their contracts but are given PRICE ADJUSTMENTs for changes in such taxes under the Federal, State, and Local Taxes clause in FAR 52.229-3. See STATE AND LOCAL TAXES.

EXCULPATORY CLAUSE A contract clause stating that one of the contracting parties is not liable upon the occurrence of some specified event. These clauses are most frequently used by the Government in an attempt to relieve itself of liability for defective specifications (see IMPLIED WARRANTY OF SPECIFICATIONS). Such clauses are not against public policy but are carefully scrutinized by the courts and BOARDs OF CONTRACT APPEALS to ensure that they are applicable to the specific problem that has been encountered by the contractor. See Cibinic & Nash, *Administration of Government Contracts* 348–63 (3d ed. 1995); Nash, *The Severin Doctrine: It's Still Barely Alive and Well*, 4 N&CR ¶ 63 (Nov. 1990); Passar, *Government Use of Disclaimers and Exculpatory Clauses in Procurement Contracts*, 1988 (unpublished L.L.M. thesis, The Geo. Wash. Univ. Nat'l Law Center, Government Contracts Program).

EXCUSABLE DELAY A delay in the performance of a contract that is caused by an event that is beyond the control of and without the fault or negligence of the contractor or its subcontractors at any tier. The TERMINATION FOR DEFAULT clauses indicate that a contractor will not be held liable if its failure to perform a contract arises from such delays. The identified excusable delays in the Default clauses for supply and service contracts in FAR 52.249-8 and -9 and in the Excusable Delays clause at FAR 52.249-10 include (1) acts of God or of the public enemy, (2) acts of the Government in either its sovereign or its contractual capacity, (3) fires, (4) floods, (5) epidemics, (6) quarantine restrictions, (7) strikes, (8) freight embargoes, and (9) unusually severe weather. The fixed-price construction Default clause in FAR 52.249-10 adds as excusable delays the following: (1) acts of another contractor in the performance of a contract with the Government and (2) delays of subcontractors or suppliers at any tier, arising from unforeseeable causes beyond the control and without the fault or negligence of the contractor and its subcontractors or suppliers. See Cibinic & Nash, *Administration of Government Contracts* 554–85 (3d ed. 1995); Finke, *Unusually Severe Weather*, 22 Pub. Cont. L.J. 495 (1993); Nash, *Excusable Delays: Labor Shortages and Loss of Key Employees*, 1 N&CR ¶ 48 (June 1987).

EXECUTIVE AGENCY Instrumentality of the Federal Government bound by the FEDERAL ACQUISITION REGULATION. Executive agencies include the executive departments (State, Justice, the Treasury, Defense, the Interior, Agriculture, Commerce, Labor, Health and Human Services, Housing and Urban Development, Transportation, Energy, Education, and Veterans Affairs), 5 U.S.C. § 101; the military departments (Army, Navy, and Air Force), 5 U.S.C. § 102; any independent establishment, 5 U.S.C. § 104(1); and any wholly owned Government corporation within the meaning of 31 U.S.C. § 9101 (such as the Export-Import Bank of the United States, the Federal Crop Insurance Corporation, FEDERAL PRISON INDUSTRIES, INC., and the Pension Benefit Guaranty Corporation). FAR 2.101. See Cibinic & Nash, chap. 1, Sec. I., *Formation of Government Contracts* (3d ed. 1998)

EXECUTIVE COMPENSATION Compensation of company officers in senior management positions. FAR 31.205-6(p)(2) provides that compensation is the total amount of taxable income paid to the employee and the total amount of elective deferred compensation earned by the employee. It also defines "officers in a senior management position" as the chief executive officer and the four most highly compensated officers in senior management positions plus the five most highly compensated officers in senior management positions in intermediate HOME OFFICEs or segments of the company. Executive compensation is limited to $250,000 by § 809 of the 1997 DOD Authorization Act, Pub. L. No. 104-201. Section 808 of the 1998 DOD Authorization Act, Pub. L. No. 105-85, requires the Administrator of Federal Procurement Policy to review commercially available surveys of executive compensation and, based on the results of the review, determine a benchmark compensation amount to apply for each fiscal year. See Worthington et al., *Executive Compensation: A Critical Examination of the Proposed "Contract Costs Act of 1997,"* 97-3 CP&A Rep.3 (Mar. 1997).

EXECUTIVE PRIVILEGE An exemption under the FREEDOM OF INFORMATION ACT which protects inter-agency or intra-agency memorandums or letters which would not be available by law to a party other than an agency in litigation with the agency from release. 5 U.S.C. § 552(b)(5). This exemption is designed to protect the decision-making process of Government agencies which require the open exchange of ideas and opinions among Government employees. See Nash & Rawicz, *Intellectual Property Series*, vol 3, 201–5 (3d ed. 1997). See also PRIVILEGED INFORMATION.

EXECUTORY ACCORD See ACCORD AND SATISFACTION.

EXPEDITED PROCEDURES Procedures used by the BOARDs OF CONTRACT APPEALS (BCAs) for the expedited disposition of any APPEAL FROM A CONTRACTING OFFICER'S DECISION, if the amount in dispute is $50,000 or less. These "small claims (expedited)" procedures are required by 41 U.S.C. § 608(a) and are often referred to as Rule 12.2 procedures because they are discussed in Uniform Rule 12.2 (see UNIFORM RULES). They apply at the sole election of the contractor. Uniform Rule 12.1(c) explains that the contractor must elect to proceed pursuant to Rule 12 within 60 days of receipt of the notice of docketing "unless such period is extended by the BCA for good cause." The Government is not only unable to choose the expedited procedure should it so desire, but it is also, for the most part, powerless to stop the contractor from electing it in appropriate circumstances. Under the expedited procedure, appeals may be decided by a single member of the agency BCA, with such concurrences as may be required by rule or regulation. Appeals must be resolved, whenever possible, within 120 days after the contractor elects to use the procedure. A decision against either party reached under the procedure is final and conclusive and may be set aside only in cases of fraud. Administrative determinations and final decisions under expedited procedures have no value as precedent for future cases. Alternatively, contractors with small claims may elect the ACCELERATED PROCEDURE.

EXPENSING OF COSTS Charging the full cost to current accounts, as compared with CAPITALIZATION. Expensing of costs permits a contractor to charge the full cost of an asset to the year it is acquired—thus maximizing its recovery. CAS 404, 48 C.F.R. § 9904.404, permits expensing of CAPITAL ASSETs with a value not exceeding $5,000, but a lesser amount may be used by contractors.

EXPERIENCE CURVE See LEARNING CURVE.

EXPERTS See INDIVIDUAL EXPERTS AND CONSULTANTS.

EXPIRED APPROPRIATION An appropriation that is no longer available for new obligations because the time available for incurring such obligations has expired. Expired appropriations are maintained by FISCAL YEAR identity for five years. During this period, obligations may be adjusted if otherwise proper and outlays are made from these accounts. Unobligated balances may not be withdrawn from expired accounts. After the five-year period has elapsed, all obligated and unobligated balances are canceled and the expired account is closed. Jones, *Glossary: Defense Acquisition Acronyms and Terms* (8th ed., Defense Systems Management College). See Cibinic & Nash, chap. 1, Sec. II., *Formation of Government Contracts* (3d ed. 1998); Nash, *Settlement =Without Funds: Life Without An "M" Account*, 8 N&CR ¶ 17 (Mar. 1994); Nash, *Reforming the Procurement Process: Part II—Additional Issues*, 7 N&CR ¶ 12 (Mar. 1993); Nash, *Postscript: Impact of "M" Account Legislation on Contract Changes*, 6 N&CR ¶ 29 (May 1992); Nash, *Cancellation of the "M" Accounts: A New Incentive for Efficient Contract Administration*, 5 N&CR ¶ 57 (Oct. 1991).

EXPORT ADMINISTRATION REGULATIONS (EAR) Regulations promulgated and administered by the Department of Commerce, Bureau of Export Administration, that control export and reexport of items and activities within the bureau's jurisdiction. These regulations are located at 15 C.F.R. Part 730.

EXPRESSLY UNALLOWABLE COST A particular item or type of cost that, under the express provisions of an applicable law, regulation, or contract, is specifically named and stated to be an UNALLOWABLE COST. FAR 31.001. FAR 31.201-6 requires that contractors identify such costs and exclude them from any billing, CLAIM, or PROPOSAL submitted to the Government. 10 U.S.C. § 2324 and 41 U.S.C. § 256 establish penalties to be assessed against contractors when it is determined by clear and convincing evidence that this requirement was not complied with in the submission of proposals for the settlement of INDIRECT COSTs. See Cibinic & Nash, *Cost-Reimbursement Contracting* 1147–48 (2d ed. 1993).

EXTENDED OVERHEAD See UNABSORBED OVERHEAD.

EXTRAORDINARY CONTRACTUAL ACTION An action taken to enter into or amend a contract without CONSIDERATION pursuant to the authority of Pub. L. No. 85-804, 50 U.S.C. §§ 1431–1435, as amended by Pub. L. No. 93-155. FAR Part 50 discusses extraordinary contractual actions and prescribes policies and procedures for the Government to use to enter into, amend, or modify contracts in order to facilitate the national defense. This power is used to give contractors additional compensation, without regard to their legal entitlement, when an actual or threatened loss under a defense contract, however caused, will impair the productive ability of a contractor whose continued performance on any defense contract or whose continued operation as a source of supply is found to be essential to the national defense. In such cases, the contract may be amended without consideration, but only to the extent necessary to avoid impairing the contractor's productive ability. An amendment without consideration may also be appropriate when a contractor suffers a loss because of Government action, in which case the contract may be adjusted in the interest of fairness. FAR 50.302-1. Contracts may also be amended or modified to correct mistakes or formalize informal commitments. FAR 50.102(c) notes that certain kinds of contractual relief formerly available only under Pub. L. No. 85-804 (such as rescission or reformation for mutual mistake) are now available under the authority of the CONTRACT DISPUTES ACT OF 1978; it also provides that this authority should be relied on in preference to Pub. L. No. 85-804. Providing indemnification to contractors is another significant use of this authority. The clause at FAR 52.250-1, Indemnification under Pub. L. No. 85-804, is inserted in a contract whenever the approving authority determines that the contractor must be indemnified against unusually hazardous or nuclear risks. FAR 50.403-3. See Larson, *Pub. L. No. 85-804: Who Pays When Private Industry Works?*, 27 Cont. Mgmt. 8 (Oct. 1987); Richardson, *The Use of the General and Residual Powers under Pub. L. No. 85-804 in the Department of Defense*, 14 Pub. Cont. L.J. 128 (1983).

EXTRAORDINARY CONTRACTUAL RELIEF See EXTRAORDINARY CONTRACTUAL ACTION.

F

FACILITIES Property used for production, maintenance, research, development, or testing. FAR 45.301. The term includes PLANT EQUIPMENT and REAL PROPERTY, but not MATERIAL, SPECIAL TEST EQUIPMENT, SPECIAL TOOLING, or AGENCY-PECULIAR PROPERTY. FAR 45.301. FAR 45.302 specifies that it is the policy of the Government that contractors provide all facilities needed to perform contracts. However, it then lists a number of situations in which the Government may provide facilities. It further specifies that when a Government agency has made the decision to provide facilities, preference is given to existing Government-owned facilities over new facilities. Government-owned facilities are one element of GOVERNMENT PRODUCTION AND RESEARCH PROPERTY, which is to be used in accordance with detailed rules in FAR Subparts 45.2 and 45.4. See Cibinic & Nash, *Administration of Government Contracts* 629–30 (3d ed. 1995).

FACILITIES CAPITAL The NET BOOK VALUE of TANGIBLE CAPITAL ASSETS and of those INTANGIBLE CAPITAL ASSETS that are subject to AMORTIZATION. FAR 31.001. This amount is one of the key elements in the computation of the COST OF CAPITAL COMMITTED TO FACILITIES.

FACILITIES CAPITAL COST OF MONEY (FCCM) The imputed cost of money committed to (1) the contractor's facilities employed in contract performance, FAR 31.205-10a, and (2) CAPITAL ASSETs under construction, FAR 31.205-10(b). The cost is imputed by using the TREASURY INTEREST RATE. The costs are allowable and must be measured and allocated according to CAS 414, Cost of Money as an Element of the Cost of Facilities Capital, or CAS 417, Cost of Money as an Element of the Cost of Capital Assets Under Construction, whether or not the contract is otherwise subject to CAS. See Cibinic & Nash, *Cost-Reimbursement Contracting* 872–75 (2d ed. 1993); McVay, *Facilities Capital Cost of Money—Now the Truth Can Be Told*, 32 Cont.

Mgmt. 10 (Sept. 1992). See also COST OF CAPITAL COMMITTED TO FACILITIES.

FACILITIES CONTRACT A contract under which the Government provides FACILITIES to a contractor or subcontractor for use in performing one or more related contracts for supplies or services. FAR 45.301. Facilities contracts may take any of the following forms: (1) facilities acquisition contracts for the acquisition, construction, and installation of facilities; (2) facilities use contracts for the use, maintenance, accountability, and disposition of facilities; or (3) consolidated facilities contracts for both facilities acquisition and use. Facilities contracts are COST CONTRACTs; the contractor receives no FEE. FAR 45.302-3 specifies that facilities may be provided as part of another contract when one of the following exceptions applies: (1) the actual or estimated cumulative acquisition cost of the facilities provided by the contracting activity to the contractor at one plant or general location does not exceed $1 million, (2) the number of items of plant equipment provided is 10 or fewer, (3) the contract performance period is 12 months or less, (4) the contract is for construction, (5) the contract is for services and the facilities are to be used in connection with the operation of a Government-owned plant or installation, or (6) the contract is for work within an establishment or installation operated by the Government. See Rosche, *Consolidated Facilities Contract—How Does It Operate?,* 34 Cont. Mgmt. 18 (Feb. 1994).

FACNET See FEDERAL ACQUISITION COMPUTER NETWORK.

FACSIMILE (FAX) Electronic equipment that communicates and reproduces both printed and handwritten material. FACSIMILE BIDs OR PROPOSALs are now accepted by many agencies but may not be considered unless permitted by the SOLICITATION. FAR 14.301(c); FAR 15.203(d).

FACSIMILE BID OR PROPOSAL A BID or PROPOSAL, or a modification or withdrawal thereof, that is transmitted to and received by the Government by FACSIMILE. Such bids or proposals may be permitted by Government agencies. FAR 14.202-7; 15.209(e). If they are permitted, the solicitation must contain the Facsimile Bids clause in FAR 52.214-31 or the Facsimile Proposals clause in FAR 52.215-5. Guidance to contracting officers on when to permit facsimile proposals is set forth in FAR 15.203(d)(1). See Cibinic, *Facsimile Bids and Proposals: On the Information Superhighway in a Horse and Buggy,*

9 N&CR ¶ 12 (Feb. 1995); Williamson, *Facsimile Bids and Proposals: A New Option for Contracting*, 19 Pub. Cont. L.J. 689 (1990).

FACT An event that has occurred. Under the TRUTH IN NEGOTIATIONS ACT (TINA), the COST OR PRICING DATA that a contractor must submit to the Government include all facts that a prudent buyer or seller would reasonably expect to affect price negotiations significantly. In this regard, facts are distinguished from judgments. A fact is objectively verifiable by audit or technical evaluation; a judgment is subjective and cannot be verified except in hindsight. While vendor quotations, nonrecurring costs, information on changes in production methods, management decisions impacting costs, data supporting projections of business prospects, unit-cost trends, and the like are considered facts, a pure estimate of the cost of future contract performance based on these facts is considered a judgment. See FAR 15.401. In the application of TINA, contractors and contracting officers have encountered continuing difficulties in drawing a firm line between facts and judgments. See Nash, *Truth in Negotiations: The FAR Implementation of FASA*, 9 N&CR ¶ 57 (Nov. 1995); Cibinic, *Cost or Pricing Data: Defining and Furnishing Data*, 9 N&CR ¶ 45 (Aug. 1995); Lovitky, *Understanding Causation and Determining the Price Adjustment in Defective Pricing Cases*, 17 Pub. Cont. L.J. 407 (1988); Lovitky, *Cost and Pricing Data Defined: An Analysis of the Scope of Contractor Disclosure Requirements Pursuant to the Truth in Negotiations Act*, 20 Nat'l Cont. Mgmt. J., Issue No. 2, p. 79 (1987).

FAILURE TO DISCLOSE INFORMATION See SUPERIOR KNOWLEDGE.

FAILURE TO MAKE A GOOD FAITH EFFORT TO COMPLY WITH THE SUBCONTRACTING PLAN For the purposes of FAR Subpart 19.7, which addresses subcontracting with small business, small disadvantaged business, and women-owned small business concerns, a willful or intentional failure to perform the contract in accordance with the subcontracting plan or a willful or intentional action to frustrate the plan. FAR 19.701. When a contractor fails to make a good faith effort to comply with a subcontracting plan, the contractor can be held liable for LIQUIDATED DAMAGES. FAR 19.705-7; 15 U.S.C. § 637(d)(4)(F).

FAILURE TO MAKE PROGRESS A failure of a contractor to perform the work required by a Government supply or service contract in a manner that provides reasonable assurance to the Government that the contract schedule will be met. The Default (Fixed-Price Supply and Service) clause in FAR 52.249-8 provides that the Government may terminate the contract for default before the completion date if the contractor's failure to make progress is such that the performance of the contract is endangered. Terminations based on failure to make progress require that the contracting officer give the contractor notice and an opportunity to "cure" the failure (a minimum of 10 days) before the Government exercises its right to terminate the contract for default. This type of TERMINATION FOR DEFAULT is distinguished from terminations based on failure to deliver supplies or perform services within the time specified in the contract, which require no CURE NOTICE. FAR 49.402-3. See Cibinic & Nash, *Administration of Government Contracts* 929–35 (3d ed. 1995).

FAILURE TO PROSECUTE THE WORK Failure of a contractor to perform the work, or any part thereof, under a construction contract with sufficient diligence to ensure completion within the contract schedule. The Default (Fixed-Price Construction) clause in FAR 52.249-10 provides that the Government may terminate the contract for default before the completion date if the contractor fails to prosecute the work. No CURE NOTICE is required for this type of TERMINATION FOR DEFAULT, but a SHOW CAUSE NOTICE is usually issued prior to termination.

FAIR AND REASONABLE PRICE A price that is fair to both parties, considering the agreed-upon conditions, promised quality, and timeliness of contract performance. FAR 15.402(a) requires contracting officers to ensure that supplies and services are purchased under negotiated contracts (see NEGOTIATION) at fair and reasonable prices. FAR 15.405(a) provides that price negotiation is the means to be used by contracting officers to arrive at this result, while FAR 15.404-1(b)(2) suggests the use of PRICE ANALYSIS to determine whether the price is fair and reasonable. FAR 14.408-2 requires contracting officers to ensure that sealed bid contracts (see SEALED BIDDING) are awarded at "reasonable" prices. It also suggests that price analysis be used to determine whether the offered price is reasonable. All of this guidance is addressed, primarily, to the issue of whether the price is too high; whereas, COST REALISM is generally addressed to the issue of whether the cost estimate is too low.

FAIR LABOR STANDARDS ACT (FLSA) A 1938 Act, 29 U.S.C. § 206, commonly known as the "Federal Wage and Hour Law." The FLSA establishes minimum-wage and maximum-hour standards.

However, if an employee is entitled under state law to higher wages or better hours than those mandated by the FLSA, the state law controls. The FLSA applies to industry generally rather than to Government contractors specifically. Federal agencies must encourage contractors to enforce FLSA requirements when applicable. FAR 22.1002-4 states that no contractor or subcontractor holding a service contract for any dollar amount shall pay any of its employees less than the minimum wage specified in § 6(a)(1) of the FLSA. See Stephenson, chap. 3, *Construction Contracting* 219–22 (1991).

FAIR MARKET PRICE The price at which bona fide sales have been consummated for assets of like type, quality, and quantity in a particular market at the time of acquisition. *Black's Law Dictionary* 597–98 (6th ed. 1990). The expectation that awards will be made at fair market prices is one of the conditions that must be met in order to SET ASIDE an acquisition or class of acquisitions for exclusive small business participation. FAR 19.502-2(b). In DOD, the expectation that award will be made at not more than 10 percent above fair market price is one of the expectations that must be met in order for an acquisition to be set aside for HISTORICALLY BLACK COLLEGES AND UNIVERSITIES and MINORITY INSTITUTIONs. DFARS 226.7003-1.

FAIR MARKET VALUE The price at which supplies would change hands between a willing buyer and a willing seller, with neither buyer nor seller under any compulsion to buy or sell and both having reasonable knowledge of the relevant facts. *Black's Law Dictionary* 597–98 (6th ed. 1990). The term arises in discussions of REASONABLENESS OF COST. In *Bruce Constr. Corp. v. United States*, 163 Ct. Cl. 97, 324 F.2d 516 (1963), in reference to the amount of an EQUITABLE ADJUSTMENT, it was held that HISTORICAL COST, rather than fair market value, is the proper measure of cost reasonableness. However, 10 U.S.C. § 2324(j) and FAR 31.201-3(a) state that contractors have the burden of proving that the costs they incurred were reasonable—that, among other things, they reflect fair market value.

FAIR USE Use of a WORK that is not an infringement of a COPYRIGHT because it is used for the purpose of criticism, comment, news reporting, teaching, scholarship, or research. 17 U.S.C. § 107. In determining whether a use is fair, a court must consider: (1) the purpose and character of the use, including whether it is commercial or educational; (2) the nature of the copyrighted work; (3) the amount and substantiality of the use in relation to the whole work; and (4) the effect of the use on the potential market for or value of the copyrighted work.

FALSE CLAIMS ACT An Act giving the Government remedies against parties that process false claims. It was originally passed at the time of the Civil War and has now been divided into two sections: the Civil False Claims Act, 31 U.S.C. § 3729, and the Criminal False Claims Act, 18 U.S.C. § 287. These acts are commonly used to address fraudulent conduct by contractors. To establish a violation of either statute, the Government must prove that (1) the contractor made or presented a claim for payment to the Government; (2) the claim was asserted against the Government; (3) the claim was false, fictitious, or fraudulent; and (4) the contractor knew that the claim was false, fictitious, or fraudulent when presenting it. The primary differences between the civil statute and the criminal statute are the level of intent required, the standard of proof the Government must meet, and the penalties the Government can inflict. Contractors can be found liable for both criminal and civil penalties. In addition, Congress has enacted a *qui tam* statute (see QUI TAM PROCEEDINGS) authorizing private individuals to bring actions for violations of the Civil False Claims Act. See Nash, *Distinguishing Mistakes From Criminal Conduct: Some Additional Views*, 11 N&CR ¶ 54 (Oct. 1997); Seyfarth et al., *The Government Contract Compliance Handbook* 1-4 through 1-6 (1996 Supp.); Dees & Bouquet, *Beyond "Diminished Value": New Challenges in the Law of Civil False Claims Act Damages*, 25 Pub. Cont. L.J. 597 (1996); Taylor & Taugher, *The California False Claims Act*, 25 Pub. Cont. L.J. 315 (1996); Nash, *An Efficient Procurement System: Striking A Balance Between Freedom and Accountability*, 9 N&CR ¶ 30 (May 1995); Lamm & Currier, *A Primer on the United States False Claims Act*, 12 Intl. Constr. L. Rev. 479 (July 1995); Cibinic & Nash, *Administration of Government Contracts* 112–16 (3d ed. 1995); LaSalle, *The Civil False Claims Act: The Need for a Heightened Burden of Proof as a Prerequisite for Forfeiture*, 28 Akron L. Rev. 497 (Spr. 1995); Lamm & Smutny, *Revisiting the Federal False Claims Act*, 26 Nat'l Cont. Mgmt. J., Issue No. 2, p. 13 (1995); Robertson, *The False Claims Act*, 26 Ariz. St. L.J. 899 (Fall 1994); Alexander, *Health Reform: False Claims Enforcement Under a New Regime*, 24 Pub. Cont. L.J. 103 (1994); Wilson, *The Government Knowledge "Defense" to Civil False Claims Actions*, 24 Pub. Cont. L.J. 43 (1994); Metzger & Goldbaum, *Retroactivity of the 1986 Amendments to the False Claims Act*, 22 Pub. Cont. L.J. 43 (1994); Waldman, *"Damage Control": A Defendant's Approach to the Damage and Penalty Provisions of the Civil False Claims Act*, 21 Pub. Cont. L.J. 131 (1992); Dever, *Double Jeopardy, False Claims, and United States v. Halper*, 20 Pub. Cont. L.J. 56 (1990); Waldman, *The 1986 Amendments to the False Claims Act: Retroactive or Prospective?*, 18 Pub. Cont. L.J. 470 (1989); Barletta &

Pollack, *Civil Litigation of Allegations of Fraud in Connection with Government Contract Claims*, 18 Pub. Cont. L.J. 235 (1988). See also PROGRAM FRAUD CIVIL REMEDIES ACT.

FALSE STATEMENTS ACT An Act, 18 U.S.C. § 1001, that prohibits any person, in any matter under the Government's jurisdiction, from "knowingly and willfully" falsifying, concealing, or covering up a material fact, or making a false, fictitious, or fraudulent statement. Considerably broader in scope than the FALSE CLAIMS ACT, the False Statements Act has been held to cover all false statements that might support fraudulent claims or that might pervert or corrupt the authorized functions of a Government agency to which the statements were made. It covers oral as well as written statements and unsworn as well as sworn statements. It also covers the omission of information on a certified statement when the information should have been included. The Act applies to matters that involve a Government agency's activity even though the false statement is not made directly to the Government. The courts have required that a statement must be material to fall within the scope of the Act; that is, it must have a natural tendency to influence or be capable of influencing the actions of a federal agency. See Seyfarth et al., *The Government Contract Compliance Handbook* 1-10–1-12 (2d ed. 1991) & 1-12–1-14 (1996 Supp.); Cibinic & Nash, *Administration of Government Contracts* 116–19 (3d ed. 1995).

FAR See FEDERAL ACQUISITION REGULATION.

FAR SECRETARIAT The Government organization, housed in the GENERAL SERVICES ADMINISTRATION, that maintains, prints, publishes, and distributes the FEDERAL ACQUISITION REGULATION. Along with the DEFENSE ACQUISITION REGULATORY (DAR) COUNCIL staff, the FAR Secretariat provides the DAR Council and the CIVILIAN AGENCY ACQUISITION COUNCIL with centralized services for keeping a synopsis of current FAR cases (proposed FAR changes) and their status, assigning FAR case numbers, maintaining official case files, assisting parties interested in reviewing the files on completed cases, and performing miscellaneous administrative tasks pertaining to the maintenance of the FAR. FAR 1.201-2.

FAR SYSTEM See FEDERAL ACQUISITION REGULATION SYSTEM.

FAST PAYMENT PROCEDURE A payment procedure that allows payment to a contractor, under limited conditions (such as individual orders not exceeding $25,000, unless the agency authorizes exceptions), before the Government verifies that supplies have been received and accepted. See FAR Subpart 13.4. When the Government intends to use the procedure, the procuring agency will include the Fast Payment Procedure clause in FAR 52.213-1 in the solicitation and contract. Under the procedure, payment may be made on the basis of the contractor's submission of an INVOICE constituting a representation that (1) the supplies have been delivered to a post office, common carrier (see CARRIER (TRANSPORTATION)), or point of first receipt by the Government; and (2) the contractor agrees to replace, repair, or correct supplies not received at destination, damaged in transit, or not conforming to purchase agreements. FAR 13.402(c) provides that title to supplies vests in the Government upon delivery to a post office or common carrier for mailing or shipment, or upon receipt by the Government if the shipment is by means other than Postal Service or common carrier. See Cibinic & Nash, *Administration of Government Contracts* 1159–60 (3d ed. 1995).

FAST PROGRAM See FEDERAL ACQUISITION SERVICES FOR TECHNOLOGY PROGRAM.

FAST-TRACK CONSTRUCTION A method of CONSTRUCTION contracting under which the contractor begins building as soon as the foundation plans are ready and a foundation permit has been issued, despite the fact that the architect-engineer has not finished designing the project. Throughout performance, the architect-engineer must keep ahead of the contractor's progress in order to supply the necessary plans and drawings before each stage of the construction is reached. This is a method of shortening the time to complete a construction project but it increases the risk of DEFECTIVE SPECIFICATIONS. See Nash, chap. 1, *Construction Contracting* 7 (1991).

FEDERAL ACQUISITION CIRCULARS (FAC) Publications of the Government that revise, amend, and update the FEDERAL ACQUISITION REGULATION. Revisions to the FAR are prepared and issued through the coordinated action of the DEFENSE ACQUISITION REGULATORY COUNCIL and the CIVILIAN AGENCY ACQUISITION COUNCIL. Each council maintains cognizance over specified portions of the FAR and is responsible for agreeing with the other council on revisions. Revisions to the FAR are submitted to the FAR SECRETARIAT and pass through a period of public notice and comment begun by publication in the FEDERAL REGISTER. See FAR Subpart 1.2. FACs were numbered sequentially (84-1 through 84-60) from the original promulgation of the FAR in 1984 until the issuance of the 1990 version of the FAR. FACs were then numbered sequentially 90-1 through 90-46 until the issuance of the 1997 version of the FAR. They are now numbered sequentially beginning with 97-1.

FEDERAL ACQUISITION COMPUTER NETWORK (FACNET) A Government-wide system for electronic commerce created by the FEDERAL ACQUISITION STREAMLINING ACT (FASA) OF 1994, Pub. L. No. 103-355. 41 U.S.C. § 426, as amended by Pub. L. No. 105-85, National Defense Authorization Act for Fiscal Year 1998, requires each executive agency to "establish, maintain, and use, to the maximum extent that is practicable and cost-effective, procedures and processes that employ electronic commerce in the conduct and administration of its procurement system." See Cibinic & Nash, chap. 3, Sec. VII., *Formation of Government Contracts* (3d ed. 1998); Godes, *Government Contracting on the Internet: Abandoning FACNET as the Government's Network for Electronic Commerce*, 26 Pub. Cont. L.J. 663 (1997); Yukins, *Managing Electronic Commerce on the Federal Acquisition Computer Network*, 27 Nat'l Cont. Mgmt. J., Issue No. 1, p. 35 (1996); Yukins, *FACNET—New Risks and New Potential*, 38 Gov't Contractor ¶ 511 (Oct. 30, 1996).

FEDERAL ACQUISITION INSTITUTE (FAI) A research and management facility dedicated to promoting Government-wide career management programs for a professional procurement workforce. Originally an organization within the OFFICE OF FEDERAL PROCUREMENT POLICY (OFPP), FAI was transferred to the GENERAL SERVICES ADMINISTRATION (GSA) in January 1984, with OFPP retaining a "policy oversight role." FAI activities include coordinating FEDERAL PROCUREMENT DATA SYSTEM (FPDS) changes with GSA's procurement activities, representing GSA on the OFPP FPDS Policy Committee, establishing and maintaining a contracting officer warrant program, and helping federal agencies develop policies, standards, criteria, and requirements designed to attract, select, motivate, and retain a more productive, better qualified professional workforce. See Livingston & Miller, *The FAI and the Contract Management Curriculum*, 33 Cont. Mgmt. 18 (June 1993).

FEDERAL ACQUISITION REFORM ACT (FARA) A 1996 Act, enacted as part of the Fiscal Year 1996 Defense Authorization Act, Pub. L. No. 104-106. The Act provides for Government-wide acquisition reform, including the repeal of the BROOKS ACT (AUTOMATIC DATA PROCESSING PROCUREMENTS), a shortening of the GENERAL ACCOUNTING OFFICE's time for issuing bid protest decisions, a revision of the PROCUREMENT INTEGRITY ACT, and the elimination of certain regulatory certification requirements. See Maloney, *FARA Provision Fosters Training for Acquisition Personnel*, 36 Cont. Mgmt. 18 (July 1996). This Act, with the INFORMATION TECHNOLOGY MANAGEMENT REFORM ACT, was renamed the CLINGER-COHEN ACT OF 1996.

FEDERAL ACQUISITION REGULATION (FAR) The primary document in the FEDERAL ACQUISITION REGULATIONS SYSTEM, containing uniform policies and procedures that govern the ACQUISITION activity of all federal agencies. The FAR is prepared, issued, and maintained jointly by the Secretary of Defense, the Administrator of General Services, and the NASA Administrator. FAR 1.103. It is published in Title 48 of the CODE OF FEDERAL REGULATIONS, in separate loose-leaf form available through the U.S. Government Printing Office, Washington, DC 20402, and in commercial versions (current paperback, loose-leaf service (part of the *Government Contracts Reporter* subscription service), or floppy disk) published by Commerce Clearing House, Inc., 4025 West Peterson Avenue, Chicago, IL 60646. In addition, the GSA has made the FAR available on the Internet at http://www.arnet.gov/far. Other Internet sites where the FAR can be found include: http://farsite.hill.af.mil (Hill AFB site); http://www.govcon.com (Govcon commercial site); and http://www.fedmarket.com (The Federal Marketplace commercial site). Changes to the FAR are made through FEDERAL ACQUISITION CIRCULARS. The FAR has 53 parts, which are grouped in 8 subchapters: General, ACQUISITION PLANNING, Contracting Methods and Contract Types, Socioeconomic Programs, General Contracting Requirements, Special Categories of Contracting, Contract Management, and Clauses and Forms.

FEDERAL ACQUISITION REGULATIONS SYSTEM The system of regulations that governs the acquisition by contract of supplies and services needed by federal agencies. The system consists of the FEDERAL ACQUISITION REGULATION (FAR), the primary document, and supplementary regulations issued by individual agencies. Such supplements (for example, the DOD FAR SUPPLEMENT and the NASA FAR SUPPLEMENT) contain regulations limited (in theory, at least) to those needed to implement FAR policies and procedures within the agency or supplement the FAR to satisfy agency-specific needs. Implementation (agency treatment expanding on FAR material) is numbered parallel to the FAR. Supplementation (agency-peculiar material with no FAR counterpart) is given numbers of 70 and up. The

FAR System does not include purely internal agency guidance that does not have a significant effect beyond the internal operating procedures of the agency and does not have a significant cost or administrative impact on contractors or offerors. FAR 1.301(a)(2). Part 1 of the FAR sets forth the rules governing the issuance of regulations in the FAR System, including administration (Subpart 1.2), agency acquisition regulations (Subpart 1.3), DEVIATIONs (Subpart 1.4), and agency and public participation (Subpart 1.5). The regulations making up the FAR system are published in Title 48 of the CODE OF FEDERAL REGULATIONS. Many of the documents making up the FAR System are available from Commerce Clearing House, Inc., 4025 West Peterson Avenue, Chicago, IL 60646 as part of the *Government Contracts Reporter* loose-leaf subscription service. In addition, many of the FAR regulations are available on the Internet, including the FAR at http://www.arnet.gov/far; the DFARS at http://www.dtic.mil/dfars; and the NFS at http://.hq.nasa.gov/office/procurement/regs/nfstoc.htm. See Cibinic & Nash, chap. 1, Sec. I., *Formation of Government Contracts* (3d ed. 1998); Nash, *Postscript: The Procurement Regulation System*, 6 N&CR ¶ 3 (Jan. 1992); Nash, *The Federal Acquisition Regulation System: Is It Shrinking?*, 5 N&CR ¶ 4 (Jan. 1991); Malloy, *FAR Revisited*, 25 Cont. Mgmt. 27 (Jan. 1985).

FEDERAL ACQUISITION REGULATORY (FAR) COUNCIL The Government organization, established by 41 U.S.C. § 421, that is charged with assisting in the direction and coordination of Government-wide procurement policy and regulatory activities. It is made up of the Administrator of the OFFICE OF FEDERAL PROCUREMENT POLICY (OFPP), the Secretary of Defense, and the administrators of GSA and NASA. DOD, GSA, and NASA are represented, through delegation, by their officials in charge of acquisition policy. The council, in a very broad sense, manages, coordinates, controls, and monitors maintenance of, issuance of, and changes in the FEDERAL ACQUISITION REGULATION (FAR). The OFPP Administrator, in conjunction with the FAR Council, ensures that procurement regulations promulgated by an executive agency are consistent with the FAR and are limited to regulations essential to implement Government-wide policies and procedures within the agency and additional policies and procedures required to satisfy the agency's specific and unique needs.

FEDERAL ACQUISITION SERVICES FOR TECHNOLOGY (FAST) PROGRAM The FAST Program is a rapid procurement, cost-reimbursable buying service managed by the GENERAL SERVICES ADMINISTRATION (GSA) for use by federal agencies.

The program will buy COMMERCIAL OFF-THE-SHELF INFORMATION TECHNOLOGY software, equipment, services, and non-complex services. The program entails a multiple-procurement-options strategy. First consideration will be given to the GSA MULTIPLE AWARD SCHEDULEs program; second will be for the buying offices to utilize other Government-wide contracts. If these options are unavailable, GSA plans to either compete the information technology requirements among holders of competitively awarded 8(a) INDEFINITE-DELIVERY/INDEFINITE-QUANTITY contracts for integration services or enter into noncompetitive definite-quantity 8(a) contracts. Under FAST, GSA will bill agency users of the service for the cost of contractor supplies, goods, and services plus a surcharge between 1 percent and 1.5 percent of the total transaction, although the fee may be slightly greater when definite-quantity contracts are involved. Buying offices are located at GSA's Central Office and in each GSA region, and federal agencies may use any GSA buying office. See the GSA FAST homepage at <http://www.gsa.gov/FAST/faq.htm>.

FEDERAL ACQUISITION STREAMLINING ACT (FASA) OF 1994 An Act, Pub. L. No. 103-355, that substantially revised federal procurement law. The Act serves to reduce paperwork, encourage the acquisition of commercial items, raise the threshold for SIMPLIFIED ACQUISITION PROCEDURES (previously called "small purchases") to $100,000, promote electronic commerce, and achieve greater efficiency and uniformity among the agencies in their procurement practices. See Nash, *Truth in Negotiations: The FAR Implementation of FASA*, 9 N&CR ¶ 57 (Nov. 1995); Humphrey & Corrao, *Changes in the Notice of Award, Debriefing, and Protest Rules After FASA*, 95-10 Briefing Papers (Sept. 1995); Cibinic, *"Accrual of a Claim:" Fixing FASA*, 9 N&CR ¶ 44 (Aug. 1995); Simchak & Gildea, *Impact of FASA on the Truth in Negotiations Act*, 95-8 Briefing Papers (July 1995); Ritenburg, *FASA's Commercial Item Preference Promises Little Streamlining Without Additional Authority*, 35 Cont. Mgmt. 4 (June 1995); Lumer & Stewart, *So You Think You Know The Federal Acquisition Streamlining Act (FASA) of 1994?*, 35 Cont. Mgmt. 4 (Mar. 1995); Wall & Gustin, *FASA Contract Financing Reforms (An Offer You Can't Refuse?)*, 95-10 CP&A Rep. 3 (Oct. 1995); Nadler & Efthymiou, *Federal Acquisition Streamlining Act Improves Bid Protest Process*, 35 Cont. Mgmt. 17 (Feb. 1995); Pennington, *Government Contract Law Reform: The Federal Acquisition Streamlining Act of 1994*, 24 Colo. Law. 29 (Jan. 1995); Welsh, *President Clinton Signs Federal Acquisition Streamlining Act*, 34 Cont. Mgmt. 4 (Dec. 1994).

FEDERAL AGENCY PROCUREMENT The acquisition (by using competitive procedures and awarding a contract) of goods and services (including construction) from non-federal sources by a federal agency using appropriated funds. For BROAD AGENCY ANNOUNCEMENTs and SMALL BUSINESS INNOVATIVE RESEARCH CONTRACTs, each proposal received constitutes a separate procurement action. FAR 3.104-3. The new PROCUREMENT INTEGRITY rules regarding disclosure and receipt of information and employment contacts apply only to conduct relating to federal agency procurement contracts. This is a substantial limitation of these rules because only competitive contracts are included in this definition (excluding sole source procurement and contract modifications). See Nash, *The New Procurement Integrity Rules*, 11 N&CR ¶ 12 (Mar. 1997).

FEDERAL AVIATION ADMINISTRATION (FAA) An organization within the DEPARTMENT OF TRANSPORTATION responsible for the control and safety of civil aviation with the United States. Section 348 of the Department of Transportation Appropriations Act of 1996, Pub. L. 104-50, directed the FAA to develop and implement a new acquisition management system and provided that it was not subject to the major laws governing procurements of the Department of Transportation. As a result, the FAA is not subject to the FEDERAL ACQUISITION REGULATION but performs its procurements under the FEDERAL AVIATION ADMINISTRATION ACQUISITION MANAGEMENT SYSTEM.

FEDERAL AVIATION ADMINISTRATION ACQUISITION MANAGEMENT SYSTEM (FAAMS) The regulation issued by the FEDEARL AVIATION ADMINISTRATION on April 1, 1996, to establish the procedures for conducting procurement under its independent authority. The current version of the FAAMS was issued in June 1997. Under this regulation, the FAA does not use SEALED BIDDING but conducts all procurements under a SCREENING procedure, soliciting information or offers through one or more SCREENING INFORMATION REQUESTs (SIRs). The regulation also establishes an independent system for resolving PROTESTs and DISPUTEs (not following the procedures of the GENERAL ACCOUNTING OFFICE or the CONTRACT DISPUTES ACT). See Allen & Yukins, *Bid Protests and Contract Disputes Under the FAA's New Procurement System*, 26 Pub. Cont. L.J. 135 (1997); Cibinic, *The Federal Aviation Administration's New Disputes Process: Authorized? Necessary?*, 10 N&CR ¶ 43 (Sept. 1996).

FEDERAL CIRCUIT COURT See COURT OF APPEALS FOR THE FEDERAL CIRCUIT.

FEDERAL CLAIMS COLLECTION ACT An Act, 31 U.S.C. chap. 37, subchapter II, that provides the basic legal framework for agency collection of debts owed to the United States, with oversight by the GENERAL ACCOUNTING OFFICE (GAO) and the DOJ. The Act authorizes compromise, suspension, or termination of collection action in limited circumstances—with the U.S. Attorney General's approval for debts exceeding $100,000 (this threshold was raised from $20,000 in 1990 by the ADMINISTRATIVE DISPUTE RESOLUTION ACT). The Act is implemented by the Federal Claims Collection Standards, issued jointly by the GAO and the DOJ, 4 C.F.R. chap. 2. Agency collection action should be aggressive and timely with effective follow-up, using all reasonable means of collection consistent with good business practice and the debtor's ability to pay. GAO, *Principles of Federal Appropriations Law*, vol. III, chap. 13 (2d ed. 1991). Most claims collection is performed by accounting officials from Government agencies. However, procedures for collecting claims on contracts are set forth in FAR Subpart 32.6.

FEDERAL COURTS ADMINISTRATION ACT OF 1992 An Act, Pub. L. No. 102-572, that, among other things, made improvements in the U.S. Claims Court, renamed by this Act to be the U.S. COURT OF FEDERAL CLAIMS. Title IX of the Act clarified the proceedings and powers of the court, as well as made certification of CLAIMs under the CONTRACT DISPUTES ACT nonjurisdictional. See House Rept. 102-1006, 102d Congress, 2d Sess. (Oct. 3, 1992); Senate Rept. 102-342 (July 27, 1992).

FEDERAL COURTS IMPROVEMENT ACT (FCIA) A 1982 Act, 28 U.S.C. § 171 et seq., 791, 794–98, 1491–92, 1494–1503, 1505, 1507–1509, that reorganized the courts dealing with Government procurement by eliminating the Court of Claims and creating the U.S. Claims Court (subsequently renamed the U.S. COURT OF FEDERAL CLAIMS) and the U.S. COURT OF APPEALS FOR THE FEDERAL CIRCUIT. The Act also conferred new jurisdiction on the Claims Court to hear preaward protests. See 28 U.S.C. § 1491(b)(1). See Hrabik, *Federal Courts Improvement Act*, 24 Duq. L. Rev. 945 (1986); Anthony & Smith, *The Federal Courts Improvement Act of 1982: Its Impact on the Resolution of Federal Contract Disputes*, 13 Pub. Cont. L.J. 201 (1983); White, *The New Government Contract Courts*, 83-11 Briefing Papers (Nov. 1983).

FEDERAL INFORMATION PROCESSING (FIP) RESOURCES AUTOMATIC DATA PROCESSING EQUIPMENT (ADPE) as defined in Pub. L. No. 99-500, the BROOKS ACT (AUTOMATIC DATA PROCESSING PROCUREMENTS), at 40 U.S.C. § 759(a)(2); any equipment or interconnected system or subsystem of equipment used in the automatic acquisition, storage, manipulation, management, movement, control, display, switching, interchange, transmission, or reception of data by a federal agency or under a contract with a federal agency, if the contract either requires use of such equipment or requires a service performed or a product produced making significant use of such equipment. The term includes computers, ancillary equipment, software, FIRMWARE and similar procedures, services, support services, and related resources. See Sochon, *Information Technology Acquisition: The New Federal Environment*, 37 Cont. Mgmt. 4 (July 1997).

FEDERAL INFORMATION PROCESSING STANDARDS PUBLICATIONS (FIPS PUBS) Official Government publications relating to standards adopted and issued under the provisions of § 5131 of the Information Technology Management Reform Act of 1996, 40 U.S.C. § 1441. FIPS PUBS, issued by the National Institute of Standards and Technology (NIST), fall into two general categories: standards, which are mandatory, and guidelines, which are informational documents. The Government Information Services Board was established by Exec. Order No. 13011, 61 Fed. Reg. 37657 (July 16, 1996), to assist NIST in developing standards and guidelines for federal information systems.

FEDERAL INFORMATION RESOURCES MANAGEMENT REGULATION (FIRMR) The regulation setting forth uniform management, acquisition, and use policies and procedures pertaining to the INFORMATION RESOURCES MANAGEMENT activities of federal agencies and those of Government contractors as directed by agencies, disestablished in 1996 by the repeal of the BROOKS ACT (AUTOMATIC DATA PROCESSING PROCUREMENTS), by Pub. L. No. 104-106. FIRMR Subchapter D established unique regulatory coverage on the acquisition of FEDERAL INFORMATION PROCESSING RESOURCES by contracting. The FIRMR system consisted of the FIRMR, the primary document, and the agency regulations that implement or supplement it. The FIRMR was prepared, issued, and maintained by the GENERAL SERVICES ADMINISTRATION.

FEDERAL LABORATORY CONSORTIUM (FLC) FOR TECHNOLOGY TRANSFER The organization that carries out the formal mission of promoting and strengthening TECHNOLOGY TRANSFER across the federal research system under 15 U.S.C. § 3701 et seq. Membership is mandatory for most federal laboratories. The FLC was created in 1971 to facilitate technology transfer between DOD and state and local governments. In 1974, the FLC was expanded to include other federal agencies on a voluntary basis. See Duncombe, *Federal Technology Transfer: A Look at the Benefits and Pitfalls of One of the Country's Best Kept Secrets*, 37 Fed. B. News & J. 608 (1990).

FEDERAL PRISON INDUSTRIES, INC. A self-supporting, wholly owned Government corporation of the District of Columbia; also referred to as UNICOR. FAR 8.601. Through the sale of its products and services to Government agencies, Federal Prison Industries provides training and employment for prisoners confined in federal penal and correctional institutions. 18 U.S.C. §§ 4121–4129. Federal Prison Industries has the authority to SET ASIDE products by placing them on the Schedule of Products Made in Federal Penal and Correctional Institutions. See FAR 8.001(a)(1). FAR 8.602 requires agencies to purchase supplies listed on the schedule at prices not to exceed current market prices and encourages agencies to use Federal Prison Industries facilities to the maximum extent practicable in purchasing supplies and services not listed on the schedule. FAR 8.601(c) states that Federal Prison Industries diversifies its products and services to prevent private industry from experiencing unfair competition from prison workshops or activities.

FEDERAL PROCUREMENT DATA SYSTEM (FPDS) A system for collecting and compiling data on federal procurement. The FPDS provides a comprehensive mechanism for assembling, organizing, and presenting contract placement data for the Federal Government. FAR 4.602. Federal agencies report data to the Federal Procurement Data Center, which collects, processes, and disseminates official statistical data on federal contracting. The data provide (1) a basis for recurring and special reports to the executive and legislative branches and the general public, (2) a means of measuring and assessing the effect of federal contracting on the nation's economy and the extent to which small business concerns are sharing in federal contracts, and (3) information for other policy and management control purposes. The data are collected and reported on Standard Form 279, Federal Procurement Data System (FPDS)—Individual Contract Action Report, FAR 53.301-279; and Standard Form 281, Federal Procurement Data

System (FPDS)—Summary of Contract Actions of $25,000 or Less. FAR 53.301-281.

FEDERAL PROCUREMENT REGULATIONS (FPR) The federal regulation that set forth uniform policies and procedures applicable to federal agencies, other than DOD and NASA, in the procurement of supplies and nonpersonal services, including construction. The FPR was superseded by the FEDERAL ACQUISITION REGULATION in 1984. The FPR was prescribed by the Administrator of General Services under the FEDERAL PROPERTY AND ADMINISTRATIVE SERVICES ACT OF 1949.

FEDERAL PROPERTY AND ADMINISTRATIVE SERVICES ACT (FPASA) OF 1949 An Act, 40 U.S.C. § 471 et seq. and 41 U.S.C. § 251 et seq., containing policies and procedures for the use and disposal of GOVERNMENT PROPERTY by all agencies and for the procurement of supplies and services, including CONSTRUCTION, by almost all federal agencies except DOD, NASA and the Coast Guard. See 41 U.S.C. § 252 for a description of the agencies covered. This Act is one of the two major acts prescribing procurement policies and procedures—the other being the ARMED SERVICES PROCUREMENT ACT. Both acts were significantly amended in 1984 by the COMPETITION IN CONTRACTING ACT and in 1994 by the FEDERAL ACQUISITION STREAMLINING ACT. See Cibinic & Nash, chap. 1, Sec. I., *Formation of Government Contracts* (3d ed. 1998).

FEDERAL PROPERTY MANAGEMENT REGULATION (FPMR) The regulation that guides and governs the federal agencies in their management of property and records. The FPMR is codified as Chapter 101 of Title 41 of the Code of Federal Regulations. It is issued by the General Services Administration.

FEDERAL REGISTER A daily publication of the Office of the Federal Register, established in 1935 by the Federal Register Act, 44 U.S.C. § 1501, as part of a central publications system for promulgating the detailed regulations issued by federal agencies. The Federal Register is the medium for notifying the public of official agency actions. Agencies' regulatory documents are filed with the Office of the Federal Register, placed on public inspection, published in the Federal Register, and then permanently codified (numerically arranged) in the CODE OF FEDERAL REGULATIONS. Publication in the Federal Register gives a regulation the force of law. In 1948, the ADMINISTRATIVE PROCEDURE ACT, 5 U.S.C. § 551 et seq., introduced the requirement that the public have an opportunity to comment on most proposed regulations (excluding procurement regulations). It stated that, absent good cause, no regulation would become final less than 30 days from its publication in the Federal Register. It also provided for publication in the Federal Register of agency statements of organization and procedural rules. Proposed procurement regulations are required to be published in the Federal Register by 41 U.S.C. § 418b. See the Office of the Federal Register publication *The Federal Register: What It Is and How to Use It* (available from the U.S. Government Printing Office, Washington, DC 20402), which provides comprehensive information on how to obtain Federal Register documents. The *Federal Register* is available on the Internet at a variety of sites, including the Government Printing Office at <http://www.access.gpo.gov>.

FEDERAL SPECIFICATIONS AND STANDARDS SPECIFICATIONS and STANDARDS issued or controlled by the General Services Administration (GSA) and listed in the *GSA Index of Federal Specifications, Standards and Commercial Item Descriptions*. This index is issued annually and available from GSA, Specification Section, Suite 800, L'Enfant Plaza, SW, Washington, DC 20407). See Cibinic & Nash, chap. 3, Sec. V., *Formation of Government Contracts* (3d ed. 1998).

FEDERAL SUPPLY SCHEDULES (FSS) A series of schedules, compiled by the GENERAL SERVICES ADMINISTRATION (GSA), of commonly used supplies and services available to Government agencies (and some cost-reimbursement contractors) at specified prices. The Federal Supply Service is converting FSS to nonmandatory sources of supply. This includes all multiple and single award schedules. Contracting officers, using competitive procedures, award INDEFINITE-DELIVERY CONTRACTs to commercial firms, requiring those firms to provide, under "schedule," specified supplies and services at stated prices for given periods of time. This process permits contracting officers outside GSA to acquire items covered by such schedules without engaging in the time-consuming process of issuing INVITATION FOR BIDS or REQUESTS FOR PROPOSALS. The schedules, often referred to as GSA schedules, allow ordering offices to issue delivery orders directly to listed contractors, receive direct shipments, make payment directly to contractors, and administer the orders. Both SINGLE-AWARD SCHEDULEs and MULTIPLE-AWARD SCHEDULEs (MASs) are established. See FAR Subpart 8.4 and Part 38; and the FPMR at 41 C.F.R. chap. 101, Subchapter E, Part 101-26. GSA can authorize other agencies to award schedule contracts and publish schedules; the DEPARTMENT OF VERTERANS AFFAIRS, for example, awards schedule contracts for medical and nonperishable subsistence items. FAR 38.101(d). See Cibinic & Nash, chap. 7, Sec. VIII., *Formation of Government Contracts* (3d ed. 1998).

FEDERAL TECHNOLOGY TRANSFER The process of shifting federally generated technology and technical know-how to state and local governments or the private sector for development and commercialization. The term "technology transfer" is used to describe the process by which technology or know-how developed for a particular purpose by one organization can be transferred to another organization for use in another area. The goal of federal technology transfer is to make technology developed in federal laboratories available to nonfederal organizations to promote economic growth through commercialization of new products or processes and improvement of existing techniques. Companies interested in a particular technology can contact a state technology transfer program, the OFFICE OF RESEARCH AND TECHNOLOGY APPLICATION of a local laboratory, the FEDERAL LABORATORY CONSORTIUM FOR TECHNOLOGY TRANSFER, or the NATIONAL INSTITUTE OF STANDARDS AND TECHNOLOGY in Washington, DC. The party contacted will try to identify a knowledgeable source within the federal network. Types of assistance available include technical assistance; access to nonclassified work; use of federal laboratory facilities or equipment; access to federal patented inventions for licensing; participation in COOPERATIVE RESEARCH AND DEVELOPMENT AGREEMENTS; and access to information, databases, and publications. See Vacketta et al., *Technology Transfer*, 94-12 Briefing Papers (Nov. 1994); Sweeney, *Commercializing Government Inventions; Utilizing the Federal Technology Transfer Act of 1986*, 20 Pub. Cont. L.J. 365 (1991); Duncombe, *Federal Technology Transfer: A Look at the Benefits and Pitfalls of One of the Country's Best Kept Secrets*, 37 Fed. B. News & J. 608 (1990).

FEDERAL TELECOMMUNICATIONS STANDARDS (FED-STDS) Official federal publications developed under delegation from the General Services Administration by the National Communications System, an interagency organization assigned national security and emergency preparedness telecommunications responsibilities. FED-STDS include the categories in the Federal Supply Class of "Telecommunications" that were not redefined as AUTOMATIC DATA PROCESSING EQUIPMENT by the PAPERWORK REDUCTION REAUTHORIZATION ACT OF 1986.

FEDERAL TELECOMMUNICATIONS SYSTEM (FTS) The umbrella of local and long-distance telecommunications services (including FTS 2000 long-distance services) provided, operated, managed, or maintained by the General Services Administration for the common use of all federal agencies and other authorized users. 41 C.F.R. § 101-35.1. Agencies must use FTS as the first source of supply for a telecommunications requirement unless the requirement falls outside the scope of FTS or the agency has an exception to the use of FTS services. 41 C.F.R. § 101-35.301-2.

FEDERAL TORT CLAIMS ACT (FTCA) A 1946 Act, 28 U.S.C. §§ 1346(b), 2401–2402, 2671–2672, 2674–2680, permitting persons injured by negligent conduct of the Government to sue for damages in U.S. District Courts. Prior to suit, 28 U.S.C. § 2675(a) requires that the injured person file for administrative relief with the agency involved. Thereafter, if relief is not granted, suit in court is permitted. 28 U.S.C. § 2680(a) precludes recovery if the Government action is the result of a discretionary function. Recovery under the FTCA is limited to actual damages; punitive damages are barred by 28 U.S.C. § 2674. See Cibinic & Nash, chap. 11, Sec. V., *Formation of Government Contracts* (3d ed. 1998). See also TORT.

FEDERALLY FUNDED RESEARCH AND DEVELOPMENT CENTER (FFRDC) A center that enables agencies to use private-sector resources to accomplish RESEARCH AND DEVELOPMENT tasks that are integral to agency missions and operations. FFRDCs are operated, managed, and/or administered by either a university or a consortium of universities, another not-for-profit organization, or an industrial firm as an autonomous firm or as an identifiable separate operating unit of a parent organization. FAR 35.017. The Government may enter into contracts with an FFRDC to facilitate long-term relationships and establish the FFRDC's mission, but an FFRDC may not compete with non-FFRDCs on agency-issued REQUESTs FOR PROPOSALS for work other than operation of the FFRDC. FAR 35.017-1. The National Science Foundation maintains a master list of FFRDCs. FAR 35.017-6. See Sanders, *Capturing Private R&D for Public Ends: The Government's Use of FFRDCs*, 26 Nat'l Cont. Mgmt. J., Issue No. 1, p. 45 (1995).

FEE The amount paid to a contractor beyond allowable costs under a COST-REIMBURSEMENT CONTRACT. In Government contracting "fee" is the term of art for PROFIT the Government agrees to pay on a cost-reimbursement contract. ("Profit" is used when the contract is a fixed-price type.) In most instances, fee reflects a variety of factors, including RISK. The FIXED FEE on COST-PLUS-FIXED-FEE CONTRACTs may not exceed certain statutory limitations. See FAR 15.404-4(c)(4). The fee may be fixed at the outset of performance, as in a cost-plus-fixed-fee contract, or it may vary within a contractually specified range (see RANGE OF INCENTIVE EFFECTIVENESS), as in a COST-PLUS-INCENTIVE-FEE CONTRACT or a COST-PLUS AWARD-FEE CONTRACT. See generally Cibinic & Nash, *Cost-Reimbursement Contracting* 571–607 (2d ed. 1993).

FEE DETERMINATION OFFICIAL (FDO) The individual responsible for reviewing the recommendations of the Performance Evaluation Board and making the final determination of the amount of AWARD FEE to be awarded to the contractor. EPAR 1516.404-272; AGAR 416.404-2. This is usually the third and last step in the procedure of establishing an award from a COST-PLUS-AWARD-FEE CONTRACT. Contract clauses typically state that the FDO's determination is binding on both parties and is not subject to appeal under the Disputes clause or any other appeal clause, but the COURT OF APPEALS FOR THE FEDERAL CIRCUIT has ruled that courts may review such fee determinations to determine if they are arbitrary or capricious, *Burnside-Ott Aviation Training Center v. Dalton*, 107 F.3d 854 (Fed. Cir. 1997). DEAR 916.405. In major procurement this official should be at the management level of the procuring agency, while in small contracts the contracting officer might perform this task. See Cibinic & Nash, *Cost-Reimbursement Contracting* 119 (2d ed. 1993).

FEE FOR PROFESSIONAL SERVICES The amount paid to a member of a profession for the performance of services. Used in this sense, the "fee" is the PRICE to be paid under a contract for PROFESSIONAL AND CONSULTANT SERVICES when the work is satisfactorily performed. 10 U.S.C. § 2306(d) and 41 U.S.C. § 254(b) provide that the fee paid for ARCHITECT-ENGINEER SERVICES may not exceed six percent of the estimated cost of construction of the work designed by the A-E. See FAR 15.404-4(c)((4)(i)(B). Neither the statutes nor the procurement regulations limits the fees paid to other professionals.

FIELD PRICING ASSISTANCE A review and evaluation of the contractor's or subcontractor's proposal by any or all field pricing support personnel. FAR 15.404-2(a)(2). Such personnel may include plant representatives, ADMINISTRATIVE CONTRACTING OFFI-

CERS, contract AUDITORs, price analysts, QUALITY ASSURANCE personnel, engineers, and small business and legal specialists. FAR 15.404-2(a) states that a contracting officer should request field pricing assistance when the information available at the buying activity is inadequate to determine a fair and reasonable price. Such requests must be tailored to reflect the minimum essential supplementary information needed to conduct a technical or cost or pricing analysis. When field pricing assistance is requested, contracting officers are encouraged to team with appropriate field experts throughout the ACQUISITION PROCESS, including negotiations. FAR 15.404-2(a)(3).

FINAL COST OBJECTIVE See COST OBJECTIVE.

FINAL DECISION See DECISION OF THE CONTRACTING OFFICER.

FINAL INDIRECT COST RATE A percentage or dollar factor, agreed to by the COST-REIMBURSEMENT CONTRACTor and the Government, expressing the ratio of INDIRECT COST incurred during a prior period to direct labor cost, manufacturing cost, or another appropriate base for the same period. For commercial contractors this rate is established after the close of the contractor's FISCAL YEAR to which it applies. In the case of cost-reimbursement research and development contracts with educational institutions, the final indirect cost rate may be predetermined; that is, it may be established for a future period on the basis of cost experience with similar contracts, together with supporting data. FAR 42.701. FAR 42.703-1 requires that a single agency must establish indirect cost rate for each BUSINESS UNIT of a contractor. This provides (1) uniformity of approach when more than one contract or agency is involved, (2) economy of administration, and (3) timely settlement under cost-reimbursement contracts. FAR 42.702. The FAR requires that final indirect cost rates be established on the basis of either a contracting officer's or an auditor's determination procedure. FAR 42.705. See Cibinic & Nash, *Cost-Reimbursement Contracting* 1091–94 (2d ed. 1993).

FINAL PAYMENT The last payment the Government makes on a contract when the parties believe all obligations under the contract have been closed out. The Government makes final payment upon completion and acceptance of all work required under a contract, once the disbursing officer receives a properly executed and duly certified VOUCHER or INVOICE showing the total amount agreed upon, less amounts previously paid. The contract may require the contractor to give a RELEASE of CLAIMs and liabilities before the Government makes final payment. The various Changes clauses in FAR 52.243-1 et seq., the Suspension of Work clause, FAR 52.242-14, and the Government Delay of Work clause, FAR 52.242-17, expressly bar claims not asserted by the contractor before final payment. Whether final payment has occurred for the purposes of these clauses depends on the totality of the facts and circumstances of a particular case. See Cibinic & Nash, *Administration of Government Contracts* 923–25 (3d ed. 1995); Nash, *Releases Accompanying Final Payment: Don't Give Up the Farm*, 1 N&CR ¶ 76 (Oct. 1987).

FINAL PROPOSAL REVISION An offer submitted to the Government in a competitive negotiated procurement (see NEGOTIATION) after DISCUSSIONs have been conducted. FAR 15.307(b). The contracting officer is required to request such revisions from all offerors still in the COMPETITIVE RANGE and to establish a common cut-off date for receipt of final proposal revisions. Prior to FAC 97-02, September 30, 1997, final proposal revisions were called BEST AND FINAL OFFERS. See Cibinic & Nash, chap. 6, *Formation of Government Contracts* (3d ed. 1998).

FINANCIAL ACCOUNTING STANDARDS BOARD (FASB) A private organization that establishes standards of financial accounting and reporting. Those standards govern the preparation of financial reports and provide for the guidance and education of the public, including issuers, auditors, and users of financial information. The FASB follows certain precepts in conducting its activities: objectivity in decisionmaking, careful weighing of the views of its constituents, promulgation of standards only when expected benefits exceed perceived costs, introduction of changes in ways that least disrupt the continuity of reporting practice, and review of the effects of past decisions. [FASB, High Ridge Park, P.O. Box 3821, Stanford, CT 06906]

FINANCIAL INABILITY A contractor's incapacity to perform for economic reasons: the contractor cannot buy materials, pay its workforce, keep its plant open, or prevent foreclosure. Such inability is generally the responsibility of the contractor, but it may be excusable if caused by an event outside the control of the contractor and may even be compensable if the Government caused it. Financial inability is distinguished from "financial difficulty" (which means economic hardship, but not to the level of incapacity) and from "commercial impracticability" (see IMPRACTICABILITY OF PERFORMANCE).

If financial inability is excusable, it may be raised as a defense against TERMINATION FOR DEFAULT or as an excuse for failing to continue performance. Nagle, *Financial Inability in Government Contracts*, 17 Pub. Cont. L.J. 320 (1987).

FINANCING The obtaining by a contractor of the money necessary for performance of a contract. FAR Part 32 governs contract financing. FAR 32.106 states the following order of preference for obtaining financing: (1) private financing without Government guarantee on reasonable terms (the contractor is not required to obtain private financing from other agencies), (2) customary contract financing (see FAR 32.113), (3) loan guarantees, (4) unusual contract financing (see FAR 32.114), and (5) ADVANCE PAYMENTs (see FAR 32.402(d) for exceptions). FAR 32.104 states that Government financing should be provided only to the extent actually needed for prompt and efficient performance, considering the availability of private financing. FAR 32.107, however, provides that if a contractor or offeror meets the RESPONSIBILITY standards prescribed for prospective contractors, the contracting officer shall not treat the contractor's need for financial assistance as a handicap for a contract award. See Wall & Gustin, *FASA Contract Financing Reforms (An Offer You Can't Refuse?)*, 95-10 CP&A Rep. 3 (Oct. 1995); Kisinger, *A Banker's View of Government Contractors*, 33 Cont. Mgmt. 20 (Aug. 1993); Dakin, *Government's Policies Toward Contractor Financing*, 32 Cont. Mgmt. 11 (Dec. 1992); Chierchella et al., *Financing Government Contracts*, 86-7 Briefing Papers (June 1986).

FINANCING INSTITUTION An institution dealing in money—as distinguished from other commodities—as the primary function of its business activity. A financing institution may be an individual or a partnership as well as a corporate organization, but it may not be a SURETY, a trust, or an ordinary corporation that incidentally provides financing to its suppliers or to others with whom it deals. The ASSIGNMENT OF CLAIMS Act permits the assignment of contract proceeds only to a bank, trust company, or other financing institution. See FAR Subpart 32.8; GAO, *Principles of Federal Appropriations Law*, vol. III, chap. 12 (2d ed. 1991); Schooner & Schooner, *Look Before You Lend: A Lender's Guide to Financing Government Contracts Pursuant to the Assignment of Claims Act*, 48 Bus. Law. 535 (1993).

FINANCING PAYMENT A Government disbursement of monies to a contractor under a contract clause or other authorization before acceptance of supplies or services by the Government. FAR 32.902.

Such payments are not subject to the PROMPT PAYMENT ACT. Financing payments include (1) ADVANCE PAYMENTs; (2) PROGRESS PAYMENTs based on costs under the Progress Payments clause at FAR 52.232-16; (3) progress payments based on a percentage or stage of completion, other than those made under the Payments under Fixed-Price Construction Contracts clause at FAR 52.232-5 or the Payments under Fixed-Price Architect-Engineer Contracts clause at FAR 52.232-10; and (4) interim payments on cost-type contracts. Financing payments do not include INVOICE PAYMENTs or payments for partial deliveries. FAR 32.902. Generally, the due date for the designated payment office to make financing payments is the 30th day after the designated billing office has received a proper request. FAR 32.906. No interest penalty is paid to a contractor as a result of delayed contract financing payments. FAR 32.907-2. See Cibinic & Nash, *Administration of Government Contracts* 1143–47 (3d ed. 1995); OMB Circular No. A-125, *Prompt Payment*, Aug. 19, 1982.

FINE A payment required to be made as a result of misconduct. FAR 31.205-15 makes fines UNALLOWABLE COSTs. Fines are generally specified as criminal sanctions under Title 18 of the United States Code or state law. See Cibinic & Nash, *Cost-Reimbursement Contracting* 876–78 (2d ed. 1993). See *Ingalls Shipbuilding v. Dalton*, 119 F.3d 972 (Fed. Cir. 1997).

FIRM-FIXED-PRICE (FFP) CONTRACT A type of contract providing for a price that is not subject to adjustment on the basis of the contractor's cost experience in performing the contract. FAR 16.202-1. FFP contracts are generally subject to adjustment in accordance with contract clauses providing for EQUITABLE ADJUSTMENTs or PRICE ADJUSTMENTs. They place maximum RISK and full responsibility on the contractor for all costs and resulting profit or loss. They provide maximum incentive for the contractor to control costs and perform effectively and impose a minimum administrative burden upon the contracting parties unless changes are issued or unforeseen events occur during performance. FAR 16.103(b) provides that firm-fixed-price contracts are the preferred type of contract when the risk involved is minimal or can be predicted with an acceptable degree of certainty. An FFP LEVEL-OF-EFFORT CONTRACT may be used for investigation or study in a specific research and development area. FAR 16.207-2. See Cibinic & Nash, chap. 8, Sec. II., *Formation of Government Contracts* (3d ed. 1998).

FIRMWARE Software that is embedded in a hardware device that allows reading and executing the software but does not allow modification. National Communications System Technology and Standards Division, *Telecommunications: Glossary of Telecommunication Terms*, Federal Standard 1037C (Aug. 1996).

FIRST ACTUAL REDUCTION TO PRACTICE The embodiment of an invention in a physical form and the demonstration of workability by subsequent testing. The amount of testing is dependent on the complexity of the invention and the environment in which it is claimed to work. Thus, the testing necessary to establish reduction to practice may be mere observation, laboratory testing, or testing in an actual operational environment. If first actual reduction to practice of an invention occurs in the performance of a Government contract containing a Patent Rights clause, the invention will be a SUBJECT INVENTION and Government will get rights (at least a royalty-free license) to any PATENT that issues on the invention. See Nash & Rawicz, *Intellectual Property in Government Contracts*, vol. 1 (3d ed. 1997).

FIRST ARTICLE TESTING Testing and evaluating first articles for conformance with specified contract requirements before or in the initial stage of production. FAR 9.301. The first articles may be preproduction models or prototypes, initial production samples, test samples, first lots, pilot lots, or pilot models. The procedures governing first article testing are set forth in FAR Subpart 9.3. First article testing and approval ensures that the contractor can furnish a product that conforms to all contract requirements for acceptance. Contracts imposing a first article testing requirement upon the contractor will contain the First Article Approval—Contractor Testing clause at FAR 52.209-3 or the First Article Approval—Government Testing clause at FAR 52.209-4. Failure to deliver or gain approval of first articles may result in TERMINATION FOR DEFAULT. See Cibinic & Nash, *Administration of Government Contracts* 598 (3d ed. 1995).

FIRST IN, FIRST OUT (FIFO) An inventory costing method in which stock acquired earliest is assumed to be sold first, leaving stock acquired more recently in inventory. Under FIFO, inventory is valued near current replacement costs. CAS 411, 48 C.F.R. § 9904.411, identifies FIFO as one of the inventory costing methods that a contractor must use in accounting for acquisition costs of material.

FISCAL YEAR (FY) **FOR CONTRACTORS**—The accounting period for which annual financial statements are regularly prepared, generally a period of 12 months, 52 weeks, or 53 weeks. FAR 31.001. CAS 406, 48 C.F.R. § 9904.406, provides criteria for selecting the time periods to be used as cost accounting periods for contract cost estimating, accumulating, and reporting. The standard is intended to reduce the effects of variations in the flow of costs within each cost accounting period; enhance objectivity, consistency, and verifiability; and promote uniformity and comparability in contract cost measurements. **FOR THE GOVERNMENT**—The period running from October 1 through September 30. Thus, the period running from October 1, 1996, through September 30, 1997 is designated FY97. Generally, APPROPRIATIONs are made for each fiscal year.

FIXED-CEILING-PRICE CONTRACT See FIXED-PRICE REDETERMINATION—RETROACTIVE CONTRACT.

FIXED COSTS Costs of an enterprise that cannot be varied with the amount of work performed. Fixed costs are generally compared to VARIABLE COSTS when analyzing INDIRECT COSTs of a contractor. If the fixed costs comprise a large part of such indirect costs, the contractor's OVERHEAD RATEs can be expected to increase significantly if the amount of work performed declines.

FIXED FEE The FEE agreed upon for the performance of a COST-PLUS-FIXED-FEE CONTRACT. 10 U.S.C. § 2306(d) and 41 U.S.C. § 254(b) provide that fixed fees may not exceed 10 percent of the ESTIMATED COST except in the case of contracts for experimental, developmental, or research work, where the limitation is 15 percent. Fixed fees are negotiated in accordance with FAR 404-4 as supplemented by agency FAR supplements. See Cibinic & Nash, *Cost-Reimbursement Contracting* 571–607 (2d ed. 1993); Cibinic, *Increasing the Fixed Fee in Equitable Adjustments to Cost-Reimbursement Contracts: A Fuzzy Standard*, 9 N&CR ¶ 47 (Sept. 1995).

FIXED-PRICE CONTRACT A type of contract providing for a firm pricing arrangement established by the parties at the time of contracting. The policies on the use of this type of contract are set forth in FAR Subpart 16.2. Whereas a FIRM-FIXED-PRICE CONTRACT is not subject to adjustment on the basis of the contractor's cost experience in performing the contract, other types of fixed-price contracts are subject to PRICE ADJUSTMENT on the basis of economic conditions or the contractor's performance of the contract. These types of contracts are

FIXED-PRICE CONTRACTs WITH ECONOMIC PRICE ADJUSTMENT, FIXED-PRICE-INCENTIVE CONTRACTs, FIXED-PRICE REDETERMINATION—PROSPECTIVE CONTRACTs, and FIXED-PRICE REDETERMINATION—RETROACTIVE CONTRACTs. See Cibinic & Nash, chap. 8, Sec. II., *Formation of Government Contracts* (3d ed. 1998); Curry, *Management of Fixed-Price/Subcontracts with Progress Payments*, 32 Cont. Mgmt. 23 (Sept. 1992).

FIXED-PRICE CONTRACT WITH ECONOMIC PRICE ADJUSTMENT A type of contract providing for upward or downward revision of the stated contract price upon the occurrence of a specified contingency. FAR 16.203-1. Adjustments may reflect increases or decreases in established prices for specific items, in the contractor's actual costs of LABOR or material, or in specific indexes of labor or material costs. FAR 16.203-2 provides that a fixed-price contract with economic price adjustment may be used when (1) there is serious doubt that market or labor conditions will remain stable during an extended period of contract performance, and (2) contingencies (see CONTINGENCY) that would otherwise be included in the contract price can be identified and covered separately in the contract. FAR 14.408-4 provides that when the Government proposes inclusion of an economic price adjustment clause in the INVITATION FOR BID (IFB), bids will be evaluated on the basis of the quoted prices without adding any amount for price adjustment. However, if no such clause is included in the IFB, the FAR provides that bids proposing economic price adjustment must be rejected unless they propose a ceiling price—in which case they will be evaluated at the ceiling. Economic price adjustment is sometimes called "escalation," but that is a misnomer because the price can be lowered as well as raised. See Cibinic & Nash, chap. 8, Sec. II., *Formation of Government Contracts* (3d ed. 1998).

FIXED-PRICE-INCENTIVE (FPI) CONTRACT A type of contract that provides for adjusting PROFIT and establishing the final contract price by a formula based on the relationship of final negotiated TOTAL COST to total TARGET COST. FAR 16.403. The final price is subject to a CEILING PRICE negotiated at the outset. There are two forms of fixed-price-incentive contracts: firm target and successive target. FAR 16.403-1 provides that a firm target is appropriate when the parties can negotiate at the outset a firm target cost, a TARGET PROFIT, a profit adjustment formula, and a ceiling price that will both give the contractor a fair and reasonable incentive and ensure that the contractor assumes an appropriate share of the RISK. FAR 16.403-2 provides that successive targets are appropriate when available cost or pricing information is not sufficient to permit the negotiation of a realistic firm target cost and profit before award. Standard clauses are provided for these types of contracts: the Incentive Price Revision—Firm Target clause in FAR 52.216-16 and the Incentive Price Revision—Successive Targets clause in FAR 52.216-17. See Cibinic & Nash, chap. 8, Sec. IV., *Formation of Government Contracts* (3d ed. 1998); McVay, *Caution! Slippery Fixed-Price Incentive Contract Ahead!,* 26 Nat'l Cont. Mgmt. J., Issue No. 1, p. 15 (1995).

FIXED-PRICE LEVEL-OF-EFFORT CONTRACT A FIRM-FIXED-PRICE CONTRACT requiring (1) the contractor to provide a specified level of effort over a stated period of time, on work that can be stated only in general terms; and (2) the Government to pay the contractor a fixed dollar amount. FAR 16.207-1. Such a contract is suitable for investigation or study in a specific research and development area. The product of the contract is usually a report showing the results achieved through application of the required level of effort. Payment, however, is based on the effort expended rather than the results achieved. FAR 16.207-2. Fixed-price level-of-effort contracts may be used only when (1) the work required cannot otherwise be clearly defined, (2) the required level of effort is identified and agreed upon in advance, (3) there is a reasonable assurance that the intended result cannot be achieved by expending less than the stipulated effort, and (4) the contract price is $100,000 or less (unless higher-level approval is obtained). FAR 16.207-3. See Cibinic & Nash, chap. 8, Sec. V., *Formation of Government Contracts* (3d ed. 1998).

FIXED-PRICE REDETERMINATION–PROSPECTIVE (FPRP) CONTRACT A type of contract that contains a firm-fixed-price for an initial period of contract delivery or performance and provides for the negotiation of a new firm-fixed-price for subsequent contract work. The contract specifies the time or times when new prices will be negotiated. FPRP contracts may be used to acquire production or services in quantity in cases when it is possible to negotiate a firm-fixed-price for an initial period but not for the entire amount of goods or services needed. The initial period should be as long as possible, and each subsequent period should be at least 12 months. FAR 16.205-2. An FPRP contract may be used only when (1) a FIRM-FIXED-PRICE CONTRACT is not feasible and a FIXED-PRICE-INCENTIVE CONTRACT would not be more appropriate, (2) the contractor's accounting system will permit price redetermination, (3) the prospective pricing periods can be made to conform with operation of the contractor's accounting system, and (4) there is reasonable assurance that price redetermination will take place promptly at the specified times. FAR 16.205-3. See Cibinic & Nash, chap. 8, Sec. II., *Formation of Government Contracts* (3d ed. 1998).

FIXED-PRICE REDETERMINATION–RETROACTIVE (FPRR) CONTRACT A type of contract under which a CEILING PRICE is negotiated before contract performance and a final fixed price within that ceiling is determined, based on an assessment of the contractor's performance and its actual audited costs, after the work is completed. Because FPRR contracts provide no positive incentive for the contractor to control costs (other than the ceiling price, which may contain a sizable margin for error and uncertainty), FAR 16.206-2 limits their use. They may be used only for research and development estimated at $100,000 or less when a FIRM-FIXED-PRICE CONTRACT cannot be negotiated and the dollar amount involved and short performance period make any other fixed-price contract type impracticable. FAR 16.206-3 further narrows the conditions for use to situations in which the contractor's accounting system is adequate for price redetermination, there is reasonable assurance that price redetermination will take place promptly as specified, and the head of the contracting activity or a higher-level official grants approval in writing. See Cibinic & Nash, chap. 8, Sec. II., *Formation of Government Contracts* (3d ed. 1998).

FLOW-DOWN CLAUSES Clauses prescribed by the Government that a PRIME CONTRACTOR incorporates into SUBCONTRACTs. These clauses "flow down" rights and responsibilities of the prime contractor to the subcontractor. Mandatory flow-down clauses are those prime contract clauses that specifically require the inclusion of their text in all subcontracts entered into in support of the prime contract. Other clauses, although not mandatory, should be flowed down to ensure that the subcontractor will provide adequate assistance or cooperation to enable the prime contractor to meet its contractual requirements with the Government. Failure to flow down certain clauses may expose the prime contractor to financial risk if the Government takes certain actions under the prime contract and the subcontract does not obligate the subcontractor to respond in accordance with those actions. See Meagher & Friery, *Revisiting Subcontract Flow-Down Provisions*, 38 Gov't Contractor ¶ 361 (July 31, 1996); Ellenson, *Flow-Down Clauses in Subcontracts*, 33 Cont. Mgmt. 10 (Nov. 1993); Hoe et al., *Flow Down Clauses in Subcontracts*, 85-5 Briefing Papers (May 1985).

FLY AMERICA ACT An Act, Section 5 of the International Air Transportation Fair Competitive Practices Act of 1974, 49 U.S.C.

§ 40118, requiring federal employees and their dependents, consultants, contractors, grantees, and others to use U.S.-flag air carriers for U.S. Government-financed international air travel and transportation of their personal effects or property, to the extent that service by these carriers is available. FAR 47.402. "International air transportation" means transportation by air between a place in the United States and a place outside the United States, or between two places both of which are outside the United States. FAR 47.401. Contracting officers must insert the clause at FAR 52.247-63, Preference for U.S. Flag Air Carriers, in solicitations and contracts unless the contract is awarded under simplified acquisition procedures or is a contract for commercial items.

FLYAWAY COSTS A DOD term that attempts to encompass the total acquisition cost of an aircraft program. It includes costs related to the development and production of a useable end item of military hardware, as well as the cost of creating the basic unit (airframe, hull, chassis, etc.), an allowance for CHANGES, propulsion equipment, electronics, armament, and other installed GOVERNMENT-FURNISHED EQUIPMENT, and nonrecurring "start-up" production costs. The term equates to rollaway and sailaway costs, for non-aircraft programs. See also AVERAGE UNIT PROCUREMENT COST OBJECTIVES. Jones, *Glossary: Defense Acquisition Acronyms and Terms* (8th ed., Defense Systems Management College).

F.O.B. An abbreviation for "free on board." FAR 47.001. This term is used with the designation of a physical point to determine the responsibility and basis for payment of freight charges and, unless otherwise agreed, the point at which TITLE for supplies passes to the buyer or consignee. The policies on designation of contracts as F.O.B. ORIGIN or F.O.B. DESTINATION are set forth in FAR Subpart 47.3. Contract clauses providing a variety of payment and evaluation arrangements for transportation costs are set forth in FAR 52.247-29 through 52.247-59. See U.C.C. § 2-319.

F.O.B. DESTINATION Free on board at destination, or where the seller or consignor delivers the supplies on the seller's or consignor's conveyance to a specified delivery point. FAR 47.001. In this case, unless the contract provides otherwise, the cost of shipping and the risk of loss are borne by the seller or consignor. Guidance on the use of this technique is set forth in FAR 47.303-6 and -7. Various clauses are provided for this type of arrangement in FAR 52.247-34, -35, -41, -42, -45, -49, and -54.

F.O.B. ORIGIN Free on board at the place of origin, or where the seller or consignor places the supplies on the conveyance by which they are to be transported. FAR 47.001. Unless the contract provides otherwise, the cost of shipping and the risk of loss are borne by the buyer or consignee. Guidance on the use of this technique is set forth in FAR 47.303-1 through -5. Various clauses are provided for this type of arrangement in FAR 52.247-29 through -33, -45, -46, -47, and -59.

FOLLOW ON CONTRACT A type of sole source award made to a contractor who has previously been awarded a design or manufacturing contract for the same item or who has previously performed the services being procured. 41 U.S.C. § 253(d)(1)(B) and 10 U.S.C. § 2304(d)(1)(B) specifically permit sole source contracting for follow-on contracts for the continued development of production of a major system or highly specialized equipment when it is likely that award to a source other than the original source would result in substantial duplication of cost to the Government, which is not expected to be recovered through competition, or unacceptable delays in fulfilling the agency's needs. See Cibinic & Nash, *Cost-Reimbursement Contracting* 166–69 (2d ed. 1993).

FOLLOWER COMPANY See LEADER-COMPANY CONTRACTING.

FORBEARANCE The postponement of the decision to terminate for default (see TERMINATION FOR DEFAULT) while the contracting officer is investigating the reasons for the contractor's failure to meet the contract requirements. With regard to the Government's WAIVER of its right to terminate a contract for late delivery, the contracting officer has a reasonable period of forbearance to investigate the facts and determine what course of action best serves the Government's interests. During the forbearance period, the Government may terminate at any time, without prior notice. The facts and circumstances of each case determine the length of time constituting a reasonable forbearance period; no clear demarcation exists between reasonable forbearance and waiver. Once the forbearance period expires, the Government waives its right to a termination for default and must reestablish a delivery schedule if it wishes to terminate. See Cibinic & Nash, *Administration of Government Contracts* 728 (3d ed. 1995); Carberry & Johnstone, *Waiver of the Government's Right to Terminate for Default in Government Defense Contracts*, 17 Pub. Cont. L.J. 470, 482 (1988).

FORCE MAJEURE A term, derived from insurance law, meaning superior or irresistible force, such as lightning, earthquakes, storms, flood, sunstroke, and freezing. Force majeure is at times thought of as an "act of God"—one occasioned exclusively by violence of nature without the interference of any human agency. Force majeure clauses are common in commercial construction contracts to protect the parties if part of the contract cannot be performed as a result of causes that are outside the control of the parties and could not have been avoided by the exercise of due care. *Black's Law Dictionary* 645 (6th ed. 1990). In Government contracting, the clauses granting the Government the right to terminate for default (see TERMINATION FOR DEFAULT) generally contain EXCUSABLE DELAY provisions that are in the nature of force majeure clauses.

FOREIGN CARRIER See CARRIER (TELECOMMUNICATIONS).

FOREIGN CORRUPT PRACTICES ACT (FCPA) An Act that prohibits the payment of bribes by United States companies and nationals to foreign officials to obtain or attempt to retain business. The penalties for criminal violations may reach $2 million for companies and $100,000 or more, with up to five years' imprisonment, for individuals. The FCPA also requires that publicly held companies maintain certain books and records to reflect certain transactions and dispositions of assets. FCPA issues often arise with regard to agents or foreign sales representatives. 15 U.S.C. § 78dd-1, -2. See McGrath et al., *The Foreign Corrupt Practices Act: A Trap for the Unwary*, 37 Cont. Mgmt. 45 (Mar. 1997).

FOREIGN END PRODUCT An article, material, or supply that, pursuant to the BUY AMERICAN ACT and its related statutes and regulations, is not a DOMESTIC END PRODUCT. FAR 25.101.

FOREIGN MILITARY FINANCING PROGRAM The program through which the United States provides funds to its allies to purchase American military articles and services. See Green & McGrath, *Audits and Investigations of Commercial Contracts under the Foreign Military Financing (FMF) Program*, 94-7 CP&A Rep. 3 (July 1994).

FOREIGN MILITARY SALES (FMS) Government-to-Government sales of U.S. defense items, as authorized under the Foreign Assistance Act of 1961 and the ARMS EXPORT CONTROL ACT. In the normal situation, FMS transactions involve DOD contracts with U.S. contractors for the furnishing of military equipment to a foreign government. Although recipient governments generally pay cash for the full costs associated with such sales, some programs involve loans or other arrangements to permit the purchase. A MEMORANDUM OF UNDERSTANDING may be established to define the relationship between the foreign government and the United States. The process typically entails a letter of request from the foreign country and a letter of offer and acceptance, DD Form 1513, DFARS 253.303-1513, which may require congressional approval. The Arms Export Control Act requires that FMS activities be conducted at no cost to the U.S. Government, that all costs be collected from the recipient government, and that payments be made in advance of delivery. FMS are considered a component of the U.S. Security Assistance Program, which provides defense articles, defense services, and military training to U.S. allies and friendly foreign nations. See DFARS Subpart 225.73; DOD Manual 5105.38-M, *Security Assistance Management*, and DOD Manual 7290.3-M, *Foreign Military Sales Financial Management*; DSMC, *Program Manager's Notebook* (1995). See also Seyfarth et al., chap. 20, *The Contract Compliance Handbook* (2d ed. 1991 & 1996 Supp.); Morgan, *Foreign Military Sales Cash Procurements: Additional Liability Considerations*, 25 Pub. Cont. L.J. 617 (1996); Reuter, *The ABCs of FMS*, 30 Cont. Mgmt. 29 (Oct. 1990); Grossman, *Foreign Military Sales*, 87-12 Briefing Papers (Nov. 1987).

FOREIGN OFFER An offered price for a FOREIGN END PRODUCT, including transportation to destination and duty (whether or not a duty-free entry certificate is issued). FAR 25.101.

FOREIGN OWNERSHIP, CONTROL, OR INFLUENCE (FOCI) Situation in which the degree of ownership, control, or influence over an offeror, bidder, contractor, or subcontractor by a foreign interest (Government, organization, or individual) is such that a reasonable basis exists for concluding that CLASSIFIED INFORMATION or special nuclear material might be compromised. DOE has procedures that require certain offerors, bidders, contractors, or subcontractors to submit information that helps in determining whether award of a contract, or continued performance of a contract, may pose an undue risk to the common defense and security because of FOCI. DEAR Subpart 904.70; DEAR 952.204-74.

FORFEITURE The loss of benefits received under a contract as a result of illegal conduct. For example, in one case of BRIBERY and CONFLICT OF INTEREST, the contractor was required to forfeit the entire contract price after completion of the work. *K & R Eng'g Co. v. United States*, 222 Ct. Cl. 340, 616 F.2d 469 (1980). 18 U.S.C. § 218 permits the voiding or rescission of a contract where there has been a violation of the criminal law against BRIBERY, the giving or receiving of GRATUITIES, or a CONFLICT OF INTEREST. This statute is implemented in FAR Subpart 3.7. 28 U.S.C. § 2514 also requires forfeiture of any claim filed in the courts that is tainted with FRAUD.

FORM, FIT, AND FUNCTION DATA Data that relate to items, components, or processes and are sufficient to enable physical and functional interchangeability, as well as data identifying source, size, configuration, mating and attachment characteristics, functional characteristics, and performance requirements. For COMPUTER SOFTWARE, the term means data identifying source, functional characteristics, and performance requirements but specifically excluding the source code, algorithm, process, formulae, and flowcharts of the software. FAR 27.401. The term has a slightly different meaning in DFARS 252.227-7013. Pursuant to 10 U.S.C. § 2320, the Rights in Technical Data—Noncommercial Items clause in DFARS 252.227-7013 provides that the Government acquires UNLIMITED RIGHTS in form, fit, and function data prepared in the performance of a contract. Under the Rights in Data—General clause at FAR 52.227-14, such data are furnished with unlimited rights and the contractor may protect qualifying LIMITED RIGHTS DATA and RESTRICTED RIGHTS computer software by withholding them from delivery to the Government and delivering form, fit, and function data instead. FAR 27.404. See Simchak & Vogel, *Rights in Technical Data and Computer Software* 43 (1995).

FORMAL ADVERTISING The term used, before the COMPETITION IN CONTRACTING ACT (CICA) of 1984, to describe the procurement technique now referred to as SEALED BIDDING. Under the statutes and regulations preceding passage of CICA, there was an expressed preference for formal advertising. Formal advertising, like sealed bidding, entailed drafting and publicizing an INVITATION FOR BIDS, holding a public BID OPENING, and awarding the contract to the lowest responsive and responsible bidder (see RESPONSIVENESS and RESPONSIBILITY). Formal advertising was aimed at securing the most advantageous contract for the Government by maximizing free and open competition; preventing favoritism, collusion, and fraud; and giving all interested parties an opportunity to compete. Nash & Cibinic, *Federal Procurement Law,* vol. I, 222 (3d ed. 1977).

FORMS Government documents used in the procurement process and governed by the policies in FAR Part 53. This Part gives rules for using forms, prescribes STANDARD FORMS (SFs), references OPTIONAL FORMS (OFs) and agency-prescribed forms used in acquisition, and illustrates all these forms (SFs in 53.301, OFs in 53.302, and selected agency forms in 53.303, in numerical order). Forms may be copied from the FAR. Executive agencies obtain forms (both SFs and OFs) from the General Services Administration; contractors and other parties can obtain them from the U.S. Government Printing Office, Washington, DC 20402. Agency forms can be obtained from the prescribing agency. FAR 53.107. See also Ferguson & Moss, *FAR Part 53—It's a Matter of Forms*, 24 Cont. Mgmt. 8 (Apr. 1984).

FORWARD PRICING RATE AGREEMENT A pricing arrangement that constitutes a written understanding negotiated between a contractor and the Government before costs have been incurred. The purpose is to make certain rates (including LABOR, INDIRECT COST, material obsolescence and usage, spare parts provisioning, and material handling) available during a specified period for use in pricing contracts or contract modifications. These rates represent reasonable projections of specific costs that are not easily estimated for, identified with, or generated by a specific contract, contract end item, or task. FAR 15.401. In determining whether to establish such an agreement, the administrative contracting officer should consider whether the benefits to be derived from it are commensurate with the effort of establishing and monitoring it. FAR 42.1701(a). See Cibinic & Nash, *Cost-Reimbursement Contracting* 569–70 (2d ed. 1993).

FRAGMENTATION OF A BASE The removal of individual elements from an appropriate base for distributing INDIRECT COSTs that has been accepted by the Government. The fragmentation of a base is prohibited. FAR 31.203(c). This requires contractors to allocate indirect costs to UNALLOWABLE COSTs as well as ALLOWABLE COSTs. See Lynch, *Allocation of Home Office Expenses to Segments and Business Unit G&A Expenses to Final Cost Objectives*, 22 Pub. Cont. L.J. 339 (1993).

FRAGMENTATION OF REMEDIES A requirement that a contractor obtain remedies from different administrative agencies or courts for events that have occurred on a single contract. One of the major difficulties that led to the passage of the CONTRACT DISPUTES ACT (CDA) OF 1978 was the complaint that disputes "ARISING UNDER THE CONTRACT" had to be appealed to BOARDs OF CONTRACT APPEALS (BCAs), while claims for Government BREACH OF CONTRACT could be taken only to the Court of Claims. This problem was resolved in the CDA by permitting contractors to elect to take all claims "RELATING TO THE CONTRACT" to either the appropriate BCA or the CLAIMS COURT (now the U.S. COURT OF FEDERAL CLAIMS). Fragmentation of remedies still exists with regard to some claims of contractors involving both contract breach and tortious conduct (see TORT) by the Government. In such cases, contract claims must be processed under the CDA while tort claims must be taken to a U.S. District Court pursuant to the FEDERAL TORT CLAIMS ACT.

FRANCHISE AGREEMENTS Typically refers to a special privilege conferred by a government on an individual or corporation, which would not otherwise belong to citizens as a common right. The term also refers to the selling or granting of the privilege to use a name or to sell products or services. Franchises typically entail elaborate agreements under which franchises conduct business in accordance with methods prescribed by the franchiser, and the franchiser assists through promotion, advertising, and advisory services. *Black's Law Dictionary* 658–59 (6th ed. 1990). Pursuant to a U.S. COURT OF FEDERAL CLAIMS advisory opinion, cable television franchise agreements for the construction, installation, or capital improvement of cable systems at military installations shall be considered contracts for purposes of the FEDERAL ACQUISITION REGULATION. Pub. L. No. 104-201, § 833; *In the Matter of the Dept. of Defense Cable Television Franchise Agreements*, 36 Fed. Cl. 171 (1996).

FRAUD An intentional perversion of truth for the purpose of inducing someone to rely upon it and part with something of value or surrender a legal right. The three necessary elements of a cause of action for fraud are (1) false representation of a present or past fact on the part of the defendant, (2) a plaintiff's action in reliance upon that misrepresentation, and (3) damage resulting to the plaintiff from the action that was based on the misrepresentation. *Black's Law Dictionary* 660 (6th ed. 1990). A fraudulent representation is a FALSE STATEMENT as to a material fact that another party believes and relies upon, and that induces that other party to act to his or her injury. The speaker must know the statement to be false or must make the statement with utter disregard for its truth or falsity and must intend that the other party will rely upon the statement. Fraud and corruption offenses, typically characterized as white-collar crimes, fall into two main areas: (1) fraud and false statement offenses, which involve deceptive conduct (see FALSE CLAIMS ACT and FALSE STATEMENTS ACT); and (2) public corruption offenses, which involve BRIBERY or illegal gratuities (see GRATUITY). See Seyfarth et al., *The Government*

Contract Compliance Handbook 1-4 through 1-6 and app. Y (1996 Supp.). See also Davidson, *10 U.S.C. § 2408: An Unused Weapon in the Procurement Fraud Wars*, 26 Pub. Cont. L.J. 181 (1997); Cox, *FASA and False Certifications: Procurement Fraud on the Information Superhighway*, 25 Pub. Cont. L.J. 1 (1995); Mackay, *The Major Fraud Act After Seven Years: An Update*, 64 Fed. Cont. Rep. 260 (Sept. 25, 1995); Wilson, *The Government Knowledge "Defense" to Civil False Claims Actions*, 24 Pub. Cont. L.J. 43 (1994); McGanny, *Winning the War on Procurement Fraud: Victory at What Price?*, 26 Colum. J.L. & Soc. Probs. 249 (Win. 1993); Nash, *Litigating Contract Claims and Fraud Claims: Is There A Rational Process?*, 7 N&CR ¶ 32 (June 1993); Mackay, *Major Fraud Against the United States*, Army Law. 7 (Sept. 1992); Berry, *Defense of Businesses, Individual Officers and Employees in Corporate Criminal Investigations*, 19 Pub. Cont. L.J. 648 (1990); Smith, *Statutes Countering Contract Administration Fraud*, 87-5 Briefing Papers (Apr. 1987); Cibinic & Elmer, *Government Contract Fraud*, 16 Pub. Cont. L.J. 331 (1986).

FREE ON BOARD See F.O.B.

FREEDOM OF INFORMATION ACT (FOIA) An Act, 5 U.S.C. § 552, part of the Administrative Procedure Act, passed in 1966, that provides a mechanism for members of the public (including contractors) to gain access to AGENCY RECORDs maintained by the Government. The Act requires public disclosure unless records fall within any of nine exemptions listed in the Act. The exemption most relevant to information submitted by contractors is Exemption 4, covering "TRADE SECRETs and commercial or financial information obtained from a person and privileged or confidential." Even if information falls within this exemption, an agency may release it unless such release would constitute an abuse of discretion. However, an abuse of discretion would normally be found if the information fell within the scope of the TRADE SECRETS ACT. Exec. Order No. 12600, 52 Fed. Reg. 23781 (June 23, 1987) requires agencies to notify persons that have submitted information to the Government when a FOIA request for that information is received. See Adler, *Litigation under the Federal Open Government Laws* (17th ed. 1992). And see DOJ *Freedom of Information Case List*, which includes the Justice Department Guide to the FOIA and is available from the U.S. Government Printing Office, Washington, DC 20402. The FAR's limited treatment of FOIA is in Subpart 24.2. DOD and NASA, however, provide expanded FOIA coverage. See DOD Directive 5400.7, *DOD Freedom of Information Act Program*, September 29, 1997, and NFS Subpart 18-24.2. See also

Nash, *Obtaining Government Information in Electronic Format: A New Statutory Provision*, 11 N&CR ¶ 32 (July 1997); Winters, *Revitalize the Sanctions Provisions of the Freedom of Information Act Amendments of 1974*, 84 Geo. L.J. 617 (Fall 1996); Roberts, *The Critical Mass Ripple in the FOIA Lake*, 36 Cont. Mgmt. 19 (June 1996); Marmelstein, *ADRA, FOIA & Confidentiality: Balancing the Policy Issues*, 31 Procmt. Law. 7 (Fall 1995); Manos, *Protecting Proprietary Information*, 94-13 Briefing Papers (Dec. 1994); Maffei, *The Impact on FOIA After Critical Mass*, 22 Pub. Cont. L.J. 757 (1993); Nash & Cibinic, *Competitive Negotiation: The Source Selection Process* 534-47 (1993); Gorelick & Enzinna, *Restrictions on the Release of Government Information*, 20 Pub. Cont. L.J. 427 (1991).

FRINGE BENEFIT A compensation, in addition to an employee's regular wage and salary, that includes vacations, sick leave, holidays, military leave, employee insurance, and supplemental unemployment compensation. Fringe benefits are allowable to the extent that they are reasonable and required by law, agreement, or established policy. FAR 31.205-6(m). See Oyer, *Allocation of Fringe Benefit Costs to Government Contracts*, 97-8 CP&A Rep. 3 (Aug. 197); Cibinic & Nash, *Cost-Reimbursement Contracting* 815–17 (2d ed. 1993).

FRONT-END LOADING The inclusion in a BID or PROPOSAL of inflated prices on items to be delivered early in the performance of the contract and unduly low prices on later items. Front-end loading, or front loading, is a form of unbalanced bidding (see UNBALANCED BID) that is aimed at enabling the bidder to recover money in advance of the performance of the work. Front-end loading may be permissible so long as the bid will clearly result in the lowest overall cost to the Government. But it will cause a bid to be found nonresponsive (see RESPONSIVENESS) if it cannot be justified on the basis of substantial mobilization or equipment costs or when it is so egregious as to amount, substantively, to an ADVANCE PAYMENT. See Cibinic & Nash, chap. 5, Sec. III., *Formation of Government Contracts* (3d ed. 1998); Shnitzer, *Government Contract Bidding* 11–21 (3d ed. 1987 & Supp. 1991); Nash, *Unbalanced Bidding in Long-Term Contracts: The Comptroller General's Accounting Lapse*, 9 N&CR ¶ 54 (Oct. 1995).

FRUSTRATION OF PURPOSE A legal doctrine that excuses a party to a contract from performing its contractual obligations in situations when the objectives of the contract have been utterly defeated by circumstances arising after the contract was formed. In such situations, performance is excused even though there is no impediment to actual performance. *Black's Law Dictionary* 670–71 (6th ed. 1990). This doctrine is rarely used in Government contracting.

FULFORD DOCTRINE A legal rule that permits a contractor's APPEAL FROM A CONTRACTING OFFICER'S DECISION assessing EXCESS COSTS OF REPROCUREMENT following a TERMINATION FOR DEFAULT to "revive" the issue of the propriety of the default termination itself, even though the contractor failed to file a timely appeal of the default termination. The name is derived from the decision of the ARMED SERVICES BOARD OF CONTRACT APPEALS in *Fulford Manufacturing Co.*, ASBCA 2144 (May 20, 1955). One result of the rule is that, upon default of a contract, a contractor may choose not to litigate the issue of whether the Government properly terminated the contract. But if the Government later charges the contractor for the excess costs of reprocurement, the contractor may appeal that cost assessment and simultaneously challenge the Government's termination action. See Cibinic & Nash, *Administration of Government Contracts* 998–1004 (3d ed. 1995); Williamson & Medill-Jones, *Government Damages for Default*, 89-7 Briefing Papers 9 (June 1989); Cibinic, *Another Attack on the Fulford Doctrine: So Much for Judicial Economy*, 2 N&CR ¶ 1 (Jan. 1988).

FULL AND OPEN COMPETITION A procurement in which all responsible sources (see RESPONSIBILITY) are permitted to compete for a contract. FAR 6.003. Under 10 U.S.C. § 2304(a) and 41 U.S.C. § 253(a), full and open competition is the established norm in Government contracting. However, 10 U.S.C. § 2304(c) and 41 U.S.C. § 253(c) provide for seven circumstances permitting other than full and open competition: (1) only one responsible source (see RESPONSIBILITY); (2) UNUSUAL AND COMPELLING URGENCY; (3) INDUSTRIAL MOBILIZATION, or the need to maintain engineering, developmental, or research capability; (4) international agreement; (5) statutory authorization or requirement; (6) risk of compromising the national security; and (7) protecting the public interest. See FAR 6.302 for additional guidance on these exceptions to the full and open competition rule. The statutes and regulations also provide substantial guidance on the type of COMPETITIVE PROCEDURES that meet the requirement for full and open competition. See FAR 6.102. FAR Subpart 6.1 prescribes the policy and procedures to be used to promote and provide for full and open competition. FAR Subpart 6.2 describes limited exceptions for full and open competition after exclusion of sources. FAR 6.303 provides guidance on the preparation of justifications and on obtaining approvals (see JUSTIFICATION

AND APPROVAL) when full and open competition is not obtained. See Cibinic & Nash, chap. 3, Sec. II., *Formation of Government Contracts* (3d ed. 1998).

FULL COST All significant expenses incurred in operating a data processing facility. This term is used in conjunction with the procedures set forth in OMB Circular No. A-130, *Management of Federal Information Resources*, February 6, 1996. The term includes the following cost elements: (1) personnel—salaries, overtime, fringe benefits, training, and travel; (2) equipment—depreciation, leased costs, and direct expenses; (3) software; (4) supplies; (5) contracted services—consulting, maintenance, and data entry; (6) space occupancy—rentals, depreciation, furniture, equipment, heating and air conditioning, utilities, security, and custodial services; (7) intra-agency services and overhead, whether billed or allocated; and (8) interagency services, whether reimbursed or estimated.

FULL FUNDING APPROPRIATIONS enacted that are sufficient in total to complete a useful segment of a capital project before any obligations may be incurred for that segment (as opposed to INCREMENTAL FUNDING). Full funding is frequently required before a contract may be awarded. DFARS Subpart 232.7. This principle applies to both regular appropriations and ADVANCE APPROPRIATIONS. GAO, *Principles of Budgeting for Capital Asset Acquisitions*, 10 Budget of the United States Government, Fiscal Year 1998 (1997).

FULL-SCALE DEVELOPMENT The final development phase of a MAJOR SYSTEM. This is the term in the FAR that is synonymous with the DOD term FULL-SCALE ENGINEERING DEVELOPMENT. FAR 34.005-5 provides that, whenever practicable, full-scale development contracts should require contractors to submit priced proposals for production that are based on the latest quantity, schedule, and LOGISTICS requirements and other considerations that will be used in making the production decision.

FULL-SCALE ENGINEERING DEVELOPMENT (FSED) The third phase in the pre-1995 DOD MAJOR SYSTEM ACQUISITION process, in which the SYSTEM and the principal items necessary for its support were fully developed, engineered, designed, fabricated, tested, and evaluated. Systems in this phase had to be approved before entering the production phase. This phase is now known as the ENGINEERING AND MANUFACTURING DEVELOPMENT phase.

DFARS 235.001. Its objectives are to (1) translate a promising design approach into a stable, producible, and cost-effective system design; (2) validate the manufacturing or production process; and (3) demonstrate through testing that the system will meet stated requirements. DOD Regulation 5000.2-R, *Mandatory Procedures for Major Defense Acquisition Programs (MDAPs) and Major Automated Information System (MAIS) Acquisition Programs*, Mar. 15, 1996, 1.5.3.

FUNCTIONAL SPECIFICATIONS Specifications that describe work to be performed in terms of the end purpose or the Government's ultimate objective, rather than in terms of the way in which the work is to be performed. Functional specifications are broader descriptions of the work than PERFORMANCE SPECIFICATIONS and are aimed at permitting more open competition on the ways of accomplishing the Government's purpose. 10 U.S.C. § 2305(a)(1) and 41 U.S.C. § 253a(a) state a preference for functional specifications. See FAR 11.002(a). A functional specification may include a statement of the qualitative nature of the product and, when necessary, will contain the minimum essential characteristics the product must exhibit in order to satisfy its intended use. See Cibinic & Nash, chap. 3, Sec. V., *Formation of Government Contracts* (3d ed. 1998).

FUNDED PENSION COST The portion of PENSION PLAN costs for a current or prior cost accounting period that has been paid to a funding agency. FAR 31.001. FAR 31.205-6(j) provides detailed guidance on the allowability of pension costs and generally requires that such costs be funded to be allowable. See Cibinic & Nash, *Cost-Reimbursement Contracting* 811–14 (2d ed. 1993).

FUTURE CONTRACT SAVINGS Savings resulting from a VALUE ENGINEERING CHANGE PROPOSAL (VECP) on future contract units scheduled for delivery during the three-year period following acceptance of the first unit incorporating the VECP. FAR 48.104-1 contains guidance on Government-contractor sharing arrangements for such savings. The calculation of these savings is based on an estimate made by the CONTRACTING OFFICER as prescribed in paragraph (g) of the Value Engineering clause in FAR 52.248-1. If the INSTANT CONTRACT is a multiyear contract (see MULTIYEAR CONTRACTING), future contract savings include savings on quantities funded after VECP acceptance. See Cibinic & Nash, *Administration of Government Contracts* 309–10 (3d ed. 1995).

FUTURE YEARS DEFENSE PROGRAM (FYDP) An official DOD document (formerly the Five-Year Defense Program) that summarizes forces and resources associated with programs approved by the Secretary of Defense. Its three parts entail the organizations affected, appropriations accounts (such as RESEARCH, DEVELOPMENT, TEST, AND EVALUATION, OPERATIONS AND MAINTENANCE, etc.), and the eleven major force programs (such as strategic forces, airlift/sealift, research and development, etc.). Under the current DOD PLANNING, PROGRAMMING, AND BUDGETING SYSTEM cycle, the FYDP is updated when the services submit their program objective memoranda to the Office of the Secretary of Defense (OSD), when the services submit their budgets to OSD, and when the President submits the national budget to Congress. Jones, *Glossary: Defense Acquisition Acronyms and Terms* (8th ed., Defense Systems Management College).

G

GATEWAY AIRPORT An airport used by a traveler at the beginning or end of a trip. "Gateway airport abroad" means the airport from which the traveler last embarks en route to the United States or at which the traveler first debarks in travel from the United States. "Gateway airport in the United States" means the last U.S. airport from which the traveler's flight departs or the first U.S. airport at which the traveler's flight arrives. FAR 47.401. These terms are used in the FAR Subpart 47.4 implementation of the FLY AMERICA ACT, which requires that federal employees and their dependents, consultants, contractors, grantees, and others use U.S.-flag air carriers for U.S. Government-financed international air travel and transportation of their property or personal effects, to the extent that service by these carriers is available.

GENERAL ACCOUNTING OFFICE (GAO) A Government agency that is part of the legislative branch and that investigates matters relating to the receipt, disbursement, and application of public funds. Headed by the COMPTROLLER GENERAL, GAO evaluates the performance of Government programs (and typically issues reports when the assessment is negative), and issues decisions concerning PROTESTs against award. See FAR Subpart 33.1. GAO has broad powers to AUDIT contractors under the EXAMINATION OF RECORDS clause and occasionally investigates contractors in the course of auditing Government programs. GAO maintains a network of 10 regional and field offices and has five divisions: four program divisions (Accounting and Information Management; General Government; Health, Education and Human Resources; National Security and International Affairs; and Resources, Community, and Economic Development). See Brittin, *The Comptroller General's Dual Statutory Authority to Decide Bid Protests*, 22 Pub. Cont. L.J. 636 (1993); Hordell, *Everyone Has Heard of the United States General Accounting Office—But What Does It Do?,* 36 Fed. B. News & J. 328 (1989); Schnitzer, *GAO Bid Protests*, 86-12 Briefing Papers (Nov. 1986).

GENERAL AND ADMINISTRATIVE (G&A) EXPENSE Any management, financial, or other expense incurred by or allocated to a BUSINESS UNIT for the general management and administration of the business unit as a whole. FAR 31.001. G&A expenses should not include those management expenses whose beneficial or causal relationship to COST OBJECTIVEs can be more directly measured by a base other than a cost input base representing the total activity of a business unit during a cost accounting period. G&A expenses commonly include expenses of a company's general and executive offices; executive compensation; the cost of staff services such as legal, accounting, public relations, financial, and similar expenses; and other miscellaneous expenses related to the overall business. CAS 410, 48 C.F.R. § 9904.410, deals with the allocation of business unit G&A expenses to FINAL COST OBJECTIVEs. See Cibinic & Nash, *Cost-Reimbursement Contracting* 690–92 (2d ed. 1993). See also ALLOCATION OF COST.

GENERAL APPROPRIATION See APPROPRIATION.

GENERAL CONTRACTOR A contractor with the entire responsibility for performing a contract for CONSTRUCTION. This term is used in the construction industry to designate the contractor that bids for a construction contract and bears the entire risk if the contract cannot be performed at the contract price. See Nash, chap. 1, *Construction Contracting* 3–5 (1991).

GENERAL PROVISIONS The standard clauses that are used by Government agencies in various types of contracts. Most of these clauses are set forth in FAR Part 52, and guidance on their use is set forth in the PROVISION AND CLAUSE MATRIX in FAR Part 52.301. The term also includes clauses specified in FAR Supplements for agency-wide use. FAR 52.102-1 provides that general provisions will be incorporated by reference to the regulations "to the maximum practical extent" rather than by placing the full text of the clauses in the contract document. See Lumer, *So You Think You Know Provisions and Clauses?,* 34 Cont. Mgmt. 23 (Nov. 1994).

GENERAL SCOPE See SCOPE OF THE CONTRACT.

GENERAL SERVICES ADMINISTRATION (GSA) An agency in the executive branch with the function of procuring supplies and services (including construction) that are used in common by many agencies. GSA procures (1) common-use supplies and services under direct contracts and in conjunction with the FEDERAL SUPPLY

SCHEDULES, (2) TELECOMMUNICATIONS SERVICES, and (3) office buildings. With DOD and NASA, GSA has responsibility for the promulgation of the FEDERAL ACQUISITION REGULATION. GSA also supports the FAR Secretariat, the focal point for managing the FAR. See National Archives and Records Administration, *U.S. Government Manual Office of the Federal Register* (GPO 1996/97).

GENERAL SERVICES ADMINISTRATION BOARD OF CONTRACT APPEALS (GSBCA) The BOARD OF CONTRACT APPEALS for the GENERAL SERVICES ADMINISTRATION (GSA) and certain other federal agencies. As the second largest board, the GSBCA has 12 ADMINISTRATIVE JUDGEs. The GSBCA resolves disputes involving GSA as well as the Departments of the Treasury, Commerce, and Education; the Federal Communications Commission and Nuclear Regulatory Commission; and the SMALL BUSINESS ADMINISTRATION. In the past, the GSBCA also had jurisdiction to rule on PROTESTs involving any agency procuring FEDERAL INFORMATION PROCESSING RESOURCES under the BROOKS ACT (AUTOMATIC DATA PROCESSING PROCUREMENTS). However, the Brooks Act was repealed by Pub. L. No. 104-106, removing GSBCA's jurisdiction over ADP procurement protests. In 1996, jurisdiction over transportation rate reviews and travel and relocation expense cases were delegated to the GSBCA pursuant to § 201 of Pub. L. No. 104-53. See Tolle & Duffey, *GSBCA Bid Protests*, 87-4 Briefing Papers (Mar. 1987).

GENERAL WAGE DETERMINATION See WAGE DETERMINATION.

GENERALLY ACCEPTED ACCOUNTING PRINCIPLES (GAAP) Accounting principles that are generally accepted by commercial organizations doing business in the United States. Under FAR 31.201-2, such principles are a factor to be considered in determining whether a cost is an ALLOWABLE COST, if none of the COST ACCOUNTING STANDARDS apply. In such cases, unless the FAR's selected COST PRINCIPLES applying to commercial contractors in FAR 31.205 specifically deal with an accounting issue, the GAAP will likely prevail. Thus, pronouncements of the FINANCIAL ACCOUNTING STANDARDS BOARD and the extensive body of uncodified GAAP found in general practice or individual industry practice are used in determining the allowable costs of Government contracts. See generally Cibinic & Nash, chap. 5, *Cost-Reimbursement*

Contracting (2d ed. 1993); Apostolou & Crumbley, *Handbook of Governmental Accounting and Finance* 3–63 (2d ed. 1992).

GENERALLY ACCEPTED AUDITING STANDARDS (GAAS) Audit standards that articulate the minimum requirements (as opposed to aspirational goals) for the work of auditors, both Government and private. There are 10 generally accepted auditing standards: three general standards, which require minimum training and proficiency, independence, and due professional care; three field work standards, which mandate adequate planning, understanding of the internal control structure, and the need for sufficient competent evidential matter; and four reporting standards, which require stating whether the financial statements comply with the GENERALLY ACCEPTED ACCOUNTING PRINCIPLES (GAAP), identifying where GAAP has not been consistently followed, regarding informative disclosures as adequate, and containing an expression of opinion regarding the financial statement. See McDonald, *Auditing Standards: What Lawyers Need to Know*, 31 Procurement Law. 18 (Win. 1996). Standards for DEFENSE CONTRACT AUDIT AGENCY auditors are found in Chapter 2 of the CONTRACT AUDIT MANUAL.

GIFT Any GRATUITY, favor, discount, entertainment, hospitality, loan, forbearance, or other item having monetary value. It includes services as well as gifts of training, transportation, local travel, lodgings, and meals, whether provided in-kind, by purchase of a ticket, payment in advance, or reimbursement after the expense has been incurred. 5 C.F.R. § 2535(b). The federal STANDARDS OF CONDUCT contain extensive guidance on gifts to Government employees and, generally, prohibit gifts of any magnitude. See Cibinic & Nash, chap. 1, Sec. VII., *Formation of Government Contracts* (3d ed. 1998); Cibinic & Nash, *Administration of Government Contracts* 89–91 (3d ed. 1995).

GLOBAL SETTLEMENT A settlement between a contractor and the Government resolving criminal, civil, and administrative disputes with the Government through simultaneous, coordinated, comprehensive agreements. The term is generally used to describe the settlement of administrative proceedings involving a SUSPENSION or DEBARMENT as well as the settlement of any criminal charges arising out of a contractor's actions. See Stubbs, *Fighting Fraud Illustrated: The Robins AFB Case*, 38 A.F. L. Rev. 141 (1994); D'Aloisio, *Accusations of Criminal Conduct by Government Contractors: The Remedies, Problems, and Solutions*, 17 Pub. Cont. L.J. 265, 300–310

(1987); Bennett & Kriegel, *Negotiating Global Settlements of Procurement Fraud Cases*, 16 Pub. Cont. L.J. 30 (1986).

GOALS AND TIMETABLES A series of annual goals by LABOR category that a contractor establishes in an attempt to increase its minority employment as part of its AFFIRMATIVE ACTION commitment to the Government. These goals and timetables are not a firm contractual commitment but, rather, are an agreement to use best efforts to meet them. See FAR Subpart 22.8; 41 C.F.R. § 60-1 and 60-2. See also DFARS Subpart 222.8; DEAR Subpart 922.8; GSAR Subpart 522.8; NFS Subpart 18-22.8.

GOLDEN PARACHUTE COSTS Costs paid to an employee of a contractor in excess of normal severance pay and contingent on a change in management control over, or ownership of, the contractor or a substantial portion of the contractor's assets. Such costs are UNALLOWABLE COSTs under 10 U.S.C. § 2324(e)(1)(K) and 41 U.S.C. § 256(e)(1)(K). See Cibinic & Nash, *Cost-Reimbursement Contracting* 610 (2d ed. 1993).

GOOD FAITH AND FAIR DEALING See DUTY OF GOOD FAITH AND FAIR DEALING.

GOODS All things (including specially manufactured goods) that are movable at the time of identification to the contractor for sale, other than the money in which the price is to be paid, investment securities, and things in action. U.C.C. § 2-105. Article 2 of the UNIFORM COMMERCIAL CODE governs contracts for the sale of goods throughout the United States, except in Louisiana. Government contracts for goods are called "supply contracts" and generally are not subject to Article 2 of the U.C.C. See SUPPLIES.

GOODWILL An intangible ASSET resulting when the price paid by an acquiring company exceeds the sum of the identifiable individual assets acquired less liabilities assumed, based upon their fair values. FAR 31.205-49 specifies that costs resulting from such goodwill are UNALLOWABLE COSTs. See Cibinic & Nash, *Cost-Reimbursement Contracting* 864–65 (2d ed. 1993).

GOVERNMENT BILL OF LADING See BILL OF LADING.

GOVERNMENT CLAIM See CLAIM.

GOVERNMENT CONTRACTOR DEFENSE A legal defense to a product liability claim (brought by or on behalf of a person injured by the product) that is available to Government contractors under certain scenarios. The defense permits the contractor to enjoy the Government's SOVEREIGN IMMUNITY from liability for the injury. The contractor escapes liability if (1) the U.S. Government approved reasonably precise specifications for the contractor, (2) the contractor's equipment conformed to those specifications, and (3) the supplier warned the Government about the dangers in the use of the equipment that were known to the supplier but not to the Government. See Biagini, *The Government Contractor Defense: Limiting Product Liability in the New Procurement Environment*, 39 Gov't Contractor ¶ 169 (Apr. 1997); Wagner, Note, *Tate v. Boeing Helicopters: Government Contractors Increasingly at Risk Despite the Government Contractor Defense*, 23 N. Ky. L. Rev. 377 (Spr. 1996); Loy, Note, *The Government Contractor Defense: Is It a Weapon Only for the Military?*, 83 Ky. L.J. 505 (1994); Moore, *Recent Development: The Third Circuit Expands the Government Defense to Include Nonmilitary Contractors*, 72 Wash. U. L.Q. 1435 (1994); Goodhue, *Product Liability: The Government Contractor Defense*, 33 Cont. Mgmt. 4 (Feb. 1993); Michaels, *The Government Contractor Defense: The Limits of Immunity after Boyle*, 33 A.F. L. Rev. 147 (1990); Dempsey & Barsy, *Government Contractor Liability for Design Defects after Boyle*, 19 Pub. Cont. L.J. 405 (1990); Haizlip, *The Government Contractor Defense in Tort Liability: A Continuing Genesis*, 19 Pub. Cont. L.J. 116 (1989); Vacketta et al., *The "Government Contractor Defense" in Environmental Actions*, 89-13 Briefing Papers (Dec. 1989).

GOVERNMENT DELAY OF WORK See COMPENSABLE DELAY.

GOVERNMENT-FURNISHED EQUIPMENT (GFE) Items in the possession of, or acquired by the Government, and delivered or otherwise made available to a contractor. FAR Part 45. See Cibinic & Nash, chap. 7, *Administration of Government Contracts* (3d ed. 1995). See also GOVERNMENT-FURNISHED PROPERTY.

GOVERNMENT-FURNISHED MATERIAL (GFM) Property furnished to a contractor by the Government that may be incorporated into or attached to a deliverable end item or that may be consumed or expended in performing a contract. Material includes assemblies, components, parts, raw and processed materials, and small tools and supplies that may be consumed in normal use in performing a contract. FAR 45.301. The material in the possession of or directly acquired by the Government and subsequently made available to the contractor constitutes Government-furnished material. See Cibinic & Nash, chap. 7, *Administration of Government Contracts* (3d ed. 1995). See also GOVERNMENT-FURNISHED PROPERTY.

GOVERNMENT-FURNISHED PROPERTY (GFP) Property in the possession of or directly acquired by the Government that is subsequently made available to the contractor. FAR 45.101. GFP is included in the broad term GOVERNMENT PROPERTY, which is subject to the policies and procedures of FAR Part 45. See Tomanelli, *Rights & Obligations Concerning Government-Furnished Property*, 24 Pub. Cont. L.J. 413 (1995); Tomanelli, *The Duty to Eliminate Competitive Advantage Arising from Contractor Possession of Government-Furnished Property*, 142 Mil. L. Rev. 141 (Fall 1994); Tomanelli, *Competitive Advantage Arising from Contractor Possession of Government-Furnished Property*, 23 Pub. Cont. L.J. 243 (1994). See Cibinic & Nash, chap. 7, *Administration of Government Contracts* (3d ed. 1995). See also GOVERNMENT-FURNISHED MATERIAL.

GOVERNMENT INFORMATION TECHNOLOGY SERVICES BOARD (GITSB) A board established to ensure continued implementation of the INFORMATION TECHNOLOGY recommendations of the NATIONAL PERFORMANCE REVIEW and to identify and promote the development of innovative technologies, standards, and practices among agencies, state and local governments, and the private sector. The board is required to seek the view of experts from industry, academia, and state and local governments. The board is intended to assist in: (1) creating opportunities for cross-agency cooperation and intergovernmental approaches in using information resources to support common operational areas and to develop and provide shared Government-wide infrastructure services; (2) developing shared Government-wide information infrastructure services to be used for innovative, multiagency information-technology projects; (3) creating and utilizing AFFINITY GROUPS for particular business or technology areas; and (4) developing standards and guidelines pertaining to federal information systems. The board is composed of individuals from agencies based on their proven expertise or accomplishments in fields necessary to achieve its goals. Exec. Order No. 13011, 61 Fed. Reg. 37657 (July 16, 1996).

GOVERNMENT — OWNED, CONTRACTOR — OPERATED PLANT (GOCO) An industrial or research and development facility that is owned by the Government but operated by a contractor. The procedures used in contracting for the operation of GOCOs are set forth in FAR Subpart 17.6 dealing with MANAGEMENT AND OPERATING CONTRACTs.

GOVERNMENT PERFORMANCE AND RESULTS ACT OF 1993 An Act, Pub. L. No. 103-62, codified at 31 U.S.C. § 1115 et seq. and 39 U.S.C. § 2801 et seq., that seeks to improve the efficiency and effectiveness of federal programs, eliminate wasteful management and performance practices, and establish accountability for results. The Act mandates that, beginning in FY94, various agencies must establish pilot programs aimed toward program performance measurement, reporting, and goal setting. The Act requires agency heads to submit strategic plans to the OFFICE OF MANAGEMENT AND BUDGET, then requires annual performance plans and reports on program performance. According to Senate Report 103-58, this Act will provide the information necessary to strengthen program management in the Federal Government. GAO, *Executive Guide: Effectively Implementing the Government Performance and Results Act*, GAO/GGD-96-118 (June 1996).

GOVERNMENT PRINTING Printing, binding, and blankbook work for the use of an executive department, independent agency, or establishment of the Government. FAR 8.801. 44 U.S.C. § 501 et seq. requires that such printing be done by the U.S. Government Printing Office with specified exceptions. See FAR 8.802.

GOVERNMENT PRINTING OFFICE (GPO) The entity that handles all printing, binding, and blankbook work for Congress, the Executive Office of the President, the Judiciary (except the Supreme Court), and every executive department, independent office, and establishment of the Government. Among its major publications are the *Congressional Record*, FEDERAL REGISTER, and COMMERCE BUSINESS DAILY. In addition, the GPO sells Government publications and documents in printed and electronic formats through its Washington, DC and regional bookstores. For information about obtaining publications, contact GPO, North Capitol & H Streets, Washington, DC 20401; (202)512-1800, <http://www.access.gpo.gov>.

GOVERNMENT PRODUCTION AND RESEARCH PROPERTY Government-owned FACILITIES, Government-owned SPECIAL TEST EQUIPMENT, and special blank sidetooling to which the Government has title or the right to acquire title. FAR 45.301. The CONTRACTING OFFICER must, "to the maximum practical extent," eliminate COMPETITIVE ADVANTAGE accruing to a contractor possessing such property under the procedures in FAR Subpart 45.2. Contractors are authorized to use such property under the procedures in FAR Subpart 45.4. See Cibinic & Nash, *Administration of Government Contracts* 630–36 (3d ed. 1995).

GOVERNMENT PROPERTY All property owned by or leased to the Government or acquired by the Government under the terms of the contract. FAR 45.101. Government property includes both GOVERNMENT-FURNISHED PROPERTY and CONTRACTOR-ACQUIRED PROPERTY. FAR Part 45 contains detailed guidance on the policies and procedures relating to Government property. FAR 45.103 provides that contractors are responsible and liable for Government property in their possession unless the contract provides otherwise. FAR Subpart 45.5 contains detailed guidance on the management of Government property in the possession of contractors. See Cibinic & Nash, chap. 7, *Administration of Government Contracts* (3d ed. 1995); Allen & Stockton, *Government Property*, 94-4 Briefing Papers (Mar. 1994); Cleary, *Government-Furnished Property: Government-Furnished Problems*, 22 Nat'l Cont. Mgmt. J., Issue No. 2, p. 1 (1989); Rindner, *For Beginners Only: Button, Button, Who Owns the Button?*, 29 Cont. Mgmt. 16 (Aug. 1989); Day & Keogh, *A Risk Analysis of Financing Federal Government Equipment Leases*, 18 Pub. Cont. L.J. 544 (1989).

GOVERNMENT-PURPOSE LICENSE RIGHTS (GPLR) The right to use, duplicate, and disclose TECHNICAL DATA, in whole or in part and in any manner, for Government purposes only, and to have or permit others to do so for Government purposes only. This right was included in the DOD data policy from 1988 to 1995 when it was replaced by GOVERNMENT PURPOSE RIGHTS. Under GPLR, Government purposes included competitive procurement but did not include the right to have or permit others to use technical data for commercial purposes. DFARS 227.402-72(a)(2) provided that, to encourage commercial utilization of technologies developed under Government contracts, the Government—instead of insisting on UNLIMITED RIGHTS—could agree to accept technical data subject to GPLR for a limited period of time. After that period, the Government was entitled to unlimited rights. DOD policy was that the Government should not agree to accept GPLR when technical data were likely to be needed to permit competitive procurement involving large numbers of potential competitors (for items such as spares) or when technical data had to be published. GPLR could also be used when the technical data pertained to items, components, or processes developed with mixed funding. See DFARS 227.472-72(c). Contractors were required to notify the Government if they desired to negotiate agreements calling for GPLR. See Simchak & Vogel, *Rights in Technical Data and Computer Software* 81–84 (1995).

GOVERNMENT PURPOSE RIGHTS (GPR) The right to use, modify, reproduce, release, perform, display or disclose TECHNICAL DATA or COMPUTER SOFTWARE within the Government without restriction or outside the Government for U.S. Government purposes. This right was included in the DOD data and software policy in 1995 to replace GOVERNMENT-PURPOSE LICENSE RIGHTS. Under GPR, the Government obtains the right to use technical data and computer software for all Government purposes, including competitive procurement but not for commercial purposes. Under the Rights in Technical Data—Noncommercial Items clause in DFARS 252.227-7013 and the Rights in Noncommercial Computer Software and Noncommercial Computer Software Documentation clause in DFARS 252.227-7014, the Government obtains GPR to all technical data and computer software developed with MIXED FUNDING if the contractor marks the data with a legend denoting such rights. These clauses provide that such rights expire at the end of five years after execution of the development contract, with the Government obtaining UNLIMITED RIGHTS thereafter. However, either party may request a different period and longer periods are encouraged when the contractor needs more time to apply the data or software to commercial products, DFARS 227.7103-5(b)(2) and DFARS 227.7203-5(b)(2). This regulation permits the negotiation of such longer periods during contract performance without CONSIDERATION from either party. See Simchak & Vogel, *Rights in Technical Data and Computer Software* 84-85 (1995).

GOVERNMENT VERSUS CONTRACTOR PERFORMANCE See A-76 POLICY.

GOVERNMENT VESSEL A vessel owned by the U.S. Government and operated directly by the Government or for the Government by an agent or contractor, including a privately owned U.S.-flag vessel under bareboat charter to the Government. FAR 47.501. Such a vessel is included in the definition of U.S.-flag vessel for the purpose of the cargo preference regulations in FAR Subpart 47.5.

GOVERNMENT-WIDE AGENCY CONTRACT (GWAC) Multi-agency contracts typically for various information technology resources that other specified federal agencies can use. The host agency normally adds a small administrative fee. Because of savings attributable to not having to incur major procurement costs when using GWAC, other agencies are often willing to pay the fee. Multiagency contracts permit AGGREGATION of agency demand to encourage vendors to offer the best possible prices, while reducing the overhead associated with multiple acquisitions, particularly by smaller agencies. Each GWAC has its own particular rules and conditions. For example, in 1996, the National Institutes of Health (NIH) selected a number of computer resellers to establish a "virtual computer store" to allow employees at NIH and HHS to shop electronically for everything from desktop computers to office automation software. Under this multiple-award contract, contractors provided a broad range of commercial, off-the-shelf personal computer equipment, including laptops, software, peripherals, and operating system software with recognizable names, with each vendor's catalogue of products and prices accessible on the World Wide Web. Pursuant to § 5124 of the CLINGER-COHEN ACT OF 1996, an agency may "enter into a contract that provides for multiagency acquisitions of information technology in accordance with guidance issued by the Director [of the OFFICE OF MANAGEMENT AND BUDGET]." 40 U.S.C. § 5124(a)(2). See also FAR Subpart 16.5, INDEFINITE-DELIVERY CONTRACTS.

GOVERNMENT-WIDE COMMERCIAL PURCHASE CARD A purchase card, similar in nature to a commercial credit card, issued to authorized agency officials for their use in acquiring SUPPLIES and SERVICES. FAR 13.101. These cards are given to agency officials who are not CONTRACTING OFFICERs, with limitations on their use. FAR 13.301(a). FAR 13.003(f) encourages their use on MICRO-PURCHASEs to the maximum extent practicable, and they are also used by some agencies for purchases of larger dollar amounts. This card is also known as the international merchant purchase authorization card or IMPAC. See the General Services Administration's IMPAC homepage on the Internet at <http://www.gsa.gov/impac/>.

GRANT A legal instrument for transferring money, property, or services to the recipient in order to accomplish a public purpose of support or stimulation where there will be no substantial involvement between the federal agency and the recipient during performance. Federal Grant and Cooperative Agreement Act of 1977, 31 U.S.C. § 6304. This act distinguishes federal assistance relationships, or grants and COOPER-

ATIVE AGREEMENTs, from procurement relationships, or procurement contracts. Unlike a procurement contract, which is a legal instrument for acquiring supplies or services for the direct benefit of or use by the Federal Government, a grant—like a cooperative agreement—has, as its main purpose, support or stimulation. A grant differs from a cooperative agreement in that, under a cooperative agreement, there is substantial involvement between the federal agency and the recipient during performance of the contemplated activity, whereas under a grant there is not. Cappalli, *I Federal Grants and Cooperative Agreements* 1-136 and 1-137 (1982). Grants are not subject to the FEDERAL ACQUISITION REGULATION. The term "grant" is an ambiguous term in that it is used to refer to agreements with private organizations (such as research grants) as well as arrangements where the Federal Government provides funds to state and local governments. With regard to the latter use, there are three general types of grants: (1) categorical grants, (2) block grants, and (3) revenue-sharing grants (currently not in use). See Walker, *Enforcing Grants and Cooperative Agreements as Contracts Under the Tucker Act*, 26 Pub. Cont. L.J. 683 (1997); Tidwell, *Federal Grants—An Alternative Source to Enhance Research and Development Funding*, 34 Cont. Mgmt. 17 (Sept. 1994); Brody, *Confidentiality Clauses in Research Contracts and Grants: Are They "Unconstitutional Conditions"?*, 22 Pub. Cont. L.J. 447 (1993); Gabig, *Federal Research Grants: Who Owns the Intellectual Property?*, 16 Pub. Cont. L.J. 187 (1986); Riley, *III Federal Contracts, Grants and Assistance* 85–86 (1984).

GRATUITY Something acquired without bargain or inducement; something given freely or voluntarily in return for a favor or a service. *Black's Law Dictionary* 699–700 (6th ed. 1990). 18 U.S.C. § 201 makes it a crime to offer or solicit GIFTs, as well as to accept a gift, and, for practical purposes, prohibits all gifts to public officials made to influence or appear to influence acts. The statute requires only a showing of wrongful purpose in offering or accepting a thing of value for or because of an official act. FAR Subparts 3.1 and 3.2 spell out the Government's policy on gratuities offered to or solicited by contracting personnel. See Cibinic & Nash, chap. 1, Sec. VII., *Formation of Government Contracts* (3d ed. 1998); Nash, *Postscript: Gratuities*, 6 N&CR ¶ 71 (Dec. 1992); Nash, *Gratuities: Is There A New Look?*, 6 N&CR ¶ 4 (Jan. 1992); Seyfarth et al., *The Government Contract Compliance Handbook* 1–16 (2d ed. 1991) and chap. 7 (1996 Supp.); Kenney & Sweeney, *Gratuities*, 90-3 Briefing Papers (Feb. 1990).

GROSS MISTAKE AMOUNTING TO FRAUD A mistake so serious or uncalled for as not to be reasonably expected, or justifiable, in the case of a responsible contractor; a mistake that cannot be reconciled in good faith. *Catalytic Eng'g & Manufacturing Corp.*, ASBCA 15257, 72-1 BCA ¶ 9342. This type of mistake overcomes the finality of ACCEPTANCE OF WORK in the Inspection of Supplies—Fixed-Price clause, FAR 52.246-2, and the Inspection of Construction clause, FAR 52.246-12. See Cibinic & Nash, *Administration of Government Contracts* 873-76 (3d ed. 1995).

GSA See GENERAL SERVICES ADMINISTRATION.

GSA ADVANTAGE! An electronic catalog intended to maximize item visibility, facilitate customer learning about available products, and simplify the ordering process. GSA Advantage! is an on-line ordering system that allows agencies to search through all General Services Administration sources of supply and select the item that is the best value for their requirements, without having to know a complex paperwork or logistics system. This on-line catalog can be found on the Internet at <http://www.gsa.gov/>. See Cibinic & Nash, chap. 3, Sec. IV., *Formation of Government Contracts* (3d ed. 1998); Gormley, *Reinventing Acquisition: GSA Trends Easier Procurements, Better Prices*, 36 Cont. Mgmt. 56 (June 1996).

GSA MOTORPOOLS See INTERAGENCY FLEET MANAGEMENT SYSTEM.

GSA SCHEDULE See FEDERAL SUPPLY SCHEDULES.

GSA STORES STOCK Supply distribution facilities operated by the General Services Administration (GSA) that maintain an inventory of stock items that constitute a mandatory source for executive agencies located within the United States. See 41 C.F.R. § 101-26.301. FAR 8.001(a)(1) requires agencies to requisition supplies from GSA stock before taking other procurement action. See Cibinic & Nash, chap. 3, Sec. IV., *Formation of Government Contracts* (3d ed. 1998); Nash & Cibinic, *Competitive Negotiation: The Source Selection Process* 37 (1993).

GUARANTEED LOAN A loan, revolving credit fund, or other financial arrangement made pursuant to Regulation V of the Federal Reserve Board (sometimes called a "V loan") under which funds are distributed, collected, and administered by the lending institution and the federal guaranteeing agency is obligated, on demand of the lender, to purchase a stated percentage of the loan and to share any losses in the amount of the guaranteed percentage. FAR 32.301. Government funds are not involved except for the purchase of the guaranteed portion of the loan for the settlement of losses. Section 301 of the Defense Production Act of 1950, 50 U.S.C. app. § 2061 et seq., authorizes loan guarantees for contract performance or other operations related to the national defense, subject to amounts annually authorized by Congress. FAR 32.106 states that guaranteed loans are a preferred form of FINANCING over unusual contract financing and ADVANCE PAYMENTs.

GUIDELINES FOR THE ACQUISITION OF INVESTIGATIONS See ANNOUNCEMENT OF OPPORTUNITY.

H

HAMILTON STIPULATION A stipulation, relating to an uncertified CLAIM before a BOARD OF CONTRACT APPEALS (BCA), that the contracting officer was aware of the claim, considered it, and would have denied it formally had it been properly certified at the time of submission. The CONTRACT DISPUTES ACT (CDA) OF 1978 states that a contractor's demand or assertion seeking payment of a sum exceeding $100,000 does not become a claim until certified. However, in *United States v. Hamilton Enterprises*, 711 F.2d 1038 (Fed. Cir. 1983), the U.S. COURT OF APPEALS FOR THE FEDERAL CIRCUIT held that "there was substantial compliance with the certification requirements" of the CDA, even though the contractor had not certified and therefore had not formally asserted its claim until it appealed the contracting officer's denial. Thus, the stipulation generates a sufficient basis for jurisdiction by a BCA to overcome the untimely certification and the lack of a final DECISION OF THE CONTRACTING OFFICER. Because of the statutory change to the certification requirement by Pub. L. No. 102-572, § 907, it is unlikely that the Hamilton stipulation will be used in the future. See CERTIFICATION OF CLAIM.

HEAD OF THE AGENCY The Secretary, Attorney General, Administrator, Governor, Chairperson, or other chief official of an executive agency, including any deputy or assistant chief official of the EXECUTIVE AGENCY. Some statutes and regulations provide that actions may only be taken by heads of agencies. For example, FAR DEVIATIONs must be approved by heads of an agency. FAR 1.403; FAR 1.404. If the statute or regulation provides that the power may be delegated, the delegee is called an AUTHORIZED REPRESENTATIVE. FAR 2.101.

HEAD OF THE CONTRACTING ACTIVITY (HCA) The official with overall responsibility for managing the CONTRACTING ACTIVITY. FAR 2.101. Examples of contracting activities are the Naval Sea Systems Command, the Air Force Material Command,

NASA's Goddard Space Flight Center, and General Service Administration's Federal Supply Service. Some actions in the procurement process may be taken only by the HCA (not a contracting officer).

HEALTH CARE SERVICES See NONPERSONAL HEALTH CARE SERVICES.

HELIUM ACT See BUREAU HELIUM DISTRIBUTOR.

HHS See DEPARTMENT OF HEALTH AND HUMAN SERVICES.

HIGH-VALUE ITEM A contract end item that (1) has a high cost (normally exceeding $100,000 per unit), such as an aircraft, an aircraft engine, a communication system, a computer system, a missile, or a ship; and (2) is designated by the contracting officer as a high-value item. FAR 46.802. FAR 46.803 states the Government policy to relieve the contractor of liability for loss of or damage to such items. This is done by including in the contract the Limitation of Liability—High-Value Item clause in FAR 52.246-24.

HISTORICAL COST The ACTUAL COST incurred by a contractor in performing the work. In *Bruce Constr. Corp. v. United States*, 163 Ct. Cl. 97, 324 F.2d 516 (1963), it was held that the measure for determining the amount of an EQUITABLE ADJUSTMENT is reasonable cost (see REASONABLENESS OF COST) plus an allowance for profit, and that historical cost, rather than FAIR MARKET VALUE, was presumed to be the proper measure of reasonable cost. This rule gives greater weight to a particular contractor's actual cost than to the determination of what the cost would have been to other contractors in general. 10 U.S.C. § 2324(j) seeks to overcome the presumption of validity of historical costs with regard to indirect cost rulings by providing that contractors have the burden of proof of reasonableness when litigating such costs. FAR 31.201-3(a) carries this logic further by stating that contractors have the burden of proof when any cost is challenged as unreasonable. See Cibinic & Nash, *Administration of Government Contracts* 682–86 (3d ed. 1995).

HISTORICALLY BLACK COLLEGES AND UNIVERSITIES (HBCUS) Institutions that the Secretary of Education has determined meet the requirements of 34 C.F.R. § 608.2. In furtherance of the Government policy of placing a fair proportion of its acquisitions with HBCUs, MINORITY INSTITUTIONs (MIs), and SMALL DISADVANTAGED BUSINESS CONCERNs (SDBCs), § 1207 of Pub. L. No. 99-661, § 806 of Pub. L. No. 100-180, and § 831 of Pub. L. No.

101-189, now located at 10 U.S.C. § 2323, established an objective for DOD to award a total of 5 percent of its total contract dollars during each fiscal year 1987 through 1993 (since extended to the fiscal year 2000) to HBCUs, MIs, and SDBCs and of maximizing the number of such entities participating in DOD prime contracts and subcontracts. DFARS 226.7003 See Ginsburg & Benton, *One Year Later: Affirmative Action in Federal Government Contracting After Adarand*, 45 Am. U. L. Rev. 1903 (1996); Lambert & Shillito, *DOD Implements Congressional Mandate to Meet a Five Percent Contract Goal for Minorities*, 27 Cont. Mgmt. 16 (Oct. 1987). See also Conway-Jones & Jones, *Department of Defense Procurement Practices After Adarand: What Lies Ahead for the Largest Purchaser of Goods and Services and Its Base of Small Disadvantaged Business Contractors*, 39 How. L.J. 391 (1995); *An Inventory of the Capabilities of the Historically Black Colleges and Universities and Other Minority Institutions (HBCUs/MIs): A NAFEO/DOD Survey* (1989) (available from the National Association for Equal Opportunity in Higher Education, 400 12th Street, N.E., Washington, DC 20002; (202)543-9111).

HOME OFFICE An office responsible for directing or managing two or more, but not necessarily all, SEGMENTs of an organization. FAR 31.001. A home office typically establishes policy for and provides guidance to the segments in their operations. It usually performs management, supervisory, or administrative functions and may also perform support service functions. An organization that has intermediate levels, such as groups, may have several home offices reporting to a common home office. An intermediate organization may be both a segment and a home office. CAS 403, Allocation of Home Office Expenses to Segments,48 C.F.R. § 9904.403, requires that, to the maximum extent practicable, home office expenses must be allocated directly to segments on the basis of the beneficial or causal relationship between supporting and receiving activities. If these expenses are not allocated directly to segments, they are to be grouped in logical and homogeneous expense pools and allocated in accordance with detailed rules in the standard. See Cibinic & Nash, *Cost-Reimbursement Contracting* 694–702 (2d ed. 1993). In pricing claims for Government delay, home office expenses are generally computed using the EICHLEAY FORMULA.

HORIZONTAL MERGER GUIDELINES A document, issued by the DEPARTMENT OF JUSTICE (DOJ) in 1984 and revised and released jointly by the DOJ and the Federal Trade Commission (FTC) in 1992, detailing the agencies' enforcement policies regarding horizontal mergers in the private sector and describing how the federal antitrust laws (§ 7 of the CLAYTON ACT, § 1 of the Sherman Act, and § 5 of the FTC Act) can impact them. It also outlines the analytical framework the Government will utilize in determining whether or not to challenge a horizontal merger. The guidelines are reprinted in 4 Trade Reg. Rep. (CCH) ¶ 13,104 (Apr. 2, 1992) and can also be found on the Internet at <gopher://justice2.usdoj.gov:70/00/ atr/Guidelines/merger.txt>. See Leo, *Mergers in a Declining Industry: Should the Merger Guidelines be Reassessed?*, 28 Conn. L. Rev. 347 (1996); Hershey, *Avoiding Antitrust Problems: A Guide for Government Contractors*, 34 Cont. Mgmt. 4 (Jan. 1994); Victorino et al., *Antitrust Implications of Defense Industry Business Combinations*, 93-7 Briefing Papers and 1995 Revision Note (June 1993); Wilkinson & Bernstein, *Mergers in the Defense Industry: Application of the 1992 Horizontal Merger Guidelines*, 23 Pub. Cont. L.J. 1 (1993).

HOTLINE A system by which employees may report suspected instances of improper conduct. DOD operates a hotline and requires that contractors performing contracts expected to exceed $5 million display DOD hotline posters prominently in common work areas (or, alternatively, that they establish a comparable internal mechanism and encourage employee reporting). DFARS Subpart 203.70; 252.203-7002. See Whitlock, *How to Establish a Hot Line Reporting System That Works*, 29 Cont. Mgmt. 48 (Nov. 1989); Nadler, *Corporate Ethics: Guidelines for an Effective Hot Line Program*, 29 Cont. Mgmt. 4 (Aug. 1989); Seyfarth et al., chap. 2, *The Government Contract Compliance Handbook* (2d ed. 1991 & 1996 Supp.).

HUD See DEPARTMENT OF HOUSING AND URBAN DEVELOPMENT.

I

IDENTICAL BIDS Bids for the same LINE ITEM that are determined to be identical in unit price or total line item amount, with or without the application of evaluation factors (such as, discounts or transportation cost). FAR 3.302. FAR 3.303(d) requires the reporting of such bids as possible ANTITRUST VIOLATIONS when there is some reason to suspect collusion between the bidders.

IDIQ CONTRACT See INDEFINITE QUANTITY CONTRACT.

IDLE CAPACITY The unused capacity of partially used facilities. FAR 31.205-17. It is the difference between (1) what a facility could achieve under 100 percent operating time on a one-shift basis (or, in some cases, a multiple-shift basis) less operating interruptions resulting from time for repairs, setups, unsatisfactory materials, and other normal delays; and (2) the extent to which the facility was actually used to meet demands during the cost accounting period. Costs of idle capacity are costs of doing business and are a factor in the normal fluctuations of use or overhead rates from period to period. Such costs are ALLOWABLE COSTs, provided the capacity is necessary or was originally reasonable and is not subject to reduction or elimination by subletting, renting, or sale, in accordance with sound business, economic, or security practices. See Cibinic & Nash, *Cost-Reimbursement Contracting* 854–57 (2d ed. 1993).

IDLE FACILITIES Completely unused facilities that are excess to the contractor's current needs. FAR 31.205-17. The costs of idle facilities are UNALLOWABLE COSTs unless the facilities (1) are necessary to meet fluctuations in workload; or (2) were necessary when acquired and are now idle because of changes in requirements, production economies, reorganization, termination, or other causes that could not reasonably have been foreseen. See Cibinic & Nash, *Cost-Reimbursement Contracting* 854–57 (2d ed. 1993).

"ILITIES" A slang term commonly used within DOD for the operational and support requirements a program must address (such as availability, maintainability, vulnerability, reliability, and logistic supportability). Jones, *Glossary: Defense Acquisition Acronyms and Terms* (8th ed., Defense Systems Management College).

IMMEDIATE-GAIN ACTUARIAL COST METHOD Any of several ACTUARIAL COST METHODs under which actuarial gains and losses are included as part of the unfunded ACTUARIAL LIABILITY of a PENSION PLAN, rather than as part of the normal cost of the plan. FAR 31.001. Actuarial gains and losses under a pension plan whose costs are measured by this actuarial cost method must be amortized over a 15-year period in equal annual installments, beginning with the date of the actuarial valuation. CAS 413, Adjustment and Allocation of Pension Costs, 48 C.F.R. § 9904.413-50(a)(2).

IMPAC CARD See GOVERNMENT-WIDE COMMERCIAL PURCHASE CARD.

IMPAIRMENT OF LONG-LIVED ASSETS Loss of value of long-lived assets to the extent that their value may not be recoverable. Long lived assets include land, buildings, and equipment that are held for use and, as such, are subject to the write-down provisions of Statement of Financial Accounting Standards (SFAS) No. 121, *Accounting for the Impairment of Long-Lived Assets and for Long-Lived Assets to be Disposed of* (Mar. 1995). When events and circumstances indicate that the value in the financial statements may not be fully recoverable, SFAS No. 121 requires that the asset be written down to its fair value. Once an impaired asset has been written down under the provisions of SFAS No. 121, GENERALLY ACCEPTED ACCOUNTING PRINCIPLES do not permit the subsequent write up of a previously impaired asset, even if that asset later recovers any part of its value. The impairment losses recognized for financial accounting purposes pursuant to SFAS No. 121, are not ALLOWABLE COSTs for Government contract costing purposes. FAR 31.205-16(g). CAS 409, 48 C.F.R. § 9904.409, Depreciation of Tangible Capital Assets, recognizes gains and losses for Government contract purposes only upon the disposition of the asset. Accordingly, the allowable cost attributed to the loss upon disposition of an impaired long-lived asset shall be the amount that would have been allowed had the asset not been written down for financial accounting purposes. See Keevan & Ruona, *Accounting for Impaired Assets Under SFAS 121, CAS & FAR Part 31*, 97-7 CP&A Rep. 3 (July 1996).

IMPLIED AUTHORITY CONTRACTING OFFICER authority that is implied from the facts of the transaction rather than delegated in writing in accordance with FAR Subpart 1.6. Implied authority is found by the courts and boards when they determine that the Government should be bound by the acts of agency employees who do not have formal contracting officer authority. It generally flows from acts of which a contracting officer was, or should have been, aware. See Cibinic & Nash, *Administration of Government Contracts* 44–47 (3d ed. 1995); Reifel & Bastianelli, *Contracting Officer Authority*, 86-4 Briefing Papers (Mar. 1986).

IMPLIED CONTRACT A contract not created or evidenced by an explicit agreement of the parties, but inferred, as a matter of reason and justice, from the parties' acts or conduct (the circumstances surrounding the transaction making it reasonable or even necessary to assume that a contract existed between the parties by tacit understanding). Implied contracts are sometimes divided into two categories: (1) those implied in fact, which derive from the above definition; and (2) those implied in law, often referred to as "quasi-contracts." Quasi-contracts derive from obligations imposed on a person by the law, not pursuant to the person's intention and agreement, either expressed or implied, and even against the person's will and design, because circumstances between the parties are such as to render it just that one party should have a right and the other party a corresponding liability, similar to those that would arise from a contract between them. *Black's Law Dictionary* 754 (6th ed. 1990). The U.S. COURT OF FEDERAL CLAIMS has jurisdiction over contracts implied in fact but not over contracts implied in law. 28 U.S.C. § 1491(a)(1). See Cibinic & Nash, chap. 2, Sec. II., *Formation of Government Contracts* (3d ed. 1998); Boyd, *Implied-in-Fact Contract: Contractual Recovery Against the Government Without an Express Agreement*, 21 Pub. Cont. L.J. 84 (1991).

IMPLIED DUTY See IMPLIED PROMISE.

IMPLIED PROMISE A promise of a contracting party that is implied from the facts of the transaction. There are a number of implied promises that attach to most contracts, such as the implied DUTY OF GOOD FAITH AND FAIR DEALING and the implied DUTY TO COOPERATE. The Government is also held to an IMPLIED WARRANTY OF SPECIFICATIONS when it furnishes design specifications to a contractor and to an implied duty to disclose information (see SUPERIOR KNOWLEDGE) when it has vital information needed by a contractor to permit successful performance. See Nash, *Implied*

Promises by the Government: The Supreme Court Speaks in Hercules, 10 N&CR ¶ 21 (May 1996).

IMPLIED WARRANTY OF SPECIFICATIONS The warranty of the Government that its design SPECIFICATIONs can be successfully used to perform a contract. When a contractor fails to perform because such specifications are defective, it can assert a CONSTRUCTIVE CHANGE claim in order to obtain an EQUITABLE ADJUSTMENT in the contract price. See Cibinic & Nash, *Administration of Government Contracts* 267–95 (3d ed. 1995); Harrington et al., *The Owner's Warranty of the Plans and Specifications for a Construction Project*, 14 Pub. Cont. L.J. 240 (1984).

IMPOSSIBILITY OF PERFORMANCE A legal doctrine deriving from the concept that an implied condition exists under which the parties to a contract intended to dissolve their contractual obligations upon an individual's death or incapacity or upon the destruction or loss of vital and irreplaceable materials. Thus, a party encountering impossibility of performance will have a defense against a suit for BREACH OF CONTRACT. Discussion of impossibility of performance typically references concepts of IMPRACTICABILITY OF PERFORMANCE and FRUSTRATION OF PURPOSE. "Impossibility" generally means technical or physical impossibility—that is, on the basis of all human experience, a thing clearly cannot be done; "impracticability of performance" typically includes unforeseen cost increases, extreme financial difficulty, illegality, or other situations in which a court may excuse lack of performance. Schooner, *Impossibility of Performance In Public Contracts: An Economic Analysis*, 16 Pub. Cont. L.J. 229 (1986). The term "existing impossibility" refers to an impossibility of performance existing when the contract was entered into, so that the contract was to do something that was impossible from the outset; "supervening impossibility" refers to impossibility that developed after the inception of the contract. *Ballentine's Law Dictionary* (3d ed. 1969). If a party has assumed the risk of impossibility, it will be denied the use of the defense and will be held liable for breach of contract. Very few experienced contractors have been able to prove that they did not assume the risk of impossibility. See Martell & Meagher, *Impossibility of Performance/Edition III*, 88-7 Briefing Papers (June 1988); Vogel, *Impossibility of Performance—A Closer Look*, 9 Pub. Cont. L.J. 110 (1977).

IMPOUNDMENT An action by the President that prevents the obligation or expenditure of BUDGET AUTHORITY. 2 U.S.C. § 681 et al.

Deferrals and rescissions are the two types of presidential impoundment. Whenever all or part of any budget authority provided by Congress is deferred or rescinded, the President must transmit a message to Congress describing the deferral or rescission. In the case of a deferral, either house of Congress may, at any time, pass an impoundment resolution disapproving this deferral of budget authority, thus requiring that the funds be made available for obligation. When no congressional action is taken, deferrals may remain in effect until, but not beyond, the end of the FISCAL YEAR. If the funds remain available beyond the end of a fiscal year and continued deferral of their use is desired, the President must transmit a new special message to Congress. In the case of a rescission, any amount of budget authority proposed to be rescinded must be made available for obligation unless, within the prescribed 45-day period, Congress has completed action on a rescission bill rescinding all or part of the amount proposed to be rescinded. See GAO, *Principles of Federal Appropriations Law*, vol. I, 1-19–1-22 (2d ed. 1991); Jones, *Glossary: Defense Acquisition Acronyms and Terms* (8th ed., Defense Systems Management College). See DEFERRAL OF BUDGET AUTHORITY; RESCISSION OF BUDGET AUTHORITY.

IMPRACTICABILITY OF PERFORMANCE Extreme and unreasonable difficulty, expense, injury, or loss to a contracting party. *Restatement (Second) of Contracts* § 261 (1981) cmt. d. See also U.C.C. § 2-615. The *Restatement* gives as examples severe shortages of raw materials or supplies due to war, embargo, local crop failure, or unforeseen shutdown of major sources of supply, all of which cause a marked increase in costs. It warns, however, that a mere change in the degree of difficulty due to such causes as increased wages, prices of raw materials, or costs of construction, unless well beyond the normal range, does not amount to impracticability. The term derives from the legal concept of IMPOSSIBILITY OF PERFORMANCE and has the same legal effect: it excuses a party from performing a contract unless that party has assumed the risk of the event. In Government contracting, impracticability has also been treated as a type of CONSTRUCTIVE CHANGE giving a contractor that has incurred extra costs an EQUITABLE ADJUSTMENT. See Nash, *Government Contract Changes* 13-36 through 13-51 (2d ed. 1989 & Supp. 1993); Cibinic & Nash, *Administration of Government Contracts* 312–21 (3d ed. 1995); Nagle, *Financial Inability in Government Contracts*, 17 Pub. Cont. L.J. 230 (1987); Schooner, *Impossibility of Performance in Public Contracts: An Economic Analysis*, 16 Pub. Cont. L.J. 229 (1986).

IMPREST FUND A cash fund (also known as "petty cash") of a fixed amount established by an advance of funds, without charge to an APPROPRIATION, from an agency finance or disbursing officer to a duly appointed cashier, for distribution as needed from time to time in making payment in cash for relatively small amounts. FAR 13.001. Imprest funds may be used for SIMPLIFIED ACQUISITIONs when (1) the transaction does not exceed $500 or another limit approved by the HEAD OF THE AGENCY, (2) the third party draft transaction does not exceed $2,500, unless authorized at a higher level in accordance with Treasury restrictions, (3) the use of imprest funds is considered to be advantageous to the Government, and (4) the use of imprest funds complies with any additional conditions established by agencies and certain Department of the Treasury and General Accounting Office manuals. FAR 13.305-3. The use of imprest funds has been largely displaced by the use of GOVERNMENT-WIDE COMMERCIAL PURCHASE CARDs. FAR 13.301. See DFARS Subpart 213.4.

IMPROPER BUSINESS PRACTICES A broad range of activities forbidden or limited by FAR Part 3 with regard to the award and performance of Government contracts. The prohibitions and guidelines are based on the premise that Government business must be conducted in a manner above reproach and, except as otherwise authorized by statute or regulation, with complete impartiality and preferential treatment for none. Transactions relating to the expenditure of public funds should merit the highest degree of public trust and reflect an impeccable standard of conduct. FAR 3.101-1. The FAR discusses the following improper or potentially improper business practices: contractor gratuities (see GRATUITY) to Government personnel (FAR Subpart 3.2); ANTITRUST VIOLATIONs (FAR Subpart 3.3); CONTINGENT FEEs (FAR Subpart 3.4); BUYING IN (FAR 3.501); KICKBACKs (FAR 3.502); unreasonable restrictions on subcontractor sales (FAR 3.503); and contracts with Government employees or organizations owned or controlled by them (FAR Subpart 3.6). It also discusses the voiding and rescinding of contracts in relation to which improper business practices have been found (FAR Subpart 3.7) and addresses PROCUREMENT INTEGRITY (FAR 3.104). FAR Part 3, while containing some specific guidance, is incomplete in terms of total coverage of improper business practices. See STANDARDS OF CONDUCT for other applicable coverage. See also Cibinic & Nash, chap. 1, Sec. VII., *Formation of Government Contracts* (3d ed. 1998); Nash, *The New Procurement Integrity Rules,* 11 N&CR ¶ 12 (Mar. 1997) Brunsman, *Standards of Conduct and Business Ethics for Buyers*, 27 Cont. Mgmt. 18 (June 1987).

IMPROPER INFLUENCE Any influence that induces or tends to induce a Government employee or officer to give consideration to or act regarding a Government contract on any basis other than the merits of the matter. FAR 3.401.

IMPROVEMENT CURVE See LEARNING CURVE.

IMPUTED COSTS A cost that does not entail actual dollar outlays. In some circumstances, contractors are permitted to recover imputed costs. Under CAS 416, Accounting for Insurance Costs, 48 C.F.R. § 9904-416, a contractor's reserves for self-insurance may be recognized as costs even though there is neither actual payment nor the incurrence of an obligation to make payment. A specific imputed cost that is recognized throughout the Government is FACILITIES CAPITAL COST OF MONEY, CAS 414, Cost of Money as an Element of the Cost of Facilities Capital, 48 C.F.R. § 9904-414. See Cibinic & Nash, *Cost-Reimbursement Contracting* 48 (2d ed. 1993).

IMPUTED KNOWLEDGE Knowledge possessed by a Government employee that is ascribed to a CONTRACTING OFFICER by virtue of the relationship presumed to exist between the employee and the contracting officer. The principle of imputed knowledge is based on the common-law concept that a principal is charged with knowledge that an agent has a duty to deliver to the principal. Courts and boards of contract appeals (BCAs) frequently assume that responsible Government employees will convey their knowledge to the contracting officer. The imputed knowledge issue arises, for example, in cases in which a contractor has failed to give formal notice of an event as required by one of the contract's adjustment clauses (such as the CHANGEs, DIFFERING SITE CONDITIONS, or SUSPENSION OF WORK clauses) but has made a Government employee aware of the event. In such a case, the courts and BCAs frequently refuse to deny, solely on grounds that formal notice was not given to the contracting officer, contractor CLAIMs for price adjustment. See Cibinic & Nash, *Administration of Government Contracts* 55–60 (3d ed. 1995).

IN-KIND CONTRIBUTIONS Non-cash contributions provided by a performing contractor or a non-federal third party who is participating with the EPA in a cosponsored project or contract. Such contributions may be used to fulfill the contractor's obligation to share the costs of performance. EPAAR 1516.303-73(b). In-kind contributions may be in the form of personal property (equipment or supplies) or services. Such contributions must be directly beneficial, specifically identifiable, and necessary to the performance of the project or program. They must (1) be verifiable from the performer's books and records; (2) not be included as contributions under any other federal contract; (3) be necessary to accomplishment project objectives; (4) provide for types of charges that would otherwise be allowable under applicable federal cost principles appropriate to the contractor's organization; and (5) not be paid for by the Federal Government under any contract, AGREEMENT, or GRANT. EPAAR 1516.303-73(c).

INCENTIVE COMPENSATION Compensation paid to an employee to motivate good performance. FAR 31.205-6(f) specifies when the cost of such compensation by a contractor may be treated as an ALLOWABLE COST. See Cibinic & Nash, *Cost-Reimbursement Contracting* 801–3 (2d ed. 1993).

INCENTIVE CONTRACT A negotiated pricing arrangement that gives the contractor higher profits for better performance and/or lower profits for worse performance in prescribed areas (cost, delivery, or technical performance). The standard types of incentive contracts are prescribed in FAR Subpart 16.4. These include (1) contracts where the profit adjustment is made in accordance with a preestablished formula, such as FIXED-PRICE-INCENTIVE CONTRACTs (with firm or successive targets) and COST-PLUS-INCENTIVE-FEE CONTRACTs; and (2) contracts where the profit adjustment is made by unilateral determination of an officer of the Government, such as COST-PLUS-AWARD-FEE CONTRACTs. Incentive contracts are designed to achieve specific acquisition objectives by (1) establishing reasonable and attainable targets that are clearly communicated to the contractor and (2) including appropriate incentive arrangements designed to motivate contractor efforts and discourage contractor inefficiency and waste. FAR 16.401. See Cibinic and Nash, chap. 8, Sec. IV., *Formation of Government Contracts* (3d ed. 1998); Nash, *Incentive Contracts: A Bit of History*, 10 N&CR ¶ 49 (Sept. 1996); Garrett, *Performance-Based Contracting Incentives: Myths, Best Practices and Innovations*, 35 Cont. Mgmt. 6 (Feb. 1995); Fisher, *Risk Management for Incentive Contracts*, 29 Cont. Mgmt. 23 (Jan. 1989).

INCREMENTALLY FUNDED CONTRACTS Contracts in which the scope of work is greater than the funds available to the agency at the time of contract AWARD. The FAR contains no guidance on when an agency may use an incrementally funded contract. However, FAR 32.705-2(c) calls for the use of the LIMITATION OF FUNDS CLAUSE in FAR 52.232-22 when an incrementally funded COST-

REIMBURSEMENT CONTRACT is used. NASA provides guidance for using incrementally funded contracts at NFS 18-32.702-70. See Nash and Cibinic, *Competitive Negotiation: The Source Selection Process* 94–96 (1993). DOD's policy on the use of incrementally funded FIXED-PRICE CONTRACTS is located at DFARS 232.704-70. See *Principles of Budgeting for Capital Asset Acquisitions*, 10 Budget of the United States Government, Fiscal Year 1998 (GPO 1997).

INCURRED COST A cost identified through the use of the ACCRUAL METHOD of accounting and reporting, or otherwise actually paid. Although a commercial definition of incurred costs would include all costs actually paid or properly accrued, the Government guidance may limit the definition to include only ALLOWABLE COSTs. See ALLOCABLE COST; ALLOWABLE COST. The *DCAA Contract Audit Manual* 6-102.1, which, in discussing AUDIT objectives for and approaches to incurred costs, explains that the AUDITOR's objective is to examine the contractor's cost representations, in whatever form they may be presented, and express an opinion whether the incurred costs (1) are reasonable, applicable to the contract, and determined according to GENERALLY ACCEPTED ACCOUNTING PRINCIPLES and COST ACCOUNTING STANDARDS applicable in the circumstances; and (2) are not prohibited by the contract, by Government statute or regulation, or by previous agreement with or decision of a Government contracting officer. See Cibinic & Nash, *Cost-Reimbursement Contracting* 638–45 (2d ed. 1993).

INDEFINITE-DELIVERY CONTRACT A type of contract in which the time of delivery is unspecified in the original contract but established by the contracting officer during performance. FAR Subpart 16.5 contains guidance on three types of indefinite-delivery contracts: (1) DEFINITE-QUANTITY CONTRACTs, (2) REQUIREMENTS CONTRACTs, and (3) INDEFINITE-QUANTITY CONTRACTs. FAR 16.501-2 states that the appropriate type of indefinite-delivery contract may be used when the exact times and/or quantities of future deliveries are not known at the time of contract award. Indefinite-delivery contracts permit maintenance of Government stocks at minimum levels and direct shipment to users. Indefinite-delivery contracts may provide for any appropriate cost or pricing arrangement under FAR Part 16. DOD notes that for items with a shelf life of less than six months, consideration should be given to use of these contracts along with simplified purchasing requirements. DFARS 216.501. See Cibinic & Nash, chap. 8, Sec. VI., *Formation of Government Contracts* (3d ed. 1998).

INDEFINITE-QUANTITY CONTRACT A contract providing for an indefinite quantity, within stated maximum or minimum limits, of specific supplies or services to be furnished during a fixed period, with deliveries to be scheduled by placing orders with the contractor. FAR 16.504(a). Such contracts are commonly referred to as IDIQ contracts. The contractor is legally bound to such a contract because the Government promises to procure, as CONSIDERATION, a minimum quantity that is more than a nominal quantity. The contract requires the Government to order at least the quantity designated as the minimum and requires the contractor to furnish, when ordered, supplies or services up to and including the quantity designated as the maximum. The contract may also specify maximum or minimum quantities that the Government may order under each task or delivery order and the maximum that it may order during a specific period of time. An indefinite-quantity contract should be used only when a recurring need is anticipated. Funds for other than the stated minimum quantity are obligated by each task or delivery order, not by the contract itself. See Cibinic & Nash, chap. 8, Sec. VI., *Formation of Government Contracts* (3d ed. 1998); Nash, *Indefinite Quantity Contracts: Compensation for Not Ordering Minimim Quantity*, 10 N&CR ¶ 40 (Aug. 1996).

INDEMNIFICATION The agreement of a contracting party to hold the other party harmless, to secure the other party against loss or damage, or to give security for the reimbursement of the other party in case of an anticipated loss. See *Black's Law Dictionary* 769 (6th ed. 1990). The Government does not generally require contractors to indemnify the Government or protect the Government from liability, but a similar result is achieved in those cases where the Government requires the contractor to purchase INSURANCE or protect itself through SELF-INSURANCE. See, for example, the Insurance—Liability to Third Persons clause in FAR 52.228-7. FAR 31.205-19 contains the cost principle on insurance and indemnification. See Cibinic & Nash, *Cost-Reimbursement Contracting* 883–86 (2d ed. 1993). The Government indemnifies contractors against losses only in unusual circumstances. See Nash & Cibinic, *Federal Procurement Law,* vol. II, 1937–39 (3d ed. 1980), for a discussion of statutes that have permitted such indemnification. FAR Subpart 50.4 and the Indemnification under Pub. Law No. 85-804 clause at FAR 52.250-1 contain guidance on indemnifying contractors against unusually hazardous or nuclear risks. See Addicott, *Double Indemnity for Operators of Nuclear Facilities? In re: Hanford Nuclear Reservation Litigation, The Price-Anderson Act, And The Government Contractor Defense*, 72 Wash. L. Rev. 505 (1997); Baker, *Indemnification of Environmental Contractors and*

Subcontractors, 32 Cont. Mgmt. 14 (June 1992); McNett, *Nuclear Indemnity for Government Contractors under the Price-Anderson Act: 1988 Amendments*, 19 Pub. Cont. L.J. 1 (1989).

INDEPENDENT CONTRACTOR A person who, "in exercise of an independent employment, contracts to do a piece of work according to his own methods and is subject to his employer's control only as to end product or final result of his work." *Black's Law Dictionary* 770 (6th ed. 1990). An independent contractor is contracted to an employee, where the employer exercises detailed control over the employee's activities.

INDEPENDENT RESEARCH AND DEVELOPMENT (IR&D) A contractor's research and development effort that is not sponsored by, or required in performance of, a contract or grant and that consists of projects falling within the following areas: (1) BASIC RESEARCH, (2) APPLIED RESEARCH, (3) DEVELOPMENT, and (4) systems and other concept formulation studies. FAR 31.205-18(a). IR&D does not include (1) technical effort expended in developing and preparing TECHNICAL DATA specifically to support submission of an offer; or (2) manufacturing engineering effort to develop or improve manufacturing or production materials, systems, processes, methods, equipment, tools, and techniques not intended for sale. IR&D costs, together with BID AND PROPOSAL COSTS, are generally ALLOWABLE COSTs under FAR 31.205-18, subject to proper allocation under CAS 420, Accounting for Independent Research and Development Costs and Bid Proposal Costs, 48 C.F.R. § 9904.420. Additional limitations may be placed by the contracting officer on IR&D allocated to DOD contracts. DFARS 231.205-18. See Cibinic & Nash, *Cost-Reimbursement Contracting* 765–76 (2d ed. 1993); Barletta, *IR&D Cost Principle Class Deviation–NFS Final Rule*, 97-5 CP&A Rep. 17 (May 1997); Russell, *"Cooperative Arrangements" Under the "IR&D" Cost Principle (FAR 31.205-18(e))*, 94-10 CP&A Rep. 3 (Oct. 1994); Chartula et al., *IR&D Redux*, 93-2 CP&A Rep. 3 (Feb. 1993); Cibinic, *IR&D and B&P Advance Agreements and Ceilings: Gone and Slowly Fading Away*, 6 N&CR ¶ 62 (Nov. 1992); Cibinic, *IR&D and Bid & Proposal and Precontract Costs: The Troublesome Troika*, 6 N&CR ¶ 42 (July 1992); Victorino & Briggerman, *The IR&D/B&P/Selling Costs Dilemma*, 87-10 Briefing Papers (Sept. 1987).

INDIAN PREFERENCE A policy established in 1975 by section 7(b) of the Indian Self-determination and Education Assistance Act, 25 U.S.C. §§ 450–450n, 455–458e, for contracts and subcontracts entered into under the Act, as well as other contracts or subcontracts with Indian organizations or for the benefit of Indians. The policy requires that (1) preference and training/education opportunities in contract administration be given to Indians, and (2) preference in SUBCONTRACTing be given to Indian organizations and Indian-owned economic enterprises. The Indian Preference Program is used primarily by the Bureau of Indian Affairs and the Indian Health Service but may be used by other contracting activities. See also BUY INDIAN ACT.

INDIAN TRIBE Any Indian tribe, band, nation, or other organized group or community of Indians, including any Alaska native corporation as defined in 13 C.F.R. § 124.100, that is recognized as eligible for the special programs and services provided by the United States to Indians because of their status as Indians, or that is recognized as such by the State in which the tribe, band, nation, group, or community resides. FAR 19.001. See also NATIVE AMERICANS.

INDIRECT COST Any cost not directly identified with a single final COST OBJECTIVE, but identified with two or more final cost objectives, or with at least one intermediate cost objective. FAR 31.203. This term is also referred to as "overhead" or "burden." After direct costs have been determined and charged directly to the contract or other work, indirect costs are those remaining to be allocated to the several cost objectives. An indirect cost must not be allocated to a final cost objective if other costs incurred for the same purpose in like circumstances have been included as a direct cost of that or any other final cost objective. FAR Subpart 42.7 deals with establishing an indirect cost rate (see OVERHEAD RATE): the percentage or dollar factor that expresses the ratio of the indirect expense incurred in a given period to the direct labor cost, manufacturing cost, or other appropriate base for the same period. Procedures are prescribed to ensure that a single agency is responsible for negotiating BILLING RATEs and FINAL INDIRECT COST RATEs for each BUSINESS UNIT of a contractor. See Cibinic & Nash, *Cost-Reimbursement Contracting* 668–76 (2d ed. 1993); Romenius, *Streamlining the Indirect Cost Proposal Process: Assessing the Alternatives*, 97-5 CP&A Rep. 3 (May 1997); Barger, *Indirect Cost Certificates and Penalties for Unallowable Costs in Defense Contracts*, 92-2 CP&A Rep. 3 (Feb. 1992); Shirk & Thompson, *Allowability of Unsettled Overhead and Accounting System Review Costs*, 91-9 CP&A Rep. 3 (Sept. 1991).

INDIRECT COST POOL A grouping of INCURRED COSTs identified with two or more COST OBJECTIVEs but not specifically identified with any final cost objective. FAR 31.001. FAR 31.203 requires that indirect costs be accumulated by logical cost groupings, with due consideration of the reasons for incurring those costs. Each grouping should be determined to permit distribution of the grouping on the basis of the benefits accruing to the several cost objectives. In most circumstances, manufacturing OVERHEAD, selling expenses, and GENERAL AND ADMINISTRATIVE COSTS are separately grouped. The contractor must select a distribution base common to all cost objectives to which the grouping is to be allocated. The contractor's method of allocating indirect costs must comply with CAS 418, Allocation of Direct and Indirect Cost, 48 C.F.R. § 9904.418, if applicable, or GENERALLY ACCEPTED ACCOUNTING PRINCIPLES. See also ALLOCABLE COST. See Cibinic & Nash, *Cost-Reimbursement Contracting* 81–84 (2d ed. 1993).

INDUSTRIAL BASE The manufacturing industry that produces consumer products, including components and parts, and that represents the basic capability available in the United States in the event of an INDUSTRIAL MOBILIZATION during a national emergency. The "mobilization base" consists of those companies that have entered into agreements with the Government to produce specific defense items in the event the Government declares a state of national emergency or war and the economy is mobilized for war. The industrial base supports the mobilization-base planned producers and, more importantly, must expand its capability to meet the large demands DOD would make in order to defend the country. See DOD Regulation 5000.2-R, *Mandatory Procedures for Major Defense Acquisition Programs (MDAPs) and Major Automated Information System (MAIS) Acquisition Programs*, Mar. 15, 1996, Part 3.3.1.3, Industrial Capability. See also Heberling, *Defense Industrial Base Policy: Revisited*, 1 Acquisition Rev. Q. 238 (1994); Sharkey, *Reinventing the National Defense Industrial Base—A Shootout*, 34 Cont. Mgmt. 19 (June 1994); Nickolas, *The Industrial Base under Siege*, 27 Cont. Mgmt. 8 (July 1987).

INDUSTRIAL BASE FACTORS ANALYSIS An analysis prepared to assess the near-term and long-range effects of a proposed international agreement on the U.S. defense industrial base. The analysis is to address both the immediate effort and the projected development, production, and/or support of any proposed follow-on effort. Effects on prime and sub-tier industries are to be considered. This information (1) is required for all proposed international agreements for research, development, and/or production of defense items; (2) is to be provided by the cognizant DOD component when a proposed agreement is submitted for approval of authority to negotiate or conclude in accordance with DOD Directive 5530.3; and (3) will be used by the Office of the Secretary of Defense during its review of the memorandum of understanding and preparation of a final industrial base impact assessment. Jones, *Glossary: Defense Acquisition Acronyms and Terms* (8th ed., Defense Systems Management College).

INDUSTRIAL ENGINEERING The process of determining the utilization of personnel, equipment, and materials, as well as the coordination of activities and events, that will attain a desired quantity of output at a specified time and at an optimum cost. Industrial engineering may include gathering, analyzing, and acting on facts pertaining to buildings and facilities, layouts, personnel organization, operating procedures, methods, processes, schedules, time standards, wage rates, wage payment plans, costs, and systems for controlling the quality and quantity of goods and services. Jones, *Glossary: Defense Acquisition Acronyms and Terms* (8th ed., Defense Systems Management College). The techniques of industrial engineering are used when the Government makes a SHOULD-COST ANALYSIS of a contractor's proposed cost of performance.

INDUSTRIAL MOBILIZATION The use of American industry to produce supplies and services in the event of a national emergency. 10 U.S.C. § 2304(c)(3) and 41 U.S.C. § 253(c)(3) permit the awarding of contracts without FULL AND OPEN COMPETITION when it is necessary to maintain sources in order to achieve such mobilization. See FAR 6.302-3. See INDUSTRIAL BASE.

INDUSTRIAL PLANT EQUIPMENT See PLANT EQUIPMENT.

INELIGIBLE Having been excluded from the award of contracts pursuant to statute, executive order, or regulatory authority other than for DEBARMENT or SUSPENSION under FAR Subpart 9.4. FAR 9.403. Common grounds for ineligibility are violations of the DAVIS-BACON ACT, the SERVICE CONTRACT ACT OF 1965, the EQUAL EMPLOYMENT OPPORTUNITY regulations, the WALSH-HEALEY PUBLIC CONTRACTS ACT, the BUY AMERICAN ACT, and the Environmental Protection acts and executive orders. Although the FAR makes this distinction between "debarred" contractors and "ineligible" contractors, all such contractors are commonly referred to as having been debarred.

INFLUENCING OR ATTEMPTING TO INFLUENCE Making, with the intent to influence, any communication or appearance in connection with the awarding, making, entering into, extension, renewal, AMENDMENT, or MODIFICATION of any federal contract, GRANT, loan, or COOPERATIVE AGREEMENT. FAR 3.801. This is commonly referred to as "lobbying." A recipient of a federal contract, grant, loan, or cooperative agreement is prohibited from using APPROPRIATED FUNDS to pay any person for influencing or attempting to influence an officer or employee of any agency or a member of Congress or a congressional employee, in connection with any of these actions. FAR 3.802; 31 U.S.C. § 1352. See ANTI-LOBBYING ACT; LOBBYING COSTS.

INFORMATION OTHER THAN COST OR PRICING DATA Any type of information that is not required to be certified in accordance with FAR 15.406-2 and is necessary to determine price reasonableness or COST REALISM. FAR 15.401. Such information may include pricing, sales, or cost information and includes COST OR PRICING DATA for which a certification is determined inapplicable after submission. FAR 15.403-3 provides guidance on obtaining this information and provides that the contracting officer should know more information than is necessary to determine price reasonableness (see FAIR AND REASONABLE PRICE) or COST REALISM.

INFORMATION RESOURCES MANAGEMENT (IRM) The process of managing information resources to accomplish agency missions and to improve agency performance, including the reduction of information collection burdens on the public. 44 U.S.C. § 3502(7).

INFORMATION RESOURCES MANAGEMENT (IRM) NON-MANDATORY ADP SCHEDULES Nonmandatory, indefinite-quantity, multiple-award instruments used to purchase, rent, and maintain FEDERAL INFORMATION PROCESSING RESOURCES. These schedules are part of Federal Supply Class Group 70. They are often referred to as the "GSA Schedules," because the GENERAL SERVICES ADMINISTRATION negotiates them with vendors on behalf of executive agencies to help cut procurement costs and time.

INFORMATION SYSTEMS SECURITY (INFOSEC) The protection of information systems against unauthorized access to or modification of information, whether in storage, processing, or transit, and against the denial of service to authorized users or the provision of service to unauthorized users. It includes those measures necessary to detect, document, and counter such threats. National Communications System Technology and Standards Division, *Telecommunications: Glossary of Telecommunication Terms*, Federal Standard 1037C (Aug. 1996).

INFORMATION TECHNOLOGY (IT) Any equipment or any interconnected system or subsystem of equipment that is used in the automatic acquisition, storage, manipulation, management, movement, control, display, switching, interchange, transmission, or reception of data or information by an agency. FAR 2.101 (interim rule). This term includes computers, ancillary equipment, software, firmware and similar procedures, services (including support services), and related technology. FAR Part 39 (interim rule) provides for the acquisition of information technology. See also NFS Part 18-39. The CLINGER-COHEN ACT OF 1996 repealed the BROOKS ACT (AUTOMATED DATA PROCESSING PROCUREMENT) and substituted in sections 5001 through 5703 of the INFORMATION TECHNOLOGY MANAGEMENT REFORM ACT OF 1996. See McConnell, *The Process of Procuring Information Technology*, 25 Pub. Cont. L.J. 379 (1996); Cox, *FASA and False Certifications: Procurement Fraud on the Information Superhighway*, 25 Pub. Cont. L.J. 1 (1995).

INFORMATION TECHNOLOGY FUND (ITF) A fund which consists of the merger of two earlier funds: the ADP Fund, established by the BROOKS ACT (AUTOMATIC DATA PROCESSING PROCUREMENT), and the Federal Telecommunications Fund. Agencies may use the ITF for financing expenses, including personal services and other costs; for a federal information processing resources procurement by lease, purchase transfer, or otherwise; and for the efficient management, coordination, operation, and utilization of such resources. 40 U.S.C. § 757.

INFORMATION TECHNOLOGY MANAGEMENT REFORM ACT (ITMRA) A 1996 Act, part of the CLINGER-COHEN ACT OF 1996 (originally included as Division E of Pub. L. No. 104-106), that repeals the BROOKS ACT (AUTOMATED DATA PROCESSING PROCUREMENT) and substitutes new guidance on the procurement of INFORMATION TECHNOLOGY (IT). The Act provides that the director of the OFFICE OF MANAGEMENT AND BUDGET will (1) promote and improve the acquisition, use, and disposal of IT by administering a capital planning and investment system (§ 5112) and (2) encourage the use of performance-based and results-based management (§ 5113). It provides that agencies will (1) implement capital planning and investment programs (§ 5122), (2) use performance-based and results-based management procedures in the acquisition of IT (§ 5123), (3) promote multiagency acquisitions of IT (§ 5124), (4) appoint a Chief Information Officer (§ 5125), (5) ensure that there is accountability that IT systems are effective (§ 5126), and (6) use MODULAR CONTRACTING to the maximum extent practicable in acquiring IT (§ 5202). The Administrator of the Office of Federal Procurement Policy is also encouraged to authorize pilot programs using the "share-in-savings" technique (§ 5311) and the SOLUTIONS-BASED CONTRACTING technique (§ 5312).

INFORMATION TECHNOLOGY RESOURCES BOARD (ITRB) A board established to provide independent assessments to assist in the development, acquisition, and management of selected major information systems and to provide recommendations to agency heads and the OFFICE OF MANAGEMENT AND BUDGET (OMB) as appropriate. The board is required to (1) review specific information systems proposed or under development and make recommendations to a requesting agency and OMB regarding the status of systems or next steps; (2) publicize lessons learned and promising practices based on information systems reviewed by the board; and (3) seek the views of experts from industry, academia, and state and local governments on matters of concern to the board. The board includes individuals from executive branch agencies based on their knowledge of INFORMATION TECHNOLOGY or program or acquisition management within federal agencies. The board may call upon the department or agency whose project is being reviewed, or any other department or agency to provide knowledgeable representatives to the board whose guidance and expertise will assist in focusing on the primary issues presented by a specific system. Exec. Order No. 13011, 61 Fed. Reg. 37657 (July 16, 1996).

INHERENTLY GOVERNMENTAL FUNCTIONS Functions that, as a matter of policy (rather than law), are so intimately related to the public interest as to mandate performance by Government employees. These functions include activities that require the exercise of discretion in applying Government authority or the making of value judgments in making decisions for the Government. These functions typically involve interpretation and execution of federal laws; bind the Government; protect the Government's interests; affect private persons' life, liberty, or property; exert control over procurement of Government property; or exert control over the collection, control, and disbursement of federal funds. FAR 7.501. Contracts cannot be used for the performance of inherently Governmental functions. FAR 7.501(a). FAR 7.503(c) contains an extensive list of inherently Governmental functions, which includes, among others, criminal investigations, command of military forces, foreign relations, and contract award, administration, and termination. See generally, FAR Subpart 7.5, FAR 37.102(b); OMB Circular No. A-76 (revised), *Performance of Commercial Activities*, Aug. 16, 1983; OFPP Policy Letter No. 92-1, *Inherently Governmental Functions*, Sept. 23, 1992. See also Cibinic & Nash, chap. 3, Sec. IV., *Formation of Government Contracts* (3d ed. 1998).

INITIAL COSTS Preproduction and startup costs, including costs such as preproduction engineering, special tooling, special plant rearrangement, training programs, and such nonrecurring costs as initial rework, initial spoilage, and pilot runs. Such costs are generally allowable TERMINATION COSTS subject to the guidance in FAR 31.205-42. See Cibinic & Nash, *Administration of Government Contracts* 1108–10 (3d ed. 1995).

INSPECTION Examining and testing supplies or services (including, when appropriate, raw materials, components, and intermediate assemblies) to determine whether they conform to contract requirements. FAR 46.101. TESTING is the part of inspection that determines the properties or elements, including the functional operation of supplies or their components, by the application of established scientific principles and procedures. Although contracts generally make contractors responsible for performing inspection before tendering supplies to the Government, there are situations in which contracts will provide for specialized inspection to be performed solely by the Government. FAR 46.201. The standard inspection clauses in FAR 52.246-2 through -8 and -10 require the contractor to (1) provide and maintain an inspection system that is acceptable to the Government, (2) give the Government the right to perform reviews and evaluations as reasonably necessary, and (3) keep complete records of its inspection work and make them available to the Government. Regulatory guidance on inspection is contained in FAR Part 46 covering QUALITY ASSURANCE. See Cibinic & Nash, *Administration of Government Contracts* 790–833 (3d ed. 1995); Bednar, chap. 10, *Construction Contracting* 786–815 (1991); Kelleher & Cherniak, *Inspection Under Fixed-Price Construction Contracts/Edition III*, 96-7 Briefing Papers (June 1996); Jaeger, *Contractor Liability for Design Defects—A Sleeping Giant?*, 21 Pub. Cont. L.J. 331 (1992); Victorino & Ivey, *The "Inspection" Clause*, 88-10 Briefing Papers (Sept. 1988).

INSPECTOR GENERAL (IG) An officer of the United States, appointed by the President and confirmed by the Senate, to serve in each major department of the Government to independently audit and investigate the activities of that department. The Inspector General Act of 1978, 5 U.S.C. app. § 2, created Inspector General offices for Government agencies in order to establish independent and objective units to (1) conduct and supervise audits and investigations relating to the programs and operations of the agencies and organizations; (2) provide leadership and coordination and recommend policies for activities designed to promote administrative economy, efficiency, and effectiveness and to prevent and detect fraud and abuse; and (3) provide a means for keeping the head of the agency or organization and Congress informed about administrative problems and deficiencies and about the necessity for and progress of corrective action. IGs are authorized to (1) have access to records, reports, and audits; (2) make investigations and reports; (3) request information and assistance from federal, State, and local governments; (4) require production of documents by subpoena; (5) administer oaths; (6) have direct access to the head of the agency or organization; (7) select employees as necessary; (8) obtain services; and (9) enter into contracts and other arrangements for audits, studies, and analyses with public agencies and private persons. 5 U.S.C. app. § 6.

INSTANT CONTRACT The contract, in the context of VALUE ENGINEERING, under which a VALUE ENGINEERING CHANGE PROPOSAL (VECP) is submitted. FAR 48.001. The instant contract does not include increases in quantities made to the contract after acceptance of the VECP that are due to contract modification, exercise of options, or additional orders. If the contract is a multiyear contract (see MULTIYEAR CONTRACTING), the term does not include quantities funded after VECP acceptance. In a FIXED-PRICE REDETERMINATION—PROSPECTIVE CONTRACT, the term refers to quantities to be manufactured in the period for which firm prices have been established.

INSTANT CONTRACT SAVINGS The net cost reductions on the contract under which a VALUE ENGINEERING CHANGE PROPOSAL (VECP) is submitted and accepted. These reductions are equal to the INSTANT UNIT COST REDUCTION multiplied by the number of INSTANT CONTRACT units affected by the VECP, less the contractor's allowable development and implementation costs. FAR 48.104-1 contains guidance on such savings; their calculation is prescribed in paragraph (g) of the Value Engineering clause in FAR 52.248-1. See also NEGATIVE INSTANT CONTRACT SAVINGS; Cibinic & Nash, *Administration of Government Contracts* 414–15 (3d ed. 1995).

INSTANT UNIT COST REDUCTION The amount of the decrease in unit cost of performance (without deducting any contractor's development or implementation costs) resulting from using a VALUE ENGINEERING CHANGE PROPOSAL (VECP) on the INSTANT CONTRACT. FAR 48.001. In service contracts, the instant unit cost reduction is normally equal to the number of hours per line-item task saved by using the VECP on the instant contract, multiplied by the appropriate contract labor rate. The concept of instant unit cost reduction is contrasted with that of future unit cost reduction, just as INSTANT CONTRACT SAVINGS are contrasted with FUTURE CONTRACT SAVINGS.

INSURANCE Protection against a risk of loss or harm. Such protection may be obtained by purchasing an insurance policy from another party or by SELF-INSURANCE. FAR 31.205-19 specifies that most normal costs of insurance incurred by a contractor are ALLOWABLE COSTs. See Cibinic & Nash, *Cost-Reimbursement Contracting* 879–82 (2d ed. 1993). CAS 416, Accounting for Insurance Costs, 48 C.F.R. § 9904.416, governs the accounting techniques that are to be used by contractors for insurance costs and permits self-insurance in lieu of the purchase of insurance policies. FAR Subpart 28.3 sets forth the policies of the Government in dealing with insurance by contractors. See Patin, chap. 18, *Construction Contracting* 1439–1520 (1991); McDonald, *Bonds, Sureties and Insurance Under Government Contracts*, 59 Fed. Cont. Rep. 753 (June 7, 1993).

INTANGIBLE CAPITAL ASSET An asset that has no physical substance, has more than minimal value, and is expected to be held by an enterprise for continued use or possession beyond the current accounting period for the benefits it yields. FAR 31.001. The value of such assets lies in the use that can be made of them, although they cannot be seen. Examples are GOODWILL and patent rights. See Rosenberg, *Dictionary of Banking and Finance* (2d ed. 1985).

INTEGRITY See PROCUREMENT INTEGRITY.

INTERAGENCY ACQUISITION A procedure by which one Government agency (the requesting agency) obtains supplies or services from or through another (the servicing agency). FAR 17.501. The Economy Act, 31 U.S.C. § 1535, authorizes agencies to enter into mutual agreements and obtain supplies and services by interagency acquisition. The Act may not be used by an agency to circumvent conditions and limitations imposed on the use of funds. FAR 17.502. Each Economy Act order shall be supported by a DETERMINATION AND FINDINGS (D&F). The D&F shall state that (1) the use of an interagency acquisition is in the best interest of the Government, and (2) the supplies and services cannot be obtained as conveniently or economically by contracting directly with a private source. FAR 17.503. Agencies are forbidden to use interagency acquisition as a means of avoiding the requirement to obtain FULL AND OPEN COMPETITION. FAR 6.002.

INTERAGENCY ACQUISITION INTERNET COUNCIL (IAIC) An interagency group established to seek and promote ways to optimize use of the Internet in streamlining the federal acquisition process and increasing communication of federal acquisition related information to private industry and federal managers. The group is intended to make federal acquisition programs, despite workforce reductions, more friendly and accessible; establish a single face to industry; reduce paperwork; shorten the acquisition cycle; and increase competition. The IAIC homepage is at <http://www.arnet.gov/IAIC/>.

INTERAGENCY FLEET MANAGEMENT SYSTEM (IFMS) A pool of vehicles and service facilities maintained by the General Services Administration for the use of federal agencies in a given area. FAR 51.201 provides that, if it is in the Government's interest, the contracting officer may authorize the contractor under a COST-REIMBURSEMENT CONTRACT to obtain, for official purposes only, IMFS vehicles and related services, including (1) fuel and lubricants, (2) vehicle inspection, maintenance, and repair, (3) vehicle storage, and (4) commercially rented vehicles for short-term use. Complete rebuilding of major components of contractor-owned or contractor-leased vehicles requires the approval of a contracting officer. The contractor must, among other things, (1) obtain vehicle liability insurance covering bodily injury and property damage protecting the contractor and the Government against third-party claims, and (2) establish and enforce penalties for its employees who use or authorize the use of Government vehicles for other than performance of Government contracts. FAR 51.202. When a contractor is authorized to follow these procedures, the solicitation and the contract will contain the Interagency Fleet Management System Vehicles and Related Services clause in FAR 52.251-2. See also 41 C.F.R. § 101-39.

INTERDIVISIONAL WORK AUTHORIZATION (IWA) See INTERORGANIZATIONAL TRANSFER.

INTERDIVISIONAL WORK ORDER (IWO) See INTERORGANIZATIONAL TRANSFER.

INTEREST An amount paid for the use of money. Interest on borrowings by a contractor (however represented) is not an ALLOWABLE COST under a contract. FAR 31.205-20. However, interest imputed to the cost of facilities is allowable. See COST OF CAPITAL COMMITTED TO FACILITIES. The PROMPT PAYMENT ACT requires payment of an interest penalty for late Government payment of contractor INVOICEs. FAR 32.903; OMB Circular No. A-125, *Prompt Payment*, Aug. 18, 1982. FAR 32.407 requires that the contracting officer charge interest on the daily unliquidated balance of ADVANCE PAYMENTs made to the contractor. The Interest clause at FAR 52.232-17 requires that all amounts payable by the contractor to the Government bear simple interest from the date due unless paid within 30 days of becoming due. The CONTRACT DISPUTES ACT OF 1978, at 41 U.S.C. § 611, provides for the payment of interest on the amount found due and unpaid on contractor claims, running from the date the contracting officer receives the CLAIM (or the due date, if later) until the date the Government pays the contractor. When interest is paid under these provisions, it is paid at the TREASURY INTEREST RATE. See Cibinic & Nash, *Administration of Government Contracts* 1191–200 (3d ed. 1995); Nash, *Postscript II: Interest Under the Contract Disputes Act*, 11 N&CR ¶ 48 (Sept. 1997); Nash, *Postscript: Interest Under the Contract Disputes Act*, 11 N&CR ¶ 25 (June 1997); Nash, *Interest Under the Contract Disputes Act: It's Not Related to the Incurrence of Costs*, 11 N&CR ¶ 18 (Apr. 1997); Simmons, *Recovering Look-Back Interest Penalties Under Construction Contracts After Illinois Constructors*, 23 Pub. Cont. L.J. 305 (1994); Nash, *Interest Rates: Heads I Win, Tails You Lose*, 5 N&CR ¶ 13 (Mar. 1991).

INTEREST RATE See TREASURY INTEREST RATE.

INTERESTED PARTY An actual or prospective offeror whose direct economic interest would be affected by the award of a contract or by the failure to award a contract. 31 U.S.C. § 3551(2); FAR 33.101. Interested parties are parties entitled to bring PROTESTs—either to the awarding agency directly, before the GENERAL ACCOUNTING OFFICE (GAO), or to the U.S. COURT OF FEDERAL CLAIMS or a federal district court. The "interested party" standard was first applied to the courts by the addition of 28 U.S.C. § 1491(b) in 1996, Pub. L. No. 104-320. An interested party is encouraged to seek resolution within the agency before going before the GAO. FAR 33.102. To determine whether a protester is an interested party, many factors are considered, including the protester's status in relation to the procurement (prospective offeror, offeror eligible for award, nonofferor, etc.), the nature of the issues raised, and the direct or indirect benefit or relief sought by the protester. See Cibinic & Nash, chap. 11, Sec. III., *Formation of Government Contracts* (3d ed. 1998); Tolle, *A Review of the First Year of ADP Bid Protests and the GSBCA*, 16 Pub. Cont. L.J. 120, 131 (1986); Hopkins, *The Universe of Remedies for Unsuccessful Offerors on Federal Contracts*, 15 Pub. Cont. L.J. 364, 380 (1985).

INTERIM PAYMENTS Payments made by the Government to a contractor periodically during performance of a COST-REIMBURSEMENT CONTRACT. These payments provide the contractor with a flow of funds that can be used to finance contract performance. Through these payments, contractors are reimbursed for COSTS, and, if any, FEE, as performance progresses. Requests for interim payments are made on public voucher forms Standard Form 1034 and Standard Form 1035. DCAA pamphlet 7641.90, October 1991, gives guidance to contractors on the preparation of vouchers. See Cibinic & Nash, *Cost-Reimbursement Contracting* 1084–88 (2d ed. 1993).

INTERIM RATE See BILLING RATE.

INTERMEDIATE COST OBJECTIVE A COST OBJECTIVE to which costs are allocated for purposes of accumulating similar costs. Once accumulated, the costs are allocated to another intermediate cost objective or to a FINAL COST OBJECTIVE. CAS 502, Consistency in Allocating Costs Incurred for the Same Purpose by Educational Institutions, 48 C.F.R. § 9905.502-30. An example of an intermediate cost objective is a contractor's BUSINESS UNIT, to which is allocated HOME OFFICE expense. Subsequently, the business unit allocates the cost to a contract or other cost objective. See Cibinic & Nash, *Cost-Reimbursement Contracting* 658–60 (2d ed. 1993).

INTERNATIONAL MERCHANT PURCHASE AUTHORIZATION CARD (IMPAC) See GOVERNMENT-WIDE COMMERCIAL PURCHASE CARD.

INTERNATIONAL TRAFFIC IN ARMS REGULATIONS (ITAR) Regulations promulgated and administered by the Office of Defense Trade Controls, Bureau of Politico-Military Affairs, Department of State, that control the export and import of defense articles and defense services. These regulations, authorized by section 38 of the Arms Export Control Act, 22 U.S.C. § 2778, are located at 22 C.F.R. Parts 120 through 130.

INTERNET A worldwide system of computer networks by which individuals and organizations share information accessible to the ordinary user via modem, phone line, and Internet provider. Several locations (cites) on the Internet offer extensive links to various procurement information. See, for example, the Federal Acquisition Jumpstation at <http://procure.msfc.nasa.gov/fedproc/home.html> and the ACQUISITION REFORM NETWORK (ARNet) at <http://www.Arnet.gov>. See also Hernandez, *Using the Internet for Recycled Products Market Research*, 36 Cont. Mgmt. 20 (Aug. 1996); Dee & Dee, *No Help Wanted! Oh Really? Have You Searched the Web?,* 36 Cont. Mgmt. 6 (July 1996); Kestenbaum & Straight, *Internet Resources for Contracting*, 36 Cont. Mgmt. 4 (Jan. 1996) and (Dec. 1995); Cibinic, *Surfing the Procurement "Net,"* 9 N&CR ¶ 65 (Dec. 1995).

INTEROPERABILITY The ability of telecommunications resources to provide services to and accept services from other telecommunications resources and to use the services so exchanged to enable them to operate effectively together. 41 C.F.R. § 101-35.5.

INTERORGANIZATIONAL TRANSFER A transaction between a contractor and a sister division, an affiliate (see AFFILIATES), or a subsidiary. Allowance for all materials, supplies, and services that are sold or transferred between any divisions, subdivisions, subsidiaries, or affiliates of the contractor under common control shall be on the basis of cost incurred in accordance with Subpart 31.2. However, allowance may be at price (1) when it is the established practice of the transferring organization to price interorganizational transfers at other than cost for commercial work of the contractor or any division, subsidiary, or affiliate of the contractor under a common control; and (2) when the item being transferred qualifies for an exception under FAR 15.403-1 and the contracting officer has not determined the price to be unreasonable. FAR 31.205-26(e); FAR Table 15-2 at FAR 15.408. The Defense Contract Audit Agency (DCAA) instructs its auditors to give "careful consideration" to transactions between affiliated concerns. *DCAA Contract Audit Manual* 6-313.1. See Nibley et al., *Applying TINA to Interorganizational Transfers*, 90-11 CP&A Rep. 3 (Nov. 1990).

INTERPRETATION See CONTRACT INTERPRETATION.

INTERROGATORY A written question submitted to the other party to a litigation. Rule 33 of the Federal Rules of Civil Procedure and Rule 15 of the UNIFORM RULES (before the BOARDs OF CONTRACT APPEALS) permit the use of written interrogatories and require that they be answered or objected to within 30 days. Such written interrogatories are one of the major forms of DISCOVERY.

INTERVENOR A person who voluntarily interposes in an action or other proceeding with the permission of the forum or court. Intervention is a procedure by which a third person, not originally a party to a suit but claiming an interest in the subject matter, comes into the dispute in order to protect its own right or interpose its own claim. *Black's Law Dictionary* 820 (6th ed. 1990). In PROTEST proceedings before the GENERAL ACCOUNTING OFFICE (GAO) an intervenor is an awardee if the award has been made or, if no award has been made, any bidder or offeror who appears to have a substantial prospect of receiving an award if the protest is denied. 4 C.F.R. § 21.0(b). In GAO protests, agencies must notify all potential intervenors when a protest is filed, and intervenors must enter the case as soon as practicable. 4 C.F.R. § 21.3.

INVENTORY A detailed list of articles of property or goods held for sale or lease or furnished under service contracts, or raw materials or work in process or materials used or consumed in a business. *Black's Law Dictionary* 824 (6th ed. 1990). "Contractor inventory" has a special meaning under FAR Subpart 45.6, which sets forth procedures for the reporting, redistribution, and disposal of contractor inventory. There it means (1) property acquired by, and in the possession of, a contractor or subcontractor under a contract, for which TITLE is vested in the Government and that exceeds the amounts needed to complete performance under the contract; (2) property that the Government is obligated or has the option to take over as a result of (a) changes in the contract's specifications or plans or (b) termination of the contract for the convenience of the Government (see TERMINATION INVENTORY); and (3) GOVERNMENT-FURNISHED PROPERTY that exceeds the amounts needed to complete contract performance. FAR 45.601.

INVITATION FOR BIDS (IFB) The solicitation document used in SEALED BIDDING procurements. IFBs must describe the Government's requirements clearly, accurately, and completely. FAR 14.101.

IFBs must also use the UNIFORM CONTRACT FORMAT to the maximum extent practicable. FAR 14.201-1. An IFB includes all documents needed by prospective bidders for the purpose of bidding plus all terms and conditions of the prospective contract (except price) so that all bidders will submit bids on the same basis so that award can be made solely on the basis of PRICE and PRICE-RELATED FACTORS. IFBs must be publicized through distribution to prospective bidders, see FAR 14.205, posting in public places, publication of a SYNOPSIS in the COMMERCE BUSINESS DAILY, and such other means as may be appropriate. FAR 14.203. They must not include unnecessarily RESTRICTIVE SPECIFICATIONS or requirements that might unduly limit the number of bidders. Publicizing must occur a sufficient time before bid opening to enable prospective bidders to prepare and submit bids. FAR 14.101. See Cibinic & Nash, chap. 5, Sec. I., *Formation of Government Contracts* (3d ed. 1998).

INVOICE A written account or itemized statement, addressed to the purchaser, of merchandise shipped or services performed, together with the quantity and the prices and charges. An invoice is the contractor's bill or written request for payment for work or services performed under the contract. Under FAR 32.902 a "proper" invoice is a bill or written request for payment that meets the minimum standards of the Prompt Payment clauses (see PROMPT PAYMENT ACT) in FAR 52.232-25 through FAR 52.232-27. Under the DISPUTEs clause in FAR 52.233-1, a VOUCHER, invoice, or other routine request for payment that is not in dispute when submitted is not a CLAIM, although it may be converted to a claim. See FAR 33.201; Cibinic & Nash, *Administration of Government Contracts* 1148–51 (3d ed. 1995).

INVOICE PAYMENT A Government disbursement of monies, subject to the PROMPT PAYMENT ACT (PPA), to a contractor under a contract or other authorization for supplies or services that have been accepted by the Government. The term encompasses payments for partial deliveries that have been accepted by the Government and final COST or FEE payments when amounts owed have been settled between the Government and the contractor. Under the PPA, invoice payments also include all PROGRESS PAYMENTs made under the Payments under Fixed-Price Construction Contracts clause at FAR 52.232-5, and the Payments under Fixed-Price Architect-Engineer Contracts clause at FAR 52.232-10. Invoice payments do not include contract FINANCING PAYMENTs. FAR 32.902. The due date for a designated payment office to make an invoice payment is generally the 30th day after the designated billing office has received a proper invoice from the contractor, or the 30th day after the Government's acceptance of supplies delivered or services performed by the contractor, whichever is later. FAR 32.905. See OMB Circular No. A-125, *Prompt Payment*, Aug. 19, 1982; Cibinic & Nash, *Administration of Government Contracts* 1148–51 (3d ed. 1995).

ISSUE IN CONTROVERSY A material disagreement between the Government and a contractor that may result in a CLAIM or is all or part of an existing claim. FAR 33.201. Agencies are encouraged to settle all issues in controversy by mutual agreement or to use ALTERNATIVE DISPUTE RESOLUTION procedures if that is not possible. FAR 33.204.

ITAR See INTERNATIONAL TRAFFIC IN ARMS REGULATIONS.

ITEM Any individual part, component, subassembly, assembly, or subsystem integral to a major system, and other property that may be replaced during the service life of the system, and includes spare parts and replenishment spare parts, but does not include packaging or labeling associated with shipment or identification of an item. 10 U.S.C. § 2302(10) and 41 U.S.C. § 403(10). This definition is used in the statutory statement of technical data policy in 10 U.S.C. § 2320 and 41 U.S.C. § 418a, which applies to "items and processes." However, the DOD data policy in DFARS Subpart 227.71 still refers to "items, components and processes" when describing its applicability.

ITMRA See INFORMATION TECHNOLOGY MANAGEMENT REFORM ACT.

J

JAVITS-WAGNER-O'DAY ACT ("JWOD ACT") An Act, codified at 41 U.S.C. §§ 46-48c, which requires Government entities to purchase certain supplies and services from workshops for the blind and other severely disabled people ("sheltered workshops") (See BLIND OR SEVERELY DISABLED), if the supplies or services are available when required. FAR Subpart 8.7 prescribes policies and procedures for implementing the Act and the rules of the Committee for the Purchase from People Who Are Blind Or Severely Disabled.

JEWEL BEARING A piece of synthetic corundum (sapphire or ruby) of any shape, except a phonograph needle, that has one or more polished surfaces to provide supporting surfaces or low-friction contact areas for revolving, oscillating, or sliding parts in an instrument, mechanism, subassembly, or part. The FAR previously required, with certain exceptions, that contractors purchase jewel bearings used in precision instruments and similar equipment acquired under a Government contract from the Government-owned, contractor-operated William Langer Plant in Rolla, North Dakota. This requirement was removed by Pub. L No. 104-201, and the plant was given to the city of Rolla subject to the condition that the land and property be used "for economic development relating to the jewel bearing plant." See Cibinic & Nash, chap. 3, Sec. IV., *Formation of Government Contracts* (3d ed. 1998).

JOB ORDER An order issued by a contracting agency for work to be performed under the terms and conditions of a BASIC ORDERING AGREEMENT or MASTER AGREEMENT FOR REPAIR AND ALTERATION OF VESSELS. Job orders are usually FIRM-FIXED-PRICE CONTRACTs for specific items of work. FAR 16.703(d) and DFARS 216.703(d) provide guidance on the procedures to be followed in issuing orders under basic ordering agreements. Separate guidance is provided for the issuance of TASK ORDERs and DELIVERY ORDERs.

JOINT COMPUTER-AIDED ACQUISITION AND LOGISTICS SUPPORT (JCALS) A part of the CONTINUOUS ACQUISITION AND LIFE-CYCLE SUPPORT, this program supports "uniform logistic and acquisition engineering, management, materiel management, and other life-cycle functional processes." See JCALS internet site at <http://150.149.1.11>.

JOINT ENGINEERING DATA MANAGEMENT INFORMATION AND CONTROL SYSTEM (JEDMICS) A DOD program "for management of approved engineering drawings and related digital technical data in the Army, Navy, Air Force and Defense Logistics Agency." See Air Force JEDMICS internet site at <http://wpaftb1.wpafb.af.mil/jedmics.html#program>. This program will replace the ENGINEERING DATA COMPUTER ASSISTED RETRIEVAL SYSTEM.

JOINT REQUIREMENTS OVERSIGHT COUNCIL (JROC) A council within DOD is responsible to the Chairman of the Joint Chiefs of Staff for assessing military requirements in support of the defense acquisition process. The Vice Chairman of the Joint Chiefs of Staff chairs the JROC and decides all matters before it. The permanent members include the Vice Chiefs of the Army and Air Force, the Vice Chief of Naval Operations, and the Assistant Commandant of the Marine Corps. The JROC directly supports the DEFENSE ACQUISITION BOARD through the review, validation, and approval of key cost, schedule, and performance parameters at the start of the ACQUISITION PROCESS, prior to each milestone review, or as requested by the Under Secretary of Defense for Acquisition and Technology. Jones, *Glossary: Defense Acquisition Acronyms and Terms* (8th ed., Defense Systems Management College).

JOINT VENTURE A legal entity in the nature of a partnership engaged in the joint prosecution of a particular transaction for mutual profit. It is a grouping of two or more persons that, unlike a partnership, does not entail a continuing relationship between the parties. Joint ventures require a community of interest in the performance of the contract or project; a right to direct and govern the policy in connection with the contract or project; and a duty, which may be altered by agreement, to share in both PROFIT and LOSSes. *Black's Law Dictionary* 839 (6th ed. 1990). FAR 9.603 provides that the Government will recognize the integrity and validity of joint ventures. However, they are infrequently used, except in construction contracting. See Chierichella & Hutchins, *Competitor Collaborations by Government Contractors—*

Unique Considerations for FTC's "Joint Venture Project," 39 Gov't Contractor ¶ 569 (Dec. 3, 1997); Ingrao, *Joint Ventures: Their Use in Federal Government Contracting*, 20 Pub. Cont. L.J. 399 (1991); Sherrer, *Joint Ventures on Government Contracts: A Walk Through a Rose Garden Planted over Land Mines*, 19 Pub. Cont. L.J. 331 (1990).

JUDGMENT FUND A freestanding appropriation used to satisfy specified claims against the Government. 31 U.S.C. § 1304. The judgment fund has no time duration or limit on the amount that can be paid. However, it does not cover a contract adjustment negotiated without litigation or the compromise settlement of a Contract Disputes Act claim that is not incorporated into a judgment. The judgment fund is used to satisfy judgments or decisions rendered by the U.S. Court of Federal Claims and the boards of contract appeals against the Government on contractor claims, judgments under the Federal Tort Claims Act, as well as various administrative and Small Claims Act awards against the United States. See Vacketta & Kantor, *Obtaining Payment from the Government's "Judgment Fund,"* 97-3 Briefing Papers (Feb. 1997); *Nash, Settlement Without Funds: Life Without An "M" Account*, 8 N&CR ¶ 17 (Mar. 1994); Cibinic, *Claims Settlement and Funding: Pay It Now Or Pay It Later*, 7 N&CR ¶ 29 (May 1993).

JUDGMENT IN PRICING A subjective factor used to estimate the cost of future work by projecting from the FACTs at the time of the estimate to the period of performance of the prospective contract. When a contractor submits COST OR PRICING DATA as a part of a contract pricing proposal pursuant to the TRUTH IN NEGOTIATIONS ACT (TINA), FAR 15.408, paragraph 2 of Table 15-2, Instructions for Submission of a Contract Pricing Proposal, requires the submission of such judgments as part of the proposal. Thus, pricing proposals consist of facts (cost or pricing data) and judgments. In the application of TINA, it has proved to be very difficult to draw a firm line between facts and judgments. See Lovitky, *Understanding Causation and Determining the Price Adjustment in Defective Pricing Cases*, 17 Pub. Cont. L.J. 407 (1988); Lovitky, *Cost and Pricing Data Defined: An Analysis of the Scope of Contractor Disclosure Requirements Pursuant to the Truth in Negotiations Act*, 20 Nat'l Cont. Mgmt. J., Issue No. 2, p. 79 (1987).

JUDGMENT OF COURT A decision issued by a court (an individual judge, a panel of judges, or the court sitting *en banc*) that resolves, as far as that court is concerned, by ruling on the issue in that case.

JURY VERDICT METHOD A technique used by BOARDs OF CONTRACT APPEALS (BCAs) and courts to resolve conflicting evidence about the amount of a contractual adjustment, or to arrive at an amount of compensation when incomplete or conflicting evidence has been submitted. It is often viewed as a means of determining the amount in cases of conflicting testimony rather than a method of proof of quantum (see BIFURCATION OF ENTITLEMENT AND QUANTUM). The jury verdict represents a figure that, in the view of the trier of the facts, is fair in light of all the facts of the case or, put another way, is supported by consideration of the entire record. Some BCAs and courts have refused to use the technique when very little or no evidence has been submitted. See Cibinic & Nash, *Administration of Government Contracts* 716–23 (3d ed. 1995); Nash, *Postscript: The Jury Verdict Approach*, 8 N&CR ¶ 60 (Oct. 1994); Nash, *The "Jury Verdict" Approach: Equitable Technique or Contractor Bonanza?,* 5 N&CR ¶ 65 (Dec. 1991).

JUSTIFICATION AND APPROVAL (J&A) The Government document required by 10 U.S.C. § 2304(f)(1) and 41 U.S.C. § 253(f)(1) when an agency is going to award a contract without providing for FULL AND OPEN COMPETITION. In such a case, the contracting officer must justify the action in writing, certify the accuracy and completeness of the justification, and obtain the approval of appropriate individuals. FAR 6.303-1. The justification may be prepared and approved following CONTRACT AWARD in situations of UNUSUAL OR COMPELLING URGENCY if prior preparation and approval would unreasonably delay the acquisition. FAR 6.302-2 and 6.303-1(e). Justifications must (1) identify the agency, the contracting activity, the action being approved, the supplies or services sought, and the statutory authority permitting the action; (2) demonstrate that the proposed contractor's unique qualifications or the nature of the acquisition require the action; (3) describe efforts made to ensure that offers were solicited from as many potential sources as practicable; (4) determine that the anticipated cost will be fair and reasonable; (5) describe market surveys conducted; and (6) describe any other facts supporting the use of other than full and open competition. FAR 6.303-2. Depending on the size and nature of the contract, justifications must be approved in writing by an official at a level above the contracting officer, by the COMPETITION ADVOCATE for the procuring activity, or by the SENIOR PROCUREMENT EXECUTIVE of the Government agency conducting the acquisition. FAR 6.304. Justifications must be made available for public inspection as required by 10 U.S.C. § 2304(f)(4) and 41 U.S.C.

§ 303(f)(4). FAR 6.305. See Cibinic & Nash, chap. 3, Sec. I., *Formation of Government Contracts* (3d ed. 1998).

JWOD PARTICIPATING NONPROFIT AGENCIES A qualified nonprofit agency employing people who are blind or who have other severe disabilities approved by the Committee for the Purchase from People Who Are Blind Or Severely Disabled, an independent Government activity with members appointed by the President, to produce a commodity for or provide a service to the Government under the JAVITS-WAGNER-O'DAY ACT, 41 U.S.C. §§ 46-48c. Such agencies are given preference for some procurements in accordance with the procedures in FAR Subpart 8.7.

K

KEY PERSONNEL Contractor personnel that are required to be used in the performance of a contract by a Key Personnel clause. See, for example, NFS 18-52.235-71. A CONTRACTING ACTIVITY uses such clauses to ensure that in performing the contract the winning contractor will not use personnel less qualified than those described and evaluated in the winning proposal. Such clauses generally permit substitution of personnel with the approval of the CONTRACTING OFFICER. Key personnel are often used as an EVALUATION FACTOR in BEST VALUE PROCUREMENT. See Cibinic & Nash, chap. 6, Sec. I., *Formation of Government Contracts* (3d ed. 1998); Nash, *Evaluating Key Personnel: Can the Offer Be Enforced?,* 10 N&CR ¶ 39 (Aug. 1996).

KICKBACK Any money, fee, commission, credit, gift, GRATUITY, thing of value, or compensation of any kind provided, directly or indirectly, to any PRIME CONTRACTOR, prime contractor employee, SUBCONTRACTOR, or subcontractor employee for the purpose of improperly obtaining or rewarding favorable treatment in connection with a contract or subcontract. FAR 3.502-1. Kickbacks have been prohibited by statute for many years, but new legislation was enacted in the ANTI-KICKBACK ACT OF 1986. See Cibinic & Nash, *Administration of Government Contracts* 107–8 (3d ed. 1995); Arnavas, *The New Anti-Kickback Act*, 87-9 Briefing Papers 2-3 (Aug. 1987). Kickbacks by construction workers to contractors and subcontractors are prohibited by the COPELAND ANTI-KICKBACK ACT.

L

LABOR Effort expended by people in exchange for wages or salary. DIRECT LABOR is one of the principal breakdowns used in costing, pricing, and profit determination. Indirect labor is an element of INDIRECT COST. FAR Part 22 sets forth the policies of the Government regarding the application of labor laws to the ACQUISITION PROCESS. Subjects treated include convict labor (FAR Subpart 22.2); the CONTRACT WORK HOURS AND SAFETY STANDARDS ACT (FAR Subpart 22.3); the DAVIS-BACON ACT (FAR 22.403-1, 22.404); the COPELAND ANTI-KICKBACK ACT (FAR 22.403-2); the WALSH-HEALEY PUBLIC CONTRACTS ACT (FAR Subpart 22.6); EQUAL EMPLOYMENT OPPORTUNITY (FAR Subpart 22.8); the SERVICE CONTRACT ACT OF 1965 (FAR Subpart 22.10); and employment of the handicapped (FAR Subpart 22.14).

LABOR-HOUR CONTRACT A type of TIME-AND-MATERIALS CONTRACT under which the Government pays a fixed amount for each hour of work performed by specified classes of LABOR. The hourly rate includes wages, overhead (see INDIRECT COST), GENERAL AND ADMINISTRATIVE EXPENSE, and PROFIT. FAR 16.602 limits the use of this type of contract and requires that the Government maintain "appropriate surveillance" to ensure that the contractor is using efficient methods of performance. See Cibinic & Nash, chap. 8, Sec. V., *Formation of Government Contracts* (3d ed. 1998).

LABOR RELATIONS The process of dealing with employees. FAR 31.205-21 states that the costs incurred by a contractor in conducting labor relations are ALLOWABLE COSTs. See Cibinic & Nash, *Cost-Reimbursement Contracting* 822 (2d ed. 1993). FAR 22.101-1 establishes the basic policy of procuring agencies to remain impartial concerning any dispute between LABOR and contractor management. It also states that Government agencies should maintain sound relations with industry and labor to keep abreast of events that might adversely affect the Government ACQUISITION PROCESS and to ensure that the Government obtains needed supplies and services without DELAY. See Stephenson, chap. 3, *Construction Contracting* (1991).

LABORERS OR MECHANICS Employees of construction contractors or subcontractors at any tier composed of (1) those workers whose duties are manual or physical in nature (including workers who use tools or who are performing the work of a trade) rather than mental or managerial; (2) apprentices, trainees, helpers, and, in contracts subject to the CONTRACT WORK HOURS AND SAFETY STANDARDS ACT, watchmen and guards; (3) working foremen who devote more than 20 percent of their time during a workweek to performing the duties of a laborer or mechanic; and (4) any other person who performs the duties of a laborer or mechanic, regardless of any contractual relationship alleged to exist between the contractor and that individual. FAR 22.401. The DAVIS-BACON ACT requires that construction contractors and subcontractors pay this class of workers the PREVAILING WAGE RATE in the locality. See Stephenson, chap. 3, *Construction Contracting* 225–27 (1991).

LAST IN, FIRST OUT (LIFO) An INVENTORY costing method in which sales are made from the most recently acquired stock, leaving the earliest acquired items in stock. The LIFO method attempts to match the most recent costs of acquiring inventory with sales. CAS 411, 48 C.F.R. § 9904.411, identifies LIFO as one of the inventory cost methods that a contractor must use in accounting for ACQUISITION COSTs of material.

LATE BID A bid received in the office designated in the INVITATION FOR BIDS after the exact time for BID OPENING. FAR 14.304-1. A late bid, late modification of a bid, or late withdrawal of a bid will not be considered unless it is received before CONTRACT AWARD, and then only if the bid was sent (1) by registered or certified mail not later than five calendar days before the bid receipt date specified, (2) by regular mail (or telegram or FACSIMILE if authorized by the SOLICITATION) and the Government determines that the late receipt was caused solely by the Government's mishandling after receipt at the Government installation, (3) by U.S. Postal Service Express Mail Next-Day Service not later than two working days before the bid receipt date specified, or (4) by an electronic commerce method authorized by the solicitation and received by the Government not later than 5:00 p.m. one working day before the bid receipt day specified. The only acceptable evidence of mailing is a U.S. or Canadian Postal Service postmark. The only acceptable evidence to establish time of receipt at the Government installation is the installation's time/date stamp. The term "postmark" means a printed, stamped, or other impression (other than a postage meter machine impression) that is readily identifiable without further action as having been supplied and affixed on the date of mailing by an employee of the Postal Service. Bidders should therefore request the postal clerk to place a hand cancellation bull's-eye postmark on both the receipt and the envelope or wrapper. See Cibinic & Nash, chap. 5, Sec. I., *Formation of Government Contracts* (3d ed. 1998).

LATE PROPOSAL An offer received in the office designated in the REQUEST FOR PROPOSALS after the exact date specified for receipt of proposals. FAR 15.208(b). A late offer, late modification of an offer, late revision, or late withdrawal of an offer will not be considered unless it is received before CONTRACT AWARD, and then only if the offer was sent (1) by registered or certified mail not later than five calendar days before the offer receipt date specified, (2) by regular mail (or telegram or FACSIMILE if authorized by the SOLICITATION) and the Government determines that the late receipt was caused solely by the Government's mishandling after receipt at the Government installation, (3) by U.S. Postal Service Express Mail Next-Day Service not later than two working days before the offer receipt date specified, or (4) by an electronic commerce method authorized by the solicitation and received by the Government not later than 5:00 p.m. one working day before the offer receipt day specified. FAR 15.215-1(c)(3)(i). The only acceptable evidence of mailing is a U.S. or Canadian Postal Service postmark. The only acceptable evidence to establish time of receipt at the Government installation is the installation's time/date stamp. The term "postmark" means a printed, stamped, or other impression (other than a postage meter machine impression) that is readily identifiable without further action as having been supplied and affixed on the date of mailing by an employee of the Postal Service. Bidders should therefore request the postal clerk to place a hand cancellation bull's-eye postmark on both the receipt and the envelope or wrapper. See Cibinic & Nash, chap. 6, Sec. III., *Formation of Government Contracts* (3d ed. 1998).

LATENT Not readily discoverable by observation on INSPECTION; hidden or concealed. "Latent" can refer to a type of deficiency potentially found in solicitations or contracts (a latent AMBIGUITY) or in contract performance (LATENT DEFECT). "Latent" is an antonym of PATENT.

LATENT AMBIGUITY See AMBIGUITY.

LATENT DEFECT A defect in the contract work that is not discoverable by the Government by the use of reasonable INSPECTION methods. A latent defect overcomes the finality of acceptance in the Inspection of Supplies—Fixed-Price clause, FAR 52.246-2, and the Inspection of Construction clause, FAR 52.246-12. See Cibinic, *Latent Design Defects: Fitting A Square Peg Into A Round Hole*, 10 N&CR ¶ 46 (Sept. 1996); Martorelli, *State Statutes of Repose and Government Claims for Latent Defects in Design and Construction*, 25 Pub. Cont. L.J. 199 (1996); Cibinic & Nash, *Administration of Government Contracts* 868–72 (3d ed. 1995); Cibinic, *Latent Defects: Late-Breaking Developments*, 8 N&CR ¶ 54 (Sept. 1994); Jaeger, *Contractor Liability for Design Defects Under the Inspection Clause: Latent Design Defects—A Sleeping Giant?,* 21 Pub. Cont. L.J. 331 (1992); Victorino & Ivey, *The "Inspection" Clause*, 88-10 Briefing Papers 8 (Sept. 1988).

LEADER-COMPANY CONTRACTING An acquisition technique used to establish a SECOND SOURCE for a product that is being or has been developed by a single contractor. It is often called "leader/follower" procurement. FAR 17.401 states that leader-company contracting is an extraordinary acquisition technique used only in special circumstances. Under this technique, a developer or sole producer of a product or system is designated to be the leader company and to furnish assistance and know-how to one or more designated follower companies, which subsequently become sources of supply. Leader-company contracting is intended to do one or more of the following: (1) reduce delivery time; (2) achieve geographic dispersion of suppliers; (3) maximize use of scarce tooling and equipment; (4) ensure uniformity and reliability in equipment, compatibility or standardization of components, and interchangeability of parts; (5) eliminate problems in use of PROPRIETARY DATA; and (6) facilitate the transition from development to production to subsequent competitive acquisition of end items or major components. FAR 17.401. Leader-company contracting should be used only when (1) the leader company has the necessary production know-how, (2) no other source can meet the Government's requirements without assistance from a leader company, (3) the assistance is limited to that which is essential to produce the item, and (4) its use is authorized in accordance with agency procedures. FAR 17.402. This technique is unpopular with leader companies because it requires them to foster their own competition. DOD encourages the use of SMALL DISADVANTAGED BUSINESS CONCERNs as follower companies. DFARS 217.401. NASA does not use leader-company contracting. NFS Subpart 18-17.4.

LEADER/FOLLOWER See LEADER-COMPANY CONTRACTING.

LEARNING CURVE A technique for projecting the amount of direct LABOR or material that will be used to manufacture a product on a repetitive basis. The learning curve concept originated in the observation that organizations performing repetitive tasks tend to exhibit a rate of improvement due to increased manual dexterity and improved manufacturing methodology. (Thus, it is more aptly called an "improvement curve.") Learning or improvement curve theories include the "Boeing" or "unit curve" theory and the "Northrop" or "cumulative average" theory. The Boeing theory holds that as the total quantity of units produced doubles, the cost per unit decreases by some constant percentage (the rate of learning). The Northrop theory holds that as the total quantity of units produced doubles, the *average* cost per unit decreases by some constant percentage (the rate of learning). See Federal Acquisition Institute and Air Force Institute of Technology, *Contract Pricing Reference Guide*, vol. II (May 1996); Loving, *Learning Curves: Uses and Misuses in Direct Labor Hour Projections*, 35 Cont. Mgmt. 15 (Sept. 1995).

LEASE A contract with the owner of real or personal property to permit another party to use that property for a specified period of time. Leases are contracts subject to the CONTRACT DISPUTES ACT OF 1978. 41 U.S.C. § 602. FAR Subpart 7.4 provides guidance on the decision of a contracting officer whether to lease rather than purchase equipment. FAR Subpart 8.11 provides guidance on leasing of motor vehicles. See RENTAL COSTS for the treatment of the costs incurred by a contractor for leases. See Herman, *Drafting Compliance with Laws Clauses in Leases (with Forms)*, 12 Prac. Real Est. Law. 27 (Jan. 1996); Whelan & Strauss, *Leases*, 49 Bus. Law. 1857 (Aug. 1994); Day & Keogh, *A Risk Analysis of Financing Federal Government Equipment Leases*, 18 Pub. Cont. L.J. 544 (1989).

LEGAL FEES The amount paid to a lawyer for professional services. FAR 31.205-47 sets forth detailed rules governing whether such fees paid by contractors are ALLOWABLE COSTs. Generally, such fees are allowable when incurred in performing normal functions required for the performance or termination of a contract, but are unallowable in the PROSECUTION OF CLAIMS and in the defense of a number of specified claims. However, small businesses can recover legal fees for prosecution of claims under the EQUAL ACCESS TO JUSTICE ACT (EAJA). See Vacketta et al., *Recovery of Legal Costs*, 93-12 Briefing Papers (Nov. 1993); Tobin & Stiffler, *Recovering Legal Fees Under*

EAJA/Edition II, 91-7 Briefing Papers (June 1991); Connelly & Schooner, *Recovery of Costs for Defense Against the Government's Charge of Illegality*, 16 Pub. Cont. L.J. 94 (1986).

LEGAL PROCEEDING Action, including investigation, by one of the parties to a contract to enforce legal rights against another party. FAR 31.205-47 makes the costs of legal and other proceedings (see LEGAL PROCEEDING COSTS) unallowable unless specific conditions are met. Legal proceedings for which costs are unallowable include criminal proceedings, civil proceedings for FRAUD or similar misconduct, DEBARMENT and SUSPENSION proceedings, prosecution or defense of contract CLAIMs, merger and reorganization proceedings, antitrust suits (see ANTITRUST VIOLATIONS), and WHISTLEBLOWER suits. See Cibinic & Nash, *Cost-Reimbursement Contracting* 823–33 (2d ed. 1993).

LEGAL PROCEEDING COSTS The costs incurred in LEGAL PROCEEDINGs including, but not limited to, administrative and clerical expenses; the cost of legal services, whether performed by in-house or private counsel; the cost of the services of accountants, consultants, or others retained by the contractor to assist it; the cost of employees, officers, and directors; and any similar costs that bear a direct relationship to the proceedings. FAR 31.205-47. This cost principle was written with this broad definition to ensure that the full costs of legal proceedings were UNALLOWABLE COSTs when the proceeding fell within its coverage. See Cibinic & Nash, *Cost-Reimbursement Contracting* 823–33 (2d ed. 1993).

LETTER CONTRACT A written preliminary contractual instrument authorizing the immediate commencement of activity under its terms and conditions, pending DEFINITIZATION of a pricing arrangement for the work to be done. FAR 16.603-1. Letter contracts are a means of permitting contractors to commence work immediately after a requirement is identified. They are strongly disfavored (10 U.S.C. § 2326 places restrictions on their use) and may not be used unless the HEAD OF THE CONTRACTING ACTIVITY determines that no other instrument is suitable. FAR 16.603-3. A letter contract must specify the maximum liability of the Government and must be superseded by a definitive contract within a specified time. Letter contracts contain a negotiated definitization schedule including (1) dates for submission of the contractor's price proposal and related information; (2) a date for the start of negotiations; and (3) a target date for definitization, which should be either within 180 days after the date of the letter contract or before completion of 40 percent of the work to be performed, whichever occurs first. FAR 16.603-2. See the Contract Definitization clause in FAR 52.216-25. See Cibinic & Nash, chap. 8, *Formation of Government Contracts* (3d ed. 1998).

LETTER OF CREDIT An instrument, issued by a bank or other financing institution, permitting the Government to withdraw funds up to a specified amount if a contractor does not meet its obligations under a contract. OFPP Policy Letter No. 91-4, *Use of Irrevocable Letters of Credit*, Nov. 8, 1991, requires contracting officers to permit contractors to meet MILLER ACT obligations by providing irrevocable letters of credit in lieu of PERFORMANCE BONDs and PAYMENT BONDs on contracts over $100,000. For construction contracts from $25,000 to $100,000, FAR 28.102-1 states a preference for the use of an irrevocable letter of credit to provide payment protection.

LETTER OF INTENT A letter customarily employed as a preliminary understanding of parties that intend to enter into a contract. *Black's Law Dictionary* 904 (6th ed. 1990). In Government procurement, such instruments take the form of LETTER CONTRACTs in almost all cases.

LETTER OF OFFER AND ACCEPTANCE (LOA) The instrument that creates a contractual relationship between the U.S. Government and a foreign purchaser in a FOREIGN MILITARY SALES transaction. The LOA lists supplies or services to be purchased, estimated costs, terms and conditions of the transaction, and payment schedules. The purchaser, an authorized representative of the foreign government, must sign, date, and return the LOA before its expiration date. See Reuter, *The ABCs of FMS*, 30 Cont. Mgmt. 29 (Oct. 1990).

LETTER OF REQUEST (LOR) The instrument used as the first step in initiating a FOREIGN MILITARY SALES transaction. The LOR is used to request defense articles and services, as well as planning and review data, price and availability data, or an actual LETTER OF OFFER AND ACCEPTANCE. It includes a statement of what is desired, with sufficient detail to enable DOD or another agency to provide a firm basis for a price estimate. The foreign state forwards the LOR through the U.S. Embassy, the designated Security Assistance Office, or the foreign state's in-country representative in the United States. See Reuter, *The ABCs of FMS*, 30 Cont. Mgmt. 29 (Oct. 1990).

LEVEL-OF-EFFORT CONTRACT A type of contract stating the work in terms of an amount of effort (usually labor-hours or labor-years) to be performed by specified classes of employees over a given period of time. There are four types of level-of-effort contracts: the FIXED-PRICE LEVEL-OF-EFFORT CONTRACT, the TIME-AND-MATERIALS CONTRACT, the LABOR-HOUR CONTRACT, and the TERM CONTRACT. See Cibinic & Nash, chap. 8, Sec. V., *Formation of Government Contracts* (3d ed. 1998).

LIABILITIES Obligations of a business that have been incurred but not yet paid, such as notes payable and accounts payable. A company's BALANCE SHEET lists all ASSETs and liabilities in order to show the company's NET WORTH.

LICENSE A legal instrument granting permission to do a particular thing, to exercise a certain privilege, to carry on a particular business, or to pursue a certain occupation. When granted by an appropriate government body, licenses are permits allowing a person, firm, or corporation to pursue some occupation or business, subject to regulation. *Black's Law Dictionary* 919–20 (6th ed. 1990). Under the Permits and Responsibilities clause in FAR 52.236-7, construction contractors bear the responsibility for obtaining necessary licenses and permits and complying with any federal, state, and municipal laws, codes, and regulations applicable to the performance of the work on fixed-price construction or dismantling, demolition, or removal-of-improvements contracts. FAR 36.507. The TECHNICAL DATA and COMPUTER SOFTWARE policies of the Government give the Government a license (of varying scope depending on the circumstances) to use the data and software. See DFARS 227.7103-4; DFARS 227.7203-4. See also UNLIMITED RIGHTS; LIMITED RIGHTS; RESTRICTED RIGHTS; GOVERNMENT-PURPOSE RIGHTS. The standard Patents Rights clauses in FAR 52.227-11 and -12 give the Government a royalty-free license to use INVENTIONs made under the contract. See PATENT RIGHTS; PATENT LICENSE.

LICENSE RIGHTS See GOVERNMENT-PURPOSE LICENSE RIGHTS; GOVERNMENT-PURPOSE RIGHTS; DIRECT LICENSE.

LICENSE TO USE INVENTION See PATENT LICENSE.

LIFE-CYCLE COST The TOTAL COST to the Government of acquiring, operating, supporting, and (if applicable) disposing of the ITEMs being acquired. FAR 7.101. Procuring agencies are expected to consider the life-cycle cost of a product in the ACQUISITION PLANNING process. FAR 7.105. However, the FAR contains no guidance on the use of life-cycle costs to improve the procurement process. Life-cycle COST ANALYSIS is the structured study of estimates and elements to identify cost drivers, total cost to the Government, cost-risk items, and cost-effective changes; it is a SYSTEM ENGINEERING tool with application to all elements of the system. DOD policy establishes life-cycle cost as a parameter equal in importance to technical requirements and schedules. DSMC, *Program Manager's Notebook* (1995); Part 3 of DOD Regulation 5000.2-R, *Mandatory Procedures for Major Defense Acquisition Programs (MDAPs) and Major Automated Information System (MAIS) Acquisition Programs*, Mar. 15, 1996.

LIMITATION OF COST (LOC) CLAUSE A key clause used in all fully funded COST-REIMBURSEMENT CONTRACTs to meet the requirements of the ANTI-DEFICIENCY ACT by limiting the OBLIGATION of the Government to an amount no greater than the contract's estimated cost plus any required FEE, unless the contract is modified to state a greater amount. FAR 32.705-2(a). The clause requires the contractor to notify the contracting officer, in writing, whenever the contractor has reason to believe that (1) the costs the contractor expects to incur under the contract within a specified period (usually one to three months), when added to all costs previously incurred, will exceed a specified percentage (usually 75 to 85 percent) of the estimated cost; or (2) the total cost for the performance of the contract, exclusive of fee, will be either greater or substantially less than had been previously estimated. In the absence of the specified notice, the Government is not obligated to reimburse the contractor for any costs in excess of the estimated cost. The clause obligates the contractor to use its BEST EFFORTS to perform the work specified and all obligations under the contract within the ESTIMATED COST and provides that the contractor has no further obligation until the estimated cost is increased. The basic clause is set forth in FAR 52.232-20. See Cibinic & Nash, *Cost-Reimbursement Contracting* 931–34 (2d ed. 1993); Madden & Walsh, *The Limitation of Cost & Funds Clauses*, 85-11 Briefing Papers (Nov. 1985).

LIMITATION OF FUNDS (LOF) CLAUSE A clause used in all incrementally funded COST-REIMBURSEMENT CONTRACTs. FAR 32.705-2(c). The clause requires the contractor to notify the contracting officer in writing when it appears that additional funds must be allotted to the contract to complete performance. The clause is set forth in FAR 52.232-22. The LOF clause and the LIMITATION OF COST CLAUSE are the basis for the contractor's freedom from performance risks. Even if the contract contains a completion-type STATEMENT

OF WORK, with definitive performance requirements and fixed performance dates, these clauses operate to relieve the contractor from any legal obligation to complete the work when the funds are exhausted. See *Ball Brothers Research Corp.*, NASABCA 1277-6, 80-2 BCA ¶ 14,526; Cibinic & Nash, *Cost-Reimbursement Contracts* 934–36 (2d ed. 1993); Madden & Walsh, *The Limitation of Cost & Funds Clauses*, 85-11 Briefing Papers (Nov. 1985).

LIMITED RIGHTS The right of the Government to reproduce and use TECHNICAL DATA with the express limitation that they will not, without written permission of the contractor, be used for purposes of manufacture nor disclosed outside the Government (except for purposes listed in the contract). FAR 27.401. The Rights in Technical Data—Noncommercial Items clause in DFARS 252.227-7013 contains a similar definition using terminology that gives the Government a copyright license as well as a trade-secret license ("the rights to use, modify, reproduce, release, perform, display, or disclose"). In either regulation, limited rights are those rights that a contractor is entitled to assert in LIMITED RIGHTS DATA. The rights are basically designed to give the contractor protection against use of data DEVELOPED AT PRIVATE EXPENSE (FAR policy) or DEVELOPED EXCLUSIVELY AT PRIVATE EXPENSE (DOD policy) by competitors. See Simchak & Vogel, chap. 4, *Rights in Technical Data and Computer Software* (1995); Burgett et al., *Government Rights in Data and Software/Edition II*, 95-11 Briefing Papers (Oct. 1995); Nash, *Removal of Limited Rights Legends from Technical Data: Playing Hardball*, 1 N&CR ¶ 85 (Nov. 1987).

LIMITED RIGHTS DATA DATA (other than COMPUTER SOFTWARE) that embody TRADE SECRETs or are commercial or financial and confidential or privileged, to the extent that such data pertain to items, components, or processes DEVELOPED AT PRIVATE EXPENSE, including minor modifications thereof. FAR 27.401. The FAR also contains an alternative, general definition that may be used in contracts for research work: data developed at private expense that embody trade secrets or are commercial or financial and confidential or privileged. FAR 27.404. Under the Rights in Data—General clause at FAR 52.227-14, the contractor may protect qualifying limited rights data and restricted computer software by withholding them from delivery to the Government and delivering FORM, FIT, AND FUNCTION DATA instead. This term is not used in the DOD technical data regulation in DFARS Subpart 227.71. See Simchak & Vogel, chap. 4, *Rights in Technical Data and Computer Software* (1995).

LINE ITEM A single-line entry on a form for the reporting, redistribution, and disposal of contractor INVENTORY that indicates a quantity of property having the same description and condition code from any one contract at any one reporting location. FAR 45.601. Line items in contracts are called CONTRACT LINE ITEMS.

LIQUIDATED DAMAGES An express provision in a contract stating a sum for which one of the parties will be liable upon BREACH OF CONTRACT or failure to perform. FAR Subpart 11.5 contains the policies and procedures governing the use of liquidated damages to cover late performance of Government contracts. FAR 11.502 states that liquidated damages clauses should be used only when both (1) the time of delivery or performance is such an important factor that the Government can reasonably expect to suffer damage if delivery or performance is delinquent, and (2) the extent or amount of damage would be difficult or impossible to ascertain or prove. The rate of liquidated damages used must be reasonable because liquidated damages fixed without any reference to probable actual damages may be held to be a PENALTY and, therefore, unenforceable. In construction contracts, liquidated damages should be assessed for each day of DELAY; and the rate should, at a minimum, cover (1) the estimated cost of INSPECTION and superintendence for each day of delay in completion; and (2) specific losses due to the failure to complete the work, such as the cost of substitute FACILITIES, RENTAL COSTS, or continued payment of quarters allowance. FAR 11.503. 15 U.S.C. § 637(d)(4)(F) allows a CONTRACTING OFFICER to assess liquidated damages when a contractor fails to make a good-faith effort to comply with a subcontracting plan. FAR 19.705-7. See Cibinic & Nash, *Administration of Government Contracts* 1048–71 (3d ed. 1995); Margulies, chap. 11, *Construction Contacting* 1048–71 (1991); Cibinic, *Performance-Based Service Contracting: Negative Incentives—Liquidated Damages or Penalties?*, 11 N&CR ¶ 40 (Aug. 1997); Cibinic, *Liquidated Damages or Penalty? A Rose by Any Other Name*, 8 N&CR ¶ 46 (Aug. 1994); Witte, *Default, Liquidated Damages Changes, Excusable Delay and Contractor Fraud*, 27 Cont. Mgmt. 36 (Oct. 1987).

LIST OF PARTIES EXCLUDED FROM PROCUREMENT AND NONPROCUREMENT PROGRAMS A list (formerly referred to as the Consolidated List of Debarred, Suspended and Ineligible Contractors), containing the names of contractors proposed for DEBARMENT, debarred, or suspended (see SUSPENSION) by agencies, as well as contractors declared ineligible under other statutory or regulatory authority. This list is compiled, maintained, and distributed by the General Services Administration, in accordance with FAR 9.404. An electronic version of the list is updated daily and a printed version is published monthly. Agencies may not solicit offers from, award contracts to, or consent to subcontracts with contractors on the list unless the head of the agency determines that there is a compelling reason to do so. FAR 9.405. Contractors may not award subcontracts of $25,000 or more to a firm on the list without compelling reason and written notice to the Government. FAR 9.405-2(b). See the Protecting the Government's Interests When Subcontracting with Contractors Debarred, Suspended or Proposed for Debarment clause at FAR 52.209-6. This list is located on the internet at www.arnet.gov/epls.

LOAN GUARANTEE See GUARANTEED LOAN.

LOBBYING ACT See ANTI-LOBBYING ACT.

LOBBYING COSTS Costs incurred by a contractor to influence the outcome of legislation. Legislative lobbying costs are considered UNALLOWABLE COSTs if associated with any of the following: (1) attempts to influence the outcome of a federal, state, or local election, referendum, initiative, or similar procedure, through contributions, endorsements, publicity, or similar activities; (2) establishing, administering, contributing to, or paying the expenses of a political party, political campaign, or political action committee; (3) any attempt to influence the introduction of federal, state, or local legislation, or the enactment or modification of any pending federal, state, or local legislation (a) through communication with a member or employee of Congress or a state legislature, or with a Government official or employee in connection with a decision to sign or veto enrolled legislation, or (b) by preparing, distributing, or using publicity or propaganda, or (c) by urging the public to contribute to or participate in a mass demonstration, march, rally, fund-raising drive, lobbying campaign, or letter-writing or telephone campaign; or (4) legislative liaison activities, gathering information regarding legislation, and analyzing the effect of legislation, when such activities are in support of, or in knowing preparation for, an effort to engage in unallowable activities. FAR 31.205-22. Lobbying costs are considered ALLOWABLE COSTs, however, if they involve (1) presentation of technical and factual information on a topic directly related to contract performance, (2) efforts to influence state legislation to directly reduce contract cost or avoid impairment of contract performance, and (3) any activity specifically authorized by statute to be funded under the contract.

FAR 31.205-22(b). See Kenney & Schroer, *The Lobbying Disclosure Act of 1995*, 96-5 Briefing Papers (Apr. 1996); Cibinic & Nash, *Cost-Reimbursement Contracting* 782–83 (2d ed. 1993).

LOGISTICS The science of planning, obtaining, maintaining, and transporting materials, personnel, and FACILITIES. More specifically, logistics refers to those aspects of military operations that deal with (1) design and development, acquisition, storage, movement, distribution, maintenance, evacuation, and disposition of materials; (2) movement, evacuation, and hospitalization of personnel; (3) acquisition, maintenance, operation, and disposition of facilities; and (4) acquisition or furnishing of services. Jones, *Glossary: Defense Acquisition Acronyms and Terms* (8th ed., Defense Systems Management College).

LONG-LEAD ITEMS; LONG-LEAD-TIME MATERIALS Those components of a system, materials, or pieces of equipment for which the times to design and fabricate are the longest and, therefore, to which an early commitment of funds may be desirable in order to meet the earliest possible date of system completion. For planning purposes, long-lead items might be ordered during engineering management development to arrive in time for the start of production. Jones, *Glossary: Defense Acquisition Acronyms and Terms* (8th ed., Defense Systems Management College).

LOSS The failure to earn a PROFIT on a contract because the costs of performance (both DIRECT COSTs and INDIRECT COSTs) have exceeded the amount paid to the contractor under the terms of the contract. FAR 31.205-23 states that losses on other contracts are UNALLOWABLE COSTs. See Cibinic & Nash, *Cost-Reimbursement Contracting* 888 (2d ed. 1993).

LOSS OF EFFICIENCY A reduction in expected productivity that can result from a variety of causes such as adverse weather, restricted access to the jobsite, out-of-sequence work, and excess or unavailability of human resources. A Government contractor may use several clauses as a basis for a claim for loss of efficiency: the Changes clause, FAR 52.243-4, the DIFFERING SITE CONDITIONS clause, FAR 52.236-2, and the SUSPENSION OF WORK clause, FAR 52.242-14. See Finke, *Claims for Construction Productivity Losses*, 26 Pub. Cont. L.J. 311 (1997); Ginsberg & Bannon, *Loss of Efficiency*, 85-12 Constr. Briefings (Dec. 1985).

LOSS OF USEFUL VALUE A termination cost, pertaining to SPECIAL TOOLING and special machinery and equipment, which is generally allowable provided that (1) the special tooling or special machinery and equipment is not reasonably capable of use in the contractor's other work, (2) TITLE is transferred to the Government or the Government's interest is protected by other means deemed appropriate by the contracting officer, and (3) "the loss of useful value for any one terminated contract is limited to that portion of the ACQUISITION COST that bears the same ratio to the total acquisition cost as the terminated portion of the contract bears to the entire terminated contract and other Government contracts for which the special tooling or special machinery and equipment was acquired." FAR 31.205-42(d). See Cibinic & Nash, *Cost-Reimbursement Contracting* 911–14 (2d ed. 1993).

LOW-RATE INITIAL PRODUCTION Production of the minimum quantity of a WEAPON SYSTEM necessary to (1) provide production-configured or representative articles for OPERATIONAL TEST AND EVALUATION, (2) establish an initial production base for the system, and (3) permit an orderly increase in the production rate for the system sufficient to lead to full-rate production upon successful completion of operational testing. 10 U.S.C. § 2400(b). Under this statute, MAJOR DEFENSE ACQUISITION PROGRAMs may not proceed beyond this point until operational test and evaluation is completed. Guidance on this procedure is contained in paragraph 1.4.4.1 of DOD Regulation 5000.2-R, *Mandatory Procedures for Major Defense Acquisition Programs (MDAPs) and Major Automated Information System (MAIS) Acquisition Programs*, Mar. 15, 1996.

LOWEST OVERALL COST The least expenditure of funds over the life of a system or item. Lowest overall cost is calculated on the basis of purchase price, LEASE or rental prices, or service prices of the contract actions involved, as well as other identifiable and quantifiable costs directly related to the acquisition and use of the system or item (for example, personnel, maintenance and operation, site preparation, energy consumption, installation, conversion, system startup, contractor support, and the PRESENT VALUE discount factor). The quantifiable cost of conducting the contracting action and other administrative costs directly related to the ACQUISITION PROCESS are also included. The costs considered in deriving lowest overall cost for a telecommunication acquisition include such elements as personnel, purchase price or rentals, maintenance, site preparation and installation, programming, and training. See Gabig & Bean, *A Primer on Federal Information Systems Acquisitions: Part Two of a Two-Part Article*, 17 Pub. Cont. L.J. 553, 588 (1988).

LOWEST PRICE TECHNICALLY ACCEPTABLE A competitive negotiation source selection process where the non-price factors of a proposal are evaluated to determine which proposals are "technically acceptable" and award is made to the offeror of the technically acceptable proposal with the lowest price. FAR 15.101-2(a) states that this process is appropriate when BEST VALUE is expected to result from the use of this process. Thus, the "best value" decision is made in planning the procurement not in evaluating the proposals (as in the TRADEOFF PROCESS). In the lowest price technically acceptable process the non-price factors are all evaluated on an acceptable/unacceptable basis with no gradations or scores for higher levels of achievement. Thus, no tradeoffs are made in the source selection decision. See Cibinic & Nash, Chap. 6, Sec. I., *Formation of Government Contracts* (3d ed. 1998).

LOWEST RESPONSIVE, RESPONSIBLE BIDDER The bidder in a sealed bid procurement (see SEALED BIDDING) that is entitled to award of the contract. 10 U.S.C. § 2305(b)(3) and 41 U.S.C. § 253b(c) require award to the responsible source (see RESPONSIBILITY) whose bid conforms to the solicitation (see RESPONSIVENESS) and is most advantageous to the Government, considering only PRICE and other PRICE-RELATED FACTORS included in the SOLICITATION. Detailed guidance is set forth in FAR Part 14. See Cibinic & Nash, chap. 5, Sec. III., *Formation of Government Contracts* (3d ed. 1998).

M

MAILBOX RULE A common-law rule providing that an ACCEPTANCE OF an OFFER becomes effective (creates a binding contract) when it is transmitted rather than when it is received. *Restatement (Second) of Contracts* § 63 (1981). In Government contracting, the time of acceptance is subject to the mailbox rule unless the SOLICITATION provides for a different time. However, there is some authority holding that acceptance is not binding until the document is received by the offeror. *Rhode Island Tool Co. v. United States*, 130 Ct. Cl. 698 (1955). See Cibinic & Nash, chap. 5, Sec. I., *Formation of Government Contracts* (3d ed. 1998).

MAINTENANCE AND OPERATING CONTRACT See MANAGEMENT AND OPERATING CONTRACT.

MAJOR AUTOMATED INFORMATION SYSTEM (MAIS) ACQUISITION PROGRAM An automated information system (AIS) acquisition program specifically designated by the Assistant Secretary of Defense (Command, Control, Communications, and Intelligence), or estimated to require program costs in any single year in excess of $30 million in FY96 constant dollars, total program costs in excess of $120 million in FY96 constant dollars, or total LIFE-CYCLE COSTS in excess of $360 million in FY96 constant dollars. MAISs do not include highly sensitive classified programs (as determined by the Secretary of Defense). For the purpose of determining whether an AIS is a MAIS, the following must be aggregated and considered a single AIS: the separate AISs that constitute a multi-element program, the separate AISs that make up an EVOLUTIONARY or incrementally developed program, or the separate AISs that make up an a multi-component AIS program. Jones, *Glossary: Defense Acquisition Acronyms and Terms* (8th ed., Defense Systems Management College). See DOD Regulation 5000.2-R, *Mandatory Procedures for Major Defense Acquisition Programs (MDAPs) and Major Automated Information System (MAIS) Acquisition Programs*, Mar. 15, 1996.

MAJOR DEFENSE ACQUISITION PILOT PROGRAM The program under which the Secretary of Defense may designate up to six major defense acquisition programs and conduct those programs in accordance with standard commercial industrial practices in order to determine the potential for making the ACQUISITION PROCESS more efficient and effective. The program permits the Secretary of Defense to waive or limit the applicability of laws prescribing procurement procedures; source preference requirements; contractor performance requirements; cost allowability, cost accounting, or AUDITing requirements; or management, testing, evaluation, or reporting requirements. The program was created by § 809 of the FY 91 Defense Authorization Act, Pub. L. No. 101-510, codified at 10 U.S.C. § 2430.

MAJOR DEFENSE ACQUISITION PROGRAM A program designated as such by the Secretary of Defense or a program that will exceed $300 million for research, development, test, and evaluation or $1.8 billion for total procurement (calculated in FY90 constant dollars). 10 U.S.C. § 2430. These programs are subject to the detailed reporting and management requirements in chapter 144 of title 10 U.S. Code. See DOD Regulation 5000.2-R, *Mandatory Procedures for Major Defense Acquisition Programs (MDAPs) and Major Automated Information System (MAIS) Acquisition Programs*, Mar. 15, 1996. See also ACQUISITION CATEGORIES.

MAJOR SYSTEM A combination of elements that will function together to produce the capabilities required to fulfill a mission need. These elements include hardware, equipment, software, or any combination of these, but exclude construction or other improvements to REAL PROPERTY. A major system must meet one of the following guidelines: (1) DOD estimates that the costs of test, research, development, and evaluation will exceed $75 million; (2) DOD expects to spend more than $300 million on the acquisition; (3) a civilian agency estimates total expenditures exceeding $750,000; or (4) the agency head designates the system as such (all dollar amounts in FY80 constant dollars). 10 U.S.C. § 2302(9); 41 U.S.C. § 403(9); FAR 34.001. Special procedures are generally used for the procurement of major systems and they are subject to FAR Part 34. See MAJOR SYSTEM ACQUISITION.

MAJOR SYSTEM ACQUISITION The process used to acquire a MAJOR SYSTEM. Contracts formed as part of this process will be for one or more of the four phases of major system development: (1) concept exploration—relatively short contract periods of performance at low dollar levels; (2) demonstration—contractors submit priced proposals, funded by the Government, for full-scale system development; (3) full-scale development—contractors should be in a position to submit priced proposals for production based on the latest quantity, schedule, and LOGISTICS requirements, as well as any other factor used in making the production decision; and (4) full production—production of successfully tested major systems selected from the full-scale development phase. FAR Part 34 reflects the guidelines in OMB Circular No. A-109, *Major Systems Acquisitions*, Apr. 5, 1976. See OFPP Pamphlet No. 1, *A Discussion of the Application of OMB Circular No. A-109*, Aug. 1976; NASA Management Instruction 7110.14, *Major Systems Acquisitions*; DOD Directive 5000.1, *Defense Acquisition*, Mar. 15, 1996, DOD Regulation 5000.2-R, *Mandatory Procedures for Major Defense Acquisition Programs (MDAPs) and Major Automated Information System (MAIS) Acquisition Programs*, Mar. 15, 1996.

MAKE ITEM An item to be produced or work effort to be performed by the PRIME CONTRACTOR or its AFFILIATES, subsidiaries, or divisions. FAR 15.407-2(b). See also BUY ITEM. Such items are reviewed by the contracting officer when a contractor is required to submit a MAKE-OR-BUY PROGRAM under the requirements of FAR 15.407-2.

MAKE-OR-BUY PROGRAM That part of a contractor's written plan for a contract identifying (1) those major items to be produced or work efforts to be performed in the prime contractor's FACILITIES (MAKE ITEMs) and (2) those to be subcontracted (BUY ITEMs). FAR 15.407-2. The Government may reserve the right to review and agree on the contractor's make-or-buy program when necessary to ensure (1) negotiation of reasonable contract prices, (2) satisfactory performance, or (3) implementation of socioeconomic policies. FAR 15.407-2. Make-or-buy programs are required to be submitted by contractors on negotiated acquisitions over $10 million, with certain exceptions. FAR 15.407-2(c).

MANAGEMENT AND OPERATING (M&O) CONTRACT An agreement under which the Government contracts for the operation, maintenance, or support, on its behalf, of a Government-owned or Government-controlled research, development, special production, or testing establishment wholly or principally devoted to one or more major programs of the contracting federal agency. FAR 17.601. An M&O contract is characterized both by its purpose and by the special relationship it creates between the Government and contractor. Certain criteria generally apply: (1) the situation requires the use of Government FACILITIES (in the interest of NATIONAL DEFENSE or MOBILIZATION readiness, for example, or to perform the agency's mission adequately, or because private enterprise is unable or unwilling to use its own facilities for the work); (2) because of the nature of the work, or because it is to be performed in Government facilities, the Government must maintain a close relationship with the contractor and the contractor's personnel in such important areas as safety, security, cost control, and site conditions; (3) the conduct of the work is wholly or at least substantially separate from the contractor's other business, if any; and (4) the work is closely related to the agency's mission and is of a long-term or continuous nature, and there is a need to ensure its continuity and to have special protection covering the orderly transition of personnel and work in the event of a change in contractors. FAR 17.604. The FAR coverage on this subject, Subpart 17.6, was written principally with the needs of DOE in mind; the subpart's provisions do not apply to DOD. DFARS Subpart 217.6. See Madsen et al., *Management Contractors and Environmental Damage: Who Shall Pay?,* 37 Fed. B. News & J. 601 (1990). See also GOVERNMENT-OWNED CONTRACTOR-OPERATED PLANT.

MANUFACTURING ENGINEERING Developing and deploying new or improved materials, systems, processes, methods, equipment, pilot production lines, tools, and techniques to be used in providing products or services. FAR 31.205-25 specifies that the costs of such work incurred by a contractor are ALLOWABLE COSTs. FAR 31.205-18(a) provides that such work is not a part of a contractor's INDEPENDENT RESEARCH AND DEVELOPMENT effort. See Cibinic & Nash, *Cost-Reimbursement Contracting* 779–81 (2d ed. 1993).

MANUFACTURING TECHNOLOGY Activities whose objectives are (1) to establish or improve, in a timely manner, the manufacturing processes, techniques, or equipment required to support current and projected programs; and (2) to assure the ability to produce, reduce lead time, ensure economic availability of end items, reduce costs, increase efficiency, improve reliability, or enhance safety and anti-pollution measures. Brechtel, *Subcontracts: Government and Industry Issues* (NCMA 1989). DOD has established special programs to encourage contractors to develop and utilize better manufacturing technology. See DOD Instruction 4200.15, *Manufacturing Technology Program*, May 24, 1985.

MARCH-IN The right of the Government under 35 U.S.C. § 203 to require a contractor or subcontractor that has made a SUBJECT INVENTION to grant another party a LICENSE to use that invention if it is determined that the contractor has not achieved PRACTICAL APPLICATION of the invention or that a license is needed for public purposes. The conditions for exercising this right are set forth in the Patent Rights clauses in FAR 52.227-11, -12, and -13. This compulsory license right has not been exercised in any reported instance, but its exercise is subject to appeal in the COURT OF FEDERAL CLAIMS. 35 U.S.C. § 203(2).

MARKET ACCEPTANCE Acceptance of an ITEM by commercial buyers or other Government agencies under current or recent contracts for the same or similar requirements. Section 8002(c) of the FEDERAL ACQUISITION STREAMLINING ACT OF 1994 provides that agencies may require offerors to demonstrate that offered products have achieved market acceptance or otherwise meet the contract SPECIFICATIONs. FAR 11.103 contains guidance on the use of this procedure.

MARKET ANALYSIS The process of analyzing prices and trends in the competitive marketplace to compare product availability and offered prices with market alternatives and establish the reasonableness of offered prices. Market analysis is one of the elements of PRICE ANALYSIS that is undertaken by the contracting officer to ensure that the contract is being awarded at a FAIR AND REASONABLE PRICE. See also MARKET RESEARCH; MARKET SURVEY.

MARKET PRICE See ESTABLISHED CATALOG OR MARKET PRICE.

MARKET RESEARCH Collecting and analyzing information about capabilities within the market to satisfy agency needs. FAR 2.101. The process is used by the contracting officer in order to take the most suitable approach to acquiring, distributing, and supporting supplies and services. FAR Part 10. Market research is required by 10 U.S.C. § 2305(a)(1)(A)(ii) and 41 U.S.C. § 253a(a)(1)(B). It involves determining if COMMERCIAL ITEMs or NONDEVELOPMENTAL ITEMs are available to meet the Government's needs or could be modified to meet those needs. FAR 10.002(b). Techniques for conducting market research include: contacting knowledgeable individuals in industry and Government; reviewing the results of recent market research; publishing formal requests for information; querying Government databases; participating in interactive, on-line communications among industry personnel, acquisition personnel, and customers; obtaining source lists from other contracting activities; reviewing catalogs and other product literature, and conducting interchange meetings and PRESOLICITATION CONFERENCEs. FAR 10.002(b)(2). See Cibinic & Nash, chap. 3, Sec. IV., *Formation of Government Contracts* (3d ed. 1998).

MARKET SURVEY An attempt by a contracting agency to ascertain whether there are unknown qualified sources capable of satisfying the Government's requirements. This testing of the marketplace may range from written or telephone contact with federal and other experts regarding similar or duplicate requirements (and the results of any market test recently undertaken) to more formal "sources sought" announcements in scientific journals or the COMMERCE BUSINESS DAILY or SOLICITATIONS FOR INFORMATION OR PLANNING PURPOSES. See MARKET RESEARCH. See Cibinic & Nash, chap. 3, Sec. IV., *Formation of Government Contracts* (3d ed. 1998).

MARKETING CONSULTANT Any independent contractor that furnishes advice, information, direction, or assistance to an offeror or any other contractor in support of the preparation or submission of an OFFER for a Government contract. A contractor is *not* a marketing consultant when rendering the following: services excluded from the definition of ADVISORY AND ASSISTANCE SERVICES by FAR Subpart 37.2; routine engineering and technical services (such as installation, operation, or maintenance of systems, equipment, software, components, or FACILITIES); routine legal, actuarial, auditing, and accounting services; or training services. FAR 9.501. FAR 9.505-4(c) warns that contractors can improperly obtain proprietary or source selection information from marketing consultants. FAR Subpart 9.5 therefore directs contracting officers to address this type of ORGANIZATIONAL CONFLICT OF INTEREST in the procurement process. The FAR coverage implements OFPP Policy Letter No. 89-1, *Conflict of Interest Policies Applicable to Consultants*, Dec. 8, 1989.

MASTER AGREEMENT FOR REPAIR AND ALTERATION OF VESSELS A form of BASIC ORDERING AGREEMENT used for the repair and alteration of ships. It is not a contract but, rather, a written instrument of understanding that establishes in advance the terms and conditions on which a contractor will effect repairs, alterations, or additions to vessels, under the provisions of job orders awarded by contracting activities from time to time. JOB ORDERs (fixed-price contracts entered into with contractors that have previously executed master agreements) apply to specific acquisitions. They set forth the scope of work, price, delivery date, and additional matters peculiar to the acquisition, and they incorporate by reference or append the appropriate clauses from the master agreement. DFARS 217.7101.

MASTER SOLICITATION As used in the context of SEALED BIDDING, the term refers to a document containing special clauses and provisions that have been identified as essential for the acquisition of a specific type of supply or service that is acquired repetitively. The master solicitation may be requested by, and is provided to, potential sources who retain it for continued and repetitive use. FAR 14.203-3.

MATERIAL Property that may be incorporated into or attached to a deliverable end ITEM or that may be consumed or expended in the performance of a contract. FAR 45.301. The term includes assemblies, components, parts, raw and processed materials, and small tools and supplies that may be consumed in normal use in the performance of a contract. FAR 45.303-1 provides that contractors must ordinarily be required to furnish all material necessary to perform their contracts but that the Government should provide material when necessary to achieve significant economy, standardization, or expedited production. FAR 45.505-3 contains the requirements for contractor management and control of GOVERNMENT-FURNISHED MATERIAL, including material to which title has passed to the Government as the result of the payment provisions of the contract. CAS 411, 48 C.F.R. § 9904.411, sets forth rules that govern accounting for costs of material by charging it directly to a contract, allocating it to an INDIRECT COST POOL, or placing it in inventory (see MATERIAL INVENTORY RECORD).

MATERIAL INSPECTION AND RECEIVING REPORT (MIRR) A DOD form used to document the INSPECTION and acceptance (see ACCEPTANCE OF WORK) of supplies and services. DFARS Appendix F sets forth procedures and instructions for using, preparing, and distributing (1) the Material Inspection and Receiving Report (DD Forms 250 series) and (2) suppliers' commercial shipping/packing lists used as evidence of Government procurement QUALITY ASSURANCE (QA). MIRRs are used to document QA, acceptance of supplies and services, and shipments. They are used by receiving, status control, technical, contracting, inventory control, requisitioning, and paying activities. The procedures of Appendix F apply to supplies or services procured by DOD when the contract includes the Material Inspection and Receiving Report clause at DFARS 252.246-7000.

MATERIAL INVENTORY RECORD Any record of a contractor used for the accumulation of actual or STANDARD COSTs of a category of MATERIAL recorded as an ASSET for subsequent allocation to one or more COST OBJECTIVEs. CAS 411, 48 C.F.R. § 9904.211-30. CAS 411 provides that the cost used in this record will be the purchase price of the item of material adjusted by extra charges incurred or discounts earned. It then permits that one of the following methods must be used consistently to charge material costs to a contract: FIRST-IN, FIRST-OUT; MOVING AVERAGE COST; WEIGHTED AVERAGE COST; STANDARD COST; or LAST-IN, FIRST-OUT.

MATERIAL MANAGEMENT AND ACCOUNTING SYSTEM (MMAS) The contractor's system for planning, controlling, and accounting for the acquisition, use, and disposition of MATERIAL. Such systems may be manual or automated and may be integrated with planning, engineering, estimating, purchasing, INVENTORY, accounting, and other systems; or they may be essentially stand-alone systems. DFARS 252.242-7202. DOD policy requires that all contractors have a system that reasonably forecasts material requirements; ensures that the costs of purchased and fabricated material charged or allocated to a contract are based on VALID TIME-PHASED REQUIREMENTS; and maintains a consistent, equitable, and unbiased logic for costing of material transactions. DFARS 252.242-7004. See Nash, *Material Management Accounting Systems: What Cost Perfect Knowledge?,* 5 N&CR ¶ 36 (June 1991); Lemmer, *Material Management and Accounting*, 88-6 Briefing Papers (May 1988).

MATERIAL REQUIREMENTS PLANNING (MRP) SYSTEM Any form of computerized manufacturing management and scheduling system. The DEFENSE CONTRACT AUDIT AGENCY (DCAA) describes an MRP system as one that identifies, initiates procurement of, and maintains current and future materials necessary to support production operations. MRP is a method of INVENTORY control, not inventory costing. DCAA identifies the following features as common to the various MRP design configurations: (1) highly automated systems with extensive use of data processing, (2) a master production schedule that maintains a balance between requirements and replenishments, (3) a netting process that involves a netting formula derived from requirements and replenishments, and (4) dynamic scheduling of items in the production process. *DCAA Contract Audit Manual* 5-702. Concern that deficiencies in these systems, or in their use, caused overcharging led DOD to issue compliance guidelines and DCAA to publish extensive guidance on MRPs. See Office of the Assistant Secretary of Defense,

Contractor Material Requirements Planning System, *reprinted in*, 48 Fed. Cont. Rep. 936 (Dec. 14, 1987); Defense Contract Audit Agency, Audit Program for Evaluation of Material Management and Accounting Systems, *reprinted in*, 49 Fed. Cont. Rep. 427, 482 (Mar. 14, 1988). See also *House Panel Votes to Require Certification of MRP Systems*, 49 Fed. Cont. Rep. 579 (Mar. 28, 1988); Fordham & Polakoff, *MRP and the DOD Solution*, 28 Cont. Mgmt. 16 (Oct. 1988); Holter, *MRP and Government Contract Costing: Are They Compatible?,* 21 Nat'l Cont. Mgmt. J., Issue No. 1, p. 1 (1987).

MATRIX See PROVISION AND CLAUSE MATRIX.

MAXIMUM FEE Dollar amount negotiated at the inception of a COST-PLUS-INCENTIVE-FEE CONTRACT as the maximum amount of PROFIT that the contractor is entitled to receive. After contract performance the FEE payable to the contractor is determined in accordance with a contract-specified fee adjustment formula based on the relationship of total ALLOWABLE COST to total TARGET COST. When total allowable cost is *less* than the range of cost within which the fee adjustment formula operates (see RANGE OF INCENTIVE EFFECTIVENESS), the contractor is paid the total allowable cost plus the maximum fee. FAR 16.404-1. See Cibinic & Nash, *Cost-Reimbursement Contracting* 77-91 (2d ed. 1993).

MEASUREMENT OF COST Accounting methods and techniques used in defining the components of cost, determining the basis for cost measurement, and establishing criteria for use of alternative cost measurement techniques. 48 C.F.R. § 9903.302-1(a). Such measurement is one type of COST ACCOUNTING PRACTICE. Examples of cost accounting practices that involve measurement of costs are (1) the use of HISTORICAL COST, MARKET VALUE, or PRESENT VALUE; (2) the use of STANDARD COST or ACTUAL COST; or (3) the designation of those items of cost that must be included in or excluded from TANGIBLE CAPITAL ASSET or PENSION PLAN costs.

MEDIATION A voluntary, flexible technique for resolving DISPUTEs: the contracting parties present their positions to a mediator who then works with them in negotiating a settlement. Generally, each party appoints a PRINCIPAL with the authority to settle the dispute. The positions of the parties can be presented to the mediator separately or in a joint session. Similarly, the negotiation can be conducted between the principals, with the mediator assisting, or by the mediator walking offers of settlement back and forth between the parties. Mediation is now one of the most widely used ALTERNATIVE DISPUTE RESOLUTION methods. See Nash, *Resolving Disputes: Is Hardball the Way to Go?*, 11 N&CR ¶ 38 (Aug. 1997); Nagle, *ADR: A Different Wrinkle*, 10 N&CR ¶ 44 (Sept. 1996); Nash, *Alternative Dispute Resolution: A Proposed Agreement*, 9 N&CR ¶ 23 (Apr. 1995) (containing a proposed mediation agreement).

MEMORANDUM OF UNDERSTANDING (MOU) An executive agreement with a foreign government. MOUs are used by DOD and NASA in situations where they have joint programs with foreign governments. Specific MOUs are negotiated with each country. They frequently contain provisions that waive the requirements of the BUY AMERICAN ACT to acquisitions of certain supplies mined, produced, or manufactured in designated foreign countries (because the agency has determined that it would be inconsistent with the public interest to apply its restrictions). See FAR 25.103. DOD policies for applying the domestic preference laws and programs to offers of products from "qualifying" foreign countries can be found at DFARS Subpart 225.872.

MENTOR FIRM See MENTOR-PROTÉGÉ PILOT PROGRAM.

MENTOR-PROTÉGÉ PILOT PROGRAM A test program that encourages major DOD contractors to act as "mentors" to SMALL DISADVANTAGED BUSINESS CONCERNs (SDBCs). The program seeks to increase the participation of SDBCs as subcontractors and suppliers under DOD contracts, other Federal Government contracts, and commercial contracts by furnishing them with assistance aimed at enhancing their performance. It provides mentor firms with incentives including reimbursement equal to the total amount of PROGRESS PAYMENTs made under the program to a Protégé firm, reimbursement for the costs of the assistance furnished, or recognition of costs as "credits" in lieu of subcontract awards toward subcontracting participation goals. The program was created by section 831 of the FY91 Defense Authorization Act, Pub. L. No. 101-510, and is implemented by DFARS 219.71. DOD policy and procedures for implementation of the program are contained in Appendix I to chap. 2, Policies and Procedures for the DOD Pilot Mentor-Protégé Program. A mentor firm must (1) have DOD contracts of at least $100 million, (2) demonstrate the capability to assist in the development of protege firms, and (3) be approved by the Secretary of Defense. A protégé firm must be a small business concern owned and controlled by socially and ECONOMICALLY DISADVANTAGED INDIVIDUALS as defined by the SMALL BUSINESS ACT. 15 U.S.C. § 637(d)(3)(C).

MERGER See BUSINESS COMBINATION.

MERGER GUIDELINES See HORIZONTAL MERGER GUIDELINES.

METHODS OF PROCUREMENT A broad term describing the way the Government procures supplies and services including construction. The Government uses two basic methods of procurement: SEALED BIDDING (see FAR Part 14) and NEGOTIATION (see FAR Part 15). Any contract awarded without using sealed bidding procedures is a negotiated contract. FAR 15.000. The SIMPLIFIED ACQUISITION PROCEDURES of FAR Part 13 are a subset of negotiation. Procurement methods can also be characterized as those meeting the statutory requirement for FULL AND OPEN COMPETITION and those not meeting this requirement. Those meeting the requirement are said to use COMPETITIVE PROCEDURES; those not meeting it include sole source acquisition (see SOLE SOURCE), use of UNSOLICITED PROPOSALs, and various other processes. FAR Part 17 discusses special contracting methods, including MULTIYEAR CONTRACTING (covering more than one year but not more than five years of requirements), OPTIONs (under which the Government has the unilateral right to increase the quantity or extend the term of the contract), LEADER-COMPANY CONTRACTING (under which a developer or sole proprietor furnishes assistance and know-how to another contractor so that the latter can become a source of supply), and INTERAGENCY ACQUISITION.

METRIC CONVERSION ACT OF 1975 An Act designating the metric system as the preferred system of weights and measures for United States trade and commerce requiring all agencies to use the metric system in their acquisitions, unless it is impracticable to do so or is likely to cause significant inefficiencies or loss of markets to United States firms. FAR 11.002.

MICRO-PURCHASE An acquisition of supplies or services (except construction), the aggregate amount of which does not exceed $2,500. Micro-purchases for construction are limited to $2,000. FAR 2.101. Micro-purchases may be made from any source using any simplified technique (they are not SET-ASIDE for SMALL BUSINESS). FAR 13.003(b). Agency heads are encouraged to delegate micro-purchase authority to individuals who will be using the supplies or services being purchased. FAR 13.201(a). They are also encouraged to use GOVERNMENT-WIDE COMMERCIAL PURCHASE CARDs in carrying out these purchases. FAR 13.201(b). See Cibinic & Nash, chap. 7, Sec. II., *Formation of Government Contracts* (3d ed. 1998).

MILESTONE PAYMENTS See PERFORMANCE-BASED PAYMENTS.

MILESTONES FOR THE ACQUISITION CYCLE Designated steps of the planned acquisition identified in the ACQUISITION PLAN, including (1) acquisition plan approval; (2) STATEMENT OF WORK; (3) SPECIFICATIONs; (4) data requirements; (5) completion of acquisition-package preparation; (6) purchase request; (7) justification and approval for OTHER THAN FULL AND OPEN COMPETITION where applicable and/or any required DETERMINATION AND FINDING approval; (8) issuance of SYNOPSIS; (9) issuance of solicitation; (10) evaluations of proposals, AUDITs, and field reports; (11) beginning and completion of negotiations; (12) contract preparation, review, and clearance; and (13) CONTRACT AWARD. FAR 7.105(b)(19). See Cibinic & Nash, chap. 3, Sec. I., *Formation of Government Contracts* (3d ed. 1998).

MILITARY AND STATE SECRETS DOCTRINE A privilege, belonging to the Federal Government and which must be formally asserted by it, that protects military and state secrets by protecting evidence containing information pertaining to national security from discovery in a litigation context. See *United States v. Reynolds*, 345 U.S. 1 (1953).

MILITARY DEPARTMENT See DEPARTMENT OF DEFENSE.

MILITARY SPECIFICATIONS (MIL-SPECS) AND STANDARDS (MIL-STDS) SPECIFICATIONs and STANDARDs, unique to DOD, that are prepared, maintained, and controlled by the Secretary of Defense. In 1994, the Secretary of Defense issued a new DOD policy advocating a greater use of performance and commercial specifications in lieu of military specifications. The intent of the policy was not to eliminate military specifications altogether, but to curtail the automatic development and imposition of unique military specifications as the cultural norm at DOD. As a result, the ORDER OF PRECEDENCE for contract specifications in FAR 11.101 is now (1) documents mandated by law; (2) performance-oriented documents; (3) detailed design-oriented documents; and (4) standards, specifications and related publications issued by the Government outside the defense or federal series. See Cibinic & Nash, chap. 3, Sec. V., *Formation of Government Contracts* (3d ed. 1998). From 1994 to 1996, 2,676 military specifications and standards were canceled. See DOD, *MilSpec Reform: Results of the First Two Years* (1996). Unclassified MIL-SPECs and MIL-STDs, along with related standardization documents and VOLUNTARY STANDARDs adopted by DOD, are listed in the *Department of Defense Index of Specifications and Standards (DODISS)*. The DODISS is available from the DOD Single Stock Point, Standardization Documents Desk, Building 4D, 700 Robbins Avenue, Philadelphia, PA 19111-5094.44.

MILITARY STANDARD REQUISITIONING AND ISSUE PROCEDURE (MILSTRIP) A procedure used by the military departments to requisition material or place Government material under supply control. When authorized by the terms of a contract, contractors may also use MILSTRIP, which uses uniform codes and punch-card formats to standardize procedures for requisitioning, receiving, and returning material and permit the maximum utilization of AUTOMATIC DATA PROCESSING EQUIPMENT. MILSTRIP applies when DOD contractors requisition from General Services Administration supply sources. The Defense Logistics Standard Systems Office is responsible for MILSTRIP. See DOD Manual 4000.25-1-M, *Military Standard Requisitioning and Issue Procedures*.

MILLER ACT A 1935 Act, 40 U.S.C. § 270a et seq., requiring the execution of separate PERFORMANCE BONDs and PAYMENT BONDs as a prerequisite to award of CONSTRUCTION contracts exceeding $100,000. See FAR 28.102. The Act protects the Government by requiring the performance bond and gives some classes of persons furnishing LABOR and materials the right to recover under a payment bond. A performance bond SURETY under the Miller Act is liable for all monetary sums arising from the contract that the Government has with the contractor, not to exceed the bond's PENAL AMOUNT. Miller Act jurisdiction for laborers and materialmen suing for compensation under the payment bond is limited to actions against the contractor or its sureties and grants no right of action against a subcontractor. The FEDERAL ACQUISITION STREAMLINING ACT OF 1994 required that the FAR provide alternatives to payment bonds for contracts exceeding $25,000 but not greater than $100,000. See FAR 28.102(b). See Cibinic, *The Miller Act and Construction Contracts under $100,000: The Right and Left Hands Playing Different Tunes*, 10 N&CR ¶ 22 (May 1996). See also DFARS 228.102-1 regarding waivers for cost-reimbursement-type construction contract bonding requirements. Patin, chap. 17, *Construction Contracting* 1222–334 (1991). See Zielke, *Arbitrating Miller Act Claims and Problems in*

Enforcing and Award under the Federal Arbitration Act, 24 Pub. Cont. L.J. 401 (1995).

MINIMUM FEE Dollar amount negotiated at the inception of a COST-PLUS-INCENTIVE-FEE CONTRACT as the minimum amount of PROFIT that the contractor is entitled to receive. After contract performance the FEE payable to the contractor is determined in accordance with a contract-specified fee adjustment formula based on the relationship of total ALLOWABLE COST to total TARGET COST. When total allowable cost is *greater* than the range of cost within which the fee-adjustment formula operates (see RANGE OF INCENTIVE EFFECTIVENESS), the contractor is paid the total allowable cost plus the minimum fee. FAR 16.404-1. The minimum fee is usually a positive number (i.e., the contractor is guaranteed to make a profit). However, if a high MAXIMUM FEE is negotiated, the contract must also provide for a low minimum fee. This low minimum fee may be zero (in which case the contractor would be paid total allowable cost only). In rare cases, it may be a negative fee (the contractor would be paid total allowable cost *minus* the minimum fee; in other words, its losses would be limited). FAR 16.404-1(b)(3). See Cibinic & Nash, *Cost-Reimbursement Contracting* 84-85 (2d ed. 1993).

MINIMUM NEEDS A misnomer for the rule that contracting agencies may not use SPECIFICATIONs or conditions that are unduly restrictive (see RESTRICTIVE SPECIFICATIONS). See FAR 11.002, which provides that plans, DRAWINGS, specifications, STANDARDs, or PURCHASE DESCRIPTIONs must state only the Government's actual "minimum needs" and describe the supplies and/or services in a manner designed to promote FULL AND OPEN COMPETITION. The term is misleading because it suggests that Government agencies must buy supplies and services that are minimally effective. This clearly is not so because agencies are generally entitled to buy supplies or services that provide the BEST VALUE, determined by the technical and economic judgment of the procuring agency. See Nash, *Minimum Needs: A Contentious Term?,* 11 N&CR ¶ 10 (Feb. 1997).

MINITRIAL A flexible, voluntary, and nonjudicial procedure wherein members of top management (called "PRINCIPALS") hear a short presentation of the factual and legal positions of the parties in a contract dispute and engage in nonbinding negotiations to resolve a CLAIM. In most cases they are aided by a NEUTRAL ADVISOR who acts as a mediator. This procedure permits either party to withdraw at any time without prejudicing the litigation process. Management officials of both parties meet to resolve the dispute rather than permit a third party—a judge or arbitrator—to control the process. This technique is expressly recognized by the ADMINISTRATIVE DISPUTE RESOLUTION ACT. The minitrial process is one of the most widely used ALTERNATIVE DISPUTE RESOLUTION options in dealing with Government contract claims. See FAR 33.201. See also Mayer, *Alternative Dispute Resolution Procedures—How to Do More for Less Cost*, 34 Cont. Mgmt. 11 (Feb. 1994); Nash, *Alternate Disputes Resolution: An Update*, 7 N&CR ¶ 25 (May 1993); Page & Lees, *Roles of Participants in the Mini-Trial*, 18 Pub. Cont. L.J. 54 (1988) (includes the text of a minitrial agreement used by the Corps of Engineers); Nash, *The Minitrial Comes of Age*, 3 N&CR ¶ 64 (Sept. 1989); Crowell et al., *Applying Alternate Dispute Resolution to Contract Claims*, 1 Admin. L.J. 553 (1987) (issue devoted to a Colloquium on Improving Dispute Resolution: Options for the Federal Government).

MINOR INFORMALITIES OR IRREGULARITIES IN BIDS Immaterial DEFECTs or variations from the exact requirements of an INVITATION FOR BID that can be corrected or waived without prejudice to other bidders. FAR 14.405. A defect or variation is immaterial when the effect on price, quantity, quality, or delivery is negligible in comparison with the total cost or scope of the supplies or services being acquired. Such defects or variations are of so little import that they do not keep a bid from being responsive (see RESPONSIVENESS). The contracting officer must give the bidder an opportunity to cure any DEFICIENCY resulting from a minor informality or irregularity, or must waive the deficiency, whichever is to the advantage of the Government. Examples of minor informalities or irregularities include failure of a bidder to return the required number of copies of signed bids and failure to furnish required information concerning number of employees. See Cibinic & Nash, chap. 5, Sec. II., *Formation of Government Contracts* (3d ed. 1998).

MINORITY INSTITUTION (MI) An institution meeting the requirements prescribed by the Secretary of Education at 34 C.F.R. § 637.4. The term also includes any nonprofit research institution that was an integral part of a HISTORICALLY BLACK COLLEGE OR UNIVERSITY (HBCU) before Nov. 14, 1986. DFARS 252.226-7000. In furtherance of the Government policy of placing a fair proportion of its acquisitions with MIs, HBCUs, and SMALL DISADVANTAGED BUSINESS CONCERNs, section 1207 of Pub. L. No. 99-661, section 806 of Pub. L. No. 100-180, and section 844 of Pub. L. No. 100-456 established the DOD objectives of (1) awarding a total of 5 percent of its total contract dollars during each of the fiscal years 1987 through 2000 to MIs and HBCUs, and (2) maximizing the number of such entities participating in DOD prime contracts and subcontracts. See 10 U.S.C. § 2323. See also DFARS 226.7000; *An Inventory of the Capabilities of the Historically Black Colleges and Universities and Other Minority Institutions (HBCUs/MIs): A NAFEO/DOD Survey* (1989); Lambert & Shillito, *DOD Implements Congressional Mandate to Meet a Five Percent Contract Goal for Minorities*, 27 Cont. Mgmt. 16 (Oct. 1987).

MISCHARGING The improper charging of a cost to a Government contract. FAR 31.205-15 makes such costs incurred by contractors—including the costs of identification, measurement, and correction—UNALLOWABLE COSTs. Mischarging can arise through improper ALLOCATION OF COSTs or through charging of EXPRESSLY UNALLOWABLE COSTs to a contract. It constitutes criminal conduct under the FALSE CLAIMS ACT. See Graham, *Mischarging: A Contract Dispute or a Criminal Fraud?,* 15 Pub. Cont. L.J. 208 (1985).

MISREPRESENTATION Either a FALSE STATEMENT of a substantive FACT or any conduct that intentionally deceives or misleads another person so that, with respect to a substantive fact material to proper understanding of the matter at hand, the other person believes what is not true. *Black's Law Dictionary* 1001 (6th ed. 1990). 41 U.S.C. § 601 defines "misrepresentation of fact" for the purposes of the CONTRACT DISPUTES ACT (CDA) OF 1978 as a false statement or misleading conduct that leads to a belief of a substantive fact material to proper understanding made with the intent to deceive or mislead 41 U.S.C. § 604 provides that if any CLAIM under the CDA is unsupported because of misrepresentation, the contractor is liable to the Government for the amount of the claim plus the cost to the Government in reviewing the claim. See FAR 33.209 providing that the contracting officer shall refer such situations to the agency official responsible for investigating FRAUD. The normal remedies for misrepresentation are DISQUALIFICATION before the contract award or RESCISSION after the contract award. (See also FALSE STATEMENTS ACT.) See Cibinic & Nash, chap. 1, Sec. VII., *Formation of Government Contracts* (3d ed. 1998); Cibinic & Nash, *Administration of Government Contracts* 133–34 (3d ed. 1995).

MISTAKE A belief that is not in accord with the existing facts (but not an error in business judgment). Mistakes made by contractors may be discovered either before or after contract awards. Before award, the

CONTRACTING OFFICER has an obligation to examine all bids and then notify the offeror of any suspected mistake and to request verification that no mistake was made (see DUTY OF VERIFICATION). In SEALED BIDDING procurement, mistakes discovered before award entitle the contractor either to withdraw the bid or to correct bids that are responsive in accordance with the guidance in FAR 14.407-3. In negotiated procurement (see NEGOTIATION), mistakes may be corrected during the procurement process in accordance with the procedures in FAR 15.306. If a mistake is discovered after award, the contractor may receive REFORMATION if there was a MUTUAL MISTAKE or a UNILATERAL MISTAKE about which the contracting officer was or should have been on notice. FAR 14.407-4. See Cibinic & Nash, *Administration of Government Contracts* 321–47 (3d ed. 1995); Cibinic, *Distinguishing Mistakes From Criminal Conduct: Delayed Second Opinion*, 11 N&CR ¶ 57 (Nov. 1997); Nash, *Reformation to Correct a Mistake in a Bid or Proposal: What "Mistakes" Qualify?*, 10 N&CR ¶ 11 (Feb. 1996); Cibinic, *Corrections of Mistakes in Proposals: To Discuss or Not to Discuss*, 8 N&CR ¶ 4 (Jan. 1994); Arnavas & Ganther, *Preventive Preaward Actions*, 90-9 Briefing Papers (Aug. 1990); Gammon & Allen, *Postaward Relief for Mistakes in Bids*, 88-11 Briefing Papers (Oct. 1988); Rudland, *Rationalizing the Bid Mistake Rules*, 16 Pub. Cont. L.J. 446 (1987).

MITIGATION The alleviation, reduction, abatement, or diminution of a PENALTY or punishment imposed by law. The doctrine of "mitigation of damages" imposes on a party injured by BREACH OF CONTRACT or TORT the obligation to exercise reasonable diligence and ordinary care in attempting to minimize its damages or avoid aggravating the injury. *Black's Law Dictionary* 1002 (6th ed. 1990). In effect, this obligation limits contract damages to the amount that would have been suffered if they had been mitigated.

MIXED FUNDING The situation where an ITEM, component, process, or COMPUTER SOFTWARE has been DEVELOPED partially at private expense and partially at Government expense. 10 U.S.C. § 2320(a)(2)(E) provides that the rights to TECHNICAL DATA pertaining to items or processes developed with mixed funding should be negotiated as early as possible in the ACQUISITION PROCESS. Under the 1988 DOD data policy, such rights were only negotiated when requested by the contractor. Under the 1995 DOD data policy, as well as the computer software policy, the Government automatically obtains GOVERNMENT PURPOSE RIGHTS when development has been accomplished with mixed funding.

MOBILIZATION The initial effort to perform a CONSTRUCTION contract by hiring necessary personnel and moving the necessary equipment and facilities on to the site of the work. Contracting agencies frequently include a separate bid item for mobilization on major construction projects in order to permit the contractor to be paid promptly for this effort. When this is done, DFARS 236.570(b)(2) prescribes the use of the Payment for Mobilization and Preparatory Work clause in DFARS 252.236-7003 or the Payment for Mobilization and Demobilization clause in DFARS 252.236-7004.

MOBILIZATION BASE See INDUSTRIAL MOBILIZATION.

MODEL PROCUREMENT CODE (MPC) A model code containing basic rules for contracting by state and local governments that was adopted by the American Bar Association (ABA) in 1979. The MPC provides (1) the statutory principles and policy guidance for managing and controlling the procurement of supplies, services, and construction for public purposes; (2) administrative and judicial remedies for the resolution of controversies relating to public contracts; and (3) a set of ethical standards governing public and private participants in the procurement process. The MPC, which is based on established principles of state and federal law, is currently adopted by 14 states and a large number of municipalities. See Cushman, *The ABA Model Procurement Code: Implementation, Evolution, and Crisis of Survival*, 25 Pub. Cont. L.J. 173 (1996); vom Baur, *A Personal History of the Model Procurement Code*, 25 Pub. Cont. L.J. 149 (1996). Copies of the Model Procurement Code for State and Local Governments, Annotations to the Model Procurement Code, Recommended Regulations, and Ordinance for Local Governments may all be purchased from the ABA. [American Bar Association, 750 North Lake Shore Drive, Chicago, IL 60611]

MODIFICATION Any written change in the terms of a contract. FAR 43.101. Modifications are either bilateral or unilateral. A *bilateral* modification (SUPPLEMENTAL AGREEMENT) is a contract modification that is signed by both the contractor and the contracting officer. Bilateral modifications are used to (1) make negotiated equitable adjustments resulting from the issuance of a CHANGE ORDER, (2) definitize LETTER CONTRACTs, and (3) reflect other agreements of the parties modifying the terms of the contract. A *unilateral* modification is a contract modification that is signed only by the contracting officer. Unilateral modifications may be used, for example, to (1) make ADMINISTRATIVE CHANGEs, (2) issue change orders, (3) make changes authorized by clauses other than a Changes clause, and (4) issue TERMINATION NOTICEs. FAR 43.103. Most Government contracts contain a Changes clause permitting the contracting officer to make unilateral changes in designated areas, within the general SCOPE OF THE CONTRACT. FAR 43.201. Jackson & Alerding, *Expanding Contracting Opportunities Without Competition*, 27 Pub. Cont. L.J. 205 (1997); Schminky, *Proper Funding of Contract Modifications Under the Antecedent Liability Rule*, 26 Pub. Cont. L.J. 221 (1997). See also CHANGE and EQUITABLE ADJUSTMENT.

MODIFIED COVERAGE A type of COST ACCOUNTING STANDARDS (CAS) coverage that requires only that the contractor comply with the following cost accounting standards: 48 C.F.R. § 9904.401, Consistency in Estimating, Accumulating, and Reporting Costs; 48 C.F.R. § 9904.402, Consistency in Allocating Costs Incurred for the Same Purpose; 48 C.F.R.§ 9904.405, Accounting for Unallowable Costs; and 48 C.F.R. § 9904.406, Cost Accounting Standard—Cost Accounting Period. Modified coverage may be applied to a covered contract of less than $25 million awarded to a business unit that received less than $25 million in net CAS-covered awards in the immediately preceding cost accounting period, as well as to covered contracts of BUSINESS UNITs that received more than $25 million in net CAS-covered contracts in the immediately preceding cost accounting period, where no single contract award exceeded $1 million. 48 C.F.R. § 9903.201-2(b)(1). See Cibinic & Nash, *Cost-Reimbursement Contracting* 622 (2d ed. 1993).

MODIFIED TOTAL COST METHOD A variation of the TOTAL COST METHOD used to establish the amount of DAMAGES or EQUITABLE ADJUSTMENT due a contractor. The modified method results in the contractor being compensated for the difference between its actual expenses and its bid price, with modifications for possible inaccuracies or errors in bidding. See *Servidone Constr. Corp. v. United States*, 931 F.2d 860 (Fed. Cir. 1991); Shea, *Proving Productivity Losses in Government Contracts*, 18 Pub. Cont. L.J. 414 (Mar. 1989).

MODULAR CONTRACTING The acquisition of a MAJOR SYSTEM of INFORMATION TECHNOLOGY in successive acquisitions of interoperable modules. FAR 39.002. Section 35 of the CLINGER-COHEN ACT OF 1996, 41 U.S.C. § 431, provides that this technique be used to acquire a major system of information technology "to the maximum extent practicable." FAR 39.102(a) explains that buying an information technology system in discrete increments is intended to balance the need of the Government for fast access to a rapidly changing technology with stability in program development and management of contract performance and risk. Guidance on the use of this type of contracting is contained in FAR Subpart 39.1. See Nash, *Modular Contracting: Some Helpful Guidance*, 11 N&CR ¶ 55 (Oct. 1997); Nash, *Selecting the Acquisition Strategy: Help From the New Information Technology Statute?,* 10 N&CR ¶ 30 (June 1996).

MOST FAVORED CUSTOMER The status that earns the largest discount that a contractor gives to its customers. The Government expects contractors on the FEDERAL SUPPLY SCHEDULES to sell supplies to the Government at prices not exceeding those given to a contractor's most favored customer. GSAR 538.270. However, some hold that the Government should receive this treatment only if it is in fact the contractor's largest and best customer, on the basis of past experience or reasonable projection. See Goodrich & Mann, *Avoiding Disaster in Federal Supply Schedule Contracts*, 15 Pub. Cont. L.J. 1 (1984); Kaufman, *The Myth of the Most Favored Customer*, 18 Pub. Cont. L.J. 29 (1988). MULTIPLE-AWARD SCHEDULE (MAS) contracts contain a price reduction clause under which the Government is entitled to receive a reduction in price (or an increase in discount) if during the term of the contract the contractor makes any changes in its discount or pricing practices which would result in a less advantageous relationship between the Government and the customer or category of customers upon which the contract discount or price was predicted. GSAR 538.272. See Hutchinson, *Tips On Selling IT Services Through GSA's MAS Program*, 39 Gov't Contractor ¶ 491 (Oct. 15, 1997); Kenney & Kirby, *"Most Favored Customer" Provisions*, 86-3 Briefing Papers (Feb. 1986).

MOVING AVERAGE COST An inventory costing method under which an average unit cost is computed after each acquisition by adding the cost of the newly acquired units to the cost of the units of INVENTORY on hand and dividing this figure by the new total number of units. FAR 31.001. This method is one of the acceptable methods of charging material in a contractor's inventory to contracts under CAS 411, 48 C.F.R. § 9904.211.

MULTIPLE AWARD PREFERENCE A statutory preference that DELIVERY ORDER CONTRACTs and TASK ORDER CONTRACTs be awarded to multiple contractors rather than a single contractor. 10 U.S.C. § 2304a(d)(3); 41 U.S.C. § 253h(d)(3). The preference is implemented in FAR 16.504(c). It requires multiple awards to the maximum extent practicable unless (1) only one contractor is able to supply unique or specialized supplies or services, (2) more favorable terms can be obtained by a single award, (3) multiple award contracts would be too costly to administer, (4) tasks likely to be ordered are so integrated that only one contractor can reasonably perform the work, (5) the total estimated value of the contract is less than the SIMPLIFIED ACQUISITION THRESHOLD, or (6) multiple awards would not be in the best interest of the Government. The preference is especially strong for contracts for ADVISORY AND ASSISTANCE SERVICES that exceed three years and $10,000,000. FAR 16.504(c)(2). See Cibinic, *Task and Delivery Order Contracting: Unique Multiple Award Arrangements*, 10 N&CR ¶ 17 (Apr. 1996); Edwards, *The New Rules for Multiple Award Task Order Contracting*, 9 N&CR ¶ 35 (June 1995).

MULTIPLE-AWARD SCHEDULE (MAS) A schedule in the FEDERAL SUPPLY SCHEDULES system that contains prices for comparable supplies or services being offered by more than one supplier. These contracts cover items at either the same or different prices for delivery to a single geographic area. An MAS permits the Government to use industry distribution FACILITIES effectively and to select among comparable supplies and services when there are no prescribed STANDARDs or SPECIFICATIONs. Agencies are expected to make a best value decision when ordering from these schedules. FAR 8.404. Because agencies may select from among several contractors, contractors do not know what volume of sales to expect; consequently, although the agencies benefit, the sources suffer because of the possibility that few, if any, orders might be placed with them. MAS contracts differ from most Government contracts in that (1) items procured through them are not designed or manufactured to Government specifications, nor are they produced exclusively or principally for Government use; and (2) the Government makes no commitment to purchase any items covered by them. The contractor must sell to any authorized user of the MAS at the prices and on the terms and conditions provided in the contract and Government agencies may negotiate lower prices with MAS contractors. The Government, however, incurs no obligation to buy anything. See Cibinic & Nash, chap. 7, Sec. VIII., *Formation of Government Contracts* (3d ed. 1998); Cibinic, *Multiple Award Schedules: What Are They?*, 11 N&CR ¶ 60 (Nov. 1997); Hutchinson, *Tips On Selling IT Services Through GSA's MAS Program*, 39 Gov't Contractor ¶ 491 (Oct. 15, 1997); Sherry & Burke, *The New Wave of MAS Protests*, 39 Gov't Contractor ¶ 432 (Sept. 10, 1997); Vacketta & Handler, *GSA's MAS Explosion*, 39 Gov't

Contractor ¶ 408 (Aug. 20, 1997); Efron et al., *The GSA Multiple Award Schedule Program*, 94-11 Briefing Papers (Oct. 1994); Sherry, *Reinventing MAS Contracting & Pricing: Some Basic Problems & Simple Solutions*, 94-2 CP&A Rep. 3 (Feb. 1994); Peiffer, *MFC Pricing: The Hidden Discount*, 23 Pub. Cont. L.J. 129 (1993); Sherry & Begun, *Resolving the Unresolvable: Federal Courts Tackle the Multiple Award Schedule Program*, 22 Pub. Cont. L.J. 669 (1993); Brams & Kelly, *Multiple Award Schedule Contracting: A Practical Guide to Surviving Its Shortcomings, Ambiguities, and Pitfalls*, 19 Pub. Cont. L.J. 441 (1990); Kaufman, *What GSA Is Entitled to Know about an MAS Contractor's Commercial Discounts*, 15 Pub. Cont. L.J. 244 (1985).

MULTIPLE YEAR CONTRACT A contract for work to be performed over more than one FISCAL YEAR. Such contracts are commonly used by Government agencies to obtain better prices by stabilizing workloads. They can be accomplished by the use of OPTIONS for additional years, multiyear contracts, or multiple year INDEFINITE-QUANTITY CONTRACTs. See Cibinic & Nash, chap. 8, Sec. VI., *Formation of Government Contracts* (3d ed. 1998); Nash, *Postscript: Multiyear Procurement*, 10 N&CR ¶ 54 (Oct. 1996); Cibinic, *Multiple-Year Task and Delivery Order Contracts: Can Annual Funds Be Used?,* 10 N&CR ¶ 31 (June 1996); Nash, *Option Quantities in Multiyear Contracts: They Just Keep Going . . . And Going . . . And Going*, 8 N&CR ¶ 7 (Feb 1994).

MULTIYEAR APPROPRIATION See APPROPRIATION.

MULTIYEAR CONTRACTING A special type of REQUIREMENTS CONTRACT covering more than one year but not more than five years of requirements, even though the total funds to be obligated are not available at the time of CONTRACT AWARD. FAR 17.101; FAR 17.102-2. FAR 17.102-3 states that these contracts are intended to achieve—by permitting early planning and ECONOMIES OF SCALE—lower costs, STANDARDIZATION, administrative simplicity, and stability, among other things. Multiyear contracts may not cover more than five years of requirements unless authorized by statute. Each program year is annually budgeted and funded and, at the time of award, funds need only have been appropriated for the first year. The contractor is protected against loss resulting from cancellation by contract provisions that allow reimbursement of costs included in a CANCELLATION CEILING. If funds do not become available to support requirements for the succeeding years, the agency must cancel the contract. See FAR Subpart 17.1. Multiyear contracts are subject to the restrictions contained in 10 U.S.C. § 2306b and 41 U.S.C. § 254c. See Cibinic & Nash, chap. 8, Sec. VI., *Formation of Government Contracts* (3d ed. 1998); Nash, *Multiyear Procurement: The Different Faces of Congress*, 9 N&CR ¶ 40 (July 1995); Nash, *Option Quantities in Multiyear Contracts: They Just Keep Going . . . And Going. . . And Going*, 8 N&CR ¶ 7 (Feb. 1994); Phillips & Saunders, *Multiyear Contracts for Major Systems*, 22 Pub. Cont. L.J. 161 (1993).

MUTUAL MISTAKE A MISTAKE common to both parties to a contract. Mutual mistakes can occur when the parties include terms in the contract that do not conform to or express their actual intent or agreement (called mistakes in integration) or when the parties labor under the same misconception about a fundamental fact on which the contract is based (called mistakes in BASIC ASSUMPTION). Nash, *Postscript II: Mutual Mistake of Basic Assumption*, 8 N&CR ¶ 47 (Aug. 1994); Cibinic, *Postscript: Mutual Mistake of Basic Assumption*, 6 N&CR ¶ 5 (Jan. 1992); Nash, *Mutual Mistake of Basic Assumption: Fitting the Remedies to the Facts*, 4 N&CR ¶ 36 (June 1990). Both types of mutual mistake have led to contract REFORMATION by the BOARDs OF CONTRACT APPEALS or the courts or through EXTRAORDINARY CONTRACTUAL ACTIONs. FAR 33.205 states that such mistakes should now be dealt with under the DISPUTEs procedures. See Cibinic & Nash, *Administration of Government Contracts* 322–30 (3d ed. 1995).

N

NAFTA See NORTH AMERICAN FREE TRADE AGREEMENT.

NASA See NATIONAL AERONAUTICS AND SPACE ADMINISTRATION.

NASA-DEFENSE PURCHASE REQUEST NASA Form 523, used by NASA contracting offices for requesting procurement of supplies or services from all DOD components. See NFS Subpart 18-17.70.

NASA FAR SUPPLEMENT (NFS) The NASA acquisition regulation, which establishes agency-wide policies and procedures for implementing and supplementing the FEDERAL ACQUISITION REGULATION. All agency-wide policies and procedures that govern the contracting process, control contracting relationships, or require publication in the FEDERAL REGISTER for public comment are included in the NFS. NFS 18-1.301. The NFS is normally amended quarterly by NASA FAR Supplement Directives (NFSDs), which are analogous to FEDERAL ACQUISITION CIRCULARS. Amending the NFS by inserting pages transmitted by a NFSD produces a new version of the NFS. The version number appears on the cover. NFS 18-1.105-2(c). A procurement notice (PN) may be used to make urgent amendments between NFSD issuances. NFS 18-1.270-2. PNs are distributed only within NASA, but any regulatory changes dealing with matters other than internal administrative matters are published in the Federal Register simultaneously with PN distribution. PNs are usually incorporated in the NFS within three to four months of issuance (when the next NFSD is published). The numbering schemes used in the NFS and in its formally published C.F.R. version are slightly different. The NFS omits the C.F.R. title number and inserts a hyphen after the C.F.R. chapter; for example, 48 C.F.R. § 1801.102 is the same as NFS 18-1.102, and 48 C.F.R. § 1815.405-2 is the same as NFS 18-15.405-2. The NFS cites or incorporates provisions of some of NASA's non-procurement documents and handbooks. See also NASA MANAGEMENT INSTRUCTION. The NFS can be purchased as part of the loose-leaf–bound subscription edition of the FEDERAL ACQUISITION REGULATIONS SYSTEM available from the U.S. Government Printing Office, Washington DC 20402.

NASA MANAGEMENT INSTRUCTION (NMI) A formal document that governs some aspect of NASA operations. Some NMIs establish regulations that apply to all personnel, including procurement personnel. Under such circumstances, the NMI may be referenced in the NASA FAR SUPPLEMENT (NFS); for example, NMI 1210.2, NASA Competition Advocacy Program, is referenced at NFS Subpart 18-6.5. Instructions for obtaining NMIs and a related document series, NASA Handbooks, are available from the NASA Information Center, Code DB-4, Washington, DC 20546; (202) 453-1000.

NASA PROCUREMENT REGULATION (NPR) The original regulation issued under the ARMED SERVICES PROCUREMENT ACT to govern NASA procurement practices. It was based on and very similar to the ARMED SERVICES PROCUREMENT REGULATION and was in effect from the inception of NASA until Apr. 1, 1984, the beginning of the FEDERAL ACQUISITION REGULATIONS SYSTEM. The NPR still applies to any NASA contracts written before Apr. 1984 and not subsequently rewritten to meet FAR requirements. The loose-leaf NPR, published by NASA as NHB 5100.2, is out of print. However, it still appears in the July 1, 1984, printing of 41 C.F.R. chap. 18. See the current 41 C.F.R. Subtitle A for more details on the public availability of pre-FAR procurement regulations.

NASA RESEARCH ANNOUNCEMENT (NRA) A BROAD AGENCY ANNOUNCEMENT used to announce NASA research interests and solicit proposals reflecting those interests. The NRA process is oriented to those research procurements for which it would be impossible to draft a sufficiently detailed REQUEST FOR PROPOSAL without constraining the technical responses. Special preparation and evaluation procedures apply. NFS 18-35.016-70, NFS Subpart 18-70.2. See Cibinic & Nash, chap. 7, Sec. V., *Formation of Government Contracts* (3d ed. 1998).

NATIONAL AERONAUTICS AND SPACE ADMINISTRATION (NASA) An independent civilian agency of the U.S. Government, established by the National Aeronautics and Space Act of 1958, 42 U.S.C. § 2452. Its basic mission is to conduct aeronautic and space activities for peaceful purposes in conjunction with the scientific and engineering communities and to widely disseminate information on the results of those efforts. NASA consists of a headquarters in Washington, DC, and a number of research and engineering field installations throughout the country. NASA contracts fall under the coverage of the FEDERAL ACQUISITION REGULATION (FAR) and the NASA FAR SUPPLEMENT (NFS). There are no lower-level acquisition regulations of general applicability. Before the FAR and the NFS went into effect in Apr. 1984, NASA contracts were governed by the NASA PROCUREMENT REGULATION. See National Archives and Records Administration, *U.S. Government Manual Office of the Federal Register* (GPO 1996/97).

NATIONAL CONTRACT MANAGEMENT ASSOCIATION (NCMA) An organization composed of individuals who are engaged in public and commercial contracting through Government agencies and companies or are in related fields of endeavor. NCMA's mission is to increase the effectiveness of public contract management by (1) helping members improve their skills through educational programs and contact with knowledgeable persons in the field; (2) establishing a uniform code of ethics; (3) providing a forum for the interchange of ideas; (4) introducing new literature, ideas, and improvements; (5) encouraging a professional attitude toward contract management and procurement; and (6) enabling members to share in the range of experience and knowledge represented by the membership as a whole. NCMA publishes a semiannual Journal as well as the monthly *Contract Management* magazine, and it administers a certification program for contract professionals. [NCMA, 1912 Woodford Road, Vienna, VA 22182; (703) 448-9231]

NATIONAL DEFENSE Any activity related to programs for military or atomic energy production or construction, military assistance to any foreign nation, stockpiling, or space. See FAR 2.101, but note that the Space Act, 42 U.S.C. § 2452, does not give the NATIONAL AERONAUTICS AND SPACE ADMINISTRATION a military role in space.

NATIONAL INDUSTRIAL SECURITY PROGRAM A program, established by Exec. Order No. 12829, 58 Fed. Reg. 3479 (Jan 8, 1993), for the purpose of safeguarding CLASSIFIED INFORMATION released to contractors, licensees, or grantees of Government agencies. The Executive Order provided for the issuance and maintenance of a *National Industrial Security Program Manual*, which sets out the specific requirements, restrictions, and other safeguards necessary to protect the classified information.

NATIONAL INSTITUTE OF STANDARDS AND TECHNOLOGY (NISA) The organization (formerly known as the Bureau of Standards) responsible for establishing technical standards for products manufactured and sold in the United States. NIST operates certain FEDERAL TECHNOLOGY TRANSFER programs, such as the Regional Centers for the Transfer of Manufacturing Technology. These programs transfer know-how and technologies developed by NIST and other federal organizations to small and mid-sized manufacturing companies. The organization's authority was extended to cover technology by the Omnibus Trade and Competitiveness Act of 1988, 19 U.S.C. § 2901 et seq. See Duncombe, *Federal Technology Transfer: A Look at the Benefits and Pitfalls of One of the Country's Best Kept Secrets*, 37 Fed. B. News & J. 608 (1990).

NATIONAL PERFORMANCE REVIEW An initiative of the Clinton-Gore Administration created in 1993 "to reform the way the Federal Government works." Headed by Vice President Gore, National Performance Review's interagency task force examined the problems of Government agencies and published reports containing hundreds of proposed recommendations. The task force then began to implement many initiatives contained in the reports. See *The Best Kept Secrets in Government*, Sept. 1996; *Reinvention's Next Steps: Governing in a Balanced Budget World*, Mar. 1996; *Common Sense Government: Works Better and Costs Less*, Sept. 1995; *By the People*, (video) Sept. 1994; *Creating a Government That Works Better and Costs Less: Status Report*, Sept. 1994; *From Red Tape to Results: Creating a Government That Works Better and Costs Less*, Sept. 1993; available from the Government Printing Office. NPR materials and information are also located on the Internet at <http://www.npr.gov>.

NATIONAL SECURITY AND EMERGENCY PREPAREDNESS (NSEP) Those physical, technical, and administrative characteristics of telecommunications systems that will ensure a prescribed level of survivability in times of national or other emergency mission needs of the Government that uses them. 41 C.F.R. § 101-35.5.

NATIONAL SECURITY INDUSTRIAL ASSOCIATION (NSIA) A not-for-profit, nonpolitical, nonlobbying association established in 1944 to foster a close working relationship and effective two-way communication between Government (primarily defense) and its supporting industry. Conceived by James Forrestal, the first Secretary of Defense, NSIA was an association of some 400 industrial, research, legal, and educational organizations of all sizes and representing all segments of industry interested in and related to national security. In 1997 NSIA merged with the American Defense Preparedness Association (ADPA). It is now known as the National Defense Industrial Association (NDIA). NDIA will represent over 900 defense companies and 25,000 individual members. [NDIA, 2111 Wilson Boulevard, Suite 400, Arlington, VA 22201-3061; (703) 522-1820] NDIA's internet site is located at <http://www.adpansia.org>.

NATIONAL SECURITY SYSTEM Any telecommunications or information system operated by the United States Government, the function, operation, or use of which (1) involves intelligence activities, (2) involves cryptologic activities related to national security, (3) involves command and control of military forces, (4) involves equipment that is an integral part of a weapon or WEAPON SYSTEM, or (5) is critical to the direct fulfillment of military or intelligence missions, excluding routine administrative or business applications. FAR 39.002. These systems are not subject to the procedures of the CLINGER-COHEN ACT OF 1996 pertaining to the acquisition of INFORMATION TECHNOLOGY, except for the provisions of Section 5141(b) of that Act. Acquisitions of national security systems are conducted in accordance with 40 U.S.C. § 1412, with regard to requirements for performance- and results-based management, the role of the agency chief information officer in acquisitions, and accountability. FAR 39.001; OMB Circular No. A-130, *Management of Federal Information Resources*, Dec. 12, 1985; Exec. Order No. 13011, 61 Fed. Reg. 37657 (July 16, 1996).

NATIVE AMERICANS American Indians, Eskimos, Aleuts, and native Hawaiians. FAR 19.001. These persons are presumed to be socially and economically disadvantaged for the purposes of determining the ownership of a SMALL DISADVANTAGED BUSINESS CONCERN. See FAR 52.219-8.

NATIVE HAWAIIAN ORGANIZATION Any community service organization serving native Hawaiians in, and chartered as a not-for-profit organization by, the State of Hawaii that is controlled by native Hawaiians and whose business activities will principally benefit native Hawaiians. FAR 19.001. Any SMALL BUSINESS CONCERN that is at least 51 percent owned and controlled by a native Hawaiian organization is a SMALL DISADVANTAGED BUSINESS CONCERN.

NEAR-EXCESS FOREIGN CURRENCY See EXCESS FOREIGN CURRENCY.

NEGATIVE INSTANT CONTRACT SAVINGS The increase in the INSTANT CONTRACT cost or price when the acceptance of a VALUE ENGINEERING CHANGE PROPOSAL results in an excess of the contractor's allowable development and implementation costs over the amount resulting from the INSTANT UNIT COST REDUCTION multiplied by the number of instant contract units affected. FAR 48.001. The Value Engineering clause in FAR 52.248-1 provides that the contract price will be increased when such negative savings (increased costs) occur.

NEGLIGENCE The failure to use such care as a reasonably prudent and careful person would use under similar circumstances. Generally, all persons, including contractors, are liable for personal injury or property damage that occurs because of the negligence of their employees. Similarly, the Government is liable for the negligence of its employees under the FEDERAL TORT CLAIMS ACT unless they are performing a DISCRETIONARY FUNCTION. Most contractors protect against claims for negligence of their employees by INSURANCE, but FAR 28.308 permits SELF-INSURANCE under prescribed circumstances. The Government does not carry insurance but utilizes self-insurance for the negligence of its employees. See Braude, chap. 15, *Construction Contracting* (1991).

NEGOTIATION A method of contracting that uses either competitive or other-than-competitive procedures that permits BARGAINING with the offerors after receipt of PROPOSALs. Any contract awarded without the use of SEALED BIDDING procedures is a negotiated contract. FAR 15.000. Contracting by negotiation is a flexible process that includes the receipt of proposals from offerors, discussion of deficiencies or weaknesses with the offeror, and usually affords offerors an opportunity to revise their offers before award of a contract. In negotiation, award can be made on the basis of technical excellence, management capability, personnel qualifications, prior experience, PAST PERFORMANCE, and other factors bearing on quality, as well as cost. In sealed bidding, only PRICE and PRICE-RELATED FACTORS are considered. Negotiation also permits the use of COST-REIMBURSEMENT CONTRACTs, which provide for payment to the contractor of allowable incurred costs. Prior to the passage of the COMPETITION IN CONTRACTING ACT, negotiation had to be justified. It is now an equally acceptable method of contracting as long as FULL AND OPEN COMPETITION is achieved, in which case it is called the COMPETITIVE PROPOSALS method of contracting. FAR 6.502. See generally Cibinic & Nash, chap. 6, *Formation of Govern-*

ment Contracts (3d ed. 1998); Nash & Cibinic, *Competitive Negotiation: The Source Selection Process* (1993). See also Nash, *Competitive Negotiation: A Better System?*, 6 N&CR ¶ 1 (Jan. 1992); Nash, *Competitive Negotiation vs. Sealed Bidding: Some Limitations on Agency Discretion*, 5 N&CR ¶ 68 (Dec. 1991); Nash, *Evaluation of Risk in Competitive Negotiated Procurement: A Key Element in the Process*, 5 N&CR ¶ 22 (Apr. 1991).

NET BOOK VALUE The stated value of a TANGIBLE CAPITAL ASSET after subtracting DEPRECIATION from the cost of the asset. Net book value of assets is used to compute the COST OF CAPITAL COMMITTED TO FACILITIES under CAS 414, 48 C.F.R. § 9904.414.

NET WORTH The amount stated on a company's BALANCE SHEET when LIABILITIES are subtracted from ASSETs. This amount provides a rough appraisal of the amount of funds a company has retained in its business and thus gives an indication of the financial capability of the company. It is used in making the determination of whether the company is a responsible contractor (see RESPONSIBILITY).

NETWORK ANALYSIS SYSTEM A recognized scheduling system, such as the CRITICAL PATH METHOD, that shows the duration, sequential relationships, and interdependence of various work activities. DFARS 236.102. DFARS 236.273 states that procedures approved by the HEAD OF THE CONTRACTING ACTIVITY must be used for preparing and using both contractor-prepared and Government-prepared network analysis systems in DOD construction contracts. See Margulies, chap. 8, *Construction Contracting* 662–67 (1991).

NEUTRAL See NEUTRAL ADVISOR.

NEUTRAL ADVISOR An individual who functions specifically to aid parties in resolving controversies through ALTERNATIVE DISPUTE RESOLUTION procedures. 5 U.S.C. § 571(9). Neutral advisors have been used extensively in MINITRIALs. The ADMINISTRATIVE DISPUTE RESOLUTION ACT contains detailed provisions regarding the meaning of "neutral" at 5 U.S.C. § 573. These provisions require an interagency committee established by the President to develop procedures that permit agencies to obtain the services of neutrals on an expedited basis. The Act also permits agencies to enter into contracts with neutral advisors.

NO-SETOFF COMMITMENT A contractual agreement that, to the extent permitted by the Assignment of Claims Act, 31 U.S.C. § 3727, payments by the Government to the ASSIGNEE under an ASSIGNMENT OF CLAIMS will not be reduced to liquidate the contractor's indebtedness to the Government that is independent of the contract. FAR 32.801. The Act authorizes such a commitment during a war or other national emergency by DOD, the General Services Administration, NASA, the Coast Guard, or any other agency designated by the President. When this commitment is made, Alternate I to the Assignment of Claims clause in FAR 52.232-23 is included in the contract. See Cibinic & Nash, *Administration of Government Contracts* 1178–80 (3d ed. 1995).

NO-YEAR APPROPRIATION See APPROPRIATION.

NOLO CONTENDERE A Latin phrase meaning "I will not contest it." As a plea in a criminal proceeding, it has an effect similar to pleading guilty; however, in pleading *nolo contendere*, the defendant neither admits nor denies the charges, and the plea cannot be used against the defendant in a civil action based on the same acts. *Black's Law Dictionary* 1048 (6th ed. 1990). A plea of *nolo contendere* is treated as a conviction for the commission of a crime and can be used as a cause for DEBARMENT. FAR 9.403. If legal proceedings for a contractor's violation of law or regulation result in a conviction entered upon a plea of *nolo contendere*, costs related to the proceedings are unallowable. FAR 31.205-47. See Connelly & Schooner, *Recovery of Costs for Defense Against the Government's Charge of Illegality*, 16 Pub. Cont. L.J. 94 (1986).

NONAPPROPRIATED FUNDS Monies derived from sources other than congressional APPROPRIATIONs. An example would be funds derived from the sale of supplies and services to military and civilian personnel and their dependents and used to support or provide recreational, religious, or educational programs or programs to improve welfare or morale. The Department of the Treasury's fiscal records do not account for nonappropriated funds. See Jones, *Glossary: Defense Acquisition Acronyms and Terms* (8th ed., Defense Systems Management College); Adelson, *Protests Against Procurement by Nonappropriated Fund Instrumentalities*, 95-12 Briefing Papers (Nov. 1995).

NONAPPROPRIATED FUNDS INSTRUMENTALITY (NAFI) An organization operated with NONAPPROPRIATED FUNDS. Such instrumentalities may include post or base exchanges, officers and noncommissioned officers clubs, theaters, bowling alleys, and similar facilities at military installations. They are not subject to the FEDERAL ACQUISITION REGULATION but frequently follow procedures essentially the same as those set forth in that regulation. See Adelson, *Protests Against Procurement by Nonappropriated Fund Instrumentalities*, 95-12 Briefing Papers (Nov. 1995)

NONCOMMON CARRIER See CARRIER (TELECOMMUNICATIONS).

NONCOMPENSABLE DELAY See DELAY.

NONDEVELOPMENTAL ITEM (NDI) Any previously developed item of supply used exclusively for Government purposes by a federal agency, a state or local government, or a foreign government with which the United States has a mutual defense cooperation agreement; or any item described above that requires only minor modification or modifications of a type customarily available in the commercial marketplace in order to meet the requirements of the procuring agency; or any item of supply being produced that does not meet the above requirements solely because the item is not yet in use. FAR 2.101. 10 U.S.C. § 2377 and 41 U.S.C. § 2645 state the congressional preference for the acquisition of commercial and nondevelopmental items by the DOD and other agencies. These statutes are implemented in FAR 7.102, 7.103, and 11.002. See DFARS 207.105. See also DOD Regulation 5000.2-R, *Mandatory Procedures for Major Defense Acquisition Programs (MDAPs) and Major Automated Information System (MAIS) Acquisition Programs,* Part 3.3.1.1. See also OFF-THE-SHELF ITEM.

NONPERSONAL HEALTH CARE SERVICES Services of physicians, dentists, and other health care providers obtained by the Government through nonpersonal health care services contracts. Under these contracts, the Government may evaluate the quality of the professional and administrative services provided, but retains no control over the medical aspects of the services, such as professional judgments, diagnosis for specific medical treatments, etc. FAR Subpart 37.4; 10 U.S.C. § 2304; 41 U.S.C. § 253.

NONPERSONAL SERVICES CONTRACT A contract under which the personnel rendering services are not subject, either by the contract's terms or by the manner of its administration, to the supervision and control usually prevailing in relationships between the Government and its employees. FAR 37.101. Such contracts are not subject to the restrictions imposed on PERSONAL SERVICES CONTRACTS. See Ritenburg, *Contracting for the Services of Specific Individuals: Avoiding "Personal Services Contracts,"* 10 N&CR ¶ 10 (Feb. 1996).

NONPROFIT ORGANIZATION A domestic university or other institution of higher education or an organization of the type described in the Internal Revenue Code of 1954, 26 U.S.C. § 501(c)(3), and exempt from taxation under the Internal Revenue Code, 26 U.S.C. § 501(a). Also, a domestic scientific or educational organization qualified under a state nonprofit organization statute. FAR 27.301. Such organizations are entitled to use a PATENT RIGHTS clause in their contracts that permits them to retain TITLE to SUBJECT INVENTIONs (giving the Government a LICENSE) in accordance with 35 U.S.C. § 200–212. See FAR Subpart 27.2. FAR 45.301 defines the term differently: any corporation, foundation, trust, or institution operated for scientific, educational, or medical purposes, not organized for profit, and no part of the net earnings of which inures to the benefit of any private shareholder or individual. This definition determines when a nonprofit educational institution is entitled to be bound by a less stringent clause when accounting for FACILITIES. See FAR 45.302-7. See also Apatoff et al., *Special Rules for Educational and Nonprofit Institutions*, 95-2 Briefing Papers (Apr. 1995).

NONRECURRING COSTS Costs that are incurred by a contractor and are not expected to recur on future work. In MULTIYEAR CONTRACTING nonrecurring production costs, including plant and equipment relocation, plant rearrangement, SPECIAL TOOLING and SPECIAL TEST EQUIPMENT, preproduction engineering, initial spoilage and rework, and special workforce training, are recoverable upon CANCELLATION of the multiyear contract. FAR 17.101. When the Government has paid NONRECURRING COSTs, they may be recovered through RECOUPMENT, in accordance with agency procedures, from contractors that sell, LEASE, or LICENSE the resulting products or technology to buyers other than the Federal Government. See FAR 35.001 and FAR 35.003. See Nash, *Recoupment: A Policy Enigma*, 6 N&CR ¶ 18 (Mar. 1992); Victorino & McQuade, *Nonrecurring Costs Recoupment*, 90-10 Briefing Papers (Sept. 1990).

NONSEVERABLE PRODUCTION AND RESEARCH PROPERTY GOVERNMENT PRODUCTION AND RESEARCH PROPERTY that cannot be removed after erection or installation without substantial loss of value or damage to the property or to the premises where it is installed. FAR 45.301. FAR 45.309 states that the Government should not provide Government production and research property to contractors when it will be installed or constructed on land not owned by the Government in such a way that it becomes nonseverable. The FAR further suggests special legal arrangements that can be made when such property must be provided.

NORTH AMERICAN FREE TRADE AGREEMENT (NAFTA) A treaty, passed by Congress in late 1993, with the goal of integrating the services, industries, and manufacturing economies of the United States, Canada, and Mexico. Part 4, chap. 10, articles 1001 through 1025, of NAFTA deal with Government procurement. The restrictions of the BUY AMERICAN ACT do not apply to offers from companies selling under NAFTA when the contract will be for construction materials with a value of at least $6,500,000 or for Canadian end products with a value above $25,000 or Mexican end products with a value above $50,000. FAR 25.402(a)(3). See Shea, *NAFTA and the FAR—An Opportunity for Businesses in NAFTA Countries*, 36 Cont. Mgmt. 11 (June 1996); Roldan, *Acquisition and NAFTA: An Overview on Government Procurement*, 35 Cont. Mgmt. 10 (May 1995); Sampliner & O'Shea, *Rules of Origin for Foreign Acquisitions under the Trade Agreements Act of 1979, NAFTA, and the New GATT Accords*, 23 Pub. Cont. L.J. 207 (1994).

NOTICE OF AWARD A method of ACCEPTANCE OF OFFER that the Government uses to make an immediate award of a contract. FAR 14.408, FAR 15.504. A notice of award is usually given by telegram or FACSIMILE, and FAR 14.408-1(c)(2) requires that it be followed as soon as possible by the formal award using Standard Form 33, Solicitation, Offer, and Award, FAR 53.301-33, or Standard Form 26, Award/Contract, FAR 53.301-26. FAR 36.304 contains additional guidance on the use of notices of award in construction contracts. See Cibinic & Nash, chap. 5, Sec. III. & chap. 6, *Formation of Government Contracts* (3d ed. 1998); Humphrey & Corrao, *Changes in the Notice of Award, Debriefing, and Protest Rules after FASA*, 95-10 Briefing Papers (Sept. 1995).

NOTICE OF INTENT TO DISALLOW COSTS See DISALLOWANCE.

NOTICE OF INTENTION TO MAKE A SERVICE CONTRACT A notice, submitted by contracting officers to the Wage and Hour Division of the DEPARTMENT OF LABOR (DOL), requesting a

WAGE DETERMINATION under the SERVICE CONTRACT ACT OF 1965. This notice is required to be submitted on all service contracts and modifications over $2,500. FAR 22.1007. It is prepared on Standard Form 98, FAR 53.301-98, in accordance with the instructions in FAR 22.1008. FAR 22.1012 contains detailed procedures governing situations when DOL does not provide a timely response to the notice.

NOTICE TO PROCEED A Government notice that directs the contractor to proceed with the performance of the work called for by a contract. In CONSTRUCTION contracting, it is common practice to require completion of performance in a specified number of days after issuance of the notice to proceed. In such cases, the NOTICE OF AWARD must specify the date of commencement of work or advise that a notice to proceed will be issued. FAR 36.213-4.

NOVATION A legal agreement executed by a contractor (transferor), a successor in interest (transferee), and the Government, by which the transferor guarantees performance of the contract, the transferee assumes all OBLIGATIONs under the contract, and the Government recognizes the transfer of the contract and related ASSETs. FAR 42.1201. Under the common law, a novation is an agreement where a contracting party accepts a new party *in place of* the prior party (relieving the prior party of any further obligations). However, in Government contracting a novation is merely an ASSIGNMENT OF CONTRACT (with the prior party retaining all obligations in the event the new party fails to perform). Although 41 U.S.C. § 15 prohibits assignment of Government contracts, the Government may, in its interest, recognize a third party as the successor in interest to a Government contract when the third party's interest in the contract arises out of the transfer of all the contractor's assets or the entire portion of the assets involved in performing the contract. FAR 42.1204. A format for novation agreements can be found at FAR 42.1204(e). There are now statutory limitations on the RESTRUCTURING COSTS that are permitted in novation agreements. 10 U.S.C. § 2324. See Manos, *Novation Agreements in Corporate Restructuring: The Government's Stealth Weapon*, 26 Pub. Cont. L.J. 339 (1997); Cibinic, *Novation Agreements: Is You Is or Is You Ain't My Baby?,* 4 N&CR ¶ 56 (Sept. 1990); Mullin, *Novation Agreements in Response to Merger and Consolidation in the Aerospace Industry*, 29 A.F. L. Rev. 69 (1988).

O

OBJECT CODE The version of a COMPUTER PROGRAM that is built into or inserted into a COMPUTER to enable the computer to perform an operation or a series of operations. Object code is in a machine-readable form, usually magnetic or optical, and may be stored in the form of a disk, tape, compact disk, computer chip, etc. It is compiled from the SOURCE CODE. Under copyright law, the object code generally may not be copied except for use in the computer for which it was bought or for archival purposes. 17 U.S.C. § 117.

OBLIGATION A definite commitment by the Government to spend APPROPRIATED FUNDS. A binding contract is an obligation. Obligations may not be made prior to the enactment of an APPROPRIATION or other statutory authority. See ANTI-DEFICIENCY ACT. See also Cibinic & Nash, chap. 1, Sec. II., *Formation of Government Contracts* (3d ed. 1998); GAO, *Principles of Federal Appropriations Law*, vol. II, chap. 7 (2d ed. 1991).

OF VALUE See THING OF VALUE.

OFF-THE-SHELF ITEM An ITEM produced and placed in stock by a contractor, or stocked by a distributor, before orders or contracts are received for its sale. The item may be commercial or may be produced to military or federal specification or description. FAR 46.101. "Off-the-shelf" also refers to procurement of existing systems or equipment without a research, development, test, and evaluation program or with only minor development to make the system suitable for Government needs. The item may be a commercial system, commercial equipment, or something already in the Government's inventory. Off-the-shelf items are also known as NONDEVELOPMENTAL ITEMs. Use of such items reduces research and development costs and speeds the ACQUISITION PROCESS. The PACKARD COMMISSION's 1986 report on defense management states: "Rather than relying on excessively rigid military specifications, DOD should make much greater use of components, systems, and services available 'off the shelf.' It should develop new or custom-made items only when it has been established that those readily available are clearly inadequate to meet military requirements."

OFFER A response to a SOLICITATION that, if accepted, would bind the offeror to perform the resultant contract. FAR 2.101. Responses to an INVITATION FOR BIDS, in SEALED BIDDING, are offers that are called BIDs or "sealed bids." Responses to a REQUEST FOR PROPOSALS, in NEGOTIATION, are offers that are called PROPOSALs. Responses to a REQUEST FOR QUOTATIONS, in negotiation, are called QUOTATIONs or "quotes" and are *not* offers. Quotations cannot be accepted by the Government to create a binding contract because they are informational in character and used for planning purposes. FAR 13.004. An offer may also take the form of an UNSOLICITED PROPOSAL, submitted upon the initiative of the submitter. Generally, the Government structures each procurement so that offers are made by prospective contractors and ACCEPTANCE OF AN OFFER is made by the Government. However, in SIMPLIFIED ACQUISITION PROCEDURES, the offer is generally made by the Government by sending the prospective contractor a PURCHASE ORDER.

OFFEROR The party that makes an OFFER and looks for acceptance from the offeree. *Black's Law Dictionary* 1082 (6th ed. 1990). In Government contracting offeror is the generic term for prospective contractors that submit BIDs or PROPOSALs.

OFFICE OF FEDERAL PROCUREMENT POLICY (OFPP) A Government organization, located in the Executive Office of the President (in the OFFICE OF MANAGEMENT AND BUDGET), that is responsible for providing overall executive branch guidance and direction of Government procurement policy and prescribes policies and regulations to be followed by executive agencies in acquiring goods, services, and FACILITIES. 41 U.S.C. § 405. The OFPP leadership role in the procurement process entails, among other things, chairing the FEDERAL ACQUISITION REGULATORY COUNCIL, which formulates Government-wide regulations (the FEDERAL ACQUISITION REGULATION); providing for the General Services Administration's (GSA) FEDERAL PROCUREMENT DATA SYSTEM; providing for a FEDERAL ACQUISITION INSTITUTE at GSA; consulting with agencies (including the SMALL BUSINESS ADMINISTRATION); developing innovative procurement methods and procedures to be tested by selected executive agencies, issuing policy regarding CONFLICT-

OF-INTEREST standards for individuals providing consultant services; establishing and maintaining the COST ACCOUNTING STANDARDS BOARD; and serving as advocate for the acquisition of COMMERCIAL PRODUCTs. See National Archives and Records Administration, *U.S. Government Manual Office of the Federal Register* (GPO 1996/97).

OFFICE OF FEDERAL PROCUREMENT POLICY (OFPP) POLICY LETTERS Policy guidance issued by the OFFICE OF FEDERAL PROCUREMENT POLICY to implement procurement policy in the form of letters that are numbered sequentially by the year of issuance (thus, 91-2 would be the second policy letter issued in 1991). These letters are usually implemented, subsequent to their issuance, in the FEDERAL ACQUISITION REGULATION. OFPP publishes a pamphlet containing all letters still in effect. See OFPP Pamphlet No. 6, *Procurement Policy Letters* (Dec. 1992) (an electronic version was updated in March 1997, see internet site at <http://www.arnet.gov/References/FWD_Index.html>.

OFFICE OF GOVERNMENT ETHICS (OGE) An office of the executive branch of the Government with the responsibility for issuing uniform STANDARDS OF CONDUCT for all Government employees. Exec. Order No. 12674, 54 Fed. Reg. 15159 (Apr. 12, 1989), as amended by Exec. Order No. 12731, 55 Fed. Reg. 42547 (Oct. 17, 1990). See the U.S. Government Manual; Alstott, *The New Standards of Ethical Conduct*, 33 Cont. Mgmt. 10 (Feb. 1993).

OFFICE OF INFORMATION AND REGULATORY AFFAIRS (OIRA) The office, within the OFFICE OF MANAGEMENT AND BUDGET, that oversees the federal regulations and information requirements and develops policies to improve Government statistics and information management. Pursuant to the PAPERWORK REDUCTION ACT OF 1980 and the CLINGER-COHEN ACT OF 1996, the Administrator of OIRA is charged with providing leadership and oversight for the Government's INFORMATION RESOURCES MANAGEMENT activities.

OFFICE OF MANAGEMENT AND BUDGET (OMB) A Government agency, in the Executive Office of the President, that serves as the President's principal arm for exercising the managerial functions of the presidency. 31 U.S.C. § 501. OMB strives to improve Government organization, information, and management systems and devises programs for developing career executive talent throughout the

Government. OMB assists the President in preparing the annual budget and in overseeing its execution. The PAPERWORK REDUCTION ACT OF 1980 imposes a requirement on federal agencies to obtain OMB's approval before collecting information from 10 or more members of the public. The information collection and record-keeping requirements contained in the FEDERAL ACQUISITION REGULATION have been approved by OMB. FAR 1.106. See National Archives and Records Administration, *U.S. Government Manual Office of the Federal Register* (GPO 1996/97).

OFFICE OF MANAGEMENT AND BUDGET (OMB) CIRCULARS Policy guidelines issued by the OFFICE OF MANAGEMENT AND BUDGET to federal agencies to promote efficiency and uniformity in Government activities. The CODE OF FEDERAL REGULATIONS contains an indexed list of these circulars at 5 C.F.R. § 1310.5. OMB Circulars can be obtained from the Office of Administration, Publications Unit, Room G-236, New Executive Office Building, Washington, DC 20503. The contents of OMB Circulars are frequently incorporated into the FEDERAL ACQUISITION REGULATION, but the documents continue to remain in effect as circulars. Relevant OMB Circulars and their FAR references include A-76, *Policies for Acquiring Commercial or Industrial Products and Services Needed by the Government*, FAR Subpart 7.3; A-109, *Major Systems Acquisitions*, FAR Part 34; and A-125, *Prompt Payment*, FAR Subpart 32.9.

OFFICE OF RESEARCH AND TECHNOLOGY APPLICATION (ORTA) An office within a federal laboratory that serves as a federal mechanism for FEDERAL TECHNOLOGY TRANSFER. Created by the Stevenson-Wydler Technology Innovation Act, 15 U.S.C. §§ 3701–3714, ORTAs are responsible for identifying and assessing technologies, know-how, or ideas that may have commercial or other outside applications, as well as cooperating with state and local governments and other federal organizations involved in technology transfer. See Nash, *Transfer of Technology from the Government to the Private Sector: Can it Be Effectively Accomplished?*, 6 N&CR ¶ 40 (July 1992); Duncombe, *Federal Technology Transfer: A Look at the Benefits and Pitfalls of One of the Country's Best Kept Secrets*, 37 Fed. B. News & J. 608 (1990).

OFFICIAL An officer as defined in 5 U.S.C. § 2104, an employee as defined in 5 U.S.C. § 2105, a member of the uniformed services as defined in 5 U.S.C. § 2101(3), or a special Government employee as defined in 18 U.S.C. § 202. FAR 3.104-3. This term is used in the PROCUREMENT INTEGRITY rules that went into effect on January 1, 1997 to define the class of employers subject to the Act if they have participated in a procurement and have had access to CONTRACTOR BID OR PROPOSAL INFORMATION or SOURCE SELECTION INFORMATION. See Nash, *The New Procurement Integrity Rules*, 11 N&CR ¶ 12 (Mar. 1997).

OFFSET The right of a contractor to deduct the amount of understated COST OR PRICING DATA submitted in support of price negotiations on the same transaction from DEFECTIVE COST OR PRICING DATA for which the Government has a claim. Offsets are permitted only when the Government has a legitimate claim for PRICE REDUCTION and then only up to the amount of the Government's claim. FAR 15.407-1. The term offset is also used to mean SETOFF.

OMBUDSMAN An employee of an agency with the authority to hear complaints from OFFERORs or CONTRACTORs, investigate the matter, and propose or implement a solution if the complaint is warranted or explain the matter if the complaint has no merit. 10 U.S.C. § 2304c(d) and 41 U.S.C. § 253j(d) require agencies to establish an ombudsman to hear complaints pertaining to the issuance of ORDERs on multiple award DELIVERY ORDER CONTRACTs and TASK ORDER CONTRACTs. See FAR 16.505(b)(4), which requires this ombudsman to be a senior agency official who is independent of the contracting officer and permits the COMPETITION ADVOCATE to serve in this position. NASA has also created an agency ombudsman and an ombudsmen at each CONTRACTING ACTIVITY to hear any complaint related to a contract or proposed contract. See Cibinic & Nash, chap. 11, Sec. II., *Formation of Government Contracts* (3d ed. 1998); Cibinic, *The Year of the Ombudsmen: A New Wrinkle On Protests,* 10 N&CR ¶ 1 (Jan. 1996).

OMISSIONS AND MISDESCRIPTIONS Omissions or erroneous descriptions of the details of the work in the contract SPECIFICATIONs and DRAWINGS. Since the Government provides the specifications and drawings to the contractor, it is frequently held liable for errors or misdescriptions under the IMPLIED WARRANTY OF SPECIFICATIONS. Some Government agencies attempt to avoid this liability by including an EXCULPATORY CLAUSE in the contract. See, for example, the Contract Drawings, Maps, and Specifications clause in DFARS 252.236-7001, which states that DOD is not liable for omissions and misdescriptions of details of work that are "manifestly necessary to carry out the intent of the drawings and specifications, or which are customarily performed." Such clauses have been effective when the omission or misdescription is in the details of the work. See Cibinic & Nash, *Administration of Government Contracts* 356–58 (3d ed. 1995).

OPERATING REVENUE Amounts accrued or charged to customers, clients, and tenants for the sale of products manufactured or purchased for resale, for services, and for rental of property held primarily for leasing to others. CAS 403, 48 C.F.R. § 9904.403-30. This term is used in connection with the COST ACCOUNTING STANDARDS in 48 C.F.R. chap. 99. Operating revenue includes both reimbursable costs and fees under COST-REIMBURSEMENT CONTRACTs and percentage-of-completion sales accruals, except that it includes only the fees for those management contracts under which the contractor acts essentially as an agent of the Government in erecting or operating Government-owned facilities. Operating revenue excludes incidental interest, dividends, royalties, rental income, and proceeds from the sale of ASSETs used in the business.

OPERATIONAL TEST AND EVALUATION The field test, under realistic combat conditions, of any ITEM of (or key component of) weapons, equipment, or munitions for the purpose of determining their effectiveness and suitability for use in combat by typical military users and the evaluation of the results of such testing. 10 U.S.C. § 139(2)(A). 10 U.S.C. § 2399 requires the completion of operational test and evaluation before a MAJOR DEFENSE ACQUISITION PROGRAM can proceed beyond LOW-RATE INITIAL PRODUCTION. To ensure that this testing is carried out independently, 10 U.S.C. § 139 establishes a separate director of operational test and evaluation in DOD. The procedures for meeting these requirements are set forth in Part 3.4 of DOD Regulation 5000.2-R, *Mandatory Procedures for Major Defense Acquisition Programs (MDAPs) and Major Automated Information System (MAIS) Acquisition Programs*, Mar. 15, 1996.

OPTION A unilateral right in a contract by which, within a specified period, the Government may elect to purchase additional supplies or services called for by the contract or may elect to extend the contract. FAR 17.201. Options are the most frequently used technique in Government contracting to buy goods and services over periods of time longer than the single year for which APPROPRIATIONs are normally made. Since they generally obligate the contractor to a firm pricing structure for a number of years, they are a useful means of preventing

BUYING-IN. When exercising an option, the contracting officer must provide the contractor written notice within the time period specified in the contract. The contracting officer may exercise an option only after determining that (1) funds are available, (2) the requirement covered by the option fulfills an existing Government need, and (3) exercise of the option is the most advantageous method of fulfilling the Government's need, price and other factors considered. FAR 17.207. See the contract clauses at FAR 52.217-3 through -9, which deal with evaluation exclusive of options, evaluation of options, options for increased quantity, and options to extend services or the term of the contract. See also Bruntel & Moosally, *Exercising Options*, 93-11 Briefing Papers (Oct. 1993) and 1995 Revision Note; Nash, *Options: They Seem to Be Many-Splendored Things*, 4 N&CR ¶ 60 (Oct. 1990); Vacketta & Frulla, *"Option" Clauses*, 88-13 Briefing Papers (Dec. 1988).

OPTIONAL FORMS (OFs) Forms used in the procurement process that may be altered at the option of the agency. FAR 53.302 illustrates those few optional forms relevant to procurement, of which the most commonly used is OF 347, Order for Supplies and Services. FAR 53.302-347. OFs are distinguished from STANDARD FORMS by the fact that the latter cannot be altered or substituted for without receipt, in advance, of an exception (an approved departure from the established design, content, printing specifications, or conditions for use). FAR 53.103. Agencies may computer-generate OFs without exception approval, provided that there is no change to the name, content, or sequence of the data elements and that the form carries the OF number and edition date. FAR 53.105. Holders of the loose-leaf edition of the FAR may photocopy the sample OFs from FAR 53.302. Executive agencies obtain OFs through the General Services Administration Supply Catalog (Office Products). Contractors may obtain them from the U.S. Government Printing Office, Washington, DC 20402. See Ferguson & Moss, *FAR Part 53—It's a Matter of Forms*, 24 Cont. Mgmt. 8 (Apr. 1984).

"OR EQUAL" See BRAND-NAME-OR-EQUAL DESCRIPTION.

ORAL PRESENTATION A presentation by an offeror during SOURCE SELECTION usually in lieu of submission of a written technical proposal, to demonstrate its capability to perform a proposed contract. FAR 15.102. The most common use of oral presentations is to present a summary of the methods the OFFEROR will use to perform the contract, followed by questions and answers or the solution of a SAMPLE TASK. Some agencies have also used oral presentations to supplement written proposals. The advantage of the oral presentation is that it permits the agency evaluators to speak directly with the KEY PERSONNEL who will perform the contract if it is awarded to the offeror. See Cibinic & Nash, chap. 6, *Formation of Government Contracts* (3d ed. 1998); Edwards, *Streamlining Source Selection with Oral Presentations* (The Geo. Wash. Univ. Law School, Government Contracts Program 1997); Nash, *Postscript III: Oral Presentations*, 9 N&CR ¶ 64 (Dec. 1995); Nash, *Postscript II: Oral Presentations*, 9 N&CR ¶ 48 (Sept. 1995); Nash, *Postscript: Oral Presentations*, 9 N&CR ¶ 29 (May 1995); Cibinic, *Oral Presentations in Competitive Negotiation: Delayed Second Opinion*, 8 N&CR ¶ 49 (Sept. 1994); Nash, *Oral Presentations in Competitive Negotiation: Could They Be Used in Lieu of Written Proposals?*, 8 N&CR ¶ 48 (Aug. 1994); Corbin, *Oral Presentations During Source Selection: Presentations Versus Discussions*, 33 Cont. Mgmt. 16 (Sept. 1993).

ORDER See JOB ORDER.

ORDER OF PRECEDENCE The hierarchy of various parts of the contract in the CONTRACT INTERPRETATION process. In the absence of a specific contract clause stating an order of precedence, the general rule of common law is that, when contracts contain inconsistencies, specific provisions will prevail over general provisions and written or typed provisions will prevail over general provisions. This general rule does not apply, however, when a specific provision conflicts with a standard Government contract clause required by statute or regulation. Cibinic & Nash, *Administration of Government Contracts* 162–66 (3d ed. 1995). The Order of Precedence clauses in FAR 52.214-29 and FAR 52.215-33 state that inconsistencies in the SOLICITATION or CONTRACT are to be resolved by giving precedence in the following order: (1) the schedule (excluding the SPECIFICATIONs); (2) representations and other instructions; (3) contract clauses; (4) other documents, exhibits, and attachments; and (5) the specifications. See UNIFORM CONTRACT FORMAT. See Cibinic, *Order of Precedence: Resolving the Battle of the Documents*, 4 N&CR ¶ 23 (Apr. 1990).

ORGANIZATION COSTS Costs of organization or reorganization of a business, including but not limited to incorporation fees and costs of attorneys, accountants, brokers, promoters, organizers, management consultants, and investment counselors, whether or not employees of the contractor. FAR 31.205-27. Organization costs in connection with the following are UNALLOWABLE COSTs: (1) planning or executing the organization or reorganization of the corporate structure of a business, including mergers and acquisitions; (2) resisting or planning to resist the reorganization of the corporate structure of a business or a change in the controlling interest in the ownership of a business; and (3) raising capital (NET WORTH plus long-term liabilities). Also unallowable are certain "reorganization" costs, including the cost of any change in the contractor's financial structure (except the administrative costs of short-term borrowings for working capital) resulting in alterations in the rights and interests of security holders, whether or not additional capital is raised. See Cibinic & Nash, *Cost-Reimbursement Contracting* 890–92 (2d ed. 1993).

ORGANIZATIONAL CONFLICT OF INTEREST (OCI) A CONFLICT OF INTEREST of a Government contractor that arises or might arise because the nature of the work to be performed may, absent some restriction on future activities, result in an UNFAIR COMPETITIVE ADVANTAGE to the contractor, impair the contractor's objectivity in performing the contract work, or make the contractor unable or potentially unable to render impartial assistance or advice to the Government. FAR 9.501. The contracting officer is responsible for resolving any significant potential conflicts before the award is made. FAR 9.504 and FAR 9.507. The FAR coverage on OCI also implements OFPP Policy Letter No. 89-1, *Conflict of Interest Policies Applicable to Consultants*, Dec. 8, 1989. In addition, some agencies have unique or additional statutory OCI requirements. According to DOE's OCI regulations, an OCI exists when an offeror or a contractor has past, present, or currently planned interests that (1) either directly or indirectly, through a client relationship, relate to the work to be performed under a DOE contract; and (2) may diminish the offeror's or contractor's capacity to give impartial, technically sound assistance and advice or may give the offeror or contractor an unfair COMPETITIVE ADVANTAGE. Offerors and contractors include chief executives and directors who will or do become involved in the contract performance and proposed consultants or subcontractors who may perform services similar to the services provided by the prime contractor. DEAR 909.570-3. See Woodruff, *Organizational Conflicts of Interest: Not What It's Said to Be*, 16 Pub. Cont. L.J. 213 (1986); Taylor, *Organizational Conflicts of Interest in Department of Defense Contracting*, 14 Pub. Cont. L.J. 158 (1983); Taylor, *Organizational Conflicts of Interest/Ed. II*, 84-8 Briefing Papers (Aug. 1984); Madden et al., *Organizational Conflicts of Interest/Ed. III*, 94-8 Briefing Papers (July 1994) and 1995 Revision Note.

ORIGINAL COMPLEMENT OF LOW-COST EQUIPMENT A group of items acquired for the initial outfitting of a TANGIBLE CAPITAL ASSET or an operational unit or as a new addition to either. FAR 31.001. The items in the group individually cost less than the minimum amount established by the contractor for CAPITALIZATION of the classes of assets acquired, but in the aggregate they represent a material investment. Under the COST PRINCIPLES in FAR Part 31, the group, as a complement, is expected to be held for continued service beyond the current accounting period. Initial outfitting is completed when the unit is ready and available for normal operations. These costs must be capitalized if in total they exceed the threshold in the contractor's capitalization policy, CAS 404.40. See Cibinic & Nash, *Cost-Reimbursement Contracting* 847 (3d ed. 1993).

ORIGINAL SOURCE An individual who has direct and independent knowledge of information on which a qui tam action (see QUI TAM PROCEEDING) is based and has voluntarily provided the information to the Government before filing the action. 31 U.S.C. § 3730(e)(4)(B). Courts have no jurisdiction over qui tam actions based on public disclosure of allegations or transactions unless the action is brought by a person who is an original source. 31 U.S.C. § 3730(e)(4)(A). See Vogel, *The Public Disclosure Bar Against Qui Tam Suits*, 24 Pub. Cont. L.J. 477 (1995); Fentin, *The False Claims Act—Finding Middle Ground Between Opportunity & Opportunism: The "Original Source" Provision of 31 U.S.C. § 3730(e)(4)*, 17 W. New Eng. L. Rev. 255 (1995); Victorino et al., *"Qui Tam" Lawsuits*, 89-10 Briefing Papers (Sept. 1989).

OTHER THAN FULL AND OPEN COMPETITION The exclusion of a source that would be required to be included under the statutory exceptions to the FULL AND OPEN COMPETITION requirement. 10 U.S.C. § 2304(c) and 41 U.S.C. § 253(a) provide for seven circumstances permitting contracting without full and open competition: (1) only one responsible source; (2) UNUSUAL AND COMPELLING URGENCY; (3) INDUSTRIAL MOBILIZATION, or the need to maintain engineering, developmental, or research capability; (4) international agreement; (5) statutory authorization or requirement; (6) risk of compromising the national security; and (7) protecting the public interest. FAR Subpart 6.3 provides guidance for contracting without providing for full and open competition. See Cibinic & Nash, chap. 3, Sec. II., *Formation of Government Contracts* (3d ed. 1998).

OTHER TRANSACTIONS A form of CONTRACT, used by DOD, that is not a procurement contract, GRANT, or COOPERATIVE AGREEMENT, and is thus not subject to many of the statutes and regulations governing those types of instruments. This instrument has been used primarily by the Defense Advanced Research Projects Agency pursuant to 10 U.S.C. § 2371, giving authority to use it for basic, applied, and advanced research projects, and 10 U.S.C. § 845, giving authority to use it for prototypes. See Cibinic & Nash, chap. 1, Sec. I, *Formation of Government Contracts* (3d ed. 1998); Dunn & Dees, *Debate on Extension of "Other Transactions" Authority*, 39 Gov't Contractor ¶ 421 (Aug. 27, 1997); Cibinic, *Postscript II: Cooperative Agreements and "Other Transactions,"* 10 N&CR ¶ 2 (Jan. 1996); Cibinic, *Postscript: Cooperative Agreements*, 9 N&CR ¶ 53 (Oct. 1995); Kuyath, *The Untapped Potential of the Department of Defense's "Other Transactions" Authority*, 24 Pub. Cont. L.J. 521 (1995); Bierbower, *"Other Transactions": A Better Mechanism for Federally Funded Research & Development?*, 31 Procmt. Law. 25 (Fall 1995).

OUTSOURCING The transfer of activities that are being performed by federal employees at federal facilities to private contractor employees at federal or private facilities. Outsourcing decisions are governed by the policies and procedures contained in OMB Circular No. A-76 (revised), *Performance of Commercial Activities*, Aug. 4, 1983, and its *Revised Supplemental Handbook*, Mar. 1996. Circular A-76 requires federal agencies to compare the cost of contracting and the cost of in-house performance to determine whether commercial activities should be outsourced. Outsourcing is limited to those activities that are not defined as INHERENTLY GOVERNMENTAL FUNCTIONS. Such activities are those that are so intimately related to the public interest that they must be performed by Government employees. They typically involve the discretionary exercise of Government authority or the performance of monetary transactions for the Government. Detailed guidance is provided by OFPP Policy Letter No. 92-1, *Inherently Governmental Functions*, Sept. 23, 1992. See Dover, *Outsourcing & Privatization: Recent Developments*, 97-4 Briefing Papers (Mar. 1997).

OVERHEAD See INDIRECT COST.

OVERHEAD RATE A percentage rate that is derived by dividing a contractor's INDIRECT COST POOL for an accounting period by the ALLOCATION BASE used to allocate INDIRECT COSTs to contracts performed during the period (see ALLOCATION OF COST). CAS 418, 48 C.F.R. § 9904.418, provides guidance on the selection of allocation bases that equitably allocate indirect costs. See Cibinic & Nash, *Cost-Reimbursement Contracting* 668–76 (2d ed. 1993).

OVERRUN An amount by which the ACTUAL COST of performance exceeds the amount budgeted for the work. Programs are said to be overrun when the original budget is exceeded. Contracts are said to be overrun when the original price or cost estimate is exceeded or when the total costs incurred exceed the price or estimated cost as adjusted in accordance with contract clauses (depending on the usage of the term). The procedures for dealing with COST OVERRUNs on COST-REIMBURSEMENT CONTRACTs are set forth in the LIMITATION OF COST CLAUSE. See Christensen, *Cost Overrun Optimism: Fact or Fiction?*, 1 Acquisition Rev. Q. 25 (Win. 1994); Cibinic, *Notice of Cost Overruns: Tell It Like It Is*, 7 N&CR ¶ 5 (Jan. 1993).

OVERTIME Time worked by a contractor's employee in excess of the employee's normal workweek or workday. FAR 22.103-1. "Normal workweek" means, generally, a workweek of 40 hours. FAR 22.103-2 provides that contractors must perform Government contracts, so far as is practicable, without using overtime, particularly as a regular employment practice, except when lower overall costs to the Government will result or when overtime is necessary to meet urgent program needs. Any approved overtime, extra-pay shifts, and multishifts should be scheduled to achieve these objectives. FAR 22.103-2. The contracting officer must review any contractor requests for overtime. FAR 22.103-4. The CONTRACT WORK HOURS AND SAFETY STANDARDS ACT requires that LABORERS OR MECHANICS employed by construction contractors be paid premium wages (not less than one-and-one-half times the basic rate) for overtime hours. See FAR Subpart 22.3. This requirement is implemented by including the Contract Work Hours and Safety Standards Act—Overtime Compensation clause in FAR 52.222-4 in such contracts. See Oyer, *Uncompensated Overtime—The Debate Continues*, 92-9 CP&A Rep. 3 (Sept. 1992); Bauder, *Uncompensated Overtime: Is It in the Government's Best Interest?,* 29 Cont. Mgmt. 10 (July 1989); Cibinic, *Uncompensated Overtime: White Collar Sweatshops?,* 3 N&CR ¶ 21 (Mar. 1989).

P

PACKAGING See BUNDLING.

PACKARD COMMISSION The popular name of the President's Blue Ribbon Commission on Defense Management, which published its final report, *A Quest for Excellence*, in June 1986. Chaired by David Packard, the commission made a number of significant recommendations on reorganizing the Joint Chiefs of Staff, the defense command structure, and the defense acquisition process, including creating the position of Under Secretary of Defense for Acquisition. The commission's acquisition task force suggested (1) streamlining acquisition organization and procedures, (2) using technology to reduce costs, (3) balancing cost and performance, (4) stabilizing programs, (5) expanding the use of COMMERCIAL PRODUCTs, and (6) enhancing the quality of acquisition personnel. The commission's preliminary report is called *A Formula for Action: A Report to the President on Defense Acquisition* (Apr. 1986). See Cavanaugh & Kalkowski, *The Packard Commission: A Blueprint for Change*, 26 Cont. Mgmt. 14 (Apr. 1986).

PAPERWORK REDUCTION ACT OF 1980 An Act, 44 U.S.C. § 3501 et seq., whose major purpose is to minimize the federal paperwork burden for individuals, small businesses, state and local governments and other persons. Among other objectives, it seeks to "ensure that automatic data processing and telecommunications technologies are acquired and used by the Federal Government in a manner which improves service delivery and program management." The Act created the Office of Information and Regulatory Affairs in the OFFICE OF MANAGEMENT AND BUDGET to "implement policies and oversee, review, and approve the acquisition and use of automatic data processing telecommunications and other technology for managing information." It directed each executive agency to designate a senior official (see DESIGNATED SENIOR OFFICIAL) to ensure that all automatic data processing and telecommunications acquisitions are conducted properly.

PAPERWORK REDUCTION REAUTHORIZATION ACT OF 1986 An Act, 44 U.S.C. § 101 and 3503, whose purpose is to maximize the usefulness of information collected, maintained and disseminated by the Federal Government. The Act (1) defined AUTOMATIC DATA PROCESSING EQUIPMENT for purposes of the BROOKS ACT (AUTOMATIC DATA PROCESSING PROCUREMENTS) (repealed in 1996 by Pub. L. No. 104-106); (2) defined the term information resources management; (3) required agencies, through the OFFICE OF MANAGEMENT AND BUDGET, to develop or revise five-year automatic data processing plans each year; and (4) created the INFORMATION TECHNOLOGY FUND.

PARALLEL PROCEEDING A simultaneous proceeding, whether administrative, civil, or criminal, brought by the Government in another forum against a contractor litigating a contract CLAIM before a BOARD OF CONTRACT APPEALS (BCA). This situation raises complex strategic decisions for both the Government and the contractor. For example, when the contractor is litigating an affirmative claim before a BCA, Government counsel may move to stay the BCA action pending the outcome of a criminal action. See the President's Council on Integrity and Efficiency booklet, *Guidelines for Civil Fraud Remedies and Parallel Proceedings* (Sept. 1985); McCastlain & Schooner, *To Stay or Not to Stay: Difficult Decisions for Boards of Contract Appeals Confronted with Parallel Proceedings*, 16 Pub. Cont. L.J. 418 (1987) (which concludes with an analytical guide stressing four considerations: BCA jurisdiction, commonality of issues, prejudice to the parties, and the question whether the equities favor one party over the other); Barletta & Pollack, *Civil Litigation of Allegations of Fraud in Connection with Government Contract Claims*, 18 Pub. Cont. L.J. 235 (1988).

PARENT COMPANY A company that, for the purposes of bidding, owns or controls the activities and basic business policies of the bidder. To own the bidder, the company must own more than 50 percent of the voting rights in the bidder's company. To control the bidder without owning it, the company must be able to formulate, determine, or veto basic policy decisions of the bidder through the use of dominant minority voting rights, use of proxy voting, or otherwise.

PAROL EVIDENCE RULE A rule of evidence that prohibits the introduction of extrinsic evidence to contradict terms of an integrated agreement. Thus, in the absence of FRAUD, DURESS, MUTUAL MISTAKE, or something of the kind, the parol evidence rule will preclude a party from presenting prior written or oral agreements to prove that the words of a contract have a meaning contrary to their clear meaning. Restatement (Second) Contracts § 215 (1981). However, the rule is of limited effect in preventing the use of extrinsic evidence in Government contract controversies because it does not apply when the sole issue is interpretation of ambiguous language. See Cibinic & Nash, Administration of Government Contracts 187–218 (3d. ed. 1995).

PARTIAL PAYMENT A payment made, as authorized by the contract, upon delivery and Government acceptance of one or more complete units (or one or more distinct items of service) as called for by the Government under the contract, even though other quantities remain to be delivered. Partial payments are permitted on any contract where the unit of work is priced in a separate CONTRACT LINE ITEM. Although partial payments are not generally considered FINANCING PAYMENTs, they can help contractors participate in Government contracts without, or with only minimal, contract financing. FAR 32.102(d). A payment made against a termination claim before final settlement of the total termination claim is also called a "partial payment." Under contracts authorizing partial payments on termination SETTLEMENT PROPOSALs before settlement, contractors may request partial payment at any time after submission of interim or final settlement proposals. FAR 49.112-1. FAR 49.602-4 prescribes use of Standard Form 1440, Application for Partial Payment, in FAR 53.301-1440. See also TERMINATION FOR CONVENIENCE.

PARTIAL SET-ASIDE See SET-ASIDE (n).

PARTIAL TERMINATION The termination of a part, but not all, of the work that has not been completed and accepted under a contract. FAR 49.001. The Government is entitled to require the contractor to complete unterminated work. See Cibinic & Nash, *Administration of Government Contracts* 1083 (3d ed. 1995). See also FAR 49.603-2; FAR 49.603-5; FAR 49.603-7.

"PARTICIPATED PERSONALLY AND SUBSTANTIALLY" A key term, under the PROCUREMENT INTEGRITY provisions of the FAR, that refers to an individual's active and significant involvement in activities directly related to the procurement. 41 U.S.C. § 423; FAR 3.104-3. Such individuals are subject to the procurement integrity rules. To participate "personally" means to be involved directly and includes the participation of a subordinate when the subordinate was directed by the supervisor in the matter. To participate "substantially" means to be involved in a significant way. Substantial participation requires more than official responsibility or knowledge, perfunctory involvement, or involvement on an administrative or peripheral issue. A finding of substantiality should be based not only on the effort devoted to a matter, but also on the importance of the effort. While a series of peripheral involvements may be insubstantial, the single act of approving or participating in a critical step may be substantial. An employee whose responsibility is to review a procurement solely for compliance with administrative procedures or budgetary considerations and who reviews a document involved in the procurement for such a purpose should not be regarded as having participated substantially in the procurement. See Nash, *The New Procurement Integrity Rules*, 11 N&CR ¶ 12 (Mar. 1997).

PARTIES EXCLUDED FROM FEDERAL PROCUREMENT AND NONPROCUREMENT PROGRAMS See LIST OF PARTIES EXCLUDED FROM FEDERAL PROCUREMENT AND NONPROCUREMENT PROGRAMS.

PARTNERING A procedure, adopted at the beginning of performance of a contract, to encourage the employees of the contractor and the Government to work together to achieve the contract objectives. Partnering involves the development of a cooperative management team, representing both the Government and the contractor, that seeks to identify common goals and objectives. Both sides work to bring about a "mutual win" situation and discourage an "us against them" attitude. The goal is to avoid litigation that involves unnecessary expense, delay, and disruption. See Edelman et al., *Partnering*, Army Corps of Engineers Pamphlet 91-ADR-P-4 (Dec. 1991); Nash, *Partnering: A New Corps of Engineering Effort to Avoid Disputes*, 5 N&CR ¶ 32 (June 1991).

PAST PERFORMANCE An EVALUATION FACTOR used to assess an offeror's capability, comprising of three elements: "(1) observations of the historical facts of a company's work experience—what work it did, when and where it did it, whom it did it for, and what methods it used; (2) qualitative judgments about the breadth, depth, and relevance of that experience based on those observations; and (3) qualitative judgments about how well the company performed, also based on those observations." Edwards, *How to Evaluate Past Performance: A Best Value Approach* (The Geo. Wash. Univ. Law School, Government Contracts Program 1996). FAR 15.304(c)(2) makes past performance a mandatory evaluation factor for negotiated competitive acquisitions expected to exceed $1 million. The solicitation must describe the approach for evaluating past performance, including evaluating offerors with no relevant performance history, and provide offerors an opportunity to identify past contracts (including federal, state, and local government and private) for efforts similar to the Government requirement. A contractor's past performance is evaluated on the basis of PAST PERFORMANCE INFORMATION that is obtained by checking references on single procurements or from data banks. See Pushkar et al., *Past Performance Evaluations*, Briefing Papers 94-6 (May 1994). Firms lacking relevant performance history or for whom no information is available may not be evaluated favorably or unfavorably on this factor. FAR 15.305(a)(2)(iv); 41 U.S.C. § 405(j)(2). See Nash, *Best Value Procurement: Random Musings on the Current State of the Art*, 11 N&CR ¶ 44 (Sept. 1997); Nash, *Past Performance Evaluations: Are They Fair?*, 11 N&CR ¶ 21 (May 1997); Subramanian, *The Implications of the FAR Rewrite for Meaningful Discussions of Past Performance*, 26 Pub. Cont. L.J. 445 (1997); Kelman, *Past Performance as an Evaluation Factor—Strengthening the Government's Best Value Decisions*, 38 Gov't Contractor ¶ 463 (Oct. 2, 1996); Cibinic, *Customer Relations: Valid Procurement Tool, Means for Extortion, or Open Door to Cronyism?*, 10 N&CR ¶ 37 (July 1996); Pachter & Shaffer, *Past Performance as an Evaluation Factor—Opening Pandora's Box*, 38 Gov't Contractor ¶ 280 (June 12, 1996); Nash, *Postscript II: Past Performance*, 9 N&CR ¶ 47 (Aug. 1995); Clark & Blum, *Changing the Way the Government Uses Past Performance Information*, 34 Cont. Mgmt. 4 (Nov. 1994); Cibinic, *Postscript: Past Performance*, 8 N&CR ¶ 33 (June 1994); Pushkar et al., *Past Performance Evaluations*, 94-6 Briefing Papers (May 1994); Cibinic, *Consideration of Past Performance in Contract Awards: "What is Past is Prologue*," 6 N&CR ¶ 8 (Feb. 1992).

PAST PERFORMANCE INFORMATION Relevant information, for future SOURCE SELECTION purposes, regarding a contractor's actions under previously awarded contracts, including the contractor's record of conforming to SPECIFICATIONs and standards of good workmanship, record of containing and forecasting costs on cost-reimbursable contracts, adherence to contract schedules, history of reasonable and cooperative behavior, commitment to customer satisfaction, and concern for the interest of the customer. FAR 42.1501 and OFPP Policy Letter No. 92-5, *Past Performance Information*, Jan. 11, 1993, require agencies to collect this information on major contracts and to make the data available for use in evaluating offerors on negotiated procurements. Agency evaluations of a contractor's past performance must be provided to the contractor as soon as practicable after completion of the evaluation. The contractor will then be given at least 30 days to submit comments, rebutting statements, or additional information. FAR 42.1503(b). See West & Mehta, *How the Skeletons in Your Closet Can Scare Away Government Business: The Use of Past Performance Information in the Source Selection Process*, 36 Cont. Mgmt. 4 (Dec. 1996); Nash, *Performance Information Systems: Is More Information Better?*, 7 N&CR ¶ 6 (Jan. 1993); Nash, *Evaluation of Risk in Competitive Negotiated Procurements: A Key Element in the Process*, 5 N&CR ¶ 22 (Apr. 1991).

PATENT (adj) Readily discoverable by observation or inspection. The adjective "patent" can refer to the type of deficiency potentially found in solicitations or contracts (patent AMBIGUITY) or in contract performance (PATENT DEFECT). Patent means "open or manifest" and is an antonym for LATENT.

PATENT (n) A grant of some privilege, property, or authority made by the Government to one or more individuals. A patent is the instrument by which the Government grants or conveys to an inventor the exclusive right to make, use, and sell an invention for 20 years from the date of filing with the Patent Office. *Black's Law Dictionary* 1125 (6th ed. 1990). The Government honors rights in patents and complies with the stipulations of law in using or acquiring such rights. FAR 27.104(g). 28 U.S.C. § 1498(a) provides that the Government will pay reasonable compensation if it, or its contractors with AUTHORIZATION AND CONSENT, infringe a patent. FAR Subpart 27.2 prescribes policy with respect to PATENT RIGHTS in inventions made during the performance of Government contracts, the granting of authorization and consent to infringe patents, patent infringement liability of contractors through PATENT INDEMNIFICATION, royalties payable in connection with performing Government contracts, and security requirements covering patent applications containing classified subject matter filed by contractors. FAR 31.205-30 makes the costs of obtaining patents that are required by a contract ALLOWABLE COSTs. See Hildebrant, *Recovering Patent-Related Costs Under Government Contracts*, 97-1 CP&A Rep. 3 (Jan. 1997).

PATENT AMBIGUITY See AMBIGUITY.

PATENT DEFECT A defect in the contract work that is discoverable by the Government by the use of reasonable INSPECTION methods. In accordance with the Inspection of Supplies—Fixed-Price clause in FAR

52.246-2 and the Inspection of Construction clause in FAR 52.246-12, Government ACCEPTANCE OF WORK containing patent defects is conclusive on the Government—with the result that the Government cannot require the contractor to correct such defective work at the contractor's own expense. The fact that the Government did not inspect the work is not relevant to the determination of whether a defect was patent. The issue is whether the defect *could have been discovered* had the Government conducted a reasonable inspection. A patent defect is the opposite of a LATENT DEFECT. See Cibinic & Nash, *Administration of Government Contracts* 866–84 (3d ed. 1995); Nash, *Design Defects in Manufacturing Contracts: Is the Contractor Liable?,* 8 N&CR ¶ 5 (Feb. 1994); Victorino & Ivey, *The "Inspection" Clause*, 88-10 Briefing Papers 8 (Sept. 1988).

PATENT INDEMNIFICATION The promise of a contractor to reimburse the Government for any amount the Government is required to pay an owner of a PATENT for use of that patent during performance of the contract. FAR 27.203 states the policy of the Government to obtain patent indemnification from all contractors (including construction contractors) furnishing supplies or services that normally are or have been sold or offered for sale to the public in the commercial open market or are the same as such supplies or services except for minor modifications. Such indemnification is necessary because the Government is primarily liable for paying compensation to the owner of a patent under 28 U.S.C. § 1498(a). See AUTHORIZATION AND CONSENT. The Government obtains patent indemnification by using the Patent Indemnification clauses in FAR 52.227-3 and -4. If the contract work contains some commercial supplies and services and some work made to the design of the Government, the FAR requires the contracting officer to segregate the commercial work and to provide for indemnification for that work only.

PATENT INFRINGEMENT Selling, making, or using a patented invention without the consent of the owner of the PATENT. Under the patent laws, the owner of a patent can usually obtain an injunction against patent infringement or damages for infringement. Such injunctions are not permitted against the Government because the only remedy for infringement by the Government or its contractors with AUTHORIZATION AND CONSENT is reasonable compensation under the provisions of 28 U.S.C. § 1498(a). See Nash & Rawicz, *Intellectual Property in Government Contracts*, vol. 1 (3d ed. 1997); McGrath, *The Unauthorized Use of Patents by the United States Government or Its Contractors*, 18 AIPLA L.J. 349 (1991).

PATENT LICENSE An agreement of the owner of a PATENT to permit another party to make, use, or sell an invention to the extent the owner has such a right. The Government obtains a license in all SUBJECT INVENTIONs under its policy on PATENT RIGHTS. In addition, 10 U.S.C. § 2386 gives DOD the right to acquire patent licenses. FAR 31.205-37 makes the costs incurred by contractors for licenses ALLOWABLE COSTs unless the Government has license rights or the patent is invalid, unenforceable, or expired.

PATENT RIGHTS The rights of the Government in PATENTs resulting from inventions made during the performance of Government contracts (see SUBJECT INVENTIONs). 35 U.S.C. § 202 requires the Government to permit all SMALL BUSINESS CONCERNs and NONPROFIT ORGANIZATIONs to take TITLE to all subject inventions and provides that the Government will have, at a minimum, a nonexclusive, nontransferable, irrevocable, paid-up LICENSE to practice the invention on its own behalf. This, in effect, divides the rights in a patent—giving the contractor commercial rights to it and the Government the right to use it for Government purposes. A presidential memorandum "Government Patent Policy," Feb. 18, 1983, requires that this policy be followed with regard to large contractors to the extent authorized by law. This policy is implemented in FAR Subpart 27.3. See Geary, *Protecting the Patent Rights of Small Business: Does the Bayh-Dole Act Live Up to Its Promise?*, 22 Pub. Cont. L.J. 101 (1992); Nash, *Patent Rights: Parallel Development Projects*, 1 N&CR ¶ 32 (Apr. 1987).

PAY-AS-YOU-GO See BUDGET ENFORCEMENT ACT OF 1990.

PAY-AS-YOU-GO COST METHOD A method of recognizing PENSION PLAN costs only when benefits are paid to retired employees or their beneficiaries. FAR 31.001. For pay-as-you-go pension plans, the entire cost assignable to a cost accounting period may be assigned to the COST OBJECTIVEs of that period only if the payment of benefits can be compelled. Otherwise, the assignable cost is limited to the amount of benefits actually paid. CAS 412, Cost Accounting Standard for Composition and Measurement of Pension Costs, 48 C.F.R. § 9904.412-40(c). See Mizoguchi, *Post-Retirement Benefits: Accounting for and Recovering the Cost of Health Care for Retirees*, 24 Pub. Cont. L.J. 357 (1995).

PAYMENT The satisfaction of the Government's OBLIGATION to compensate the contractor in accordance with the terms of a contract.

The Government's payment obligation is not dealt with in any single part of the FAR but is scattered through various parts. Most of the clauses setting forth the requirements for payment are contained in FAR 52.216 or FAR 52.232. See, for example, the standard Allowable Cost and Payment clause in FAR 52.216-7, which is used in cost-reimbursement contracts; the Payments clause in FAR 52.232-1, which is used in fixed-price supply contracts; and the Payments under Fixed-Price Construction Contracts clause in FAR 52.232-5. Payment may be made in the form of PROGRESS PAYMENTs, PARTIAL PAYMENTs, and FINAL PAYMENTs. The PROMPT PAYMENT ACT uses the terms INVOICE PAYMENTs and FINANCING PAYMENTs. See Cibinic & Nash, *Administration of Government Contracts* 1135–76 (3d ed. 1995); Nash, chap. 12, *Construction Contracting* 897–927 (1991); Murphy, *The Case Against Limiting the Base for Computing Progress Payments to Allowable Costs*, 95-3 CP&A Rep. 3 (Mar. 1995); Nash, *Application of the Prompt Payment Act to Interim Payments on Cost Reimbursement Contracts*, 6 N&CR ¶ 26 (Apr. 1992).

PAYMENT BOND A promise of a SURETY assuring payment to all persons supplying LABOR or materials in the work provided for in a contract. FAR 28.001. This bond is purchased by a prospective contractor in accordance with the requirement of the Government. The MILLER ACT requires such bonds for construction contracts exceeding $100,000, and they may occasionally be required for other contracts as well. FAR 28.102-1, FAR 28.103. The PENAL AMOUNT of Miller Act payment bonds must be (1) 50 percent of the contract price if that price does not exceed $1 million, (2) 40 percent of the contract price if that price is more than $1 million but not more than $5 million, or (3) $2.5 million if the contract price is more than $5 million. FAR 28.102-2. The bond is furnished on Standard Form 25-A, FAR 53.301-25-A. In lieu of furnishing a payment bond a contractor may deposit securities. FAR 28.204. See Patin, chap. 17, *Construction Contracting* 1222–1309 (1991).

PAYMENT DATE For the purposes of the PROMPT PAYMENT ACT, the date on which a Government check for payment to a contractor is dated or; for an ELECTRONIC FUNDS TRANSFER, the SPECIFIED PAYMENT DATE. FAR 32.902.

PEER OR SCIENTIFIC REVIEW A process of proposal review that utilizes a group of experts in the field represented by the proposal to evaluate the proposal for merit. FAR 6.102(d)(2) provides that the award of basic and applied research contracts in response to a BROAD AGENCY ANNOUNCEMENT using a peer or scientific review is a competitive procedure. See NFS Subpart 18-72.4.

PENAL AMOUNT The amount of money specified in a BOND (or a percentage of the bid price in a BID BOND) as the maximum payment for which the SURETY is obligated. FAR 28.001. For example, on CONSTRUCTION contracts, the penal amount of performance bonds must normally be 100 percent of the original contract price, unless the contracting officer determines that a lesser amount would be adequate for the protection of the Government. The penal amount of payment bonds must equal (1) 50 percent of the contract price if that price is not more than $1 million, (2) 40 percent if the contract price is between $1 million and $5 million, or (3) $2.5 million if the contract price exceeds $5 million. FAR 28.102-2.

PENAL SUM See PENAL AMOUNT.

PENALTY A punishment for the commission of a criminal act or the BREACH OF a CONTRACT. FAR 31.205-15(a) makes the costs of penalties resulting from violations of, or failure to comply with, federal, state, local, or foreign laws and regulations unallowable (see UNALLOWABLE COST) unless they are incurred as a result of compliance with specific TERMS AND CONDITIONS of a contract or written instructions from a contracting officer. FAR 31.205-47, dealing with the allowability of the costs of legal and other proceedings, states that penalties do not include restitution, reimbursement, or compensatory damages. If LIQUIDATED DAMAGES are found to constitute a penalty, the Government may not enforce them.

PENSION PLAN A DEFERRED COMPENSATION plan established and maintained by one or more employers to provide systematically for the payment of benefits to plan participants after their retirements, provided that the benefits are paid for life or are payable for life at the option of the employee. FAR 31.001. Additional benefits, such as permanent and total disability payments, death payments, and survivorship payments to beneficiaries of deceased employees, may be an integral part of a pension plan. Pension plans are generally either the insured type (insured under a contract with a life insurance company) or the trustee type (self-insured under a formal trust agreement with a trustee). The allowability of costs (see ALLOWABLE COST) incurred by a contractor to fund pension plans is governed by FAR 31.205-6(j). The allocability of such costs (see ALLOCABLE COST) is covered in

CAS 412 and CAS 413, 48 C.F.R. § 9904.412 and 48 C.F.R. § 9904.413. See *DCAA Contract Audit Manual* 7-600; Pompeo, *Segment Closure Pension Accounting Under Gould*, 97-9 CP&A Rep. 3 (Sept. 1997); McQuade & Buss, *The New CAS 412 & 413: Significant Pension Accounting Changes*, 95-4 CP&A Rep. 3 (Apr. 1995).

PERFORMANCE-BASED CONTRACTING A method of acquisition in which all aspects of the acquisition are structured around the purpose of the work to be performed rather than either the manner by which it is to be done or broad and imprecise statements of work. FAR 37.101. OFPP Policy Letter No. 91-2, *Service Contracting*, Apr. 9, 1991, requires that federal agencies use performance-based contracting methods to the maximum extent practicable when acquiring services. Performance-based contracting emphasizes objective, measurable performance requirements and quality standards in developing STATEMENTs OF WORK, selecting contractors, determining contract type and incentives, and performing contract administration. FAR 37.601 encourages the use of measurable performance standards, price or fee reduction provisions for nonperformance of services and performance incentives in such contracts. See OFPP *A Guide to Best Practices for Performance-Based Service Contracting* (Interim ed., Apr. 1996); Nash, *Performance-Based Service Contracting: The New FAR Guidance*, 11 N&CR ¶ 56 (Nov. 1997); Cibinic, *Performance-Based Service Contracting: Negative Incentives—Liquidated Damages or Penalties?*, 11 N&CR ¶ 40 (Aug. 1997).

PERFORMANCE-BASED PAYMENTS Contract FINANCING PAYMENTS on fixed-price-type contracts that are not payments for accepted items but are based on objective performance measures, accomplishment of defined events, or other quantifiable measures of results (milestones). FAR 32.1002. Guidance on the use of these payments is set forth in FAR Subpart 32.10. FAR 32.1000 states that PROGRESS PAYMENTs based on a percentage of completion (used in construction, architect-engineer, and shipbuilding contracts) are not subject to this guidance. These payments may not be used on COST-REIMBURSEMENT CONTRACTS (FAR 32.1000(a)), RESEARCH AND DEVELOPMENT contracts (FAR 32.1000(c)), contracts awarded using COMPETITIVE PROCEDURES (FAR 32.1000(d) or contracts with other types of financing payments (FAR 32.1003(c)). When used, they may not exceed 90 percent of the contract price of the entire contract or an item delivered under the contract. FAR 32.1004(b)(2).

PERFORMANCE-BASED SERVICE CONTRACTING (PBSC) See PERFORMANCE-BASED CONTRACTING.

PERFORMANCE BOND A promise of a SURETY, sometimes referred to as a "completion bond," assuring the Government that once the contract is awarded, the contractor will perform its OBLIGATIONs under the contract. FAR 28.001. This bond is purchased by a prospective contractor in accordance with the requirements of the Government. The MILLER ACT generally requires performance bonds for construction contracts exceeding $100,000, and they may occasionally be required for other contracts as well. FAR 28.102-1, 28.103. The PENAL AMOUNT of a Miller Act performance bond must be 100 percent of the original contract price, unless the contracting officer determines that a smaller amount will adequately protect the Government. FAR 28.102-2. In lieu of a performance bond a contractor may deposit securities. FAR 28.204. See Patin, chap. 17, *Construction Contracting* 1310–34 (1991).

PERFORMANCE EVALUATION The periodic evaluation of the performance of a contractor in carrying out its OBLIGATIONs on Government contracts. Contracting activities evaluate the performance of construction contractors by preparing Standard Form 1420, Performance Evaluation—Construction Contracts in FAR 53.301-1420, for contracts of $500,000 or more, or more than $10,000 if the contract was terminated for default. Before making determinations of RESPONSIBILITY, contracting officers may consider these performance evaluations in accordance with agency instructions. FAR 36.201. In DOD, DD Form 2626, Performance Evaluation, is used; information from this form is entered into a computerized system maintained by the Office of the Chief of Engineers. In addition, a Construction Contractor Appraisal Support System is maintained by the Army Corps of Engineers' North Pacific Division in Portland, Oregon. DFARS 236.201. See Yasenchak, *A CM Report: System Provides Contractor Performance Histories*, 28 Cont. Mgmt. 50 (Nov. 1988). Performance evaluations are also required by FAR 42.1502(a) for all major nonconstruction contracts (see PAST PERFORMANCE INFORMATION).

PERFORMANCE EVALUATION PLAN A plan unilaterally established by the Government to be used in determining the amount of AWARD FEE earned by the contractor in cost-plus-award-fee MANAGEMENT AND OPERATING CONTRACTS. The plan sets forth the criteria on which the contractor will be evaluated for performance relating to any technical, schedule, management, and COST OBJECTIVEs selected for evaluation. The plan includes the criteria to be considered under each area evaluated and includes the percentage of award fee available for each area. DEAR 970.5204-54.

PERFORMANCE PURCHASING The concept that the Government describes its requirements in terms of how a product or service should perform rather than in terms of the design of that product or service. Functional terms rather than design terms set the requirements. This type of purchasing enables the vendor community to offer the latest technology to meet performance requirements and keeps both parties, Government and contractor, focused on the desired outcome of the procurement. See also PERFORMANCE-BASED CONTRACTING.

PERFORMANCE RISK ASSESSMENT GROUP A group of experienced Government personnel that may be appointed by the SOURCE SELECTION ADVISORY COUNCIL chairperson to assess performance risk. AFFARS Appendix BB.

PERFORMANCE SCHEDULE See DELIVERY OR PERFORMANCE SCHEDULE.

PERFORMANCE SPECIFICATIONS Technical requirements that set forth the operational characteristics desired for an ITEM. They indicate what the final product must be capable of accomplishing rather than how the product is to be built or what its measurements, tolerances, or other design characteristics must be. When the contract contains performance specifications, the contractor accepts general responsibility for product design and engineering and for achieving the stated performance requirements. See Cibinic & Nash, chap. 3, Sec. V., *Formation of Government Contracts* (3d ed. 1998). Performance specifications are preferred over DESIGN SPECIFICATIONS. FAR 11.101(a).

PERSONAL CONFLICT OF INTEREST A number of types of conduct proscribed by law and regulation, on grounds that the conduct would compromise or appear to compromise the complete impartiality of the procurement process. Prohibitions apply to Government employees, former Government employees, and members of Congress. As a rule, no Government employee may solicit or accept a GRATUITY (18 U.S.C. § 201(c); 10 U.S.C. § 2207; 5 U.S.C. § 7353; 5 C.F.R. § 2635, Subpart B; FAR 3.101-2 and Subpart 3.2) or offer or accept a bribe (see BRIBERY) 18 U.S.C. § 201(b)). Nor, as a rule, may a Government employee have a financial interest in an organization with which he or she is dealing (18 U.S.C. § 208; 5 C.F.R. § 2635, Subpart D). Discussion of future employment or business opportunities with a contractor seeking a Government contract is considered a financial interest under 18 U.S.C. § 208, 5 C.F.R. § 2635.603(b), and is also dealt with in competitive procurements by 41 U.S.C. § 423(c), FAR 3.104-4(c). Award of a contract to a Government employee or to a business substantially owned or controlled by a Government employee is also prohibited by FAR 3.601. Post-employment restrictions are contained in 18 U.S.C. § 207 and 41 U.S.C. § 423(d) (see REVOLVING DOOR). As a rule, no member of Congress may be awarded a Government contract or personally benefit from award of a contract (41 U.S.C. § 22). See DFARS Part 203 and DOD Directive 5500.7, *Standards of Conduct*, Aug. 30, 1993; American B. Ass'n., *Personal Conflicts of Interest in Government Contracting*, A.B.A. Sec. Pub. Cont. L. 1991; Darley, *Personal Conflicts of Interest Digest*, 20 Pub. Cont. L.J. 302 (1991). OFPP Policy Letter No. 89-1, *Conflict of Interest Policies Applicable to Consultants*, Dec. 8, 1989, provides guidelines concerning the conditions or circumstances wherein a person is unable, or potentially unable, to render impartial ADVISORY AND ASSISTANCE SERVICES to the Government because of other activities or relationships with other persons, or wherein a person has an unfair COMPETITIVE ADVANTAGE. See also PROCUREMENT INTEGRITY.

PERSONAL PROPERTY Property of any kind, or interest in it, with the exception of REAL PROPERTY, RECORDS of the Federal Government, naval battleships, cruisers, aircraft carriers, destroyers, and submarines. FAR 45.601. More generally, all property other than real property; everything that is the subject of ownership, not coming under the denomination of real estate. *Black's Law Dictionary* 1216 (6th ed. 1990). Instructions on contractor reporting of excess personal property are set forth in FAR 45.608-8. Such reports, when required by the contract, are submitted on Standard Form 120, Report of Excess Personal Property, FAR 53.301-120.

PERSONAL SERVICES CONTRACT A contract that, by its express terms or as administered, makes the contractor personnel appear to be, in effect, Government employees. FAR 37.101. Government agencies may not award personal services contracts unless specifically authorized by statute to do so, because such contracts tend to circumvent the civil service laws requiring the Government to obtain its employees by direct hire using established competitive procedures. FAR 37.104(b). FAR 37.104(c) provides that the key indicator of a personal services contract is "relatively continuous supervision and control" of contractor employees by Government officials. FAR 37.104(d) provides a list of other elements that may indicate that a personal services contract exists. See also DFARS 237.104; Ritenburg, *Contracting for the Services of Specific Individuals: Avoiding "Personal Services Contracts,"* 10 N&CR ¶ 10 (Feb. 1996).

PETTY CASH See IMPREST FUND.

PILOT ACQUISITION PROGRAM See MAJOR DEFENSE ACQUISITION PILOT PROGRAM.

PILOT MENTOR-PROTÉGÉ PROGRAM See MENTOR-PROTÉGÉ PILOT PROGRAM.

PLAINTIFF The party bringing suit in a court. In the U.S. COURT OF FEDERAL CLAIMS, the contractor is always the plaintiff even though the suit may be based on a Government CLAIM under the CONTRACT DISPUTES ACT OF 1978. In such cases, the Government is referred to as the DEFENDANT. (If such a case were appealed to a BOARD OF CONTRACT APPEALS, the contractor would be referred to as the appellant and the Government would be called the respondent.)

PLANNING, PROGRAMMING AND BUDGETING SYSTEM (PPBS) A system by which DOD, the Organization of the Joint Chiefs of Staff, the Unified and Special Commands, and the defense agencies plan, program, and budget, in order "to provide the operational commanders in chief the best mix of forces, equipment, and support attainable within fiscal constraints." The PPBS is also one of three major decision making support systems for defense acquisition. It entails a formal, systematic structure for making decisions on policy, strategy, and the development of forces and capabilities to accomplish anticipated missions. PPBS is a cyclic process containing three distinct, but interrelated phases: planning, which produces Defense Planning Guidance; programming, which produces approved program objectives memoranda for the military departments and defense agencies; and budgeting, which produces the DOD portion of the President's budget. Jones, *Glossary: Defense Acquisition Acronyms and Terms* (8th ed., Defense Systems Management College). *The Planning, Programming, and Budgeting System (PPBS)*, DOD Directive 7045.14 (May 22, 1984; change 1 July 28, 1990). See also Philips & Saunders, *Multiyear Contracts for Major Systems*, 22 Pub. Cont. L.J. 161, 164–69 (1993).

PLANT CLEARANCE All actions relating to the screening, redistribution, and disposal of contractor INVENTORY from a contractor's plant or work site. "Contractor's plant" includes any GOVERNMENT-OWNED, CONTRACTOR-OPERATED PLANT. FAR 45.601. FAR Subpart 45.6 contains guidance on the procedures to be followed in the plant clearance process. For this function, Government agencies normally appoint a plant clearance officer to act as the authorized representative of the contracting officer. The plant clearance period is the period beginning on the effective date of contract completion or termination and ending 90 days (or later, if agreed to) after the contracting officer receives acceptable inventory schedules for each property classification.

PLANT EQUIPMENT Personal property of a capital nature (including equipment, machine tools, test equipment, furniture, vehicles, and accessory and auxiliary items) for use in manufacturing supplies, in performing services, or for any administrative or general plant purpose. It does not include SPECIAL TEST EQUIPMENT or SPECIAL TOOLING. FAR 45.101. The contracting officer must approve in advance any contractor use of active plant equipment, and such approval may be granted only when in the Government's interest. FAR 45.407. The DFARS categorizes plant equipment as "industrial plant equipment (IPE)" or "other plant equipment (OPE)." IPE means plant equipment in federal stock group 34 with an acquisition cost of $15,000 or more used for cutting, abrading, grinding, shaping, forming, joining, heating, treating, or otherwise altering the physical properties of materials, components, or end items entailed in manufacturing, maintenance, supply, processing, assembly, or research and development (R&D) operations. OPE excludes items categorized as IPE. It is that part of plant equipment, regardless of dollar value, that is used in, or in conjunction with, the manufacture of components or end items for maintenance, supply, processing, assembly, or R&D operations. DFARS 245.301. Before acquiring IPE, DOD contracting offices must notify the Defense Industrial Plant Equipment Center, which will determine whether existing, reallocable Government-owned equipment can fill the requirement. DFARS 245.302-1(b)(1)(A)(1).

POOL OF CONTRACTORS See DEFENSE PRODUCTION POOL; DEFENSE RESEARCH & DEVELOPMENT POOL.

POOL OF COSTS See INDIRECT COST POOL.

POST-AWARD DEBRIEFING See DEBRIEFING.

PRACTICAL APPLICATION The manufacture (in the case of a composition or product), the practice (in the case of a process or method), or the operation (in the case of a machine or system) of an invention, under conditions establishing that the invention is being utilized and that its benefits are, to the extent permitted by law or Government regulations, available to the public on reasonable terms. FAR 27.301. The Patent Rights clauses in FAR 52.227-11, -12, and -13 provide that the Government may require the contractor to LICENSE others to use a SUBJECT INVENTION, to which it has obtained TITLE, in the United States if it does not bring the invention to the point of practical application. See MARCH-IN.

PREAWARD DEBRIEFING See DEBRIEFING.

PREAWARD SURVEY An evaluation, usually conducted by the cognizant CONTRACT ADMINISTRATION OFFICE, of a prospective contractor's capability to perform a proposed contract. FAR 9.101. A preaward survey is normally required when the information on hand or readily available to the contracting officer is not sufficient to make a determination regarding RESPONSIBILITY. The surveying activity begins by checking whether the prospective contractor is debarred, suspended, or ineligible (see PARTIES EXCLUDED FROM FEDERAL PROCUREMENT AND NONPROCUREMENT PROGRAMS), in which case the surveying activity notifies the contracting officer and does not proceed with the preaward survey. FAR 9.106-1. The following standard forms (SFs) are used for preaward surveys: SF 1403 (General), SF 1404 (Technical), SF 1405 (Production), SF 1406 (Quality Assurance), SF 1407 (Financial Capability), and SF 1408 (Accounting System). FAR 53.301-1403 through 1408. At NASA, a preaward survey board reviews the preaward survey report before action is taken by the contracting officer. NFS 18-9.106-70. See Cibinic & Nash, chap. 3, Sec. VII., *Formation of Government Contracts* (3d ed. 1998).

PRE-BID CONFERENCE A meeting of the contracting officer with prospective bidders during the SOLICITATION period of a SEALED BIDDING procurement. FAR 14.207 provides that such conferences may be used, usually in complex acquisitions, as a means of briefing prospective bidders and explaining complicated specifications and requirements to them as early as possible after the INVITATION FOR BIDS (IFB) has been issued and before bids are submitted. They are not to be used, however, as a substitute for amending a defective or ambiguous IFB. Notice of the conference must be provided to all prospective bidders. See Cibinic & Nash, chap. 3, Sec. VII., *Formation of Government Contracts* (3d ed. 1998).

PRECIOUS METALS Uncommon and highly valuable metals characterized by their superior resistance to corrosion and oxidation. FAR 45.601. Included are silver, gold, and the platinum group metals—latinum, palladium, iridium, osmium, rhodium, and ruthenium. FAR 45.607-2 prescribes special procedures to be used for such metals when contractors dispose of unused inventory and SCRAP at the end of contract performance.

PRECONTRACT COSTS Costs incurred by a contractor before the effective date of the contract. FAR 31.205-32 specifies that such costs are ALLOWABLE COSTs if they would have been allowable after the date of the contract, and if they were incurred in anticipation of contract award and were necessary to comply with the contract schedule. See Cibinic, *Independent Research and Development, Bid and Proposal, and Precontractual Costs: The Troublesome Troika*, 6 N&CR ¶ 42 (July 1992); Wiener, *The Allowability of Precontract Costs*, 91-11 CP&A Rep. 3 (Nov. 1991); Hordell, *The Precontract Cost Principle (FAR 31.205-32)*, 89-1 CP&A Rep. 13 (Jan. 1989); Cibinic, *Precontract Costs: A Risky Business*, 1 N&CR ¶ 29 (Apr. 1987).

PREEMPTION The situation where federal law overrides and supersedes state or local law. 17 U.S.C. § 301 states that the Copyright Act, Title 17 of the United States Code, preempts state law with regard to any of the exclusive rights within the general scope of the Act.

PREJUDICE A showing of harm. Prejudice is an essential element in every viable PROTEST. To prevail in a protest, the protester must not only show a significant error in the procurement process but also that the error prejudiced it. See *LaBarge Prods., Inc. v. West*, 46 F.3d 1547 (Fed. Cir. 1995). To establish prejudice the protester must demonstrate some probability that it would receive the award. See Cibinic, *Protests: The "No Prejudice" Rule*, 11 N&CR ¶ 20 (May 1997).

PRELIMINARY DESIGN REVIEW (PDR) A review, conducted during SYSTEMs acquisition, of each configuration item to (1) evaluate the progress, technical adequacy, and risk resolution of the selected design approach; (2) determine the item's compatibility with the performance and engineering requirements of the development SPECIFICATION; and (3) establish the existence and compatibility of the physical and functional interfaces among the item and other items of equipment, FACILITIES, computer programs, and personnel. Part 15 of DOD Instruction 5000.2, *Defense Acquisition Management Policies and Procedures*, Feb. 23, 1991, provided guidance on PDRs. They are no longer covered by DOD Regulation 5000.2-R, *Mandatory Procedures for Major Defense Acquisition Programs (MDAPs) and Major Automated Information System (MAIS) Acquisition Programs*, Mar. 15, 1996. However, PDRs are a standard step in the process of developing systems for DOD.

PRELIMINARY INJUNCTION An interim remedy granted by a court ordering a party not to proceed with a proposed action. The COURT OF FEDERAL CLAIMS and district courts may use this remedy in a BID PROTEST to afford a party relief. 28 U.S.C. § 1491(b)(2). In granting such relief, the court is required to consider the interests of NATIONAL DEFENSE and national security. See Nash & Cibinic, chap. 11, *Competitive Negotiation: The Source Selection Process* (1993).

PREPRODUCTION TEST A test of design-qualified hardware using production tooling and processes that will be used to produce the operational hardware. The Government should not accept production hardware before satisfactory completion of this test, whose objectives include instilling confidence that the hardware works, proves reliable, can be maintained and supported by the agency, and is not over-designed. Jones, *Glossary: Defense Acquisition Acronyms and Terms* (8th ed., Defense Systems Management College). Preproduction testing is more commonly called FIRST ARTICLE TESTING.

PREPROPOSAL CONFERENCE A meeting of the contracting officer with prospective offerors during the SOLICITATION period of a procurement by NEGOTIATION. Such conferences may be held, generally in complex acquisitions, to brief prospective offerors and to explain or clarify complicated SPECIFICATIONs and requirements. FAR 15.201 Adequate notice of the conference should be given to all prospective offerors. Technical and legal personnel should be invited to attend and prospective offerors should be invited to submit questions in advance. See Cibinic & Nash, chap. 3, Sec. VII., *Formation of Government Contracts* (3d ed. 1998). See also PRESOLICITATION CONFERENCE.

PREQUALIFICATION Determination of the RESPONSIBILITY of an OFFEROR prior to SOLICITATION; in other words, determination of an offeror's eligibility to *compete* for a Government contract. Prequalification has frequently been thought an undue restriction on

FULL AND OPEN COMPETITION and therefore has been rejected as a means of easing the administrative burden of evaluating large numbers of offerors. FAR Subpart 9.2, which implements 41 U.S.C. § 253c and 10 U.S.C. § 2319, sets forth conditions that agencies must meet in establishing a prequalification system. For a discussion of situations in which the use of a prequalification system has been upheld or rejected by the Comptroller General, see Cibinic & Nash, chap. 4, Sec. I., *Formation of Government Contracts* (3d ed. 1998); Nash, *Prequalification: Can It Be Used To Improve The Procurement Process?,* 10 N&CR ¶ 16 (Apr. 1996). See also Jackson, *Prequalification and Qualification: Discouragement of New Competitors,* 19 Pub. Cont. L.J. 702 (1990).

PRESENT VALUE The value in current dollars of work to be performed in the future. This value is determined by discounting the price of work to be paid for in the future by a rate commensurate with the interest rate on the funds for the period before payment is required. Making a determination of present value is a beneficial way of comparing competing offers that call for payment by the Government at varying times. Thus, it is a way of dealing with UNBALANCED BIDs. OMB Circular No. A-104 (revised), *Comparative Cost Analysis for Decisions to Lease or Purchase General-Purpose Real Property*, June 1, 1986, provides guidance on present value calculations in another context.

PRESIDENT'S BLUE RIBBON COMMISSION ON DEFENSE MANAGEMENT See PACKARD COMMISSION.

PRESOLICITATION CONFERENCE A meeting held by the contracting officer with prospective offerors as a preliminary step in negotiated acquisitions (see NEGOTIATION) in order to develop or identify interested sources, request preliminary information based on a general description of the supplies or services involved, explain complicated SPECIFICATIONs and requirements, and aid prospective contractors in preparing proposals without undue expenditure of effort, time, and money. FAR 15.201.

PRESOLICITATION NOTICE A notice sent by the contracting officer to business concerns on the SOLICITATION MAILING LIST and published by SYNOPSIS. In many procurement situations such notice must be given 15 days before issuance of a solicitation. See 41 U.S.C. § 416(a). The requirement for a presolicitation synopsis is implemented in FAR Subpart 5.2. In SEALED BIDDING, the notice

(1) briefly describes the requirement and furnishes other essential information to enable concerns to determine whether they have an interest in the INVITATIONS FOR BIDs (IFBs); (2) specifies the final date for requesting a complete bid set; and (3) notifies concerns that, if no bid is to be submitted, they should advise the issuing office in writing if they want to receive future IFBs for similar supplies or services. Drawings, plans, and specifications normally will not be furnished with the notice. This procedure is particularly suitable when either the solicitation mailing list or the IFB is lengthy. FAR 14.205-4(c). In negotiated procurements (see NEGOTIATION), a presolicitation notice may also be used to develop or identify interested sources, request preliminary information based on a general description of the requirement, explain complicated specifications and requirements, and aid prospective contractors in subsequent proposal preparation. FAR 15.201. The notice states whether a PRESOLICITATION CONFERENCE is contemplated and requests an expression of interest in the planned acquisition by a specific date. In a complex acquisition, the notice may request information on management, engineering, and production capabilities. See FAR 36.213-2 regarding the use of presolicitation notices in construction contracting. See also Cibinic & Nash, chap. 3, Sec. VII., *Formation of Government Contracts* (3d ed. 1998).

PREVAILING PARTY A party that succeeds on any significant issue in litigation and thereby achieves some of the benefit sought by the individual or corporation bringing the suit. Under the EQUAL ACCESS TO JUSTICE ACT (EAJA), courts and agencies award fees and other expenses to small businesses that are prevailing parties in adversary adjudications. A party may be deemed to have prevailed if that party obtains a settlement of the dispute; victory following a trial on the merits is not a prerequisite. A party is also deemed a prevailing party if it has established entitlement to relief on the merits, and a court remands the dispute to an agency for further proceedings consistent with the court's opinion. See 28 U.S.C. § 2412, 5 U.S.C. § 504. See also Richmond, *Eligibility Under the Equal Access to Justice Act in Government Contract Litigation*, Army Law. 17 (Mar. 1995); Hinchey, *Prevailing Subcontractor Denied Recovery of EAJA Fees*, 15 Constr. Law. 81 (Apr. 1993); Nash, *Equal Access To Justice Act: A Statute That Is Working Well*, 2 N&CR ¶ 20 (Apr. 1988); Kinlin, *Equal Access to Justice Act*, 16 Pub. Cont. L.J. 266 (1986).

PREVAILING WAGE RATE The rate of wages, including fringe benefits, paid to a majority of the workers in a geographic area for the same type of work on similar projects. DOL ascertains the prevailing wage rates in order to establish WAGE DETERMINATIONs for construction contracts under the DAVIS-BACON ACT and for service contracts under the SERVICE CONTRACT ACT. See 29 C.F.R. § 1.2 and 29 C.F.R. § 4.3. See also Cibinic & Nash, chap. 10, Sec. VII., *Formation of Government Contracts* (3d ed. 1998).

PRICE A monetary amount paid, received, or asked for in exchange for supplies or services, expressed in terms of a single item of, or unit of measure for, the supplies or services. The term "price" is usually associated with a FIXED-PRICE CONTRACT, which calls for the payment of a negotiated amount, established at the outset or by redetermination, for satisfactorily completed work—rather than a COST-REIMBURSEMENT CONTRACT, which calls for payment of the contractor's ALLOWABLE COSTs plus any negotiated FEE.

PRICE ADJUSTMENT An adjustment to the price that is called for by the terms of a contract. Most price adjustments are EQUITABLE ADJUSTMENTs that contain an adjustment of PROFIT as well as an amount commensurate with the change in costs that has occurred. However, the Suspension of Work clause in FAR 52.242-14 and the Government Delay of Work clause in FAR 52.242-17 call for price adjustments that exclude profit and reflect only the costs incurred by the contractor during the time the contracting officer unreasonably delayed performance. See Cibinic & Nash, chap. 8, *Administration of Government Contracts* (3d ed. 1995); Cibinic, *Profit in Retroactive Pricing: Rethinking the Risk Factor*, 9 N&CR ¶ 32 (May 1995); Cibinic, *Accounting for Price Adjustments*, 8 N&CR ¶ 30 (May 1994); Howlett, *New Guidance for Economic Price Adjustment Clauses*, Army Law. 51 (May 1993).

PRICE ANALYSIS The process of examining and evaluating a prospective PRICE without performing COST ANALYSIS; that is, without evaluating the separate cost elements and PROFIT of the offeror included in that price. FAR 15.404-1(b). Price analysis may be accomplished by (1) comparing offers with one another; (2) comparing prior proposed prices and contract prices with current proposed prices for the same or similar end items; (3) using yardsticks (dollars per pound or per horsepower, or other units) to highlight significant inconsistencies that warrant additional inquiry; (4) comparing offers with competitive published price lists, published market prices of commodities, similar indexes, and discount or rebate arrangements; (5) comparing proposed prices with independently developed Government estimates; or (6) comparing proposed prices with prices of the same or similar items obtained through MARKET RESEARCH. FAR 15.404-1(b)(2). The contracting officer is responsible for selecting and using whatever price analysis techniques will ensure a FAIR AND REASONABLE PRICE. See Cibinic & Nash, chap. 9, Sec. III., *Formation of Government Contracts* (3d ed. 1998); Cibinic, *Cost and Price Analysis: Understanding the Terms*, 9 N&CR ¶ 5 (Jan. 1995).

PRICE COMPETITION The competition that is achieved on a Government procurement when price will be a significant element in the SOURCE SELECTION. COST OR PRICING DATA may not be required to be submitted by contractors when there is ADEQUATE PRICE COMPETITION. FAR 15.403-1. See Cibinic & Nash, chap. 9, Sec. I., *Formation of Government Contracts* (3d ed. 1998).

PRICE NEGOTIATION MEMORANDUM (PNM) A Government document that summarizes the process of negotiating a contract's price and the outcome of that process and that serves as a record of the decisions made in determining a price to be fair and reasonable. FAR 15.406-3 requires the Government's contracting officer to prepare a PNM promptly at the conclusion of each negotiation of an initial or revised PRICE. The memorandum, which is included in the contract file, must (1) document the purpose of the negotiation, (2) describe the acquisition, (3) give information on participants in the negotiation, (4) give the status of the contractor's purchasing system, (5) if COST OR PRICING DATA were not required, state the exemption used, (6) if cost or pricing data were required, give a statement about reliance, (7) summarize the contractor's proposal and any field pricing assistance recommendations, (8) state the most significant facts or considerations controlling the establishment of the prenegotiation objectives, (9) discuss and quantify the impact of direction given by Congress, (10) state the basis for the PROFIT or FEE, and (11) provide documentation of fair and reasonable pricing. See Cibinic & Nash, chap. 9, Sec. VI., *Formation of Government Contracts* (3d ed. 1998).

PRICE REASONABLENESS See FAIR AND REASONABLE PRICE.

PRICE REDETERMINABLE CONTRACT See FIXED-PRICE REDETERMINATION–PROSPECTIVE CONTRACT; FIXED-PRICE REDETERMINATION—RETROACTIVE CONTRACT.

PRICE REDUCTION The amount by which the Government is entitled to adjust a contract formed by NEGOTIATION if CERTIFIED COST

OR PRICING DATA required under the TRUTH IN NEGOTIATIONS ACT are found not to be ACCURATE, COMPLETE, AND CURRENT. This adjustment consists of any significant amount by which the negotiated price, including PROFIT or FEE, was increased because of the DEFECTIVE COST OR PRICING data. In arriving at this price reduction, the contracting officer is to consider the time when the cost or pricing data became reasonably available to the contractor and the extent to which the Government relied on the defective data. FAR 15.407-1(b)(2). OFFSETs against the amount of the reduction are required for understated cost or pricing data up to (but not exceeding) the amount of the reduction. FAR 15.407-1(b)(4). See Wall, *Surviving Commercial Pricing Rules*, 23 Pub. Cont. L.J. 533 (1994); Lovitky, *Understanding Causation and Determining Price Adjustments in Defective Pricing Cases*, 17 Pub. Cont. L.J. 407 (1988); Vacketta et al., *The "Price Reductions" Clause*, 85-12 Briefing Papers (Dec. 1985).

PRICE-RELATED FACTORS EVALUATION FACTORS other than price that affect a contract's overall cost to the Government and can be quantified in dollars; the term is used mainly in the context of SEALED BIDDING procurements, which must be awarded solely on the basis of price and the price-related factors included in the SOLICITATION. See FAR 14.101(e). Price-related factors are added to the price to determine the low bidder. Examples of price-related factors that may be applicable in evaluating bids are (1) foreseeable costs or DELAYs to the Government resulting from such factors as differences in INSPECTION procedure, locations of supplies, and transportation costs; (2) changes made or requested by a bidder in any of the provisions of the INVITATION FOR BIDS, if the changes do not constitute grounds for rejection; (3) advantages or disadvantages to the Government that might result from making more than one award ($500 is assumed to be the administrative cost to the Government for issuing and administering each contract awarded under a solicitation); (4) the applicability of federal, state, and local taxes; and (5) the origin of supplies and, if foreign, the application of the BUY AMERICAN ACT, 41 U.S.C. § 10, or any other factor affecting foreign purchases. FAR 14.201-8. See Cibinic & Nash, chap. 6, *Formation of Government Contracts* (3d ed. 1998).

PRICING See CONTRACT PRICING.

PRICING ARRANGEMENT A basis agreed to by contractual parties for the payment of amounts for specified performance. Such an arrangement usually takes the form of a specific TYPE OF CONTRACT, either cost reimbursement or fixed price.

PRIME CONTRACT A contract entered into directly between the Government and a contractor (the PRIME CONTRACTOR). "Prime" is used to distinguish that contract from any SUBCONTRACT entered into between the prime contractor and a supplier or vendor called a subcontractor, or between such a subcontractor and another, lower-level subcontractor. FAR 3.502-1; FAR 44.101. There is PRIVITY OF CONTRACT between the Government and prime contractors, but not between the Government and subcontractors.

PRIME CONTRACTOR A person or organization entering into a contract directly with the United States. FAR 3.502-1. This term is synonymous with CONTRACTOR. In construction contracting, the prime contractor is usually called the GENERAL CONTRACTOR.

PRINCIPAL A person with authority to act for an organization. In agency law, principals are those who delegate authority to agents to act in their behalf. In ALTERNATIVE DISPUTE RESOLUTION proceedings, principals are the representatives of the parties with the authority to negotiate a binding settlement of the matter in DISPUTE. See Nash, *Alternate Disputes Resolution: An Update*, 7 N&CR ¶ 25 (May 1993).

PRIOR COURSE OF DEALING The dealings between the contracting parties on transactions prior to the current contract. Under U.C.C. § 1-205(1), "prior course of dealing" or "course of dealing" refers to a sequence of interactions between parties to a particular transaction that may fairly be regarded as establishing a basis for interpreting their statements and other conduct. The concept is similar to, yet more specific than, "course of business," which refers to what is usually and normally done in the management of trade or business. When the parties to a contract interpretation dispute have interpreted the provisions of a similar, previously performed contract, the courts and boards of contract appeals presume that the parties intended the same meaning for the provisions in the disputed contract. See Cibinic & Nash, *Administration of Government Contracts* 199–209 (3d ed. 1995).

PRIORITIES AND ALLOCATIONS A method for implementing the DEFENSE PRIORITIES AND ALLOCATIONS SYSTEM (DPAS), which ensures that critical materials and FACILITIES are to be used for national defense in the event of an emergency. FAR Subpart 11.6. Certain contracts and orders are accorded preferential treatment by being designated as RATED ORDERS under the DPAS regulation that guides the DEPARTMENT OF COMMERCE's Office of Industrial Resource Administration in developing, coordinating, and administering a system of priorities and allocations with respect to industrial resources, pursuant to Title I of the Defense Production Act of 1950, 50 U.S.C. app. § 2061 et seq.

PRISON INDUSTRIES See FEDERAL PRISON INDUSTRIES, INC.

PRIVATELY OWNED U.S.-FLAG COMMERCIAL VESSEL A vessel that is (1) registered and operated under the laws of the United States, (2) used in commercial trade of the United States, and (3) owned and operated by U.S. citizens, including a vessel under voyage or time charter to the Government; or a Government-owned vessel under bareboat charter to and operated by U.S. citizens. FAR 47.501. Such vessels are included in the definition of U.S.-FLAG VESSELs for purposes of the cargo preference regulations in FAR Subpart 47.5.

PRIVATIZATION The process of changing a public entity or enterprise to private control and ownership. It does not include a determination as to whether a support service should be obtained through public or private resources when the Government retains full responsibility and control over the delivery of those services. OMB Circular No. A-76, *Revised Supplementary Handbook*, Mar. 1996. It is a form of OUT-SOURCING that usually involves the actual transfer of ownership or control of ASSETs, such as land, FACILITIES, or equipment from the Federal Government to private entities. See OMB Circular No. A-76 (revised), *Performance of Commercial Activities*, Aug. 4, 1983; OFPP Policy Letter No. 92-1, *Inherently Governmental Functions*, Sept. 23, 1992; Dover, *Outsourcing & Privatization: Recent Developments*, 97-4 Briefing Papers (Mar. 1997); Smith, *The Limits of Privatization: Privacy in the Context of Tax Collection*, 47 Case W. Res. L.R. 627 (1997); Sabatino, *Privatization and Punitives: Should Government Contractors Share the Sovereign's Immunities from Exemplary Damages?*, 58 Ohio St. L.J. 175 (1997); Jones et al., *The Process of Developing a Cost-Effective Public-Private Partnership: The Team Approach*, 21 Pub. Cont. L.J. 442 (1992).

PRIVILEGED INFORMATION Information not subject to the disclosure requirements of the FREEDOM OF INFORMATION ACT. The most commonly used privileges include the ATTORNEY WORK-PRODUCT PRIVILEGE, the EXECUTIVE PRIVILEGE, and the

TRADE-SECRET PRIVILEGE. See Nash & Rawicz, *Intellectual Property in Government Contracts*, vol. 3, 184-210 (3d ed. 1997).

PRIVITY OF CONTRACT The legal relationship and responsibilities between parties to the same contract. The Government has privity of contract with the PRIME CONTRACTOR; the prime contractor has privity of contract with the first-tier SUBCONTRACTOR, but there is generally no privity of contract between the Government and subcontractors. The result is that CLAIMs of subcontractors against the Government under the CONTRACT DISPUTES ACT OF 1978 must be asserted by the prime contractor or in the name of the prime contractor. This proves problematic because the Act requires prime contractors to certify claims of more than $100,000 submitted by their subcontractors. Thus, under this "sponsorship" system, contract disputes are certified by the prime contractor, even though it may take a passive role in litigating the dispute. See Singer, *Asserting Government Control over Subcontractors*, Army Law. 11 (Sept. 1994); Pachter, *Certification of Subcontractor Claims*, 19 Pub. Cont. Newsl. 3 (Fall 1983). See also SPONSORSHIP OF SUBCONTRACTOR CLAIMS.

PROBABLE COST The Government's best estimate of the costs that a contractor will incur in performing a COST-REIMBURSEMENT CONTRACT. FAR 14.404-1(d)(2)(i). The probable cost must be ascertained by making a COST REALISM ANALYSIS during the evaluation of each proposal and must be used in making the source selection decision.

PROCUREMENT All stages of the process of acquiring property or services, beginning with determination of a need for the property or services and ending with contract completion and closeout. 41 U.S.C. § 403(2). "Procurement" also means the acquisition (and directly related matters) of PERSONAL PROPERTY and nonpersonal services (including CONSTRUCTION) from non-federal sources by such means as purchasing, renting, leasing (including the leasing of REAL PROPERTY), contracting, bartering, and condemnation, donation, and requisition (but not by seizure). The synonymous term ACQUISITION is usually used in the FEDERAL ACQUISITION REGULATIONS SYSTEM, whereas "procurement" is used in the United States Code. Contracting is a subset of procurement.

PROCUREMENT AUTOMATED SOURCE SYSTEM (PASS) A system, initiated by the SMALL BUSINESS ADMINISTRATION (SBA) in 1977, to provide a single automated database of small, women-owned, and minority-owned firms. The system helps federal agency procurement offices, prime contractors, and major sub-contractors meet their respective small business procurement goals. In 1996, the PASS database contained approximately 200,000 firms, of which more than 34,000 were minority owned, more than 49,000 were women owned, and more than 47,000 were veteran owned. The user fee for PASS in 1996 was $38 per hour. Questions about PASS, as well as company profiles intended for inclusion in the PASS database, should be directed to regional or district SBA offices.

PROCUREMENT CONTRACT A contract between the Government and a private party to provide supplies or services (including construction). 31 U.S.C. § 6301 et seq. distinguishes between procurement contracts, GRANTs, and COOPERATIVE AGREEMENTs and contains guidance as to when each type of instrument should be used. In this sense, procurement contracts are those instruments governed by the FEDERAL ACQUISITION REGULATION (FAR). The coverage of the CONTRACT DISPUTES ACT OF 1978 is also limited to procurement contracts and contracts for the disposal of PERSONAL PROPERTY.

PROCUREMENT EXECUTIVE See SENIOR PROCUREMENT EXECUTIVE.

PROCUREMENT INSTRUMENT IDENTIFICATION (PII) NUMBERS A system of identifying numbers that are assigned to DOD SOLICITATIONs, contracts, and related instruments. DFARS 204.7000. The basic PII number remains unchanged throughout the life of the instrument; it consists of 13 alphanumeric characters. The first six positions begin with the capital letters assigned to the department preparing the instrument (e.g., "DA" for Department of the Army, "F" for Air Force) and identify the activity preparing the instrument. The seventh and eighth positions contain the last two digits of the fiscal year in which the PII number is assigned. The ninth position contains a capital letter indicating the type of instrument code (e.g., "A" for blanket purchase agreement, "B" for invitation for bids). Finally, the tenth through the thirteenth positions represent the serial number of the instrument. DFARS 204.7003. NASA has a similar system, called ACQUISITION INSTRUMENT IDENTIFICATION.

PROCUREMENT INTEGRITY Rules of conduct, contained in the 1989 amendments to the OFFICE OF FEDERAL PROCUREMENT POLICT ACT, 41 U.S.C. § 423, that were formalized for the purpose of upholding the integrity of the Government procurement process. These rules were revised by section 4304 of the CLINGER-COHEN ACT OF 1996, Pub. L. No. 104-106. The 1989 rules, implemented by FAR 3.104, were as follows. During the conduct of any federal agency procurement, no COMPETING CONTRACTOR could knowingly (1) offer or discuss a future business or employment opportunity with an agency PROCUREMENT OFFICIAL, (2) offer or give anything of value to a procurement official, or (3) solicit or obtain, before contract award, PROPRIETARY INFORMATION or SOURCE SELECTION INFORMATION about the procurement. No procurement official could knowingly discuss future business or employment opportunities, receive gratuities (see GRATUITY), or disclose proprietary or source selection information. No person with access to proprietary or source selection information about a procurement could disclose that information improperly. In addition, the employment and post-employment activities of Government officials, civilian and military, were further restricted. The procurement integrity provisions also required CERTIFICATION by competing contractors and the contracting officer. Detailed guidance on these rules and their application was contained in FAR 3.104. The new rules (1) prohibit disclosure of CONTRACTOR BID OR PROPOSAL INFORMATION or source selection information before the award of a FEDERAL AGENCY PROCUREMENT contract, (2) prohibit obtaining such information, (3) require agency OFFICIALs to report contacts by bidders or offerors relating to non-federal employment and reject such possibility or disqualify themselves from further work on the procurement, and (4) prohibit a limited group of employees who have participated in actions over $10 million from accepting compensation from the contractor for one year after their participation. They also remove all certification requirements. The new rules became effective January 1, 1997 and are now set forth in FAR 3.104-4. See Arnavas, *The Procurement Integrity Act/ Ed. II*, 97-12 Briefing Papers (Nov. 1997); Nash, *The New Procurement Integrity Rules*, 11 N&CR ¶ 12 (Mar. 1997); Rector, *Disclosure & Receipt of Procurement Information Under the Revised Procurement Integrity Act*, 39 Gov't Contractor ¶ 68 (Feb. 12, 1997); Pushkar & Levy, *Guidelines & Observations on the Procurement Integrity Rules Affecting the Hiring of Government Employees*, 39 Gov't Contractor ¶ 15 (Jan. 15, 1997); Nash, *Job Discussions During the Procurement Process*, 7 N&CR ¶ 20 (Apr. 1993); Gerich et al., *The Revised Procurement Integrity Rule*; Arnavas & Marsh, *The Procurement Integrity Act*, 91-9 Briefing Papers (Aug. 1991); Cibinic, *Procurement Integrity Update*, 5 N&CR ¶ 44 (Aug. 1991); Wallick et al., *Procurement Integrity: Pondering Some Imponderables*, 19 Pub. Cont. L.J. 349 (1990); Nash, *Procurement*

Integrity: Additional Thoughts, 4 N&CR ¶ 24 (Apr. 1990); Cibinic, *Procurement Integrity: The Certification Trap*, 3 N&CR ¶ 77 (Nov. 1989); Cibinic, *Procurement Integrity: The Iron Curtain Closes*, 3 N&CR ¶ 49 (July 1989).

PROCUREMENT OFFICIAL Any civilian or military official or employee of an agency who, as defined under the original PROCUREMENT INTEGRITY prohibitions of the OFFICE OF FEDERAL PROCUREMENT POLICY ACT, 41 U.S.C. § 423, had "PARTICIPATED PERSONALLY AND SUBSTANTIALLY" in the conduct of the relevant agency procurement, including all officials and employees responsible for reviewing or approving the procurement. The term included participation in the following activities: (1) developing ACQUISITION PLANs; (2) developing specifications, STATEMENT OF WORK, purchase descriptions, or purchase requests; (3) developing solicitation or contract provisions; (4) evaluating or selecting a contractor; and (5) negotiating or awarding a contract or a MODIFICATION to a contract. This term is not used in the revised procurement integrity rules that became effective on January 1, 1997. The term was defined in FAR 3.104-4 prior to its revision on January 2, 1997, and is operative for contracts entered into prior to the revision of the Act. NASA regulations provided a more detailed list of potential procurement officials, including DOD personnel, who participated in preaward surveys or technical evaluations. NFS 18-3.104-5.

PROCUREMENT SYSTEM The integration of the PROCUREMENT process, the professional development of procurement personnel, and the management structure for carrying out the procurement function. 41 U.S.C. § 403(3).

PROCURING CONTRACTING OFFICER (PCO) A contracting officer in a Government buying office who enters into contracts and signs them on behalf of the Government. This term is used by DOD and other major agencies. In such agencies, after contract execution, an ADMINISTRATIVE CONTRACTING OFFICER typically assumes responsibility for CONTRACT ADMINISTRATION. Generally, a PCO is responsible for creating and publicizing the SOLICITATION, selecting the source, negotiating and executing the contract, negotiating and executing certain contract MODIFICATIONs, determining whether exceptions to requirements for submission of certified COST OR PRICING DATA apply, and settling certain defective pricing issues. A PCO is not normally involved in contract terminations, which are usually handled by a TERMINATION CONTRACTING OFFICER. In many agencies, particularly those with decentralized contracting offices, all of the contracting officer functions are handled by the same person.

PRODUCIBILITY The relative ease of manufacturing an item, product, or system. This relative ease is governed by the characteristics and features of a design that enable economical fabrication, assembly, INSPECTION, and testing using available manufacturing techniques.

PRODUCIBILITY ENGINEERING AND PLANNING (PEP) Production engineering tasks performed to ensure a smooth transition from development into production. PEP, a systems and planning engineering approach, assures that an item can be produced in the required quantities and in the specified period of time, efficiently and economically, and will meet the necessary performance objectives within its design and specification constraints. As an essential part of all engineering design, PEP is intended to identify potential manufacturing problems and suggest design and production changes or schedule trade-offs that would facilitate the production process. Jones, *Glossary: Defense Acquisition Acronyms and Terms* (8th ed., Defense Systems Management College).

PRODUCIBILITY REVIEW A review, study, or analysis of the design of a specific hardware item or system to determine the relative ease of producing it using available production technology considering the elements of fabrication, assembly, inspection, and test. Jones, *Glossary: Defense Acquisition Acronyms and Terms* (8th ed., Defense Systems Management College).

PRODUCT SUBSTITUTION Delivery to the Government of a product that does not meet the contract requirements. Such substitution can occur by mismarking products, deviation from specifications, and other types of conduct that indicate an intention to deceive the Government in the performance of the contract. Such conduct subjects contractors to criminal sanctions under the FALSE CLAIMS ACT. See Cibinic & Nash, chap. 1, Sec. VII., *Formation of Government Contracts* (3d ed. 1998); Seyfarth et al., chap. 18, *The Government Contract Compliance Handbook*, (2d ed. 1991 & 1996 Supp.); *Review of Significant Product Substitution Cases Within DOD*, 7050.1-R Inspector Gen. Rep. (Sept. 1987).

PRODUCTION ENGINEERING See MANUFACTURING ENGINEERING.

PRODUCTION READINESS A SYSTEM's readiness to proceed into production. A system is ready for production when the production design and the managerial and physical preparations necessary for a viable production effort have progressed to the point where a production commitment can be made without incurring unacceptable schedule, performance, cost, or other risks. A production readiness review was called for during the development phase (see ACQUISITION PROCESS) to determine whether the design was ready for production and whether the producer had planned adequately for the production phase. DOD Instruction 5000.2, *Defense Acquisition Management Policies and Procedures*, Parts 6 and 15, Feb. 23, 1991. The term is no longer used in DOD Regulation 5000.2-R, *Mandatory Procedures for Major Defense Acquisition Programs (MDAPs) and Major Automated Information System (MAIS) Acquisition Programs*, Mar. 15, 1996, but the concept is still contained in paragraph 4.3.1 of that regulation.

PRODUCTION SURVEILLANCE A function of CONTRACT ADMINISTRATION used to determine contractor progress and to identify any factors that may delay performance. Production surveillance involves Government review and analysis of the contractor's performance plans, schedules, controls, and industrial processes and the contractor's actual performance under them. FAR 42.1101. Although the contractor is responsible for timely contract performance, the Government maintains surveillance as necessary to protect its interests. FAR 42.1103. The office administering the contract determines the extent of surveillance on the basis of the criticality (degree of importance to the Government) of the supplies or services and consideration of the following factors: (1) contract requirements for reporting production progress and performance, (2) the contractor performance schedule, (3) the contractor's production plan, (4) the contractor's history of contract performance, (5) the contractor's experience with the contract supplies or services, (6) the contractor's financial capability, and (7) any supplementary written instructions from the contracting office. FAR 42.1104.

PROFESSIONAL AND CONSULTANT SERVICES Services by members of a recognized profession, such as the legal, accounting, and engineering professions. FAR 31.205-33 specifies that the costs of contracting for such services incurred by contractors are generally ALLOWABLE COSTs subject to specified conditions. The Government may contract for such services with the individual professionals or with organizations, but such contracts may be subject to the rules governing PERSONAL SERVICES CONTRACTS. See OFPP, *Study* *of Professional Services Contracting.* 10 U.S.C. § 2331 states a preference that DOD contracts for professional services be for stated tasks rather than for hours of services provided. If the professional services are ARCHITECT-ENGINEER SERVICES, special contracting procedures must be used. All other types of professional services are subject to the normal procurement rules. See Victorino & Molinski, *Competing for Professional Services Contracts*, 94-10 Briefing Papers (Sept. 1994).

PROFESSIONAL EMPLOYEE Any person meeting the definition of "employee employed in a bona fide . . . professional capacity" given in 29 C.F.R. Part 541. The term embraces members of the professions that have a recognized status based upon professional knowledge acquired by prolonged study. These professions include, among others, accountancy, actuarial computation, architecture, dentistry, engineering, law, medicine, nursing, pharmacy, the sciences (for example, biology, chemistry, and physics), and teaching. To be a professional employee, a person must not only be a professional but must also be involved essentially in discharging professional duties. FAR 22.1102. When the amount of a SERVICE CONTRACT formed by NEGOTIATION is expected to exceed $500,000 and the contract work will require meaningful numbers of professional employees, offerors must submit for evaluation a total compensation plan for those employees. FAR 22.1103.

PROFIT The amount realized by a contractor after the costs of performance (both direct and indirect) are deducted from the amount to be paid under the terms of the contract. On an annual basis, profit is computed by subtracting total costs of a contractor from the total amount received from sales. In procurements by NEGOTIATION where there is COST ANALYSIS, the Government negotiates a projected amount of profit in accordance with FAR 15.404-4. FAR 15.404-4(a)(2) states that it is in the Government's interest to offer contractors opportunities for financial rewards sufficient to (1) stimulate efficient contract performance, (2) attract the most capable and qualified contractors, and (3) maintain a viable industrial base. Just as actual costs may differ from estimated costs, the contractor's actual realized profit may differ from the negotiated profit because of such factors as efficiency of performance and incurrence of costs not allowed by the Government (see ALLOWABLE COST and TYPE OF CONTRACT). In COST-REIMBURSEMENT CONTRACTs, the amount of projected profit included in the contract by negotiation is called FEE. FAR 15.404-4(c)(4) imposes limitations on negotiated FIXED FEEs on

COST-PLUS-FIXED-FEE CONTRACTs. See Cibinic & Nash, chap. 9, Sec. V., *Formation of Government Contracts* (3d ed. 1998); Murphy, *Managing for Improved Profitability Through Effective Use of the Federal Government's Procurement Regulations and Common Sense Management*, 21 Pub. Cont. L.J. 294 (1992).

PROFIT CENTER The smallest organizationally independent segment of a company charged by management with PROFIT and LOSS responsibilities. FAR 31.001. INDIRECT COSTs are normally accumulated and reported for each profit center.

PROFIT OBJECTIVE The amount that the contracting officer, in preparing to negotiate PRICE based on COST ANALYSIS, concludes is the appropriate negotiated PROFIT or FEE for a procurement. FAR Subpart 15.404-4 provides overall guidance to agencies in establishing profit objectives and FAR 15.404-4(b) requires each agency making noncompetitive awards totaling $50 million or more a year to have a structured approach to establishing such objectives. See the WEIGHTED GUIDELINES APPROACH used by DOD. In establishing a profit objective for a prospective CONTRACT AWARD, the contracting officer must consider all pertinent information (including audit data) available before negotiation. The profit objective need not be computed using precise mathematical calculations, however, particularly with respect to subelements of the major profit factors. *DCAA Contract Audit Manual* 9-902.

PROGRAM DECISION MEMORANDUM (PDM) A memorandum, issued as the last step in the programming phase of PLANNING, PROGRAMMING, AND BUDGETING SYSTEM. PDMs record the program review decisions of the Defense Resources Board and are signed by the Secretary of Defense and distributed to DOD components and the OFFICE OF MANAGEMENT AND BUDGET. A PDM is issued for each service and forms the basis for budget submissions.

PROGRAM EXECUTIVE OFFICER (PEO) The Government official in DOD with immediate supervisory authority over PROGRAM MANAGERs. PEOs report directly to the SENIOR PROCUREMENT EXECUTIVE of the procuring agency. They were established to ensure that the reporting chain between program managers and senior procurement executives was not excessive. PEOs must meet specific experience and training requirements including 10 years' experience in an acquisition position. 10 U.S.C. § 1735(c).

PROGRAM FRAUD CIVIL REMEDIES ACT A 1986 Act, 31 U.S.C. § 3801 et seq., that allows federal agencies to adjudicate small-dollar cases, arising out of false claims and false statements made to the Government, that previously would have required court litigation. Agencies may assess civil penalties of up to $5,000 per false claim or false statement, as well as double damages for those claims that the Government has paid. Liability for false claims requires the establishment of four elements: (1) there must be a claim, (2) the claim must be made to an authority, (3) the claim must be false, and (4) the defendant must know or have reason to know that the claim is false. 31 U.S.C. § 3802(a)(1). There is a ceiling of $150,000 on claims that can be prosecuted under the Act. 31 U.S.C. § 3803(c)(1). See Brown & Boyd, *The Program Fraud Civil Remedies Act: The Administrative Adjudication of Fraud Against the Government*, 50 Fed. Cont. Rep. 691 (Oct. 24, 1988); Bellman, *The Program Fraud Civil Remedies Act*, 88-4 Briefing Papers (Mar. 1988). See also FALSE CLAIMS ACT; FALSE STATEMENTS ACT.

PROGRAM MANAGER (PM) An individual who manages a system acquisition (typically a MAJOR SYSTEM ACQUISITION) program. PMs are tasked with developing acquisition strategies, promoting FULL AND OPEN COMPETITION, and sustaining effective competition between alternative major system concepts and sources (as long as it is economically beneficial and practicable to do so). See FAR 34.004; FAR 34.005-1. In DOD the PM is responsible to, and reports directly to, the PROGRAM EXECUTIVE OFFICER on all program matters.

PROGRAM OBJECTIVE MEMORANDUM (POM) A memorandum, created during the programming phase of PLANNING, PROGRAMMING, AND BUDGETING SYSTEM, that identifies major issues required to be resolved during the year. Each military department and defense agency must prepare and submit to the Secretary of Defense a POM consistent with both the programmatic and fiscal strategy and guidance stated in the defense guidance. DOD Instruction 7045.7, May 23, 1984.

PROGRAM OPPORTUNITY NOTICE (PON) A type of BROAD AGENCY ANNOUNCEMENT used by DOE to inform potential offerors of scientific and technological areas in which DOE wants to accelerate demonstration of the technical, operational, economic, and commercial feasibility and environmental acceptability of particular energy technologies, systems, subsystems, and components. DEAR 917.7201-1(a). At a minimum, each PON must include the goal of the demonstration effort, the time schedule for award, evaluation criteria, PROGRAM POLICY FACTORS, amount of cost detail required, and proposal submission information. DEAR 917.7201-1(b).

PROGRAM POLICY FACTORS Factors that, while not appropriate indicators of a proposal's individual merit (technical excellence, offeror's ability, cost, etc.), are essential to the process of choosing which of the proposals received will best achieve the program objectives. All program policy factors should be predetermined and specified in the PROGRAM OPPORTUNITY NOTICE or PROGRAM RESEARCH AND DEVELOPMENT ANNOUNCEMENT to notify offerors that factors essentially beyond their control will affect the selection process. DEAR 917.7203(b).

PROGRAM RESEARCH AND DEVELOPMENT ANNOUNCEMENT (PRDA) A type of BROAD AGENCY ANNOUNCEMENT used by DOE to inform potential offerors of DOE's interest in entering into arrangements for research, development, and related activities in the energy field. A PRDA is used only when (1) RESEARCH AND DEVELOPMENT (R&D) is required in support of a specific project within an energy program with the objective of advancing the general scientific and technological base, and this objective is best achieved through a diversity of possible approaches, the involvement of a broad spectrum of organizations, the application of unique qualifications or capabilities of many individual proposers, and the fostering of new and creative solutions; (2) it is anticipated that choices will have to be made among dissimilar concepts, ideas, or approaches; and (3) a broad range of organizations exist that would be capable of contributing toward the overall R&D goals of the program. DEAR 917.7301-1(c). DOE may accept—for award or support—all, none, or any number or part of the proposals submitted. DEAR 917.7301-1(d).

PROGRESS PAYMENT A payment made as costs are incurred by the contractor while work progresses under the contract. FAR 32.102(b). Progress payments are made on the basis of either a percentage of completion of the work or the incurrence of costs. Progress payments made on the basis of percentage of completion to construction contractors and architect-engineers are considered to be INVOICE PAYMENTs, which are subject to the PROMPT PAYMENT ACT. FAR 32.903. FAR Subpart 32.5 sets forth the policy and procedures for making progress payments based on costs. The payments are made under FAR guidelines using the CUSTOMARY PROGRESS PAYMENTs rate, the cost base and frequency of payment established in the contract's Progress Payments clause, and either the ordinary liquidation method (see FAR 32.503-8) or the alternate method (see FAR 32.503-9). Any other progress payments based on costs are considered UNUSUAL PROGRESS PAYMENTs and may be used only when authorized in exceptional cases. See FAR 32.501-1 and -2. The Progress Payment Not Included clause at FAR 52.232-15 is used to warn offerors that no progress payments will be included in the contract. See Cibinic & Nash, *Administration of Government Contracts* 1138–43 (3d ed. 1995); Murphy, *The Case Against Limiting the Base for Computing Progress Payments to Allowable Costs*, 95-2 CP&A Rep. 3 (Mar. 1995); Nash, *Postscript: Timely Payment of Subcontractors*, 7 N&CR ¶ 60 (Nov. 1993); Nash, *Timely Payment of Subcontractors: Is the Government Responsible?,* 7 N&CR ¶ 34 (June 1993); Paulini, *Administering Progress Payments—A Complex, Time Consuming Process*, 31 Cont. Mgmt. 12 (Aug. 1991). See also FINANCING.

PROJECT MANAGER (PM) An official responsible for planning and controlling assigned projects to achieve program goals. Typical duties that relate to the Government procurement process include establishing program objectives; developing requirements, including PURCHASE REQUESTs containing SPECIFICATIONs and STATEMENTS OF WORK; obtaining required approvals; scheduling, estimating, budgeting, and controlling projects; coordinating project planning with the contracting officer; and functioning as the CONTRACTING OFFICER REPRESENTATIVE or CONTRACTING OFFICER TECHNICAL REPRESENTATIVE. See also PROGRAM MANAGER.

PROJECT WAGE DETERMINATION See WAGE DETERMINATION.

PROJECTED AVERAGE LOSS The estimated long-term average loss per period for periods of comparable exposure to risk of loss. FAR 31.001. When a contractor has a SELF-INSURANCE program, costs of actual losses are not ALLOWABLE COSTs if they exceed projected average losses. FAR 31.205-19. See CAS 416, Accounting for Insurance Costs, 48 C.F.R. § 9904.416.

PROMISSORY ESTOPPEL A legal doctrine binding a person to a promise when another party has relied on the promise to its detriment and the person making the promise could have reasonably foreseen the reliance. *Restatement (Second) of Contracts* § 90 (1981). The court usually gives damages for breach of the promise commensurate with the costs incurred in reliance on the promise. The COURT OF FEDERAL

CLAIMS has ruled that it has no jurisdiction over claims of BREACH OF CONTRACT based on promissory estoppel. See Nash, *Promissory Estoppel: A Theory Without a Home in Government Contracts*, 3 N&CR ¶ 52 (July 1989).

PROMPT PAYMENT ACT (PPA) A 1983 Act, 31 U.S.C. § 3901 et seq., requiring solicitations and contracts to specify payment procedures, payment due dates, and INTEREST penalties for late INVOICE PAYMENTs. The Act is implemented by FAR Subpart 32.9 and OMB Circular No. A-125, *Prompt Payment*, Dec. 12, 1989. The Government must make invoice payments and contract FINANCING PAYMENTs as close as possible to, but not later than, the due dates specified in the contract (generally no longer than 30 days after receipt of a proper INVOICE). The detailed procedures followed are set forth in the Prompt Payment clause in FAR 52.232-25, the Prompt Payment for Fixed-Price Architect-Engineer Contract clause in FAR 52.232-26, and the Prompt Payment for Construction Contracts clause in FAR 52.232-27. Determination of the date of payment is based on receipt of a proper invoice or contract financing request and satisfactory contract performance. Checks are mailed and electronic funds transfers are made on or about the same day the payment action is dated. Agencies pay an interest penalty for late invoice payments or improperly taken discounts for prompt payment. See Cibinic & Nash, *Administration of Government Contracts* 1147–59, 1192–95 (3d ed. 1995); Schimpf, *Understanding the Prompt Payment Act*, 32 Cont. Mgmt. 40 (Aug. 1992); Renner, *Prompt Payment Act: An Interest(ing) Remedy for Government Late Payment*, 21 Pub. Con. L.J. 177 (1992); Nash, chap. 12, *Construction Contracting* 912–14 (1991); Rosen et al., *Prompt Payment Act Amendments of 1988*, 90-4 Briefing Papers (1990).

PROPERTY Tangible things of value. In FAR Part 45, providing guidance on GOVERNMENT PROPERTY, property is defined as all property, both real and personal. FAR 45.101. It includes FACILITIES, MATERIAL, SPECIAL TOOLING, SPECIAL TEST EQUIPMENT, and AGENCY-PECULIAR PROPERTY.

PROPERTY ADMINISTRATOR An AUTHORIZED REPRESENTATIVE of the contracting officer assigned to administer contract requirements and obligations relating to GOVERNMENT PROPERTY. FAR 45.501.

PROPOSAL An OFFER in a negotiated procurement (see NEGOTIATION). FAR 2.101. Proposals for new contracts are submitted in response to a REQUEST FOR PROPOSALS (RFPs) or a BROAD AGENCY ANNOUNCEMENT. The term "proposal" is generally used in FAR Part 15 to mean the offer submitted by an offeror in a negotiated procurement plus all the information that the RFP requires to be submitted with the offer. Proposal is also defined in FAR 31.001 as any offer or other submission used as a basis for pricing a contract, contract MODIFICATION, or termination settlement (see TERMINATION FOR CONVENIENCE) or for securing payments thereunder. Proposals for contract modifications or termination settlements are submitted pursuant to clauses of the contract. When proposals are submitted without prior request from a Government agency they are called UNSOLICITED PROPOSALs. See Nash, *The Technical Proposal: Is It Fish Or Fowl?*, 11 N&CR ¶ 22 (May 1997); Cibinic, *Oral Communications: Interviews, Presentations, Or Discussions But Not Proposals*, 10 N&CR ¶ 63 (Dec. 1996).

PROPOSAL EVALUATION In contracting by NEGOTIATION, the process by which the Government assesses an offeror's PROPOSAL (both the offer and the other information submitted in response to the REQUEST FOR PROPOSALS) to determine the relative merits of the offer and the offeror's ability to successfully accomplish a prospective contract. The Government conducts both a cost or price evaluation (using COST ANALYSIS or PRICE ANALYSIS), a PAST PERFORMANCE evaluation, and a TECHNICAL EVALUATION. FAR 15.305. 10 U.S.C. § 2305(b)(1) and 41 U.S.C. § 253b(a) require agencies to evaluate competitive proposals solely on the basis of factors specified in the SOLICITATION. They require that the solicitation describe the SOURCE SELECTION system to be used by listing all significant EVALUATION FACTORS and stating their RELATIVE IMPORTANCE. This statutory language essentially leaves procuring agencies free to use any proposal evaluation system they choose, and a wide variety of systems have been adopted. The agency manuals, handbooks, and documents that provide instructions on proposal evaluation demonstrate that there is no consensus on the procedures to be followed or the scoring systems to be used. Some call for evaluation by individual evaluators, while others require evaluation by teams. As to the scoring systems, some agencies use numerical scoring on all evaluation factors, including cost or price, whereas others require comparison of raw data on cost or price and narrative analysis of quality factors such as technical merit and management ability. See Cibinic & Nash, chap. 6, *Formation of Government Contracts* (3d ed. 1998); Nash, *Comparative Evaluations: A Very Red (Scarlet?) Herring*, 11 N&CR ¶ 59 (Nov. 1997); Jones, *Sample Tasks in Evaluation of Proposals*, Army Law. 32

(Sept. 1991); Nash, *Source Selection: A Variety of Agency Guidance*, 3 N&CR ¶ 60 (Aug. 1989); Nash, *Source Selection: The "Solicitation-Evaluation-Decision" Linkage*, 1 N&CR ¶ 56 (July 1987).

PROPOSAL MODIFICATION A change made to a PROPOSAL before the SOLICITATION closing date and time, made in response to an AMENDMENT, or made to correct a MISTAKE at any time before award. FAR 15.001. Proposal modifications must be submitted by the time specified or they will be treated as LATE PROPOSALs. FAR 15.208.

PROPOSAL REVISION A change to a PROPOSAL made after the SOLICIATION closing date, at the request of the contracting officer, as a result of DISCUSSIONs. FAR 15.001. Proposal revisions are made to document understandings reached during negotiations. FAR 15.307(b). At the conclusion of discussions, each offeror still in the COMPETITIVE RANGE must be given the opportunity to submit a FINAL PROPOSAL REVISION.

PROPRIETARY DATA TECHNICAL DATA submitted to the Government under a contract and subject to protection by the contractor. Under FAR Subpart 27.4 and DFARS Subpart 227.71 such data are subject to LIMITED RIGHTS if they are DEVELOPED AT PRIVATE EXPENSE or DEVELOPED EXCLUSIVELY AT PRIVATE EXPENSE, respectively. Under the DFARS the data can also be delivered subject to GOVERNMENT PURPOSE RIGHTS. See Simchak & Vogel, *A Few Words of Advice: Protecting Intellectual Property When Contracting with the Department of Defense According to the 1988 Regulations*, 23 Pub. Cont. L.J. 141 (1994); Witte, *Safeguards of Proprietary Data*, 26 Cont. Mgmt. 37 (June 1986). Restrictions on disclosure of proprietary data by Government employees are set forth in the PROCUREMENT INTEGRITY provisions (which now call it CONTRACTOR BID OR PROPOSAL INFORMATION) and the TRADE SECRETS ACT.

PROPRIETARY INFORMATION Information contained in a bid or proposal, COST OR PRICING DATA, or any other information submitted to the Government by a contractor and designated as proprietary. This term was used in the PROCUREMENT INTEGRITY Act, 41 U.S.C. § 423, prior to its amendment by the CLINGER-COHEN ACT OF 1996, to identify a class of information that could not be disclosed. The amended act uses the term CONTRACTOR BID OR PROPOSAL INFORMATION. FAR 52.215-1(e) provides that all information in a proposal may be marked as proprietary information. FAR 15.609 provides that all information in UNSOLICITED PROPOSALS may be marked as proprietary information. NASA has a more restrictive policy defining "proprietary information" as "information (data) that constitutes a TRADE SECRET and/or information that is commercial or financial and confidential or privileged." NFS 18-5.202(a). This information is also subject to protection from release in accordance with the FREEDOM OF INFORMATION ACT. See Manos, *Protecting Proprietary Information*, 94-13 Briefing Papers (Dec. 1994).

PROSECUTION OF CLAIMS The assertion by a contractor of a CLAIM for additional compensation or other benefit from the Government in a court or BOARD OF CONTRACT APPEALS. The fees and expenses of attorneys incurred in this effort are barred from being included in a judgment by 28 U.S.C. § 2412(a)(1). FAR 31.205-47(f) provides that costs of legal, accounting, and consulting services and directly associated costs incurred by contractors for such efforts are UNALLOWABLE COSTs. See Nash, *Postscript II: More Reflections on Reflectone*, 10 N&CR ¶ 35 (July 1996); Cibinic, *Allowable Contract Administration Costs vs. Unallowable Claim Costs: Bill Strong Reversed*, 9 N&CR ¶ 27 (Apr. 1995); Cibinic, *Costs Associated with Claims by or Against the Government: Reshuffling the Deck*, 4 N&CR ¶ 33 (May 1990). See also EQUAL ACCESS TO JUSTICE ACT; PROFESSIONAL AND CONSULTANT SERVICES.

PROSPECTIVE PRICING Pricing of a contract before the work is begun. It is the policy of the Government to use prospective pricing whenever possible. See LETTER CONTRACT.

PROTECTIVE ORDER An order of a court or administrative tribunal limiting the scope of the disclosure of PRIVILEGED INFORMATION. Protective orders are used to ensure that information obtained in DISCOVERY is not improperly used. They are issued under Rule 26(c) of the Federal Rules of Civil Procedure, Rule 14 of the UNIFORM RULES (in cases before the BOARDs OF CONTRACT APPEALS), and Rule 21.4 of the GENERAL ACCOUNTING OFFICE (in PROTESTs). See Cibinic, *Protective Orders: Expert Witnesses Exiled to Siberia*, 7 N&CR ¶ 64 (Nov. 1993); Peterson, *In-House Counsel and Protective Orders in Bid Protests*, 21 Pub. Cont. L.J. 53 (1991).

PROTÉGÉ FIRM See MENTOR-PROTÉGÉ PILOT PROGRAM.

PROTEST An objection, submitted by an INTERESTED PARTY in writing, protesting an agency solicitation for offers, the cancellation of a SOLICITATION, or the award or proposed award of a contract. FAR 33.101. Protests are also known as "bid protests," "award protests," or "protests against award." Protests can be made to (1) the procuring agency, before or after award, FAR 33.103; (2) the GENERAL ACCOUNTING OFFICE (GAO), within 10 calendar days after the grounds for the protest are known or should have been known, see GAO Bid Protest Regulations for detailed timing rules, 4 C.F.R. Part 21, FAR 33.104; (3) the UNITED STATES COURT OF FEDERAL CLAIMS, 28 U.S.C. § 1491(b)(1); and (4) the U.S. District Court, if the protester has suffered an "injury in fact" within six years of the date the cause of action arose (see SCANWELL ACTION). See FAR 52.233-2 and -3. See also Cibinic & Nash, chap. 11, *Formation of Government Contracts* (3d ed. 1998); Nash, *Protests & Debriefings: A Tangled Web*, 11 N&CR ¶ 47 (Sept. 1997); Cibinic, *Bid Protests: Additional Authority for the Courts*, 11 N&CR ¶ 14 (Mar. 1997); Lieberman, *Bid Protests at the Court of Federal Claims and the General Accounting Office: A Comparison*, 67 Fed. Cont. Rep. 382 (Mar. 31, 1997); Schnitzer, *The 1996 GAO Bid Protest Rules*, 96-13 Briefing Papers (Dec. 1996); Nash, *Protests in the General Accounting Office: The New Discovery Rules*, 10 N&CR ¶ 57 (Nov. 1996); Adelson, *The New Bid Protest Procedures—A Cautionary Note*, 36 Cont. Mgmt. 4 (June 1996); Allen & Harrington, *Pursuing a Classified Protest at the GAO*, 31 Procrmt. Law 21 (Fall 1995); Adelson, *Protests Against Procurements by Nonappropriated Fund Instrumentalities*, 95-12 Briefing Papers (Nov. 1995); American B. Ass'n, *The Protest Experience under the Competition in Contracting Act*, A.B.A. Sec. Pub. Cont. L. 1989; Shnitzer, *How to Recognize a Protestable Issue*, 93-3 Briefing Papers (Feb. 1993); Brittin, *The Comptroller General's Dual Statutory Authority to Decide Bid Protests*, 22 Pub. Cont. L.J. 636 (1993); Shnitzer, *The New GAO Protest Rules*, 92-4 Briefing Papers (Mar. 1992).

PROVISION A written term or condition used only in SOLICITATIONs and applying only before contract award. FAR 52.101. Solicitation provisions are distinguished from CLAUSEs, which are terms and conditions in contracts. FAR Subpart 52.2 sets forth the text of all FAR provisions and clauses (as do DFARS Subpart 252.2 and NFS Subpart 18-52.2 for DFARS and NASA provisions and clauses, respectively), each in its own separate subsection. The subpart is arranged by subject matter in the same order as, and keyed to, the parts of the FAR. All FAR provision numbers begin with "52.2." The next two digits correspond with the number of the FAR subject part in which the provision is prescribed. The number is completed by a hyphen and a sequential number assigned within each section of FAR Subpart 52.2. For example, FAR 52.223-1 contains the Clean Air and Water Certification provision prescribed at FAR 23.105(a), whereas FAR 52.223-2 contains the Clean Air and Water provision prescribed at FAR 23.105(b). The FAR provision number will be followed by the provision's title and, in solicitations, its effective date. FAR Subpart 52.1 contains instructions for using provisions, and FAR Subpart 52.3 contains an extensive PROVISION AND CLAUSE MATRIX.

PROVISION AND CLAUSE MATRIX A comprehensive chart in FAR Subpart 52.3 that provides menus of the solicitation PROVISIONs and contract CLAUSEs suitable for contracts of various types and purposes. The matrix (1) lists all FAR-prescribed provisions and clauses by number and title; (2) tells users where in the FAR each provision or clause is prescribed; (3) distinguishes provisions from clauses; (4) codes all the provisions and clauses to indicate whether they can be incorporated by reference or must be set forth in full text; (5) designates the section of the UNIFORM CONTRACT FORMAT in which each provision or clause should appear; and (6) categorizes the provisions and clauses as *required*, *required when applicable*, or *optional* in terms of each applicable type or purpose of contract.

PROVISIONAL PAYMENT An interim payment made by the Government to a contractor to provide compensation during the negotiation and settlement of CLAIMs or EQUITABLE ADJUSTMENT proposals. The FAR contains no guidance on such payments, but they are used by agencies to provide financing to contractors that have incurred substantial costs in performing work not covered by the contract because the contract has not been modified to reflect the value of the claim or adjustment. Provisional payments are made pursuant to MODIFICATIONs that generally limit such payments to an amount commensurate with the Government's evaluation of the value of the claim or proposal. See Cibinic & Nash, *Administration of Government Contracts* 1146–47 (3d ed. 1995); Nash, *Provisional Payments: Another Technique*, 3 N&CR ¶ 18 (Feb. 1989); Nash, *Provisional Payments: A Well Kept Secret*, 2 N&CR ¶ 67 (Nov. 1988).

PUBLIC INTEREST In the interest of the United States. This term is frequently used when broad authority is granted to an officer of the Government. For example, 10 U.S.C. § 2304(c)(7) and 41 U.S.C. § 253(c)(7) permit award of contracts without FULL AND OPEN

COMPETITION when the HEAD OF THE AGENCY determines that such action would be in the public interest. Further, FAR 14.209 instructs that invitations for bids should not be cancelled unless cancellation is clearly in the public interest, and FAR 25.102 explains that the BUY AMERICAN ACT requires purchase of domestic end products except where the agency head determines that domestic preference would be inconsistent with the public interest.

PUBLIC LAW 85-804 See EXTRAORDINARY CONTRACTUAL ACTION.

PUBLIC RELATIONS All functions and activities dedicated to (1) maintaining, protecting, and enhancing the image of a concern or its products; or (2) maintaining or promoting reciprocal understanding and favorable relations with the public. FAR 31.205-1. Public relations costs are ALLOWABLE COSTs only in specified circumstances. See FAR 31.205-1(d). See also ADVERTISEMENT.

PUBLICIZING CONTRACT ACTIONS The dissemination to the public of information about proposed contract actions and awards. The primary purposes of making such information available are to enhance competition and to improve small business access to acquisition opportunities. Contracting officers are required by 15 U.S.C. § 637(e) and 41 U.S.C. § 416 to disseminate information on proposed contract information by (1) synopsizing in the COMMERCE BUSINESS DAILY (CBD) proposed contract actions expected to exceed $25,000; and (2) for contract actions between $10,000 and $25,000, displaying in a public place, including an electronic bulletin board or other electronic means, a notice or copy of the solicitation. In addition, other methods of publicizing contract actions which the contracting officer may use include (1) preparing and displaying periodic handouts listing proposed contracts, (2) assisting local trade associations in disseminating information to their members, (3) making brief announcements of proposed contracts to newspapers, trade journals, magazines or other mass media outlets, and (4) placing paid advertisements in newspapers or other communications media. See FAR Part 5. NASA is required to make all its synopses available on the Internet in addition to publication in the CBD. NASA Midrange acquisitions with annual sales up to $500,000 are made available only on the Internet. NFS 18-5.201.

PUNITIVE DAMAGES Damages that are awarded in a civil action, in addition to COMPENSATORY DAMAGES, to punish a DEFENDANT for gross or willful misconduct. Punitive damages are generally not recoverable in BREACH OF CONTRACT actions. *Restatement (Second) of Contracts* § 355 (1981). They are recoverable in TORT actions between private parties but not in actions under the FEDERAL TORT CLAIMS ACT.

PURCHASE CARD See GOVERNMENT-WIDE COMMERCIAL PURCHASE CARD.

PURCHASE DESCRIPTION A description of the essential physical characteristics and functions required to meet the Government's requirements. When used in a general sense, the term embraces SPECIFICATIONs, STANDARDs, and other means of describing the Government's requirements. It can be used more narrowly, however, to denote a description developed for a given procurement when no existing specification is appropriate. Purchase descriptions must describe the supplies or services to be acquired in a manner designed to permit FULL AND OPEN COMPETITION. They must not specify a product or feature of a product peculiar to one manufacturer, thereby precluding consideration of products from other companies, unless the particular product or feature is essential to the Government's requirements and other companies' similar products or products lacking the particular feature would not meet the Government's MINIMUM NEEDS. FAR 11.104. See FAR 11.105 for drafting requirements of purchase descriptions for service contracts.

PURCHASE ORDER (PO) An OFFER by the Government to buy supplies or services, including construction and research and development, upon specified terms and conditions, using SIMPLIFIED ACQUISITION PROCEDURES. FAR 13.001. See FAR 13.302. A binding contract may be formed upon either (1) written acceptance of the purchase order by the contractor (see BILATERAL CONTRACT) or (2) the contractor's undertaking performance of the work (see UNILATERAL CONTRACT). FAR 13.302-3. Standard Form 44 can be used for small, over-the-counter purchases. FAR 13.306. Standard Form 1449 or Optional Form 347, Order for Supplies or Services, FAR 53.302-347 may also be used as a purchase order, or an agency form/format may be used. FAR 13.307. Purchase orders are generally issued on a FIRM-FIXED-PRICE CONTRACT basis; but they may provide for ECONOMIC PRICE ADJUSTMENT when used to buy COMMERCIAL ITEMS. FAR 12.207. They should reflect any trade or prompt payment discounts that are offered. FAR 13.302-1(a)(5). Unpriced purchase orders may be used in limited circumstances. FAR 13.302-2. Guidance on the modification of purchase orders is set forth in FAR 13.302-3 and DFARS 213.503. See Cibinic & Nash, chap. 7, Sec. II., *Formation of Government Contracts* (3d ed. 1998).

PURCHASE REQUEST A document that, when submitted to a contracting office, officially initiates a particular procurement action; sometimes called a requisition or request for contract. Purchase requests provide the official basis for deciding how a procurement will be conducted and how a contract will be awarded. They contain a description of the requirement, required authorizations, and necessary administrative details that enable the contracting officer to prepare and issue a SOLICITATION and develop a contract document. The heart of the procurement request is the SPECIFICATION, STATEMENT OF WORK, or PURCHASE DESCRIPTION, which tells what must be delivered or accomplished.

Q

QUALIFICATION REQUIREMENT See PREQUALIFICATION.

QUALIFIED BIDDERS LIST (QBL) A list of bidders who have had their products examined and tested and who have satisfied all applicable qualification requirements for those products or have otherwise satisfied all applicable qualification requirements. FAR 9.201. These lists are used infrequently in the procurement process. FAR Subpart 9.2 sets forth the procedures that must be used to establish QBLs and to use them in the procurement process. See also PREQUALIFICATION.

QUALIFIED MANUFACTURERS LIST (QML) A list of manufacturers who have had their products examined and tested and who have satisfied all applicable qualification requirements for those products. FAR 9.201. These lists are used when an agency determines that manufacturers must have special capabilities to enable them to meet the Government requirements. FAR Subpart 9.2 sets forth the procedures that must be used to establish QMLs and to use them in the procurement process. See also PREQUALIFICATION.

QUALIFIED PRODUCTS LIST (QPL) A list of products that have been examined and tested and have satisfied all applicable qualification requirements. FAR 9.201. These lists are used on procuremenmts to restrict offerors on procurements to those products on the lists. FAR Subpart 9.2 sets forth the procedures that must be used to establish QPLs and to use them in the procurement process. See also PREQUALIFICATION.

QUALITY ASSURANCE (QA) Tasks performed by persons *outside* an organization to monitor or improve the quality of the organization's output. In Government contracting, QA refers to the various functions, including INSPECTION, performed by the Government to determine whether a contractor has fulfilled its contract obligations pertaining to quality and quantity. FAR 46.101. Government contracting QA may also be defined as a planned, systematic pattern of actions taken to provide adequate confidence that sufficient technical requirements are established, that products and services conform to those requirements, and that satisfactory performance is achieved. DFARS 246.101. The term QUALITY CONTROL is sometimes used interchangeably with quality assurance; for example, the General Services Administration (GSA) has a quality control division in each of its 10 regions that ensures the quality of the products and services GSA procures. See Zupa et al., *Quality Assurance Requirements*, 93-13 Briefing Papers (Dec. 1993).

QUALITY CONTROL (QC) Tasks performed by persons *within* an organization to improve the quality of the organization's output. FAR 46.105 states the Government policy that contractors have the fundamental responsibility for control of the quality of the work they perform. The INSPECTION requirements of most Government contracts call for the contractor to provide a QC system that ensures that the work meets contract requirements. FAR Subpart 46.3. QC can be seen as consisting of four steps: (1) setting cost, performance, safety, and reliability standards (or noting the standards that apply to a given contract); (2) comparing the offered product or service with those standards; (3) taking corrective action when necessary; and (4) planning for improvements.

QUANTUM The amount owed by one party to the other party as a result of a CLAIM on the contract. This amount is generally determined by computing the EQUITABLE ADJUSTMENT or PRICE ADJUSTMENT called for by a contract clause. On occasion, it is determined by computing DAMAGES for BREACH OF CONTRACT. BOARDS OF CONTRACT APPEALS frequently delay the determination of quantum until they have decided whether the claim has merit. See BIFURCATION OF ENTITLEMENT AND QUANTUM.

QUANTUM MERUIT A Latin expression meaning "as much as he deserves." Quantum meruit is an equitable doctrine, and it implies a promise to pay a reasonable amount for work completed or materials or services provided. The doctrine is based on the concept that there should not be unjust enrichment by one contracting party for the labor and materials expended by the other party. *Black's Law Dictionary* 1243 (6th ed. 1990). The term is traditionally used by courts to describe an action for the value of services performed. When RATIFICATION of an unauthorized contractual commitment is not permissible due to improprieties in the procurement, the contracting officer may recommend that payment be made for services rendered on a quantum merit basis (the reasonable value of work or LABOR), provided there is a showing that the Government received a benefit. GSAR 501.602-3. See Cibinic & Nash, *Administration of Government Contracts* 695–97 (3d ed. 1995); Cibinic, *Invalid or Unauthorized Commitments: Up the Creek Without a Contract*, 1 N&CR ¶ 64 (Aug. 1987). See also QUANTUM VALEBENT.

QUANTUM VALEBANT A Latin expression meaning "as much as they were worth." The term is traditionally used by the courts to describe an action for the value of goods delivered. When RATIFICATION of an unauthorized contractual commitment is not permissible due to improprieties in the procurement, the contracting officer may recommend that payment be made for goods furnished on a quantum valebant basis (the reasonable value of goods sold and delivered), provided there is a showing that the Government received a benefit. GSAR 501.602-3. See Cibinic, *Invalid or Unauthorized Commitments: Up the Creek Without a Contract*, 1 N&CR ¶ 64 (Aug. 1987).

QUASI-CONTRACT See IMPLIED CONTRACT.

QUI TAM PROCEEDINGS A legal procedure named for a Latin phrase meaning (in its entirety) "who sues for the king as well as for himself in the matter." Under the 1986 amendments to the FALSE CLAIMS ACT, any person may bring a civil action under the Act "for the person and for the United States," and the action is brought in the name of the United States." 31 U.S.C. § 3730(b). The qui tam plaintiff files a civil complaint, typically against an employer/contractor. If DOJ intervenes, it bears primary responsibility for prosecuting the action. If DOJ fails to intervene, the qui tam plaintiff may continue the suit to conclusion. Qui tam plaintiffs are given a share of the Government's monetary recovery against the contractor and are granted WHISTLEBLOWER protection. 31 U.S.C. § 3730(h). See Cibinic & Nash, chap. 1, Sec. VII., *Formation of Government Contracts* (3d ed. 1998); Cibinic, *Litigation Costs: Employee Allegations of Improper Conduct*, 11 N&CR ¶ 53 (Oct. 1997); Cibinic, *Fraud, Forfeiture, and Collateral Estoppel*, 11 N&CR ¶ 46 (Sept. 1997); Callahan, *Double Dippers or Bureaucracy Busters? False Claims Act Suits by Government Employees*, 49 Wash. U. J. & Contemp. L. 97 (1996); Kovacic, *Whistleblower Bounty Lawsuits as Monitoring Devices in Government Contracting*, 29 Loy. L.A. L. Rev. 1799 (1996); Vogel, *The Public Disclosure Bar Against Qui Tam Suits*, 24 Pub. Cont. L.J. 477 (1995); Salcido, *Screening Out Unworthy Whistleblower Actions: An Historical Analysis of the Public Disclosure Jurisdictional Bar to Qui Tam Actions*

Under the False Claims Act, 24 Pub. Cont. L.J. 237 (1995); Ryland, *The Government Contractor's Dilemma: Voluntary Disclosures as the Source of Qui Tam Litigation*, 22 Pub. Cont. L.J. 764 (1993); Vogel, *Eligibility Requirements for Relators Under Qui Tam Provisions of the False Claims Act*, 21 Pub. Cont. L.J. 593 (1992); Brady, *Recent Developments in the Area of "Qui Tam" Lawsuits: A New Weapon for Challenging Those Who May Be Submitting False Claims*, 37 Fed. B. News & J. 592 (1990); Victorino et al., *"Qui Tam" Lawsuits*, 89-10 Briefing Papers (Sept. 1989); Waldman, *The 1986 Amendments to the False Claims Act: Retroactive or Prospective?,* 18 Pub Cont. L.J. 469 (1989); Graham, *The Qui Tam Amendments: Privatizing the Civil Prosecution Function*, 49 Fed. Cont. Rep. 659 (Apr. 4, 1988).

QUOTATION A statement of current prices for items being procured under SMALL PURCHASE PROCEDURES, made in response to Standard Form 18, Request for Quotations, FAR 53.301-18, or to an oral request for quotations. FAR 13.004. Quotations are also solicited, on occasion, on major procurements when competition is not contemplated. A quotation does not constitute a binding OFFER; therefore, issuance by the Government of an order in response to a supplier's quotation does not establish a contract. FAR 13.004.

R

RACKETEER INFLUENCED AND CORRUPT ORGANIZATIONS (RICO) ACT An Act, 18 U.S.C. §§ 1961–1968, that does not penalize on the basis of a specific crime, but imposes additional criminal and civil penalties on persons who engage in a pattern of racketeering activity, defined as the violation of two or more of more than 30 specified federal and state statutes during a 10-year period. Crimes that can serve as predicates for a RICO violation include BRIBERY, the furnishing of an illegal GRATUITY, and mail and wire FRAUD, but not false claims or false statements (see FALSE CLAIMS ACT and FALSE STATEMENTS ACT). To establish a RICO criminal violation, the Government must prove the existence of an enterprise that affected interstate or foreign commerce and employed an individual who knowingly and willfully participated, directly or indirectly, in the affairs of the enterprise through a pattern of racketeering activity. See Seyfarth et al., *The Government Contract Compliance Handbook* 1-42 and 1-43 (2d ed. 1991 & 1996 Supp.).

RANGE OF INCENTIVE EFFECTIVENESS (RIE) Under a COST-PLUS-INCENTIVE-FEE CONTRACT, the dollar range of possible cost outcomes under which the contractor has a monetary incentive to control costs through sound management. The contract specifies a MAXIMUM FEE and a MINIMUM FEE which place limits on the sharing required by the incentive formula. The RIE is the range of costs within these limits. If the ALLOWABLE COSTS incurred falls outside of the RIE, the contract becomes, in effect, a COST-PLUS-FIXED-FEE CONTRACT. See Cibinic & Nash, chap. 8, Sec. IV., *Formation of Government Contracts* (3d ed. 1998).

RATED ORDER A prime contract or resulting SUBCONTRACT or PURCHASE ORDER for products, services, or materials (including CONTROLLED MATERIALS) that is placed by a delegate agency (one authorized by delegation from the DEPARTMENT OF COMMERCE) under the provisions of the DEFENSE PRIORITIES AND ALLOCATIONS SYSTEM in support of an authorized program (one approved by the Federal Emergency Management Agency. Such orders receive preferential treatment. FAR 11.601; 50 U.S.C. app. § 2061 et seq. Rated orders receive ratings of DX and DO; DX ratings have priority. Contractors and suppliers may be directed to accept rated orders, rearrange production or delivery schedules to accommodate them, or improve shipments against them. See FAR 11.603.

RATIFICATION The act, by an official who has the authority to do so, of approving an unauthorized commitment. FAR 1.602-3(a). An unauthorized commitment is an agreement that is not binding solely because the Government representative who made it lacked the authority to enter into that agreement on behalf of the Government. Unless a higher-level official is designated by the agency, the HEAD OF THE CONTRACTING ACTIVITY (HCA) may ratify any unauthorized commitment if (1) supplies or services have been provided to and accepted by the Government, (2) the official could have entered into a HCA or higher-level contractual commitment at the time it was made and still has the authority to do so, (3) the contract would have been proper if made by an appropriate contracting officer, (4) the contracting officer reviewing the unauthorized commitment determines the price to be fair and reasonable, (5) the contracting officer recommends payment and legal counsel concurs, (6) funds are available and were available at the time the unauthorized commitment was made, and (7) the ratification is in accordance with any other limitations prescribed under agency procedures. FAR 1.602-3(c). Ratification can also be accomplished outside of the FAR procedures. Courts and boards of contract appeals also find that ratification has occurred in the course of contract performance. See Cibinic & Nash, chap. 1, Sec. III., *Formation of Government Contracts* (3d ed. 1998); Nash, *Authority of Unauthorized Representatives: It Ain't Necessarily So*, 5 N&CR ¶ 56 (Oct. 1991).

REAL PROPERTY Land and rights in land, ground improvements, utility distribution systems, and buildings and other structures. FAR 45.101. Real property does not include foundations and other work necessary for installing SPECIAL TOOLING, SPECIAL TEST EQUIPMENT, or PLANT EQUIPMENT. Real property purchases are not covered by the FEDERAL ACQUISITION REGULATION or the CONTRACT DISPUTES ACT OF 1978. However, construction contracts are not considered real property for this purpose.

REASONABLE PRICE See FAIR AND REASONABLE PRICE.

REASONABLENESS OF COST One of the elements in the determination of whether a cost is an ALLOWABLE COST. A cost is reasonable if, in its nature and amount, it does not exceed that which would be incurred by a prudent person in the conduct of competitive business. The Government attaches no presumption of reasonableness to the incurrence of costs by a contractor. If an initial review of the facts results in the challenge of a specific cost by the contracting officer or the contracting officer's representative, the burden of proof is on the contractor. What is reasonable depends on a variety of considerations and circumstances, including (1) the type of cost generally recognized as ordinary and necessary for the conduct of the contractor's business or the performance of the contract; (2) generally accepted sound business practices, arm's-length bargaining, and federal and state laws and regulations; (3) the contractor's responsibilities to the Government, other customers, the owners of the business, employees, and the public at large; and (4) any significant deviations from the contractor's established practices. FAR 31.201-3. See Cibinic & Nash, *Cost-Reimbursement Contracting* 726–47 (2d ed. 1993).

RECORD Under the Privacy Act of 1974, 5 U.S.C. § 552a, any item, collection, or grouping of information about an individual (1) that is maintained by an agency, including the individual's education, financial transactions, medical history, and criminal or employment history; and (2) that contains the name, identifying number, symbol, or other identifying particular, such as a fingerprint, voice print, or photograph assigned to the individual. FAR 24.101. "Records" also denotes books, papers, maps, photographs, machine-readable materials, or other documentary materials, regardless of physical form or characteristic, made or received by an agency of the U.S. Government under federal law or in connection with the transaction of public business, and preserved or appropriated for preservation by that agency or its legitimate successor either as evidence of the organization, functions, policies, decisions, procedures, operations, or other activities of the Government or because of the informational value of the data in them. Library and museum material made or acquired and preserved solely for reference or exhibition purposes, extra copies of documents preserved only for convenience of reference, and stocks of publications and of processed documents are not included. 44 U.S.C. § 3301. The term AGENCY RECORDS is used in conjunction with the FREEDOM OF INFORMATION ACT. See FAR Subpart 4.7 regarding contractor records. See also West & Kassel, *Access to Contractor Records*, 88-5 Briefing Papers (Apr. 1988).

RECORD DRAWINGS Drawings submitted by a contractor or subcontractor at any tier to show the CONSTRUCTION of a particular structure or work as actually completed under the contract. FAR 36.102. When these drawings are required to be prepared, FAR 36.521 requires the use of alternate versions of the Specifications and Drawings for Construction clause in FAR 52.236-21. Record drawings are frequently called as-built drawings. They are often used, in conjunction with AS-PLANNED DRAWINGS, to prove DELAY.

RECORDS DISPOSITION Any disposal by destruction or donation of RECORDs no longer necessary for the conduct of business; transfer of records to federal agency storage facilities or records centers; transfer to the National Archives of the United States of records determined to have sufficient historical or other value to warrant continued preservation; or transfer of records from one federal agency to any other federal agency. 44 U.S.C. § 2901(5). Electronic records may be destroyed only in accordance with a records disposition schedule approved by the Archivist of the United States. 36 C.F.R. § 1234.32. See *Records Management Handbook: Disposition of Federal Records* (National Archives and Records Administration 1996).

RECORDS MAINTENANCE AND USE Any activity involving location of RECORDs of a federal agency; storage, retrieval, and handling of records kept at office file locations by or for a federal agency; processing of mail by a federal agency; or selection and use of equipment and supplies associated with records and copying. 44 U.S.C. § 2901(4).

RECORDS MANAGEMENT The planning, controlling, directing, organizing, training, promoting, and other managerial activities involved in RECORDs creation, RECORDS MAINTENANCE AND USE, and RECORDS DISPOSITION in order to achieve (1) adequate and proper documentation of the policies and transactions of the Federal Government, and (2) effective and economical management of agency operations. 44 U.S.C. § 2901(2). The HEAD OF THE AGENCY is responsible for complying with the records management policies and guidance provided by the Administrator of the General Services Administration and the Archivist of the United States for all media (paper, electronic, or other). See 44 U.S.C. § 2904.

RECOUPMENT The recovery by the Government, pursuant to contract provisions, of Government-funded NONRECURRING COSTS from contractors that sell, LEASE, or LICENSE the resulting products or technology to buyers other than the Federal Government. FAR 35.001. Contract clauses calling for recoupment were widely used on DOD contracts in the 1970s and 1980s but are no longer used except on FOREIGN MILITARY SALES (FMS) contracts. Section 4303 of the CLINGER-COHEN ACT amended the Arms Export Control Act, 22 U.S.C. § 2761(e)(2), to permit the President to waive recoupment on foreign military sales. DOD Directive 2140.2, *Recoupment of Non-recurring Costs (NC) on Sales of U.S. Items*, Jan. 13, 1993. See Nash, *Postscript: Recoupment*, 6 N&CR ¶ 60 (Oct. 1992); Victorino & McQuade, *Nonrecurring Costs Recoupment*, 90-10 Briefing Papers (Sept. 1990).

RECOVERED MATERIALS Materials that have been collected or recovered from solid waste. FAR 23.402. FAR Subpart 23.4 sets forth the Government policy to encourage contractors to use such materials in the performance of their contracts. See RESOURCE CONSERVATION AND RECOVERY ACT.

RECRUITMENT COSTS The costs of locating and hiring new employees necessary for the performance of the contractor's work. FAR 31.205-34 specifies that such costs, typically including help-wanted ADVERTISING, operating costs of an employment office, aptitude and testing programs, recruiter and prospective employee travel costs, and fees paid to employment agencies, are ALLOWABLE COSTs with certain specified limitations. See Cibinic & Nash, *Cost-Reimbursement Contracting* 836–38 (2d ed. 1993).

RECURRING COSTS Production costs, such as LABOR and materials, that vary with the quantity being produced. FAR 17.103. Such costs are distinguished from NONRECURRING COSTS.

REDETERMINABLE CONTRACT See FIXED-PRICE REDETERMINATION—PROSPECTIVE CONTRACT and FIXED-PRICE REDETERMINATION—RETROACTIVE CONTRACT.

REDUCTION TO PRACTICE See FIRST ACTUAL REDUCTION TO PRACTICE.

REFORMATION An equitable remedy used to reframe written contracts to reflect the real agreement between contracting parties when, through either MUTUAL MISTAKE or UNILATERAL MISTAKE coupled with actual or equitable FRAUD by any party, the writing fails to represent the contract the parties made. If the writing does not conform to the parties' agreement, by mistake of fact as to the writing's contents or by mistake of law with regard to the writing's legal effect, the writing can be reformed to accord with the agreement. *Black's Law Dictionary* 1281 (6th ed. 1990). Usually a court will not grant reformation unless it can determine from the conduct of the parties the terms of the agreement that they would have agreed to but for the mistake. See, however, *National Presto Industries, Inc. v. United States*, 167 Ct. Cl. 749, 338 F.2d 99 (1964), *cert. denied,* 380 U.S. 962 (1960), where the court granted reformation in the contract price without clear evidence of the price that would have been agreed to. See also Nash, *Reformation to Correct a Mistake in a Bid or Proposal: What "Mistakes" Qualify?,* 10 N&CR ¶ 11 (Feb. 1996); Cibinic & Nash, *Administration of Government Contracts* 343–46 (3d ed. 1995); Nash, *Contract Reformation: A Means of Getting Rid of Nasty Clauses*, 4 N&CR ¶ 58 (Oct. 1990).

REJECTION OF BID The determination by the contracting officer that a bid does not conform to the essential requirements of an INVITATION FOR BIDS. Such bids must be rejected because they are not responsive (see RESPONSIVENESS). FAR 14.404-2. All bids may be rejected, and the invitations for bids cancelled before award but after BID OPENING, for reasons including, but not limited to, the following: (1) cancellation is in the public interest, (2) bids were collusive or submitted in bad faith, (3) the supplies or services being procured are no longer needed, or (4) the SPECIFICATIONs have been revised. FAR 14.404-1. See Cibinic & Nash, chap. 5, Sec. II., *Formation of Government Contracts* (3d ed. 1998).

REJECTION OF WORK The Government's refusal to accept work that does not conform to the requirements of a contract. The right of rejection is the initial right granted to the Government in the standard INSPECTION clauses used in Government contracts. FAR 46.407 states that contracting officers should reject supplies or services not conforming in all respects to contract requirements, but contractors ordinarily should be given an opportunity to correct or replace nonconforming supplies or services when correction or replacement can be accomplished within the required delivery schedule. FAR 46.407(d) permits contracting officers to decide not to reject work when the nonconformance is minor, but FAR 46.407(f) requires that an EQUITABLE ADJUSTMENT reducing the price or other CONSIDERATION be obtained when this is done. See Cibinic & Nash, *Administration of Government Contracts* 833–52 (3d ed. 1995).

"RELATING TO THE CONTRACT" Having a connection with a contract. This term of art is used in the CONTRACT DISPUTES ACT OF 1978 to broaden the scope of the DISPUTEs process to include claims that cannot be resolved through a contract clause providing for the type of relief sought, such as claims for BREACH OF CONTRACT or for correction of MISTAKEs. Prior to the Act, the disputes process covered only claims "ARISING UNDER THE CONTRACT." The effect of this broadened scope is to make the current Disputes clause in FAR 52.233-1 an ALL DISPUTES CLAUSE. FAR 33.205 emphasizes the all-encompassing scope of the current clause by stating that many claims previously submitted under Pub. L. No. 85-804 should be handled through the disputes procedures. See Cibinic & Nash, *Administration of Government Contracts* 1244–46 (3d ed. 1995).

RELATIVE IMPORTANCE The relationship of the EVALUATION FACTORS and subfactors in a BEST VALUE PROCUREMENT. The REQUEST FOR PROPOSALS must state the relative importance of the evaluation factors and significant subfactors in order to provide prospective offerors with information on which evaluation factors the agency believes to be most important in satisfying the agency's procurement objectives. FAR 15.304(d). The statement of relative importance does not control the ultimate source selection decision because that is made on the basis of trade-offs between the proposals received. See Nash, *Best Value Procurement: Random Musings on the Current State of the Art*, 11 N&CR ¶ 44 (Sept. 1997); Edwards, *The Relative Importance of Source Selection Evaluation Factors: Analysis of a Misunderstood Rule*, 10 N&CR ¶ 34 (July 1996); Nash, *Evaluating Competitive Proposals: Relative Importance of the Factors*, 6 N&CR ¶ 17 (Mar. 1992); Nash, *Source Selection: The Request for Proposal Language*, 2 N&CR ¶ 57 (Sept. 1988).

RELEASE An agreement of a contracting party that the other party will not be liable if CLAIMs are asserted in the future. An unconditional general release by a contractor bars all existing contractor claims, including pending claims as well as known and unknown claims. The contractor, however, may preserve its rights to specific claims by expressly excepting those claims when the release is executed. The contract may require the contractor to give a release of claims and liabilities before the Government makes final payment. FAR 43.204(c)(2) states that contracting officers should insert releases in SUPPLEMENTAL AGREEMENTs settling claims. See Cibinic & Nash, *Administration of Government Contracts* 1227–31 (3d ed. 1995).

RELOCATION COSTS The costs incident to the permanent change of duty or assignment of an existing employee or upon recruitment of a new employee. FAR 31.205-35 specifies that such costs incurred by contractors are ALLOWABLE COSTs if the assignment is for a period of not less than 12 months and if specified limitations are met. Allowable relocation costs include travel and transportation costs, cost of finding a new home, closing costs, mortgage interest differential payments, rental differential payments, and the cost of canceling an unexpired lease. See Cibinic & Nash, *Cost-Reimbursement Contracting* 838–40 (2d ed. 1993).

REMEDY The right of a contracting party when the other party does not fulfill its contractual obligations. In general, contracting parties have remedies for BREACH OF CONTRACT by the other party. However, in Government contracts most of the remedies available to the parties are spelled out in contract clauses. Thus, the Government has remedies for nonperformance under the TERMINATION FOR DEFAULT clause and for defective performance under the INSPECTION clause of the contract. The contractor's remedies are generally for EQUITABLE ADJUSTMENT or PRICE ADJUSTMENT under a variety of clauses. Prospective contractors also have remedies against the Government through the PROTEST procedures. See Taylor, *Subcontractor Remedies*, 86-8 Briefing Papers (July 1986).

REMEDY COORDINATION OFFICIAL (RCO) A person or entity that coordinates within an agency the administration of criminal, civil, administrative, and contractual remedies resulting from investigations of FRAUD or corruption related to procurement activities. The term was created by § 836(a) of the FY91 Defense Authorization Act, Pub. L. No. 101-510. See FAR 32.006-2. If an agency RCO finds substantial evidence that a contractor's request for advance, partial, or PROGRESS PAYMENT under a contract is based on fraud, the RCO must recommend that the head of the agency reduce or suspend further payments to that contractor. 10 U.S.C. § 2307(h)(1). See Knight & Ochs, *Withholding Payments under the FY 1991 DOD Authorization Act*, 90-12 CP&A Rep. 3 (Dec. 1990).

REMOTE TERMINAL EMULATION (RTE) A technique for validating the performance of FEDERAL INFORMATION PROCESSING RESOURCES equipment and teleprocessing systems when it is not practical to conduct BENCHMARKs with the total proposed network of computers, terminal devices, and data communications facilities. RTE was originally developed in the 1960s by computer hardware manufacturers to test the functions and performance of their interactive systems. RTE, as originally formulated, emulated a set of dumb terminals attached to a large host processor. The General Services Administration subsequently developed standards for RTE, which it published in a 1979 handbook (now out of print), *Use and Specification of Remote-Terminal Emulation in ADP System Acquisition.* The material is somewhat dated and no longer mandatory, but it still provides useful information and guidance on RTE. The disadvantages of using RTE are the same as for any other benchmark test and are compounded by the fact that the procedure is much more complex.

RENEGOTIATION The recovery from a contractor of an amount determined to reflect "excessive profits" made in the performance of defense contracts. 50 U.S.C. § 1213 et seq. Renegotiation began in 1942 and ended in 1976 and was carried out, after 1950, by an independent Government agency known as the Renegotiation Board. Essentially covering defense and space-related contracts, renegotiation considered a contractor's business in a single, composite assessment each fiscal year. In most cases, the most difficult and complex part of renegotiation was determining the extent to which the contractor's PROFITs were excessive. Contractors were entitled, under the statute, to DE NOVO review of the Renegotiation Board's decision in the Court of Claims. See Cibinic & Nash, *Federal Procurement Law*, vol. II, 1996–2026 (3d ed. 1980).

RENTAL COSTS The costs paid to the owner of real or personal property for the use of that property. FAR 31.205-36 sets forth the rules on when such costs incurred by a contractor are ALLOWABLE COSTs. The cost principle focuses on the reasonableness of the rental costs, considering the following factors: (1) rental costs of similar property; (2) market conditions in the area; (3) type, estimated life, and value of the property; (4) alternatives to the leased asset; and (5) the provisions of the lease. The allowability of rental costs of AUTOMATIC DATA PROCESSING EQUIPMENT is discussed in FAR 31.205-2. See Faulconer, *Limitations on Contractor Recovery of Lease Costs: Considerations and Concerns*, 26 Pub. Cont. L.J. 623 (1997); Cibinic & Nash, *Cost-Reimbursement Contracting* 859–62 (2d ed. 1993).

RENTAL EQUIVALENT An evaluation factor, equal to the amount of rent that would normally be charged, that is added to a competitor's offered price to overcome the UNFAIR COMPETITIVE ADVANTAGE gained from the rent-free use of GOVERNMENT PRODUCTION OR RESEARCH PROPERTY. FAR 45.202-1. This amount is computed in accordance with the Use and Charges clause in FAR 52.245-9. The rental equivalent is generally calculated by the contracting officer issuing the supply contract on which the property will be used. In the alternative, rent can be charged by the contracting officer having cognizance over the FACILITIES CONTRACT governing the property. FAR 45.202-2. See Tomanelli, *The Duty to Eliminate Competitive Advantage Arising from Contractor Possession of Government-Furnished Property*, 142 Mil. L. Rev. 141 (Fall 1994).

REPAIRS AND MAINTENANCE The total endeavor to obtain the expected service during the life of TANGIBLE CAPITAL ASSETs. CAS 404, Capitalization of Tangible Assets, 48 C.F.R. § 9904.404-30. Maintenance is the regularly recurring activity of keeping assets in normal or expected operating condition. Repair is the activity of putting them back into normal or expected operating condition. Under CAS 409, Depreciation of Tangible Capital Assets, 48 C.F.R. § 9904.409, the costs of repairs and maintenance must be taken into account in estimating the service life of a TANGIBLE CAPITAL ASSET and determining appropriate DEPRECIATION charges. 48 C.F.R. § 9904.409-50(a).

REPOSITORY See DATA REPOSITORY.

REPUDIATION Rejection, disclaimer, or renunciation. Repudiation of a contract is the refusal to perform a duty or obligation owed to the other party. It may consist of words or actions. Repudiation of a contract before the performance is due serves as an anticipatory BREACH OF CONTRACT but does not constitute a breach unless the other party elects to treat it as such. *Black's Law Dictionary* 1303 (6th ed. 1990). If the contractor, at any time, repudiates the contract, the Government can terminate the contract for default (see TERMINATION FOR DEFAULT). *Fairfield Scientific Corp.*, ASBCA 21151, 78-1 BCA ¶ 13,082, *aff'd*, 78-2 BCA ¶ 13,429. Repudiations may be withdrawn, however, if the withdrawal occurs before the termination action. U.C.C. § 2-611. Repudiation is sometimes called ANTICIPATORY REPUDIATION. See Cibinic & Nash, *Administration of Government Contracts* 953–61 (3d ed. 1995).

REPURCHASE AGAINST CONTRACTOR'S ACCOUNT See EXCESS COSTS OF REPROCUREMENT.

REQUEST FOR CONTRACT See PURCHASE REQUEST.

REQUEST FOR EQUITABLE ADJUSTMENT (REA) A request by one of the contracting parties for an EQUITABLE ADJUSTMENT under a contract clause providing for such adjustment. Under the CONTRACT DISPUTES ACT OF 1978, an REA is distinguished from a CLAIM—primarily because interest will begin to run upon the submission of a claim but not upon the submission of an REA. Most REAs are submitted by contractors under the CHANGEs clause of the contract, which generally requires that such requests be submitted within 30 days of receipt of a CHANGE ORDER. However, this time limitation is enforced only when the Government has been prejudiced by late submission of the request. See Cibinic and Nash, *Administration of Government Contracts* 476–85 (3d ed. 1995). The Government can also submit an REA to a contractor when the CONTRACTING OFFICER determines that a downward adjustment in the price is warranted. See Nash, *Postscript III: More Reflections on Reflectone*, 10 N&CR ¶ 45 (Sept. 1996); Nash, *Postscript II: More Reflections on Reflectone*, 10 N&CR ¶ 35 (July 1996); Nash, *Postscript: Further Reflections on Reflectone*, 9 N&CR ¶ 59 (Nov. 1995).

REQUEST FOR INFORMATION (RFI) A request for information used when the Government does not presently intend to award a contract but needs to obtain price, delivery, other market information, or capabilities for planning purposes. Responses to these notices are not offers and cannot be accepted by the Government to form a binding contract. There is no required format for RFIs. FAR 15.201(e).

REQUEST FOR PROPOSALS (RFP) A SOLICITATION document used in negotiated procurements (see NEGOTIATION) to communicate Government requirements to prospective contractors and to solicit PROPOSALs from them. RFPs must contain the information necessary to enable prospective contractors to prepare proposals properly. FAR 15.203. See McKenna, *Pathways to Excellence: Continuing to Improve the RFP Process: An Electronic Bulletin Board for RFP's—And More!*, 34 Cont. Mgmt. 4 (Mar. 1994). RFPs contain essentially all the terms and conditions of the prospective contract and are prepared using the UNIFORM CONTRACT FORMAT shown at FAR 15.204-1. When an RFP so states, the Government reserves the right to award a contract on the basis of initial offers received, without any written or oral DISCUSSION with offerors. An RFP can be compared with a REQUEST FOR QUOTATIONS (RFQ), the other type of solicitation document used in negotiated procurement. An RFP is intended to result in a contracting action, whereas an RFQ solicits information rather than binding offers. Compare Standard Form 33, Solicitation, Offer and

Award, FAR 53.301-33 with Standard Form 18, Request for Quotations, FAR 53.301-18.

REQUEST FOR QUOTATIONS (RFQ) A solicitation document (usually Standard Form 18, FAR 53.301-18) used in SIMPLIFIED ACQUISITIONs to communicate Government requirements to prospective contractors. FAR 13.307(b)(1). As it is merely a request for information, quotes submitted in response to it are not OFFERs, and consequently may not be accepted by the Government to form a binding contract. (A contract comes into being only when the supplier accepts the Government's order in response to its quotation or the parties mutually agree to a subsequent contract.) An RFQ is also used by some agencies to obtain price, delivery, or other information on sole source procurements. For simplified acquisitions, quotations may be solicited orally rather than in writing whenever economical and practical. FAR 13.106-1(c).

REQUEST FOR TECHNICAL PROPOSALS (RFTP) A solicitation document used in the first step of TWO-STEP SEALED BIDDING. FAR 14.503-1 requires that RFTPs include, at a minimum, the following: (1) a description of the supplies or services required; (2) a statement of intent to use the two-step method; (3) the requirements of the proposal; (4) the evaluation factors; (5) a statement that proposals are not to include prices or pricing information; (6) the time by which proposals must be received; (7) a statement that, in the second step, only bids based on proposals determined to be acceptable, either initially or as a result of discussions, will be considered for award, and that each bid in the second step must be based on the bidder's own proposal; (8) a statement that offerors should submit proposals acceptable without additional explanation, and that proposals may be evaluated as submitted or after discussion; (9) a statement that a notice of unacceptability will be forwarded to unsuccessful offerors following proposal evaluation; and (10) a statement about whether multiple proposals may be submitted. Requests for technical proposals are also used in negotiated procurements (see NEGOTIATION) when ALTERNATIVE SOURCE SELECTION PROCEDURES are used. DFARS 215.613.

REQUIRED SOURCES OF SUPPLIES AND SERVICES Mandatory sources from which the Government must (frequently in accordance with statutory requirements) buy specific products or services. Such sources are designated in FAR Part 8. Agencies must satisfy requirements for supplies and services from or through the following sources, listed in descending order of priority.

SUPPLIES— from (1) agency inventories; (2) EXCESS PERSONAL PROPERTY from other agencies; (3) FEDERAL PRISON INDUSTRIES, INC.; (4) procurement lists of products available from the Committee for Purchase from PEOPLE WHO ARE BLIND OR SEVERELY DISABLED; (5) wholesale supply sources, such as stock programs of the General Services Administration, the Defense Logistics Agency, the Department of Veterans Affairs, and military inventory control points; (6) mandatory FEDERAL SUPPLY SCHEDULES (FSS); (7) optional FSS; and (8) commercial sources. **SERVICES**— from (1) procurement lists of services available from the Committee for Purchase from People Who Are Blind or Severely Disabled; (2) mandatory FSS; (3) optional FSS; (4) Federal Prison Industries, Inc.; and (5) commercial sources. FAR 8.001. See Cibinic & Nash, chap. 3, Sec. IV., *Formation of Government Contracts* (3d ed. 1998).

REQUIREMENTS CONTRACT A contract that provides for filling all actual purchase requirements of designated Government activities for specific supplies or services during a specified contract period, with deliveries to be scheduled as orders are placed. FAR 16.503. The contractor is legally bound to such a contract because the Government's promise to buy its requirements constitutes CONSIDERATION. A requirements contract may be used when the Government anticipates recurring requirements but cannot predetermine the precise quantities of supplies or services that designated Government activities will need. Generally, a requirements contract is appropriate for items or services that are COMMERCIAL PRODUCTs or COMMERCIAL-TYPE PRODUCTs. Funds are obligated by each DELIVERY ORDER, not by the contract itself. FAR 16.503. Requirements contracts are a type of INDEFINITE-DELIVERY CONTRACT. They may permit faster deliveries than the other two types—DEFINITE-QUANTITY CONTRACTs and INDEFINITE-QUANTITY CONTRACTs—when production lead time is involved, because a contractor is usually willing to maintain limited stocks when the Government will obtain all of its actual purchase requirements from the contractor. Requirements-type contracts have been used to purchase all supplies and services in excess of those that can be provided by a Government activity or to purchase a stated percentage of the activity's requirements. See Cibinic & Nash, chap. 8, Sec. VI., *Formation of Government Contracts* (3d ed. 1998).

REQUISITION See PURCHASE REQUEST.

RESCISSION OF CONTRACT The relieving of a party from all obligations under a contract. Rescission is a remedy for MUTUAL

MISTAKE, when REFORMATION is not possible, and for other defects in contract formation such as DURESS, FRAUD, MISREPRESENTATION, and UNCONSCIONABILITY. AVOIDANCE is used to mean rescission when the party to the contract exercises the right on its own initiative. See Cibinic & Nash, *Administration of Government Contracts* 346–47 (3d ed. 1995).

RESCISSION OF BUDGET AUTHORITY An action by the President that rescinds all or part of any BUDGET AUTHORITY. 2 U.S.C. § 683. A rescission is a type of Presidential IMPOUNDMENT. This action is taken whenever the President determines that all or part of any budget authority will not be required to carry out the full objectives or scope of programs for which it is provided or that such budget authority should be rescinded for fiscal policy or other reasons, or whenever all or part of budget authority provided for only one fiscal year is to be reserved from obligation for such FISCAL YEAR. A rescission must be communicated to the Congress by the President in a special message. Any amount of budget authority proposed to be rescinded must be made available for obligation unless, within the prescribed 45-day period, the Congress has completed action on a rescission bill rescinding all or part of the amount proposed to be rescinded. Funds made available for obligation under this procedure may not be proposed for rescission again. See IMPOUNDMENT; DEFERRAL OF BUDGET AUTHORITY.

RESEARCH Effort directed toward increasing knowledge by study and experimentation. Research is generally divided into BASIC RESEARCH and APPLIED RESEARCH. Most research is procured using BROAD AGENCY ANNOUNCEMENT (BAA) procedures. FAR Part 35 provides guidance on contracting for research. Research is also supported by GRANTs and COOPERATIVE AGREEMENTs. DFARS 235.001 does not distinguish between basic and applied research but defines "research" as all scientific study and experimentation directed toward increasing knowledge and understanding in those fields of the physical, engineering, environmental, and life sciences related to long-term national security needs. Research, according to the DFARS, provides fundamental knowledge required for the solution of military problems. It forms part of the base for subsequent exploratory and advanced developments in defense-related technologies and for new or improved military functional capabilities in areas such as communications, detection, tracking, surveillance, propulsion, mobility, guidance and control, navigation, energy conversion, materials and structures, and personnel support. See also RESEARCH AND DEVELOPMENT.

RESEARCH AND DEVELOPMENT (R&D) Effort that constitutes either RESEARCH or DEVELOPMENT or both. FAR Part 35 prescribes policies and procedures that apply Government-wide to R&D contracting and the PROVISION AND CLAUSE MATRIX in FAR 52.300 provides guidance on the solicitation provisions and contract clauses to be used in R&D contracts. R&D contracts are to be used only to acquire supplies or services for the direct benefit or use of the Federal Government. If the goal is to stimulate or support R&D for some other public purpose, GRANTs or COOPERATIVE AGREEMENTs are appropriate. Further, it is important to distinguish R&D contracting from INDEPENDENT RESEARCH AND DEVELOPMENT, which is defined and discussed at FAR 31.205-18. In many agencies, the funds to support R&D are contained in a separate APPROPRIATION (such as the research, development, test, and engineering appropriation for DOD).

RESEARCH, DEVELOPMENT, TEST, AND EVALUATION (RDT&E) See RESEARCH AND DEVELOPMENT; TEST AND EVALUATION.

RESEARCH OPPORTUNITY ANNOUNCEMENT (ROA) The DEPARTMENT OF ENERGY's (DOE) term for BROAD AGENCY ANNOUNCEMENT. ROAs are a form of competitive solicitation under which DOE's broad missions and program-level research objectives are defined and proposals are requested from all offerors capable of satisfying DOE's needs. The proposals are evaluated by PEER OR SCIENTIFIC REVIEW against stated evaluation criteria. Selection for award is based on that evaluation, on the importance of the research to program objectives, and on the funds available. DEAR 935.016-1.

RESEARCH TAX CREDIT A tax credit against corporate income taxes in the amount of 25 percent of additional costs of research funded by a company. 26 U.S.C. § 44F(a). Costs incurred on COST-REIMBURSEMENT CONTRACTs are not funded by a company, but costs incurred on a FIXED-PRICE CONTRACT have been held to be funded by a company. See Nash, *Fixed-Price Research and Development Contracts: A Taxing Issue*, 10 N&CR ¶ 8 (Feb. 1996).

RESIDUAL VALUE The proceeds, less removal and disposal costs, if any, realized upon disposition of a TANGIBLE CAPITAL ASSET.

FAR 31.001. Residual value usually is measured by the net proceeds from the sale or other disposition of the ASSET, or its fair value if the asset is traded in on another asset. The estimated residual value is a current forecast of the residual value. CAS 409, Depreciation of Tangible Capital Assets, 48 C.F.R. § 9904.409, requires that DEPRECIATION be computed on the acquisition cost of an asset, less its estimated residual value.

RESOURCE CONSERVATION AND RECOVERY ACT (RCRA) A 1976 Act, 42 U.S.C. § 6901 et seq., that establishes Government policy on conservation of resources. The Act requires agencies responsible for drafting or reviewing SPECIFICATIONs to ensure that Government specifications and STANDARDs do not exclude the use of RECOVERED MATERIALS, do not require the item to be manufactured from virgin materials, but do require the use of recovered materials to the maximum extent possible without jeopardizing the intended end use of the item. FAR 23.401. Recovered materials are materials that have been collected or recovered from solid waste. FAR 23.402. The Government's policy is to acquire items composed of the highest percentage of recovered materials practicable, consistent with maintaining a satisfactory level of competition, without adversely affecting performance requirements or exposing suppliers' employees to undue hazards from the recovered materials. FAR 23.403. See the April 1992 issue of *Public Contract Management*, dedicated entirely to environmental contracting issues. See also *A CM Report: Recycled Materials: Procurement Guidelines for Government Agencies*, 29 Cont. Mgmt. 36 (May 1989); Hall & Davis, *Environmental Compliance at Federal Facilities*, 88-9 Briefing Papers (Aug. 1988).

RESPONDENT In a contract DISPUTE, the party that must file an ANSWER to a COMPLAINT presented by an APPELLANT before a BOARD OF CONTRACT APPEALS. The contracting agency is always the respondent because the contractor is required to initiate appeals before the boards of contract appeals.

RESPONSIBILITY The status of a prospective contractor determining that it has the capability, tenacity, and perseverance to perform a contract. 10 U.S.C. § 2305(b) and 41 U.S.C. § 253(b) require that contracts be awarded to responsible contractors only. FAR 9.103(b) implements this requirement by stating contracting officers should make an "affirmative determination" of responsibility before making an award. The contracting officer's signature on a contract constitutes a determination that the prospective contractor is responsible with respect to that contract. If a contracting officer makes a determination of nonresponsibility, a written statement must be included in the contract file giving the reasons for such determination. FAR 9.105-2. FAR 9.104-1 lists the general standards a contractor must meet to be considered responsible: (1) have or be able to obtain adequate financial resources to perform the contract; (2) be able to comply with the required or proposed delivery or performance schedule, taking into consideration all existing commercial and Government business commitments; (3) have a satisfactory performance record; (4) have a satisfactory record of integrity and business ethics; (5) have or be able to obtain the necessary organization, experience, accounting and operational controls, and technical skills; (6) have or be able to obtain the necessary production, construction, and technical equipment and facilities; and (7) be otherwise qualified and eligible to receive an award under applicable laws and regulations. A PREAWARD SURVEY can be used when the information available is insufficient to permit the contracting officer to make a determination regarding responsibility. FAR 9.105-1. If the prospective contractor is a SMALL BUSINESS CONCERN, the SMALL BUSINESS ADMINISTRATION can issue a CERTIFICATE OF COMPETENCY overriding a determination of nonresponsibility in almost all procurements. FAR Subpart 19.6. See Cibinic & Nash, chap. 4, Sec. I., *Formation of Government Contracts* (3d ed. 1998); Cibinic, *Responsiveness vs. Responsibility: Don't Add to the Confusion*, 11 N&CR ¶ 5 (Jan. 1997); Ginsburg & Patin, chap. 2, *Construction Contracting* 60–87 (1991).

RESPONSIBLE OFFICIAL The contracting officer or other official designated under agency procedures to administer the collection of CONTRACT DEBTs and applicable interest. FAR 32.601. In most contracting agencies, the responsible official is not the contracting officer but a fiscal officer. However, the contracting officer is charged with collecting contract debts if that can be done by WITHHOLDING of payments during performance of the contract.

RESPONSIVENESS An objective, nondiscretionary determination by the contracting officer, at the time of opening of sealed bids (see SEALED BIDDING), that a bid conforms to the INVITATION FOR BIDS (IFBs). 10 U.S.C. § 2305(b)(3) and 41 U.S.C. § 253(b)(c) require a bid to conform in all material respects to the IFB in order to be considered for award. This requirement for compliance ensures that all bidders stand on an equal footing and maintains the integrity of the sealed bidding system. FAR 14.301. Any bid that fails to conform to the IFB's essential requirements must be rejected. FAR 14.404-2. Bids should be filled out, executed, and submitted in accordance with the IFB's instructions. If a bidder uses its own bid form or a letter to submit a bid, the bid may be considered only if (1) the bidder accepts all the terms and conditions of the IFB and (2) award on the bid would result in a binding contract with terms and conditions that do not vary from those of the IFB. FAR 14.301. Bids are still considered responsive if they contain MINOR INFORMALITIES—variations from the exact requirements of the IFB that can be corrected or waived without being prejudicial to other bidders. FAR 14.405. The concept of responsiveness does not apply to procurements by NEGOTIATION. See Cibinic & Nash, chap. 5, Sec. II., *Formation of Government Contracts* (3d ed. 1998); Ginsburg & Patin, chap. 2, *Construction Contracting* 88–127 (1991).

REPROCUREMENT See EXCESS COSTS OF REPROCUREMENT.

RESTATEMENT OF THE LAW OF CONTRACTS A methodical summary of the common law of contracts, prepared and adopted by the American Law Institute. The first *Restatement* was adopted in 1932, the second in 1981. The *Restatement* is composed of statements of each legal rule, followed by comments and factual examples. It attempts to state the current legal rules being applied by the courts of the various states. The *Restatement* is frequently cited by the courts and either followed or distinguished. [American Law Institute, 4025 Chestnut St., Philadelphia, PA 19104; <http://www.ali.org>]

RESTRICTED COMPUTER SOFTWARE Computer software that was DEVELOPED AT PRIVATE EXPENSE and that is a TRADE SECRET; that is commercial or financial and confidential or privileged; or that is published copyrighted computer software, including minor modifications of such software. FAR 27.401. Under the Rights in Data—General clause in FAR 52.227-14, the contractor is entitled to assert RESTRICTED RIGHTS in such software.

RESTRICTED DATA Defined in § 2 of the Atomic Energy Act of 1954, 42 U.S.C. § 2014(a), as all data concerning (1) the design, manufacture, or utilization of atomic weapons; (2) the production of special nuclear material; or (3) the use of special nuclear material in the production of energy, except for data declassified or removed from the restricted data category pursuant to § 142. DEAR 904.401.

RESTRICTED RIGHTS Rights that the Government has in COMPUTER SOFTWARE that was developed at PRIVATE EXPENSE in accordance with the various clauses in this area. (The comparable term relating to TECHNICAL DATA is LIMITED RIGHTS). Under the Rights in Data—General clause in FAR 52.227-14, this is the right to (1) use the software in the computer or computers for which it was acquired; (2) use it in a backup computer; (3) copy it for archival purposes; (4) modify, adapt, or combine it with other software; (5) disclose it to or reproduce it for support service contractors, and use it in a replacement computer. Under the Rights in Noncommercial Computer Software and Noncommercial Computer Software Documentation (JUN 1995) clause in DFARS 252.227-7014 (1995 DOD policy), these rights are to (1) use a COMPUTER PROGRAM with one computer at a time; (2) transfer a computer program to another Government agency; (3) make a minimum number of copies of the software for safekeeping (archive), backup, or modification purposes; (4) modify the software; (5) permit service contractors to use the software to diagnose or correct deficiencies in a computer program, or modify the software to enable a computer program to be combined with, adapted to, or merged with other computer programs, and permit contractors or subcontractors performing emergency repairs or overhaul to use the software to perform such work and to modify the software to reflect the work done. Under the Rights in Technical Data and Computer Software clause in DFARS 252.227-7013 (OCT 1988) clause (pre-1995 DOD policy), these were rights, at a minimum, to (1) use the software with the computer for which or with which it was acquired, including use at any Government installation to which the computer was transferred by the Government; (2) use it with a backup computer if the computer for which or with which it was acquired was inoperative; (3) copy computer programs for safekeeping (archiving) or backup purposes; and (4) modify it or combine it with other software, subject to the provision that those portions of the derivative software incorporating restricted rights software are subject to the same restricted rights. In addition, restricted rights include any other specific rights not inconsistent with the minimum rights in (1) through (4) (pre-1995 policy) that were listed or described in a contract or described in a licensing agreement made a part of a contract. The DOD clause provided a somewhat different set of restricted rights when the software was "commercial computer software." See Schwartz, *The Acquisition of Technical Data Rights by the Government*, 23 Pub. Cont. L.J. 513 (1994); Simchak & Vogel, *A Few Words of Advice: Protecting Intellectual Property When Contracting with the Department of Defense*, 23 Pub. Cont. L.J. 141 (1994); Taylor & Burgett, *Government Rights in Data and Software*, 88-3 Briefing Papers (Feb. 1988).

RESTRICTIVE LEGENDS Markings on TECHNICAL DATA or COMPUTER SOFTWARE that restrict the rights of the Government to use such data or software. Under the policy in FAR Subpart 27.4, the contractor may use either a LIMITED RIGHTS legend or a RESTRICTED RIGHTS legend in appropriate circumstances. Under the 1995 DOD policy, the legends can be limited rights, restrictive rights, or GOVERNMENT-PURPOSE RIGHTS. Under the pre-1995 DOD policy in DFARS Subpart 227.4, the legends could be limited rights, restricted rights, or GOVERNMENT-PURPOSE LICENSE RIGHTS. If any data delivered under the contract are marked with these notices and use of the notices is not authorized by the contract, or if the data bear any other restrictive or limiting markings not authorized by the contract, the contracting officer may, at any time, either return the data to the contractor or cancel and ignore the markings subject to the VALIDATION procedures in 10 U.S.C. § 2321 and 41 U.S.C. § 253d. See FAR 27.404(h); DFARS 227.7103-12 and 227.7203-12; DFARS 227.473-3 (pre-1995 version); Nash, *Removal of Limited Rights Legends from Technical Data: Playing Hardball*, 1 N&CR ¶ 85 (Nov. 1987).

RESTRICTIVE SPECIFICATIONS Specifications that unnecessarily exclude a potential contractor from competing for a procurement. 10 U.S.C. § 2305(a)(1)(B)(ii) and 41 U.S.C. § 253a(a)(2)(B) permit restrictive provisions or conditions only to the extent necessary to satisfy the needs of the agency. Thus, the specifications must describe the supplies or services in a manner designed to promote FULL AND OPEN COMPETITION. PERFORMANCE SPECIFICATIONS containing unnecessary design requirements, specifications including arbitrary requirements not related to the Government's needs, and specifications written around a specific product are examples of restrictive specifications. See Cibinic & Nash, chap. 3, Sec. V., *Formation of Government Contracts* (3d ed. 1998); Milton, Note, *Standards of Review of Specifications in Government Procurement: An Equal Protection Analog*, 58 Geo. Wash. L. Rev. 573 (Feb. 1990).

RESTRUCTURING COSTS The costs, both direct and indirect, of restructuring a contractor's organization. Allowable restructuring costs may include severance pay, early retirement incentive payments, employee retraining costs, employee relocation expense, and relocation and rearrangement of plant and equipment. DFARS 231.205.70(b)(4). Restructuring activities are defined as nonroutine, nonrecurring, or extraordinary activities to combine facilities, operations, or workforce in order to eliminate redundant capabilities, improve future operations, and reduce overall costs. DFARS 231.205.70(b)(3). Restructuring costs are either internal or external. Internal restructuring costs are those that involve the facilities or workforce of only one of the companies involved in a business combination or, when there has been no business combination, the costs of restructuring a single company. The allowability of internal restructuring costs are governed by the FAR Part 31 COST PRINCIPLES. External restructuring costs are costs incurred as a result of external restructuring activities that result from a business combination that affects the operations of companies not previously under common ownership or control. External restructuring costs are allowable only when audited savings for DOD resulting from the restructuring will exceed the costs allowed by a margin of at least two to one (when FY97 funds are involved). If the business combination will result in the presentation of a critical capability that might otherwise be lost to DOD, the savings need only exceed the costs. DFARS 231.205.70(c). See Carlton & Andre, *Recovery of Restructuring Costs*, 97-10 Briefing Papers (Sept. 1997); Cibinic, *Restructuring Costs: More Madness*, 11 N&CR ¶ 16 (Apr. 1997); Metzger, *The Renewed Debate Over "Restructuring Costs,"* 38 Gov't Contractor ¶ 347 (July 24, 1996); Cibinic, *Restructuring Costs Update*, 9 N&CR ¶ 18 (Mar. 1995); Cibinic, *Restructuring Costs: Trying to Make Sense Out of a Mess*, 8 N&CR ¶ 64 (Nov. 1994).

RETAINAGE A percentage of the PROGRESS PAYMENT due under a CONSTRUCTION contract that is retained either routinely or because the contractor failed to make satisfactory progress. Such retainage is permitted by paragraph (e) of the Payments under Fixed-Price Construction Contracts clause in FAR 52.232-5. FAR 32.103 provides that retainage should not be used as a substitute for good contract management and the contracting officer should not withhold funds without cause. Determinations of whether and how much to retain are made on a case-by-case basis and are based on the contracting officer's assessment of the contractor's performance and of the likelihood that such performance will continue. The amount of retainage withheld will normally not exceed 10 percent of the amount due in accordance with the terms of the contract and may be adjusted as the contract approaches completion to recognize better than expected performance, the ability to rely on alternative safeguards, and other factors. Upon completion of all contract requirements, retained amounts must be paid promptly. See Nash, chap. 12, *Construction Contracting* 898–906 (1991).

RETENTION OF RECORDS Retention by contractors of documents connected with Government contracts. Such retention is required by various contract clauses, including the EXAMINATION OF RECORDS CLAUSE. FAR Subpart 4.7 gives guidance on the requirements for records retention and the methods that may be used to satisfy these requirements. See Godzac & Jordan, *Records Retention—Beginning with the End in Mind*, 34 Cont. Mgmt. 10 (Nov. 1994); Skupsky, *Records Retention Procedures: Your Guide to Determining How Long to Keep Your Records and How to Safely Destroy Them!* (1990).

REVERSE ENGINEERING The process of developing DESIGN SPECIFICATIONS by inspection and analysis of a product. The UNIFORM TRADE SECRETS ACT provides that reverse engineering is a proper means of obtaining a person's TRADE SECRETs. See Nash, *Postscript: Reverse Engineering*, 5 N&CR ¶ 16 (Mar. 1991); Nash, *Reverse Engineering: The Government Is Using It to Work Around Proprietary Data*, 4 N&CR ¶ 26 (Apr. 1990).

REVOLVING DOOR The practice of Government employees leaving Government service to join private industry. Restrictions on the activities of such employees are contained in 18 U.S.C. § 207. These provisions are amplified and interpreted by regulations issued by the OFFICE OF GOVERNMENT ETHICS at 5 C.F.R. § 2637 and § 2641. They deal primarily with any former Government employee representing companies with which the employee has dealt and assisting foreign entities before the Government or any companies in trade negotiations. They also bar senior-level employees, for one year, from communicating with or making an appearance before the agency for which he or she worked. Restrictions barring employment of specified individuals, are contained in the PROCUREMENT INTEGRITY rules. The revolving-door problem is especially serious when it involves the employment of any former Government employee by any contractors seeking that individual's knowledge about specific procurements or seeking to obtain an advantage by that employee's special contacts. See Levy et al., *A Contractor's Guide to Hiring Government Employees*, 96-8 Briefing Papers (July 1996); Roberts, *The "Revolving Door": Issues Related to the Hiring of Federal Government Employees*, 43 Ala. L. Rev. 343 (1992); Darley, *New "Revolving Door" Issues for Federal Officials under the OFPP Policy Act Amendments of 1988: A Quick Overview*, 18 Pub. Cont. L.J. 432 (1989); Darley, *Conflict of Interest Restrictions Applicable to Separating and Former Department of Defense Personnel*, 17 Pub. Cont. L.J. 388 (1988); Cohen, *The Revolving Door: A Job Hunting Primer*, 29 A.F. L. Rev. 157 (1988);

Brown, *The Current State of the Federal Law on Post Government Employment Restrictions*, 35 Fed. B. News & J. 434 (1988).

RIGHTS IN TECHNICAL DATA The Government's rights to make various uses of TECHNICAL DATA. Very broadly speaking, if the Government has funded or will fund development of an item, component, or process, the Government generally obtains UNLIMITED RIGHTS in the technical data. If, in contrast, a contractor or subcontractor developed the item, component, or process at private expense, the Government generally obtains only LIMITED RIGHTS in the technical data. The distinction is important because data delivered with unlimited rights may be disclosed to competing contractors, whereas LIMITED RIGHTS DATA are considered proprietary and must be protected. DOD also obtains GOVERNMENT-PURPOSE RIGHTS to technical data pertaining to items, components, or processes developed with MIXED FUNDING. DFARS 227.7103-5. All of these rights are license rights with the contractor retaining title to the technical data. FAR 227.7103-4(a). See Lewis, *Technical Data Rights in Government Contractor Value Engineering Change Proposals*, Army Law. 12 (Nov. 1994); Schwartz, *The Acquisition of Technical Data Rights by the Government*, 23 Pub. Cont. L.J. 513 (1994); Nash, *Government Rights in Technical Data: Recent Court Decisions*, 3 N&CR ¶ 83 (Dec. 1989); Taylor & Burgett, *Government Rights in Data and Software*, 88-3 Briefing Papers (Feb. 1988); Nash, *Proprietary Rights in the Competitive Era*, Gov't Executive 51 (Apr. 1987).

RISK The assumption of possible monetary loss or gain in view of the job or work to be done. FAR 16.104 requires that risk be one of the elements to be considered in negotiating a FAIR AND REASONABLE PRICE, as well as in determining the TYPE OF CONTRACT under which performance will occur. The contractor's assumption of greater cost risks should result in a proportionate increase in compensation. The contractor assumes the greatest cost risk in a FIRM-FIXED-PRICE CONTRACT, in which the contractor has full responsibility for the performance costs and the resulting profit or loss. Under a COST-PLUS-FIXED-FEE CONTRACT, the contractor bears minimal responsibility for the performance costs because the negotiated FEE is fixed. FAR 15.404-4(d)(1)(ii) requires that this risk also be assessed in negotiating the contractor's PROFIT. Complex requirements, particularly those unique to the Government, usually lead to the Government's assuming greater risk. FAR 16.104. See Cibinic, chap. 5, *Construction Contracting* 406–99 (1991); Nash, *Evaluation of Risk in*

Competitive Negotiated Contracts: A Key Element in the Process, 5 N&CR ¶ 22 (Apr. 1991).

RISK ALLOCATION The apportionment of the risk of financial loss on a contract by the TYPE OF CONTRACT or the contract clauses. FAR 16.103 calls for the use of a type of contract that does not allocate undue risks to the contractor. The standard contract clauses also balance the allocation of risk by providing that the Government will grant EQUITABLE ADJUSTMENTs or PRICE ADJUSTMENTs upon the occurrence of specified events. The term "risk allocation" is also used to denote the resolution of a contractual DISPUTE by apportioning the damages incurred by one party to the contractual parties in accordance with each share of the risk of the occcurence that led to the assessment of damages. This has occurred when there was joint fault, joint negligence, or concurrent delays. See Cibinic & Nash, *Administration of Government Contracts* 373–79 (3d ed. 1995).

RISK MANAGEMENT Generally, all plans and actions taken to identify, assess, mitigate, and continuously track, control, and document program risks. Jones, *Glossary: Defense Acquisition Acronyms and Terms* (8th ed., Defense Systems Management College). Risk management is an organized method of identifying and measuring risk and developing, selecting, and managing options for handling relevant risks. The OFFICE OF MANAGEMENT AND BUDGET suggests three principles for managing risk when agencies procure CAPITAL ASSETS: (1) avoiding or limiting the amount of development work; (2) making effective use of competition and financial incentives; and (3) establishing a performance-based acquisition management system that provides for accountability for program successes and failures, such as an EARNED VALUE system. *Principles of Budgeting for Capital Asset Acquisitions*, 10 Budget of the United States Government, Fiscal Year 1998 (GPO 1997). FAR Part 39 discusses risk management in the context of INFORMATION TECHNOLOGY procurements, suggesting that reasonable risk taking is appropriate as long as risks are controlled and mitigated. Appropriate risk management and mitigation techniques include prudent project management, use of MODULAR CONTRACTING, thorough ACQUISITION PLANNING tied to budgeting planning, continuous collection and evaluation of risk-based assessment data, prototyping prior to implementation, post-implementation reviews, and focusing on risks and returns using quantifiable measures. FAR 39.102.

RISK ANALYSIS A detailed examination of each identified program risk that refines the description of the risk, isolates the cause, and determines the impact of the program risk in terms of its probability of occurrence, its consequences, and its relationship to other risk areas or processes. This analysis assumes that risk is a measure of the inability to achieve program objectives within defined cost and schedule constraints. Risk is associated with all aspects of the program, e.g., technology, design processes, WORK BREAKDOWN STRUCTURE elements, etc. Risk has two components: (1) the probability of failing to achieve a particular outcome and (2) the consequences of failing to achieve that outcome. Jones, *Glossary: Defense Acquisition Acronyms and Terms* (8th ed., Defense Systems Management College).

ROYALTY Compensation for the use of property. In Government procurement, royalties are generally paid by contractors for the use of PATENTs or COPYRIGHTs. FAR 31.205-37 provides that patent royalties are ALLOWABLE COSTs if they are arrived at through arm's-length bargaining, unless the Government has a LICENSE in the patent. To ascertain whether a contractor has licensed a patent to which the Government has rights, FAR 27.204 requires the reporting of royalties on most contracts. See the Royalty Information clause in FAR 52.227-6. There are no similar provisions with regard to contractor payment of royalties for the use of copyrights. The Government also assesses royalties against contractors as part of its RECOUPMENT policy. See Nash, *Royalties for Successful Development: A New Form of Profit!*, 1 N&CR ¶ 62 (Aug. 1987).

RULE 4 FILE See APPEAL FILE.

RULE OF TWO A judgmental rule that requires a small business SET-ASIDE on contracts over $100,000 when the contracting officer determines that there is a reasonable expectation that (1) offers will be obtained from at least two responsible (see RESPONSIBILITY) SMALL BUSINESS CONCERNS offering the products of different small business concerns, and (2) award will be made at FAIR MARKET PRICEs. FAR 19.502-2(b). This rule is based on the assumption that two competing concerns will provide sufficient competition to ensure a FAIR AND REASONABLE PRICE. The rule generates considerable controversy in the acquisition community. Critics have asserted that it is unfair to reserve a contract or all contracts in a given category for small business whenever only two small business offerors express an interest, with no regard to whether the contract could be awarded at a lower price to a large firm or to what effect this has on the overall percentage of the contracts set aside in a particular industry.

See Ciummo, *The "Rule of Two" Gets A Boost*, 30 Cont. Mgmt. 12 (May 1990).

RULE 12 PROCEDURES See EXPEDITED PROCEDURES.

S

SALIENT CHARACTERISTICS Those qualities of an ITEM that are essential to ensure that the intended use of the item can be satisfactorily realized. The term is mainly used in connection with describing a Government requirement with a BRAND-NAME-OR-EQUAL DESCRIPTION. DFARS 211.270-1 requires that such descriptions contain a statement of the salient physical, functional, or other characteristics of the referenced product that an equal product must have in order to meet the Government's needs. The FAR contains no such requirement.

SALVAGE Property that, because of its worn, damaged, deteriorated, or incomplete condition or specialized nature, has no reasonable prospect of sale or use as serviceable property without major repairs, but has some value in excess of its SCRAP value. FAR 45.501. FAR 45.505-8 requires contractors to maintain records of all salvage generated from GOVERNMENT PROPERTY.

SAMPLE TASK A hypothetical task that is given to offerors during SOURCE SELECTION to evaluate their understanding of the work and ability to perform the work. Sample tasks are given in the solicitation with written solutions to be submitted with the proposal or are given during ORAL PRESENTATIONs with verbal solutions to be given during the presentation. FAR 15.102(c). Agencies are not required to identify WEAKNESSes or deficiencies (see DEFICIENCY) that they detect in the responses to sample tasks. See Nash, *Use of Sample Tasks to Evaluate Proposals: A Fair Technique?*, 6 N&CR ¶ 53 (Sept. 1992).

SCANWELL ACTION A PROTEST filed in a U.S. District Court after the award of a contract (or before award in a few circuits). The case *Scanwell Laboratories, Inc. v. Shaffer*, 424 F.2d 859 (D.C. Cir. 1970), established that an unsuccessful offeror may challenge the award of a Government contract on the grounds of arbitrary or capricious action not in compliance with the Administrative Procedure Act, 5 U.S.C. § 552. The courts and congressional committee reports acknowledge the Scanwell doctrine as a judicial REMEDY; it is a settled feature of Government contracting. District courts also have jurisdiction over PROTESTs under 28 U.S.C. § 1491(b). See Mason, *Bid Protests and the U.S. District Courts—Why Congress Should Not Allow the Sun to Set on This Effective Relationship*, 26 Pub. Cont. L.J. 567 (1997); Pachter, *The Need for a Comprehensive Judicial Remedy for Bid Protests*, 16 Pub. Cont. L.J. 47 (1986); Hopkins, *The Universe of Remedies for Unsuccessful Offerors on Federal Contracts*, 15 Pub. Cont. L.J. 365 (1985).

SCREENING The process by the FEDERAL AVIATION ADMINISTRATION to determine which offeror provides the BEST VALUE to the Government. For less complex procurements, screening is done in a single step, soliciting offers from all vendors (essentially the same as the solicitation of COMPETITIVE PROPOSALs in a competitive negotiation). In more complex procurements, screening can be done in three steps, soliciting qualification information in the first step, soliciting screening information from qualified vendors in the second step, and soliciting offers from the remaining vendors in the third step. See Federal Aviation Administration Management System 3.2.2.3.1.2. See Cibinic & Nash, Chap. 7, Sec. IX., *Formation of Government Contracts* (3d ed. 1998).

SCREENING INFORMATION REQUEST (SIR) A request by the FEDERAL AVIATION ADMINISTRATION for documentation, information, presentations, proposals, or binding offers. The SIR is used in each step of the SCREENING process for a different purpose and will solicit different information depending on that purpose. When it is used to obtain qualification information, it is tailored to obtain all information necessary to determine that the potential vendor is qualified to perform the work to be procured. When it is used to obtain screening information, it is tailored to obtain information about the key discriminators that will be used to select the winning contractor. When it is used to obtain offers, it is written as a solicitation of a binding offer. Federal Aviation Administration Management System 3.2.2.3.1.2. See Cibinic & Nash, Chap. 7, Sec. IX., *Formation of Government Contracts* (3d ed. 1998).

SCHEDULE CONTRACT; SCHEDULES See FEDERAL SUPPLY SCHEDULES.

SCIENTIFIC AND TECHNICAL INFORMATION REPORTS Reports documenting the work accomplished under a RESEARCH

AND DEVELOPMENT (R&D) contract. FAR 35.010 provides that such reports must be required in order to make a permanent record of the work accomplished. Agencies are encouraged to make R&D contract results available to other Government activities and to the private sector, and R&D contracts should require that contractors send copies of scientific and technical reports to the Defense Technical Information Center (DTIC) or the National Technical Information Service. These activities provide a central service for the interchange of scientific and technical information. Scientific and technical information reports announcing current publications that address aeronautics, space, and supporting disciplines are available from NASA. NFS 18-35.003-70. The DTIC provides DOD information to qualified requesters. See DFARS 235.010.

SCOPE OF THE CONTRACT All work that was fairly and reasonably within the contemplation of the parties at the time the contract was made. Nearly all Government contracts contain a Changes clause that permits the contracting officer to make unilateral changes in designated areas, within the general scope of the contract. FAR 43.201. Changes beyond the scope of the contract are CARDINAL CHANGEs. The determination of whether changes lie beyond the contract's general scope typically entails comparing the total work performed by the contractor with the work called for by the original contract. If the function of the work as changed is generally the same as the work originally called for, the changes fall within the contract's general scope. See Cibinic & Nash, *Administration of Government Contracts* 384–91 (3d ed. 1995); Nash, chap. 4, *Government Contract Changes* (2d ed. 1989 & Supp. 1993); Willmeth, *Determining Whether Modifications are Within the Scope of the Contract*, 29 A.F. L. Rev. 93 (1988).

SCRAP Personal property that has no value except for its basic material content. FAR 45.501. FAR 45.505-8 requires contractors to maintain records of scrap generated from GOVERNMENT PROPERTY. See also FAR 45.607, which discusses sorting and disposal of scrap and recovery of PRECIOUS METALS.

SEALED BIDDING A method of contracting that, through an INVITATION FOR BIDS, solicits the submission of competitive bids, followed by a public opening of the bids (see BID OPENING). A contract is awarded to the responsive and responsible bidder (see RESPONSIVENESS; RESPONSIBILITY) whose bid is most advantageous to the Government, considering price and PRICE-RELATED FACTORS. FAR 14.103-2. Prior to the COMPETITION

IN CONTRACTING ACT, sealed bidding was called "formal advertising" and was the preferred method of contracting. Under CICA it is merely one of the COMPETITIVE PROCEDURES that meets the requirement to obtain FULL AND OPEN COMPETITION. 41 U.S.C. § 252(c). Sealed bidding is a highly structured form of procurement that is governed by the rules in FAR Part 14. See Cibinic & Nash, chap. 5, *Formation of Government Contracts* (3d ed. 1998); Nash, *Competitive Negotiation vs. Sealed Bidding: Some Limitations on Agency Discretion*, 5 N&CR ¶ 68 (Dec. 1991).

SECOND SOURCE An alternative source for a supply or service, obtained to foster competition. When quantities of work are sufficient to permit economical performance by two sources, it is the Government's policy to obtain second sources. See DUAL SOURCE. See also Kirshner, *Second Sourcing in the Department of Defense*, 1982 (unpublished L.L.M. thesis, The Geo. Wash. Univ. Nat'l Law Center, Government Contracts Program).

SECRETARY The head of an agency with cabinet status. Exceptions are DOJ, whose head is called the Attorney General, and DOD, where there is a Secretary of Defense (with cabinet status) as well as Secretaries of the Departments of the Army, Navy, and Air Force (without cabinet status). The term is similar to the broader term HEAD OF THE AGENCY. It is used primarily in statutes governing the activities of a single cabinet-level department. Some decisions are permitted to be made only by the Secretary or at the "secretarial level." When handling extraordinary contractual actions to facilitate the national defense, "secretarial level" means a level at or above the level of a deputy assistant agency head, or a contract adjustment board. FAR 50.001; DFARS 250.001. Acquisitions conducted without providing for FULL AND OPEN COMPETITION because it is not in the public interest, under the authority of 10 U.S.C. § 2304(c)(7) or 41 U.S.C. § 253(c)(7), require a written determination by the Secretary of Defense, the Secretary of the Army, the Secretary of the Navy, the Secretary of the Air Force, the Secretary of Transportation for the Coast Guard, the Administrator of NASA, or the head of any other executive agency. This authority may not be delegated. FAR 6.302-7.

SECTION 8(A) See 8(a) PROGRAM.

SECTION 800 PANEL A committee of 13 members established by DOD as directed by Section 800 of the National Defense Authorization Act of 1991, Pub. L. No. 101-510. The panel was charged with the task of reviewing all laws affecting DOD procurement "with a view toward streamlining the defense acquisition process." The panel submitted its report in January 1993, recommending amendment of 163 statutes and repeal of 135 statutes. This report contained a detailed analysis of the recommendations and served as the basis for the FEDERAL ACQUISITION STREAMLINING ACT OF 1994 and the CLINGER-COHEN ACT OF 1996. Among the more important recommendations were raising the threshold for SIMPLIFIED ACQUISITION from $25,000 to $100,000, broadening the definition of COMMERCIAL ITEMs, and making many of the socioeconomic statutes inapplicable to simplified acquisitions and purchases of commercial items.

SECTION 807 PANEL A committee of Government and industry members established by DOD in accordance with Section 807 of the National Defense Authorization Act for 1992 and 1993, Pub. L. No. 102-190. This panel was given the task of negotiating a DOD technical data policy that complied with 10 U.S.C. § 2320. The panel's report was forwarded to Congress in April 1994 and served as the basis for the new DOD technical data and computer software policy which was adopted in 1995. See Nash, *The New DOD "Rights in Software Policy: Half A Loaf*, 10 N&CR ¶ 12 (Mar. 1996); Nash, *The New DOD Policy on Technical Data and Computer Software*, 8 N&CR ¶ 22 (Apr. 1994).

SEGMENT One of two or more divisions, product departments, plants, or other subdivisions of an organization that reports directly to a HOME OFFICE and are usually identified with responsibility for PROFIT or production. See FAR 31.001. The term includes GOVERNMENT-OWNED, CONTRACTOR-OPERATED PLANTs as well as JOINT VENTUREs and subsidiaries (domestic and foreign) in which the organization has a majority ownership. The term also includes those joint ventures and subsidiaries (domestic and foreign) in which the organization has less than a majority of ownership, but over which it exercises control. A contractor's cost accounting system must, to the maximum extent practicable, allocate HOME OFFICE expenses directly to segments, based on the relationship between the expenses and the segments that incur them or benefit from them. See CAS 403, 48 C.F.R. § 9904.403.

SEGMENT CLOSING In the allocation of pension costs to SEGMENTs of an organization, the term means a segment has (1) been sold or ownership otherwise transferred, (2) discontinued operations, or (3) discontinued doing or actively seeking Government business under contracts subject to CAS 413. 48 C.F.R. § 9904.413-30. If a segment is closed, the contractor is required to adjust previously determined pension costs by determining the difference between the actuarial accrued liability for the segment and the market value of the assets allocated to the segment. 48 C.F.R. § 9904.413-50.

SELECTED ACQUISITION REPORTS (SARs) Standard, comprehensive summary status reports on selected DOD ACQUISITION PROGRAMs, required by 10 U.S.C. § 2432 to be submitted by DOD to Congress. SARs provide key cost, schedule, and technical information in a concise, summary form, generally limited to no more than 20 pages. They are required for MAJOR DEFENSE ACQUISITION PROGRAMs in which the eventual expenditure for research, development, test, and evaluation will exceed $300 million or the total expenditure will exceed $1.8 billion. (Both thresholds are calculated in FY90 constant dollars.) In addition to an initial filing, programs may require quarterly or annually submission of SARs. See DOD Instruction 5000.2-M, *Defense Acquisition Management Documentation and Reports*, Feb. 23, 1991, Part 17.

SELECTED COSTS A type of cost, incurred by a contractor, that is dealt with specifically in the FAR COST PRINCIPLES. FAR 31.205 discusses the allowability (see ALLOWABLE COST) or unallowability (see UNALLOWABLE COST) of 51 selected costs: PUBLIC RELATIONS and ADVERTISEMENT costs; AUTOMATIC DATA PROCESSING EQUIPMENT leasing costs; BAD DEBTS; BONDING COSTS; CIVIL DEFENSE COSTS; compensation for personal services (see PERSONAL SERVICES CONTRACT); contingencies (see CONTINGENCY); contributions or DONATIONs; cost of money (see COST OF MONEY FACTORS); DEPRECIATION; ECONOMIC PLANNING COSTS; employee morale, health, welfare, food service, and dormitory costs and credits; ENTERTAINMENT costs; FINEs, penalties, and MISCHARGING costs; gains and losses on disposition of depreciable property or other capital ASSETs; IDLE CAPACITY and IDLE FACILITIES costs; INDEPENDENT RESEARCH AND DEVELOPMENT costs and BID AND PROPOSAL COSTS; INSURANCE and INDEMNIFICATION; INTEREST and other financial costs; LABOR RELATIONS costs; legislative LOBBYING COSTS; LOSSes on other contracts; REPAIRS AND MAINTENANCE costs; manufacturing and production engineering costs (see MANUFACTURING ENGINEERING); MATERIAL costs; ORGANIZATION COSTS; other business expenses; plant protection costs; PATENT costs; plant reconversion costs; PRECONTRACT COSTS; PROFESSIONAL AND CONSULTANT SERVICES costs; RE-

CRUITMENT COSTS; RELOCATION COSTS; RENTAL COSTS; ROYALTY and other costs for use of patents; SELLING costs; service and WARRANTY costs; SPECIAL TOOLING and SPECIAL TEST EQUIPMENT costs; TAXES; termination costs (see TERMINATION FOR CONVENIENCE and TERMINATION FOR DEFAULT); TRADE, BUSINESS, TECHNICAL, AND PROFESSIONAL ACTIVITY COSTS; TRAINING AND EDUCATION COSTS; TRANSPORTATION costs; TRAVEL COSTS; costs related to legal and other proceedings (see LEGAL FEES); deferred RESEARCH AND DEVELOPMENT costs; GOODWILL; executive LOBBYING COSTS; costs of alcoholic beverages; and asset valuations resulting from BUSINESS COMBINATIONs.

SELECTIVE APPLICATION See TAILORING.

SELF-CERTIFICATION The certification by a firm that it qualifies as a SMALL BUSINESS CONCERN. This is the initial step in determining whether a contractor is a small business. The contracting officer is bound to accept the self-certification unless another bidder or INTERESTED PARTY challenges the contractor's small business representation in a SIZE PROTEST, or the contracting officer has reason to question the representation. FAR 19.301(b). See SIZE STATUS.

SELF-COMPLIANCE See SELF-GOVERNANCE.

SELF-GOVERNANCE A program adopted by contractors, with the encouragement of DOD, to ensure that they fulfill their responsibility to avoid improper business practices. Contractors should have STANDARDS OF CONDUCT and internal control systems designed to (1) promote those standards, (2) facilitate the timely discovery and disclosure of improper conduct in connection with Government contracts, and (3) ensure that corrective measures are promptly carried out. DFARS 203.7000. A self-governance program is an ongoing, internally created and managed effort designed to ensure that the contractor complies with both corporate and contractual requirements. Self-governance programs typically include a CODE OF ETHICS, an education and training program, and systematic reviews of existing practices and procedures. Programs may also include screening of employees for drug or alcohol abuse, review of the records of new employees for evidence of prior misconduct, AUDITs, hotlines, and disciplinary actions. See Seyfarth et al., *The Government Contract Compliance Handbook* 2-1 and 2-2 (1996 Supp.); Pendergast & Gold,

Surviving Self-Governance: Common Interests Approach to Protecting Privileges under the DOD Voluntary Disclosure Program, 22 Pub. Cont. L.J. 195 (1993); Mur, *Ethics in Government Contracting: Putting Your House in Order*, 20 Nat'l Cont. Mgmt. J., Issue No. 2, p. 15 (1987); Victorino & Kadue, *Compliance Programs*, 86-11 Briefing Papers (Oct. 1986). See also CONTRACTOR RISK ASSESSMENT GUIDE.

SELF-INSURANCE Assumption or retention of the risk of loss by the contractor, whether voluntarily or involuntarily. FAR 31.001. CAS 416, 48 C.F.R. § 9904.416, which contains rules governing the accounting for insurance costs, provides that self-insurance costs will generally be measured on an actuarial basis rather than an actual-loss basis. Under the FAR COST PRINCIPLES, self-insurance includes the deductible portion of purchased insurance. FAR 31.001. FAR 28.308 requires that the contractor submit information on any proposed self-insurance program to the ADMINISTRATIVE CONTRACTING OFFICER and obtain approval of the program when it is anticipated that (1) 50 percent or more of the self-insurance costs to be incurred at a SEGMENT of a contractor's business will be allocable (see ALLOCABLE COST) to negotiated Government contracts and (2) self-insurance costs at the segment for the fiscal year will be $200,000 or more. To qualify for a self-insurance program, a contractor must demonstrate its ability to sustain the potential losses involved. See also INSURANCE.

SELLING COSTS All efforts to market a contractor's products or services. FAR 31.205-38. Selling costs are generally unallowable under FAR 31.205-38, unless they constitute "direct selling efforts" or are made allowable by other COST PRINCIPLES of FAR 31.205. The principle activities that fall under the generic term "selling" include (1) advertising (see ADVERTISEMENT) (FAR 31.205-1): (2) corporate image enhancement, including broadly targeted sales efforts, other than advertising (includes PUBLIC RELATIONS, FAR 31.205-1, and ENTERTAINMENT, FAR 31.205-14): (3) BID AND PROPOSAL COSTS (FAR 31.205-18); (4) market planning (FAR 31.205-12); and (5) direct selling (FAR 31.205-38). See Oyer, *Allocability of Direct Selling Costs—Cost/Benefit Relationships*, 96-2 CP&A Rep. 3 (Feb. 1996); Cibinic and Nash, *Cost-Reimbursement Contracting* 753–58 (2d ed. 1993).

SENIOR PROCUREMENT EXECUTIVE An individual appointed pursuant to § 16 of the OFFICE OF FEDERAL PROCUREMENT

POLICY ACT, 41 U.S.C. § 414, who is responsible for managing the direction of the acquisition system of an executive agency, including implementation of the agency's unique acquisition policies, regulations, and standards. FAR 2.101. Each agency must appoint a senior procurement executive to ensure that there is clear authority for carrying out efficient and effective procurement policies.

SENSITIVE INFORMATION Any information that, in the event of loss, misuse, or unauthorized access or modification, could adversely affect the national interest, the conduct of federal programs, or the privacy to which individuals are entitled under the Privacy Act, 5 U.S.C. § 552a, but that has not been specifically authorized, under criteria established by an executive order or an act of Congress, to be kept secret in the interest of national defense or foreign policy. DFARS 252.239-7016. Contractors must agree to secure such information during telecommunications. DFARS 239.7402(b).

SERVICE CONTRACT A contract that directly engages the time and effort of a contractor to perform an identifiable task rather than to furnish an end item of supply. FAR 37.101. Guidance on service contracting is contained in FAR Part 37. See also NFS Part 18.37. A service contract may be either a PERSONAL SERVICES CONTRACT or a NONPERSONAL SERVICES CONTRACT and can cover services performed by either professional or nonprofessional personnel on either an individual or an organizational basis. Service contracts include those for (1) maintenance, overhaul, repair, servicing, rehabilitation, salvage, modernization, or modification of supplies, systems, or equipment; (2) routine recurring maintenance of real property; (3) housekeeping and base services; (4) ADVISORY AND ASSISTANCE SERVICES; (5) operation of Government-owned equipment, facilities, and systems; (6) communications services; (7) ARCHITECT-ENGINEER SERVICES; (8) transportation and related services; and (9) RESEARCH AND DEVELOPMENT. See also SERVICE CONTRACT ACT OF 1965.

SERVICE CONTRACT ACT (SCA) OF 1965 An Act, 41 U.S.C. §§ 351–357, requiring that contractors pay not less than the PREVAILING WAGE RATE and provide safe conditions of work under contracts for the performance of services in the United States through the use of SERVICE EMPLOYEEs. Prevailing wage rates are established by DOL upon receipt of a Standard Form 98 from a contracting officer. FAR 22.1007, FAR 22.1008. Examples of services subject to the Act include (1) motor pool operation, parking, taxicab, and ambulance services; (2) packing, crating, and storage; (3) custodial, janitorial, housekeeping, and guard services; (4) food service and lodging; (5) laundry, dry cleaning, linen supply, clothing alteration, and repair services; (6) snow, trash, and garbage removal; (7) aerial spraying and aerial reconnaissance for fire detection; (8) some support services at installations, including grounds maintenance and landscaping; (9) certain specialized services requiring specific skills, such as drafting, illustrating, graphic arts, stenographic reporting, or mortuary services; (10) electronic equipment maintenance and operation and engineering support services; (11) maintenance and repair of all types of equipment, such as aircraft, engines, electrical motors, vehicles, and electronic, office and related business and construction equipment; (12) operation, maintenance, or logistics support of a federal facility; and (13) data collection, processing, and analysis services. FAR 22.1003-5. Service contracts over $2,500 must contain provisions regarding minimum wages and fringe benefits, safe and sanitary working conditions, notification to employees of the minimum allowable compensation, and equivalent federal employee classifications and wage rates. FAR Subpart 22.10. See Cibinic & Nash, chap. 10, Sec. VII., *Formation of Government Contracts* (3d ed. 1998); Fontana, *Employer Obligations Under the Service Contract Act: Just Another Minimum Wage Law?*, 25 Pub. Cont. L.J. 483 (1996); Vecchio, *Understanding the Service Contract Act*, 34 Cont. Mgmt. 22 (Feb. 1994); Ginsburg et al., *The Service Contract Act*, 90-7 Briefing Papers (June 1990).

SERVICE EMPLOYEE Any person engaged in the performance of a SERVICE CONTRACT other than those in a bona fide executive, administrative, or professional capacity. FAR 22.1001. Service employees are those employees given the protection of the SERVICE CONTRACT ACT OF 1965.

SERVICEABLE OR USEABLE PROPERTY Property that has a reasonable prospect of use or sale either in its existing form or after minor repairs or alterations. FAR Subpart 45.6 provides policies and procedures for reporting, redistribution, and disposal of this property.

SERVICES See SERVICE CONTRACT.

SET-ASIDE (n) An acquisition exclusively or partially reserved for the participation of SMALL BUSINESS CONCERNs pursuant to the SMALL BUSINESS ACT, 15 U.S.C. § 644. A set-aside restricts the competition to small business concerns that qualify under the applicable standards. A total set-aside restricts the entire procurement, whereas a partial set-aside restricts only a stated portion of the procurement. The contracting officer makes the initial determination of whether an acquisition should be set aside and must document why a set-aside is inappropriate when the procurement is not set aside. FAR 19.501(c). FAR 19.502-5 provides that the following, in and of themselves, do not make a set-aside inappropriate: (1) a large percentage of previous contracts for the required items have been with small business concerns, (2) the item is on the QUALIFIED PRODUCTS LIST, (3) the contract is classified; and (4) small businesses are already receiving a fair portion of the agency's contracts. See Heggs, *Practitioner's Viewpoint What To Expect After Adarand*, 25 Pub. Cont. L.J. 451 (1996); Newman, *Affirmative Action and the Construction Industry*, 25 Pub. Cont. L.J. 433 (1996); Black, *An Evaluation of Federal Contract Set-Aside Goals in Reducing Socioeconomic Discrimination*, 20 Nat'l Cont. Mgmt. J., Issue No. 2, p. 87 (1987).

SET-ASIDE (v) To reserve an acquisition exclusively or partially for the participation of a special class of contractors. The SMALL BUSINESS ACT, at 15 U.S.C. § 644, authorizes procuring agencies to set aside procurements or portions of procurements for the exclusive participation of SMALL BUSINESS CONCERNs. See also SET-ASIDE (n).

SETOFF The reduction of contract payments by the amount of a contractor's indebtedness to the Government. The Government's right of setoff applies to debts arising from unrelated as well as related transactions and to noncontractual as well as contractual debts. There is no requirement that the Government's claim be judged by a court before setoff may be used. See GAO, *Principles of Federal Appropriations Law*, vol. III, chap. 13 (2d ed. 1991); FAR 32.611 and FAR 32.612. However, it has been held that setoff (but not WITHHOLDING) can only be made in accordance with the procedures of the DEBT COLLECTION ACT and the CONTRACT DISPUTES ACT OF 1978. See Cibinic & Nash, *Administration of Government Contracts* 1176–81 (3d ed. 1995); Nash, chap. 12, *Construction Contracting* 907–11 (1991); Cibinic, *Withholding, Offset and Debt Collection: A Double Whammy for the Debt Collection Act*, 7 N&CR ¶ 44 (Aug. 1993); Cibinic, *Postscript II: Debt Collection by Offset*, 3 N&CR ¶ 80 (Nov. 1989); Cibinic & Nash, *Debt Collection by Offset: What's Wrong?*, 1 N&CR ¶ 5 (Jan. 1987). See also NO-SETOFF COMMITMENT.

SETTLEMENT AUTHORITY The authority to settle contractual DISPUTEs by agreement. FAR 33.210 provides that the contracting officer has the authority to settle all CLAIMs arising under or related to the contract that are subject to the CONTRACT DISPUTES ACT OF 1978. Exceptions are (1) claims involving penalties or forfeitures prescribed by statute or regulation that another federal agency is specifically authorized to administer, settle, or determine; and (2) claims involving FRAUD. If a contracting officer is unable to settle a claim but renders a decision, the settlement authority varies thereafter. If the DECISION OF THE CONTRACTING OFFICER on a claim is the subject of an appeal to an agency BOARD OF CONTRACT APPEALS (BCA), the contracting officer retains settlement authority and may not delegate that authority to a Government trial attorney. If the decision of the contracting officer is appealed to the COURT OF FEDERAL CLAIMS or the decision of a BCA is appealed to the COURT OF APPEALS FOR THE FEDERAL CIRCUIT, settlement authority resides with the Attorney General and is normally delegated to DOJ attorneys. See Cibinic & Nash, *Administration of Government Contracts* 1284–89 (3d ed. 1995); Latham, *Government Contract Disputes* 5-23 and 5-24 (1986).

SETTLEMENT PROPOSAL A proposal for effecting settlement of a contract terminated by the Government in whole or in part, submitted by a contractor or subcontractor in the proper form, and supported by the data. A settlement proposal is included within the general meaning of the word CLAIM under the FALSE CLAIMS ACT. FAR 49.001. Settlement proposals are submitted by contractors in TERMINATIONs FOR CONVENIENCE, as well as by cost-reimbursement contractors in TERMINATIONs FOR DEFAULT. In the case of a termination for default, however, the costs of preparing the proposal are not ALLOWABLE COSTs. FAR 49.403. FAR 49.602 discusses the forms and procedures necessary for settling terminated prime contracts. See Seidman & Banfield, *Preparing Termination for Convenience Settlement Proposals for Fixed-Price Contracts*, 97-11 Briefing Papers (Oct. 1997); Fish, *When a Termination for Convenience Settlement Proposal Constitutes a Claim Under the Contract Disputes Act*, 26 Pub. Cont. L.J. 423 (1997); Cibinic & Nash, *Administration of Government Contracts* 1090–96 (3d ed. 1995).

SEVERANCE PAY A payment in addition to regular salaries and wages by contractors to workers whose employment is being involuntarily terminated. Severance pay, or dismissal wages, must meet the requirements of FAR 31.205-6(g) to be an ALLOWABLE COST. The FAR distinguishes between normal turnover severance pay, which is allowable, and mass severance pay, which is unallowable. See Cibinic & Nash, *Cost-Reimbursement Contracting* 803–7 (2d ed. 1993).

SEVERELY DISABLED See BLIND OR SEVERELY DISABLED.

SEVERIN DOCTRINE A legal rule preventing contractors from recovering damages on behalf of subcontractors for BREACH OF CONTRACT by the Government if the contractor has no liability to the subcontractor. The rule originated with the case of *Severin v. United States*, 99 Ct. Cl. 435 (1943), which held that a clause in a subcontract completely exculpating the contractor from liability barred any CLAIM on behalf of the subcontractor against the Government because the contractor could not prove that it (rather than the subcontractor) had suffered any damages. The rule does not apply to claims for compensation under contract clauses. See Cibinic & Nash, *Administration of Government Contracts* 1256–57 (3d ed. 1995); Nash, *The Severin Doctrine: It's Still Barely Alive and Well*, 4 N&CR ¶ 63 (Nov. 1990).

"SHALL" The imperative term used in the FEDERAL ACQUISITION REGULATIONS SYSTEM. FAR 2.101. When a regulation uses the term "shall," it denotes that the regulation must be followed unless the contracting officer has obtained a DEVIATION. If a mandatory clause is omitted from the contract without a deviation, it is included in the contract by operation of the CHRISTIAN DOCTRINE.

SHARE-IN SAVINGS CONTRACTING An acquisition method under which an agency enters into a contract for an INFORMATION TECHNOLOGY solution for improving mission-related or administrative processes with payment to be made to the contractor in the form of a share of the savings derived from the new technology. Section 5311 of the CLINGER-COHEN ACT OF 1996, 40 U.S.C. § 1491, permits the Administrator of the Office of Federal Procurement Policy to authorize the heads of two executive agencies to carry out pilot programs using such contracts, with no more than five contracts for each program. The statute contains no guidance on the duration of such contracts or the percentage share of the savings that may be negotiated.

SHARED-SAVING PROJECT A project where an agency enters into a contract to achieve energy savings by permitting the contractor to make energy audits, install energy saving equipment and train personnel in exchange for a share of the energy savings resulting from such measures. This type of contract is permitted by 42 U.S.C. § 8287, which contains quite detailed guidance on their form. Such contracts may be for periods up to 25 years. FAR 41.102(b)(7) states that FAR 41, providing guidance on acquisition of utilities, does not apply to such contracts.

SHARING ARRANGEMENT The method by which an agency determines a contractor's fair share of ACQUISITION SAVINGS resulting from the application of an accepted VALUE ENGINEERING CHANGE PROPOSAL. The contractor is entitled to a percentage share of any net acquisition savings realized on the instant contract, concurrent contracts, and future contracts (see CONCURRENT CONTRACT SAVINGS and FUTURE CONTRACT SAVINGS). FAR 48.104 provides guidance for determining the Government/ contractor shares of such savings.

SHARING BASE The number of affected end items on contracts of the contracting office accepting a VALUE ENGINEERING CHANGE PROPOSAL. FAR 48.001. The sharing base is one of the elements in the computation of ACQUISITION SAVINGS.

SHARING PERIOD The period beginning with acceptance of the first unit incorporating the VALUE ENGINEERING CHANGE PROPOSAL (VECP) and ending at the later of (1) three years after the first unit affected by the VECP is accepted or (2) the last scheduled delivery date of an item affected by the VECP under the contract delivery schedule in effect at the time the VECP is accepted. FAR 48.001. The sharing period is one of the elements in the computation of FUTURE CONTRACT SAVINGS.

SHELTERED WORKSHOP See BLIND OR SEVERELY DISABLED.

SHOP DRAWINGS Drawings submitted by a construction contractor or subcontractor showing in detail the proposed fabrication and assembly of structural elements or the installation of materials or equipment. FAR 36.102. The standard Specifications and Drawings for Construction clause in FAR 52.236-21 contains detailed procedures for the submission of shop drawings when they are required by the contract. These procedures require the contracting officer to give approval or disapproval of such drawings, but the clause states that approval does not relieve the contractor of the responsibility for errors or omissions in the drawings (see OMISSIONS AND MISDESCRIPTIONS). See Parrott, *The Shop Drawing Submittal Process*, 96-9 Constr. Briefings (Aug. 1996).

SHORT FORM RESEARCH CONTRACT (SFRC) A form of contract used by DOD to purchase RESEARCH on a cost-reimbursement basis (see COST-REIMBURSEMENT CONTRACT) from educational institutions or domestic nonprofit organizations.

DFARS 235.015-71. SFRCs need not follow the UNIFORM CONTRACT FORMAT but must include certain FAR and DFARS clauses. DFARS 235.015-71 (h) and (i). Contractors must use DD Form 2222-2, Short Form Research Contract—Research Proposal, DFARS 253.303-2222-2, when submitting research proposals for SFRC awards. DFARS 235.015-71(d). The contracting officer may award a SFRC on the basis of FULL AND OPEN COMPETITION if the contract is based on a BROAD AGENCY ANNOUNCEMENT. The contracting officer may award the contract on the basis of other than full and open competition if it is based on an UNSOLICITED PROPOSAL for research work or if it is necessary to award the contract to establish or maintain an essential engineering research or development capability. DFARS 235.015-71(e).

SHOULD-COST ANALYSIS See SHOULD-COST REVIEW.

SHOULD-COST REVIEW A technique aimed at establishing a PRICE on the basis of what it *should* cost the contractor to produce, assuming reasonable economy and efficiency of operation. It is a specialized form of COST ANALYSIS that does not assume that a contractor's historical costs reflect efficient and economical operation, but instead evaluates the economy and efficiency of the contractor's existing workforce, methods, materials, facilities, operating systems and management. A should-cost review is performed at the contractor's plant, employing a multi-functional team of Government procurement, contract administration, pricing, AUDIT, and engineering representatives. The objective is to reduce the cost of performance of Government contracts by promoting both short- and long-range improvements in the contractor's economy and efficiency; quantifying the findings in terms of their impact on cost; and developing a realistic price objective for negotiation. The scope of a should-cost review can range from a large-scale review of the contractor's entire operation, including plantwide overhead and major subcontractors, to a small-scale tailored review examining specific contractor operations. FAR 15.407-4. In establishing a should-cost review, the contracting officer should identify the specific elements of a contractor's operations that have the greatest potential for cost savings. DOD requires a should-cost review for major systems contracts over $100 million when (1) some initial production has already taken place, (2) the contract will be awarded on a sole source basis, (3) there are future requirements for substantial quantities of like items, (4) the work is sufficiently defined to permit an effective analysis, and (5) major changes in the system are unlikely. DFARS 215.810. See Cibinic & Nash, *Cost-Reimbursement Contracting* 568 (2d ed. 1993).

SHOULD-COST REVIEW TEAM An integrated team of Government procurement, contract administration, pricing, AUDIT, and engineering representatives formed to conduct a coordinated, in-depth SHOULD-COST REVIEW at the contractor's plant. The team normally consists of a team leader, a deputy team leader, a DEFENSE CONTRACT AUDIT AGENCY representative, an operations and administration officer, and three subteams—technical, management, and pricing. See *DCAA Contract Audit Manual* 9-1303 and 9-1304.

SHOW CAUSE NOTICE A preliminary written notice given to the contractor by the contracting officer when TERMINATION FOR DEFAULT appears to be appropriate. FAR 49.402-3(e)(1). It (1) notifies the contractor of the possibility of termination, (2) indicates the contractual liabilities of default termination, and (3) asks the contractor to show cause why the contract should not be terminated for default. The notice may state that failure of the contractor to show cause may be taken as admission that there is no valid cause. The notice may also invite the contractor to discuss the matter at a meeting or conference. A suggested format for a show cause notice is set forth in FAR 49.607. See Cibinic & Nash, *Administration of Government Contracts* 994–96 (3d ed. 1995). See also CURE NOTICE.

SIGNIFICANT REVISION A revision to the FAR or one of its agency supplements that alters the meaning of any coverage having a significant cost or administrative impact on contractors or offerors, or a significant effect beyond the internal operating procedures of the issuing agency. Significant revisions do not include editorial, stylistic, or other revisions that have no impact on the basic meaning of the coverage being revised. FAR 1.501-1. Public comments must be solicited on proposed revisions to the FAR SYSTEM unless the proposed coverage does not constitute a significant revision. FAR 1.501-3.

SIMPLIFIED ACQUISITION PROCEDURES The methods used for making purchases of supplies not exceeding the SIMPLIFIED ACQUISITION THRESHOLD using the procedure prescribed in FAR Part 13. These simplified procedures are intended to (1) reduce administrative costs, (2) improve opportunities for SMALL BUSINESS CONCERNS and SMALL DISADVANTAGED BUSINESS CONCERNs, (3) promote efficiency and economy in contracting, and (4) avoid unnecessary burdens for agencies and contractors. FAR

13.003. Simplified purchases may be made using IMPREST FUNDS, FAR 13.305; PURCHASE ORDERS, FAR Subpart 13.302; BLANKET PURCHASE AGREEMENTs, FAR Subpart 13.303; GOVERNMENT-WIDE COMMERCIAL PURCHASE CARDs, or any other authorized method. FAR 13.103. These procedures must be used to the maximum extent practicable for all purchases not exceeding the simplified acquisition threshold ($100,000), unless requirements can be met by using required sources of supply. FAR 13.003. The contracting officer is required to SET ASIDE all purchases exceeding $2,500 but not exceeding $100,000 (except foreign purchases) for SMALL BUSINESS. FAR 13.003. See Cibinic & Nash, chap. 7, Sec. II., *Formation of Government Contracts* (3d ed. 1998); Cibinic, *Simplified Acquisition: Specifying the Basis for Award*, 11 N&CR ¶ 52 (Oct. 1997); Cibinic, *Simplified Acquisition: Late Quotations*, 11 N&CR ¶ 19 (Apr. 1997); Cibinic, *Simplified Acquisition: Keep It Simple*, 9 N&CR ¶ 4 (Jan. 1996); .

SIMPLIFIED ACQUISITION THRESHOLD The maximum dollar value of an acquisition that may use SIMPLIFIED ACQUISITION PROCEDURES. The threshold was established at $100,000 by the FEDERAL ACQUISITION STREAMLINING ACT OF 1994, Pub. L No. 103-355.

SIMPLIFIED CONTRACT FORMAT A standardized format used in lieu of the UNIFORM CONTRACT FORMAT when obtaining supplies or services using a FIRM-FIXED-PRICE CONTRACT or a FIXED-PRICE CONTRACT WITH ECONOMIC PRICE ADJUSTMENT in SEALED BID procurements. The recommended format is the Solicitation/Contract form (Standard Form 1447), followed by the contract schedule, clauses, a list of documents and attachments (if necessary), and representations and instructions. The contracting officer, however, has flexibility in organizing and preparing the documentation. See FAR 14.201-9.

SINGLE-AWARD SCHEDULE A schedule in the FEDERAL SUPPLY SCHEDULES series for which there is only one contract made with a supplier for any given item at a stated price, for delivery to points within a geographic area as defined in the schedule. Award of a single-award schedule contract is appropriate if there are adequate commercial descriptions or specifications to permit competitive offers. The procedures to be followed in ordering from these schedules are set forth in FAR Subpart 8.4. See Cibinic & Nash, chap. 7, Sec. VIII., *Formation of Government Contracts* (3d ed. 1998).

SINGLE PROCESS INITIATIVE A DOD policy designed to implement a single process in a contractor's plant or facility in order to reduce the cost of performance of all DOD contracts at that plant or facility. A single process is implemented by processing a "block change" modification to all contracts with the plant or facility consolidating or eliminating multiple processes, specifications and standards. See the DOD Single Process Initiative homepage at <http://www.acq.osd.mil/ar/single.htm>. See also *Navy Single Process Initiative (SPI) Handbook* (Apr. 1, 1997); *Single Process Initiative Guidance for Army Component Team Leaders* (U.S. Contracting Support Agency, Oct. 1996).

SINGLE SOURCE See SOLE SOURCE.

SITE OF WORK The physical place or places where construction called for in the contract will remain when work is completed, and nearby property used by the contractor or subcontractor during construction that is so close it can reasonably be included in the site. FAR 22.401. Fabrication plants, mobile factories, batch plants, borrow pits, job headquarters, tool yards, and the like are parts of the site of work, provided they are dedicated exclusively, or nearly so, to performance of the contract or project, and are close enough to the actual construction location that it would be reasonable to include them. The site of work does not include permanent HOME OFFICEs, branch plant establishments, fabrication plants, or tool yards of a contractor or subcontractor whose locations and continuance in operation are determined wholly without regard to a particular federal contract or project. The DAVIS-BACON ACT is applicable only to LABORERS OR MECHANICS employed directly on the site of work.

SIZE APPEAL See SIZE PROTEST.

SIZE PROTEST The protest by an offeror or interested party challenging another offeror's representation of itself as a SMALL BUSINESS CONCERN. Such protests must be filed within five days after BID OPENING or receipt of notice of an apparent successful offeror. FAR 19.302(d)(1). Size protests are referred to the SMALL BUSINESS ADMINISTRATION (SBA) regional office where the principal office of the challenged offeror is located. FAR 19.302(c). Once the contracting officer receives a protest, he or she may not award the contract until SBA makes a size determination or 10 business days transpire after SBA's receipt of the protest, whichever occurs first. When the contracting officer determines in writing that award must be made to protect the public interest, the award need not be stayed, although the contracting officer must notify the SBA. FAR 19.302(h). The contracting officer may stay the award longer than 10 days, until SBA's determination is received, unless the delay would prove disadvantageous to the Government. Appeals from adverse size determinations by the SBA must be filed with the SBA Office of Hearings and Appeals in Washington, DC. FAR 19.302(i). See Hordell & Hoffman, *Small Business Size Appeals/Edition III*, 96-9 Briefing Papers (Aug. 1996); Patin, chap. 4, *Construction Contracting* 335–43 (1991). See also SIZE STATUS.

SIZE STANDARDS See SMALL BUSINESS CONCERN.

SIZE STATUS The characteristics of a firm that qualify it to obtain the benefits of being a SMALL BUSINESS CONCERN. The size status of a concern is determined, in the first instance, by SELF-CERTIFICATION that a firm meets size standards established by the SMALL BUSINESS ADMINISTRATION and set forth at FAR 19.102. If the status is challenged, the size is determined through the SIZE PROTEST procedures. See Cibinic, *Date of Small Business Size Status: "This Could Be the Start of Something Big,"* 8 N&CR ¶ 19 (Mar. 1994).

SMALL AND DISADVANTAGED BUSINESS UTILIZATION SPECIALIST (SADBUS) A Government employee with the responsibility of ensuring the utilization of SMALL BUSINESS CONCERNs and SMALL DISADVANTAGED BUSINESS CONCERNs (SDBCs) in accordance with agency regulations. FAR 19.201. Agencies frequently use titles such as small business specialist or small business/disadvantaged business specialist in lieu of SADBUS. See, for example, NFS 18-19.201(c). The duties assigned to this function vary from agency to agency. Within DOD, DFARS 219.201(d) specifies that the SADBUS must (1) make sure that programs affecting small business concerns, HISTORICALLY BLACK COLLEGES AND UNIVERSITIES (HBCUs), MINORITY INSTITUTIONs (MIs), and LABOR SURPLUS AREA (LSA) CONCERNs are implemented; (2) advise contracting, program, and requirements personnel on all matters affecting small businesses, HBCUs, MIs, and LSA concerns; (3) advise and inform small businesses, SDBCs, HBCUs, MIs, and LSA concerns about acquisition procedures and proposed acquisitions and instruct them in preparing proposals and interpreting solicitation provisions and contract clauses; (4) maintain outreach programs designed to locate small businesses, SDBCs, HBCUs, and MIs and to develop information on their technical competence; (5) ensure that small business concerns are offered financial assistance available under existing regulations and that they obtain payment under their contracts; (6) help contracting officers determine when subcontracting plans are needed, whether they are acceptable, and whether they are being complied with; and (7) monitor performance against small and disadvantaged business program goals and recommend action to correct deficiencies. NASA prescribes slightly different duties. NFS 18-19.201(c).

SMALL BUSINESS ACT An Act, 15 U.S.C. § 631 et seq., that in 1963 created the SMALL BUSINESS ADMINISTRATION (SBA). The SBA is jointly responsible with the federal procuring agencies for promoting policies and taking actions to ensure that SMALL BUSINESS CONCERNs and SMALL DISADVANTAGED BUSINESS CONCERNs obtain their fair share of Government procurements. The 1978 amendments gave added emphasis to the 8(a) PROGRAM by providing for business development assistance, establishing new eligibility standards, and requiring prime contractors to submit formal plans for subcontracting to small businesses and 8(a) firms.

SMALL BUSINESS ADMINISTRATION (SBA) A Government agency that counsels SMALL BUSINESS CONCERNs and helps contracting personnel ensure that a fair proportion of contracts for supplies and services is placed with small business. FAR 19.201(a). The SBA is authorized to (1) define specific small business size standards; (2) make loans; (3) enter into contracts with the Government and arrange for performance by subcontracting to small business (see 8(a) PROGRAM); (4) engage in determinations that certain interests would be served by awarding all or part of a contract to small business; (5) determine the SIZE STATUS of small business concerns; (6) certify the competency, including capacity and credit, of small businesses to perform particular contracts (see CERTIFICATE OF COMPETENCY; and (7) assist and encourage small business to undertake joint research and development programs (see SMALL BUSINESS INNOVATIVE RESEARCH CONTRACT). FAR Part 19. SBA regulations are at 13 C.F.R. Parts 101 through 140. See National Archives and Records Administration, *U.S. Government Manual Office of the Federal Register* (GPO 1996/97); Lambert & Shillito, *New Developments in Small Business*, 29 Cont. Mgmt. 24 (Mar. 1989).

SMALL BUSINESS COMPETITIVENESS DEMONSTRATION PROGRAM A program to improve the small business policies of the

Government, enacted by the Business Opportunity Development Reform Act of 1988, 15 U.S.C. § 644. This program is in effect from January 1, 1989, through September 30, 1997, and is intended to (1) show the competitive capabilities of small business on unrestricted Government contracts, and (2) target for expansion small business SET-ASIDEs in industries that historically demonstrate low small business involvement. As long as selected agencies maintain awards for selected industries—construction, refuse systems, architect-engineer services, and non-nuclear ship repair—at a level of at least 40 percent small business those agencies will use FULL AND OPEN COMPETITION rather than set-asides. However, the agencies must designate industries with which they have had low small business involvement for special efforts to increase that involvement. This program calls for participation by the following agencies: the Departments of Agriculture, Defense, Energy, Health and Human Services, the Interior, Transportation, and Veterans Affairs; the Environmental Protection Agency; the General Services Administration; and the National Aeronautics and Space Administration. The program creates a new category of small business concern known as EMERGING SMALL BUSINESS. FAR Subpart 19.10. See Nash, *Small Business: The Machinery Gets a Major Retuning*, 3 N&CR ¶ 44 (June 1989).

SMALL BUSINESS CONCERN A concern, under the SMALL BUSINESS ACT, 15 U.S.C. § 632, that is independently owned and operated and not dominant in its field of operation. The SMALL BUSINESS ADMINISTRATION is responsible for further definition of the term and does this through its Small Business Size Standards Regulations, 13 C.F.R. Part 121, incorporated in FAR 19.102. The definition of a small business varies by industry. To qualify, a contractor must fall within the size standard applicable to the industry under the STANDARD INDUSTRIAL CLASSIFICATION, which divides industries into 89 major groups and then into subgroups. Depending on the industry in question, the standard applied is based on either dollar volume (average ANNUAL RECEIPTS for the preceding three fiscal years) or number of employees. See Lambert & Shillito, *New Developments in Small Business*, 29 Cont. Mgmt. 24 (Mar. 1989); Kennedy & Trilling, *Pathways and Pitfalls for Small Business: Federal Procurement Socioeconomic Programs*, 22 Nat'l Cont. Mgmt. J., Issue No. 1, p. 55 (1988); Seidman, *An Overview of Small and Disadvantaged Business Contracting*, 19 Nat'l Cont. Mgmt. J., Issue No. 1, p. 5 (1985). See also SIZE STATUS; SIZE PROTEST.

SMALL BUSINESS INNOVATIVE RESEARCH (SBIR) CONTRACT A contract issued pursuant to the Small Business Innovation Development Act of 1982, 15 U.S.C. § 638. This act requires agencies with a budget for "extramural" research and development of more than $100 million to expend 2.5 percent of their budget with small businesses on SBIR contracts. These contracts are issued in two phases: Phase I for $100,000 to demonstrate the feasibility of the innovation and Phase II for $750,000 for development of the innovation. Procedures for these contracts are contained in 13 C.F.R. Part 121. Contracts issued under the SBIR program meet the COMPETITIVE PROCEDURES requirement of the COMPETITION IN CONTRACTING ACT. 10 U.S.C. § 2302(2); 41 U.S.C. § 259(b). The Rights in Data—SBIR Program clause at FAR 52.227-20 is used in the contracts to give SBIR contractors special rights in the TECHNICAL DATA developed under them. See Cibinic & Nash, chap. 7, Sec. VI., *Formation of Government Contracts* (3d ed. 1998).

SMALL BUSINESS REGULATORY FAIRNESS ACT (SBRFA) A law mandating congressional review of executive agency rules; requiring agencies—when a rule is expected to have a significant economic impact on a substantial number of SMALL BUSINESSes—to publish information to assist small businesses in complying with the rule; authorizes small businesses to seek judicial review of agency compliance with statutorily required regulatory flexibility (or RegFlex) analysis; establishing a SMALL BUSINESS ADMINISTRATION OMBUDSMAN; creating citizen review panels; and allowing small businesses to recover their legal fees in certain challenges to agency regulations. Pub. L. No. 104-194.

SMALL CLAIMS PROCEDURES See EXPEDITED PROCEDURES.

SMALL DISADVANTAGED BUSINESS CONCERN (SDBC) A SMALL BUSINESS CONCERN that is at least 51 percent unconditionally owned by one or more individuals who are both socially and economically disadvantaged (see SOCIALLY DISADVANTAGED INDIVIDUALS and ECONOMICALLY DISADVANTAGED INDIVIDUALS); or a publicly owned business with at least 51 percent of its stock unconditionally owned by, and its management and daily business controlled by, one or more socially and economically disadvantaged individuals. FAR 19.001. This term also means a small business concern that is at least 51 percent unconditionally owned by an economically disadvantaged INDIAN TRIBE or NATIVE HAWAIIAN

ORGANIZATION, or a publicly owned business with at least 51 percent of its stock unconditionally owned by one of these entities, its management and daily business controlled by members of an economically disadvantaged Indian tribe or Native Hawaiian organization, and that meets the requirements of 13 C.F.R. Part 124. Individuals must certify that they are members of named groups that are considered socially and economically disadvantaged—Black Americans, Hispanic Americans, NATIVE AMERICANS, ASIAN-PACIFIC AMERICANS, and SUBCONTINENT-ASIAN AMERICANS—in order to qualify for SDBC benefits and other minority aid programs. The defense authorization or appropriation acts of 1987 and the following years have established the goal that 5 percent of all DOD procurements be awarded to SDBCs and have authorized less than FULL AND OPEN COMPETITION and premiums not to exceed 10 percent of the FAIR MARKET PRICE. In DOD procurements, SDBCs include HISTORICALLY BLACK COLLEGES AND UNIVERSITIES and other MINORITY INSTITUTIONS. See DFARS 226.7003; Lambert & Shillito, *DOD Implements Congressional Mandate to Meet a Five Percent Contract Goal for Minorities*, 27 Cont. Mgmt. 16 (Oct. 1987).

SMALL PURCHASE PROCEDURES See SIMPLIFIED ACQUISITION PROCEDURES.

SOCIALLY DISADVANTAGED INDIVIDUALS Individuals who have been subjected to racial or ethnic prejudice or cultural bias because of their identity as members of a group without regard to their qualities as individuals. FAR 19.001. Businesses owned by such individuals who are also ECONOMICALLY DISADVANTAGED INDIVIDUALS are given special preferences in Government procurement. See Thomas, *So You Think You Know Federal Minority Contracting Law?* 37 Cont. Mgmt. 8 (Jan. 1997).

SOCIOECONOMIC PROGRAMS Programs that are incorporated into the procurement process to foster the achievement of national goals. Although federal procurement policy endeavors to obtain supplies and services economically, efficiently, and in a timely manner, the Government also utilizes its purchasing power as a means of promoting public policies. Government contracts attempt to further such national goals as fostering small business, overcoming regional unemployment, assisting minority workers, giving preference to domestic and other special sources, ensuring fair treatment of employees, maintaining integrity and fair competitive practices, and protecting the environment. See FAR Part 19, Small Business and Small Disadvantaged Business

Concerns; FAR Part 22, Application of Labor Laws to Government Acquisitions; FAR Part 23, Environment, Conservation, Occupational Safety, and Drug-Free Workplace; FAR Part 24, Protection of Privacy and Freedom of Information; and FAR Part 25, Foreign Acquisition. See Cibinic & Nash, chap. 10, *Formation of Government Contracts* (3d ed. 1998); Black, *Socioeconomic Contract Goal Setting Within the Department of Defense: Promises Still Unfulfilled*, 22 Nat'l Cont. Mgmt. J., Issue No. 2, p. 67 (1989); Horowitz & Wickersty, *Socio-Economic Procurement Requirements*, 85-3 Briefing Papers (Mar. 1985).

SOFTWARE See COMPUTER SOFTWARE.

SOFTWARE DOCUMENTATION See COMPUTER SOFTWARE DOCUMENTATION.

"SOLD IN SUBSTANTIAL QUANTITIES TO THE GENERAL PUBLIC" See COMMERCIALITY.

SOLE SOURCE The only source known to be able to perform a contract, or the one source among others that, for justifiable reason, is found to be most advantageous for the purpose of contract award. A sole source acquisition means a contract for the purchase of supplies or services that is entered into, or proposed to be entered into, by an agency after soliciting and negotiating with only one source. FAR 6.003. Such an acquisition is normally justified only when there is just one responsible source (see RESPONSIBILITY) and no other supplies or services will satisfy agency requirements. FAR 6.302-1. Justifying a procurement without obtaining FULL AND OPEN COMPETITION does not automatically permit contracting with a sole source because FAR 6.301(d) requires contracting officers to solicit offers from as many potential sources as is practicable in these circumstances. See Cibinic & Nash, chap. 3, Sec. II., *Formation of Government Contracts* (3d ed. 1998).

SOLICITATION A document, sent to prospective contractors by a Government agency, requesting the submission of OFFERs or of information. This generic term includes INVITATIONs FOR BIDS (IFBs), REQUESTs FOR PROPOSALS (RFPs), and REQUESTs FOR QUOTATIONS (RFQs). The term is also used to denote the process of issuing such documents and obtaining responses. See Cibinic & Nash, chaps. 5 & 6, *Formation of Government Contracts* (3d ed. 1998); Nagle, *How to Review a Federal Contract and Research Federal Contract Law* 14–47 (1990).

SOLICITATION MAILING LIST A list of known or potential sources for each type of supply or service, including construction, that an agency acquires. Each CONTRACTING ACTIVITY must maintain such lists. FAR 14.205-1. An application (Standard Form 129, FAR 53.301-129) to be placed on a solicitation mailing list (sometimes called a bidders mailing list) must be signed by the actual supplier, dealer, or manufacturer and not by an agent. Contracting activities should notify prospective contractors when they are placed on the mailing list or if they fail to meet the criteria for inclusion on the list. FAR 14.205-1(b). If solicitation mailing lists become excessively long, the Government may reduce the number of concerns on the list, rotate or use different portions of the list for separate acquisitions, or send PRESOLICITATION NOTICEs rather than complete bid sets. FAR 14.205-4. Concerns failing to submit an offer, to respond to a presolicitation notice, or to otherwise respond to a solicitation may be removed from the mailing list without notice. FAR 14.205-2. See *CM Update: GSA Replacing System Used to Maintain Centralized Bidder's Mailing List*, 28 Cont. Mgmt. 33 (Jan. 1988).

SOLICITATION PROVISION See PROVISION.

SOLUTIONS-BASED CONTRACTING An acquisition method under which the acquisition objectives are defined by the Federal Government user of the technology to be acquired, a streamlined contractor selection process is used, and industry sources are allowed to provide solutions that attain the objectives effectively. Section 5312 of the CLINGER-COHEN ACT OF 1996, 40 U.S.C. § 1492, permits the Administrator of the Office of Federal Procurement Policy to authorize the heads of any executive agency to carry out a pilot program to test the feasibility of using solutions-based contracting for the acquisition of INFORMATION TECHNOLOGY. See Nash, *Solutions-Based Contracting: A Better Way to Buy Information Technology?*, 11 N&CR ¶ 17 (Apr. 1997).

SOURCE CODE The version of a COMPUTER PROGRAM that is written in a human-readable programming language. In order to be used in a COMPUTER, the program must be converted into OBJECT CODE. Creation of the source code is the initial step in writing a computer program after its design has been formulated. Modifications or adaptations of the program are also generally made to the source code initially and then converted to object code.

SOURCE SELECTION The process of selecting a contractor through competitive negotiation. Source selection procedures are designed to (1) maximize competition; (2) minimize the complexity of the solicitation, evaluation, and selection process; (3) ensure the impartial and comprehensive evaluation of proposals; and (4) ensure selection of the source whose proposal is most advantageous and realistic and whose performance is expected to best meet stated Government requirements. Agency heads or their designees (see HEAD OF THE AGENCY) are responsible for source selection. The contracting officer is responsible for selecting the source unless another official is designated as the source selection authority (SSA). FAR 15.303. Source selection typically entails determining EVALUATION FACTORS, developing REQUESTs FOR PROPOSALS, evaluating proposals, determining the COMPETITIVE RANGE, conducting written or oral DISCUSSIONs, requesting PROPOSAL REVISIONS, selecting the source, and awarding the contract. Almost all of the major agencies have source selection directives or manuals outside of the FEDERAL ACQUISITION REGULATIONS SYSTEM, which contain detailed guidance on the procedures followed in FORMAL SOURCE SELECTIONs. See generally Nash & Cibinic, *Competitive Negotiation: The Source Selection Process* (1993); Cibinic & Nash, chap. 6, *Formation of Government Contracts* (3d ed. 1998).

SOURCE SELECTION ADVISORY COUNCIL (SSAC) A panel of senior Government personnel appointed by a SOURCE SELECTION AUTHORITY to advise on the conduct of the source selection process and prepare a comparative analysis of the evaluation results on a competitively negotiated procurement (see NEGOTIATION). SSACs are used on major procurements under agency policies, which are generally promulgated by handbooks or regulations outside of the FAR system.

SOURCE SELECTION AUTHORITY (SSA) The Government official in charge of selecting a source or sources in a competitive negotiated acquisition (see NEGOTIATION). The title is most often used in the FORMAL SOURCE SELECTION process, when the official is someone other than the contracting officer. FAR 15.303. The agency head or a designee formally designates the source selection authority, who (1) establishes an evaluation group structure, (2) approves a SOURCE SELECTION PLAN, and (3) considers the recommendations of evaluation and advisory groups in making the source selection decision. See Nash & Cibinic, *Competitive Negotiation: The Source Selection Process* (1993); Schnitzer & Humphrey,

The Scope of the Source Selection Official's Discretion, 94-5 Briefing Papers (Apr. 1994); Nash, *The Source Selection Official in Competitive Negotiations: Who Should It Be?*, 7 N&CR ¶ 50 (Sept. 1993).

SOURCE SELECTION BOARD (SSB) A panel of agency officials that oversees the evaluation of PROPOSALs submitted on competitively negotiated procurements. SSBs are generally responsible for ensuring that the evaluations submitted to the SOURCE SELECTION AUTHORITY are consistent and represent a fair evaluation of the proposals submitted. SSBs are used most frequently on major procurements, and the procedures that they follow vary in accordance with agency procedures, which are generally found in handbooks or regulations outside the FAR system.

SOURCE SELECTION EVALUATION BOARD (SSEB) A synonym for SOURCE SELECTION BOARD.

SOURCE SELECTION INFORMATION Information of the following types that is prepared for use by a federal agency for the purpose of evaluating a BID or PROPOSAL to enter into a FEDERAL AGENCY PROCUREMENT contract, if that information has not been previously made available to the public or disclosed publicly: (1) bid prices in SEALED BIDDING or lists of such bid prices before bid opening; (2) proposed costs or prices on negotiated procurements (see NEGOTIATION) and lists of such cost or prices; (3) SOURCE SELECTION PLANs; (4) TECHNICAL EVALUATION plans; (5) technical evaluations of proposals; (6) cost or price evaluations of proposals; (7) COMPETITIVE RANGE determinations; (8) rankings of bids, proposals, or competitors; (9) reports and evaluations of source selection panels, boards or advisory councils; and (10) other information marked with the legend "Source Selection Information—See FAR 3.104." This information may not be disclosed pursuant to the PROCUREMENT INTEGRITY provisions of the Office of Federal Procurement Policy Act, 41 U.S.C. § 423. The definition was slightly different in the statute and regulations in effect prior to January 1, 1997. FAR 3.104-5 provides guidance on the treatment of this information. See Arnavas & Marsh, *The Procurement Integrity Act*, 91-9 Briefing Papers (Aug. 1991).

SOURCE SELECTION OFFICIAL (SSO) A synonym for SOURCE SELECTION AUTHORITY.

SOURCE SELECTION PLAN A plan formulated by an agency to specify the key elements of a proposed SOURCE SELECTION. The source selection plan must identify those milestones at which a decision should be made. The plan should address all technical, business management, and other significant considerations that will control the procurement. The specific content of plans can vary, depending on the nature, circumstances, and stage of the acquisition. FAR 7.105. See Cibinic & Nash, chap. 6, *Formation of Government Contracts* (3d ed. 1998).

SOVEREIGN ACTS DOCTRINE A defense employed by the Federal Government to avoid liability when the Government acts as a sovereign in a way that affects a contractor's performance of a Government contract. See Schwartz, *Assembling Winstar: Triumph of the Ideal of Congruence in Government Contracts Law?*, 26 Pub. Cont. L.J. 481 (1997); Cibinic, *Supreme Court Decides Winstar: "Unmistakablility" Doctrine And "Sovereign Acts" Defense Deliberated*, 10 N&CR ¶ 42 (Aug. 1996); Cibinic, *Sovereignty: The Winstar Case*, 9 N&CR ¶ 58 (Nov. 1995); Nash, *Postscript: The Sovereign Power of Congress To Abrogate Contract Terms*, 7 N&CR ¶ 45 (Aug. 1993); Morgan, *Identifying Protected Government Acts under the Sovereign Acts Doctrine: A Question of Acts and Actors*, 22 Pub. Cont. L.J. 223 (1993); Cibinic, *Sovereignty: Is Our Government an Honest Person?*, 6 N&CR ¶ 72 (Dec. 1992).

SOVEREIGN IMMUNITY A legal doctrine that precludes a litigant from asserting an otherwise meritorious cause of action against a sovereign or a party with sovereign attributes unless the sovereign consents to suit. Sovereignty is the supreme, absolute, and uncontrollable power by which any independent state is governed. Sovereignty entails the power to make laws, regulate, collect taxes, wage war or make peace. Historically, governments (whether federal, state, city, or other) have been immune from TORT (injury to person or property) liability arising from activities that were governmental in nature. *Black's Law Dictionary* 1396 (6th ed. 1990). The Government has waived its sovereign immunity to permit certain types of actions against the Government through a wide variety of statutes, such as the FEDERAL TORT CLAIMS ACT (tort actions), the TUCKER ACT (actions based on the Constitution, statutes, regulations, or contracts, express or implied in fact), the CONTRACT DISPUTES ACT OF 1978 (disputes concerning claims arising under or relating to contracts), 28 U.S.C. § 1498 (use of PATENTs and COPYRIGHTs), and the EQUAL ACCESS TO JUSTICE ACT (recovery of ATTORNEY'S FEES). See Cibinic, *Sovereignty: The Winstar Case*, 9 N&CR ¶ 58 (Nov. 1995).

SPARES ACQUISITION INTEGRATED WITH PRODUCTION (SAIP) A technique used to acquire spare and repair parts combined with procurement of identical items produced for the primary system, subsystem, or equipment. DFARS 217.7502. SAIP minimizes the cost of spares by avoiding the charges normally associated with separate material orders and manufacturing actions. SAIP is appropriate where ECONOMIES OF SCALE achieved by combining spares orders with installation orders substantially exceed any added administrative costs.

SPEARIN DOCTRINE A rule creating an IMPLIED WARRANTY OF SPECIFICATIONS when the Government furnishes specifications that are not suitable for their intended purpose or are defective. *United States v. Spearin*, 248 U.S. 132 (1918). Cibinic & Nash, *Administration of Government Contracts* 267 (3d ed. 1995); Golden & Thomas, *The Spearin Doctrine: The False Dichotomy Between Design and Performance Specifications*, 25 Pub. Cont. L.J. 47 (1995).

SPECIAL DRAWING RIGHTS (SDRs) An international reserve asset that serves as the official unit of account with the International Monetary Fund (IMF) and which is intended to stimulate and facilitate international trade. A "drawing right" is a grant of credit, arranged by the IMF, from one member nation to another member nation. The IFM frequently attaches conditions for the granting of funds or credit through the exercise of SDRs. See Folsom et al., *International Business Transactions in a Nutshell* 185-87 (5th ed. 1996). The SDR is, in effect, a universal currency. Janik, *A U.S. Perspective on the GATT Agreement on Government Procurement*, 20 Geo. Wash. J. Int'l L. & Econ. 491, 494 n. 31 (1987). SDRs are an element in determining the threshold amount to which the TRADE AGREEMENTS ACT OF 1979, an exception to the BUY AMERICAN ACT, applies. The Trade Agreements Act excludes from its coverage contracting actions involving less than 150,000 SDRs (typically between $150,000 and $200,000), a figure set by the U.S. Trade Representative and published in the FEDERAL REGISTER. See FAR 25.402.

SPECIAL TEST EQUIPMENT Single or multipurpose integrated test units engineered, designed, fabricated, or modified to accomplish special-purpose testing in performing a contract. FAR 45.101. Special test equipment consists of items or assemblies of equipment, including standard or general-purpose items or components that are so interconnected and interdependent that they become a new functional entity for special testing purposes. It does not include MATERIAL, SPECIAL TOOLING, FACILITIES, or PLANT EQUIPMENT used for general plant testing purposes. FAR 45.307 permits agencies to provide existing special test equipment to contractors. It has traditionally been the policy of the Government to permit contractors to include the full cost of special test equipment needed for a specific contract in the price of that contract. FAR 31.205-40 specifies that such costs incurred by a contractor are ALLOWABLE COSTs. See Hill, *The Special Tooling and Special Test Equipment Cost Principle (FAR 31.205-40)*, 89-7 CP&A Rep. 14 (July 1989).

SPECIAL TOOLING Jigs, dies, fixtures, molds, patterns, taps, gauges, other equipment and manufacturing aids, and all components and replacements of these items that are of such a specialized nature that, without substantial modification or alteration, their use is limited to the development or production of particular supplies or parts thereof or to the performance of particular services. FAR 45.101. It does not include MATERIAL, SPECIAL TEST EQUIPMENT, FACILITIES (except foundations and similar improvements necessary for installing special tooling), general or special machine tools, or similar capital items. FAR 45.306 permits agencies to provide existing special tooling to contractors and provides guidance on when contractors should be permitted to retain title to special tooling required for contract performance. When existing Government tooling is not available, it has traditionally been the policy of the Government to include the full cost of special tooling in the contract price. FAR 31.205-40 specifies that such costs incurred by a contractor are ALLOWABLE COSTs. See Hill, *The Special Tooling and Special Test Equipment Cost Principle (FAR 31.205-40)* 89-7 CP&A Rep. 14 (1989).

SPECIFIC APPROPRIATION See APPROPRIATION.

SPECIFICATION A description of the technical requirements for a material, product, or service that includes the criteria for determining whether these requirements are met. Specifications may be prepared to cover a group of products, services, or materials, or a single product, service, or material. Specifications should state only the Government's actual minimum needs and be designed to promote FULL AND OPEN COMPETITION, with due regard to the nature of the supplies or services to be acquired. FAR 11.002. For some purposes, specifications are classified as FUNCTIONAL SPECIFICATIONS, DESIGN SPECIFICATIONS, and PERFORMANCE SPECIFICATIONS. See National Cont. Mgmt. Assoc., *Specifications and Standards*; Nash, *Opening Up the Specifications: The Risks and the Benefits*, 11 N&CR ¶ 41 (Aug. 1997); Allen & Villet, *Implied Warranty of Specifications*,

91-8 Briefing Papers (July 1991); Beran, *Specifications: The Duty Trilogy, Government and Contractor Responsibilities*, 27 Cont. Mgmt. 4 (Aug. 1987), 12 (Sept. 1987), and 11 (Oct. 1987). See also STANDARD; MILITARY SPECIFICATIONS AND STANDARDS.

SPECIFIED PAYMENT DATE For the purposes of the PROMPT PAYMENT ACT, this date, which is used in the context of ELECTRONIC FUNDS TRANSFER (EFT), is distinguished from the PAYMENT DATE, which applies only to payment by paper check. The specified payment date is the date that the Government places in the EFT transaction instruction, which is given to the Federal Reserve System, as the date on which the funds are to be transferred to the contractor's account by the financial agent. If no date is specified, the specified payment date is three business days after the payment office, typically the DISBURSING OFFICE, releases the EFT payment transaction instruction. FAR 32.902.

SPONSORSHIP OF SUBCONTRACTOR CLAIMS A process of permitting SUBCONTRACTORs to appeal adverse DECISIONs OF THE CONTRACTING OFFICER wherein the prime contractor permits the subcontractor to use the prime's name or agrees to appeal for the benefit of the subcontractor. The sponsorship system is a means of preserving the technical concept of PRIVITY OF CONTRACT by permitting appeals and suits to be brought by or in the name of the prime contractor even though the prime has no real interest in the matter and plays a passive role. Sponsorship means that the subcontractor may have its attorney prosecute the appeal, but the paperwork must be done in the name of the prime contractor and the prime contractor must certify the claim as required by the CONTRACT DISPUTES ACT OF 1978. See *United States v. Johnson Controls, Inc.*, 713 F.2d 1541 (Fed. Cir. 1983); Pachter, *Certification of Subcontractor Claims*, 19 Pub. Cont. Newsl. 3 (Fall 1983). If sponsorship occurs in a claim for BREACH OF CONTRACT, the SEVERIN DOCTRINE will bar the claim if the contractor is totally absolved of liability to the subcontractor. See Cibinic & Nash, *Administration of Government Contracts* 1253–57 (3d ed. 1995); Thrasher, *Subcontractor Dispute Remedies: Asserting Subcontractor Claims Against the Federal Government*, 23 Pub. Cont. L.J. 39 (1993).

SPREAD-GAIN ACTUARIAL COST METHOD Any of several projected benefit actuarial cost methods under which actuarial gains and losses are included as part of the current and future normal costs of a PENSION PLAN. FAR 31.001. Actuarial gains and losses under a pension plan whose costs are measured by this actuarial cost method must be included as part of current and future normal cost and spread over the remaining average working lives of the workforce. 48 C.F.R. § 9904.413-50.

STANDARD A document that establishes engineering and technical limitations and applications of items, materials, processes, methods, designs, and engineering practices. It includes any related criteria deemed essential to achieve the highest practical degree of uniformity in materials or products, or interchangeability of parts used in those products. Standards may be used in SPECIFICATIONs, INVITATIONs FOR BIDS, REQUESTs FOR PROPOSALS, and contracts. A voluntary standard is a standard established by a private-sector body and available for public use. The term does not include private standards of individual firms. See OMB Circular No. A-119 (revised), *Federal Participation in the Development and Use of Voluntary Standards*, Oct. 20, 1993.

STANDARD COST Any cost computed with the use of preestablished measures. FAR 31.001. A standard cost is a goal or baseline cost that is used to expedite the costing of transactions; it is determined from historical experience or derived from the best information available. Except for costs attributable to precise and highly predictable operations, ACTUAL COSTs will almost always vary from standard costs due to factors that affect performance, such as employee fatigue, unforeseen interruptions, and other delays (called VARIANCEs). See *Cost Analysis: Contract Pricing Reference Guide*, vol. III (Dec. 1993). Guidance on the use of standard costs for estimating, accumulating, and reporting costs of direct material and direct LABOR is contained in CAS 407, 48 C.F.R. § 9904.407.

STANDARD FORMS (SFs) Forms prescribed by the FAR for use throughout the Government in the contracting process. FAR Part 53 illustrates SFs for Government procurement prescribed elsewhere in the FAR and contains requirements and information generally applicable to SFs, OPTIONAL FORMS, and agency-prescribed forms. Unless provided in the FAR instructions for use of a standard form, agencies may not alter any standard form prescribed by the FAR, or use any form other than the standard form prescribed by the FAR for a particular purpose, without receiving, in advance, an exception (an approved departure from the form's established design, content, printing specifications, or conditions for use). Executive agencies obtain SFs through the General Services Administration Supply Catalog (Office Products).

Contractors may obtain them from the U.S. Government Printing Office, Washington, DC 20402. See Ferguson & Moss, *FAR Part 53—It's a Matter of Forms*, 24 Cont. Mgmt. 8 (Apr. 1984).

STANDARD INDUSTRIAL CLASSIFICATION (SIC) A classification system dividing industries into 89 major groups, each with subgroups. The Government's SIC Manual classifies and defines the entire field of economic activities by these industry categories. It is the source used by the SMALL BUSINESS ADMINISTRATION in defining size standards for the purpose of small business qualification.

STANDARDIZATION The adoption of a single product or group of products to be used by different organizations or all parts of one organization. Standardization of weapons has been the DOD policy for many years. It is also the policy of DOD and the North Atlantic Treaty Organization to (1) achieve the closest practicable cooperation among forces; (2) facilitate the most efficient use of research, development, and production resources; and (3) agree to adopt on the broadest possible basis the use of (a) common or compatible operational, administrative, and logistic procedures and criteria, (b) common or compatible technical procedures and criteria, (c) common, compatible, or interchangeable supplies, components, weapons, or equipment, and (d) common or compatible tactical doctrines with corresponding organizational compatibility. Jones, *Glossary: Defense Acquisition Acronyms and Terms* (8th ed., Defense Systems Management College).

STANDARDS OF CONDUCT The rules applicable to Government employees and individuals dealing with the Government. The primary standards are set forth in the following sections of title 18 U.S.Code: § 201, Bribery and Gratuities; § 202, Definitions; § 203, Compensation of Members of Congress and Government Officers; § 204, Practice in U.S. Claims Court and Court of Appeals for the Federal Circuit by Members of Congress; § 205, Activities of Officers and Employees in Claims Against and Other Matters Affecting Government; § 206, Exemption of Retired Officers of the Uniformed Services; § 207, Post-Employment Restrictions (see REVOLVING DOOR); § 208, Acts Affecting a Personal Financial Interest (see PERSONAL CONFLICT OF INTEREST); § 209, Supplementation of Salary of Government Employees; § 210, Offer to Procure Appointive Public Office; § 211, Acceptance or Solicitation to Obtain Appointive Public Office; § 212, Offer of Loan or Gratuity to Bank Examiner; § 213, Acceptance of Loan or Gratuity by Bank Examiner; § 214, Offer for Procurement of Federal Reserve Bank Loan and Discount of Commercial Paper; § 215,

Receipt of Commissions or Gifts for Procuring Loans; § 216, Penalties and Injunctions; § 217, Acceptance of Consideration for Adjustments of Farm Indebtedness; and § 218, Voiding Contracts Violating These Criminal Provisions. Other standards are set forth in other parts of the criminal code (see, particularly, the FALSE CLAIMS ACT and the FALSE STATEMENTS ACT). Guidance on these standards is set forth in the regulations of the Office of Government Ethics, 5 C.F.R. § 2600 et seq. See Alstott, *The New Standards of Ethical Conduct,* 33 Cont. Mgmt. 10 (Feb. 1993); Brunsman, *Standards of Conduct and Business Ethics for Buyers*, 27 Cont. Mgmt. 18 (June 1987). See also PROCUREMENT INTEGRITY.

STANDING PRICE QUOTATIONS A method of obtaining prices for simplified acquisitions or commercial items without obtaining individual quotations for each purchase. FAR 13.103. It reduces paperwork in that authorized individuals merely issue a PURCHASE ORDER against it. Standing price quotations may be used if the pricing information is current and the Government obtains the benefit of maximum discounts before award. This procedure is used extensively by the Department of Veterans Affairs. See Cibinic & Nash, chap. 7, Sec. II., *Formation of Government Contracts* (3d ed. 1998).

STATE AND LOCAL TAXES TAXES imposed by a state or local government. Such taxes include income taxes, sales and use taxes, franchise taxes, EXCISE TAXes, and property taxes. FAR 31.205-41 specifies the rules governing whether such taxes paid by contractors are ALLOWABLE COSTs. Contractors are frequently not subject to such taxes when working on federal contracts. See FAR Subpart 29.3. Contractors normally bear the risk of determining what taxes of this nature apply to their contracts but are given PRICE ADJUSTMENTs for changes in such taxes under the Federal, State, and Local Taxes clause in FAR 52.229-3. See Johnson, *Price Adjustment Clauses for State and Local Taxes in Federal Government Contracts: Aerospace and Taxes Charged to Contracts Through Overhead*, 26 Pub. Cont. L.J. 599 (1997); Weckstein & Kempler, *Tax Considerations in Government Contracting*, 85-10 Briefing Papers (Oct. 1985); Cavin, *Federal Immunity of Government Contractors From State and Local Taxation: A Survey of Recent Decisions and Their Impact on Government Procurement Policies*, 61 Denver L.J. 797 (1984).

STATE SECRETS DOCTRINE See MILITARY AND STATE SECRETS DOCTRINE.

STATEMENT OF WORK (SOW) The portion of a contract that describes the actual work to be done by the contractor by means of (1) SPECIFICATIONs or other minimum requirements, (2) quantities, (3) performance dates, (4) time and place of performance of services, and (5) quality requirements. Jones, *Glossary: Defense Acquisition Acronyms and Terms* (8th ed., Defense Systems Management College). The SOW is set forth in Section C of the UNIFORM CONTRACT FORMAT. It plays a key role in the solicitation because it serves as the basis for the contractor's response. It also serves as a baseline against which progress and subsequent contractual changes are measured during contract performance. The FAR uses the term WORK STATEMENT in referring to the SOW for a RESEARCH AND DEVELOPMENT contract.

STATUTE OF LIMITATIONS A law prescribing limitations to the right of action on certain described causes of action, declaring that no suit may be maintained on such causes of action unless brought within a specified period of time after the right accrued. *Black's Law Dictionary* 927 (6th ed. 1990). Under 28 U.S.C. § 2501, the limitation period for CLAIMs against the Government in the COURT OF FEDERAL CLAIMS is six years after the right of action accrues. Under 28 U.S.C. § 2415(a), the limitation period for claims filed by the Government is six years after the right of action accrues, or one year after the final decision in any applicable administrative proceeding required by contract or law, whichever is later. Under the CONTRACT DISPUTES ACT OF 1978, 41 U.S.C. § 605(a), the limitation period for claims by both the contractor and the Government is six years after the accrual of the claim. See GAO, *Principles of Federal Appropriations Law*, vol. III, chap. 13 (2d ed. 1991); West & Cassidy, *Contract-Related Statutes of Limitations*, 97-7 Briefing Papers (June 1997); Cibinic, *Accrual of a Claim: Fixing FASA*, 9 N&CR ¶ 44 (Aug. 1995); Arnavas, *To Claim or Not To Claim: Legislators and Regulators Are Being Forced To Fix Court Initiated Problems*, 8 N&CR ¶ 63 (Nov. 1994).

STEVEDORING Loading cargo from a point of rest on a pier or lighter and storing it aboard a vessel, or breaking out and discharging cargo from any space in a vessel to a point of rest dockside or in a lighter. DFARS 247.270-2. Normally, stevedoring services will be contracted for by means of an INDEFINITE-QUANTITY CONTRACT. DFARS 247.270-3. Because conditions vary at different ports and sometimes within the same port, standard technical provisions covering all phases of stevedoring operations are impractical. If car loading and unloading or other dock and terminal work will be performed under a stevedoring contract, technical provisions appropriate for that work should be added to the contract as separate items of work. DFARS 247.270-4.

STOCK OPTION An option to buy stock in a corporation. FAR 31.205-6(i) provides that the costs of such options, when given by contractors to employees as compensation, are ALLOWABLE COSTs only when they meet the rules governing DEFERRED COMPENSATION.

STOCK RECORD A perpetual INVENTORY record that shows by nomenclature the quantities of each item received and issued and the balance on hand. FAR 45.501. FAR 45.505-3 requires that contractors maintain such records for MATERIAL that is furnished by the Government or to which the Government has title.

STOP-WORK ORDER A unilateral order of the contracting officer requiring the contractor to stop all or any part of the work called for under the contract. Stop-work orders may be issued if the contract contains the Suspension of Work clause in FAR 52.242-14 (mandatory in fixed-price construction and architect-engineer contracts) or the Stop-Work Order clause in FAR 52.242-15 (optional in contracts for supplies, services, or research and development (R&D)). These clauses give the contractor an adjustment in the price to compensate for costs incurred because of the order (plus profit under the Stop-Work Order clause). FAR 42.1303 provides that stop-work orders may be used in negotiated, fixed-price or cost-reimbursement supply, R&D, or service contracts if work stoppage is required for reasons such as advancements in the state-of-the-art, production or engineering breakthroughs, or realignment of programs. Generally, a stop-work order will be issued only if it is advisable to suspend work pending a decision by the Government but a supplemental agreement providing for the suspension is not feasible. Issuance of a stop-work order must be approved at a level higher than the contracting officer. A stop-work order may not be used in place of a TERMINATION NOTICE after a decision to proceed with a TERMINATION FOR DEFAULT has been made. See Cibinic & Nash, *Administration of Government Contracts* 586–89 (3d ed. 1995).

SUBCONTINENT-ASIAN AMERICANS United States citizens whose origins are in India, Pakistan, Bangladesh, Sri Lanka, Bhutan, or Nepal. FAR 19.001. These persons are presumed to be socially and economically disadvantaged for the purpose of determining the ownership of a SMALL DISADVANTAGED BUSINESS CONCERN. See FAR 52.219-8.

SUBCONTRACT A contract or contractual action entered into by a PRIME CONTRACTOR or SUBCONTRACTOR for the purpose of obtaining supplies, materials, equipment, or services under a PRIME CONTRACT. FAR 3.502-1. Subcontracts include purchase orders as well as changes and modifications to purchase orders. The FAR addresses situations in which the Government must consent to a prime contractor's subcontract (FAR Subpart 44.2) and the procedures to be used in making a CONTRACTOR PURCHASING SYSTEM REVIEW (FAR Subpart 44.3). Consent to subcontract is required when subcontract work is complex, the dollar value is substantial, or the Government's interest is not adequately protected by competition and the type of prime contract or subcontract. FAR 44.102. 10 U.S.C. § 2306(e) and 41 U.S.C. § 254(b) require contractors to give notice (but not to obtain consent) on COST CONTRACTs and COST-PLUS-FIXED-FEE CONTRACTs for (1) all cost-plus-fixed-fee subcontracts and (2) all fixed-price subcontracts over $100,000 or 5 percent of the estimated cost of the prime contract. Successful offerors in both negotiated and sealed bidding acquisitions that exceed or are expected to exceed $500,000 (or $1 million for construction contracts) and that have substantial subcontracting possibilities must provide formal SUBCONTRACTING PLANs for Government review. 15 U.S.C. § 637(d); FAR 19.704. Although a subcontractor lacks PRIVITY OF CONTRACT with the Federal Government, prime contractors pass on significant Government requirements to subcontractors, such as the requirements for submission of COST OR PRICING DATA and the TERMINATION FOR CONVENIENCE clause. See Patin & Ginsburg, chap. 16, *Construction Contracting* 1111–207 (1991); Hale, *Subcontractor Claims: Strategies for the Prime*, 95-7 Briefing Papers (July 1995).

SUBCONTRACT APPROVAL The contracting officer's written consent for the prime contractor to enter into a particular subcontract. FAR 44.102 requires consent to subcontract when the subcontract work is complex, the dollar value is substantial, or the Government's interest is not adequately protected by competition and the type of prime contract or subcontract. Consent requirements may be waived when the CONTRACTOR's PURCHASING SYSTEM has been reviewed and approved. FAR Subpart 44.2.

SUBCONTRACTING PLAN A plan, adopted by a contractor, to further the Government's program under the SMALL BUSINESS ACT by subcontracting parts of the contract work. Successful offerors under both negotiated and sealed bidding acquisitions that are expected to exceed $500,000 (or $1 million for construction) and that have subcontracting possibilities must provide formal subcontracting plans. 15 U.S.C. § 637(d). FAR 19.704 provides that the subcontracting plans must include (1) percentage goals for using SMALL BUSINESS CONCERNs, SMALL DISADVANTAGED BUSINESS CONCERNs, and WOMEN-OWNED SMALL BUSINESS as subcontractors; (2) the name of an individual who will administer the offeror's subcontracting program; (3) a description of the efforts the offeror will make to ensure that small business has an equitable opportunity to compete for subcontracts; (4) assurances that the offeror will include the clause at FAR 52.219-8, Utilization of Small Business Concerns, Small Disadvantaged and Women-Owned Business Concerns, in all subcontracts; (5) assurances that the offeror will (a) cooperate in studies or surveys, (b) submit periodic reports to allow the Government to determine the extent of the offeror's compliance, and (c) submit Standard Form 294, Subcontracting Report for Individual Contracts, and Standard Form 295, Summary Subcontract Report, at FAR 53.301-294 and -295; and (6) a recitation of the records the offeror will maintain to demonstrate procedures adopted to comply with the plan. DFARS 215.605 states that subcontracting plans will be an evaluation factor in source selection for RESEARCH AND DEVELOPMENT, MAJOR SYSTEM ACQUISITIONs, and other complex or sensitive acquisitions. FAR 19.702(c) provides that any contractor or subcontractor failing to comply in good faith with the requirements of a subcontracting plan is in material BREACH OF CONTRACT. Further, 15 U.S.C. § 637(d)(4)(F) directs that a contractor's failure to make a good faith effort to comply with the requirements of the subcontracting plan must result in the imposition of LIQUIDATED DAMAGES. See FAR 19.705-7.

SUBCONTRACTOR Any supplier, distributor, vendor, or firm that furnishes supplies or services to a prime contractor or another subcontractor. See FAR 44.101. For the purposes of the ANTI-KICKBACK ACT OF 1986, it means any person, other than a PRIME CONTRACTOR, who offers to furnish or furnishes supplies, materials, equipment, or services of any kind under a prime contract or a subcontract entered into in connection with a prime contract, and includes any person who offers to furnish or furnishes general supplies to the prime contractor or a higher-tier subcontractor. FAR 3.502-1.

The term "first-tier subcontractor" means a subcontractor holding a subcontract with a prime contractor. FAR 22.801. Second- or third-tier subcontractors hold a subcontract with a subcontractor. When the term "subcontractor" is used in a contract clause, the context of the clause must be analyzed to determine whether the term means only first-tier subcontractors or subcontractors at every tier.

SUBCONTRACTOR CLAIMS See SPONSORSHIP OF SUBCONTRACTOR CLAIMS.

SUBJECT INVENTION Any invention of a contractor conceived or first actually reduced to practice in the performance of work under a Government contract. 35 U.S.C. § 201(e); FAR 27.301. Under its PATENT RIGHTS policy, the Government obtains a LICENSE to use such inventions. The determination of whether an invention is a subject invention is not dependent on the relative financial contributions of the parties in funding the work that led to the invention; rather, it depends on whether either of two events—CONCEPTION or FIRST ACTUAL REDUCTION TO PRACTICE—occurred during contract performance. See Nash & Rawicz, *Intellectual Property in Government Contracts*, vol. 1 (3d ed. 1997).

SUBROGATION The substitution of one person in the place of another with reference to a lawful claim, demand, or right, so that the one substituted succeeds to the rights of the other in relation to the debt or claim and its rights, remedies, and securities. *Black's Law Dictionary* 1427 (6th ed. 1990). A SURETY that carries out its obligation under the BOND and pays for the completion of the work after the contractor has been unable to perform is entitled to the rights of subrogation. The SURETY's right to recover under the doctrine of subrogation is limited to the contract balance at the time the Government was notified of the SURETY's interest. See Nash, *The Rights of Performance Bond Sureties: It Depends On the Circumstances*, 6 N&CR ¶ 57 (Oct. 1992).

SUBSTANTIAL COMPLETION SUBSTANTIAL PERFORMANCE of contract requirements in a construction contract, though not complete performance. Substantial completion is often found when the contractor completes construction of the structure but fails to complete punch list items, install ornamental features, finish site cleanup, etc. The doctrine of substantial completion bars the Government from assessing LIQUIDATED DAMAGES or terminating the contract without providing a reasonable period of time to correct the deficiencies. The doctrine does not bar the Government, however, from insisting on strict compliance and full completion of the work or from obtaining an EQUITABLE ADJUSTMENT in the contract price if strict compliance is not attained. The term has also been used to decide DISPUTEs under service contracts for services. See Cibinic & Nash, *Administration of Government Contracts* 919–24 (3d ed. 1995); Jackson & DeLancey, *Substantial Completion in Construction Contracts*, 96-4 Briefing Papers (Mar. 1996).

SUBSTANTIAL COMPLIANCE The timely delivery of supplies on a supply contract that substantially comply with the contract requirements. When a contractor has met the test of substantial compliance, the Government may not issue a summary TERMINATION FOR DEFAULT. In order to meet the test of substantial compliance, (1) the contractor must demonstrate that it had reasonable grounds to believe that the delivery would conform to the contract requirements, and (2) any defects must be minor in nature and extent and susceptible to correction within a reasonable time. Other relevant considerations include the usability of the items, the nature of the product, and the urgency of the Government's requirement. See Cibinic & Nash, *Administration of Government Contracts* 912–18 (3d ed. 1995); Venema, *Substantial Compliance in Fixed-Price Supply Contracts: A Call for Commercial Reasonableness*, 17 Pub. Cont. L.J. 187 (1987).

SUBSTANTIAL PERFORMANCE Performance short of full performance but nevertheless performance in good faith and in compliance with the contract, except perhaps for minor and relatively unimportant deviations. *Ballentine's Law Dictionary* 1232 (3d ed. 1969) Substantial performance is synonymous with SUBSTANTIAL COMPLETION.

SUBSTANTIALLY JUSTIFIED A position of the Government regarding a DISPUTE that is clearly reasonable. Under the EQUAL ACCESS TO JUSTICE ACT (EAJA), a court or an agency must award ATTORNEY'S FEES and other expenses to individuals with net worth of no more than $2 million, profit-making small businesses with no more than $7 million net worth or 500 employees, and tax-exempt organizations that prevail in adversary adjudications in which the Government's position during settlement negotiations and litigation was not substantially justified. If the Government, during litigation concerning the recovery of attorney's fees and expenses, can demonstrate that its prior position was substantially justified, the prevailing party cannot recover under the EAJA. In determining substantial justification, the courts and boards of contract appeals evaluate the issue of reasonableness of the Government's position based on what support in law and fact the Government offers in defending its case. See Nash, *Equal Access to Justice Act: A Statute That Is Working Well*, 2 N&CR ¶ 20 (Apr. 1988); Kinlin, *Equal Access to Justice Act*, 16 Pub. Cont. L.J. 266, 273 (1986).

SUBSTITUTED CONTRACT A method of resolving a disputed issue under a contract whereby the parties agree to discharge all obligations under the original contract and substitute a new contract in its place. If the performance is not rendered under the new contract, the nonbreaching party may sue only for breach of the new contract. *Restatement (Second) of Contracts* § 279 (1981). This should be contrasted with an ACCORD AND SATISFACTION where the nonbreaching party has the election of suing for breach of the original contract if the other party breaches the accord. Substituted contracts are normally accomplished by execution of a bilateral MODIFICATION. See Cibinic & Nash, *Administration of Government Contracts* 1219–20 (3d ed. 1995).

SUCCESSOR IN INTEREST See NOVATION.

SUITABLE FOR INTENDED USE The condition of property such that it can be used by a contractor in a manner that facilitates expeditious and economical performance. GOVERNMENT PROPERTY furnished to a contractor need not be perfect, but it must be given to the contractor in a condition suitable for its intended use under the contract. To recover for a claim for defective GOVERNMENT-FURNISHED PROPERTY (GFP), the contractor must demonstrate that (1) the property was furnished as GFP, (2) the property was unsuitable, (3) the unsuitability related to the property's intended purpose, and (4) the unsuitability caused the contractor's injury (cost overrun, late delivery, etc.). Cibinic & Nash, *Administration of Government Contracts* 641–45 (3d ed. 1995); FAR 52.245-2.

SUM CERTAIN The monetary amount being claimed by a contractor under the CONTRACT DISPUTES ACT OF 1978. Under this act a CLAIM entails, among other things, a written demand for the payment of money in a "sum certain." FAR 33.201. When the recovery of money is the essence of the contractor's request for relief, the contracting officer need not issue a final decision (see DECISION OF THE CONTRACTING OFFICER) unless the contractor's claim specifies the amount of recovery sought—a sum certain—in a finite amount not subject to qualification or conditions. The reasoning behind this rule is that the contracting officer cannot determine whether the Act's requirement for certification of claims of $100,000 or more applies to the contractor's claim unless the claim is made in a specific dollar amount. See Nash, *The Contract Disputes Act: No Claim, No Jurisdiction*, 5 N&CR ¶ 66 (Dec. 1991).

SUPERIOR KNOWLEDGE A legal rule providing that a contracting party has an obligation to disclose vital information to the other party. Generally, the Government must disclose to offerors or contractors information it possesses that (1) is relevant to contradictory information in the solicitation or contract and should be disclosed to keep the offeror or contractor from being misled; or (2) may materially affect an offer, and the offeror lacks the information or is relying on erroneous assumptions; and (3) it knows the contractor does not know. Failure to disclose such information may result in the Government's assuming responsibility for the contractor's increased costs through the CONSTRUCTIVE CHANGE doctrine. To establish that the Government breached its duty to disclose its superior knowledge, the contractor must prove that the Government possessed such knowledge, that the knowledge was vital to contract performance, that the information was unknown and not reasonably available to the contractor, and that the contractor was misled by the nondisclosure. See Cibinic & Nash, *Administration of Government Contracts* 255–67 (3d ed. 1995), 448–50; Nash, chap. 14, *Government Contract Changes* (2d ed. 1989 & Supp. 1993); Eshelman & Sanford, *The Superior Knowledge Doctrine: An Update*, 22 Pub. Cont. L.J. 477 (1993); Beran, *Specifications: The Duty Trilogy—Government and Contractor Responsibilities, Part Two: The Duty to Disclose Superior Knowledge*, 27 Cont. Mgmt. 12 (Sept. 1987).

SUPPLEMENTAL AGREEMENT A contract MODIFICATION that is accomplished by the mutual action of the parties. FAR 43.101.

SUPPLIES All property except land or interest in land. Supplies include, but are not limited to, public works, buildings, and facilities; ships, floating equipment, and vessels of every character, type, and description, together with parts and accessories; aircraft and aircraft parts, accessories, and equipment; machine tools; and the alteration or installation of any of the foregoing. FAR 2.101. This FAR definition is misleading in that it includes public works, buildings, and facilities within the scope of the term. However, the PROVISION AND CLAUSE MATRIX in FAR 52.300 provides separate provisions and clauses for supply contracts and construction contracts. The inspection clauses used for supply contracts define supplies as including, but not limited to, raw materials, components, intermediate assemblies, end products, and lots of supplies (see, for example, the Inspection of Supplies—Fixed Price clause in FAR 52.246-2. However, the Inspection of Supplies—Cost-Reimbursement clause in FAR 52.246-3 defines supplies to include data if the contract does not include a Warranty of Data clause. The term "supplies" is a term used primarily in Government contracting; the synonymous term in commercial contracting is GOODS.

SURETY The individual or corporation that has agreed to be legally liable for the debt, default, or failure of a principal to satisfy a contractual obligation. FAR 28.001. Contractors purchase BONDs from sureties when such bonds are specified by the Government to be a condition of award. The types of sureties referred to in the FAR include (1) an individual surety—one person who is liable for the entire PENAL AMOUNT of the bond; (2) a corporate surety that is licensed under various insurance laws and that, under its charter, has legal power to act as surety for others; and (3) a cosurety—one of two or more sureties that are jointly liable for the penal amount of the bond. FAR 28.201 requires agencies to obtain adequate security for bonds (including coinsurance and reinsurance agreements) required or used with a contract for supplies or services (including construction). The FAR discusses corporate sureties (FAR 28.202), individual sureties (FAR 28.203), and alternatives in lieu of sureties (FAR 28.204). See Standard Form 28, Affidavit of Individual Surety, FAR 53.301-28; SF 1414, Consent of Surety, FAR 53.301-1414; and Standard Form 1415, Consent of Surety and Increase of Penalty, FAR 53.301-1415. See also Donohue & Thomas, *Surety Bond Basics*, 96-3 Constr. Briefings (Feb. 1996); Nash, *Sureties' Obligations: The Duty To Deal in Good Faith*, 3 N&CR ¶ 55 (Aug. 1989); Cibinic, *In Defense of Corporate Surety Bonds*, 2 N&CR ¶ 75 (Dec. 1988); Nash, *Rights of Sureties: They're Growing*, 2 N&CR ¶ 42 (July 1988); Nash, *Dealing with Performance Bond Sureties*, 1 N&CR ¶ 35 (Apr. 1987); Patin, chap. 17, *Construction Contracting* (1991).

SURPLUS PROPERTY Contractor inventory not required by any federal agency. FAR 45.601. FAR 45.610 sets forth the procedures to be followed in disposing of surplus property resulting from Government contracts.

SURPLUS STRATEGIC AND CRITICAL MATERIALS Inventories of metals and ores, such as cobalt, industrial diamond stones, lead, nickel, tin, and zinc, that exceed National Defense Stockpile requirements. FAR 8.002 requires Government agencies to satisfy their requirements for such materials from or through surplus holdings that are maintained by the National Defense Stockpile Center.

SUSPENDED COSTS An indirect or direct cost under a COST-REIMBURSEMENT CONTRACT that lacks adequate explanation or documentary support for definitive AUDIT approval or disapproval, and that is not paid until the required data is received and a determination is made as to its allowability. Audit guidance and procedures on suspension of costs are provided in *DCAA Contract Audit Manual* 6-900 (Jan. 1997). DCAA Form 1, Notice of Contract Costs Suspended And/Or Disapproved, is used by the AUDITOR to indicate a suspended cost. See also NASA Form 456. See Cibinic & Nash, *Cost-Reimbursement Contracting* 1119–20 (2d ed. 1993); FAR 42.803.

SUSPENSION An action taken by the HEAD OF AN AGENCY, or a designee authorized by the agency head, to disqualify a contractor temporarily from Government contracting and Government-approved subcontracting. A contractor so disqualified is "suspended." FAR 9.403. Causes for suspension include adequate evidence of or indictment for (1) commission of a FRAUD or criminal offense related to obtaining or performing a public contract; (2) violation of antitrust statutes; (3) commission of embezzlement, theft, forgery, making FALSE STATEMENTs, and the like; (4) violation of the Drug-Free Workplace Act of 1988, 41 U.S.C. § 701 et seq.; (5) intentionally affixing a "Made in America" label to a product sold or shipped to the United States. but not made in the United States; (6) commission of an unfair trade practice; and (7) commission of any other offense indicating a lack of business integrity or business honesty that seriously and directly affects the present responsibility of a Government contractor or subcontractor. FAR 9.407-2. Suspension can occur without prior notice to the contractor, but notice must be given after the decision to suspend has been made. FAR 9.407-3. No suspension can exceed 18 months unless legal proceedings are initiated within that time. FAR 9.407-4. See *Nash, Suspension and Debarment: Can They Be Punitive?*, 11 N&CR ¶ 29 (June 1997); Gordon, *Suspension and Debarment from Federal Programs*, 23 Pub. Cont. L.J. 573 (1994); Toomey et al., *Debarment & Suspension/Edition III*, 89-4 Briefing Papers (Mar. 1989); Nadler, *Suspension and Debarment of Government Contractors: The Current Climate*, 22 Nat'l Cont. Mgmt. J., Issue No. 2, p. 9 (1989);

Norton, *The Questionable Constitutionality of the Suspension and Debarment Provisions of the Federal Acquisition Regulations: What Does Due Process Require?,* 18 Pub. Cont. L.J. 633 (1989).

SUSPENSION OF WORK Government DELAY, either by order or constructively, of the work of a construction contractor or an architect-engineer. The Suspension of Work clause in FAR 52.242-14 is required to be included in fixed-price construction and ARCHITECT-ENGINEER CONTRACTs. FAR 42.1305. It permits the contracting officer to order the contractor, in writing, to suspend, delay, or interrupt performance of all or any part of the work for the period of time that the contracting officer determines appropriate for the convenience of the Government. It also give the contractor rights if performance is suspended, delayed, or interrupted for an unreasonable period of time by (1) an act of the contracting officer in the administration of the contract or (2) the contracting officer's failure to act within the time specified in the contract. In both cases a PRICE ADJUSTMENT is required to be made for any increase in the cost of performance of the contract (excluding PROFIT) that necessarily results from an unreasonable delay, and the contract is modified in writing accordingly. See Cibinic & Nash, *Administration of Government Contracts* 586–618 (3d ed. 1995); Margulies, chap. 8, *Construction Contracting* 634–47 (1991).

SYNOPSIS A notice of contract awards and proposed contract actions published in the COMMERCE BUSINESS DAILY as required by 15 U.S.C. § 637(e) and 41 U.S.C. § 416. Guidance on synopsis requirements is contained in FAR Subpart 5.2 and FAR Subpart 5.3. When a synopsis of a proposed contract action is required, it must be published 15 days before issuance of the SOLICITATION. FAR 5.203. However, when buying COMMERCIAL ITEMs, the agency may combine the synopsis with the solicitation (see COMBINED SYNOPSIS/SOLICITATION). FAR 12.603. The format for the synopsis of proposed contract actions is contained in FAR 5.207. FAR 5.206 also encourages contractors to place synopses of subcontract opportunities in the Commerce Business Daily.

SYSTEM ENGINEERING A logical sequence of activities and decisions that transforms an operational need into a description of SYSTEM performance parameters and a preferred system configuration. System engineering is a disciplined approach to coordinating all aspects of a system, ensuring that its individual parts will function as intended in the operational environment and meet contract requirements. It is a process for identifying and assessing each technical and other variable involved in total system design. A contractor that performs system engineering is barred from contracting for manufacturing work on that system by the ORGANIZATIONAL CONFLICT OF INTEREST rules. See DOD Regulation 5000.2-R, *Mandatory Procedures for Major Defense Acquisition Programs (MDAPs) and Major Automated Information System (MAIS) Acquisition Programs*, Part 4.3, Mar. 15, 1996.

SYSTEM OF RECORDS A group of any records under the control of any agency from which information is retrieved by the name of an individual or by some number, symbol, or other identifying particular assigned to the individual. FAR 24.101. The Privacy Act of 1974, 5 U.S.C. § 552a, requires that contracts for the maintenance of such systems must comply with its provisions. FAR Subpart 24.1 provides guidance on the implementation of this requirement. NFS 18-24.102 provides examples of systems of records to which the Privacy Act applies.

T

TAILORING The process by which individual sections, paragraphs, or sentences of the SPECIFICATIONs, STANDARDs, and related documents selected for use in a procurement are reviewed and modified so that each one that is selected contains an accurate statement of the Government's needs, is not unduly restrictive (see RESTRICTIVE SPECIFICATIONS), and incorporates COMMERCIAL ITEMs or NONDEVELOPMENTAL ITEMs. FAR 11.002(c) requires specifications and standards to be selectively applied and tailored in their application. Selective application is the process of reviewing and choosing from the many available specifications, standards, and related documents only those relevant to a particular acquisition. Such tailoring need not be made a part of the basic specification or standard but will vary with each application, depending on the nature of the acquisition. FAR 12.302 also permits tailoring of contract clauses used in the procurement of commercial items.

TAKEOVER AGREEMENT An agreement, between the Government and the SURETY that has furnished a PERFORMANCE BOND, that the surety will complete the performance of a contract that has been terminated for default (see TERMINATION FOR DEFAULT). Guidance on entering into such an agreement is contained in FAR 49.404. Since the surety is liable to the Government for the consequences of the contractor's default, it is not required to enter into a takeover agreement. However, FAR 49.404(c) provides that the contracting officer will normally enter into such an agreement if the surety offers to complete the contract. If a surety enters into a takeover agreement, it gives up any financial protection that it has pursuant to the ceiling amount in the bond (see PENAL AMOUNT) but it gains access to the COURT OF FEDERAL CLAIMS and the BOARDs OF CONTRACT APPEALS to pursue CLAIMs against the Government. See Nash, *The Rights Of Performance Bond Sureties: It Depends On The Circumstances*, 6 N&CR ¶ 57 (Oct. 1992); Nash, *Dealing with Performance Bond Sureties*, 1 N&CR ¶ 35 (Apr. 1987).

TANGIBLE CAPITAL ASSET An ASSET that has physical substance, has more than minimal value, and is expected to be held by an enterprise for continued use or possession beyond the current accounting period for the services it yields. FAR 31.001. Such assets may take the form, for example, of cash, land, or buildings. Rosenberg, *Dictionary of Banking and Finance* (2d ed. 1985). CAS 404, 48 C.F.R. § 9904.404, sets forth criteria that contractor policies on the CAPITALIZATION of tangible assets must meet. CAS 409, 48 C.F.R. § 9904.409, provides guidance on the DEPRECIATION of tangible capital assets.

TANKER A vessel used primarily for the carriage of bulk liquid cargoes such as liquid petroleum products, vegetable oils, and molasses. FAR 47.501. Under the Preference for Privately Owned U.S.-Flag Commercial Vessels clause in FAR 52.247-64, contractors must compute shipments in these vessels separately in determining whether they have met the requirement that at least 50 percent of the gross tonnage shipped be in U.S.-FLAG VESSELs.

TARGET COST The negotiated amount of cost included in INCENTIVE CONTRACTs. See FAR Subpart 16.4. The target cost serves as the baseline for adjusting the contractor's TARGET PROFIT (in a FIXED-PRICE-INCENTIVE CONTRACT) or TARGET FEE (in a COST-PLUS-INCENTIVE-FEE CONTRACT). In these types of contracts the negotiated PROFIT or FEE will be adjusted, upon completion of the contract, by a formula based on the relationship of total ALLOWABLE COSTs to total target costs. The formula provides, within limits, for increases in profit or fee when total allowable costs are less than target costs, and decreases in fee when total allowable costs exceed target costs. The adjustment is intended to provide an incentive for the contractor to manage the contract effectively. FAR 16.401(a)(2). Before this adjustment is made, the parties must adjust the target cost to reflect all EQUITABLE ADJUSTMENTs and PRICE ADJUSTMENTs called for by the contract.

TARGET FEE The amount of FEE the contractor will receive if its total ALLOWABLE COSTs equal total TARGET COSTs in a COST-PLUS-INCENTIVE-FEE CONTRACT. In this type of contract, under the contract sharing arrangement, the final fee paid to the contractor is adjusted downward if actual costs exceed the target costs and upward if actual costs are less than target costs. This adjustment is limited, however, by the RANGE OF INCENTIVE EFFECTIVENESS resulting from the MINIMUM FEE and MAXIMUM FEE contained in the contract. FAR 16.405-1.

TARGET PRICE The sum of the TARGET COST and the TARGET PROFIT in a FIXED-PRICE-INCENTIVE CONTRACT.

TARGET PROFIT The amount of PROFIT the contractor will receive if its total ALLOWABLE COSTs equal total TARGET COSTs in a FIXED-PRICE-INCENTIVE (FPI) CONTRACT. In FPI contracts with a firm target, the parties work with a target cost and CEILING PRICE. The target profit is adjusted in accordance with the contract SHARING ARRANGEMENT until costs reach the ceiling, at which point (the "point of total cost assumption") the contractor absorbs all additional costs. FAR 16.403-1. In FPI contracts with successive targets, the parties negotiate at the outset the production point at which a firm target cost and target profit will be negotiated. FAR 16.403-2. The target profit is either established in the competitive process or negotiated based on a structured profit formula, following agency guidance such as the WEIGHTED GUIDELINES METHOD in DFARS 215.971.

TASK ORDER An order for services issued under a TASK ORDER CONTRACT. When such orders are issued under multiple award contracts, each awardee must be given a fair opportunity to be considered. FAR 16.505(b). However, the failure to receive such fair consideration is not subject to PROTEST but may be referred to the agency OMBUDSMAN. 10 U.S.C. § 2304c and 41 U.S.C. § 253j. See Cibinic & Nash, chap. 8, Sec. VI, *Formation of Government Contracts* (3d ed. 1998); Victorino & Chierichella, *Multiple Award Task and Delivery Order Contracts*, 96-10 Briefing Papers (Sept. 1996); Edwards, *The New Rules for Multiple Award Task Order Contracting*, 9 N&CR ¶ 35 (June 1995).

TASK ORDER CONTRACT A contract for services that does not procure or specify a firm quantity, but provides for the issuance of orders for the performance of tasks during the period of the contract. FAR 16.501-1. 10 U.S.C. § 2304a and 41 U.S.C. § 253h contain special rules for task order contracts requiring that they include (1) the period of the contract, including options; (2) the maximum quantity or dollar value of the services that may be procured; and (3) a STATEMENT OF WORK that reasonably describes the general scope, nature, complexity, and purposes of the services to be procured under the contract. 10 U.S.C. § 2304(a)(d) and 41 U.S.C. § 253j(d) establish a preference for multiple award contracts (see MULTIPLE AWARD

PREFERENCE). These requirements are implemented in FAR 16.504. See Cibinic & Nash, chap. 3, Sec. II.; chap. 8, Sec. VI., *Formation of Government Contracts* (3d ed. 1998); Cibinic & Nash, *Cost-Reimbursement Contracting* 130–34 (2d ed. 1993).

TAXES Mandatory amounts paid to governments to support their operation. Guidance on taxes is contained in FAR Part 29. See EXCISE TAXes and STATE AND LOCAL TAXES. Most general taxes, other than federal income and excess profits taxes and taxes related to refinancing or reorganization, are allowable costs under FAR 31.205-41. However, this provision contains a number of specific rules. See Cibinic & Nash, *Cost-Reimbursement Contracting* 899–903 (2d ed. 1993); The MAC Group, *The Impact on Defense Industrial Capability of Changes in Procurement and Tax Policy, 1984–1987*, 22 Nat'l Cont. Mgmt. J., Issue No. 2, p. 37 (1989); Weckstein & Kempler, *Tax Considerations in Government Contracting*, 85-10 Briefing Papers (Oct. 1985).

TEAM AGREEMENT An agreement in which (1) two or more companies form a partnership or JOINT VENTURE to act as a potential PRIME CONTRACTOR, or (2) a potential prime contractor agrees with one or more other companies to have them act as SUBCONTRACTORs under a specified Government contract or ACQUISITION PROGRAM. FAR 9.601. Team agreements enable the companies involved to complement each other's capabilities and offer the Government the best combination of performance, cost, and delivery for the system or product being acquired. The agreements prove particularly appropriate in complex RESEARCH AND DEVELOPMENT acquisitions. Companies normally form a team agreement before the offer is submitted. FAR 9.602. See Walker et al., *A Virtual Approach to Success: Teaming*, 35 Cont. Mgmt. 4 (May 1995); Porterfield, *Understanding the Use of Teams in Winning Contract Award*, 34 Cont. Mgmt. 23 (Dec. 1994); Eger, *Contractor Team Arrangements under the Antitrust Laws*, 17 Pub. Cont. L.J. 595 (1988).

TECHNICAL ANALYSIS The examination and evaluation—by personnel having specialized knowledge, skills, experience, or capability in engineering, science, or management—of proposed quantities and kinds of materials, LABOR, processes, SPECIAL TOOLING, FACILITIES, and associated factors set forth in a PROPOSAL, in order to determine and report on the need for and reasonableness of the proposed resources, assuming reasonable economy and efficiency. FAR 15.404-1. FAR 15.404-1(e) explains that, when COST OR

PRICING DATA are required, the contracting officer should generally request a technical analysis of proposals, asking that requirements, logistics, or other qualified personnel review and assess, at a minimum, (1) the quantities and kinds of materials proposed, (2) the need for the number and kinds of labor hours and the labor mix, (3) the special tooling and facilities proposed, (4) the reasonableness of proposed scrap and spoilage factors, and (5) any other data that may be pertinent to the COST ANALYSIS or PRICE ANALYSIS.

TECHNICAL DATA DATA (other than COMPUTER SOFTWARE) of a scientific or technical nature. FAR 27.401. Because under the FAR data policy the term "computer software" includes COMPUTER PROGRAMs, COMPUTER DATABASEs, and COMPUTER SOFTWARE DOCUMENTATION, this is a narrow definition of technical data. Under both the 1988 and 1995 DOD policies, the term "technical data" is more fully described as follows: "Recorded information, regardless of the form or method of the recording, of a scientific or technical nature (including computer software documentation). The term does not include computer software or data incidental to contract administration, such as financial or management information." However, because of the differences in the DOD definitions of computer software and computer software documentation in these two policies, the term "technical data" actually has a significantly different meaning. In the 1988 DOD policy, it included the SOURCE CODE for computer programs as well as the documentation of the design of the program, but did not include computer databases. In the 1995 DOD policy, it includes computer databases but excludes source code and design documentation. Thus, the term has a different meaning in each of the three major data policies. Burgett et al., *Government Rights in Data and Software/Edition II*, 95-11 Briefing Papers (Oct. 1995). The Government obtains LIMITED RIGHTS, UNLIMITED RIGHTS, GOVERNMENT-PURPOSE LICENSE RIGHTS, or GOVERNMENT-PURPOSE RIGHTS to technical data in accordance with the clauses used. See Mayner, *Understanding The New DFARS Technical Data Rights Regs: How Will They Affect Selling Software To The Government?*, 37 Cont. Mgmt. 3 (Aug. 1997); Schwartz, *The Acquisition of Technical Data Rights by the Government*, 23 Pub. Cont. L.J. 513 (1994); Victorino & McQuade, *Enforcing Data Rights*, 91-10 Briefing Papers (Sept. 1991); Nash, *Removal of Limited Rights Legends from Technical Data: Playing Hardball*, 1 N&CR ¶ 85 (Nov. 1987); Vacketta & Holmes, *Government Rights in Technical Data*, 84-12 Briefing Papers (Nov. 1984).

TECHNICAL DATA PACKAGE (TDP) A relatively complete package of design and manufacturing information adequate for supporting an ACQUISITION STRATEGY, production, engineering, and logistics support. The description, typically incorporated into the contract, defines the required design configuration and procedures to ensure adequacy of item performance. It consists of all applicable TECHNICAL DATA, such as drawings, associated lists, specifications, standards, performance requirements, quality assurance provisions, and packaging details. The TDP is one of the traditional logistic support elements. Jones, *Glossary: Defense Acquisition Acronyms and Terms* (8th ed., Defense Systems Management College).

TECHNICAL DIRECTION Government guidance of a contractor's effort toward certain areas of endeavor or lines of inquiry that fall within the contract STATEMENT OF WORK. Technical direction is generally provided in writing by the CONTRACTING OFFICER TECHNICAL REPRESENTATIVE (COTR), with a copy to the contracting officer. The COTR coordinates such direction with the contractor to ensure that it does not impose work beyond the contract requires. The FAR contains no standard technical direction clause, but a number of agencies have adopted agency clauses. See Cibinic & Nash, *Cost-Reimbursement Contracting* 975–79 (2d ed. 1993).

TECHNICAL EVALUATION The evaluation of the technical aspects of a PROPOSAL submitted in a COMPETITIVE PROPOSALS procurement or a TWO-STEP SEALED BIDDING procurement. Such evaluation is conducted by Government employees (or occasionally by contractor employees) skilled in the fields of technology addressed in the proposal. FAR 15.305(a)(3) contains minimal guidance on evaluation of proposals in competitive negotiations. FAR 14.503-1(e) discusses evaluation of technical proposals in two-step procurements. Evaluation must be done against the criteria contained in the solicitation. See Cibinic & Nash, chap. 6, *Formation of Government Contracts* (3d ed. 1998).

TECHNICAL LEVELING An unfair practice of helping (such as by pointing out weaknesses resulting from an offeror's lack of diligence, competence, or inventiveness in preparing the proposal) an offeror to bring its PROPOSAL up to the level of other proposals through successive rounds of DISCUSSION. Prior to FAC 97-02, September 30, 1997, FAR 15.610(d) prohibited the contracting officer and other Government procurement personnel from engaging in technical leveling. See Nash, *Technical Leveling: Confusion and Clarification*, 1

N&CR ¶ 2 (Jan. 1987), for a critique of this definition suggesting that technical leveling should be defined as "helping an offeror to bring its proposal up to the level of other proposals by coaching or providing solutions or approaches desired by the agency." See also Nash, *Postscript: Understanding the Meaning of "Technical Leveling,"* 4 N&CR ¶ 62 (Nov. 1990). FAR 15.306(e)(1) now merely prohibits favoring one offeror over another in the conduct of discussions. Furthermore, FAR 15.306(d)(3) suggests giving specific suggestions to offerors as to potential improvements in their proposals. Thus, technical transfusion is no longer prohibited in any significant manner. See Feldman, *Traversing the Tightrope Between Meaningful Discussions and Improper Practices in Negotiated Federal Acquisitions: Technical Transfusion, Technical Leveling, and Auction Techniques*, 17 Pub. Cont. L.J. 211, 238 (1987). See also AUCTION; SOURCE SELECTION, TECHNICAL TRANSFUSION.

TECHNICAL PROPOSAL A proposal submitted in response to a REQUEST FOR PROPOSALS. This ambiguous term can cover all types of information from proposed plans for performing a proposed contract to mere information relating to an offeror's PAST PERFORMANCE or experience. FAR 15.204-5(b) permits the RFP instructions in Section L to call for the submission of technical proposals in separate volumes. Technical proposals are frequently used to assess an offeror's understanding of the work. See Nash, *The Technical Proposal: Is It Fish Or Fowl?*, 11 N&CR ¶ 22 (May 1997); Cibinic, *Oral Communications: Interviews, Presentations, Or Discussions But Not Proposals*, 10 N&CR ¶ 63 (Dec. 1996); Nash, *Postscript II: Oral Presentations*, 9 N&CR ¶ 48 (Sept. 1995); Nash, *Streamlining Source Selection By Improving The Quality Of Evaluation Factors*, 8 N&CR ¶ 56 (Oct. 1994).

TECHNICAL TRANSFUSION Government disclosure of technical information pertaining to a PROPOSAL that results in improvement of a competing proposal. Prior to FAC 97-02, September 30, 1997, FAR 15.610(e)(1) prohibited such conduct. FAR 15.306(e)(3) now prohibits revealing an offeror's technical solution, including unique technology, innovative and unique uses of COMMERCIAL ITEMs, or any other information that would compromise an offeror's intellectual property to another offeror. See Feldman, *Traversing the Tightrope Between Meaningful Discussions and Improper Practices in Negotiated Federal Acquisitions: Technical Transfusion, Technical Leveling, and Auction Techniques*, 17 Pub. Cont. L.J. 211, 227 (1987). See also AUCTION; SOURCE SELECTION.

TECHNOLOGY TRANSFER See FEDERAL TECHNOLOGY TRANSFER.

TELECOMMUNICATIONS FACILITIES Equipment such as data equipment, radios, telephones, teletypewriters, FACSIMILE equipment, cables, and switches, used for producing TELECOMMUNICATIONS SERVICES. National Communications System Technology and Standards Division, *Telecommunications: Glossary of Telecommunications Terms*, Federal Standard 1037C (Aug. 1996). Executive agencies are authorized to enter into multiyear contracts for telecommunications resources, including facilities, subject to certain conditions. 41 C.F.R. § 101-35.6.

TELECOMMUNICATIONS SERVICES Any service provided by a telecommunications provider, including the transmission, emission, or reception of signals, signs, writing, images, sounds, or intelligence of any nature, by wire, cable, satellite, fiber optics, laser, radio, or any other electronic, electric, electromagnetic, or acoustically coupled means. National Communications System Technology and Standards Division, *Telecommunications: Glossary of Telecommunications Terms*, Federal Standard 1037C (Aug. 1996). The term includes the telecommunications facilities and equipment necessary to provide such services. DFARS 239.7401. The General Service's Administration provides both local and long distance telecommunications service for federal agencies, including service at locations where consolidation can bring better prices or where meeting a common need (for example, national security) cannot be cost justified by individual agencies. The objective is to have a single telecommunications service to meet the needs of all agencies at a location. 41 C.F.R. § 101-35. DOD's policy is to acquire telecommunications services from both common and noncommon carriers (see CARRIER (TRANSPORTATION)), normally on a competitive basis. DFARS 239.7402. See Galloway & Schloth, *Telecommunications Procurement*, 86-10 Briefing Papers (Sept. 1986).

TERM CONTRACT A type of COST-PLUS-FIXED-FEE CONTRACT in which the scope of work is described in general terms and the contractor's obligation is stated in terms of a specified level of effort for a stated period of time. FAR 16.306(d)(2). This is contrasted to a COMPLETION FORM CONTRACT in which the scope of work is stated as a definite goal or target with a specified end product. In the term-type contract, the contractor earns the fixed fee when the level of effort has been completed—without regard to the work accomplished.

In the completion form contract, the fixed fee is not earned until the end result is accomplished. See Cibinic & Nash, *Cost-Reimbursement Contracting* 71–74 (2d ed. 1993).

TERMINATION CONTRACTING OFFICER (TCO) A contracting officer (CO) who settles terminated contracts. FAR 49.001. After the CO issues a notice of termination, the TCO is responsible for negotiating any settlement with the contractor, including a no-cost settlement if appropriate. FAR 49.101(d). See TERMINATION FOR CONVENIENCE; TERMINATION FOR DEFAULT. In accordance with the termination clause and the notice of termination, the TCO (1) directs the action required of the prime contractor; (2) examines the SETTLEMENT PROPOSAL of the prime contractor and, when appropriate, the settlement proposals of the subcontractors; (3) promptly negotiates settlement with the contractor and enters into a settlement agreement; and (4) if a complete settlement cannot be negotiated, promptly settles the contractor's settlement proposal by determination for the elements that cannot be agreed upon. FAR 49.105. In DOD, TCOs are frequently specialists with no other responsibilities. In other agencies, the TCO functions are usually handled by the CO who was responsible for initiation of the procurement. See Nash, *Negotiating Out of a Contract: A Seldom Used Solution*, 7 N&CR ¶ 70 (Dec. 1993); Nash, *Authority of Authorized Representatives: It Ain't Necessarily So*, 5 N&CR ¶ 56 (Oct. 1991).

TERMINATION COSTS Costs incurred by a contractor solely attributable to the termination, such as termination settlement expenses and subcontractor claims, or costs which the contractor incurred planning to charge them to the contract or amoritize them over the life of the contract. FAR 31.205-42. See Cibinic & Nash, *Cost-Reimbursement Contracting* 906–27 (2d ed. 1993).

TERMINATION FOR CONVENIENCE The right of the Government to terminate or cancel performance of work under a contract, in whole or in part, if the CONTRACTING OFFICER determines that termination is in the Government's interest. The courts have placed limits on this right, but there is considerable confusion as to the extent of these limits. The right to terminate for convenience is made a part of almost all Government contracts by inclusion of the standard Termination for the Convenience of the Government clauses in FAR 52.249-1 through -5. The parties may settle cost-reimbursement and fixed-price contracts terminated for the convenience of the Government by negotiated agreement, determination of the TERMINATION

CONTRACTING OFFICER (only when settlement cannot be reached by agreement), costing out (in cost-reimbursement contracts), or a combination of these methods. FAR 49.103. If the parties are unable to agree on a settlement, the Government must pay the contractor the costs incurred in performing the terminated work, the costs of settling and paying SETTLEMENT PROPOSALs under terminated subcontracts, and a fair and reasonable PROFIT on work performed (but not on terminated work). The contracting officer is required to enter into a no-cost settlement if it is known the contractor will accept one, GOVERNMENT PROPERTY was not furnished, and the contractor does not have any outstanding payments, debts or obligations due to the Government. FAR 49.101. See Petrillo & Conner, *Convenience Termination After Krygoski*, 67 Fed. Cont. Rep. 447 (Apr. 14, 1997); McGovern, *Significant Cost Recovery Issues in Termination for Convenience Cases*, 37 Cont. Mgmt. 4 (Apr. 1997); Cibinic, *Convenience Terminations: What Are the Limits ?*, 10 N&CR ¶ 52 (Oct. 1996); Cibinic & Nash, *Administration of Government Contracts* 1073–134 (3d ed. 1995); Holland, *Terminations for Convenience: A Contractor's Guide* (Holbrook & Kellogg 1995); Seidman & Banfield, *Maximizing Termination for Convenience Settlements*, 95-5 Briefing Papers (Apr. 1995); Nash, *Negotiating Out of a Contract: A Seldom Used Solution*, 7 N&CR ¶ 70 (Dec. 1993); Martell & Featherstun, *Convenience Termination: More Selected Problems*, 91-13 Briefing Papers (Dec. 1991).

TERMINATION FOR DEFAULT The right of the Government to completely or partially terminate a contract because of the contractor's actual or anticipated failure to perform its contractual obligations (also called "default termination"). FAR 49.401. This right is included in almost all Government contracts by the inclusion of the standard default clauses in FAR 52.249-8 through -10. See FAR 49.504 for guidance on the use of these clauses. Procedures for administering default terminations are set forth in FAR Subparts 49.1 and 49.4. Under fixed-price supply and service contracts, the Government has the right, subject to the notice requirements for certain situations, to terminate the contract if the contractor fails to (1) deliver the supplies or perform the services within the time specified; (2) perform any other provisions of the contract; or (3) make sufficient progress, if that failure endangers performance of the contract. FAR 49.402-1. The contractor is liable to the Government for any excess costs incurred in acquiring supplies or services similar to those terminated for default and for any other damages, whether or not repurchase is effected. (see EXCESS COSTS OF REPROCUREMENT). See FAR 49.402-2, FAR 49.402-6, FAR

49.402-7. If the contractor can establish, or it is otherwise determined, that the contractor was not in default or that the failure to perform is excusable, the default clauses provide that a termination for default will be considered to have been a TERMINATION FOR CONVENIENCE, and the rights and obligations of the parties will be governed accordingly. FAR 49.401. See Cibinic & Nash, chap. 10, *Administration of Government Contracts* (3d ed. 1995); Pettit et al., *Government Contract Default Termination* (Supp. 1995); Nash, *Procedural Litigation on Default Terminations: Will It Never End?*, 8 N&CR ¶ 42 (July 1994); Cibinic, *Default Termination for Failure to Comply With "Other Provisions:" Requiring Contractors to Do the Complete Job*, 8 N&CR ¶ 24 (Apr. 1994); Nash, *Postscript: Appealing A Default Termination*, 7 N&CR ¶ 3 (Jan. 1993); Cibinic, *Appealing a Default Termination: Why, Where, and When?*, 6 N&CR ¶ 48 (Aug. 1992); Margulies, chap. 11, *Construction Contracting* 837–77 (1991).

TERMINATION INVENTORY Any property that is (1) purchased, supplied, manufactured, furnished, or otherwise acquired for the performance of a contract subsequently terminated; and (2) properly allocable to the terminated portion of the contract. FAR 45.601. Termination inventory includes GOVERNMENT-FURNISHED PROPERTY in the possession of or directly acquired by the Government and subsequently made available to the contractor, but does not include any facilities, material, or items of SPECIAL TEST EQUIPMENT or SPECIAL TOOLING that are subject to a separate contract or to a special contract requirement governing their use or disposition. After termination the contractor prepares schedules of all termination inventory in accordance with FAR Subpart 45.6, the contracting officer decides on the disposition of the inventory (FAR 49.105(6)(4)), and the contractor disposes of the inventory as directed by the contracting officer (FAR 48.104(i)).

TERMINATION LIABILITY The maximum cost the Government would incur if a contract is terminated. When a multiyear contract (see MULTIYEAR CONTRACTING) is terminated before completion of the work on the current year, the amount includes the current year termination charges plus cancellation charges for the unfunded years.

TERMINATION NOTICE A notice from the contracting officer to the contractor stating that the contract is partially or completely terminated under either a TERMINATION FOR CONVENIENCE or a TERMINATION FOR DEFAULT. FAR 49.601 provides recommended formats for notices of termination for convenience and suggests that a telegraphic notice be used. FAR 49.402-3 contains guidance on the issuance of notices of termination for default. In such cases, DELINQUENCY NOTICEs may be required or desirable prior to the issuance of the termination notice. The default termination notice is a final DECISION OF THE CONTRACTING OFFICER, which is subject to immediate appeal under the CONTRACT DISPUTES ACT OF 1978. FAR 49.402-3(g)(7). See Cibinic & Nash, *Administration of Government Contracts* 996–98; 1083–84 (3d ed. 1995).

TERMS AND CONDITIONS All the provisions of a contract. FAR 14.201-1 and FAR 15.204-1 require that the terms and conditions follow the UNIFORM CONTRACT FORMAT. See also GENERAL PROVISIONS.

TEST AND EVALUATION (T&A) A process by which a SYSTEM or components are compared with requirements and specifications through testing. The Government evaluates the results to assess the progress of design, performance, supportability, and the like. During the ACQUISITION PROCESS, T&E can be any of three types: developmental test and evaluation (DT&E), which assists the engineering design and development phase and verifies attainment of technical performance specifications and objectives; operational test and evaluation (OT&E), which estimates a system's operational effectiveness and suitability, identifies needed modifications, and provides information on tactical, organizational, and personnel requirements (see OPERATIONAL TEST AND EVALUATION); and production acceptance test and evaluation (PAT&E), which demonstrates that the items meet the requirements and specifications of the contract. Jones, *Glossary: Defense Acquisition Acronyms and Terms* (8th ed., Defense Systems Management College). 10 U.S.C. § 2399 requires DOD to conduct OT&E on all MAJOR DEFENSE ACQUISITION PROGRAMs.

TEST AND EVALUATION MASTER PLAN (TEMP) Within DOD, the TEMP documents the overall structure and objectives of the test and evaluation (T&E) program. The TEMP provides a framework within which to generate detailed T&E plans, and it documents schedule and resource implications associated with the T&E program. The TEMP identifies the necessary developmental T&E, operational T&E, and live fire T&E activities. It relates program schedule, test management strategy and structure, and required resources to critical operational issues, critical technical parameters, objectives and thresholds documented in the operational requirements document; evaluation criteria, and milestone decision points. For multiservice or joint programs, a single integrated TEMP is required. See DOD Regulation 5000.2-R, *Mandatory Procedures for Major Defense Acquisition Programs (MDAPs) and Major Automated Information System (MAIS) Acquisition Programs*, Mar. 15, 1996.

TESTING That element of INSPECTION that determines the properties or elements, including functional operation, of supplies or their components by the application of established scientific principles and procedures. FAR 46.101. Testing is part of the QUALITY CONTROL and the QUALITY ASSURANCE processes. It is done by both the contractor (and its subcontractors) and the Government to ensure that supplies meet contract requirements.

THING OF VALUE A cash payment, a gift, or any variety of benefits including automobiles, cameras, clothing, food, loans, prostitutes, vacations, or promises of future employment. An element in finding the existence of either BRIBERY or a GRATUITY is that something of value is given, offered, promised, solicited, or received. Generally, the term is broadly construed and encompasses more than just items of substantial value. Cibinic & Nash, *Administration of Government Contracts* 84–91 (3d ed. 1995).

THIRD-PARTY DRAFT An agency bank draft, similar to a check, that is used to acquire and to pay for supplies and services. FAR 13.001; Treasury Financial Manual Section 3040.70. Third-party drafts may be used to acquire and pay for MICRO-PURCHASEs of supplies and services. FAR 13.305. However, FAR 13.201(b) states that use of the GOVERNMENT-WIDE COMMERCIAL PURCHASE CARD is the preferred method of obtaining such supplemental services.

TIME-AND-MATERIALS (T&M) CONTRACT A type of contract providing for the acquisition of supplies or services on the basis of (1) direct LABOR hours at specified fixed hourly rates that include wages, overhead, GENERAL AND ADMINISTRATIVE EXPENSEs, and PROFIT; and (2) materials at cost including, if appropriate, material handling costs. FAR 16.601. A T&M contract may be used only if (1) at the time of placing the contract it is not possible to estimate accurately the extent or duration of the work or to anticipate costs with any reasonable degree of confidence; (2) the contracting officer executes a DETERMINATION AND FINDINGS concluding that no other contract type is suitable; and (3) the contract includes a CEILING PRICE that the contractor exceeds at its own risk. A T&M contract provides no positive profit incentive to the contractor for cost control or labor efficiency. See Cibinic & Nash, chap. 8, Sec. V., *Formation of Government Contracts* (3d ed. 1998).

TITLE The paramount right to property. The Government claims title to all property bought by the contractor during the performance of a contract when the PROGRESS PAYMENTs clause in FAR 52.232-16 is included in the contract. However, *Marine Midland Bank v. United States*, 231 Ct. Cl. 496, 687 F.2d 395 (1982), holds that the Government right is not title but rather a lien with priority over all other claims against the property. See also FAR 32.503-15, which gives the contractor considerable control over the property during performance of the contract. With regard to PATENTs, TECHNICAL DATA, and COMPUTER SOFTWARE, the contractor generally retains title to the rights when they are created in the performance of the contract, but the Government is given a LICENSE to use the rights. See FAR 27.302(b); DFARS 227.7103-4 and DFARS 227.7203-4.

TITLE I; TITLE II; TITLE III Categories of ARCHITECT-ENGINEER (A-E) SERVICES used by DOE. Title I requires the A-E to provide necessary topographical and other field surveys, test borings, and other subsurface investigation; to prepare preliminary studies, sketches, layout plans, and outline specifications; and to prepare reports including cost estimates for the proposed project and all related structures, utilities, and appurtenances. Title II requires the A-E to provide complete design services, including all required preliminary and final working drawings, specifications, estimates, and contract documents; to assist in securing, analyzing, and evaluating bids or proposals for construction; and to consult with DOE on all questions arising in connection with the A-E's services. Title III requires the A-E to provide complete A-E supervision and inspection of construction, to check SHOP DRAWINGs, and to furnish drawings to show that construction has actually been accomplished. DEAR 936-605(c). See also CONCEPTUAL DESIGN.

TORT Injury to a person by NEGLIGENCE or through committing an act that is proscribed by community standards. Tort is one of the common causes of action that can be used to recover DAMAGES. The FEDERAL TORT CLAIMS ACT permits persons injured by negligent conduct of the Government to sue for damages in U.S. District Court.

TOTAL COST The sum of the allowable direct and indirect costs allocable to the contract, incurred or to be incurred, less any allocable credits, plus any allocable cost of money. FAR 31.201-1. See ALLOCABLE COST; ALLOWABLE COST; COST OF MONEY FACTORS. This is the amount that is reimbursable by the Government under COST-REIMBURSEMENT CONTRACTs or is accepted in pricing of FIXED-PRICE CONTRACTs. FAR Subpart 31.2 contains detailed guidance on the computation of total costs.

TOTAL COST METHOD A method of establishing the amount of DAMAGES or EQUITABLE ADJUSTMENT that results in the contractor's being compensated for the difference between its actual expenses and its bid or estimated costs. The courts and boards of contract appeals look on this method of proving damages with disfavor, tolerating its use only when no other method of calculating damages is available. Acceptability of the method requires a demonstration that (1) the nature of the particular losses makes it impossible or highly impracticable to determine them with a reasonable degree of accuracy, (2) the contractor's bid or estimate was realistic, (3) the actual costs expended were reasonable, and (4) the contractor was not responsible for the added expenses. See Cibinic & Nash, *Administration of Government Contracts* 710–16 (3d ed. 1995); Nash, chap. 19, *Government Contract Changes* (2d ed. 1989 & Supp. 1993).

TOTAL QUALITY MANAGEMENT (TQM) A philosophy and set of guiding principles that are intended to be the foundation of a continuously improving organization by encouraging employees to focus their attention on means of improving efficiency and effectiveness by assessing whether each activity adds value to the performance of the organization. TQM has been adopted by DOD. It is the application of human resources and quantitative methods to improve (1) the materials and services supplied to an organization, (2) all the processes within an organization, and (3) the degree to which the needs of the customer are met, now and in the future. TQM integrates fundamental management techniques, existing improvement efforts, and technical tools within a disciplined approach focused on continuous process improvement. See Ante, *Subcontract Management Surveillance: Putting TQM Principles to Work*, 32 Cont. Mgmt. 10 (Nov. 1992); Hudson, *From Deming to Doing: Putting Total Quality to Work in a Government Procurement Organization*, 32 Cont. Mgmt. 18 (Nov. 1992); Yurcisin, *The Way to Quality*, 29 Cont. Mgmt. 4 (Nov. 1989).

TOTAL SET-ASIDE See SET-ASIDE (n).

TRADE AGREEMENTS ACT OF 1979 An Act, 19 U.S.C. §§ 2501–2582, requiring agencies to evaluate offers from contractors from designated countries without regard to the restrictions of the BUY AMERICAN ACT. The exemption applies only to procurements at or over the dollar equivalent of 150,000 SPECIAL DRAWING RIGHTS units. FAR 25.401 lists the 59 designated countries eligible for exemption and the 24 additional countries eligible under the CARIBBEAN BASIN ECONOMIC RECOVERY ACT. The U.S. Trade Representative has determined that these countries provide appropriate reciprocal competitive government procurement opportunities for American products and suppliers. Exceptions to the Trade Agreements Act, under which the Buy American Act does apply, are found at FAR 25.403. See Connelly et al., *Minimum Mandatory Requirements of Solicitations*, 95-4 Briefing Papers (Mar. 1995); Sampliner & O'Shea, *Rules of Origin for Foreign Acquisitions Under the Trade Agreements Act of 1979, NAFTA & The New GATT Accords*, 23 Pub. Cont. L.J. 207 (1994); Kenney et al., *Domestic Preference Provisions/Ed. II*, 94-3 Briefing Papers (Feb. 1994); Kenney & Duberstein, *Domestic Preference Provisions*, 89-3 Briefing Papers (Feb. 1989); Rothlein & Schooner, *The Trade Agreements Act: Installation Procurement and International Government Acquisition Law*, Army Law. 1 (Sept. 1983).

TRADE, BUSINESS, TECHNICAL, AND PROFESSIONAL ACTIVITY COSTS Costs incurred by a contractor as a result of membership in trade, business, technical, and professional organizations. FAR 31.205-43 makes the following costs allowable: membership costs; subscriptions to trade, business, professional, or other technical periodicals; and costs associated with meetings, conferences, symposia, or seminars, as specified below, when their principal purpose is the dissemination of trade, business, technical, or professional information or the stimulation of production or improved productivity. Allowable meeting costs are the costs of organizing, setting up, and sponsoring the meetings, symposia, etc., including rental of meeting facilities, transportation, subsistence, and incidental costs; the costs of attendance by contractor employees, including travel costs; and the costs of attendance by individuals who are not employees of the contractor, provided such costs are not also reimbursed to the individual by the employing company or organization and provided the individual's attendance is essential in achieving the purpose of the conference, meeting, symposium, or seminar. See also ALLOWABLE COST. See Cibinic & Nash, *Cost-Reimbursement Contracting* 784 (2d ed. 1993).

TRADEOFF PROCESS The competitive negotiation process where the Government evaluates both price and non-price factors and awards the contract to the offeror proposing the combination of factors which offers the BEST VALUE to the Government. FAR 15.101-1(a) states that this process is appropriate when it is in the best interest of the Government to consider award to other than the lowest price offeror or the highest technically rated offeror. In making the award decision under this process, the Government makes a tradeoff analysis of the proposals, ascertaining which offers the best overall value. Prior to FAC 97-02, September 30, 1997, this process was widely described as the best value process. See BEST VALUE PROCUREMENT. See Cibinic & Nash, chap. 6. Sec. I., *Formation of Government Contracts* (3d ed. 1998).

TRADE PRACTICE See TRADE USAGE.

TRADE SECRET Information—including a formula, pattern, device, compilation, program, method, technique, or process—that is the subject of reasonable efforts to maintain its secrecy and that derives independent economic value, actual or potential, as a result of not being generally known to and not being readily ascertainable by proper means. Uniform Trade Secrets Act. The Government is generally barred from disclosing trade secrets under the TRADE SECRETS ACT, the PROCUREMENT INTEGRITY ACT, and the FREEDOM OF INFORMATION ACT. See Nash & Rawicz, *Intellectual Property in Government Contracts*, vol. 1, 70–85 (3d ed. 1997); Nash, *Additional Protection for Trade Secrets*, 11 N&CR ¶ 28 (June 1997); Hill, *Does the New Trade Secret Law Improve Owner's Protection?*, 37 Cont. Mgmt. 4 (Mar. 1997).

TRADE SECRETS ACT An Act, 18 U.S.C. § 1905, making it a crime for an employee of the United States to publish or disclose trade secrets and other confidential information obtained as a result of Government employment. The Act has not led to any significant amount of criminal prosecution, but it is important in establishing a standard barring disclosure of information under the FREEDOM OF INFORMATION ACT. See Manos, *Protecting Proprietary Information*, 94-13 Briefing Papers (Dec. 1994); Nash, *The Trade Secrets Act: An Enigma*, 4 N&CR ¶ 57 (Oct. 1990).

TRADE SECRETS EXEMPTION An exemption under the FREEDOM OF INFORMATION ACT from the disclosure of TRADE SECRETS. 5 U.S.C. § 552(b)(4). See Nash & Rawicz, *Intellectual*

Property Series, vol 3, 191–92 (3d ed. 1997). See also PRIVILEGED INFORMATION.

TRADE USAGE A use of language with such regularity of observance in a place, vocation, or trade as to justify an expectation that it will be observed with respect to a particular agreement. Trade usage is distinguished from common usage or normal dictionary definitions. Evidence of trade usage, typically in conjunction with industry or trade custom or practice, may be used to interpret vague contract language. As a general rule, trade usage and trade practice or custom will not prevail over clear and unambiguous contractual language. Cibinic & Nash, *Administration of Government Contracts* 209–211 (3d ed. 1995); *Restatement (Second) Contracts* § 222 (1981).

TRAIL BOSS PROGRAM An alternative approach initiated by the General Services Administration for managing the Government's major information technology acquisitions in the 1990s. The Trail Boss Program focuses on a single manager for an acquisition and emphasizes individuals, cooperation, and accomplishment over process and procedure.

TRAINING COSTS Costs of providing vocational training intended to increase the skills of a contractor's employees. FAR 31.205-44 specifies that such costs are ALLOWABLE COSTs, with some limitations. See Cibinic & Nash, *Cost-Reimbursement Contracting* 840–43 (2d ed. 1993).

TRANSPORTATION The shipment of material, parts, components, or end items in the procurement of supplies. FAR Part 47 deals with policies and procedures for applying transportation and traffic management considerations in the acquisition of transportation or transportation-related services by contract methods other than BILLS OF LADING, transportation requests, transportation warrants, and similar transportation forms. The preferred method of transporting supplies for the Government is by commercial carrier (see CARRIER TRANSPORTATION). However, Government-owned, leased, or chartered vehicles, aircraft, and vessels may be used if they are available and not fully utilized, if their use will result in substantial economies, and if their use is in accordance with all applicable statutes, policies, and regulations. FAR 47.101.

TRANSPORTATION TERM CONTRACTS REQUIREMENTS CONTRACTs for transportation or transportation-related services. FAR 47.203. Such contracts are generally used for the transportation of household goods, office furniture, and other general freight. FAR Subpart 47.2 provides guidance on the use of such contracts. See also INDEFINITE-DELIVERY CONTRACT.

TRAVEL COSTS The cost of transportation, lodging, subsistence, and incidental expenses. FAR 31.205-46 specifies that such costs incurred by a contractor are ALLOWABLE COSTs, with some limitations, if they are incurred on official company business. See Cibinic & Nash, *Cost-Reimbursement Contracting* 817–21 (2d ed. 1993).

TREASURY INTEREST RATE The interest rate set by the Secretary of the Treasury for each six-month period on a calendar year basis. The rate is published in the FEDERAL REGISTER and is used to calculate the amount of INTEREST payable by the Government under the PROMPT PAYMENT ACT and the CONTRACT DISPUTES ACT OF 1978. The interest rates for the past decade are shown below:

Year	*Jan.–June*	*July–Dec.*
1987	7 5/8%	8 7/8%
1988	9 3/8%	9 1/4%
1989	9 ¾%	9 1/8%
1990	8 ½%	9%
1991	8 3/8%	8 1/2%
1992	6 7/8%	7%
1993	6 ½%	5 5/8%
1994	5 ½%	7%
1995	8 1/8%	6 3/8%
1996	5 7/8%	7%
1997	6 3/8%	6 3/4%

TRUTH IN NEGOTIATIONS ACT (TINA) An Act, 10 U.S.C. § 2306a, 41 U.S.C. § 254b, that was added to the ARMED SERVICES PROCUREMENT ACT in 1963 to enhance the Government's ability to negotiate fair prices by ensuring that the contracting officer has the same factual information that is available to the contractor at the time of price negotiations. TINA established the requirement for the submission of COST OR PRICING DATA and certification of their accuracy, completeness, and currency for the award of any negotiated contract expected to exceed $500,000 ($100,000 in the case of a prime contract entered into on or before Dec. 5, 1990), subject to exemptions when ADEQUATE PRICE COMPETITION or other conditions reflecting a competitive marketplace exist, as discussed at FAR 15.403-1. (see CERTIFIED COST OR PRICING DATA). It also provided for contract price adjustment as a result of submission of DEFECTIVE COST OR PRICING DATA. In 1984 the COMPETITION IN CONTRACTING ACT added these requirements to the FEDERAL PROPERTY AND ADMINISTRATIVE SERVICES ACT OF 1949 at 41 U.S.C. § 254b. Subsequently, in 1986, TINA was greatly expanded and codified at 10 U.S.C. § 2306a. The FEDERAL ACQUISITION STREAMLINING ACT OF 1994, Pub. L. No. 103-355, further modified and refined TINA requirements, including placing prohibitions on its use when there was adequate price competition or the Government was buying COMMERCIAL ITEMs. TINA is not the only remedy available to the Government for defective data; a contractor may be found liable for civil fraud under the FALSE CLAIMS ACT, 31 U.S.C. §§ 3729–3732, for knowingly submitting defective data. Certification under the Act is accomplished by the Certificate of Current Cost or Pricing Data in FAR 15.506-2. The Act is implemented by the Price Reduction for Defective Cost or Pricing Data clauses at FAR 52.215-22 and -23. The data are submitted in accordance with Table 15-2, FAR 15.408. See Cibinic & Nash, chap. 1, Sec. VII., *Formation of Government Contracts* (3d ed. 1998); Nash, *Truth in Negotiations: The FAR Implementation of FASA*, 9 N&CR ¶ 57 (Nov. 1995); Simchak & Gildea, *Impact of FASA on the Truth in Negotiations Act*, 95-8 Briefing Papers (July 1995); Kipps & Rice, *Living with TINA: A Practical Guide to the Truth in Negotiations Act* (Wash. Legal Found. 1989); Morrison & Ebert, *Truth in Negotiations/Edition III*, 89-11 Briefing Papers (Oct. 1989); Feldman, *The Truth in Negotiations Act: A Primer*, 21 Nat'l Cont. Mgmt. J., Issue No. 2, p. 67 (1988).

TUCKER ACT An Act, 28 U.S.C. § 1346(a) and § 1491, that waives SOVEREIGN IMMUNITY from suit for all CLAIMs founded upon the Constitution, statutes, regulations, or any contract, express or implied, with the U.S. Government. Originally passed in 1855 and enacted in its present form in 1887, the Tucker Act made the Court of Claims the major court resolving Government contract DISPUTEs, but gave federal district courts jurisdiction up to $10,000. The CONTRACT DISPUTES ACT OF 1978 repealed the part of the Tucker Act that gave the federal district courts jurisdiction over claims up to $10,000 and gave contractors direct access to the Court of Claims to challenge contracting officer decisions on contract disputes. See Nash & Cibinic, *Federal Procurement Law*, vol. II, 2140 (3d ed. 1980). The FEDERAL COURTS IMPROVEMENT ACT further altered the process by creating the COURT of FEDERAL CLAIMS (originally named the Claims Court) and the COURT OF APPEALS FOR THE FEDERAL CIRCUIT out of the former Court of Claims. See Nash, *Tucker Act Jurisdiction: It's Narrower than You Think*, 4 N&CR ¶ 28 (May 1990).

TURNKEY See DESIGN-BUILD.

TWO-PHASE DESIGN-BUILD CONTRACTING A method of selecting a DESIGN-BUILD contractor in which a limited number of offerors (normally five or fewer) is selected during phase one to submit detailed proposals for phase two. FAR 36.102. This selection procedure was authorized by the CLINGER-COHEN ACT OF 1996, Pub. L. No. 104-106, 10 U.S.C. § 2505a and 41 U.S.C. § 253m. It is implemented in FAR Subpart 36.3. It may be used when it is determined that three or more offers are anticipated and significant design work will be required in order to select the design-build contractor. In making this determination, the following criteria must be considered: (1) the adequacy of the definition of project requirements, (2) the time constraints for delivery of the project, (3) the capability and experience of potential contractors, (4) the suitability of the project for the two-phase method, (5) the capability of the agency to manage the project, and (6) other criteria established by the contracting activity. See Nash, *Design-Build Contracting: The New Two-Step Procedure*, 11 N&CR ¶ 13 (Mar. 1997); Nash, *Design-Build Contracting: Can The Federal Government Use This Technique Effectively?*, 8 N&CR ¶ 68 (Dec. 1994).

TWO-STEP SEALED BIDDING A method of procurement that combines competitive procedures in order to obtain the benefits of SEALED BIDDING when adequate SPECIFICATIONs are not available. FAR 14.501. One objective of this process is to permit the development of a sufficiently descriptive and not unduly restrictive statement of the Government's requirements, including an adequate TECHNICAL DATA package, so that subsequent acquisitions can be made by conventional sealed bidding. This method is especially useful in acquisitions requiring technical proposals, particularly those for complex items. Step One consists of the request for and submission, EVALUATION, and DISCUSSION of technical proposals; no pricing is involved. Step Two involves the submission of sealed bids by offerors that submitted acceptable technical proposals in Step One. See

Cibinic & Nash, chap. 5, Sec. V., *Formation of Government Contracts* (3d ed. 1998).

TYPE OF CONTRACT Categories of contracts that are differentiated according to the time the price is arrived at and the firmness of the price. FAR Part 16 describes and states the policies governing the various types of contract. Contracts are of two basic types: FIXED-PRICE CONTRACTs and COST-REIMBURSEMENT CONTRACTs. Within these two basic families are a sizable number of specific types, such as FIRM-FIXED-PRICE CONTRACTs, FIXED-PRICE-INCENTIVE CONTRACTs, COST-PLUS-INCENTIVE-FEE CONTRACTs, and COST-PLUS-FIXED-FEE CONTRACTs. Under a fixed-price contract, the contractor agrees to perform the work called for by the contract for the firm-fixed-price stated in the contract or, if the price is tentative and subject to later adjustment, for some amount under a specified price ceiling. Under a cost-reimbursement contract, the Government agrees to reimburse the contractor for the costs it incurs in performing the contract and, usually, to pay a fee representing the contractor's profit for performing the contract. Under a fixed-price contract, the contractor must complete the contract for the agreed-upon price. If costs are less than anticipated, the contractor will earn increased profits. But if costs are greater than anticipated, the contractor will incur a loss or at least not realize the profit contemplated. Whatever the situation, the responsibility is entirely the contractor's, and the contractor must deliver for the specified price regardless of how badly it may have miscalculated. Under a cost-reimbursement contract, on the other hand, the contractor agrees to use its best efforts to complete contract requirements within a TOTAL COST previously estimated and agreed upon. The contractor must notify the Government if and when it believes that the contract will not be completed within that estimate, giving a revised estimate of the cost of performance. The contractor is not obliged to continue performance or incur additional costs beyond the original estimate—if it does, it does so at its own risk—unless and until notified that the contract funding and estimate have been increased. The major test applied in the selection of contract type is the degree of uncertainty involved: solid bases for pricing lead to fixed-price arrangements, whereas uncertainties lead to cost-reimbursement or incentive arrangements. Special contract types include INDEFINITE-DELIVERY CONTRACTs, TIME-AND-MATERIALS CONTRACTs, LABOR-HOUR CONTRACTs, and LETTER CONTRACTs. For discussion of the various contract types, see Cibinic & Nash, chap. 8, *Formation of Government Contracts* (3d ed. 1998).

U

UNABSORBED OVERHEAD Overhead (see INDIRECT COST) that cannot be charged to a contract as originally anticipated because the direct costs of performance have been stopped due to a delay. During periods of Government DELAY in or SUSPENSION of a particular contract, there is a marked decrease in or cessation of DIRECT COSTs incurred for that contract. Consequently, the HOME OFFICE costs that would otherwise have been charged to that contract by means of applying the home office overhead rate to direct costs cannot be "absorbed" by that contract and must be borne by the contractor's other work. The term "unabsorbed overhead" has its roots in manufacturing accounting and is often used to describe this additional overhead burden. The EICHLEAY FORMULA is the prevalent method for calculating unabsorbed and extended overhead. See Cibinic & Braude, chap. 9, *Construction Contracting* 751–64 (1991). See also Kenyon, *Closing the Gate on Unabsorbed Overhead Claims*, 39 Gov't Contractor ¶ 559 (Nov. 26, 1997); Cibinic, *Unabsorbed Overhead in Delay Claims: Is One period's Loss Another Period's Gain?*, 11 N&CR ¶ 1 (Jan. 1997); Anderson, *Practitioner's Viewpoint: Federal Circuit Creates an Invalid Legal Test for Determining Entitlement to Unabsorbed Overhead*, 26 Pub. Cont. L.J. 353 (1997); Nash, *Postscript: The "Eichleay" Formula*, 10 N&CR ¶ 56 (Nov. 1996); Kauffman & Holman, *The "Eichleay" Formula: A Resilient Means for Recovering Unabsorbed Overhead*, 24 Pub. Con. L.J. 319 (1995); Cibinic, *Unabsorbed Overhead on Supply Contracts: An Idea Whose Time Has Come*, 8 N&CR ¶ 45 (Aug. 1994); Cibinic, *The "Eichleay" Formula: Extended vs. Unabsorbed Home Office Overhead*, 6 N&CR ¶ 68 (Dec. 1992); Nash, *The "Eichleay" Formula: Does It Spell Relief?*, 5 N&CR ¶ 62 (Nov. 1991).

UNALLOWABLE COST A cost incurred by a contractor that is not chargeable to Government contracts. Unallowable costs must be identified and excluded from any billing, claim, or proposal applicable to a Government contract. FAR 31.201-6. CAS 405, 48 C.F.R. § 9904.405, provides guidance in accounting for such costs. 10 U.S.C. § 2324 and 41 U.S.C. § 256 call for severe sanctions for claiming costs that are unallowable pursuant to statute or regulation. See Smith et al., *Accounting for Unallowable Costs Under CAS 405*, 97-6 CP&A Rep. 3 (June 1997); Cibinic, *Penalties for Unallowable Costs: A Kinder and Gentler Statute for DOD Contractors and Things to Come for Civilian Agency Contractors*, 7 N&CR ¶ 8 (Feb. 1993). See also ALLOWABLE COST and EXPRESSLY UNALLOWABLE COST.

UNAUTHORIZED COMMITMENT See RATIFICATION.

UNBALANCED BID A BID that states nominal or low prices for some work and enhanced prices for other work. For the bid to be deemed nonresponsive (see RESPONSIVENESS), it must be both mathematically unbalanced and materially unbalanced. FAR 14.404-2(g). A determination of mathematical unbalance asks whether each bid item carries its share of the cost of the work plus profit or whether the bid is based on nominal or low prices for some work and enhanced prices for other work. A determination of material unbalance asks whether there is reasonable doubt that award to the bidder submitting the mathematically unbalanced bid ultimately will result in the lowest cost. See Nash, *Unbalanced Bidding in Long-Term Contracts: The Comptroller General's Accounting Lapse*, 9 N&CR ¶ 54 (Oct. 1995); Gordon, *Unbalanced Bids*, 24 Pub. Cont. L.J. 1 (1994); Cibinic, *Unbalanced Bids and Proposals: Trying to Beat the System*, 5 N&CR ¶ 21 (Apr. 1991); Preston, *Evaluating Bids Against Cost Limitations*, 15 Pub. Cont. L.J. 463, 476–85 (1985).

UNBALANCED PRICING Pricing of a negotiated contract where the price of one or more contract line items is significantly over or understated as indicated by the application of cost or price analysis techniques. FAR 15.404-1(g) indicates that such pricing may increase performance risk or result in unreasonably high prices. Contracting officers are therefore directed to analyze all line item prices to determine if they are unbalanced and to reject the offer if the unbalancing poses an unacceptable risk to the Government. This regulation rejects the mathematical/material analysis used to deal with UNBALANCED BIDs in favor of granting the contracting officer discretion to deal with this issue on a case-by-case basis.

UNCONSCIONABILITY A bargain or contract that no person in possession of his or her senses—that is to say, not under a delusion—would make and that no fair and honest person would accept. The basic test of Unconscionability is whether, under circumstances existing when the contract was made and in light of general commercial background and commercial needs of the particular trade or case, the contract clauses are so one-sided as to oppress or unfairly surprise a party. Unconscionability generally implies an absence of meaningful choice on the part of one of the parties. Moreover, the one-sidedness often obtains when the imbalance is buried in small print or couched in language unintelligible even to a person of moderate education. *Black's Law Dictionary* 1525 (6th ed. 1990). Unconscionability is grounds for contract AVOIDANCE. U.C.C. § 2-302. See Cibinic & Nash, *Administration of Government Contracts* 341–42 (3d ed. 1995).

UNDEFINITIZED CONTRACTUAL ACTION A contract in which the parties have not fully agreed on all the TERMS AND CONDITIONS. In most cases in Government procurement, such contracts are called LETTER CONTRACTs. 10 U.S.C. § 2326 precludes agencies from entering into undefinitized contractual actions without proper justification and provides that DEFINITIZATION should occur within 180 days of the contractor's proposal to definitize and before the expenditure of more than 50 percent of the funds to be used. Procedures for complying with this statute are contained in DFARS Subpart 217.74.

UNFAIR COMPETITIVE ADVANTAGE An advantage of one competitor over another competitor that is derived from improper Government action or is created by the Government. An unfair competitive advantage exists when a contractor competing for the award of any federal contract possesses PROPRIETARY INFORMATION that was obtained from a Government official without proper authorization or SOURCE SELECTION INFORMATION that is relevant to the contract but is not available to all competitors, and such information would assist that contractor in obtaining the contract. The underlying concept is that no competitor should benefit from exclusive access to information. OFPP Policy Letter No. 89-1, *Conflict of Interest Policies Applicable to Consultants*, Dec. 8, 1989. See also FAR Subpart 9.5. An unfair competitive advantage also exists when a contractor is permitted to use GOVERNMENT PRODUCTION AND RESEARCH PROPERTY in a competitive procurement without payment of rent or addition of a RENTAL EQUIVALENT. FAR 45.201. FAR Subpart 45.2 sets forth the procedures for overcoming this type of unfair advantage by charging rent or adjusting bid prices.

UNICOR See FEDERAL PRISON INDUSTRIES, INC.

UNIFORM COMMERCIAL CODE (U.C.C.) A uniform law governing commercial transactions such as sales of GOODS, commercial paper, bank deposits and collections, LETTERs OF CREDIT, bulk transfers, warehouse receipts, BILLs OF LADING, investment securities, and secured transactions. All states except Louisiana have adopted the U.C.C. The U.C.C. is one of the Uniform Laws drafted by the National Conference of Commissioners on Uniform State Laws. *Black's Law Dictionary* 1531 (6th ed. 1990). The U.C.C.'s underlying purposes and policies are to simplify, clarify, and modernize the law governing commercial transactions; permit the continued expansion of commercial practices through custom, usage, and agreement of the parties; and make the law uniform throughout the various jurisdictions. U.C.C. § 1-102. The U.C.C. is not directly applicable to Government contracting, but it is used by analogy and for guidance when the terms of a contract or the regulations do not deal directly with a subject. See Nash & Cibinic, *Federal Procurement Law,* vol. I, 796–98 (3d ed. 1977).

UNIFORM CONTRACT FORMAT (UCF) A standardized format for structuring Government SOLICITATIONs and CONTRACTs. FAR 14.201-1; FAR 15.204-1. Its use facilitates preparation of the solicitation and contract as well as reference to and use of the documents in the solicitation and contract. Found on Standard Form 26—Award and Contract—and Standard Form 33—Solicitation, Offer and Award—the UCF is simply a table of contents for organizing contractual documents into four parts and 13 sections. In negotiated acquisitions, Part I, The Schedule, includes sections A, Solicitation/contract form; B, Supplies or services and prices/costs; C, Description/specifications/work statement; D, Packaging and marking; E, Inspection and acceptance; F, Deliveries or performance; G, Contract administration data; and H, Special contract requirements. Part II, Contract Clauses, consists of a single section I, Contract clauses. Part III, List of Documents, Exhibits, and Other Attachments, consists of a single section J, List of attachments. Part IV, Representations and Instructions, contains sections K, Representations, certifications, and other statements of offerors or quoters; L, Instructions, conditions, and notices to offerors or quoters; and M, Evaluation factors for award. In sealed bidding, the format is the same, with minor differences in language.

UNIFORM RULES A standardized set of rules of procedure for the various agency BOARDs OF CONTRACT APPEALS (BCAs). The CONTRACT DISPUTES ACT OF 1978 requires that the Administrator of the OFFICE OF FEDERAL PROCUREMENT POLICY (OFPP) issue guidelines with respect to the establishment, functions, and procedures of the agency BCAs. 41 U.S.C. § 607(h). OFPP issued "Uniform Rules of Procedure for Boards of Contract Appeals" in 1979. See 44 Fed. Reg. 12519 (Mar. 7, 1979); 44 Fed. Reg. 34227 (June 14, 1979). The rules resemble the uniform rules drafted by the National Conference of Boards of Contract Appeals Members (now called the Board of Contract Appeals Judges Association), with sections added to implement the Contract Disputes Act's small claims and subpoena provisions. OFPP intended that the various BCAs would adopt the Uniform Rules in place of their individual rules, except when a BCA's size or the nature of its docket justified a variance. Each BCA's "customized" version of the rules can be found in the loose-leaf advance sheet section of the *Board of Contract Appeals Decisions* available from Commerce Clearing House, Inc., 4025 West Peterson Avenue, Chicago, IL 60646.

UNILATERAL CHANGE A CHANGE ORDER issued by a contracting officer, without the need for agreement or acceptance by the contractor, under a Changes clause. Most Government contracts contain a Changes clause permitting the contracting officer to make unilateral changes in designated areas, within the general SCOPE OF THE CONTRACT. FAR 43.201. The contractor is bound to proceed in accordance with such a change order even if it does not agree with it. It is the policy of the Government to avoid issuing unilateral changes by attempting instead to price changes before they are issued and then issue a bilateral MODIFICATION. FAR 43.102(b). When this cannot be done, it is the policy of the Government to negotiate a maximum price in the change order. See Nash, chap. 7, *Government Contract Changes* (2d ed. 1989 & Supp. 1993). Unilateral changes are issued on Standard Form 30, Amendment of Solicitation/Modification of Contract, FAR 53.301-30. FAR 43.201(a). See also UNILATERAL MODIFICATION.

UNILATERAL CONTRACT A binding contractual agreement where the OFFER specifies that the ACCEPTANCE can be effective only if it is in the form of performance. *Restatement (Second) Contracts* § 45 (1981). In such instances, an attempted acceptance by communication or promise will be ineffective to form a contract. This is called a unilateral contract because the OFFEROR is bound while the other party is not (the offer being considered the giving of an OPTION under the *Restatement*). The term "unilateral contract" has frequently been thought to mean any contract formed by an offer from one party and acceptance in the form of performance by the other party. The contracting officer can issue a PURCHASE ORDER as a unilateral contract or as a BILATERAL CONTRACT. FAR 13.302-3. See Cibinic & Nash, chap. 2, Sec. I., *Formation of Government Contracts* (3d ed. 1998).

UNILATERAL MISTAKE A MISTAKE of only one party—generally the contractor. Relief for such mistakes may be given if they are alleged by the offeror before award, provided they are not mistakes in business judgment. See FAR 14.407, FAR 15.508. No relief is given for such mistakes alleged by a contractor after award unless the contracting officer knew or should have known of the mistake before award or failed to ask for verification (see DUTY OF VERIFICATION). See FAR 14.407-4; Cibinic & Nash, *Administration of Government Contracts* 330–40 (3d ed. 1995).

UNILATERAL MODIFICATION A MODIFICATION to a contract that is signed only by the contracting officer. Unilateral modifications are generally used to make ADMINISTRATIVE CHANGEs, issue CHANGE ORDERs, make changes authorized by clauses other than a Changes clause, and issue TERMINATION NOTICEs. FAR 43.103. The alternative to a unilateral modification is a bilateral modification.

UNILATERAL PRICE DETERMINATION A Government-directed MODIFICATION to a contract that sets forth a presumptively fair price for the supplies or services that are at issue. This presumption is rebuttable upon a contractor showing that the unilaterally determined price is either not fair or not reasonable, or both, based on certain facts, cost or price principles or assumptions, or legal theories. If a contractor does not sign the unilateral price determination but fails to object in a timely manner, the modification may have the force and effect of a bilateral agreement and may not be susceptible to subsequent legal challenge. See Jeroslow, *Avoiding Negotiation Deadlock: The Use and Care of Unilateral Price Determinations*, 86-1 Caveat Emptor 1, cited in Henson, *The Legality of the UPD*, 30 Cont. Mgmt. 9 (Aug. 1990). See also UNILATERAL CHANGE.

UNIQUE AND INNOVATIVE CONCEPT A concept that, in the opinion and to the best knowledge of the Government evaluator, is the product of original thinking submitted in confidence by one source; contains novel or changed concepts, approaches, or methods; was not submitted previously by another; and is not otherwise available within the Federal Government. FAR 6.003. In this context, the term does not mean that the source has the sole capability of performing the research. When such a concept is included in an UNSOLICITED PROPOSAL, a contracting agency may award a contract to the offeror without obtaining FULL AND OPEN COMPETITION. See FAR 15.601, which provides that a valid unsolicited proposal must contain a unique and innovative concept.

UNIT COST REDUCTION See INSTANT UNIT COST REDUCTION.

UNITED STATES CODE (U.S.C.) A consolidation and codification of all the general and permanent laws of the United States. The code provides an organized system for finding federal laws by title (50 headings, primarily alphabetical) and section. For example, Title 41, Public Contracts, contains many of the basic laws governing the procurement process. Within Title 41, sections 251 through 266 contain the procurement parts of the FEDERAL PROPERTY AND ADMINISTRATIVE SERVICES ACT OF 1949, sections 401 through 434 contain the OFFICE OF FEDERAL PROCUREMENT POLICY Act, and sections 601 through 613 contain the CONTRACT DISPUTES ACT OF 1978. Note, however, that the ARMED SERVICES PROCUREMENT ACT is codified in Title 10, Armed Forces. Whereas bills passed by Congress are sequentially numbered as public laws or statutes, the code organizes the laws by subject matter, often placing portions of new statutes in multiple U.S.C. titles. As officially published, the code is generally updated and reissued every six years; however, current versions of the code are published by commercial vendors such as West Publishing Company (United States Code Annotated or U.S.C.A.) and the Lawyer's Cooperative Publishing Company (United States Code Service or U.S.C.S.).

UNLIMITED RIGHTS The rights of the Government to use TECHNICAL DATA and COMPUTER SOFTWARE in any way. This term has a slightly different definition in each of the three major policies. Under the FAR policy it means the right, with respect to rights in DATA and COPYRIGHTS, to use, disclose, reproduce, prepare derivative works, distribute copies to the public, and perform publicly and display publicly, in any manner and for any purpose, and have others do so or permit them to do so. FAR 27.401. Under the Rights in Data—General clause in FAR 52.227-14, the Government acquires unlimited rights in (1) data first produced in the performance of a contract; (2) FORM, FIT, AND FUNCTION DATA delivered under contract; (3) data that constitute manuals or instructional and training material for installation, operation, or routine maintenance and repair of items, components, or processes delivered or furnished for use under a contract; and (4) all other data delivered under a contract, other than LIMITED RIGHTS DATA or restricted COMPUTER SOFTWARE. FAR 27.404. Under the 1995 DOD policy, the Rights in Technical Data—Noncommercial Items (Jun 1995) clause in DFARS 252.227-7013 and the Rights in Noncommercial Computer Software and Noncommercial Computer Software Documentation (Jun 1995) clause in DFARS 252.227-7014 define unlimited rights as rights to use, modify, reproduce, release, perform, display, or disclose [technical data or computer software of computer software documentation, as appropriate] in whole or in part, in any manner, and for any purpose whatsoever, and to have or authorize others to do so. Under the 1988 DOD policy, unlimited rights were the rights to use, duplicate, release, or disclose, technical data or computer software in whole or in part, in any manner and for any purpose whatsoever, and to have or permit others to do so. These DOD policies take unlimited rights in a slightly broader set of situations than does the FAR policy. See Nash, *The New DOD "Rights in Software" Policy: Half a Loaf*, 10 N&CR ¶ 12 (Mar. 1996); McAleese & Newman, *Leveraging Technical Data and Computer Software*, 36 Cont. Mgmt. 4 (Mar. 1996); Burgett et al., *Government Rights in Data and Software/Edition II*, 95-11 Briefing Papers (Oct. 1995); Nash, *Department of Defense Technical Data Policy: The New Interim Rule*, 3 N&CR ¶ 1 (Jan. 1989).

UNPRICED PURCHASE ORDER An order for supplies or services whose PRICE is not established at the time the order is issued. FAR 13.302-2. An unpriced PURCHASE ORDER may be used only when (1) the transaction is not expected to exceed the SIMPLIFIED ACQUISITION THRESHOLD; (2) it is impractical to obtain pricing before issuing the purchase order; and (3) the purchase is for repairs to equipment requiring disassembly to determine the nature and extent of repairs, or for material that is available from only one source and for which the cost cannot be readily established, or for supplies or services for which prices are known to be competitive but exact prices are not known (for example, miscellaneous repair parts or maintenance services).

UNSOLICITED PROPOSAL A written proposal that is submitted to a Government agency on the initiative of the submitter for the purpose of obtaining a contract with the Government and that is not in response to a REQUEST FOR PROPOSALS (RFP) or a BROAD AGENCY ANNOUNCEMENT. FAR 15.601. Unsolicited proposals are a means for Government agencies to obtain innovative or unique methods or approaches to accomplishing their missions from sources outside the Government but the basic policy of the Government is to encourage the submission of such methods or approaches in response to broad agency announcements. FAR 15.602. 10 U.S.C. § 2304(d)(1) and 41 U.S.C. § 253(d)(1) provide that agencies may enter into contracts based on unsolicited RESEARCH proposals without obtaining FULL AND OPEN COMPETITION. A valid unsolicited proposal must contain a UNIQUE AND INNOVATIVE CONCEPT; must be independently originated and developed, prepared without Government supervision, and sufficiently detailed for Government review, but must not be an advance proposal for a known agency requirement. FAR 15.303. Agencies are to encourage potential offerors to make preliminary contacts with appropriate agency personnel before the offerors expend extensive effort on detailed unsolicited proposals or submit PROPRIETARY DATA to the Government. Potential offerors' preliminary contacts should include inquiries into the general need for the type of effort contemplated and discussions with agency technical personnel for the limited purpose of obtaining an understanding of the agency's mission and responsibilities in relation to the contemplated effort. FAR 15.604. FAR 15.609 permits proprietary legends on unsolicited proposals and directs Government personnel to attempt to protect data in such proposals even if proprietary legends are not applied. Proprietary legends are used to restrict the proposal if the offeror does not want data included in the proposal disclosed for any purpose other than evaluation. See Cibinic & Nash, chap. 6, *Formation of Government Contracts* (3d ed. 1998).

UNUSUAL AND COMPELLING URGENCY A condition that will lead to serious injury if a procurement is not undertaken immediately. 10 U.S.C. § 2304(c)(2) and 41 U.S.C. § 253(c)(2) permit the award of a contract without FULL AND OPEN COMPETITION when such urgency exists. However, 10 U.S.C. § 2304(f)(5)(A) and 41 U.S.C. § 253(f)(5)(A) preclude the use of this exception to full and open competition if the urgency is created by lack of ACQUISITION PLANNING or concerns over the amount of funds available for the procurement. FAR 6.302-2 provides guidance on the use of this exception. Examples of unusual and compelling urgencies are provided in DFARS 206.302-2. See Cibinic & Nash, chap. 3, Sec. II., *Formation of Government Contracts* (3d ed. 1998).

UNUSUAL PROGRESS PAYMENT Any PROGRESS PAYMENT based on cost that provides payment in a higher amount than would a

CUSTOMARY PROGRESS PAYMENT. FAR 32.501. The contracting officer may provide unusual progress payments only if (1) the contract necessitates predelivery expenditures that are large in relation to contract price and in relation to the contractor's working capital and credit; (2) the contractor fully documents an actual need to supplement any private financing available, including GUARANTEED LOANs; and (3) the contractor's request is approved by the HEAD OF THE CONTRACTING ACTIVITY or a designee. FAR 32.501-2. The excess of the unusual progress payment rate approved over the customary progress payment rate should be the smallest amount possible under the circumstances. Progress payments are not considered unusual merely because they are on LETTER CONTRACTs or the definitive contracts that supersede letter contracts.

UNUSUALLY SEVERE WEATHER Adverse weather that is unusual at the time of year it occurs for the place in which it occurs. No matter how severe or destructive, if the weather is not unusual for the particular time and place or if the contractor should have reasonably anticipated it, the contractor is not entitled to relief. *Bigelow, Inc.*, ASBCA 27540, 84-3 BCA ¶ 17,531. Unusually severe weather may be cause for an EXCUSABLE DELAY. See Cibinic & Nash, *Administration of Government Contracts*, 554–56 (3d ed. 1995); Finke, *Unusually Severe Weather*, 22 Pub. Cont. L.J. 495 (1993).

URGENCY See UNUSUAL AND COMPELLING URGENCY.

U.S.-FLAG VESSEL Either a GOVERNMENT VESSEL or a PRIVATELY OWNED U.S.-FLAG COMMERCIAL VESSEL. FAR 47.501. FAR 47.503 requires that contractors and subcontractors give preference to the use of such vessels in the performance of their contracts under the terms of the Preference for Privately Owned U.S.-Flag Commercial Vessels clause in FAR 52.247-64, which implements the policies of the CARGO PREFERENCE ACTS and the Merchant Marine Act of 1936, 46 U.S.C. § 1101.

USDA See DEPARTMENT OF AGRICULTURE.

USEFUL ASSET An economically and programmatically separate segment of the asset procurement stage of a capital project that provides an asset for which the benefits exceed the costs, even if no further funding is appropriated. The total CAPITAL ASSET may include one or more useful assets, although it may not be possible to divide all procurements in this way. *Principles of Budgeting for Capital Asset*

Acquisitions, 9 Budget of the United States Government, Fiscal Year 1998 (GPO 1997).

UTILITY DISTRIBUTION SYSTEM Distribution and transmission lines, substations, or installed equipment forming an integral part of the system by which gas, water, steam, electricity, sewerage, or other utility services are transmitted between the outside building or structure in which the services are used and the point of origin, disposal, or connection with some other system, but excluding TELECOMMUNICATION SERVICES. FAR 45.501. This term is used in FAR Subpart 45.5 with regard to management of GOVERNMENT PROPERTY in the possession of contractors.

UTILITY SERVICE A service, such as the furnishing of electricity, gas, water, steam, and sewerage, that is available to the general public and performed by Government entities or private companies. FAR 41.101. Utility services are ordinarily subject to Government regulation. The term also includes services, such as snow removal and removal of garbage, rubbish, and trash, that are performed on a contractual basis and may be subject to Government or public regulation. The term "utility service" generally does not include telecommunication services. FAR Subpart 41.1 sets forth policies and procedures for the procurement of utility services.

V

V-LOAN See GUARANTEED LOAN.

VA See DEPARTMENT OF VETERANS AFFAIRS.

VALID TIME-PHASED REQUIREMENTS A part of a contractor's plan for accounting for MATERIAL that ensures that such material is (1) needed to fulfill a production plan, including reasonable quantities for scrap, shrinkage, yield, etc.; and (2) charged or billed to contracts or other COST OBJECTIVEs in a manner consistent with the need to fulfill the plan. DFARS 252.242-7004. DOD policy requires contractors to have a MATERIAL MANAGEMENT AND ACCOUNTING SYSTEM that reasonably forecasts material requirements, ensures that the costs of purchased and fabricated material charged or allocated to a contract are based on valid time-phased requirements, and maintains a consistent, equitable, and unbiased logic for the costing of material transactions. DFARS 242.7202.

VALIDATION The checking of all TECHNICAL DATA submitted by a contractor with RESTRICTIVE LEGENDS to ensure that such legends are properly applied. Validation procedures are prescribed by 10 U.S.C. § 2321 and 41 U.S.C. § 253d for contracts for MAJOR SYSTEMs; they are implemented by FAR 27.406(d) and DFARS 227.7103-4. The procedures are contained in the standard DOD Validation of Restrictive Markings on Technical Data (JUN 1995) clause in DFARS 252.227-7037. They permit a contractor to appeal any challenges of a legend through the DISPUTEs procedure and preclude the Government from removal of the legend until the appeal is resolved. DOD also uses a Validation of Asserted Restrictions—Computer Software clause, DFARS 252.227-7019, containing the same procedures.

VALUE ENGINEERING (VE) A formal technique by which contractors may (1) voluntarily suggest methods for performing more economically and may share in any resulting savings or (2) be required to establish a program or identify and submit to the Government methods for performing more economically. FAR 48.101(a). Value engineering attempts to eliminate, without impairing essential functions or characteristics, anything that increases acquisition, operation, or support costs. FAR Part 48 contains guidance on VE. The Government encourages VE by including one of the Value Engineering clauses in FAR 52.248-1 through -3 in almost all Government contracts. These clauses contain one of two approaches to submission of VALUE ENGINEERING CHANGE PROPOSALs (VECPs): an incentive or voluntary approach or a mandatory program in which the Government pays for a specific VE effort. In either case, the contractor is motivated to submit VECPs by being paid for INSTANT CONTRACT SAVINGS, CONCURRENT CONTRACT SAVINGS, FUTURE CONTRACT SAVINGS, and COLLATERAL SAVINGS in accordance with the provisions of the specific clause used in the contract. FAR 48.104-1. See Nash, chap. 9, *Government Contract Changes* (2d ed. 1989 & Supp. 1993); Cibinic & Nash, *Administration of Government Contracts* 412–29 (3d ed. 1995); Nash, *Postscript: Value Engineering*, 10 N&CR ¶ 51 (1996); Nash, *Value Engineering: Another Illusory Promise?,* 9 N&CR ¶ 20 (Mar. 1995); Connelly, *Value Engineering* 94-7 Briefing Papers (June 1994); Rozanski, *The Capital Gain Controversy over VECP Payments in Government Contracts*, 16 Pub. Cont. L.J. 321 (1987).

VALUE ENGINEERING CHANGE PROPOSAL (VECP) A change proposal that (1) requires a change to the INSTANT CONTRACT to implement and (2) results in reducing the overall projected cost to the agency without impairing essential functions or characteristics. FAR 48.001. Not qualifying as VECPs are proposals for changes in quantities of deliverable end items only, proposals for changes in research and development items or test quantities based solely on the results of previous testing, or proposals for changes to contract type only. See Nash, chap. 9, *Government Contract Changes* (2d ed. 1989 & Supp. 1993); Lewis, *Technical Data Rights in Government Contractor Value Engineering Change Proposals*, Army Law. 12 (Nov. 1994); Nash, *"Value Engineering" Clauses: Read Them Carefully!,* 8 N&CR ¶ 18 (Mar. 1994).

VARIABLE COSTS Costs of an organization that vary with the amount of work performed. Variable costs are usually contrasted with FIXED COSTs in analyzing a contractor's INDIRECT COSTs. If variable costs are a large percentage of a contractor's indirect costs, then the contractor's OVERHEAD RATEs can be expected to decrease more sharply with a decrease in volume of work than would be the case if fixed costs were a large percentage of the contractor's indirect costs.

VARIANCE The amount that a contractor's ACTUAL COSTs deviate from its STANDARD COSTs. See FAR 31.001. Variances are normally recorded for each unit of a contractor's manufacturing operation and are used to compute actual costs and to estimate future costs. They must be allocated at least annually and may be included in INDIRECT COST POOLs if they are immaterial. See CAS 407, 48 C.F.R. § 9904.407-50.

VARIATION IN QUANTITY A variation in the quantity of supplies or services ordered or estimated to be required in the performance of a contract. FAR 11.703(a) requires the use of the Variation in Quantity clause in FAR 52.211-16 in supply contracts. This clause provides for specified variations in quantity when such variation will meet the needs of the Government. FAR 11.703(c) requires the use of the Variation in Estimated Quantity clause in FAR 52.211-18 in construction contracts calling for the furnishing of work to be paid for at unit prices. This clause provides for price adjustments if the quantity of actual work varies from the estimated quantity by more than 15 percent. See Cibinic & Nash, *Administration of Government Contracts* 537–42 (3d ed. 1995); Cibinic, *Postscript II: "Variation in Estimated Quantity" Clause*, 7 N&CR ¶ 71 (Dec. 1993); Cibinic, *Postscript: "Variation in Estimated Quantity" Clause*, 6 N&CR ¶ 69 (Dec. 1992).

VENDOR A seller of goods. In Government contracting the term "vendor" generally refers to a person or organization selling goods to contractors, but can also mean a person or organization selling to the Government under SIMPLIFIED ACQUISITION PROCEDURES.

VERIFICATION See DUTY OF VERIFICATION.

VOIDABLE CONTRACT See AVOIDANCE OF CONTRACT.

VOLUNTARY DISCLOSURE Agreed-upon contractor identification of improper and illegal practices. Under an agreement between the contractor and the DOD Inspector General, contractors obligate themselves to a SELF-GOVERANCE program where they monitor compliance with federal procurement laws, adopt procedures for disclosing violations of those laws, and take corrective action. See Sherzer et al., *A Complete Guide to the Department of Defense Voluntary Disclosure Program* (1996); American Bar Ass'n, *The Department of Defense Voluntary Disclosure Program: A Description* *of the Process* (1994); Ryland, *The Government Contractor's Dilemma: Voluntary Disclosures as the Source of Qui Tam Litigation*, 22 Pub. Cont. L.J. 764 (1993); Kluber, *The Department of Defense Voluntary Disclosure Program*, 19 Pub. Cont. L.J. 504 (1990); McVey & Lemmer, *Voluntary Disclosure*, 87-6 Briefing Papers (May 1987).

VOLUNTARY REFUND A payment or credit, not required by any contractual or other legal obligation, made to the Government by a contractor or subcontractor either as a payment or as an adjustment under one or more contracts or subcontracts. DFARS 242.7100. It may be unsolicited or it may be made in response to a request by the Government. In most cases, voluntary refunds are requested after it has been determined that no contractual REMEDY is readily available for the Government to obtain the amount sought from the contractor. Acceptance of a voluntary refund does not prejudice remedies otherwise available to the Government. The refund should be made by CONTRACT MODIFICATION, if possible. Otherwise, it is made by check, which is credited to the appropriation or account for the contract. DFARS 242.7102.

VOLUNTARY STANDARD A STANDARD established by a private-sector body and available for public use. The term does not include private standards of individual firms. 41 C.F.R. § 101-29.218. See OMB Circular No. A-119 (revised), *Federal Participation in the Development and Use of Voluntary Standards*, Oct. 26. 1982. Such standards may be used to describe supplies or services being procured by the Government.

VOUCHER A document recording a business transaction, such as an expense voucher that records expenses incurred by an employee or in relation to a certain transaction. FAR 4.705-1 requires that financial and cost accounting records such as vouchers be retained by contractors for four years.

W

WAGE DETERMINATION A determination of DOL that a certain scale of WAGES is the PREVAILING WAGE in a locality. Wage determinations are issued under the DAVIS-BACON ACT and the SERVICE CONTRACT ACT OF 1965 and establish the minimum wages that Government contractors must pay their employees. Under the Davis-Bacon Act, wage determinations are either "general wage determinations"—issued periodically with no expiration date—or "project wage determinations"—issued for a specific project at the request of the procuring agency and expiring in 180 days. FAR 22.404-1. General wage determinations are published in the FEDERAL REGISTER and in the Government Printing Office document *General Wage Determinations Issued Under the Davis-Bacon and Related Acts*. The procedures for requesting project wage determinations are contained in FAR 22.404-3. Under the Service Contract Act, wage determinations are all issued for specific projects. These wage determinations are requested by use of a NOTICE OF INTENTION TO MAKE A SERVICE CONTRACT, Standard Form 98, FAR 53.301-98. The procedures for preparation and submittal of this form are contained in FAR 22.1008. See Cibinic & Nash, chap. 10, Sec. VII., *Formation of Government Contracts* (3d ed. 1998).

WAGES Compensation to employees for work. As used in regard to the DAVIS-BACON ACT, wages are the total compensation paid to employees of construction contractors, including the following: basic hourly rate of pay; any contribution irrevocably made by a contractor or subcontractor to a trustee or to a third person pursuant to a bona fide fringe benefit fund, plan, or program; and the rate of costs to the contractor or subcontractor that may reasonably be anticipated in providing bona fide fringe benefits to laborers and mechanics pursuant to an enforceable commitment to carry out a financially responsible plan or program that has been communicated in writing to the affected LABORERS OR MECHANICS. FAR 22.401. These are the elements of the compensation that must meet the minimum wage requirement of the Davis-Bacon Act. The fringe benefits enumerated in the Act include medical or hospital care, pensions on retirement or death, compensation for injuries or illness resulting from occupational activity, or insurance to provide any of the foregoing; unemployment benefits; life insurance, disability insurance, sickness insurance, or accident insurance; vacation or holiday pay; costs to defray the expense of apprenticeship or other similar programs; or other bona fide fringe benefits.

WAIVER The intentional or voluntary relinquishment of a known right, or conduct that warrants an inference that the right has been relinquished. Waiver entails the renunciation, REPUDIATION, abandonment, or surrender of some claim, right, or privilege, or of the opportunity to take advantage of some defect, irregularity, or wrong. *Black's Law Dictionary* 1580 (6th ed. 1990). If for example, the Government fails within a reasonable period to issue a TERMINATION FOR DEFAULT based on late delivery of supplies, and the contractor relies on that failure to terminate the contract and continues performance, the Government has waived its right to terminate the contract for the contractor's failure to meet the delivery date. See Cibinic and Nash, *Administration of Government Contracts* 75–76 (3d ed. 1995) Waiver of a specification entails written authorization to accept an item that departs from specified requirements but is nevertheless considered suitable either "as is" or after rework by an approved method. Jones, *Glossary: Defense Acquisition Acronyms and Terms* (8th ed., Defense Systems Management College). The parties may also waive contract requirements, such as delivery dates, testing requirements, and performance standards, or may waive potential rights regarding future claims, interest on claims, ATTORNEY'S FEES, appeal, and so forth. See Carberry & Johnstone, *Waiver of the Government's Right to Terminate for Default in Government Defense Contracts*, 17 Pub. Cont. L.J. 470 (1988).

WALSH-HEALEY PUBLIC CONTRACTS ACT A 1936 Act, 41 U.S.C. §§ 35–45, requiring that contracts over $10,000 for the manufacture or furnishing of materials, supplies, articles, or equipment include or incorporate by reference the stipulations required by the Act pertaining to such matters as minimum wages, maximum hours, child labor, convict labor, and safe and sanitary working conditions. FAR 22.602. DOL does not issue WAGE DETERMINATIONS under this Act; all contractors subject to the act must pay the minimum wages specified in the FAIR LABOR STANDARDS ACT. The Act is implemented by using the Walsh-Healey Public Contracts Act clause in FAR 52.222-20. When a contract subject to the act is awarded, the contracting officer must furnish to the contractor DOL Publication WH-1313, *Notice to Employees Working on Government Contracts*. FAR 22.608(a).

WARNER AMENDMENT A provision, 40 U.S.C. § 759(a)(3)(C), incorporated into the BROOKS ACT (AUTOMATIC DATA PROCESSING PROCUREMENTS) at 40 U.S.C. § 759(a)(3)(C) by the PAPERWORK REDUCTION REAUTHORIZATION ACT OF 1986. The Warner Amendment made the Brooks Act inapplicable to DOD procurements of FEDERAL INFORMATION PROCESSING RESOURCES or services if (1) the function, operation, or use of the equipment or services involves intelligence activities, cryptologic activities related to NATIONAL SECURITY, command and control of military forces, or equipment that is an integral part of a weapon or weapons system, or if (2) the equipment or service is critical to the direct fulfillment of military or intelligence missions (unless it is used for routine administrative and business applications, such as payroll, finance, logistics, and personnel management). When the Brooks Act was repealed by the CLINGER-COHEN ACT OF 1996, these types of INFORMATION TECHNOLOGY systems were renamed NATIONAL SECURITY SYSTEMs, which were excepted from the Act subject to the provisions of section 5141(b).

WARRANT The CONTRACTING OFFICER's (CO's) certificate of authority to enter into, administer, or terminate contracts and make related DETERMINATIONS AND FINDINGS. COs may bind the Government only to the extent of the authority delegated to them. Information about the limits of the contracting officer's authority must be readily available to the public and to agency personnel. FAR 1.602-1. COs are appointed in writing on Standard Form 1402, Certificate of Appointment, FAR 53.301-1402, which states any additional limitations on the scope of authority to be exercised beyond those contained in applicable laws or regulations. Appointing officials must maintain files containing copies of all certificates of appointment that have not been terminated. FAR 1.603-3. See Cibinic & Nash, chap. 1, Sec. III., *Formation of Government Contracts* (3d ed. 1998).

WARRANTY A promise or affirmation made by a contractor to the Government regarding the nature, usefulness, or condition of the supplies or services furnished under the contract. FAR 46.701. The principal purpose of a warranty in a Government contract is to relieve the Government of the conclusiveness of ACCEPTANCE OF WORK, which would otherwise preclude it from imposing the liability for

PATENT DEFECTs on the contractor. Other purposes of warranties are to delineate the rights and obligations of the contractor and the Government for defective items and services and to foster quality performance. Generally, a warranty should provide a contractual right to correction of defects, notwithstanding any other contract requirement pertaining to Government acceptance of the supplies or services. It should also specifically state the period of time after acceptance during which the Government may assert its right to have defects corrected. The benefits to be derived from a warranty must be commensurate with the cost of the warranty to the Government. FAR 46.702. In determining whether a warranty is appropriate for a specific acquisition, the contracting officer considers (1) the nature and use of the supplies or services, (2) warranty cost, (3) the feasibility of administration and enforcement, (4) whether warranty is customary in the trade, and (5) whether warranty costs can be offset by reduced QUALITY ASSURANCE requirements. FAR 46.703. In DOD, the chief of the contracting office must approve the use of a warranty, with certain exceptions. See DFARS 246.704. Standard warranty clauses are included in FAR 52.246-17 through -21. See Cibinic & Nash, *Administration of Government Contracts* 884–96 (3d ed. 1995); Dyer, *Breach of Warranty Damages: Consequently, Contractors Are Not Liable*, 24 Pub. Cont. L.J. 89 (1994); Kopf, *Warranties and Commercial Supply Contracts: A Need for Definitive Rules*, 17 Pub. Cont. L.J. 534 (1988).

WEAKNESS A flaw in an offeror's proposal that increases the risk of unsuccessful contract performance. FAR 15.301. Significant weaknesses must be discussed with offerors in the COMPETITIVE RANGE. FAR 15.306(d)(3). Some agencies now make a distinction between a weakness and a DEFICIENCY, but the Comptroller General has held that this distinction is not valid. See Nash, *Discussion of "Weaknesses": A Little Knowledge Is a Dangerous Thing*, 7 N&CR ¶ 59 (Oct. 1993). See also Cibinic & Nash, chap. 6, *Formation of Government Contracts* (3d ed. 1998).

WEIGHTED GUIDELINES METHOD DOD's structured technique for establishing the contracting officer's negotiating position on PROFIT. See DFARS Subpart 215.9. The technique is also used as a basis for documenting and explaining the final pricing agreement reached between buyer and seller. The weighted guidelines method ensures consideration of the relative value of appropriate profit factors, including the contractor's degree of performance risk, the risk imposed on the contractor by the type of contract, facilities investment, and working capital. DFARS 215.971-1. The contracting officer uses DD

Form 1547, Record of Weighted Guidelines Application, DFARS 253.303-1547, in computing profit. See DFARS 215.970. FAR 15.404-4 requires other agencies to have a structured system similar to the weighted guidelines method, including the profit factors discussed in FAR 15.404-4(d) (which are somewhat different from the DOD factors). DOE provides extensive guidance on its weighted guidelines at DEAR 915.970-2. See Brunsman, *Subcontracting Made Easy: Coping with the New Weighted Guidelines*, 25 Cont. Mgmt. 36 (May 1988); Nash, *Adverse Effects of New DOD Profit Policy*, 1 N&CR ¶ 3 (Jan. 1987).

WHISTLEBLOWER An employee who discloses to an outside person or entity an activity by his or her employer that the employee characterizes as illegal, immoral, or otherwise improper. The Defense Acquisition Improvement Act of 1986 provides that no one may be discharged, demoted, or otherwise discriminated against as a reprisal for disclosing to a member of Congress or to an authorized DOD or DOJ official information about a substantial violation of law related to a defense contract. 10 U.S.C. § 2409. Other statutes permit a whistleblower who has been discharged, demoted, or otherwise discriminated against as a reprisal for such disclosure to seek reinstatement, an award of twice the applicable back pay plus interest, and compensation for special damages, including litigation costs and ATTORNEY'S FEES. 10 U.S.C. § 1031(h); 31 U.S.C. § 3730(h). See Seyfarth et al., *The Government Contract Compliance Handbook* 4-7 through 4-9 (1996 Supp.)

WITHHOLDING The nonpayment of contract amounts by the contracting officer because the contractor failed to carry out some obligation under the contract. This term is sometimes used more broadly to denote SETOFF (the nonpayment of contract amounts because of debts of the contractor outside of the contract). Withholding is permitted by a number of contract clauses such as the Withholding of Funds clause in FAR 52.222-7, under which the Government may withhold funds necessary to pay contractor employees the full amount of wages required by the contract. However, withholding is a general right of the Government, even without such a clause. The amount withheld should be commensurate with the anticipated amount of damage the Government will suffer as a result of the nonperformance. See Cibinic & Nash, *Administration of Government Contracts* 1172–76 (3d ed. 1995); Nash, *Postscript III: Government Withholding of Payment*, 8 N&CR ¶ 6 (Feb. 1994); Cibinic, *Withholding, Offset, and Debt Collection: A Double Whammy for the Debt Collection Act*, 7 N&CR ¶ 44 (Aug. 1993); Nash,

Government Withholding of Payment: Handle with Care, 3 N&CR ¶ 51 (July 1989).

WOMEN-OWNED SMALL BUSINESSES SMALL BUSINESS CONCERNs that are at least 51 percent owned by women who are U.S. citizens and who also control and operate the business. FAR 19.201 states that women-owned small businesses must have the "maximum practicable opportunity" to participate as subcontractors in the contracts awarded by any agency. Contracting officers must insert in most contracts the Utilization of Small, Small Disadvantaged and Women-Owned Small Business Concerns clause in FAR 52.219-8. Contractors must provide women-owned small businesses the "maximum practicable opportunity" to participate in SUBCONTRACTs. FAR 19.702. The Women's Business Ownership Act of 1988, 15 U.S.C. § 631(h), makes an affirmative finding of discrimination in entrepreneurial endeavors based on gender and establishes a National Women's Business Council. This council makes annual recommendations to the Interagency Committee on Women's Business Enterprise and reports and makes recommendations, as it deems appropriate, to Congress and the President.

WORK A work of authorship that under the Copyright Act, Title 17 of the United States Code, is a (1) literary work, (2) musical work, (3) dramatic work, (4) pantomime or choreographic work, (5) pictorial, graphic, or sculptural work, (6) motion picture or other audiovisual work, (7) sound recording, or (8) architectural work. 17 U.S.C. § 102(a). To obtain a COPYRIGHT an author must demonstrate that his or her product is a work.

WORK BREAKDOWN STRUCTURE (WBS) A graphic display of a contract's STATEMENT OF WORK or an organizational chart depicting the necessary hardware, software, and services required in contract performance, and their relationship to each other. A WBS subdivides the work to be performed under a contract into logical segments in order to help track progress and performance cost. MIL-STD-881A, paragraph 3.4, defines a WBS as a product-oriented family tree (composed of hardware, services, and data) that results from project engineering efforts during the development and production of a defense material item and that completely defines the project or program. A WBS displays and defines the products to be developed or produced under the contract and relates the elements of work to be accomplished to each other and to the end product. WBSs are required as a part of a COST/SCHEDULE CONTROL SYSTEM used to manage major contracts. See DFARS 234.005-70 and Part 4.4.2 of DOD Regulation 5000.2-R, *Mandatory Procedures for Major Defense Acquisition Management Programs (MDAPs) and Major Automated Information System (MAIS) Acquisition Programs*, Mar. 15, 1996. See also Grskovich, *What Is C/SCSC?—In English, Please!*, 23 Nat'l Cont. Mgmt. J., Issue No. 2, p. 25 (1990); Dominic, *Understanding the C/SSR*, 30 Cont. Mgmt. 8 (Nov. 1990).

WORK FOR HIRE A WORK prepared by an employee within the scope of his or her employment or specially ordered or commissioned, and expressly agreed to in a written instrument, for use as (1) a contribution to a collective work, (2) a part of a motion picture or other audiovisual work, (3) a translation, (4) a supplementary work, (5) a test, (6) answered material for a test, or (7) an atlas. 17 U.S.C. § 101. Under 17 U.S.C. § 201(b), the employer is the author of a work for hire and therefore is the owner of the COPYRIGHT in the work.

WORK-IN-PROCESS Material that has been released to manufacturing, engineering, design, or other services under the contract and includes undelivered manufactured parts, assemblies, and products, either complete or incomplete. FAR 45.501. FAR 45.505-3 requires contractors to keep records of such material.

WORK STATEMENT The part of a RESEARCH AND DEVELOPMENT contract that describes the work to be performed by the contractor. FAR 35.005 provides that in such contracts, a clear and complete work statement concerning the area of exploration (for BASIC RESEARCH) or the end objectives (for DEVELOPMENT and APPLIED RESEARCH) is essential. The work statement should allow contractors to be innovative and creative; it must be individually tailored by technical and contracting personnel for this purpose. In basic research, the emphasis is on achieving specified objectives and knowledge rather than achieving predetermined end results prescribed in a statement of specific performance characteristics. In reviewing work statements, contracting officers should ensure that language suitable for a level-of-effort approach is not intermingled with language suitable for a task-completion approach. A level-of-effort approach requires the furnishing of technical effort and a report on the results; a task-completion approach often requires the development of a tangible end item designed to achieve specific performance characteristics. The wording of the work statement should also be consistent with the type and form of contract to be negotiated. See also STATEMENT OF WORK.

WORKERS ADJUSTMENT AND RETRAINING NOTIFICATION (WARN) ACT An Act, 29 U.S.C. § 2101 et seq., that provides that employers must give employees advance warning of plant closings or mass layoffs. Implementation of the Act requires no action by Government contracting activities. However, the Act might apply to some contracts (such as on-site support service contracts), and some of the costs of a contractor's noncompliance with the Act could be subject to reimbursement by the Government. NFS 18-22.101-72. See Cibinic, *Mass Layoffs: Duty to Warn Employees*, 11 N&CR ¶ 23 (May 1997).

WORKING CAPITAL ADJUSTMENT FACTOR Under DOD contracts, an adjustment added to the profit objective for contract-type risk for the purpose of giving general recognition to the contractor's cost of working capital under varying contract circumstances, financing policies, and the economic environment. It applies only to fixed-price contracts that provide for progress payments. Although a formula approach is used, it is not intended to be an exact calculation of the cost of working capital. See DFARS 215.971-3(a). DFARS 215.971-3(b) explains the determination of the adjustment. See also Cibinic & Nash, *Cost-Reimbursement Contracting* 600 (2d ed. 1993).

WRITTEN INTERROGATORY See INTERROGATORY.

WRITTEN OR ORAL DISCUSSIONS See DISCUSSION.

WUNDERLICH ACT A 1954 Act, 41 U.S.C. §§ 321–322, that precluded contract clauses from preventing judicial review of agency decisions on DISPUTEs. The Act codified the "arbitrary and capricious" standard of review for administrative decisions and permitted the courts to overrule administrative decisions that were not supported by "substantial evidence." The Act also provided that contractors could bargain away their right to full-scale judicial review of administrative decisions on questions of law. The purpose of the legislation was to overcome the effect of the Supreme Court decision in the case of *United States v. Wunderlich*, 342 U.S. 98 (1951), under which the decisions of Government officers rendered pursuant to the Disputes clause were held to be final in the absence of fraud on the part of the Government officers. The Act has been subsumed by the CONTRACT DISPUTES ACT OF 1978, which incorporates judicial review of agency decisions in the DISPUTEs process. See Gantt & Roberts, *Wunderlich Act Review in the Court of Claims under Bianchi, Utah, and Grace,* 3 Pub. Cont. L.J. 1 (1970).

Y

YEAR 2000 COMPLIANT The state of INFORMATION TECHNOLOGY that accurately processes date and time data from, into, and between the twentieth and twenty-first centuries, and the years 1999 and 2000 and leap year calculations. FAR 39.002. In January of 1997, language was added to the FAR that requires agencies to ensure that solicitations and contracts require Government information technology to be year 2000 compliant or require that noncompliant technology be upgraded. FAR 39.106; 10 U.S.C. § 2302 note.

Acronyms and Abbreviations Used in This Book

A-76	OMB Circular No. A-76
ABA	American Bar Association
ABC	Activity Based Costing
ACAT(s)	Acquisition Categories
ACI	Allocated Configuration Identification
ACO	Administrative Contracting Officer
ACRN	Accounting Classification Reference Number
ACTD	Advanced Concept Technology Demonstration
ACWP	Actual Cost of Work Performed
ADP	Automatic Data Processing
ADPE	Automatic Data Processing Equipment
ADPE/DS	Automatic Data Processing Equipment/Data System
ADR	Alternative Dispute Resolution
A-E	Architect-Engineer
AECA	Arms Export Control Act
AGC	Associated General Contractors of America
AIA	Aerospace Industries Association of America
AIA	American Institute of Architects

AO	Announcement of Opportunity
APB	Acquisition Program Baseline
APR	Agency Procurement Request
ASA	American Subcontractors Association
ASBCA	Armed Services Board of Contract Appeals
ASCE	American Society of Civil Engineers
ASPA	Armed Services Procurement Act
ASPM	*Armed Services Pricing Manual*
ASPR	*Armed Services Procurement Regulation*
AUPC	Average Unit Procurement Cost
B&P	Bid and Proposal
BAA	Broad Agency Announcement
BAFO	Best and Final Offer
BCA	Board of Contract Appeals
BCM	Business Clearance Memorandum
BCWP	Budgeted Cost of Work Performed
BCWS	Budgeted Cost of Work Scheduled
BEA	Budget Enforcement Act of 1990
BOA	Basic Ordering Agreement
BPA	Blanket Purchase Agreement
BPCR	Breakout Procurement Center Representative
CAAC	Civilian Agency Acquisition Council
CAAS	Contracted Advisory and Assistance Services
CACO	Corporate Administrative Contracting Officer

CAFC	Court of Appeals for the Federal Circuit
CALS	Continuous Acquisition and Life-Cycle Support
CAM	*Contract Audit Manual*
CAS	Cost Accounting Standards
CBD	*Commerce Business Daily*
CCASS	Construction Contractor Appraisal Support System
CCDR	Contractor Cost Data Reporting
CDA	Contract Disputes Act of 1978
CDRL	Contract Data Requirements List
CFR	*Code of Federal Regulations*
CICA	Competition in Contracting Act
CID	Commercial Item Description
CIO	Chief Information Officers
CIPR	Contract Insurance/Pension Review
Cl. Ct.	Claims Court
CLIN	Contract Line Item Number
CMAA	Construction Management Association of America
CMF	Cost of Money Factors
CO	Contracting Officer
COC	Certificate of Competency
CODSIA	Council of Defense and Space Industry Association
COGP	Commission on Government Procurement
Comp. Gen.	Comptroller General
COMSEC	Communications Security

COR	Contracting Officer Representative
COTR	Contracting Officer Technical Representative
COTS	Commercial Off-the-Shelf
CPAF	Cost-Plus-Award Fee
CPCM	Certified Professional Contracts Manager
CPFF	Cost-Plus-Fixed Fee
CPI	Cost Performance Index
CPIF	Cost-Plus-Incentive Fee
CPM	Critical Path Method
CPPC	Cost-Plus-a-Percentage-of-Cost
CPR	Cost Performance Report
CPSR	Contractor Purchasing System Review
CRA	Continuing Resolution Authority
CRADA	Cooperative Research and Development Agreement
CRAG	*Contractor Risk Assessment Guide*
C/SCSC	Cost/Schedule Control Systems Criteria
C/SSR	Cost/Schedule Status Report
Ct. Cl.	Court of Claims
CWAS	Contractor Weighted Average Share
CWHSSA	Contract Work Hours and Safety Standards Act
D&F	Determination and Findings
DAB	Defense Acquisition Board
DAC	Defense Acquisition Circular
DAE	Defense Acquisition Executive

DAR Council	Defense Acquisition Regulatory Council
DARPA	Defense Advanced Research Projects Agency
DARS	Defense Acquisition Regulation Summary
DAU	Defense Acquisition University
DAWIA	Defense Acquisition Workforce Improvement Act
D.C. Cir.	Court of Appeals for the District of Columbia Circuit
DCAA	Defense Contract Audit Agency
DCAM	*Defense Contract Audit Manual*
DCAS	Defense Contract Administration Service
DCMC	Defense Contract Management Command
DEAR	*Department of Energy Acquisition Regulation*
DFARS	*Department of Defense FAR Supplement*
DID	Data Item Description
DIPEC	Defense Industrial Plant Equipment Center
DISC	Defense Industrial Supply Center
DLA	Defense Logistics Agency
DLSSO	Defense Logistics Standard Systems Office
DO	Disbursing Officer
DOD	Department of Defense
DODD	DOD Directive
DODISS	DOD Index of Specifications and Standards
DOE	Department of Energy
DOI	Department of the Interior
DOJ	Department of Justice

DOL	Department of Labor
DOT	Department of Transpiration
DPA	Delegation of Procurement Authority
DPAS	Defense Priorities and Allocations System
DPSC	Defense Personnel Support Center
DSMC	Defense Systems Management College
DT&E	Developmental Test and Evaluation
DTIC	Defense Technical Information Center
EA	Evolutionary Acquisition
EAC	Estimate at Completion
EAJA	Equal Access to Justice Act
EAR	*Export Administration Regulations*
ECP	Engineering Change Proposal
EDCAR	Engineering Data Computer Retrieval System
EDI	Electronic Data Interchange
EEO	Equal Employment Opportunity
EFT	Electronic Funds Transfer
EIA	Electronics Industries Association
EOQ	Economic Order Quantity
EPA	Economic Price Adjustment
ESOP	Employee Stock Ownership Plan
F.2d	*Federal Reporter Second Series* (e.g., 614 F.2d 740)
FAC	Federal Acquisition Circular
FACNET	Federal Acquisition Computer Network

FAI	Federal Acquisition Institute
FAR	*Federal Acquisition Regulation*
FARA	Federal Acquisition Reform Act
FASA	Federal Acquisition Streamlining Act
FASB	Financial Accounting Standards Board
FAST	Federal Acquisition Services for Technology
FAX	Facsimile
FCC	Federal Communications Commission
FCCM	Facilities Capital Cost of Money
FCIA	Federal Courts Improvement Act
FCPA	Foreign Corrupt Practices Act
FDO	Fee Determination Official
FDPC	Federal Data Processing Center
Fed. Cir.	Court of Appeals for the Federal Circuit
Fed. Cl.	Court of Federal Claims
FED-STDS	Federal Telecommunications Standards
FEMA	Federal Emergency Management Agency
FFP	Firm Fixed Price
FFRDC	Federally Funded Research and Development Center
FIFO	First In, First, Out
FIPS PUBS	*Federal Information Processing Standards Publications*
FIRMR	Federal Information Resources Management
FIP	Federal Information Processing

FLC	Federal Laboratory Consortium for Technology Transfer
FLSA	Fair Labor Standards Act
FMS	Foreign Military Sales
FOCI	Foreign Ownership, Control, or Influence
FOIA	Freedom of Information Act
FPASA	Federal Property and Administrative Services Act of 1949
FPDC	Federal Procurement Data Center
FPDS	Federal Procurement Data System
FPI	Fixed-Price Incentive
FPMR	*Federal Property Management Regulation*
FPR	*Federal Procurement Regulations*
FPRA	Forward Pricing Rate Agreement
FPRP	Fixed-Price Redetermination—Prospective
FPRR	Fixed-Price Redetermination—Retroactive
FSC	Federal Supply Class
FSEC	Federal Software Exchange Center
FSED	Full-Scale Engineering Development
FSEP	Federal Software Exchange Program
FSS	Federal Supply Schedule
FTCA	Federal Tort Claims Act
FTS	Federal Telecommunications System
FY	Fiscal Year
FYDP	Future Years Defense Program

G&A	General and Administrative
GAAP	*Generally Accepted Accounting Principles*
GAO	General Accounting Office
GBL	Government Bill of Lading
GFM	Government-Furnished Material
GFP	Government-Furnished Property
GITSB	Government Information Technology Services Board
GOCO	Government-Owned, Contractor-Operated Plant
GPLR	Government-Purpose License Rights
GPO	Government Printing Office
GPR	Government Purpose Rights
GSA	General Services Administration
GSBCA	General Services Administration Board of Contract Appeals
GWAC	Government-wide Agency Contract
HBCUS	Historically Black Colleges and Universities
HCA	Head of the Contracting Activity
HHS	Department of Health and Human Services
HUD	Department of Housing and Urban Development
IAIC	Interagency Acquisition Internet Council
IFB	Invitation for Bids
IFMS	Interagency Fleet Management System
IG	Inspector General
IMIP	Industrial Modernization Incentives Program
IMPAC	International Merchant Purchase Authorization Card

INFOSEC	Information Systems Security
IPE	Industrial Plant Equipment
IR&D	Independent Research and Development
IRM	Information Resources Management
IT	Information Technology
ITAR	*International Traffic in Arms Regulation*
ITF	Information Technology Fund
ITMRA	Information Technology Management Reform Act
ITRB	Information Technology Resources Board
IWA	Interdivisional Work Authorization
IWO	Interdivisional Work Order
JCALS	Joint Computer-Aided Acquisition and Logistics Support
JEDMICS	Joint Engineering Data Management Information and Control System
JROC	Joint Requirements Oversight Council
L-H	Labor-Hour
LOA	Letter of Offer and Acceptance
LOC	Limitation of Cost
LOF	Limitation of Funds
LOR	Letter of Request
LSA	Labor Surplus Area
LTD	Live Test Demonstration
M&O	Management and Operating
MAS	Multiple-Award Schedule

MI	Minority Institution
MIL-SPEC	Military Specification
MIL-STD	Military Standard
MILSTRIP	Military Standard Requisitioning and Issue Procedure
MIRR	Material Inspection and Receiving Report
MMAS	Material Management and Accounting System
MOU	Memorandum of Understanding
MPC	*Model Procurement Code*
MRP	Material Requirements Planning
NAFI	Nonappropriated Funds Instrumentality
NASA	National Aeronautics and Space Administration
NAFTA	North American Free Trade Agreement
NASABCA	National Aeronautics and Space Administration Board of Contract Appeals
NCMA	National Contract Management Association
NDI	Nondevelopmental Item
NFS	*NASA FAR Supplement*
NFSD	*NASA FAR Supplement Directive*
NHB	*NASA Handbook*
NIST	National Institute of Standards and Technology
NMI	NASA Management Instruction
NPR	*NASA Procurement Regulation*
NRA	NASA Research Announcement
NRC	Nuclear Regulatory Commission
NSEP	National Security and Emergency Preparedness

NSF	National Science Foundation
NSIA	National Security Industrial Association
NTIS	National Technical Information Service
OCD	Operational Capability Demonstration
OCI	Organizational Conflict of Interest
OF	Optional Form
OFPP	Office of Federal Procurement Policy
OGE	Office of Government Ethics
OIRA	Office of Industrial Resource Administration
OMB	Office of Management and Budget
OPE	Other Plant Equipment
OPM	Office of Personnel Management
ORTA	Office of Research and Technology Application
OSD	Office of the Secretary of Defense
OT&E	Operational Test and Evaluation
PASS	Procurement Automated Source System
PAT&E	Production Acceptance Test and Evaluation
PBSC	Performance-Based Service Contracting
PCO	Procuring Contracting Officer
PCR	Procurement Center Representative
PDM	Program Decision Memorandum
PDR	Preliminary Design Review
PEO	Program Executive Officer
PEP	Producibility Engineering and Planning

PII	Procurement Instrument Identification
PM	Program Manager, Project Manager
PN	Procurement Notice
PNM	Price Negotiation Memorandum
PO	Purchase Order
POM	Program Objective Memorandum
PON	Program Opportunity Notice
PPA	Prompt Payment Act
PPBS	Planning, Programming and Budgeting System
PRDA	Program Research and Development Announcement
PSR	Productivity Savings Reward
QA	Quality Assurance
QBL	Qualified Bidders List
QC	Quality Control
QML	Qualified Manufacturers List
QPL	Qualified Products List
R&D	Research and Development
RCO	Remedy Coordination Official
RCRA	Resource Conservation and Recovery Act
RDT&E	Research, Development, Test, and Evaluation
REA	Request for Equitable Adjustment
RFI	Request for Information
RFP	Request for Proposals
RFQ	Request for Quotations

RFTP	Request for Technical Proposals
RICO	Racketeer Influenced and Corrupt Organization Act
RIE	Range of Incentive Effectiveness
ROA	Research Opportunity Announcement
RTE	Remote Terminal Emulation
SADBUS	Small and Disadvantaged Business Utilization Specialist
SAIP	Spares Acquisition Integrated with Production
SAR	Selected Acquisition Report
SBA	Small Business Administration
SCA	Service Contract Act of 1965
SDBC	Small Disadvantaged Business Concern
SDR	Special Drawing Right
SF	Standard Form
SFRC	Short Form Research Contract
SIC	Standard Industrial Classification
SOW	Statement of Work
SPICE	Simplified Procurement in a Competitive Environment
SRC	Special Research Contract
SSA	Source Selection Authority
SSAC	Source Selection Advisory Council
SSB	Source Selection Board
SSEB	Source Selection Evaluation Board
SSO	Source Selection Official
T&E	Test and Evaluation

T&M	Time and Materials
TCO	Termination Contracting Officer
TDP	Technical Data Package
TEMP	Test and Evaluation Master Plan
TINA	Truth in Negotiations Act
TQM	Total Quality Management
U.C.C.	*Uniform Commercial Code*
UCF	Uniform Contract Format
U.S.	*United States (Supreme Court) Reports* (e.g., 450 U.S. 785)
U.S.C.	*United States Code*
U.S.C.A.	*United States Code Annotated*
U.S.C.S.	*United States Code Service*
USDA	Department of Agriculture
VA	Department of Veterans Affairs
VE	Value Engineering
VECP	Value Engineering Change Proposal
WARN	Workers Adjustment and Retaining Notification
WBS	Work Breakdown Structure

Internet Resources

Acquisition Reform Net or ARNet
http://www-far.npr.gov or http://www.arnet.gov

Acquisition Reform Resource Center (ARRC)
http://afmc.wpafb.af.mil/organizations/hq-afmc/dp/dpe/lb-9/arrc.htm

Acquisition Systems Management (includes DOD 5000 series documents)
http://www.acq.osd.mil/api/asm

Acronyms (DSMC Homepage)
http://www.dsmc.dsm.mil/pubs/glossary/preface.htm

Advanced Technology Program (ATP)
http://www.atp.nist.gov/

Air Force Acquisition
http://www.safaq.hq.af.mil/

Air Force Acquisition Model
http://afamsun.wpafb.af.mil/prod01.htm

Air Force Contracting
http://www.safaq.hq.af.mil/contracting/

Air Force Country Store
http://www.hanscom.af.mil/Orgs/Spo/AVC/Cstore/

Air Force PDSM Program Office
http://wpaftb1.wpafb.af.mil/index.html

Alliance for Redesigning Government, Public Procurement Cluster
http://www.clearlake.ibm.com/alliance/clusters/crt/casestud.7p.html

American Bar Association, Section of Public Contract Law
http://www.abanet.org/contract/home.html

Army Acquisition Website
http://acqnet.sarda.army.mil

Army Material Command
http://amc.citi.net

ASC Contracting Business Opportunities Homepage
http://www.wpafb.af.mil/pk/index.html

Assistant Secretary of the Army for Research, Development, and Acquisition
http://www.sarda.army.mil/

Bureau of Engraving and Printing
Federal Acquisition Information
http://www.ustreas.gov/treasury/bureaus/bep/proc/jump.html

Caldwell & Bodenheimer
http://www.covesoft.com/caldwell/ctips.htm

Chamber of Commerce
http://www.chamber-of-commerce.com/

Code of Federal Regulations
http://www.access.gpo.gov/nara/cfr/cfr-table-search.html

Commerce Business Daily, CBDNet
http://cbdnet.gpo.gov/index.html

Comptroller General Bid Protest Decisions
http://www.gao.gov/decisions/bidpro/bidpro.htm

Congressional Record
http://thomas.loc.gov/home/r105query.html

Davis-Bacon Wage Determination Database
http://kirk.fedworld.gov/dbhome.htm

Defense Acquisition Deskbook
http://deskbook.osd.mil/deskbook.html

Defense Acquisition University
http://www.acq.osd.mil/dau/

Defense Advanced Research Projects Agency
http://www.arpa.mil/

Defense Contract Management Command (DCMC)
http://www.dcmc.dcrb.dla.mil/

Defense Fuel Supply Center (DFSC)
http://www.dfsc.dla.mil/

DefenseLINK (Department of Defense)
http://www.dtic.mil/defenselink/

Defense Logistics Agency
http://www.dla.mil/

Defense Logistics Agency Material Management
http://www.supply.dla.mil/

Defense Logistics Agency Systems Design Center
http://www.dsdc.dla.mil/

Defense Logistics Services Center
http://www.dlsc.dla.mil/

Defense Personnel Support Center (DPSC)
http://www.dpsc.dla.mil/

Defense Supply Center Columbus
http://www.dscc.dla.mil/

Defense Supply Center Richmond
http://www.dscr.dla.mil/

Defense Systems Management College
http://www.dsmc.dsm.mil/

Department of Defense Acquisition Workforce
http://www.dtic.dla.mil/acqed2/acqed.html

Department Of Defense Directives and Instructions
http://web7.whs.osd.mil/corres.htm

Department Of Energy Business Communications Center
http://www.pr.doe.gov/prbus.html

Department of Energy Procurement and
Assistance Data System (PADS)
http://www.pr.doe.gov/pads.html

Department of Labor, Grants and Contracts
http://dol.gov/dol/oasam/public/grants/main.htm

Department of Transportation, Procurement Information
http://www.dot.gov/ost/m60/index.html

Deputy Under Secretary of Defense (Acquisition Reform)
http://www.acq.osd.mil/ar

Directorate of Clothing & Textiles
http://ct.dpsc.dla.mil/

EDS Government Products and Services
http://www.eds-ms.com/

Electronic Commerce Program Office (ECPO)
http://www.ec.fed.gov

EPA Contracts, Grants & Financing
http://www.epa.gov/epahome/finance.htm

ESI International
http://www.esi-intl.com/

FedCenter Contract Resource Center
http://crc.fedcenter.com/

Federal Acquisition Circulars
http://www.gsa.gov/far/FAC/FACs.html

Federal Acquisition Institute
http://www.gsa.gov/staff/v/training.htm

Federal Acquisition Jumpstation
http://procure.msfc.nasa.gov/fedproc/home.html

Federal Acquisition Regulation (FAR) (see also GSA)
http://www.arnet.gov/far

Federal Acquisition Virtual Library
http://www.arnet.gov/References/References.html

Federal Aviation Administration
Office of Acquisitions
http://www.faa.gov/ara/arahome.htm

Federal Aviation Administration
Office of Acquisition
http://www.faa.gov/asu/asuhome.htm

Federal Information Exchange, Inc.
http://web.fie.com/

Federal Marketplace, Procurement Data Warehouse
http://www.fedmarket.com/

Federal Publications
http://www.fedpub.com

Federal Procurement Data System (FPDS)
http://www.gsa.gov/staff/oppe/fpds/fpds.htm

Federal Register
http://www.access.gpo.gov/su_docs/aces/aces140.html

The Federal Systems Integration and Management Center (FEDSIM)
http://www.gsa.gov/iti/lans.htm

Finance Net
http://www.financenet.gov/

Friedman & Fuller
http://www.ffgroup.com/contractor/

General Accounting Office
http://www.gao.gov

General Services Administration, GSA
http://www.gsa.gov

Glossary of EDI Terms
http://www.ecrc.gmu.edu/edistone/edigloss.html

George Washington University
Government Procurement Law LL.M.
http://www.law.gwu.edu/5-2c.htm

Government Business Resources
http://www.uscontracts.com/

Government Contractor Resource Center
http://www.govcon.com/

Government Contracts Program
George Washington University
http://www.gwprofdev.com/gcp/

Government Electronic Mail (GEM)
http://www.gsa.gov/gem.htm

Government Printing Office (GPO)
http://www.access.gpo.gov/

Government PROcurement Magazine
http://www.penton.com/corp/mags/gpro.html

Government Resource Center
http://www.cio.com/CIO/rc_govt.html

Government Solutions Procurement Search Engine
http://www.govsolutions.com/psearch.html

GSA Advantage! (electronic catalog)
http://www.gsa.gov/fssintro.htm

House of Representatives (U.S. Congress)
http://www.house.gov/

Industry Net
http://www.industry.net/

Inspector General Network
http://www.sbaonline.sba.gov/ignet/ig.html

Interagency Acquisition Internet Council (IAIC)
http://www.arnet.gov/IAIC/

ITEC Direct, The Navy's Information Technology Catalog
http://www.part.net/itec/itec.htm

IT Policy OnRamp from the Office of Information Technology (MK), General Services Administration,
http://www.itpolicy.gsa.gov/

Joint Dual-Use Program
http://www.jdupo.darpa.mil/jdupo/index.html

Legislative Branch (U.S. Government)
http://lcweb.loc.gov/global/legislative/congress.html

Library of Congress
http://lcweb.loc.gov/

NASA Headquarters Acquisition Division
http://www.hq.nasa.gov/office/procurement/acquisition/procref.htm

NASA Procurement Homepages
http://procure.msfc.nasa.gov/nasaproc.html

NASA Procurement Synopsis Search
http://www.dfrc.nasa.gov/Procure/NPSE//

National Archives and Record Administration
http://www.access.gpo.gov/nara/index.html

National Association of Purchasing Management
http://www.napm.org/

National Contract Management Association (NCMA)
http://www.ncmahq.org/

National Institute of Governmental Purchasing, Inc. (NIGP)
http://www.nigp.org

National Performance Review (NPR)
http://www.npr.gov/

National Property Management Association, Inc.
http://www.npma.org/

National Purchasing Institute
http://www.concom.com/~triddle/index.html

National Technical Information Service (NTIS)
http://www.ntis.gov/

Naval Air Warfare Center, Weapons Division
http://www.nawcwpns.navy.mil/

Naval Research Laboratory
http://www.nrl.navy.mil/

Navy Acquisition Reform
http://www.acq-ref.navy.mil/docs.html

NIH Office of Information Resources Management (OIRM)
http://www.oirm.mih.gov

Office of Federal Procurement Policy (OFPP)
http://www-far.npr.gov/OFPP.html

The Office of Information Technology Integration (ITI)
http://www.gsa.gov/iti/iti1.htm

Office of Management and Budget (OMB)
http://www.whitehouse.gov/wh/eop/omb

Outsourcing Institute
http://www.outsourcing.com/

Patent and Trademark Office Acquisitions
http://www.uspto.gov/web/offices/ac/comp/proc/acquisitions/

Postal Service (Selling to the U.S.)
http://www.usps.gov/business/

Procurement Assistance Jumpstation
http://www.fedmarket.com/procinet.html

Procurement and Funding Related Information
http://www.nttc.edu/gov/other/procurement.html

The Purchasing Station
http://management.bus.okstate.edu/faculty/christensen

San Antonio Electronic Commerce Resource Center
http://www.saecrc.org/

Small Business Administration
http://www.sbaonline.sba.gov/

Small Business Administration, Office of Advocacy
http://www.sba.gov/advo/

Small Business Innovative Research (SBIR) (DOE)
http://sbir.er.doe.gov/sbir

Senate (U.S. Congress)
http://www.senate.gov/

Standard Industrial Classification Search
http://www.osha.gov/oshstats/sicser.html

Thomas, Legislative Information, a service of the U.S. Congress
http://thomas.loc.gov/

U.S. Business Advisor
http://www.business.gov/

The White House
http://www.whitehouse.gov/wh/welcome.html

3M Federal Systems Department
http://www.mmm.com/market/government/index.html

Texts Cited in This Book

Administration of Government Contracts. 3d ed. John Cibinic, Jr., and Ralph C. Nash, Jr. Washington, DC: The George Washington University Government Contracts Program, 1995.

The Antitrust Government Contracts Handbook. William Kovacic. Chicago, IL: American Bar Association, Section of Antitrust Law, 1990.

Armed Services Pricing Manual (ASPM). Vol. I: *Contract Pricing*, Vol. 2: *Price Analysis*. Department of Defense. Chicago, IL: Commerce Clearing House, Inc., 1986 (vol. 1) and 1987 (vol. 2).

Ballentine's Law Dictionary. 3d ed. Rochester, NY: The Lawyers Cooperative Publishing Company, 1969.

Barron's Finance and Investment Handbook. 3d ed. John Downes and Jordan Elliott Goodman. New York, NY: Barron's Educational Series, Inc., 1990.

Black's Law Dictionary. 6th ed. St. Paul, MN: West Publishing Co., 1990.

Changes in Cost Accounting Practice. Wayne Davis. Washington, DC: The George Washington University Government Contracts Program (unpublished L.L.M. thesis), 1989.

A Citizen's Guide to the Federal Budget, Budget of the United States Government. Washington, DC: Executive Office of the President, Office of Management and Budget, 1997.

Competitive Negotiation: The Source Selection Process. Ralph C. Nash, Jr., and John Cibinic, Jr. Washington, DC: The George Washington University Government Contracts Program, 1993.

A Complete Guide to the Department of Defense Voluntary Disclosure Program. Harvey G. Sherzer, Scott Arnold, David A. Francis. Washington, DC: The George Washington University Government Contracts Program, 1995.

Construction Contracting. Richard J. Bednar (chapters 10 and 13), Herman M. Braude (chapters 7, 9, and 15), John Cibinic, Jr. (chapters 5 and 9), Gilbert J. Ginsburg (chapters 2 and 16), J. Richard Margulies (chapters 8, 11, and 14), Ralph C. Nash, Jr. (chapters 1, 6, and 12), Douglas L. Patin (chapters 2, 4, 16, 17, and 18), and Andrew W. Stephenson (chapter 3). Washington, DC: The George Washington University Government Contracts Program, 1991.

Contract Pricing Reference Guide. Vol 1: *Price Analysis*, Vol. 2: *Quantitative Techniques for Contract Pricing*, Vol. 3: *Cost Analysis*, Vol. 4: *Advanced Issues in Contract Pricing* (draft), Vol. 5: *Federal Contract Negotiation Techniques*. Washington, DC: Federal Acquisition Institute. 1996 (Vol. 2, Vol. 4, Vol. 5) and 1997 (Vol. 1, Vol. 3).

Cost-Reimbursement Contracting. 2d ed. John Cibinic, Jr., and Ralph C. Nash, Jr. Washington, DC: The George Washington University Government Contracts Program, 1993.

DCAA Contract Audit Manual (CAM). 2 vols. Defense Contract Audit Agency. Washington, DC: U.S. Government Printing Office, 1997.

Dictionary of Banking and Finance. 2d ed. Jerry M. Rosenberg. New York, NY: John Wiley & Sons, 1985.

The Dollars and Sense of Government Contract Funding. William A. Hill, Chicago, IL: American Bar Association, Section of Public Contract Law, 1988.

Federal Contract Management: A Manual for the Contract Professional. Norman A. Steiger. New York, NY: Matthew Bender, 1982.

Federal Contracts, Grants and Assistance. 3 vols. Dennis J. Riley. Colorado Springs, CO: Shepard's/McGraw-Hill, 1983.

Federal Grants and Cooperative Agreements. Vol. I. Richard B. Cappalli. Wilmette, IL: Callaghan & Company, 1982 (as supplemented).

Federal Procurement Law. 3d ed. Vol. I: Contract Formation. Vol. II. Contract Performance. Ralph C. Nash, Jr. and John Cibinic, Jr. Washington, DC: The George Washington University Government Contracts Program, 1977 (vol. I) and 1980 (vol. II).

Formation of Government Contracts. 3d ed. John Cibinic, Jr., and Ralph C. Nash, Jr. Washington, DC: The George Washington University Government Contracts Program, 1998.

Glossary: Defense Acquisition Acronyms and Terms. 8th ed., Wilbur D. Jones, Jr. Fort Belvoir, VA: Defense Systems Management College, 1997.

Government Contract Bidding. 3d ed. Paul Shnitzer. Washington, D.C.: Federal Publications Inc., 1987 (1991 supplement).

Government Contract Changes. 2d ed. Ralph C. Nash, Jr. Washington, DC: Federal Publications Inc., 1989 (1993 supplement).

The Government Contract Compliance Handbook. Seyfarth, Shaw, Fairweather, and Geraldson (Government Contracts Group), Washington, DC: Federal Publications Inc., 1988 (1996 supplement).

Government Contract Default Termination. Walter F. Pettit, Carl L. Vacketta, and David V. Anthony. Washington, DC: Federal Publications Inc., 1991.

Government Contract Disputes. 2d ed. Peter S. Latham. Washington, DC: Federal Publications Inc., 1986 (1991 supplement).

Government Contracts Under the Federal Acquisition Regulation. 2d ed. W. Noel Keyes. St. Paul, MN:West Publishing Co., 1997.

A Guide to Best Practices for Performance-Based Service Contracting. Washington, DC: Office of Federal Procurement Policy, 1996.

Guidelines for Civil Fraud Remedies and Parallel Proceedings. Washington, DC: Executive Office of the President. Office of Management and Budget, 1985.

Handbook of Government Accounting and Finance. Nicholas G. Apostolou and D. Larry Crumbley. New York, NY: J. Wiley & Sons, 1988.

How to Evaluate Past Performance: A Best-Value Approach. 2d ed. Vernon J. Edwards. Washington, DC: The George Washington University Government Contracts Program, 1996.

How to Review a Federal Contract and Research Federal Contract Law. James F. Nagle. Chicago, IL: American Bar Association, Section of General Practice, 1990.

Intellectual Property in Government Contracts. 3d ed. Ralph C. Nash, Jr., and Leonard Rawicz. Washington, DC: The George Washington University Government Contracts Program, 1997.

International Business Transactions in a Nutshell. 5th ed. Ralph H. Folsom, St. Paul, MN: West Publishing Co., 1996.

Litigation under the Federal Freedom of Information and Privacy Act. 15th ed. Allen Adler, editor. Washington, DC: American Civil Liberties Union, 1990.

Living with TINA: A Practical Guide to the Truth in Negotiations Act. Clarence T. Kipps, Jr., and John Lloyd Rice. Washington, DC: Washington Legal Foundation, 1988.

Manual for Practice Before the Boards of Contract Appeals. Washington, DC: Federal Bar Association (Boards of Contract Appeals Committee), 1981.

Murray On Contracts. 3d ed. John Edward Murray, Jr. Charlottesville, VA: Michie Co., 1990 (as supplemented).

Personal Conflicts in Government Contracting. L. James D'Agostino, James R. Humphries, and James W. Taylor. Chicago, IL: American Bar Association, Section of Public Contract Law, 1988.

Principles of Budgeting for Capital Asset Acquisitions, 8 Budget of the United States Government Fiscal Year 1998 (1997): Washington, DC: U.S. Government Printing Office.

Principles of Federal Appropriations Law. 2d ed. 4 vols. U.S. General Accounting Office. Washington, DC: U.S. Government Printing Office, 1991.

Program Manager's Notebook. 2d ed. Fort Belvoir, VA: Defense Systems Management College, 1989.

The Protest Experience under the Competition in Contracting Act. Chicago, IL: American Bar Association, Section of Public Contract Law, 1989.

Questions and Answers About Best-Value Source Selection. Vernon J. Edwards. Washington, DC: The George Washington University Government Contracts Program, 1994.

Records Retention Procedures: Your Guide to Determining How Long to Keep Your Records and How to Safely Destroy Them. Donald S. Skupsky. Denver, CO: Information Requirements Clearinghouse, 1990.

Restatement (Second) of Contracts. 3 vols. St. Paul, MN: American Law Institute, 1981 (as supplemented).

Rights in Technical Data and Computer Software. Matthew S. Simchak and David A. Vogel. Washington, DC: The George Washington University Government Contracts Program, 1995.

Second Sourcing in the Department of Defense. William Kirshner III, Washington, DC: The George Washington University Government Contracts Program (unpublished thesis), 1982.

Sourcebook: Federal Agency Use of Alternative Means of Dispute Resolution. Marguerite S. Millhauser. Washington, DC: Administrative Conference of the United States (Office of the Chairman), 1987.

Streamlining Source Selection with Oral Presentations. Vernon J. Edwards. Washington, DC: The George Washington University Government Contracts Program. 1996.

Study of Professional Services Contracting. Washington, DC: Office of Federal Procurement Policy, 1985.

Telecommunications: Glossary of Telecommunication Terms. National Communications System Technology and Standards Division. Washington, DC: General Services Administration, 1996.

Periodicals Cited in This Book

Acquisition Rev. Q.	*Acquisition Review Quarterly.* Published quarterly by the Defense Systems Management College, 9820 Belvoir Road, Suite G38, Fort Belvoir, VA 22060-5565. Available for purchase from the U.S. Government Printing Office (202) 512-1800.
Admin. L.J.	*Administrative Law Journal.* Published three times a year by The American University, Washington College of Law, 4801 Massachusetts Avenue, N.W., Washington, DC 20016. (202) 885-3412.
A.F. L. Rev.	*The Air Force Law Review.* Published semi annually by the Air Force Judge Advocate General School (CPD/JAL), Maxwell Air Force Base, AL 36112-5712. Available for purchase from the U.S. Government Printing Office, Washington, DC 20402. (202) 512-1800.
AIPLA	*AIPLA Law Journal.* Published quarterly by American Intellectual Property Law Association, 2001 Jefferson Davis Highway, Suite 203, Arlington, VA 22202. (703) 415-0780.
Ala. L. Rev.	*Alabama Law Review.* Published 3 times a year by The University of Alabama School of Law, Box 870382, Tuscaloosa, AL 35487-0382. (205) 348-7191.
Am U.L. Rev.	*American University Law Review.* Published 6 times a year by The American University,

	Washington College of Law, 4801 Massachusetts Avenue, N.W., Washington, DC 20016. (202) 274-0773.
Antitrust Bull.	*Antitrust Bulletin.* Published quarterly by Federal Legal Publications Inc., 157 Charles Street, New York, NY 10007. (212) 619-4949.
Army Law.	*Army Lawyer.* Published monthly by the Judge Advocate General's School, United States Army, Charlottesville, VA 22903-1781. Available for purchase from the U.S. Government Printing Office.
Briefing Papers	*Briefing Papers.* Published monthly (except January—twice monthly) by Federal Publications Inc., 1120 20th Street, N.W., Washington, DC 20036. (202) 337-7000.
Bus. Law.	*Business Lawyer.* Published quarterly by the American Bar Association, 750 North Lake Shore Drive, Chicago, IL 60611. (312) 988-5000.
Colo. Law.	*Colorado Lawyer.* Published monthly by the Colorado Bar Association, 1900 Grant Street, Ninth Floor, Denver, CO 80203. (303) 860-1115.
Conn. L. Rev.	*Connecticut Law Review.* Published quarterly by The University of Connecticut School of Law, 55 Elizabeth Street, Hartford, CT 06105-2296. (860) 241-4638.
Constr. Briefings	*Construction Briefings.* Published monthly (except January—twice monthly) by Federal Publications Inc., 1120 20th Street, N.W., Washington, DC 20036. (202) 337-7000.
Constr. Law.	*Construction Lawyer.* Published quarterly by the American Bar Association, 750 North

	Lake Shore Drive, Chicago, IL 60611. (312) 988-5000.
Cont. Mgmt	*Contract Management.* Published monthly by the National Contract Management Association, 1912 Woodford Road, Vienna, VA 22182. (703) 448-9231.
CP&A Rep.	*Government Contract Costs, Pricing & Accounting Report.* Published monthly by Federal Publications Inc., 1120 20th Street, N.W., Washington, DC 20036. 202 337-7000.
Denver L.J. (now Denver L. Rev.)	*Denver University Law Journal* (now *Denver University Law Review*). Published quarterly by the University of Denver College of Law, 7039 E. 18th Ave., Denver, CO 80220. (303) 871-6000.
Duq. L. Rev.	*Duquesne Law Review.* Published quarterly by the Duquesne University Law School, 132 Edward J. Hanley Hall, Pittsburgh, PA 15282. (412) 434-6300.
Employee Rel. L.J.	*Employee Relations Law Journal.* Published quarterly by Executive Enterprises Publishing Co. Inc., 22 West 21st Street, 10th floor, New York, NY 10010-6904. 1-800-332-8804; (212) 645-7880, ext. 208.
Fed. B. News & J. (now Fed. Lawyer)	*Federal Bar News & Journal.* (now *Federal Lawyer*) Published 10 times a year by the Federal Bar Association, 1815 H Street, N.W., Suite 408, Washington, DC 20006-3697. (202) 638-0252.
Fed. Cont. Rep.	*Federal Contracts Report.* Published weekly by The Bureau of National Affairs, Inc., 1231 25th Street, N.W., Washington, DC 20037. (202) 452-4383.
Geo. Mason U. L. Rev.	*George Mason University Law Review.* (now *George Mason Law Review*). Published 4

(now Geo. Mason L. Rev.)	times a year by the George Mason University School of Law, 3401 North Fairfax Drive, Arlington, VA 22201. (703) 993-8148.
Geo. Wash. J. Int'l L. & Econ.	*George Washington University Journal of International Law and Economics*. Published 3 times a year by The George Washington University Law School, George Washington University, 2008 G Street, N.W., Washington, DC 20052. (202) 676-3847.
Government Contractor	*Government Contractor.* Published weekly by Federal Publications Inc., 1120 20th Street, N.W., Washington, DC 20036. (202) 337-7000.
Gov't Executive	*Government Executive.* Published monthly by National Journal, Inc., 1501 M Street, N.W., Washington, DC 20005. (202) 739-8500.
How. L.J.	*Howard Law. Journal.* Published by the Howard University School of Law, 2900 Van Ness Street, N.W., Washington, DC 20008. (202) 806-8000.
Inspector Gen. Rep.	*Inspector General Reports*. Issued by the Office of Inspector General, Department of Defense, 400 Army-Navy Drive, Arlington, VA 22202. (703) 604-8937.
Loy. L.A. L. Rev.	*Loyola of Los Angeles Law Review.* Published by Loyola Law School, 919 South Albany Street, Los Angeles, CA 90015-0019. (213) 736-1000.
Mil. L. Rev.	*Military Law Review.* Published quarterly by the Judge Advocate General's School. United States Army. Charlottesville, VA 22903-1781. Available for purchase from the U.S. Government Printing Office. (202) 512-1800.
N&CR	*The Nash & Cibinic Report.* Published monthly by Federal Publications Inc., 1120

	20th Street, N.W., Washington, DC 20036. (202) 337-7000.
Nat'l Cont. Mgmt. J.	*National Contract Management Journal.* Published semiannually by the National Contract Management Association, 1912 Woodford Road, Vienna, VA 22182. (703) 448-9231.
Pub. Cont. L.J.	*Public Contract Law Journal.* Published quarterly by the Section of Public Contract Law, American Bar Association, 750 North Lake Shore Drive, Chicago, IL 60611. (312) 988-5555.
Pub. Cont. Newsl. (now Procurement Law.)	*Public Contract Newsletter* (now *Procurement Lawyer*). Published quarterly by the Section of Public Contract Law, American Bar Association, 750 North Lake Shore Drive, Chicago, IL 60611. (312) 988-5555.
Wash. L. Rev.	*Washington Law Review.* Published quarterly by Washington Law Review, 1100 N.E. Campus Parkway, University of Washington, Condon Hall, Seattle, WA 98105-6617. (202) 543-6335.
Wash. U.J. & Contemp. L	*Washington University Journal of Urban and Contemporary Law.* Published semiannually by Washington University School of Law, One Brooking Drive, St. Louis, MO 63130-4899. (314) 935-4525.
Rutgers Computer Tech. L.J.	*Rutgers Computer Technology Law Journal.* Published semiannually by the Rutgers University Law School, 15 Washington Street, Newark, NJ 07102. (873) 353-5549.